with MyAccountingLab

- **Worked Solutions**—Provide step-by-step explanations on how to solve select problems using the exact numbers and data that were presented in the problem. Instructors will have access to the Worked Out Solutions in preview and review mode.

- **Algorithmic Test Bank**—Instructors have the ability to create multiple versions of a test or extra practice for students.

- **Reporting Dashboard**—View, analyze, and report learning outcomes clearly and easily. Available via the Gradebook and fully mobile-ready, the Reporting Dashboard presents student performance data at the class, section, and program levels in an accessible, visual manner.

- **LMS Integration**—Link from any LMS platform to access assignments, rosters, and resources, and synchronize MyLab grades with your LMS gradebook. For students, new direct, single sign-on provides access to all the personalized learning MyLab resources that make studying more efficient and effective.

- **Mobile Ready**—Students and instructors can access multimedia resources and complete assessments right at their fingertips, on any mobile device.

PEARSON

College Accounting

A Practical Approach

Thirteenth Edition

Chapters 1–12
With Study Guide and Working Papers

Jeffrey Slater
North Shore Community College
Danvers, Massachusetts

PEARSON

Boston Columbus Indianapolis New York San Francisco Hoboken
Amsterdam Cape Town Dubai London Madrid Milan Munich Paris Montréal Toronto
Delhi Mexico City São Paulo Sydney Hong Kong Seoul Singapore Taipei Tokyo

For Matty: More planes and trains
For Mia: Losing to you in chess
For Sam: Watching you in flag football
For Hope: Watching you chase your pugs

Vice President, Business Publishing: Donna Battista
Acquisitions Editor: Ellen Geary
Editorial Assistant: Christine Donovan
Vice President, Product Marketing: Maggie Moylan
Director of Marketing, Digital Services and Products: Jeanette Koskinas
Senior Product Marketing Manager: Alison Haskins
Executive Field Marketing Manager: Lori DeShazo
Senior Strategic Marketing Manager: Erin Gardner
Team Lead, Program Management: Ashley Santora
Program Managers: Erin McDonagh, Nancy Freihofer
Team Lead, Project Management: Jeff Holcomb
Project Manager: Heather Pagano
Operations Specialist: Carol Melville
Creative Director: Blair Brown
Art Director: Jon Boylan

Vice President, Director of Digital Strategy and Assessment: Paul Gentile
Manager of Learning Applications: Paul DeLuca
Digital Editor: Paul DeLuca
Director, Digital Studio: Sacha Laustsen
Digital Studio Manager: Diane Lombardo
Product Manager: James Bateman
Digital Content Team Lead: Noel Lotz
Digital Content Project Leads: Martha LaChance, Elizabeth Geary
Full-Service Project Management and Composition: Laserwords
Interior Designer: Gillian Hall, The Aardvark Group
Cover Designer: Joyce Wells, Creative Circle
Cover Art: Arcady/Shutterstock and Bubaone/iStockphoto
Printer/Binder: Courier Kendallville
Cover Printer: Courier Kendallville

Library of Congress Cataloging-in-Publication Data is on file at the Library of Congress

10 9 8 7 6 5 4 3 2 1

www.pearsonhighered.com

ISBN 10: 0-13-386630-0
ISBN 13: 978-0-13-386630-8

Brief Contents

Contents

6 Banking Procedures and Control of Cash   201

7 Calculating Pay and Recording Payroll Taxes: The Beginning of the Payroll Process   239

8 Paying the Payroll, Depositing Payroll Taxes, and Filing the Required Quarterly and Annual Tax Forms: The Conclusion of the Payroll Process   275

9 Sales and Cash Receipts   313

12 Completion of the Accounting Cycle for a Merchandise Company   439

Preface

All Chapters:

- Found after each Learning Unit, Try It! Interactive questions give students the opportunity to apply the concept they just learned. Linking in the eText will allow students to practice in MyAccountingLab without interrupting their interaction with the eText. Students' performance on the questions creates a precise adaptive study plan in MyAccountingLab for additional practice.

- New discussions of modern accounting techniques and tools bring accounting practice into the 21st century, while still focusing on building basic skills and background knowledge so students can critically understand their practice.

- Updated end-of-chapter problem material gives a fresh opportunity for students and instructors to apply the concepts they have learned.

- New Demonstration Summary Problems for Chapters 6–12 walk students through a sample problem as if they were getting one-on-one help from their instructor.

- New Computer Workshops for QuickBooks and Sage 50 (formerly Peachtree) give students an opportunity to practice in real-world applications.

- New Learning Objectives align with Learning Units for easy class organization and topic coverage.

SAMPLING OF CHAPTER-SPECIFIC UPDATES

Chapter 1: Accounting Concepts and Procedures

- New discussion in Learning Unit 1-3 of Cash Basis versus Accrual Accounting. This new section reinforces the matching principle as students begin recording transactions into the expanded accounting equation. This discussion sets the framework for the text's use of the Accrual Basis of Accounting.

- New chapter-wide continuing demonstration problem.

Chapter 4: The Accounting Cycle Continued

- New learning unit added to Chapter 4. This new unit focuses on adjustments and how to record them on the worksheet. A step-by-step approach is used to place adjustments on the worksheet. The remainder of the chapter focuses on completion of the worksheet and preparing the financial statements.

Chapter 6: Banking Procedure and Control of Cash

- This chapter provides a fresh look at how technology is changing the banking process. A new focus is on the latest trends in banking and how banking apps provide easy smartphone access to banking. Mobile banking has been completely updated to provide students with the latest technology updates like computerized bank deposits and virtual checks.

Chapter 7: Calculating Pay and Recording Payroll Taxes: The Beginning of the Payroll Process

- This chapter takes a new approach to simplifying concepts. All tables, figures and rates have been updated to use the 2014 rates. The chapter also features a new presentation of the payroll register in a much more concise format to enhance student learning.

Chapter 8: Paying the Payroll, Depositing Payroll Taxes, and Filing the Required Quarterly and Annual Tax Forms: The Conclusion of the Payroll Process

- New forms are included in this chapter, along with a simplified presentation of tax deposits and new information about FUTA—its new rate and form. This chapter has also been streamlined from the previous edition. Students can more clearly see the relationship of the employee to the employer.

Visual Walkthrough

COACHING SUCCESS WITH IN-CHAPTER LEARNING TOOLS

 **TRY IT!**   Learning Unit 1-1

Record the following transactions into the basic accounting equation:

Cash + Salon Equipment = Accounts Payable + B. Rey, Capital

1. Bernie Rey invests $20,000 to open a hair salon company.
2. The hair salon company buys new salon equipment for $10,000, paying $4,000 down and charging the balance.

Calculate the ending balances.

- **Try It! Interactive Questions**

  NEW! Found at the end of each Learning Unit, these questions provide students a chance to check their understanding of key concepts in the unit. Linking in the eText will allow students to practice in MyAccountingLab without interrupting their interaction with the eText. Students' performance on the questions creates a precise adaptive study plan for additional practice.

- **Video Solutions**

  NEW! Found in the eText and MyAccountingLab, the video solutions feature the author walking through the Try It! questions on a white board. Designed to give students detailed help when they need it.

- **Coaching Tips**

  These kernels of advice are short, sweet, and to the point. These tips have been placed strategically throughout the text, where students are known to need a hint or reminder.

 **COACHING TIP**

In accounting, capital does not mean cash. Capital is the owner's current investment, or equity, in the assets of the business.

ACCOUNTING COACH   CHAPTER 1

The following Coaching Tips are from Learning Units 1-1 through 1-4. Take the Pre-Game Checkup and use the Check Your Score at the bottom of the page to see how you are doing. The Accounting Coach provides tips before each Checkup to help you avoid common accounting errors.

LU 1-1 Accounting, Business, and the Accounting Equation

Pre-Game Tips: After a transaction is recorded in the accounting equation, the sum of all the assets must equal the total of all the liabilities and owner's equity.

Pre-Game Checkup: Answer true or false to the following statements.

1. Capital is cash.
2. Accounts Payable is a liability.
3. A shift in assets means liabilities will increase.
4. Assets − Liabilities = Owner's Equity.
5. Assets represent what is owned by the business.

LU 1-2 The Balance Sheet

LU 1-3 The Accounting Equation Expanded: Revenue, Expenses, and Withdrawals

Pre-Game Tips: Revenue is recorded when earned even if cash is not received. Expenses are recorded when they happen (incurred) whether they are paid or to be paid later.

Pre-Game Checkup: Answer true or false to the following statements.

1. Revenue is an asset.
2. Withdrawals increase owner's equity.
3. As expenses go down, owner's equity goes down.
4. An advertising bill incurred but unpaid is recorded as an increase in Advertising Expense and a decrease in a liability.
5. Revenue inflows can only be in the form of cash.

LU 1-4 The Three Financial Statements

Pre-Game Tips: Net income from the income statement is

- **Accounting Coach**

  Each Learning Unit of the chapter is summarized as a "Pre-Game Tip," for students to review before taking the "Pre-Game Checkup." These True/False questions, created by Jeffrey Slater, the author, challenge the student to apply what's learned in each section and help students focus on the key topics in each chapter.

END-OF-CHAPTER PRACTICE MATERIAL

• ## Chapter Summary

Organized by Learning Objective, the Chapter Summary breaks down the key elements of each objective, and provides easy reference to the key terms.

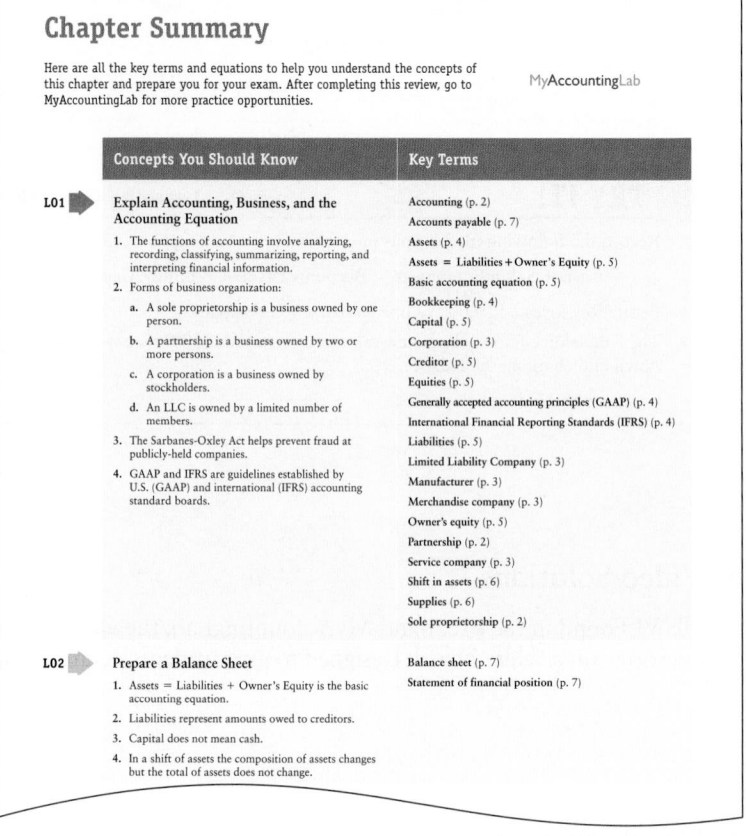

Chapter Summary

Here are all the key terms and equations to help you understand the concepts of this chapter and prepare you for your exam. After completing this review, go to MyAccountingLab for more practice opportunities.

MyAccountingLab

Concepts You Should Know	Key Terms
L01 Explain Accounting, Business, and the Accounting Equation	Accounting (p. 2)
1. The functions of accounting involve analyzing, recording, classifying, summarizing, reporting, and interpreting financial information.	Accounts payable (p. 7)
2. Forms of business organization:	Assets (p. 4)
a. A sole proprietorship is a business owned by one person.	Assets = Liabilities + Owner's Equity (p. 5)
b. A partnership is a business owned by two or more persons.	Basic accounting equation (p. 5)
c. A corporation is a business owned by stockholders.	Bookkeeping (p. 4)
d. An LLC is owned by a limited number of members.	Capital (p. 5)
3. The Sarbanes-Oxley Act helps prevent fraud at publicly-held companies.	Corporation (p. 3)
4. GAAP and IFRS are guidelines established by U.S. (GAAP) and international (IFRS) accounting standard boards.	Creditor (p. 5)
	Equities (p. 5)
	Generally accepted accounting principles (GAAP) (p. 4)
	International Financial Reporting Standards (IFRS) (p. 4)
	Liabilities (p. 5)
	Limited Liability Company (p. 3)
	Manufacturer (p. 3)
	Merchandise company (p. 3)
	Owner's equity (p. 5)
	Partnership (p. 2)
	Service company (p. 3)
	Shift in assets (p. 6)
	Supplies (p. 6)
	Sole proprietorship (p. 2)
L02 Prepare a Balance Sheet	Balance sheet (p. 7)
1. Assets = Liabilities + Owner's Equity is the basic accounting equation.	Statement of financial position (p. 7)
2. Liabilities represent amounts owed to creditors.	
3. Capital does not mean cash.	
4. In a shift of assets the composition of assets changes but the total of assets does not change.	

Discussion Questions and Critical Thinking/Ethical Case

1. What are the functions of accounting?
2. Define, compare, and contrast sole proprietorships, partnerships, and corporations.
3. How are businesses classified?
4. How has technology affected the role of the bookkeeper?
5. List the three elements of the basic accounting equation.
6. Define capital.
7. The total of the left-hand side of the accounting equation must equal the total of the right-hand side. True or false? Please explain.
8. A balance sheet tells a company where it is going and how well it performs. True or false? Please explain.
9. Revenue is an asset. True or false? Please explain.
10. Owner's equity is subdivided into what categories?
11. A withdrawal is a business expense. True or false? Please explain.

• ## Discussion Questions and Critical Thinking/Ethical Cases

The first set of end-of-chapter questions asks students to think critically about what they have just learned. They can be used in class to generate discussion or can be assigned as homework, requiring short essay answers.

Selected end-of-chapter problems are designed to be completed with Sage 50 or QuickBooks. All questions are available in MyAccountingLab.

• Concept Checks

These short exercises can be assigned as homework or discussed in class for difficult topics.

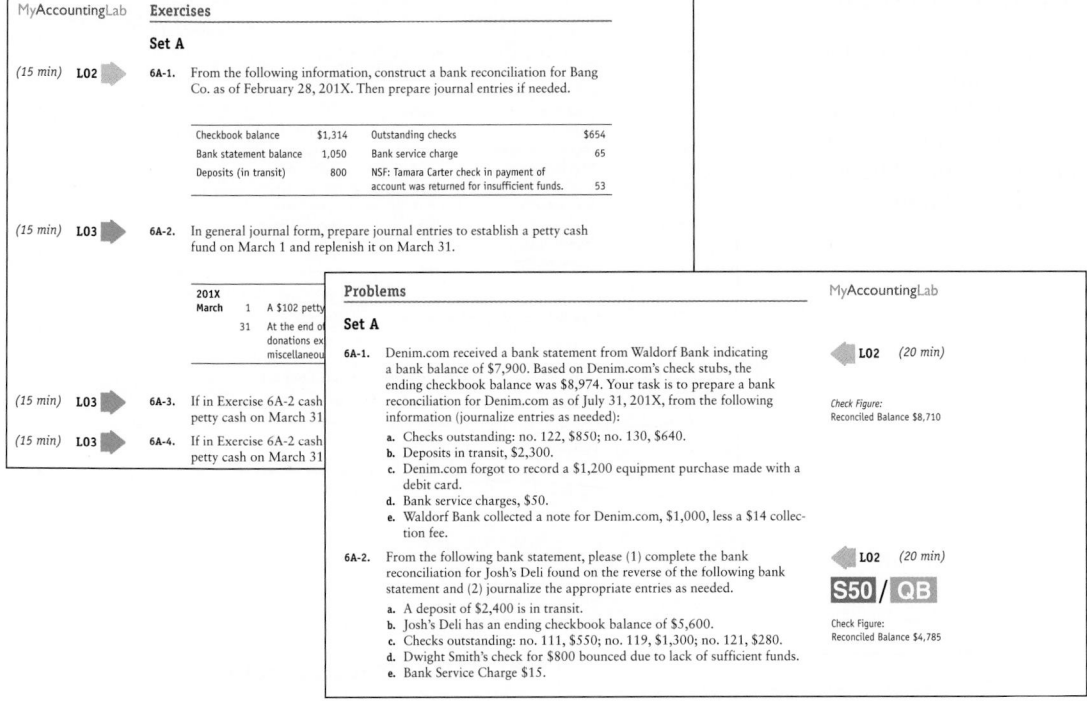

• Exercises and Problems (Sets A and B)

Each question has been updated in this new edition. Short exercises can be assigned or used in class to focus on building skills. The longer problems give students a chance to do one learning unit at a time or combine many units in one problem. These problems help put the pieces together. They're a great reinforcement of the accounting principles.

- ## Financial Report Problem

  Students use the 2013 annual financial report of the Kellogg's Company to apply theory and applications completed in the chapter.

- ## On the Job Continuing Problem

  Students follow the activities of a fictional company, *The Smith Computer Center*, and then are asked to apply concepts to solve specific accounting problems for the company. Problems can be solved manually or by using Sage 50 or QuickBooks.

Financial Report Problem

Reading the Kellogg's Annual Report

Go to http://investor.kelloggs.com/investor-relations/annual-reports/ to access the Kellogg's 2013 Annual Report and find the balance sheet of Kellogg's. Did Kellogg's Accounts Payable go up or down from 2012 to 2013? What does this change mean? Into what category does Accounts Payable fall by rules of debit and credit? Which side of the T account would make Accounts Payable increase?

LO2   *(5 min)*

ON THE JOB SMITH COMPUTER CENTER

MyAccountingLab

LO1,2,3   *(60 min)*

The Smith Computer Center created its chart of accounts as follows:

Chart of Accounts as of July 1, 201X

Assets		Revenue	
1000	Cash	4000	Service Revenue
1020	Accounts Receivable	**Expenses**	
1030	Supplies	5010	Advertising Expense
1080	Computer Shop Equipment	5020	Rent Expense
1090	Office Equipment	5030	Utilities Expense
Liabilities		5040	Phone Expense
2000	Accounts Payable	5050	Supplies Expense
Owner's Equity		5060	Insurance Expense
3000	Feldman, Capital	5070	Postage Expense
3010	Feldman, Withdrawals		

You will use this chart of accounts to complete the Continuing Problem.
The following problem continues from Chapter 1.

Assignment

1. Set up T accounts in a ledger and post the ending balances from Chapter 1.
2. Record transactions k through s in the appropriate T accounts.
3. Foot and take the balances of the T accounts where appropriate.
4. Prepare a trial balance at the end of August.
5. From the trial balance, prepare an income statement, statement of owner's

---

Mini Practice Set

Est. Time: 5 hours

Sousa Realty

Reviewing the Accounting Cycle Twice

This comprehensive review problem requires you to complete the accounting cycle for Sousa Realty twice. This practice set allows you to review Chapters 1–5 while reinforcing the relationships between all parts of the accounting cycle. By completing two cycles, you will see how the ending September balances in the ledger are used to accumulate data in October.

First, look at the chart of accounts for Sousa Realty.

Sousa Realty
Chart of Accounts

Assets	Revenue
111 Cash	411 Commissions Earned
112 Accounts Receivable	**Expenses**
114 Prepaid Rent	511 Rent Expense
115 Office Supplies	512 Salaries Expense
121 Office Equipment	513 Gas Expense

- ## Mini Practice Sets

  The in-text Sousa Realty Practice Set (Chapter 5) includes actual source documents for each transaction and The Elegant Dress Shop Practice Set (Chapter 12) enable students to complete two cycles of transactions (either manually, with Sage 50 or with QuickBooks).

• Computer Workshops

This book contains seven computer workshops to be completed with Sage 50 and QuickBooks. Detailed step-by-step instructions are available on the Student Download site, and in MyAccountingLab showing students how to take any manual problem from the end of the chapter and solve it using both types of software.

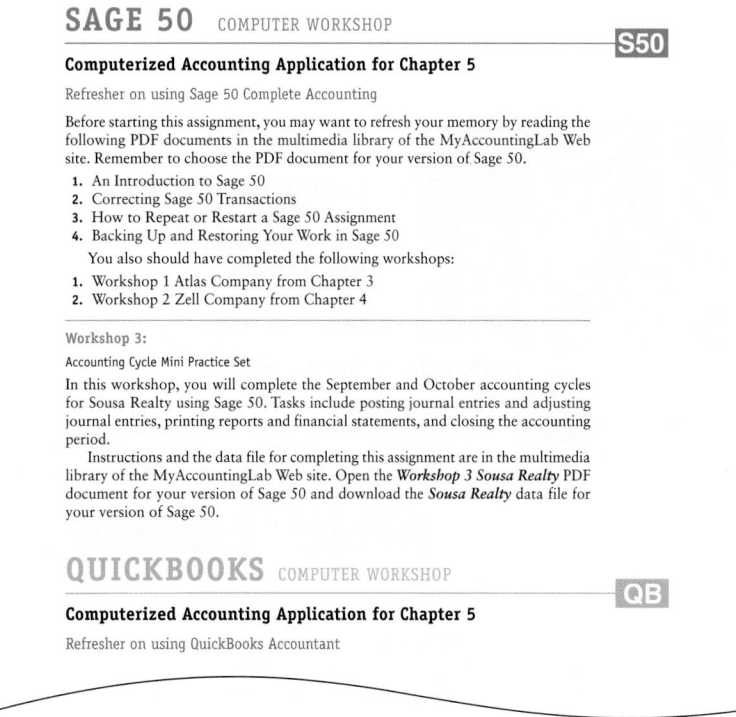

SAGE 50 COMPUTER WORKSHOP

S50

Computerized Accounting Application for Chapter 5

Refresher on using Sage 50 Complete Accounting

Before starting this assignment, you may want to refresh your memory by reading the following PDF documents in the multimedia library of the MyAccountingLab Web site. Remember to choose the PDF document for your version of Sage 50.

1. An Introduction to Sage 50
2. Correcting Sage 50 Transactions
3. How to Repeat or Restart a Sage 50 Assignment
4. Backing Up and Restoring Your Work in Sage 50

You also should have completed the following workshops:

1. Workshop 1 Atlas Company from Chapter 3
2. Workshop 2 Zell Company from Chapter 4

Workshop 3:

Accounting Cycle Mini Practice Set

In this workshop, you will complete the September and October accounting cycles for Sousa Realty using Sage 50. Tasks include posting journal entries and adjusting journal entries, printing reports and financial statements, and closing the accounting period.

Instructions and the data file for completing this assignment are in the multimedia library of the MyAccountingLab Web site. Open the *Workshop 3 Sousa Realty* PDF document for your version of Sage 50 and download the *Sousa Realty* data file for your version of Sage 50.

QUICKBOOKS COMPUTER WORKSHOP

QB

Computerized Accounting Application for Chapter 5

Refresher on using QuickBooks Accountant

SUPPLEMENTS FOR INSTRUCTORS AND STUDENTS

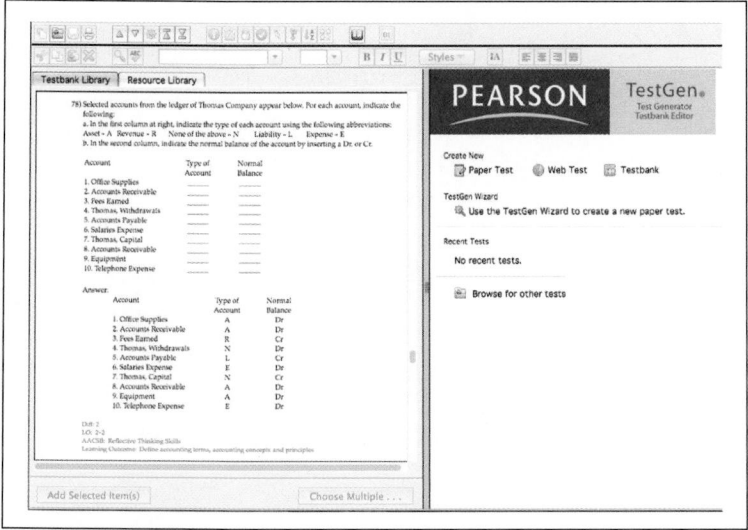

• Test Bank

NEW! The Test Bank now includes algorithmic questions. Both objective-based questions and computational problems are available throughout the over 3,000 questions in the Test Bank.

• Study Guide and Working Papers

These guides include templates to answer questions that appear in the text, including: Demonstration Summary Problems, Set A and B Exercises, Set A and B Problems, On the Job Continuing Problems, and Mini Practice Sets.

Each chapter also includes a Self-Practice Test with solutions. The Working Papers are also available in Excel Format.

• Solutions Manual

Contains solutions to all end-of-chapter questions.

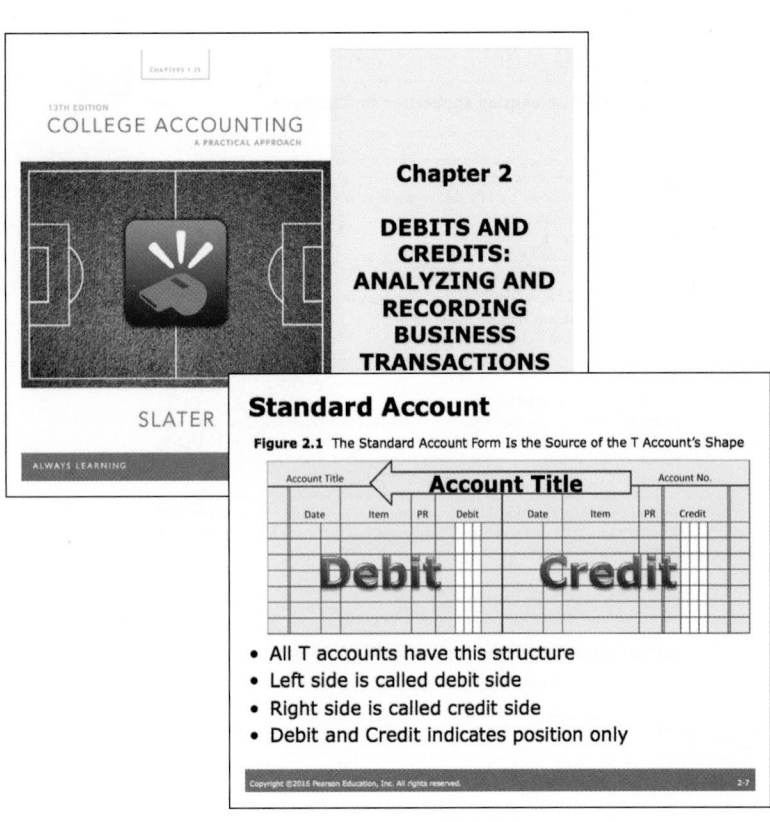

• PowerPoint Presentations

The lecture notes provided take students through the learning objectives of the chapter, using art from the text as a guide.

- Instructor PowerPoint Presentations—complete with lecture notes
- Student PowerPoint Presentations

• Instructor's Resource Manual

Each chapter of the manual is organized by Learning Objective, and offers the following resources to instructors:
- Chapter Overview
- Assignment Grid
- Summary
- Key Concepts
- Lecture Outlines

Student and Instructor Resources

MyAccountingLab

myaccountinglab.com online Homework and Assessment Manager includes:

- Pearson eText
- Student PowerPoint® Presentations
- Data Files
- Accounting Cycle Tutorial
- New! Try It! Videos
- Flash Cards
- Working Papers
- New! Learning Catalytics
- New! Dynamic Study Modules

Student Resource Web site: pearsonhighered.com/slater
The Book's Web site contains the following:

- **Data Files:** Computer Workshop files and Solutions to end-of-chapter QuickBooks and Sage 50 exercises and problems from the text, in the most recent version of each software
- **Working Papers:** In Excel Format

Students can also purchase a printed **Study Guide with Working Papers** to accompany the text.

FOR INSTRUCTORS

MyAccountingLab

myaccountinglab.com online Homework and Assessment Manager

For the instructor's convenience, the instructor resources can be downloaded from the textbook's catalog page (pearsonhighered.com/slater) and MyAccountingLab.
Available resources include the following:

- **Instructor's Resource Manual**
- **Solutions Manual**
- **Test Bank**
- **PowerPoint Presentations**
- **Working Papers**

Acknowledgments

REVIEWERS

Terry Aime, *Delgado Community College*
Cornelia Alsheimer, *Santa Barbara City College*
Barbara Anderson, *Yuba County Community College*
Julia Angel, *North Arkansas College*
Julie Armstrong, *St. Clair County Community College*
Marjorie Ashton, *Truckee Meadows Community College*
Barbara Aue, *Santa Barbara City College*
John Babich, *Kankakee Community College*
Cecil Battiste, *Valencia Community College*
Donald Benoit, *Mitchell College*
Peggy A. Berrier, *Ivy Technical State College*
Michelle Berube, *Everest University*
Becky Beydler, *State Fair Community College*
Anne Bikofsky, *College of Westchester*
Michael Bitting, *John A. Logan College*
David Bland, *Cape Fear Community College*
Suzanne Bradford, *Angelina College*
Beverly Bugay, *Tyler Junior College*
Gary Bumgarner, *Mountain Empire Community College*
Allyson Carmichael, *Florence-Darlington Technical College*
Ricardo Colon, *Lamar University*
Betsy Crane, *Victoria College*
Noel Craven, *El Camino College*
Don Curfman, *McHenry County College*
John Daugherty, *Pitt Community College*
Susan Davis, *Green River Community College*
Michael Discello, *Pittsburgh Technical Institute*
Sylvia Dorsey, *Florence-Darlington Technical College*
Sid Downey, *Cochise College*
Donna Eakman, *Great Falls College of Technology*
Steven Ernest, *Baton Rouge Community College*
John Evanson, *Williston State College*
Marilyn Ewing, *Seward County Community College*
Nancy Fallon, *Albertus Magnus College*
Nicole Fife, *Bucks County Community College*
Brian Fink, *Danville Area Community College*
Paul Fisher, *Rogue Community College*
Carolyn Fitzmorris, *Hutchinson Community College*
Trish Glennon, *Central Florida Community College*
Nancy Goehring, *Monterey Peninsula College*
Jane Goforth, *North Seattle Community College*
Lori Grady, *Bucks County Community College*
Gretchen Graham, *Community College of Allegheny County*
Marina Grau, *Houston Community College*
Mary Jane Green, *Des Moines Area Community College*
Joyce Griffin, *Kansas City Kansas Community College*

Becky Hancock, *El Paso Community College*
Toni Hartley, *Laurel Business Institute*
Raymond Hartman, *Triton Community College*
Scott Hays, *Central Oregon Community College*
Kathy Hebert, *Louisiana Technical College*
Sueanne Hely, *West Kentucky Community & Technical College*
Maggie Hilgart, *Mid-State Technical College*
Michele Hill, *Schoolcraft College*
Michelle Hoeflich, *Elgin Community College*
Mary Hollars, *Vincennes University*
Donna Jacobs, *University of New Mexico-Gallup*
Judy Jager, *Pikes Peak Community College*
Jane Jones, *Mountain Empire Community College*
Jenny Jones, *Central Kentucky Technical College*
Patrick Jozefowicz, *Southwest Wisconsin Technical College*
Mark Justice, *Blue Mountain Community College*
Dimitriy Kalyagin, *Chabot College*
Nancy Kelly, *Middlesex Community College*
Karen Kettelson, *Western Wisconsin Technical College*
Elizabeth King, *Sacramento City College*
Ken Koerber, *Bucks County Community College*
Elida Kraja, *St. Louis Community College*
David Krug, *Johnson County Community College*
Christy Land, *Catawba Valley Community College*
Ronald Larner, *John Wood Community College*
Lee Leksell, *Lake Superior College*
Lolita Lockett, *Florida Community College at Jacksonville*
Bonnie Malcolm, *Southeast Community College*
Sue Mardock, *Colby Community College*
John Masserwick, *Five Towns College*
Pam Mattson, *Tulsa Community College*
Bonnie Mayer, *Lakeshore Technical College*
Sally McMillin, *Katharine Gibbs School*
John Miller, *Metropolitan Community College*
Susan L. Miller, *Delaware County Community College*
Cora Newcomb, *Technical College of Lowcountry*
Jon Nitschke, *Great Falls Technical College*
Christine Noel, *Metropolitan Community College*
Lorinda Oliver, *Vermont Technical College*
Rukshad Patel, *College of DuPage*
Barbara Pauer, *Gateway Technical College*
Nicholas Peppes, *St. Louis Community College*
Richard Pettit, *Mountain View College*
Lisa Phillips, *City College*
Margaret Pollard, *American River College*
Shirley Powell, *Arkansas State University*

Linda Prescott, *Hillsborough Community College*
Claudia Quinn, *San Joaquin Delta College*
Jerry Rhodes, *Daymar College*
Ed Richter, *Southeast Technical Institute*
Alberta Robinson, *Indiana Business College*
Beth Sanders, *Hawaii Community College*
Bob Sanner, *Central Community College*
Debra Schmidt, *Cerritos College*
Karen Scott, *Bates Technical College*
Carolyn Seefer, *Diablo Valley College*
Pamela Shaw, *Southwestern Community College*
Jeri Spinner, *Idaho State University*
Alice Steljes, *Illinois Valley Community College*
Jack Stone, *Linn-Benton Community College*
Carolyn Strauch, *Crowder College*
Rick Street, *Spokane Community College*
Domenico Tavella, *Pittsburgh Technical Institute*
Bill Taylor, *Cossatot Community College*
Mary J. Tobaben, *Collin County Community College*
Ron J. Trucks, *Jefferson College*
Elaine Tuttle, *Bellevue Community College*
Ski Vanderlaan, *Delta College*
Andy Williams, *Edmonds Community College*
Jack Williams, *Tulsa Community College*

Supplement Authors and Invaluable Assistance

Study Guide and Working Papers: Carolyn Streuly, and Barbara Aue, *Santa Barbara Community College*
Solutions Manual: Judith Zander, *Grossmont Community College*
Instructor's Resource Manual: Carolyn Strauch, *Crowder College*
Test Bank: William Jefferson, *Metropolitan Community College*, and Daniel Kerch, *Pennsylvania Highlands Community College*
PowerPoint Presentations: Erin Dischler, *Milwaukee Area Technical College*
Sage 50/QuickBooks Problems and Computerized Workshops: Terri Brunsdon, CITP, CPA, JD/MT
Update of Chapters 7, 8, and Mini Practice Set: The Elegant Dress Shop: Linda Flowers, *Houston Community College*
Text Accuracy Checkers: Becky Beydler, *State Fair Community College*, Carolyn Streuly
Supplement Quality Assurance: Carolyn Streuly, Mary Strayer

About the Author

Jeff Slater teaches at the North Shore Community College in Danver, Massachusetts, where he was voted Teacher of the Year. Additionally, he has acted as a consultant for the federal office of personnel management, training personnel in government bookkeeping and accounting. Jeff has traveled the country speaking about class retention in Accounting courses.

He has been author or co-author of over ten college textbooks, including the following Pearson titles:

- Basic College Mathematics
- Beginning Algebra
- College Accounting
- Intermediate Algebra
- Prealgebra

Jeff lives with his wife: Shelley, and Golden Doodle: Bernie. He has two children: Abby and Russell, and four grandchildren: Matt, Mia, Sam, and Hope. In his spare time, he enjoys collecting vintage toys and vintage auto parts.

IN HIS OWN WORDS

"Talk to your students, not at them." In my 45 years of teaching I've learned that you need to show students you care about them. I love to take complicated material and break it down into simple steps to enhance learning. I believe in repetition: "Say it once, say it again." Talking about real world examples and how it relates to accounting theory makes the class come alive.

I WANT TO HEAR FROM YOU

Students know that I love what I do . . . They are my customers and they need to be served in a professional manner. Please e-mail me at jeffslater@aol.com, and I promise to get back to you within 24 hours or less.

Accounting Concepts and Procedures

CHAPTER PREVIEW: THE BIG PICTURE

Pam Sullivan has been searching the Web for the best deal on a Microsoft Surface Pro tablet. She decided the best deal for her was on eBay. She found a manufacturer-refurbished tablet that had an original price of $695 marked down to $499. Payment could be made via PayPal using a major credit card or with an electronic check. Pam wondered how eBay could keep track of all of the millions of sales transactions each day. Her accounting professor told her that eBay tracks the sale in its version of a PayPal account called the Revenue account. In this chapter we will see how a company records transactions and communicates its sales to the business world. In 2015 eBay and PayPal will become independent companies.

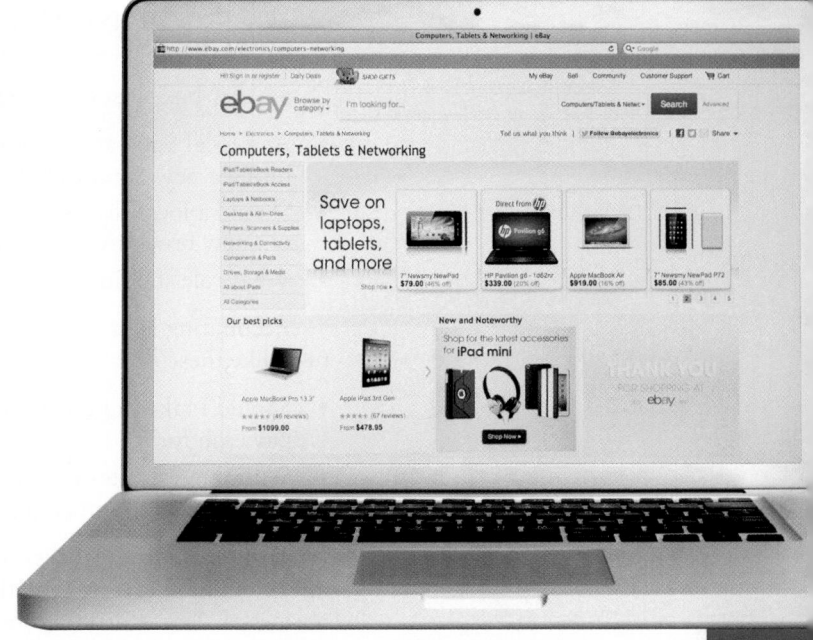

Learning Objectives

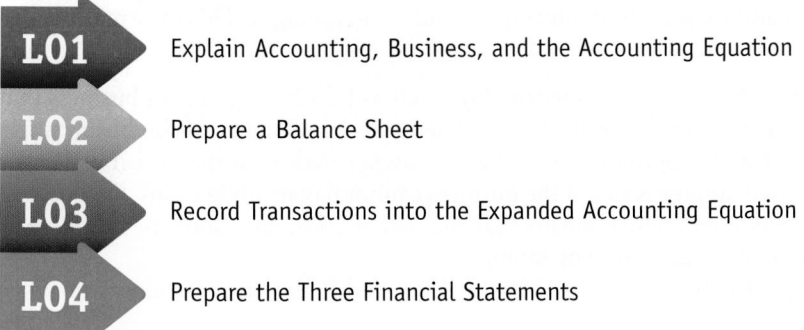

LO1   Explain Accounting, Business, and the Accounting Equation

LO2   Prepare a Balance Sheet

LO3   Record Transactions into the Expanded Accounting Equation

LO4   Prepare the Three Financial Statements

Accounting, Business, and the Accounting Equation

Accounting A system that measures the business's activities in financial terms, provides written reports and financial statements about those activities, and communicates these reports to decision makers and others.

Companies like eBay have to comply with many federal statutes. The Sarbanes-Oxley Act is a federal statute passed to prevent fraud at publicly-held companies. This act requires a closer look at the internal controls and the accuracy of the financial results of a company.

Accounting is the language of business; it provides information to managers, owners, investors, government agencies, and others inside and outside the organization. Accounting provides answers and insights to questions like these:

- Which computer software will best fit our company?
- Should I invest in Facebook or Apple stock?
- How will increasing fuel costs affect Jet Blue?
- Can Boeing pay its debt obligations?
- What percentage of the Walmart marketing budget is allocated to e-business? How does that percentage compare with that of the competition? What is the overall financial condition of Walmart?

Smaller businesses also need answers to their financial questions:

- At a local Subway, did business increase enough over the last year to warrant hiring a new Sandwich Artist?
- Should a local real estate agency spend more money to design, produce, and send out new brochures in an effort to generate more home listings and sales?
- What role should social media play in the future of business spending?

Accounting is as important to individuals as it is to businesses; it answers questions like these:

- Should I take out a loan to buy a new computer or wait until I can afford to pay cash for it?
- With interest rates fluctuating, would my money work better in a money market or in the stock market?

The accounting process analyzes, records, classifies, summarizes, reports, and interprets financial information for decision makers—whether individuals, small businesses, large corporations, or governmental agencies—in a timely fashion. It is important that students understand the "whys" of this accounting process. Just knowing the mechanics is not enough.

Types of Business Organizations

The four main categories of business organizations are (1) sole proprietorships, (2) partnerships, (3) corporations, and (4) limited liability companies. Let's define each of them and look at their advantages and disadvantages. This information also appears in Table 1.1, page 3.

Sole proprietorship A type of business organization that has one owner. The owner is personally liable for paying the business's debts.

Sole Proprietorship. A sole proprietorship, such as Jill's Nail Care, is a business that has one owner. That person is both the owner and the manager of the business. An advantage of a sole proprietorship is that the owner makes all the decisions for the business. A disadvantage is that if the business cannot pay its obligations, the business owner must pay them, which means that the owner could lose some or all of his or her personal assets (e.g., house or savings).

Sole proprietorships are easy to form. They end if the business closes or when the owner dies.

Partnership A form of business organization that has at least two owners. The partners usually are personally liable for the partnership's debts.

Partnership. A partnership, such as Hope and Sam, is a form of business ownership that has at least two owners (partners). Each partner acts as an owner of the company, which is an advantage because the partners can share the decision making and the risks of the business usually outlined in a partnership agreement. A disadvantage

TABLE 1.1 Types of Business Organizations

	Sole Proprietorship (Jill's Nail Care)	Partnerships (Hope and Sam)	Corporation (Facebook)	Limited Liability Companies (LLC)
Ownership	Business owned by one person.	Business owned by more than one person.	Business owned by stockholders.	Business owned by a limited number of members.
Formation	No formal filing or agreement necessary to form.	Requires a partnership agreement to define the terms of partnership.	Requires filing with the state to be recognized.	Requires filing with the state a document called articles of incorporation.
Liability	Owner could lose personal assets to meet obligations of business.	Partners could lose personal assets to meet obligations of partnership.	Limited personal risk. Stockholders' loss is limited to their investment in the company.	Limited personal risk. Members loss is limited to their investment.
Closing	Ends with death of owner or closing of business.	Ends with death of partner or closing of business.	Can continue indefinitely.	May end with death of member.

is that, as in a sole proprietorship, the partners' personal assets could be lost if the partnership cannot meet its obligations.

Partnerships are easy to form. They end when a partner dies or leaves the partnership, or when the partners decide to close the business.

Corporation. A corporation, such as Facebook, is a business owned by stockholders. The corporation may have only a few stockholders, or it may have many. The stockholders are not personally liable for the corporation's debts, and they usually do not have input into the business's decisions.

Corporations are more difficult to form than sole proprietorships or partnerships, as the corporation must file with the state in order to gain the protections provided by this form of business. Corporations can exist indefinitely.

Limited Liability Company (LLC). A limited liability company, such as the law firm of Battista, Tucker and Sam, LLC, is a business owned by a few members. The members are liable only to the extent of their investment in the firm and, unlike a corporation, have input into the business's decisions. Like corporations, the LLC must file with the state in which it does business in order to gain the liability protection of this form of business.

Classifying Business Organizations

Whether we are looking at a sole proprietorship, a partnership, or a corporation, the business can be classified by what it does to earn money. Companies are categorized as service, merchandise, or manufacturing businesses.

A limo service is a good example of a service company because it provides a service. The first part of this book focuses on service businesses.

Gap and Pottery Barn sell products. They are called merchandise companies. Merchandise companies can either make their own products or sell products that are made by another supplier. Companies such as Levi Strauss and Company and Ford Motor Company that make their own products are called manufacturers. (See Table 1.2, page 4.)

Definition of Accounting

Accounting (also called the accounting process) is a system that measures the activities of a business in financial terms. It provides reports and financial statements that show how the various transactions the business undertook (e.g., buying and selling goods) affected the business. This accounting process performs the following functions:

- **Analyzing:** Looking at what happened and how the business was affected.
- **Recording:** Putting the information into the accounting system.

Corporation A type of business organization that is owned by stockholders. Stockholders usually are not personally liable for the corporation's debts.

Limited Liability Company A type of business organization that is owned by a few members. Members are only liable to the extent of their investment.

Service company Business that provides a service.

Merchandise company Business that makes its own products or buys a product from a manufacturing company to sell to its customers.

Manufacturer Business that makes a product and sells it to its customers.

TABLE 1.2 Examples of Service, Merchandise, and Manufacturing Businesses

Service Businesses	Merchandise Businesses	Manufacturing Businesses
Jill's Nail Care	Pottery Barn	Hershey's
Facebook	Best Buy	Ford Motor Company
Dr. Wheeler, M.D.	Amazon.com	Toro
Accountemps	Home Depot	Levi Strauss and Company
Langley Landscaping	Gap	Brunswick

- **Classifying:** Grouping all the same activities (e.g., all purchases) together.
- **Summarizing:** Totaling the results.
- **Reporting:** Issuing the statements that tell the results of the previous functions.
- **Interpreting:** Examining the statements to determine how the various pieces of information they contain relate to each other.
- **Communication:** Providing the reports and financial statements to people who are interested in the information, such as the business's decision makers, investors, creditors, and government agencies (e.g., the Internal Revenue Service).

As you can see, a lot of people use these reports. A set of procedures and guidelines was developed to make sure that everyone prepares and interprets them the same way. These guidelines are known as generally accepted accounting principles (GAAP). International Financial Reporting Standards (IFRS) are a group of guidelines developed by the International Accounting Standards Board. The United States is considering some changes from GAAP to IFRS. No final decisions will be made until 2017.

Now let's look at the difference between bookkeeping and accounting. Keep in mind that we use the terms *accounting* and the *accounting process* interchangeably.

Computer Software and the Bookkeeper

Bookkeeping is the recording (record keeping) function of the accounting process. Today, computers are used for routine bookkeeping operations that formerly took weeks or months to complete. This book explains the processes and logical steps behind those operations, giving the reader the hands-on knowledge that a bookkeeper needs even though computers perform many tasks. Bookkeepers today need to be trained to use the latest computer software that is available, including QuickBooks, Excel, and Sage 50.

An accountant takes the bookkeeping records and prepares the financial statements that are used to analyze the company's financial position. Accounting involves many complex activities. Often, it includes the preparation of tax and financial reports, budgeting, and analyses of financial information.

The Accounting Equation: Assets, Liabilities, and Equities

Let's begin our study of accounting concepts and procedures by looking at a small business: Mia Wong's law practice. Mia decided to open her practice at the end of August. She consulted her accountant before she made her decision, and he gave her some important information. First, he told her the new business would be considered a separate business entity whose finances had to be kept separate and distinct from Mia's personal finances. The accountant went on to say that all transactions can be analyzed using the basic accounting equation: Assets = Liabilities + Owner's Equity.

Mia had never heard of the basic accounting equation. She listened carefully as the accountant explained the terms used in the equation and how the equation works.

Assets. Cash, land, supplies, office equipment, buildings, and other properties of value *owned* by a firm are called assets.

Generally accepted accounting principles (GAAP) The procedures and guidelines that must be followed during the accounting process.

International Financial Reporting Standards (IFRS) A group of accounting standards and procedures that if adopted by the U.S., could replace GAAP.

Bookkeeping The recording function of the accounting process.

Assets Properties (resources) of value owned by a business (cash, supplies, equipment, land).

Equities. The rights or financial claims to the assets are called equities. Equities belong to those who supply the assets. If you are the only person to supply assets to the firm, you have the sole rights or financial claims to them. For example, if you supply the law firm with $6,000 in cash and $8,000 in office equipment, your equity in the firm is $14,000.

Equities The rights or financial claims of creditors (liabilities) and owners (owner's equity) who supply the assets to a firm.

Relationship between Assets and Equities. The relationship between assets and equities is

Assets = Equities

(Total value of items *owned* by business)   (Total claims against the assets)

The total dollar value of the assets of your law firm will be equal to the total dollar value of the financial claims to those assets, that is, equal to the total dollar value of the equities.

The total dollar value is broken down on the left-hand side of the equation to show the specific items of value owned by the business and on the right-hand side to show the types of claims against the assets owned.

Liabilities. A firm may have to borrow money to buy more assets; when it does, it *buys assets on account* (buy now, pay later). Suppose the law firm purchases a new computer for $3,000 on account from Dell, and the company is willing to wait 10 days for payment. The law firm has created a liability: an obligation to pay that comes due in the future. Dell is called the creditor. This liability—the amount owed to Dell—gives the company the right, or the financial claim, to $3,000 of the law firm's assets. When Dell is paid, the company's rights to the assets of the law firm will end because the obligation has been paid off.

Liabilities Obligations that come due in the future. Liabilities are the financial rights or claims of creditors to assets.

Creditor Someone who has a claim to assets.

Basic Accounting Equation. To best understand the various claims to a business's assets, accountants divide equities into two parts. The claims of creditors—outside persons or businesses—are labeled *liabilities*. The claim of the business's owner is labeled owner's equity. Let's see how the accounting equation looks now.

Owner's equity Rights or financial claims to the assets of a business (in the accounting equation, assets minus liabilities).

Assets = **Equities**

1. Liabilities: rights of creditors
2. Owner's equity: rights of owner

Assets = Liabilities + Owner's Equity

The total value of all the assets of a firm equals the combined total value of the financial claims of the creditors (liabilities) and the claims of the owners (owner's equity). This calculation is known as the basic accounting equation. The basic accounting equation provides a basis for understanding the conventional accounting system of a business. The equation records business transactions in a logical and orderly way that shows their impact on the company's assets, liabilities, and owner's equity.

Basic accounting equation Assets = Liabilities + Owner's Equity.

Importance of Creditors. Another way of presenting the basic accounting equation is

Assets − Liabilities = Owner's Equity

This form of the equation stresses the importance of creditors. The owner's rights to the business's assets are determined after the rights of the creditors are subtracted. In other words, creditors have first claim to assets. If a firm has no liabilities—therefore no creditors—the owner has the total rights to assets. Another term for the owner's current investment, or equity, in the business's assets is capital.

As Mia Wong's law firm engages in business transactions (paying bills, serving customers, and so on), changes will take place in the assets, liabilities, and owner's equity (capital). Let's analyze some of these transactions.

Capital The owner's investment of equity in the company.

COACHING TIP

In accounting, capital does not mean cash. Capital is the owner's current investment, or equity, in the assets of the business.

Transaction A Aug. 28: Mia invests $6,000 in cash and $200 of office equipment into the business.

On August 28, Mia withdraws $6,000 from her personal bank account and deposits the money in the law firm's newly opened bank account. She also invests $200 of office equipment in the business. She plans to be open for business on September 1. With the help of her accountant, Mia begins to prepare the accounting records for the business. We put this information into the basic accounting equation as follows:

Assets			= Liabilities + Owner's Equity	
Cash	+	Office Equipment	=	Mia Wong, Capital
Transaction	+ $6,000	+	+ $200	=	+ $6,200

$$\$6,200 = \$6,200$$

Note that the total value of the assets, cash, and office equipment—$6,200—is equal to the combined total value of liabilities (none, so far) and owner's equity ($6,200). Remember, Mia has supplied all the cash and office equipment, so she has the sole financial claim to the assets. Note how the heading "Mia Wong, Capital" is written under the owner's equity heading. The $6,200 is Mia's investment, or equity, in the firm's assets.

Transaction B Aug. 29: Law practice buys office equipment for cash, $500.

Supplies One type of asset acquired by a firm; it has a much shorter life than equipment.

From the initial investment of $6,000 cash, the law firm buys $500 worth of office equipment (such as a computer desk), which lasts a long time, whereas supplies (such as pens) tend to be used up relatively quickly.

	Assets			= Liabilities + Owner's Equity
	Cash	+	Office Equipment	=	Mia Wong, Capital
Beginning Balance	$6,000	+	$200	=	$6,200
Transaction	−500		+500		
Ending Balance	$5,500	+	$700	=	$6,200

$$\$6,200 = \$6,200$$

Shift in assets A shift that occurs when the composition of the assets has changed but the total of the assets remains the same.

Shift in Assets. As a result of the last transaction, the law office has less cash but has increased its amount of office equipment. This shift in assets indicates that the makeup of the assets has changed, but the total of the assets remains the same.

Suppose you go food shopping at Walmart with $100 and spend $60. Now you have two assets, food and money. The composition of your assets has *shifted*—you have more food and less money than you did—but the *total* of the assets has not increased or decreased. The total value of the food, $60, plus the cash, $40, is still $100. When you borrow money from the bank, on the other hand, you increase cash (an asset) and increase liabilities at the same time. This action results in an increase in assets, not just a shift.

An accounting equation can remain in balance even if only one side is updated. The key point to remember is that the left-hand-side total of assets must always equal the right-hand-side total of liabilities and owner's equity.

Transaction C Aug. 30: Law firm buys additional office equipment on account, $300.

The law firm purchases an additional $300 worth of chairs and desks from Wilmington Company. Instead of demanding cash right away, Wilmington agrees to deliver the equipment and to allow up to 60 days for the law practice to pay the invoice (bill).

This liability, or obligation to pay in the future, has some interesting effects on the basic accounting equation. Wilmington Company accepts as payment a partial claim against the assets of the law practice. This claim exists until the law firm pays off the bill. This unwritten promise to pay the creditor is a liability called accounts payable.

Accounts payable Amounts owed to creditors that result from the purchase of goods or services on account—a liability.

Assets			=	Liabilities	+	Owner's Equity	
Cash	+	Office Equipment	=	Accounts Payable	+	Mia Wong, Capital	
$5,500	+	$700	=			$6,200	Beginning Balance
		+300		+$300			Transaction
$5,500	+	$1,000	=	$300	+	$6,200	Ending Balance

$$\$6,500 = \$6,500$$

When this information is analyzed, we can see that the law practice increased what it owes (accounts payable) as well as what it owns (office equipment) by $300. The law practice gains $300 in an asset but also takes on an obligation to pay Wilmington Company at a future date.

The owner's equity remains unchanged. This transaction results in an increase of total assets from $6,200 to $6,500.

Finally, note that after each transaction the basic accounting equation remains in balance. Now it's your turn to see if you understood what we have covered. This TRY IT! feature will be found after each learning unit. The solutions are at end of the chapter following the blueprint.

 TRY IT!   **Learning Unit 1-1**

Record the following transactions into the basic accounting equation:

Cash + Salon Equipment = Accounts Payable + B. Rey, Capital

1. Bernie Rey invests $20,000 to open a hair salon company.
2. The hair salon company buys new salon equipment for $10,000, paying $4,000 down and charging the balance.

Calculate the ending balances.

The Balance Sheet

LEARNING UNIT 1-2

 L02

In the first learning unit, the transactions for Mia Wong's law firm were recorded in the accounting equation. The transactions we recorded occurred before the law firm opened for business. A statement called a balance sheet or statement of financial position can show the financial position of a company before it opened. The balance sheet is a formal statement that presents the information from the ending balances of both sides of the accounting equation. Think of the balance sheet as a snapshot of the business's financial position as of a particular date.

Let's look at the balance sheet of Mia Wong's law practice for August 31, 201X, shown in Figure 1.1, page 8. The figures in the balance sheet come from the ending balances of the accounting equation for the law practice as shown in Learning Unit 1-1.

Note in Figure 1.1 that the assets owned by the law practice appear on the left-hand side and that the liabilities and owner's equity appear on the right-hand side. Both sides equal $6,500. This *balance* between left and right gives the balance sheet its name. In later chapters we look at other ways to set up a balance sheet.

Balance sheet A statement, as of a particular date, that shows the amount of assets owned by a business as well as the amount of claims (liabilities and owner's equity) against these assets. Also known as **statement of financial position**.

FIGURE 1.1
The Balance Sheet

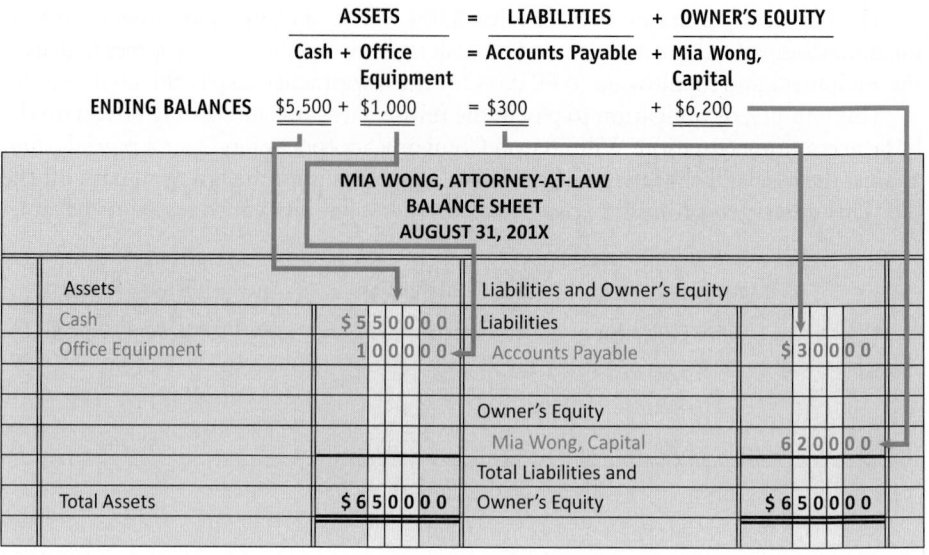

COACHING TIP

The balance sheet shows the company's financial position as of a particular date. (In our example, that date is at the end of August.)

Points to Remember in Preparing a Balance Sheet

The Heading. The heading of the balance sheet provides the following information:

- The company name: Mia Wong, Attorney-at-Law
- The name of the statement: Balance Sheet
- The date for which the report is prepared: August 31, 201X

Use of the Dollar Sign. Note that the dollar sign is not repeated each time a figure appears. As shown in Figure 1.2, the balance sheet for Mia Wong's law practice, it usually is placed to the left of each column's top figure and to the left of the column's total.

FIGURE 1.2 Partial Balance Sheet

Distinguishing the Total. If you are using a paper ledger, when adding numbers down a column, use a single line above the total and a double line beneath it. A single line means that the numbers above it have been added or subtracted. A double line indicates a total. These rules are the same for all accounting reports. With computer software today, the dollar sign and total are just a click away as the balance sheet's layout is pre-programmed.

The balance sheet gives Mia the information she needs to see the law firm's financial position before it opens for business. This information does not tell her, however, whether the firm made a profit.

 **TRY IT!**   Learning Unit 1-2

From the following prepare a balance sheet in proper form:

Flynn Company; November 30, 201X; iPads $4,000; Accounts Payable $3,000; Pete Flynn, Capital $9,000; Cash $8,000

The Accounting Equation Expanded: Revenue, Expenses, and Withdrawals

 **LEARNING UNIT 1-3**

L03

As soon as Mia Wong's office opened on September 1, she began performing legal services for her clients and earning revenue for the business. At the same time, as a part of doing business, she incurred various expenses such as rent. Mia's accountant explained there are two types of accounting systems to record business transactions: the cash basis system and the accrual basis system. In the cash basis system, revenues are recorded when cash is received, and expenses are recorded when cash is paid. Some small businesses use this method, and individuals use the cash basis to do their personal income taxes. In the accrual basis system, revenue transactions are recorded when they are earned (not when money is received), and expenses are recorded when they are incurred (or happen) whether paid in cash or not. The accountant told Mia that she would be using the accrual basis system of accounting because this system matches revenues and expenses in the same time period (not just when cash is paid). Now let's look at how the revenue transaction is recorded for Mia's business.

Revenue

A service company earns revenue when it provides services to its clients. Mia's law firm earned revenue when she provided legal services to her clients for legal fees. When revenue is earned, owner's equity is increased. In effect, revenue is a subdivision of owner's equity.

Assets are increased. The increase is in the form of cash if the client pays right away. If the client promises to pay in the future, the increase is called accounts receivable. When revenue is earned, the transaction is recorded as an increase in revenue and an increase in assets (either as cash or as accounts receivable, depending on whether it was paid right away or will be paid in the future).

Expenses

A business's expenses are the costs the company incurs in carrying on operations in its effort to create revenue. Expenses are also a subdivision of owner's equity; when expenses are incurred, they *decrease* owner's equity. Expenses can be paid for in cash or they can be charged.

Net Income/Net Loss

When revenue totals more than expenses, net income is the result; when expenses total more than revenue, net loss is the result.

Withdrawals

At some point Mia Wong may need to withdraw cash or other assets from the business to pay living or other personal expenses that do not relate to the business. We will record these transactions in an account called withdrawals. Sometimes this account is called the *owner's drawing account*. Withdrawals is a subdivision of owner's equity that records personal expenses not related to the business. Withdrawals decrease owner's equity (see Figure 1.3, page 10).

Cash basis An accounting system that records revenue when cash is received and expenses when paid. This system does not match revenues and expenses like in the accrual basis of accounting.

Accrual basis An accounting system that matches revenues when earned with expenses that are incurred.

Revenue An amount earned by performing services for customers or selling goods to customers; it can be in the form of cash or accounts receivable. A subdivision of owner's equity: As revenue increases, owner's equity increases.

Accounts receivable An asset that indicates amounts owed by customers.

Expense A cost incurred in running a business by consuming goods or services in producing revenue. A subdivision of owner's equity.

Net income When revenue totals more than expenses, the result is net income.

Net loss When expenses total more than revenue, the result is net loss.

Withdrawals A subdivision of owner's equity that records money or other assets an owner withdraws from a business for personal use.

FIGURE 1.3
Owner's Equity

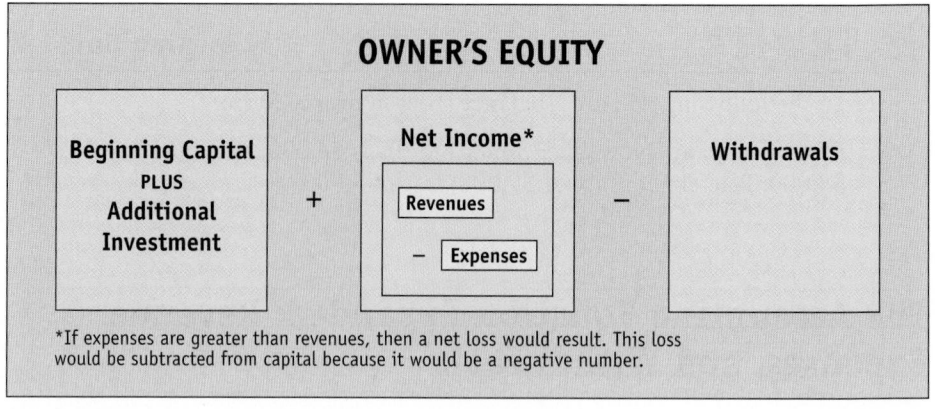

*If expenses are greater than revenues, then a net loss would result. This loss would be subtracted from capital because it would be a negative number.

It is important to remember the difference between expenses and withdrawals. Expenses relate to business operations; withdrawals are the result of personal needs outside the normal operations of the business.

Now let's analyze the September transactions for Mia Wong's law firm using an expanded accounting equation that includes withdrawals, revenues, and expenses.

Expanded accounting equation Assets = Liabilities + Capital – Withdrawals + Revenue – Expenses.

Expanded Accounting Equation

Transaction D Sept. 1–30: Provided legal services for cash, $2,000.

Transactions A, B, and C were discussed earlier, when the law office was being formed in August. See Learning Unit 1-1.

Assets			=	Liabilities	+			Owner's Equity				
Cash	+ Accts. Rec.	+ Office Equip.	=	Accts. Pay.	+	M. Wong, Capital	–	M. Wong, Withdr.	+	Revenue	– Expenses	
$5,500		+ $1,000	=	$ 300	+	$6,200						Balance Forward
+2,000										+$2,000		Transaction
$7,500		+ $1,000	=	$ 300	+	$6,200			+	$2,000		Ending Balance
		$8,500	=	$8,500								

In the law firm's first month of operation, a total of $2,000 in cash was received for legal services performed. In the accounting equation, the asset Cash is increased by $2,000. Revenue is also increased by $2,000, resulting in an increase in total owner's equity.

A revenue column was added to the basic accounting equation. Amounts are recorded in the revenue column when they are earned. They are also recorded in the assets column under Cash and/or Accounts Receivable (see also Transaction E below). Do not think of revenue as an asset. It is part of owner's equity. It is the revenue that creates an inward flow of cash and accounts receivable.

COACHING TIP

Remember: Accounts receivables result from earning revenue even when cash is not yet received.

Record an expense when it is incurred, whether it is paid immediately or is to be paid later.

Transaction E Sept. 1–30: Provided legal services on account, $3,000.

Mia's law practice performed legal work on account for $3,000. The firm did not receive the cash for these earned legal fees; it accepted an unwritten promise from these clients that payment would be received in the future.

Assets			= Liabilities +		Owner's Equity			
Cash	+ Accts. Rec.	+ Office Equip.	= Accts. Pay.	+ M. Wong, Capital	− M. Wong, Withdr.	+ Revenue	− Expenses	
$7,500		+ $ 1,000	= $ 300	+ $6,200		+ $2,000		Bal. Forward
	+$3,000					+$3,000		Transaction
$7,500 +	$3,000 +	$ 1,000	= $ 300	+ $6,200		+ $5,000		End. Bal.
		$11,500	= $11,500					

Transaction F Sept. 1–30: Received $900 cash as partial payment from previous services performed on account.

During September some of Mia's clients who had received services and promised to pay in the future decided to reduce what they owed the practice by making payment of $900. This decision is shown as follows on the expanded accounting equation:

Assets			= Liabilities	+	Owner's Equity			
Cash	+ Accts. Rec.	+ Office Equip.	= Accts. Pay.	+ M. Wong, Capital	− M. Wong, Withdr.	+ Revenue	− Expenses	
$7,500 +	$3,000 +	$ 1,000	= $ 300	+ $6,200		+ $5,000		Bal. Forward
+900	−900							Transaction
$8,400 +	$2,100 +	$ 1,000	= $ 300	+ $6,200		+ $5,000		End. Bal.
		$11,500	= $11,500					

The law firm increased the asset Cash by $900 and reduced another asset, Accounts Receivable, by $900. The *total* of assets does not change. The right-hand side of the expanded accounting equation has not been touched because the total on the left-hand side of the equation has not changed. The revenue was recorded when it was earned (see Transaction E), and the *same revenue cannot be recorded twice.* This transaction analyzes the situation *after* the revenue has been previously earned and recorded. Transaction F shows a shift in assets resulting in more cash and less accounts receivable.

Transaction G Sept. 1–30: Paid salaries expense, $700.

Assets			= Liabilities	+	Owner's Equity			
Cash	+ Accts. Rec.	+ Office Equip.	= Accts. Pay.	+ M. Wong, Capital	− M. Wong, Withdr.	+ Revenue	− Expenses	
$8,400 +	$2,100 +	$ 1,000	= $ 300	+ $6,200		+ $5,000		Bal. Forward
−700							+$700	Transaction
$7,700 +	$2,100 +	$ 1,000	= $ 300	+ $6,200		+ $5,000	− $700	End. Bal.
		$10,800	= $10,800					

As expenses increase, they decrease owner's equity. This incurred expense of $700 reduces the cash by $700. Although the expense was paid, the total of the expenses to date has *increased* by $700. Keep in mind that owner's equity decreases as expenses increase, so the accounting equation remains in balance, because expenses are deducted from Owner's Equity.

Transaction H Sept. 1–30: Paid rent expense, $400.

	Assets		=	Liabilities	+			Owner's Equity		
Cash	+ Accts. Rec.	+ Office Equip.	=	Accts. Pay.	+	M. Wong, Capital	− M. Wong, Withdr.	+ Revenue	−	Expenses
Bal. Forward	$7,700	+ $2,100	+ $ 1,000	=	$ 300	+ $6,200		+ $5,000	−	$ 700
Transaction	−400									+400
End. Bal.	$7,300	+ $2,100	+ $ 1,000	=	$ 300	+ $6,200		+ $5,000	−	$1,100
			$10,400	=	$10,400					

During September the practice incurred rent expenses of $400. This rent was not paid in advance; it was paid when it came due. The payment of rent reduces the asset Cash by $400 as well as increases the expenses of the firm, resulting in a decrease in owner's equity. The firm's expenses are now $1,100.

Transaction I Sept. 1–30: Incurred advertising expenses of $200, to be paid next month.

	Assets		=	Liabilities	+	Owner's Equity				
Cash	+ Accts. Rec.	+ Office Equip.	=	Accts. Pay.	+	M. Wong, Capital	− M. Wong, Withdr.	+ Revenue	−	Expenses
Bal. Forward	$7,300	+ $2,100	+ $ 1,000	=	$ 300	+ $6,200		+ $5,000	−	$1,100
Transaction					+200					+200
End. Bal.	$7,300	+ $2,100	+ $ 1,000	=	$ 500	+ $6,200		+ $5,000	−	$1,300
			$10,400	=	$10,400					

Mia ran an ad in the local newspaper and incurred an expense of $200. This increase in expenses caused a corresponding decrease in owner's equity. Because Mia has not paid the newspaper for the advertising yet, she owes $200. Thus her liabilities (Accounts Payable) increase by $200. Eventually, when the bill comes in and is paid, both Cash and Accounts Payable will be decreased.

Transaction J Sept. 1–30: Mia withdrew $100 for personal use.

	Assets		=	Liabilities	+			Owner's Equity		
Cash	+ Accts. Rec.	+ Office Equip.	=	Accts. Pay.	+	M. Wong, Capital	− M. Wong, Withdr.	+ Revenue	−	Expenses
Bal. Forward	$7,300	+ $2,100	+ $ 1,000	=	$ 500	+ $6,200		+ $5,000	−	$1,300
Transaction	−100						+$100			
End. Bal.	$7,200	+ $2,100	+ $ 1,000	=	$ 500	+ $6,200	− $100	+ $5,000	−	$1,300
			$10,300	=	$10,300					

By taking $100 for personal use, Mia *increased* her withdrawals from the business by $100 and decreased the asset Cash by $100. Note that as withdrawals increase, the owner's equity *decreases*. Keep in mind that a withdrawal is *not* a business expense. It is a subdivision of owner's equity that records money or other assets an owner withdraws from the business for *personal* use.

Subdivision of Owner's Equity. Take a moment to review the subdivisions of owner's equity:

- As capital increases, owner's equity increases (see transaction A).
- As withdrawals increase, owner's equity decreases (see transaction J).
- As revenue increases, owner's equity increases (see transactions D and E).
- As expenses increase, owner's equity decreases (see transactions G through I).

Mia Wong's Expanded Accounting Equation. The following is a summary of the expanded accounting equation for Mia Wong's law firm.

COACHING TIP

Revenue is shown when earned, not when cash is received.

Mia Wong
Attorney-at-Law
Expanded Accounting Equation: A summary

		Assets		=	Liabilities	+			Owner's Equity			
Cash	+	Accts. Rec.	+ Office Equip.	=	Accts. Pay.	+ M. Wong, Capital	− M. Wong, Withdr.	+	Revenue	− Expenses		
$6,000			+$200 =			+$6,200						A.
6,000		+	200 =			6,200						Balance
−500			+500									B.
5,500		+	700 =			6,200						Balance
			+300		+$300							C.
5,500	+		1,000 =		300	+ 6,200						Balance
+2,000									+$2,000			D.
7,500		+	1,000 =		300	+ 6,200		+	2,000			Balance
	+$3,000								+3,000			E.
7,500	+	3,000 +	1,000 =		300	+ 6,200		+	5,000			Balance
+900	−900											F.
8,400	+	2,100 +	1,000 =		300	+ 6,200		+	5,000			Balance
−700										+$700		G.
7,700	+	2,100 +	1,000 =		300	+ 6,200		+	5,000	− 700		Balance
−400										+400		H.
7,300	+	2,100 +	1,000 =		300	+ 6,200		+	5,000	− 1,100		Balance
					+200					+200		I.
7,300	+	2,100 +	1,000 =		500	+ 6,200		+	5,000	− 1,300		Balance
−100							+$100					J.
$7,200	+	$2,100 +	$ 1,000 =		$ 500	+ $6,200	− $100	+	$5,000	− $1,300		End. Balance
			$10,300 =		$10,300							

TRY IT!   Learning Unit 1-3

Use the expanded accounting equation to solve for the missing amount.

Assets $30,000; Liabilities ?; Owner's Capital, Beginning Balance $15,000; Revenues $10,000; Expenses $3,000; Withdrawals $1,000

The Three Financial Statements

Mia Wong would like to be able to find out if her firm is making a profit, so she asks her accountant if he can measure the firm's financial performance on a monthly basis. Her accountant replies that a number of financial statements that he can prepare, such as the income statement, will show Mia how well the law firm has performed over a specific period of time. The accountant can use the information in the income statement to prepare other reports.

The Income Statement

Income statement An accounting statement that details the performance of a firm (revenue minus expenses) for a specific period of time.

An income statement is an accounting statement that shows business results in terms of revenue and expenses. If revenues are greater than expenses, the report shows net income. If expenses are greater than revenues, the report shows net loss. An income statement typically covers 1, 3, 6, or 12 months. It cannot cover more than one year. The statement shows the result of all revenues and expenses throughout the entire period and not just as of a specific date. The income statement for Mia Wong's law firm is shown in Figure 1.4.

FIGURE 1.4
The Income Statement

MIA WONG, ATTORNEY-AT-LAW INCOME STATEMENT FOR MONTH ENDED SEPTEMBER 30, 201X			
Revenue:			
Legal Fees			$5 0 0 0 0 0
Operating Expenses:			
Salaries Expense		$7 0 0 0 0	
Rent Expense		4 0 0 0 0	
Advertising Expense		2 0 0 0 0	
Total Operating Expenses			1 3 0 0 0 0
Net Income			$3 7 0 0 0 0

Points to Remember in Preparing an Income Statement

Heading. The heading of an income statement tells the company's name, the name of the statement, and the period of time the statement covers.

The Setup. As you can see on the income statement, the inside column of numbers ($700, $400, and $200) is used to subtotal all expenses ($1,300) before subtracting them from revenue ($5,000 − $1,300 = $3,700).

Operating expenses may be listed in alphabetical order, in order of largest amount to smallest, or in a set order established by the accountant.

COACHING TIP

The income statement is prepared from data found in the revenue and expense columns of the expanded accounting equation. The inside column of numbers ($700, $400, $200) is used to subtotal all expenses ($1,300) before subtracting from revenue.

The Statement of Owner's Equity

As we said, the income statement is a business statement that shows business results in terms of revenue and expenses, but how does net income or net loss affect owner's equity? To find out, we have to look at a second type of statement, the statement of owner's equity.

Statement of owner's equity A financial statement that reveals the change in capital. The ending figure for capital is then placed on the balance sheet.

The statement of owner's equity shows for a certain period of time what changes occurred in Mia Wong, Capital. The statement of owner's equity is shown in Figure 1.5.

FIGURE 1.5
Statement of Owner's Equity—Net Income

MIA WONG, ATTORNEY-AT-LAW STATEMENT OF OWNER'S EQUITY FOR MONTH ENDED SEPTEMBER 30, 201X		
Mia Wong, Capital, September 1, 201X		$6 2 0 0 0 0
Net Income for September	$3 7 0 0 0 0	
Less: Withdrawals for September	– 1 0 0 0 0	
Increase in Capital		3 6 0 0 0 0
Mia Wong, Capital, September 30, 201X		$9 8 0 0 0 0

Comes from Income Statement

The capital of Mia Wong can be

Increased by: Owner Investment

Net Income (Revenue – Expenses) and Revenue Greater Than Expenses

Decreased by: Owner Withdrawals

Net Loss (Revenue – Expenses) and Expenses Greater Than Revenue

---

COACHING TIP

If this statement of owner's equity is omitted, the information will be included in the owner's equity section of the balance sheet.

Remember, a withdrawal is *not* a business expense and thus, is not involved in the calculation of net income or net loss on the income statement. It appears on the statement of owner's equity. The statement of owner's equity summarizes the effects of all the subdivisions of owner's equity (revenue, expenses, and withdrawals) on beginning capital. The ending capital figure ($9,800) will be the beginning figure in the next statement of owner's equity.

Suppose Mia's law firm had operated at a loss in the month of September. Suppose that instead of net income, a $400 net loss occurred and an additional investment of $700 was made on September 15. Figure 1.6 shows how the statement would look with this net loss and additional investment.

FIGURE 1.6
Statement of Owner's Equity—Net Loss

MIA WONG, ATTORNEY-AT-LAW STATEMENT OF OWNER'S EQUITY FOR MONTH ENDED SEPTEMBER 30, 201X		
Mia Wong, Capital, September 1, 201X		$6 2 0 0 0 0
Additional Investment, September 15, 201X		7 0 0 0 0
Total Investment for September*		$6 9 0 0 0 0
Less: Net Loss for September	$4 0 0 0 0	
Withdrawals for September	1 0 0 0 0	
Decrease in Capital		– 5 0 0 0 0
Mia Wong, Capital, September 30, 201X		$6 4 0 0 0 0

*Beginning capital and additional investments.

The Balance Sheet

Now let's look at how to prepare a balance sheet from the expanded accounting equation (see Figure 1.7, page 16). As you can see, the asset accounts (cash, accounts receivable, and office equipment) appear on the left side of the balance sheet.

Accounts payable and Mia Wong, Capital appear on the right side. Notice that the $9,800 of capital can be calculated within the accounting equation or can be read from the statement of owner's equity.

Main Elements of the Income Statement, the Statement of Owner's Equity, and the Balance Sheet

In this chapter we have discussed three financial statements: the income statement, the statement of owner's equity, and the balance sheet. A fourth statement, called the statement of cash flows, will not be covered at this time. Let us review what elements

FIGURE 1.7
The Accounting Equation and the Balance Sheet

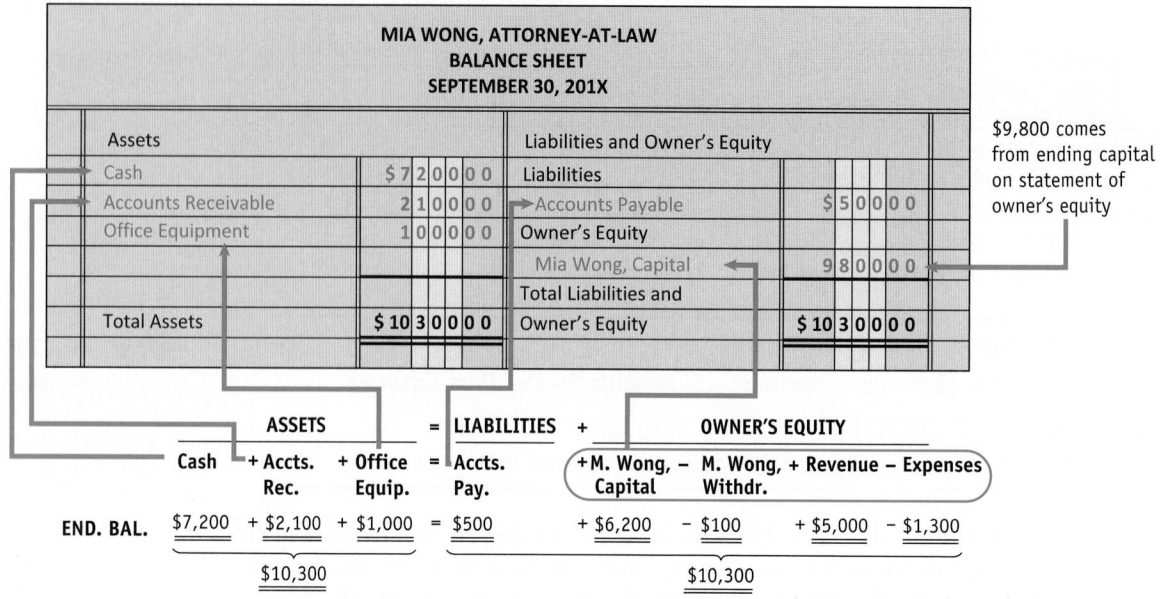

of the expanded accounting equation go into each statement and the usual order in which the statements are prepared. Figure 1.7 presents a diagram of the accounting equation and the balance sheet. Table 1.3 summarizes the following points:

- The income statement is prepared first; it includes revenues and expenses and shows net income or net loss. This net income or net loss is used to update the next statement, the statement of owner's equity.

- The statement of owner's equity is prepared second; it includes beginning capital and any additional investments, the net income or net loss shown on the income statement, withdrawals, and the total, which is the ending capital.

- The balance sheet is prepared last; it includes the final balances of each of the elements listed in the accounting equation under Assets and Liabilities. The balance in Capital comes from the statement of owner's equity.

Ending capital Beginning Capital + Additional Investments + Net Income – Withdrawals = Ending Capital. Or: Beginning Capital + Additional Investments – Net Loss – Withdrawals = Ending Capital.

TABLE 1.3 What Goes on Each Financial Statement

	Income Statement	Statement of Owner's Equity	Balance Sheet
Assets			X
Liabilities			X
Capital* (beg.)		X	
Capital (end.)		X	X
Withdrawals		X	
Revenues	X		
Expenses	X		

*Note: Additional investments go on the statement of owner's equity.

COACHING TIP

Net income is reported separately from capital on the balance sheet in the equity section in both QuickBooks and Sage 50.

▶ TRY IT!   **Learning Unit 1-4**

From the following titles identify which financial statement(s) they would be placed on (Income Statement (IS), Statement of Owner's Equity (SOE), Balance Sheet (BS)).

1. Accounts Payable
2. John Ryan, Capital (ending)
3. Accounts Receivable
4. Computer Equipment
5. Legal Fees (Revenue)
6. Office Expense
7. Advertising Expense
8. John Ryan, Withdrawals
9. Salaries Payable
10. Cash

DEMONSTRATION SUMMARY PROBLEM

 L03,4

Michael Brown opened his law office on June 1, 201X. During the first month of operation, Michael conducted the following transactions:

a. Invested $6,000 in cash into the law practice.

b. Paid $600 for office equipment.

c. Purchased additional office equipment on account, $1,000.

d. Received cash for performing legal services for clients, $2,000.

e. Paid salaries, $800.

f. Performed legal services for clients on account, $1,000.

g. Paid rent, $1,200.

h. Withdrew $500 from his law practice for personal use.

i. Received $500 from customers in partial payment for legal services performed, transaction f.

Requirements

1. Record these transactions in the expanded accounting equation.

2. Prepare the financial statements at June 30 for Michael Brown, Attorney-at-Law.

Solutions

Requirement 1

Record these transactions in the expanded accounting equation.

Tips to Expanded Accounting Equation

- **Transaction a:** The business increased its Cash by $6,000. Owner's Equity (capital) increased when Michael supplied the cash to the business. Note how the equation is now in balance.

- **Transaction b:** A shift in assets occurred when the equipment was purchased. The business lowered its Cash by $600, and a new column—Office Equipment—was increased for the $600 of equipment that was bought. The amount of capital is not touched because the owner did not supply any new funds. You do not have to touch both sides of the equation to make it balance.

- **Transaction c:** When creditors supply $1,000 of additional equipment, the business shows an increase in its debt. The business had increased what it *owes* the creditors. The end result is an increase in an asset and an increase in a liability.

(continued at the bottom of page 18)

Solution to Recording Transactions into Expanded Accounting Equation

	Cash		Accts. Rec.		Office Equip.		Accounts Payable		M. Brown, Capital		M. Brown, Withdr.		Legal Fees		Expenses
	Assets					=	**Liabilities** +		**Owner's Equity**						
a.	+$6,000								+$6,000						
BAL.	6,000					=			6,000						
b.	−600				+$600										
BAL.	5,400	+			600	=			6,000						
c.					+1,000		+$1,000								
BAL.	5,400	+			1,600	=	1,000	+	6,000						
d.	+2,000												+$2,000		
BAL.	7,400	+			1,600	=	1,000	+	6,000			+	2,000		
e.	−800														+$800
BAL.	6,600	+			1,600	=	1,000	+	6,000			+	2,000	−	800
f.			+$1,000										+1,000		
BAL.	6,600	+	1,000	+	1,600	=	1,000	+	6,000			+	3,000	−	800
g.	−1,200														+1,200
BAL.	5,400	+	1,000	+	1,600	=	1,000	+	6,000			+	3,000	−	2,000
h.	−500										+$500				
BAL.	4,900	+	1,000	+	1,600	=	1,000	+	6,000	−	500	+	3,000	−	2,000
i.	+500		−500												
End. Bal.	$5,400	+	$500	+	$1,600	=	$1,000	+	$6,000	−	$500	+	$3,000	−	$2,000
							$7,500	=	$7,500						

(Tips continued)

- **Transaction d:** Legal Fees, a subdivision of Owner's Equity, is increased when the law firm provides a service even if no money is received. The service provides an inward flow of $2,000 to Cash, an asset. Remember that Legal Fees is *not* an asset. As Legal Fees revenue increases, Owner's Equity increases. Keep in mind that revenue can provide an inflow of cash and/or accounts receivable. Cash and accounts receivable are assets. The revenue is part of Owner's Equity.

- **Transaction e:** The salary paid by Michael creates an $800 increase in Expenses and a corresponding decrease in Owner's Equity as well as a decrease in Cash. Keep in mind that as the expenses increase they do in fact lower Owner's Equity.

- **Transaction f:** Michael did the work and earned the $1,000. That $1,000 is recorded as revenue. This time the legal fees create an inward flow of assets called Accounts Receivable for $1,000. Remember that Legal Fees is *not* an asset. It is a subdivision of Owner's Equity.

- **Transaction g:** The $1,200 rent expense reduces Owner's Equity as well as Cash. Remember to think of expenses as increasing. This increase in expenses then causes Owner's Equity to decrease.

- **Transaction h:** Withdrawals are for personal use. Here the business decreases Cash by $500 while Michael's withdrawals increase by $500. Withdrawals decrease the Owner's Equity. Remember to think of withdrawals as increasing. This is the amount withdrawn by the owner for personal use, decreasing Owner's Equity.

- **Transaction i:** This transaction does not reflect new revenue in the form of Legal Fees. It is only a shift in assets: more Cash and less Accounts Receivable.

Requirement 2

Prepare the financial statements at June 30 for Michael Brown, Attorney-at-Law. Figures 1.8 and 1.9 show the completed statements for Michael.

Solutions to Preparing Financial Statements

A	MICHAEL BROWN, ATTORNEY-AT-LAW INCOME STATEMENT FOR MONTH ENDED JUNE 30, 201X		
Revenue:			
Legal Fees			$3,000
Operating Expenses:			
Salaries Expense		$ 800	
Rent Expense		1,200	
Total Operating Expenses			2,000
Net Income			$1,000

B	MICHAEL BROWN, ATTORNEY-AT-LAW STATEMENT OF OWNER'S EQUITY FOR MONTH ENDED JUNE 30, 201X		
Michael Brown, Capital, June 1, 201X			$6,000*
Net income for June		$1,000	
Less: Withdrawls for June		− 500	
Increase in Capital			500
Michael Brown, Capital, June 30, 201X			$6,500

*No additional investments were made after the $6,000. The capital balance before the investment was 0.

C	MICHAEL BROWN, ATTORNEY-AT-LAW BALANCE SHEET JUNE 30, 201X		
Assets		**Liabilities and Owner's Equity**	
Cash	$5,400	Liabilities	
Accounts Receivable	500	Accounts Payable	$1,000
Office Equipment	1,600	Owner's Equity	
		M. Brown, Capital	$6,500
Total Assets	$7,500	Total Liabilities and Owner's Equity	$7,500

FIGURE 1.8
Michael Brown's Income Statement and Statement of Owner's Equity

FIGURE 1.9
Michael Brown's Balance Sheet

Tips to Preparing Financial Statements

a. The income statement lists only revenues and expenses for a period of time. The inside column is for subtotaling. Withdrawals are not listed here.

b. The statement of owner's equity takes the net income figure of $1,000 and adds it to beginning capital less any withdrawals. This new capital figure of $6,500 will go on the balance sheet. This statement shows changes in capital for a period of time.

c. The $5,400, $500, $1,600 (Assets) and $1,000 (Liabilities) came from the totals of the expanded accounting equation. The capital figure of $6,500 came from the statement of owner's equity. This balance sheet reports assets, liabilities, and a new figure for capital at a specific date.

BLUEPRINT: FINANCIAL STATEMENTS

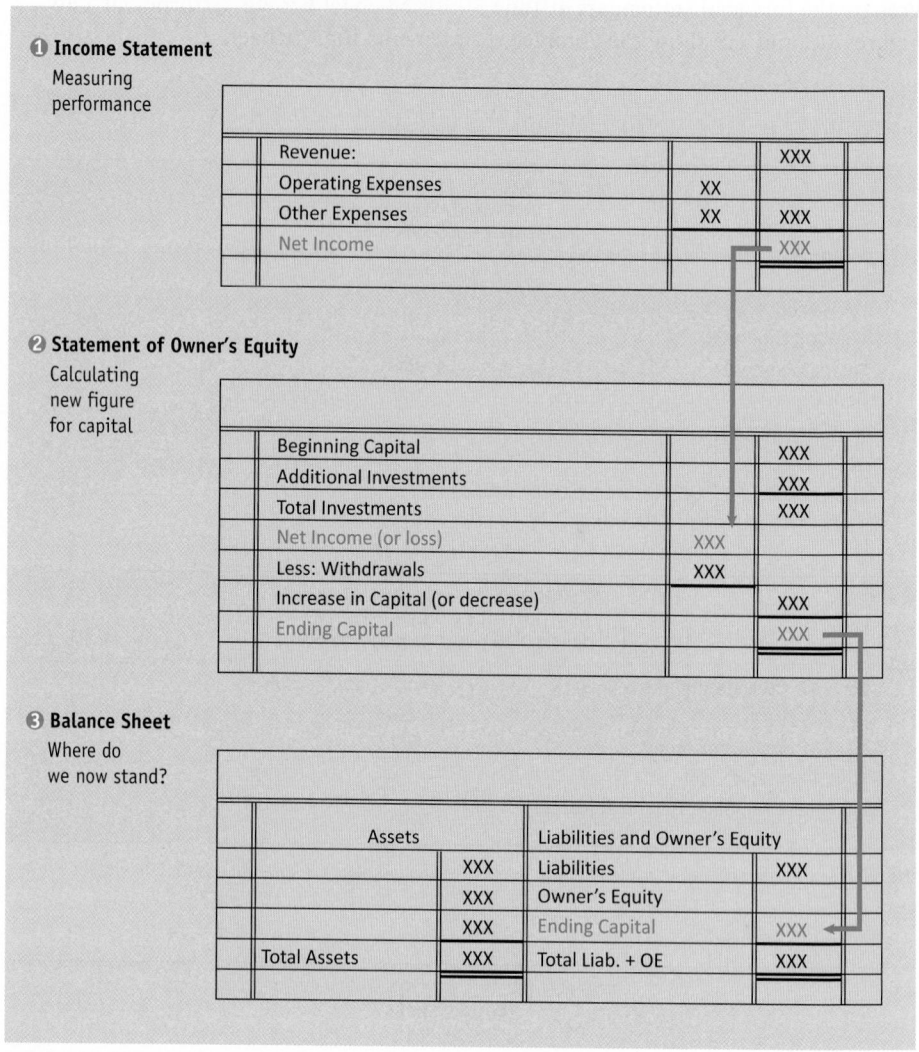

❶ Income Statement
Measuring
performance

Revenue:		XXX
Operating Expenses	XX	
Other Expenses	XX	XXX
Net Income		XXX

❷ Statement of Owner's Equity
Calculating
new figure
for capital

Beginning Capital		XXX
Additional Investments		XXX
Total Investments		XXX
Net Income (or loss)	XXX	
Less: Withdrawals	XXX	
Increase in Capital (or decrease)		XXX
Ending Capital		XXX

❸ Balance Sheet
Where do
we now stand?

Assets		Liabilities and Owner's Equity	
	XXX	Liabilities	XXX
	XXX	Owner's Equity	
	XXX	Ending Capital	XXX
Total Assets	XXX	Total Liab. + OE	XXX

MyAccountingLab    **TRY IT!**   **Solutions**

Learning Unit 1-1

	Assets	=	Liabilites + Owner's Equity
	Cash + Salon Equip.		Accounts Pay. + B. Rey, Capital

			=		
1.	+ $20,000		=		+ $20,000
2.	− $ 4,000	+ $10,000	=	+$6,000	
	$16,000	+ $10,000	=	$6,000	+ $20,000

Learning Unit 1-2

Flynn Co.
Balance Sheet
November 30, 201X

Assets		Liabilities and Owner's Equity	
Cash	$ 8,000	Liabilities	
iPads	4,000	Accounts Payable	$ 3,000
		Owner's Equity	
		P. Flynn, Capital	9,000
Total Assets	$12,000	Total Liabilities and Owner's Equity	$12,000

Learning Unit 1-3

Total Assets $30,000 Less Owner's Equity $21,000=Liabilities $9,000

The calculation of $21,000 was Owner's Capital, Beginning Balance $15,000 +Revenue of $10,000 Less Expenses and Withdrawals of $4,000

Learning Unit 1-4

1. BS
2. SOE, BS
3. BS
4. BS
5. IS
6. IS
7. IS
8. SOE
9. BS
10. BS

ACCOUNTING COACH

The following Coaching Tips are from Learning Units 1-1 through 1-4. Take the Pre-Game Checkup and use the Check Your Score at the bottom of the page to see how you are doing. The Accounting Coach provides tips before each Checkup to help you avoid common accounting errors.

LU 1-1 Accounting, Business, and the Accounting Equation

Pre-Game Tips: After a transaction is recorded in the accounting equation, the sum of all the assets must equal the total of all the liabilities and owner's equity.

Pre-Game Checkup: Answer true or false to the following statements.

1. Capital is cash.
2. Accounts Payable is a liability.
3. A shift in assets means liabilities will increase.
4. Assets − Liabilities = Owner's Equity.
5. Assets represent what is owned by the business.

LU 1-2 The Balance Sheet

Pre-Game Tips: The Balance Sheet is a formal report listing assets, liabilities, and owner's equity as of a particular date.

Pre-Game Checkup: Answer true or false to the following statements.

1. Cash is a liability.
2. Office Equipment is an asset.
3. Accounts Payable is listed under assets.
4. Capital is listed under liabilities.
5. A heading of a financial report has no particular date.

LU 1-3 The Accounting Equation Expanded: Revenue, Expenses, and Withdrawals

Pre-Game Tips: Revenue is recorded when earned even if cash is not received. Expenses are recorded when they happen (incurred) whether they are paid or to be paid later.

Pre-Game Checkup: Answer true or false to the following statements.

1. Revenue is an asset.
2. Withdrawals increase owner's equity.
3. As expenses go down, owner's equity goes down.
4. An advertising bill incurred but unpaid is recorded as an increase in Advertising Expense and a decrease in a liability.
5. Revenue inflows can only be in the form of cash.

LU 1-4 The Three Financial Statements

Pre-Game Tips: Net income from the income statement is used to update the statement of owner's equity. The ending figure for capital on the statement of owner's equity is the one used to update the balance sheet.

Pre-Game Checkup: Answer true or false to the following statements.

1. Net income occurs when expenses are greater than revenue.
2. Withdrawals will reduce owner's capital on the income statement.
3. The balance sheet lists assets, liabilities, and expenses.
4. Withdrawals are listed on the income statement.
5. Assets are listed on the income statement.

CHECK YOUR SCORE: Answers to the Pre-Game Checkup

LU 1-1
1. False—Capital represents the owner's claim to the assets.
2. True.
3. False—A shift in assets means liabilities will stay the same.
4. True.
5. True.

LU 1-2
1. False—Cash is an asset.
2. True.
3. False—Accounts Payable is listed under liabilities.
4. False—Capital is listed under owner's equity.
5. False—A heading of a financial report does have a particular date.

LU 1-3
1. False—Revenue is part of owner's equity.
2. False—Withdrawals decrease owner's equity.
3. False—As expenses go down, owner's equity goes up.
4. False—An advertising bill incurred but unpaid is recorded as an increase in Advertising Expense and an increase in a liability.
5. False—Revenue inflows can be in the form of cash and/or accounts receivable.

LU 1-4
1. False—Net income occurs when expenses are less than revenue.
2. False—Withdrawals will reduce owner's capital on the statement of owner's equity.
3. False—Expenses are listed on the income statement.
4. False—Withdrawals are listed on the statement of owner's equity.
5. False—Assets are listed on the balance sheet.

Chapter Summary

Here are all the key terms and equations to help you understand the concepts of this chapter and prepare you for your exam. After completing this review, go to MyAccountingLab for more practice opportunities.

MyAccountingLab

Concepts You Should Know	Key Terms

L01 **Explain Accounting, Business, and the Accounting Equation**

1. The functions of accounting involve analyzing, recording, classifying, summarizing, reporting, and interpreting financial information.

2. Forms of business organization:

   a. A sole proprietorship is a business owned by one person.

   b. A partnership is a business owned by two or more persons.

   c. A corporation is a business owned by stockholders.

   d. An LLC is owned by a limited number of members.

3. The Sarbanes-Oxley Act helps prevent fraud at publicly-held companies.

4. GAAP and IFRS are guidelines established by U.S. (GAAP) and international (IFRS) accounting standard boards.

Key Terms:

Accounting (p. 2)

Accounts payable (p. 7)

Assets (p. 4)

Assets = Liabilities + Owner's Equity (p. 5)

Basic accounting equation (p. 5)

Bookkeeping (p. 4)

Capital (p. 5)

Corporation (p. 3)

Creditor (p. 5)

Equities (p. 5)

Generally accepted accounting principles (GAAP) (p. 4)

International Financial Reporting Standards (IFRS) (p. 4)

Liabilities (p. 5)

Limited Liability Company (p. 3)

Manufacturer (p. 3)

Merchandise company (p. 3)

Owner's equity (p. 5)

Partnership (p. 2)

Service company (p. 3)

Shift in assets (p. 6)

Supplies (p. 6)

Sole proprietorship (p. 2)

L02 **Prepare a Balance Sheet**

1. Assets = Liabilities + Owner's Equity is the basic accounting equation.

2. Liabilities represent amounts owed to creditors.

3. Capital does not mean cash.

4. In a shift of assets the composition of assets changes but the total of assets does not change.

Key Terms:

Balance sheet (p. 7)

Statement of financial position (p. 7)

L03

Record Transactions into the Expanded Accounting Equation

1. Revenue generates an inward flow of assets. Expenses generate an outward flow of assets or a potential outward flow.

2. When revenue totals more than expenses, net income is the result; when expenses total more than revenue, there is a net loss.

3. Owner's equity can be subdivided into four elements: capital, withdrawals, revenue, and expenses.

4. Withdrawals and expenses will decrease owner's equity.

Accounts receivable (p. 9)

Accrual basis (p. 9)

Cash basis (p. 9)

Expanded accounting equation (p. 10)

Expense (p. 9)

Net income (p. 9)

Net loss (p. 9)

Revenue (p. 9)

Withdrawals (p. 9)

Assets = Liabilities + Capital − Withdrawals + Revenue − Expenses (p. 10)

 **L04**

Prepare the Three Financial Statements

1. The income statement is a statement written for a specific period of time that lists earned revenue and expenses incurred to produce the earned revenue.

2. The statement of owner's equity is a statement written for a specific period of time that reveals the causes of a change in capital. The ending figure for capital will be used on the balance sheet.

3. The balance sheet is a statement written for a specific point of time that uses the ending balances of assets and liabilities from the accounting equation and the capital from the statement of owner's equity.

4. The income statement should be prepared first because the information on it about net income or net loss is used to prepare the statement of owner's equity, which in turn provides information about capital for the balance sheet.

Ending capital (p. 16)

Income statement (p. 14)

Statement of owner's equity (p. 14)

Discussion Questions and Critical Thinking/Ethical Case

1. What are the functions of accounting?

2. Define, compare, and contrast sole proprietorships, partnerships, and corporations.

3. How are businesses classified?

4. How has technology affected the role of the bookkeeper?

5. List the three elements of the basic accounting equation.

6. Define capital.

7. The total of the left-hand side of the accounting equation must equal the total of the right-hand side. True or false? Please explain.

8. A balance sheet tells a company where it is going and how well it performs. True or false? Please explain.

9. Revenue is an asset. True or false? Please explain.

10. Owner's equity is subdivided into what categories?

11. A withdrawal is a business expense. True or false? Please explain.

12. As expenses increase they cause owner's equity to increase. Defend or reject.

13. What does an income statement show?

14. The statement of owner's equity only calculates ending withdrawals. True or false? Please explain.

15. Paul Kloss, accountant for Lowe & Co., traveled to New York on company business. His total expenses came to $350. Paul felt that because the trip extended over the weekend he would "pad" his expense account with an additional $100 of expenses. After all, weekends represent his own time, not the company's. What would you do? Write your specific recommendations to Paul.

Concept Checks

MyAccountingLab

Classifying Accounts

L01   *(5 min)*

1. Classify each of the following items as an Asset (A), Liability (L), or part of Owner's Equity (OE).

    a. iPad   _____

    b. Accounts Receivable   _____

    c. Accounts Payable   _____

    d. Smartphone   _____

    e. B. Long, Capital   _____

    f. Cash   _____

The Accounting Equation

L01   *(5 min)*

2. Complete the following statements.

    a. _____: rights of the creditors

    b. _____ are total value of items owned by a business.

    c. _____ _____ is an unwritten promise to pay the creditor.

(5 min)   **LO1** ▶   **Shift versus Increase in Assets**

3. Identify which transaction results in a shift in assets (S) and which transaction causes an increase in assets (I).

    a. Target bought computer equipment on account.

    b. Macy's bought office equipment for cash.

(5 min)   **LO2** ▶   **The Balance Sheet**

4. From the following, calculate what would be the total of assets on the balance sheet.

B. Devin, Capital	$43,000
Warehouse Equipment	3,000
Accounts Payable	6,500
Cash	31,000

(5 min)   **LO3** ▶   **The Accounting Equation Expanded**

5. From the following, which are subdivisions of owner's equity?

    a. Smartphone _____

    b. J. Penny, Capital _____

    c. Accounts Payable _____

    d. J. Penny, Withdrawals _____

    e. Accounts Receivable _____

    f. Advertising Expense _____

    g. Taxi Fees Earned _____

    h. Microsoft Tablet _____

(5 min)   **LO2** ▶   **Identifying Assets**

6. Identify which of the following are *not* assets.

    a. Sony DVD Player _____

    b. Accounts Receivable _____

    c. Accounts Payable _____

    d. Grooming Fees Earned _____

(5 min)   **LO3** ▶   **The Accounting Equation Expanded**

7. Which of the following statements are false?

    a. _____ Revenue provides only outward flows of cash.

    b. _____ Revenue is a subdivision of Assets.

    c. _____ Revenue provides an inward flow of cash or accounts receivable.

    d. _____ Expenses are part of Total Assets.

(5 min)   **LO4** ▶   **Preparing Financial Statements**

8. Indicate whether the following items would appear on the income statement (IS), statement of owner's equity (OE), or balance sheet (BS).

a. _____ Tutoring Fees Earned

b. _____ Office Equipment

c. _____ Accounts Receivable

d. _____ Office Supplies

e. _____ Legal Fees Earned

f. _____ Advertising Expenses

g. _____ J. Earl, Capital (Beg.)

h. _____ Accounts Payable

Preparing Financial Statements

LO4   *(5 min)*

9.   Indicate next to each statement whether it refers to the income statement (IS), statement of owner's equity (OE), or balance sheet (BS).

a. _____ Withdrawals found on it

b. _____ List total of all assets

c. _____ Statement that is prepared last

d. _____ Statement listing net income

Exercises

MyAccountingLab

Set A

1A-1.   Complete the following table:

LO1   *(5 min)*

	Assets	=	Liabilities	+	Owner's Equity
a.	$30,000	=	?	+	$22,000
b.	?	=	$7,000	+	$98,000
c.	$25,000	=	$11,000	+	?

1A-2.   Record the following transactions in the basic accounting equation. Treat each one separately.

LO1   *(5 min)*

$$\text{Assets} = \text{Liabilities} + \text{Owner's Equity}$$

a. Matty invests $130,000 in company.

b. Bought equipment for cash, $1,100.

c. Bought equipment on account, $950.

1A-3.   From the following, prepare a balance sheet for Rideout Co. Cleaners at the end of November 201X: Cash, $71,000; Equipment, $12,000; Accounts Payable, $15,100; B. Rideout, Capital.

LO2   *(10 min)*

1A-4.   Record the following transactions in the expanded accounting equation. Do not calculate a running balance.

LO3   *(15 min)*

Assets			=	Liabilities	+		Owner's Equity			
Cash	+ Accounts Receivable	+ Computer Equipment	=	Accounts Payable	+	B. Black, Capital	−	B. Black, Withdrawals	+ Revenues	− Expenses

a. Black invested $60,000 in a computer company.

b. Bought computer equipment on account, $7,000.

c. Black paid personal telephone bill from company checkbook, $100.

d. Received cash for services rendered, $14,300.

e. Billed customers for services rendered for month, $30,600.

f. Paid current rent expense, $3,600.

g. Paid supplies expense, $1,470.

(20 min) **LO4** ▶ **1A-5.** From the following account balances, prepare in proper form for November (a) an income statement, (b) a statement of owner's equity, and (c) a balance sheet for Frederick Realty.

Cash	$4,800	S. Frederick, Withdrawals	$ 120
Accounts Receivable	1,230	Professional Fees	3,000
Office Equipment	8,300	Salaries Expense	550
Accounts Payable	4,000	Utilities Expense	200
S. Frederick, Capital, Nov. 1, 201X	9,000	Rent Expense	800

Set B

(5 min) **LO1** ▶ **1B-1.** Complete the following table:

	Assets	=	Liabilities	+	Owner's Equity
a.	$ 27,000	=	?	+	$ 20,000
b.	?	=	$ 12,000	+	$ 73,000
c.	$ 30,000	=	$ 5,000	+	?

(5 min) **LO1** ▶ **1B-2.** Record the following transactions in the basic accounting equation. Treat each one separately.

Assets = Liabilities + Owner's Equity

a. Mandy invests $114,000 in company.
b. Bought equipment for cash, $1,600.
c. Bought equipment on account, $1,150.

(10 min) **LO2** ▶ **1B-3.** From the following, prepare a balance sheet for Rolland Co. Cleaners at the end of June 201X: Cash, $52,000; Equipment, $36,000; Accounts Payable, $11,000; B. Rolland, Capital.

(15 min) **LO3** ▶ **1B-4.** Record the following transactions in the expanded accounting equation. Do not calculate a running balance.

Assets			=	Liabilities	+		Owner's Equity		
Cash +	Accounts Receivable	+ Computer Equipment	=	Accounts Payable	+ B. Bell, Capital	− B. Bell, Withdrawals	+ Revenues − Expenses

a. Bell invested $45,000 in a computer company.
b. Bought computer equipment on account, $9,500.
c. Bell paid personal telephone bill from company checkbook, $75.
d. Received cash for services rendered, $14,100.
e. Billed customers for services rendered for month, $29,600.
f. Paid current rent expense, $3,400.
g. Paid supplies expense, $1,500.

(20 min) **LO4** ▶ **1B-5.** From the following account balances, prepare in proper form for September (a) an income statement, (b) a statement of owner's equity, and (c) a balance sheet for French Realty.

Cash	$ 2,900	S. French, Withdrawals	$ 200
Accounts Receivable	1,750	Professional Fees	3,400
Office Equipment	10,400	Salaries Expense	425
Accounts Payable	7,000	Utilities Expense	300
S. French, Capital, Sept 1, 201X	6,050	Rent Expense	475

Problems

Set A

1A-1. Morgan Amberson decided to open Morgan's Nail Spa. Morgan completed the following transactions:

 **L01** *(15 min)*

    a. Invested $16,000 cash from her personal bank account into the business.
    b. Bought store equipment for cash, $3,700.
    c. Bought additional store equipment on account, $6,050.
    d. Paid $600 cash to partially reduce what was owed from transaction C.

Check Figure:
Cash $11,700

Based on this information, record these transactions into the basic accounting equation.

1A-2. Ben Shea is the accountant for Shea's Internet Service. From the following information, his task is to construct a balance sheet as of June 30, 201X, in proper form. Could you help him?

L02 *(15 min)*

Building	$ 55,000	Cash	$38,000
Accounts Payable	14,000	Equipment	39,000
B. Shea, Capital	118,000		

Check Figure:
Total Assets $132,000

1A-3. At the end of June, Rick Fontan decided to open his own computer service. Analyze the following transactions he completed by recording their effects in the expanded accounting equation.

 **L03** *(20 min)*

    a. Invested $25,000 in his computer service.
    b. Bought new computer equipment on account, $2,500.
    c. Received cash for computer services rendered, $800.
    d. Performed computer services on account, $2,100.
    e. Paid secretary's salary, $275.
    f. Paid office supplies expense for the month, $170.
    g. Rent expenses for office due but unpaid, $1,200.
    h. Withdrew cash for personal use, $700.

Check Figure:
Total Assets $29,255

1A-4. Jody Williams, owner of Williams Home Decorating Service, has requested that you prepare from the following balances (a) an income statement for September 201X, (b) a statement of owner's equity for September, and (c) a balance sheet as of September 30, 201X.

 **L04** *(30 min)*

Cash	$2,100	Home Decorating Fees	$2,700
Accounts Receivable	1,050	Advertising Expense	255
Decorating Equipment	985	Repair Expense	45
Accounts Payable	450	Travel Expense	650
J. Williams, Capital, Sept. 1, 201X	2,500	Supplies Expense	115
J. Williams, Withdrawals	300	Rent Expense	150

Check Figure:
Total Liabilities and Owner's Equity
$4,135

1A-5. James Tanson, a retired army officer, opened Tanson's Catering Service. As his accountant, analyze the transactions listed next and present them in proper form.

 **L03,4** *(45 min)*

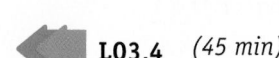

    a. The analysis of the transactions by using the expanded accounting equation.
    b. A balance sheet showing the position of the firm before opening for business on October 31, 201X.
    c. An income statement for the month of November.

d. A statement of owner's equity for November.

e. A balance sheet as of November 30, 201X.

Check Figure:
Total Assets,
Nov. 30 $24,240

201X	
Oct. 25	James Tanson invested $20,000 in the catering business from his personal savings account.
27	Bought equipment for cash from Munroe Co., $2,300.
28	Bought additional equipment on account from Ryan Co., $2,000.
29	Paid $900 to Ryan Co. as partial payment of the October 28 transaction.

(You should now prepare your balance sheet as of October 31, 201X.)

Nov. 1	Catered a graduation and immediately collected cash, $1,300.
5	Paid salaries of employees, $800.
8	Prepared desserts for customers on account, $500.
10	Received $250 cash as partial payment of November 8 transaction.
15	Paid telephone bill, $400.
17	Paid his home electric bill from the company's checkbook, $160.
20	Catered a wedding and received cash, $1,800.
25	Bought additional equipment on account, $1,200.
28	Rent expense due but unpaid, $650.
30	Paid supplies expense, $300.

Set B

(15 min) **LO1**

1B-1. Mandy Anabelle decided to open Mandy's Nail Spa. Mandy completed the following transactions:

a. Invested $21,000 cash from her personal bank account into the business.
b. Bought store equipment for cash, $3,500.
c. Bought additional store equipment on account, $5,750.
d. Paid $1,000 cash to partially reduce what was owed from transaction C.

Check Figure:
Ending Balance Cash $16,500

Based on this information, record these transactions into the basic accounting equation.

(15 min) **LO2**

1B-2. Brad Sealy is the accountant for Sealy's Internet Service. From the following information, his task is to construct a balance sheet as of November 30, 201X, in proper form. Can you help him?

Check Figure:
Total Assets $119,000

Building	$ 50,000	Cash	55,000
Accounts Payable	15,500	Equipment	14,000
B. Sealy, Capital	103,500		

(20 min) **LO3**

1B-3. At the end of April, Red Fuman decided to open his own computer service. Analyze the following transactions he completed by recording their effects into the expanded accounting equation.

a. Invested $10,000 in his computer service business.
b. Bought new computer equipment on account, $2,000.
c. Received cash for computer services rendered, $200.
d. Performed computer services on account, $2,200.

   e. Paid secretary's salary, $500.

   f. Paid office supplies expense for the month, $120.

   g. Rent expenses for office due but unpaid, $600.

   h. Withdrew cash for personal use, $900.

Check Figure:
Total Assets $12,880

1B-4. Jeanette Wu, owner of Wu Home Decorating Service has requested that you prepare from the following balances (a) an income statement for June 201X, (b) a statement of owner's equity for June, and (c) a balance sheet as of June 30, 201X.

 **L04** *(30 min)*

Cash	$1,700	Home Decorating Fees	$2,400
Accounts Receivable	600	Advertising Expense	185
Decorating Equipment	1,285	Repair Expense	40
Accounts Payable	1,140	Travel Expense	110
J. Wu, Capital, June 1, 201X	1,215	Supplies Expense	135
J. Wu, Withdrawals	400	Rent Expense	300

Check Figure:
J. Wu, Capital, $2,445
June 30, 201X

1B-5. John Thildore, a retired army officer, opened Thildore's Catering Service. As his accountant, analyze the transactions listed and present them in proper form.

   a. The analysis of the transactions by using the expanded accounting equation.

   b. A balance sheet showing the financial position of the firm before opening on October 31, 201X.

   c. An income statement for the month of November.

   d. A statement of owner's equity for November.

   e. A balance sheet as of November 30, 201X.

L03,4

S50 / **QB**

201X	
Oct. 25	John Thildore invested $25,000 in the catering business from his personal savings account.
27	Bought equipment for cash from Small Co., $1,200.
28	Bought additional equipment on account from Ryan Co., $800.
29	Paid $400 to Ryan Co. as partial payment of the Oct. 28 transaction.

(You should now prepare your balance sheet as of October 31, 201X.)

Check Figure:
Total Liabilities and Owner's Equity
Nov. 30 $30,380

Nov. 1	Catered a graduation and collected cash, $2,200.
5	Paid salaries of employees, $550.
8	Prepared desserts for customers on account, $250.
10	Received $80 cash as partial payment of Nov. 8 transaction.
15	Paid telephone bill, $50.
17	Paid his home electric bill from the company's checkbook, $120.
20	Catered a wedding and received cash, $2,500.
25	Bought additional equipment on account, $1,300.
28	Rent expense due but unpaid, $650.
30	Paid supplies expense, $550.

Financial Report Problem

L02 *(5 min)*

Reading the Kellogg's Annual Report

Go to http://investor.kelloggs.com/investor-relations/annual-reports/ to access the Kellogg's 2013 Annual Report. Find the balance sheet and calculate the following: How much did cash increase or decrease in 2013 from 2012?

ON THE JOB   SMITH COMPUTER CENTER

(45 min)   **LO3,4** ➡

The following problem continues from one chapter to the next, carrying the balances of each month forward. Each chapter focuses on the learning experience of the chapter, adds information as the business grows, and shows how critical the knowledge of accounting is to the performance of a business decision-maker.

Assignment

1. Set up an expanded accounting equation spreadsheet using the following accounts:

Assets	Liabilities	Owner's Equity
Cash	Accounts Payable	Feldman, Capital
Supplies		Feldman, Withdrawal
Computer Shop Equipment		Service Revenue
Office Equipment		Expenses (notate type)

2. Analyze and record each transaction in the expanded accounting equation.

3. Prepare the financial statements ending July 31 for Smith Computer Center.

On July 1, 201X, Thad Feldman decided to begin his own computer service business. He named the business the Smith Computer Center. During the first month, Thad conducted the following business transactions:

a. Invested $6,000 of his savings into the business.

b. Paid $1,800 (check #8095) for the computer from A-Tech, Inc.

c. Paid $3,300 (check #8096) for office equipment from Bertha and Pac Furniture, Inc.

d. Set up a new account with The Staple Store and purchased $200 in office supplies on credit.

e. Paid July rent, $500 (check #8097).

f. Repaired a system for a customer and collected $800.

g. Collected $600 for system upgrade labor charge from a customer.

h. Electric bill due but unpaid, $75.

i. Collected $1,800 for services performed on Phil's Photography computers.

j. Withdrew $175 (check #8098) to take his wife, Chelsea, out in celebration of opening the new business.

Debits and Credits: Analyzing and Recording Business Transactions

CHAPTER PREVIEW: THE BIG PICTURE

Pete Ansell was eating lunch at a local Subway. As an accounting student, Pete wondered how he could apply the accounting equation and the rules of debits and credits he had just learned to better explain how Subway is accurately reporting its financial activities. In this chapter, we learn how businesses—both small and large—like Subway are required to use the accounting equation to ensure it balances. By following the rules associated with the accounting equation, investors and creditors, when reviewing financial statements, can have confidence that businesses like Subway are accurately reporting their financial activities.

Learning Objectives

LO1   Explain T Accounts and How to Foot and Balance

LO2   Use a Chart of Accounts to Record Transactions in T Accounts According to the Rules of Debits and Credits

LO3   Prepare a Trial Balance and the Financial Statements

In Chapter 1 we used the expanded accounting equation to document the financial transactions performed by Mia Wong's law firm. Remember how long it was: The cash column had a long list of pluses and minuses, with no quick system of recording and summarizing the increases and decreases of cash or other items. Can you imagine the problem Subway would have if it used the expanded accounting equation to track the thousands of business transactions it makes each day?

LEARNING UNIT 2-1

L01

Account An accounting device used in bookkeeping to record increases and decreases of business transactions relating to individual assets, liabilities, capital, withdrawals, revenue, expenses, and so on.

Standard account A formal account that includes columns for date, explanation, posting reference, debit, and credit.

Ledger A group of accounts that records data from business transactions.

T account A skeleton version of a standard account, used for demonstration purposes.

The T Account and How to Foot and Balance

Let's look at the problem a little more closely. Each business transaction is recorded in the accounting equation under a specific account. Different accounts are used for each of the subdivisions of the accounting equation: asset accounts, liability accounts, expense accounts, revenue accounts, and so on. What is needed is a way to record the increases and decreases in specific account *categories* and yet keep them together in one place. The answer is the standard account form (see Figure 2.1). A standard account is a formal account that includes columns for date, explanation, posting reference (PR), debit, and credit. Each account has a separate form, and all transactions affecting that account are recorded on the form. All the business's account forms (which often are referred to as *ledger accounts*) are then placed in a ledger. Each page of the ledger, or tab of the electronic file, contains one account. If computers are used, the ledger may be part of a computer file. For simplicity's sake, we use the T account form. This form got its name because it looks like the letter T. Generally, T accounts are used for demonstration purposes. Each T account contains three basic parts:

1
Title of Account

2 Left side	Right side 3

All T accounts have this structure.

In accounting, the left side of any T account is called the debit side.

Left side Dr. (debit)	

Debit The left-hand side of any account. A number entered on the left side of any account is said to be debited to an account.

Just as the word *left* has many meanings, the word *debit* for now in accounting means a position, the left side of an account. Do not think of it as good (+) or bad (−).

Amounts entered on the left side of any account are said to be *debited* to an account. The abbreviation for debit, Dr., is from the Latin *debere*.

The right side of any T account is called the credit side.

	Right side Cr. (credit)

Credit The right-hand side of any account. A number entered on the right side of any account is said to be credited to an account.

Amounts entered on the right side of an account are said to be *credited* to an account. The abbreviation for credit, Cr., is from the Latin *credere*.

At this point do not associate the definition of debit and credit with the words *increase* or *decrease*. Think of debit or credit as only indicating a *position* (left or right side) of a T account.

Balancing an Account

No matter which individual account is being balanced, the procedure used to balance it is the same.

Account Title							Account No.	
Date	Item	PR	Debit	Date	Item	PR	Credit	

FIGURE 2.1
The Standard Account Form Is the Source of the T Account's Shape

COACHING TIP

If the balance is greater on the credit side, that is the side the ending balance would be on.

		Dr.	Cr.
Entries	→	5,000	400
		600	500
Footings	→	5,600	900
Balance		4,700	

In the "real" world, the T account would also include the date of the transaction.

		Dr.	Cr.	
4/2		5,000	400	4/3
4/20		600	500	4/25
		5,600	900	
Bal		4,700		

Note that on the debit (left) side the numbers add up to $5,600. On the credit (right) side the numbers add up to $900. The $5,600 and the $900 written in small type are called footings. Footings help in calculating the new (or ending) balance. The ending balance ($4,700) is placed on the debit or left side, because the balance of the debit side is greater than that of the credit side.

Remember that the ending balance does not tell us anything about increase or decrease. It only tells us that we have an ending balance of $4,700 on the debit side.

Footings The totals of each side of a T account.

Ending balance The difference between footings in a T account.

 **TRY IT!**   Learning Unit 2-1

From the following cash T account, prepare footings and calculate the ending balance:

		Cash		
		Dr.	Cr.	
4/4		7,000	300	4/6
4/24		6,000	900	4/18

The Chart of Accounts: Recording Transactions in T Accounts According to Rules of Debits and Credits

LEARNING UNIT 2-2

LO2

Can you get a queen in checkers? In a baseball game, does a runner rounding first base skip second base and run over the pitcher's mound to get to third? No. Most of us don't do such things because we follow the rules of the game. Usually we learn the rules first and reflect on the reasons for them afterward. Today people write emails instead of letters, but the rules of grammar still apply; thus, formats may change, but certain rules still need to be followed. The same is true in accounting.

Instead of first trying to understand all the rules of debit and credit and how they were developed in accounting, it is easier to learn the rules by "playing the game."

T Account Entries for Accounting in the Accounting Equation

Have patience. Learning the rules of debit and credit is like learning to play any game: The more you play, the easier it becomes. Table 2.1 shows the rules for the side on which you enter an increase or a decrease for each of the separate account categories in the accounting equation. For example, an increase is entered on the debit side in the asset account but on the credit side for a liability account.

TABLE 2.1 Rules of Debit and Credit

Account Category	Increase (Normal Balance)	Decrease
Assets	Debit	Credit
Liabilities	Credit	Debit
Owner's Equity		
Capital	Credit	Debit
Withdrawals	Debit	Credit
Revenue	Credit	Debit
Expenses	Debit	Credit

It might be easier to visualize these rules of debit and credit if we look at them in the T account form, using + to show increase and − to show decrease.

Assets	=	Liabilities	+	Owner's Equity							
				Capital −	Withdrawals +	Revenue −	Expenses				
Dr. | Cr.		Dr. | Cr.	+	Dr. | Cr.	Dr. | Cr.	Dr. | Cr.	Dr. | Cr.				
+ | −		− | +		− | +	+ | −	− | +	+ | −				

In a computerized system, the computer will record the debits and credits based on the account type.

Rules for Assets Work in the Opposite Direction to Those for Liabilities. When you look at the equation you can see that the rules for assets work in the opposite direction to those for liabilities. That is, for assets the increases appear on the debit side and the decreases are shown on the credit side; the opposite is true for liabilities. As for the owner's equity, the rules for withdrawals and expenses, which *decrease* owner's equity, work in the opposite direction to the rules for capital and revenue, which *increase* owner's equity.

Assets +	Withdrawals +	Expenses =	Liabilities +	Capital +	Revenue
Dr. | Cr.	Dr. | Cr.	Dr. | Cr.	Dr. | Cr.	Dr. | Cr.	Dr. | Cr.
+ | −	+ | −	+ | −	− | +	− | +	− | +

This setup may help you visualize how the rules for withdrawals and expenses are just the opposite of those for capital and revenue.

A **normal balance of an account** is the side that increases by the rules of debit and credit. For example, the normal balance of cash is a debit balance, because an asset is increased by a debit. We discuss normal balances further in Chapter 3.

COACHING TIP

Normal Balance	
Dr.	Cr.
Assets	Liabilities
Withdrawals	Capital
Expenses	Revenue

Normal balance of an account The side of an account that increases by the rules of debit and credit.

Balancing the Equation. It is important to remember that any amount(s) entered on the debit side of a T account or accounts also must appear on the credit side of another T account or accounts. This approach ensures that the total amount added to the debit side will equal the total amount added to the credit side, thereby keeping the accounting equation in balance.

Chart of Accounts. Our job is to analyze Mia Wong's business transactions—the transactions we looked at in Chapter 1—using a system of accounts guided by the rules of debit and credit that will summarize increases and decreases of individual accounts in the ledger. The goal is to prepare an income statement, statement of owner's equity, and balance sheet for Mia Wong's business. Sound familiar? If this system works, the rules of debit and credit and the use of accounts will give us the same answers as in Chapter 1, but with greater ease.

Mia's accountant developed what is called a chart of accounts. The chart of accounts is a numbered list of all of the business's accounts. It allows accounts to be located quickly. In Mia's business, for example, 100s are assets, 200s are liabilities, and so on. As you see in Table 2.2, each separate asset and liability account has its own number. Note that the chart may be expanded as the business grows.

Chart of accounts A numbering system of accounts that lists the account titles and account numbers to be used by a company.

TABLE 2.2 Chart of Accounts for Mia Wong, Attorney-at-Law

Balance Sheet Accounts	
Assets	**Liabilities**
111 Cash	211 Accounts Payable
112 Accounts Receivable	**Owner's Equity**
121 Office Equipment	311 Mia Wong, Capital
	312 Mia Wong, Withdrawals
Income Statement Accounts	
Revenue	**Expenses**
411 Legal Fees	511 Salaries Expense
	512 Rent Expense
	513 Advertising Expense

The Transaction Analysis: Five Steps

We will analyze the transactions in Mia Wong's law firm using a teaching device called a *transaction analysis chart* to record these five steps. (Keep in mind that the transaction analysis chart is not a part of any formal accounting system.) The five steps to analyzing each business transaction include the following:

STEP 1: Determine which accounts are affected. Example: Cash, Accounts Payable, Rent Expense. A transaction always affects at least two accounts.

STEP 2: Determine which categories the accounts belong to: assets, liabilities, capital, withdrawals, revenue, or expenses. Example: Cash is an asset.

STEP 3: Determine whether the accounts increase or decrease. Example: If you receive cash, that account increases.

STEP 4: What do the rules of debit and credit say (Table 2.1)?

STEP 5: What does the T account look like? Place amounts into accounts either on the left or right side depending on the rules in Table 2.1.

The following chart shows the five-step analysis from another perspective.

COACHING TIP

Remember that the rules of debit and credit only tell us on which side to place information. Whether the debit or credit represents increases or decreases depends on the account category: assets, liabilities, capital, and so on. Think of a business transaction as an exchange: You get something and you give or part with something.

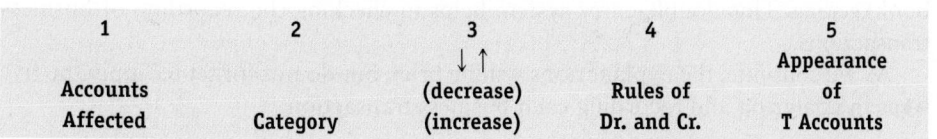

1	2	3	4	5
		↓ ↑		Appearance
Accounts		(decrease)	Rules of	of
Affected	Category	(increase)	Dr. and Cr.	T Accounts

Let us emphasize a major point: *Do not try to debit or credit an account until you go through the first three steps of the transaction analysis.*

Applying the Transaction Analysis to Mia Wong's Law Practice

Transaction A Aug. 28: Mia Wong invests $6,000 cash and $200 of office equipment in the business.

COACHING TIP

Note that in column 3 of the chart it doesn't matter if both arrows go up, as long as the sum of the debits equals the sum of the credits in the T accounts in column 5.

1 Accounts Affected	2 Category	3 ↓ ↑	4 Rules of Dr. and Cr.	5 Appearance of T Accounts
Cash	Asset	↑	Dr.	Cash 111
				(A) 6,000
Office Equipment	Asset	↑	Dr.	Office Equipment 121
				(A) 200
Mia Wong, Capital	Capital	↑	Cr.	Mia Wong, Capital 311
				6,200 (A)

Note again that every transaction affects at least two T accounts and that the total amount added to the debit side(s) must equal the total amount added to the credit side(s) of the T accounts of each transaction.

Analysis of Transaction A

STEP 1: Which accounts are affected? The law firm receives its cash and office equipment, so three accounts are involved: Cash, Office Equipment, and Mia Wong, Capital. These account titles come from the chart of accounts.

STEP 2: Which categories do these accounts belong to? Cash and Office Equipment are assets. Mia Wong, Capital is capital.

STEP 3: Are the accounts increasing or decreasing? Cash and Office Equipment, both assets, are increasing in the business. The rights or claims of Mia Wong, Capital are also increasing because she invested money and office equipment in the business.

STEP 4: What do the rules say? According to the rules of debit and credit, an increase in assets (Cash and Office Equipment) is a debit. An increase in Capital is a credit. Note that the total dollar amount of debits will equal the total dollar amount of credits when the T accounts are updated in column 5.

STEP 5: What does the T account look like? The amount for Cash and Office Equipment is entered on the debit side. The amount for Mia Wong, Capital goes on the credit side.

Compound entry A transaction involving more than one debit or credit.

Double-entry bookkeeping An accounting system in which the recording of each transaction affects two or more accounts and the total of the debits is equal to the total of the credits.

A transaction that involves more than one debit or more than one credit is called a compound entry. This first transaction of Mia Wong's law firm is a compound entry; it involves a debit of $6,000 to Cash and a debit of $200 to Office Equipment (as well as a credit of $6,200 to Mia Wong, Capital).

The name for this double-entry analysis of transactions, where two or more accounts are affected and the total of debits and credits is equal, is double-entry bookkeeping. This double-entry system helps in checking the recording of business transactions.

As we continue, the explanations will be brief, but do not forget to apply the five steps in analyzing and recording each business transaction.

Transaction B Aug. 29: Law practice bought office equipment for cash, $500.

1 Accounts Affected	2 Category	3 ↓↑	4 Rules of Dr. and Cr.	5 T Account Update
Office Equipment	Asset	↑	Dr.	Office Equipment 121
				(A) 200 |
				(B) 500 |
Cash	Asset	↓	Cr.	Cash 111
				(A) 6,000 | 500 (B)

Analysis of Transaction B

STEP 1: The law firm paid $500 cash for the office equipment it purchased. The accounts involved in the transaction are Cash and Office Equipment.

STEP 2: The accounts belong to these categories: Office Equipment is an asset; Cash is an asset.

STEP 3: The asset Office Equipment is increasing. The asset Cash is decreasing; it is being reduced to buy the office equipment.

STEP 4: An increase in the asset Office Equipment is a debit; a decrease in the asset Cash is a credit.

STEP 5: When the amounts are placed in the T accounts, the amount for Office Equipment is entered on the debit side and the amount for Cash on the credit side.

Transaction C Aug. 30: Bought more office equipment on account, $300.

1 Accounts Affected	2 Category	3 ↓↑	4 Rules of Dr. and Cr.	5 T Account Update
Office Equipment	Asset	↑	Dr.	Office Equipment 121
				(A) 200 |
				(B) 500 |
				(C) 300 |
Accounts Payable	Liability	↑	Cr.	Accounts Payable 211
				| 300 (C)

Analysis of Transaction C

STEP 1: The law firm receives office equipment totaling $300 by promising to pay in the future. An obligation or liability, Accounts Payable, is created. The accounts affected are Office Equipment and Accounts Payable.

STEP 2: Office Equipment is an asset. Accounts Payable is a liability.

STEP 3: The asset Office Equipment is increasing; the liability Accounts Payable is increasing because the law firm is increasing what it owes.

STEP 4: An increase in the asset Office Equipment is a debit. An increase in the liability Accounts Payable is a credit.

STEP 5: Enter the amount for Office Equipment on the debit side of the T account. The amount for the Accounts Payable goes on the credit side.

Transaction D Sept. 1–30: Provided legal services for cash, $2,000.

---

1 Accounts Affected	2 Category	3 ↓ ↑	4 Rules of Dr. and Cr.	5 T Account Update			
Cash	Asset	↑	Dr.			Cash 111	
				(A)	6,000	500	(B)
				(D)	2,000		
Legal Fees	Revenue	↑	Cr.			Legal Fees 411	
						2,000	(D)

Analysis of Transaction D

STEP 1: The firm earned revenue from legal services and received $2,000 in cash. The accounts affected are Legal Fees and Cash.

STEP 2: Cash is an asset. Legal Fees is revenue.

STEP 3: Cash, an asset, is increasing. Legal Fees, or revenue, is also increasing.

STEP 4: An increase in Cash, an asset, is debited. An increase in Legal Fees, or revenue, is credited.

STEP 5: Enter the amount for Cash on the debit side of the T account. Enter the amount for Legal Fees on the credit side.

Transaction E Sept. 1–30: Provided legal services on account, $3,000.

---

1 Accounts Affected	2 Category	3 ↓ ↑	4 Rules of Dr. and Cr.	5 T Account Update			
Accounts Receivable	Asset	↑	Dr.			Accounts Receivable 112	
				(E)	3,000		
Legal Fees	Revenue	↑	Cr.			Legal Fees 411	
						2,000	(D)
						3,000	(E)

Analysis of Transaction E

STEP 1: The law practice has earned revenue of $3,000 but has not yet received payment (cash). The amounts owed by these clients are called Accounts Receivable. Revenue is earned at the time the legal services are provided, regardless of whether payment is received then or will be received some time in the future. The accounts affected are Accounts Receivable and Legal Fees.

STEP 2: Accounts Receivable is an asset. Legal Fees is revenue.

STEP 3: Accounts Receivable is increasing because the law practice increased the amount owed to it for legal fees earned but not yet received. Legal Fees, or revenue, is increasing.

STEP 4: An increase in the asset Accounts Receivable is a debit. An increase in Legal Fees is a credit.

STEP 5: Enter the amount for Accounts Receivable on the debit side of the T account. The amount for Legal Fees goes on the credit side.

Transaction F Sept. 1–30: Received $900 cash from clients for services rendered previously on account.

---

1 Accounts Affected	2 Category	3 ↓ ↑	4 Rules of Dr. and Cr.	5 T Account Update
Cash	Asset	↑	Dr.	Cash 111
				(A) 6,000 | 500 (B)
				(D) 2,000
				(F) 900
Accounts Receivable	Asset	↓	Cr.	Accounts Receivable 112
				(E) 3,000 | 900 (F)

Analysis of Transaction F

STEP 1: The law firm collects $900 in cash from previous revenue earned. Because the revenue is recorded at the time it is earned, and not when the collection is received, in this transaction we are concerned only with the collection, which affects the Cash and Accounts Receivable accounts.

STEP 2: Cash is an asset. Accounts Receivable is an asset.

STEP 3: Because clients are paying what is owed, Cash (asset) is increasing and the amount owed (Accounts Receivable) is decreasing (the total amount owed by clients to Wong is going down). This transaction results in a shift in assets, more Cash for less Accounts Receivable.

STEP 4: An increase in Cash, an asset, is a debit. A decrease in Accounts Receivable, an asset, is a credit.

STEP 5: Enter the amount for Cash on the debit side of the T account. The amount for Accounts Receivable goes on the credit side.

Transaction G Sept. 1–30: Paid salaries expense, $700.

---

1 Accounts Affected	2 Category	3 ↓ ↑	4 Rules of Dr. and Cr.	5 T Account Update
Salaries Expense	Expense	↑	Dr.	Salaries Expense 511
				(G) 700 |
Cash	Asset	↓	Cr.	Cash 111
				(A) 6,000 | 500 (B)
				(D) 2,000 | 700 (G)
				(F) 900 |

Analysis of Transaction G

STEP 1: The law firm pays $700 of salaries expense by cash. The accounts affected are Salaries Expense and Cash.

STEP 2: Salaries Expense is an expense. Cash is an asset.

STEP 3: The Salaries Expense of the law firm is increasing, which results in a decrease in Cash.

STEP 4: An increase in Salaries Expense, an expense, is a debit. A decrease in Cash, an asset, is a credit.

STEP 5: Enter the amount for Salaries Expense on the debit side of the T account. The amount for Cash goes on the credit side.

Transaction H Sept. 1–30: Paid rent expense, $400.

---

1 Accounts Affected	2 Category	3 ↓ ↑	4 Rules of Dr. and Cr.	5 T Account Update
Rent Expense	Expense	↑	Dr.	Rent Expense 512
				(H) 400 │
Cash	Asset	↓	Cr.	Cash 111
				(A) 6,000 │ 500 (B)
				(D) 2,000 │ 700 (G)
				(F) 900 │ 400 (H)

Analysis of Transaction H

STEP 1: The law firm's rent expense of $400 is paid in cash. The accounts affected are Rent Expense and Cash.

STEP 2: Rent is an expense. Cash is an asset.

STEP 3: The Rent Expense increases the expenses, and the payment for the Rent Expense decreases the cash.

STEP 4: An increase in Rent Expense, an expense, is a debit. A decrease in Cash, an asset, is a credit.

STEP 5: Enter the amount for Rent Expense on the debit side of the T account. Place the amount for Cash on the credit side.

Transaction I Sept. 1–30: Received a bill for Advertising Expense (to be paid next month), $200.

---

1 Accounts Affected	2 Category	3 ↓ ↑	4 Rules of Dr. and Cr.	5 T Account Update
Advertising Expense	Expense	↑	Dr.	Advertising Expense 513
				(I) 200 │
Accounts Payable	Liability	↑	Cr.	Accounts Payable 211
				│ 300 (C)
				│ 200 (I)

Analysis of Transaction I

STEP 1: The advertising bill in the amount of $200 has come in and payment is due but has not yet been made. Therefore, the accounts involved here are Advertising Expense and Accounts Payable; the expense has created a liability.

STEP 2: Advertising Expense is an expense. Accounts Payable is a liability.

STEP 3: Both the expense and the liability are increasing.

STEP 4: An increase in an expense is a debit. An increase in a liability is a credit.

STEP 5: Enter the amount for Advertising Expense on the debit side of the T account. Enter the amount for Accounts Payable on the credit side.

Transaction J Sept. 1–30: Wong withdrew cash for personal use, $100.

---

1 Accounts Affected	2 Category	3 ↓ ↑	4 Rules of Dr. and Cr.	5 T Account Update
Mia Wong, Withdrawals	Withdrawals	↑	Dr.	Mia Wong, Withdrawals 312
				(J) 100 |
Cash	Asset	↓	Cr.	Cash 111
				(A) 6,000 | 500 (B) (D) 2,000 | 700 (G) (F) 900 | 400 (H) | 100 (J)

Analysis of Transaction J

STEP 1: Mia Wong withdraws $100 cash from business for *personal* use. This withdrawal is not a business expense. The accounts affected are Mia Wong, Withdrawals and Cash.

STEP 2: This transaction affects Mia Wong, Withdrawals and Cash accounts.

STEP 3: Mia has increased what she has withdrawn from the business for personal use. The business cash decreased.

STEP 4: An increase in Withdrawals is a debit. A decrease in Cash is a credit. (*Remember:* Withdrawals go on the statement of owner's equity; expenses go on the income statement.)

STEP 5: Enter the amount for Mia Wong, Withdrawals, on the debit side of the T account. The amount for Cash goes on the credit side.

COACHING TIP

Withdrawals are always increased by debits.

Summary of Transactions for Mia Wong								
Assets	=	**Liabilities**	+			**Owner's Equity**		
Cash 111	=	Accounts Payable 211	+	Capital	−	Withdrawals	+ Revenue	− Expenses
(A) 6,000 | 500 (B) (D) 2,000 | 700 (G) (F) 900 | 400 (H) | 100 (J)	=	| 300 (C) | 200 (I)	+	Mia Wong, Capital 311 | 6,200 (A)	−	Mia Wong, Withdrawals 312 (J) 100 |	+ Legal Fees 411 | 2,000 (D) | 3,000 (E)	− Salaries Expense 511 (G) 700 |
Accounts Receivable 112								
(E) 3,000 | 900 (F)								− Rent Expense 512
Office Equipment 121								(H) 400 |
(A) 200 | (B) 500 | (C) 300 |								− Advertising Expense 513 (I) 200 |

 **TRY IT!**   Learning Unit 2-2

Given the following partial chart of accounts for Earl Miller's law office, complete a transaction analysis box for Earl's transactions below:

Cash 111

Accounts Receivable 112

Accounts Payable 211

Legal Fees 411

Legal Expenses 511

Transaction: Earl completed legal work for $10,000. The client paid Earl $2,000 in cash and promised to pay the balance next month.

LEARNING UNIT 2-3

L03

The Trial Balance and Preparation of Financial Statements

Let us look at all the transactions we have discussed, arranged by T accounts and recorded using the rules of debit and credit. This grouping of accounts is much easier to use than the expanded accounting equation because all the transactions that affect a particular account are in one place.

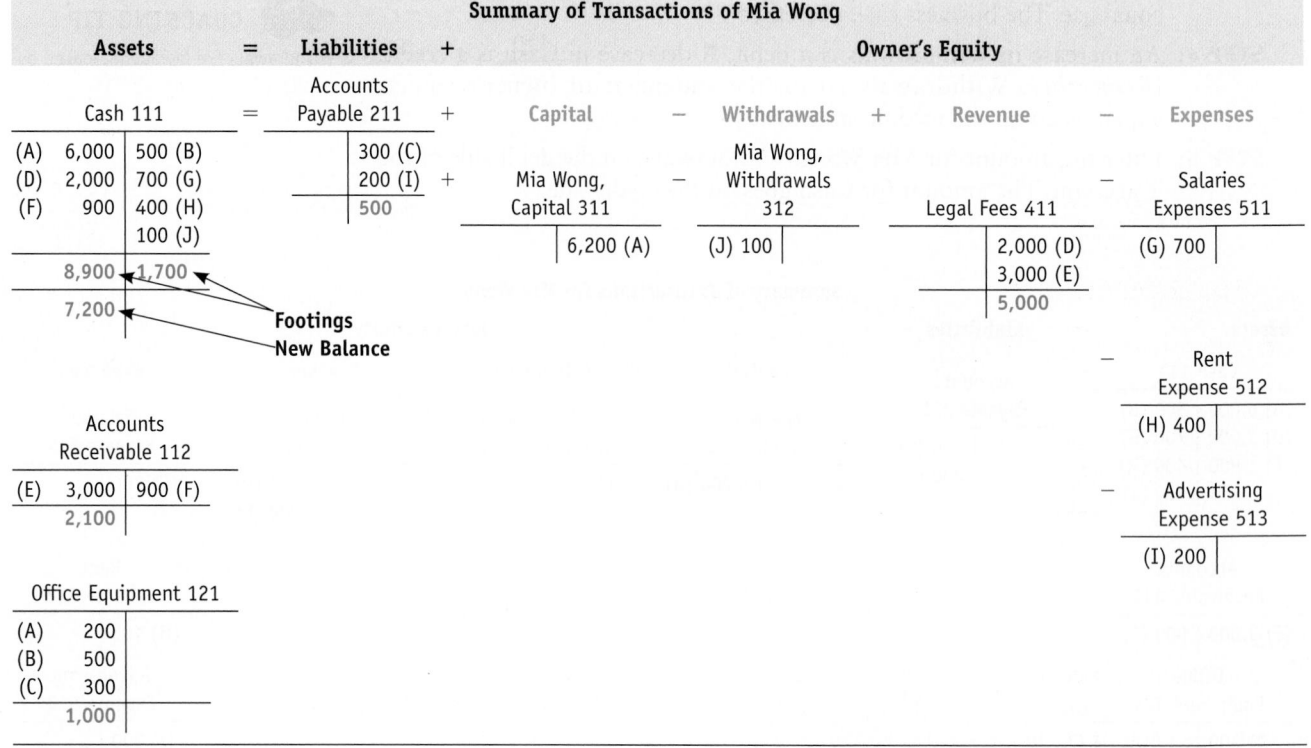

As we saw in Learning Unit 2-2, when all the transactions are recorded in the accounts, the total of all the debits should be equal to the total of all the credits. (If they are not, the accountant must go back and find the error by checking the numbers and adding every column again.)

The Trial Balance

Footings are used to obtain the totals of each side of every T account that has more than one entry. The footings are used to find the ending balance. The ending balances are used to prepare a trial balance. The trial balance is not a financial statement, although it is used to prepare financial statements. The trial balance lists all the accounts with their balances in the same order as they appear in the chart of accounts. It proves the accuracy of the ledger. For example, look at the preceding Cash account. The footing for the debit side is $8,900, and the footing for the credit side is $1,700. Because the debit side is larger, we subtract $1,700 from $8,900 to arrive at an *ending debit balance* of $7,200. Now look at the Rent Expense account. It doesn't need a footing because it has only one entry. The amount itself is the ending balance. When the ending balance has been found for every account, we should be able to show that the total of all debits equals the total of all credits.

In the ideal situation, businesses would take a trial balance every day. The large number of transactions most businesses conduct each day makes this impractical. Instead, trial balances are prepared periodically.

Keep in mind that the figure for Capital might not be the beginning figure if any additional investment has taken place during the period. You can tell by looking at the Capital account in the ledger.

A more detailed discussion of the trial balance is provided in the next chapter. For now, notice the heading, how the accounts are listed, the debits in the left column, the credits in the right, and that the total of debits is equal to the total of credits.

A trial balance of Mia Wong's accounts is shown in Figure 2.2.

Trial balance A list of the ending balances of all the accounts in a ledger. The total of the debits should equal the total of the credits.

	Dr.	Cr.
MIA WONG, ATTORNEY-AT-LAW TRIAL BALANCE SEPTEMBER 30, 201X		
Cash	7 2 0 0 0	
Accounts Receivable	2 1 0 0 0	
Office Equipment	1 0 0 0 0	
Accounts Payable		5 0 0 0 0
Mia Wong, Capital		6 2 0 0 0 0
Mia Wong, Withdrawals	1 0 0 0	
Legal Fees		5 0 0 0 0 0
Salaries Expense	7 0 0 0	
Rent Expense	4 0 0 0	
Advertising Expense	2 0 0 0	
Totals	11 7 0 0 0 0	11 7 0 0 0 0

FIGURE 2.2
Trial Balance for Mia Wong's Law Firm

Preparing Financial Statements

The trial balance is used to prepare the financial statements. The diagram in Figure 2.3 on page 46 shows how financial statements can be prepared from a trial balance. Statements do not have debit or credit columns. The left column is used only to subtotal numbers.

FIGURE 2.3 Steps in Preparing Financial Statements from a Trial Balance

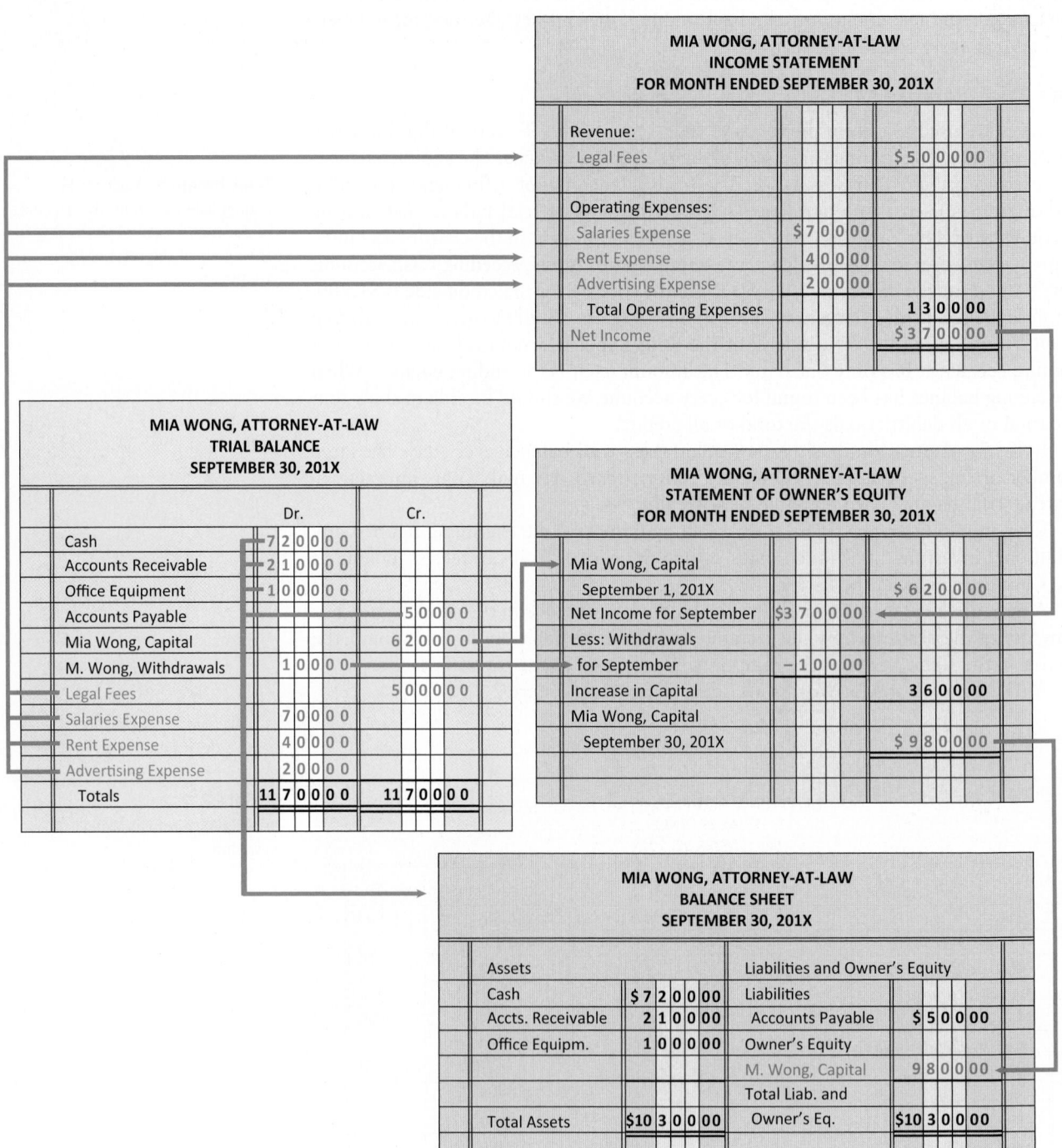

 **TRY IT!**   **Learning Unit 2-3**

From the following trial balance, prepare the three financial statements.

	Ward's Gym Trial Balance Sept. 30, 201X	
	Dr.	**Cr.**
Cash	500	
Accounts Receivable	850	
Gym Equipment	3,000	
Accounts Payable		1,000
Pete Ward, Capital		2,750
Pete Ward, Withdrawals	500	
Gym Fees		2,800
Rent Expense	700	
Advertising Expense	200	
Salaries Expense	800	
	6,550	6,550

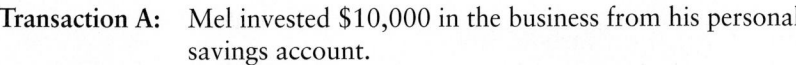

DEMONSTRATION SUMMARY PROBLEM

 L01,2,3

The chart of accounts of Mel's Delivery Service includes the following: Cash, 111; Accounts Receivable, 112; Office Equipment, 121; Delivery Trucks, 122; Accounts Payable, 211; Mel Free, Capital, 311; Mel Free, Withdrawals, 312; Delivery Fees Earned, 411; Advertising Expense, 511; Gas Expense, 512; Salaries Expense, 513; and Telephone Expense, 514. The following transactions resulted for Mel's Delivery Service during the month of July:

Transaction A:	Mel invested $10,000 in the business from his personal savings account.
Transaction B:	Bought delivery trucks on account, $17,000.
Transaction C:	Advertising bill received but unpaid, $700.
Transaction D:	Bought office equipment for cash, $1,200.
Transaction E:	Received cash for delivery services rendered, $15,000.
Transaction F:	Paid salaries expense, $3,000.
Transaction G:	Paid gas expense for company trucks, $1,250.
Transaction H:	Billed customers for delivery services rendered, $4,000.
Transaction I:	Paid telephone bill, $300.
Transaction J:	Received $3,000 as partial payment of transaction H.
Transaction K:	Mel paid home telephone bill from company checkbook, $150.

Requirements

As Mel's newly employed accountant, you must do the following:

1. Set up T accounts in a ledger.
2. Record transactions in the T accounts. (Place the letter of the transaction next to the entry.)

3. Foot and take the balance of each account where appropriate.

4. Prepare a trial balance at the end of July.

5. Prepare from the trial balance, in proper form, (a) an income statement for the month of July, (b) a statement of owner's equity, and (c) a balance sheet as of July 31, 201X.

Solutions

Requirements 1, 2, 3, 4

Set up T accounts, record transactions, foot each account, and prepare a trial balance.

General Ledger

Cash 111				Accts. Payable 211		Advertising Expense 511	
(A) 10,000	1,200	(D)		17,000 (B)		(C) 700	
(E) 15,000	3,000	(F)		700 (C)			
(J) 3,000	1,250	(G)		17,700			
	300	(I)					
	150	(K)					
28,000	5,900						
22,100							

Accts. Receivable 112			Mel Free, Capital 311		Gas Expense 512	
(H) 4,000	3,000	(J)		10,000 (A)	(G) 1,250	
1,000						

Office Equipment 121		Mel Free, Withdrawals 312		Salaries Expense 513	
(D) 1,200		(K) 150		(F) 3,000	

Delivery Trucks 122		Delivery Fees Earned 411		Telephone Expense 514	
(B) 17,000			15,000 (E)	(I) 300	
			4,000 (H)		
			19,000		

Tips to Recording Transactions

A. Cash	Asset	↑	Dr.
Mel Free, Capital	Capital	↑	Cr.
B. Delivery Trucks	Asset	↑	Dr.
Accts. Payable	Liability	↑	Cr.
C. Advertising Expense	Expense	↑	Dr.
Accts. Payable	Liability	↑	Cr.
D. Office Equipment	Asset	↑	Dr.
Cash	Asset	↓	Cr.
E. Cash	Asset	↑	Dr.
Del. Fees Earned	Revenue	↑	Cr.
F. Salaries Expense	Expense	↑	Dr.
Cash	Asset	↓	Cr.
G. Gas Expense	Expense	↑	Dr.
Cash	Asset	↓	Cr.

H. Accts. Receivable	Asset	↑	Dr.
Del. Fees Earned	Revenue	↑	Cr.
I. Tel. Expense	Expense	↑	Dr.
Cash	Asset	↓	Cr.
J. Cash	Asset	↑	Dr.
Accts. Receivable	Asset	↓	Cr.
K. Mel Free, Withdrawals	Withdrawals	↑	Dr.
Cash	Asset	↓	Cr.

Mel's Delivery Service
Trial Balance
July 31, 201X

	Dr.	Cr.
Cash	22,100	
Accounts Receivable	1,000	
Office Equipment	1,200	
Delivery Trucks	17,000	
Accounts Payable		17,700
Mel Free, Capital		10,000
Mel Free, Withdrawals	150	
Delivery Fees Earned		19,000
Advertising Expense	700	
Gas Expense	1,250	
Salaries Expense	3,000	
Telephone Expense	300	
Totals	46,700	46,700

Tips to Taking the Balance of an Account and Preparation of a Trial Balance

3. Footings: Cash   Add left side, $28,000.

Add right side, $5,900.

Take difference, $22,100, and stay on side that is larger.

Accounts Payable   Add $17,000 + $700 and stay on same side.

Total is $17,700.

4. Trial balance is a list of the ledger's ending balances. The list is in the same order as the chart of accounts. Each account has only one number listed as either a debit or a credit balance.

Requirement 5

Prepare an Income Statement, Statement of Owner's Equity, and a Balance Sheet from the Trial Balance (see Figure 2.4, page 50). When the Statement of Owner's Equity is prepared, assume the initial investment represents the beginning figure for capital and that no additional investments were made.

FIGURE 2.4
Financial Statements

4a.

MEL'S DELIVERY SERVICE INCOME STATEMENT FOR MONTH ENDED JULY 31, 201X		
Revenue:		
Delivery Fees Earned		$ 19 0 0 00
Operating Expenses:		
Advertising Expense	$ 7 0 0 00	
Gas Expense	1 2 5 0 00	
Salaries Expense	3 0 0 0 00	
Telephone Expense	3 0 0 00	
Total Operating Expenses		5 2 5 0 00
Net Income		$ 13 7 5 0 00

b.

MEL'S DELIVERY SERVICE STATEMENT OF OWNER'S EQUITY FOR MONTH ENDED JULY 31, 201X		
Mel Free, Capital		
July 1, 201X		$ 10 0 0 0 00
Net Income for July	$13 7 5 0 00	
Less: Withdrawals for July	– 1 5 0 00	
Increase in Capital		$ 13 6 0 0 00
Mel Free, Capital		
July 31, 201X		$ 23 6 0 0 00

c.

MEL'S DELIVERY SERVICE BALANCE SHEET JULY 31, 201X				
Assets		Liabilities and Owner's Equity		
Cash	$22 1 0 0 00	Liabilities		
Accounts Receivable	1 0 0 0 00	Accounts Payable	$17 7 0 0 00	
Office Equipment	1 2 0 0 00			
Delivery Trucks	17 0 0 0 00			
		Owner's Equity		
		Mel Free, Capital	23 6 0 0 00	
		Total Liab. and		
Total Assets	$41 3 0 0 00	Owner's Equity	$41 3 0 0 00	

Tips to Prepare Financial Statements from a Trial Balance

Trial Balance

		Dr.	Cr.
Balance Sheet	Assets	X	
	Liabilities		X
Statement of Owner's Equity	Capital		X
	Withdrawals	X	
Income Statement	Revenues		X
	Expenses	X	
		XX	XX

Net income of $13,750 on the income statement goes on the statement of owner's equity.

Ending capital of $23,600 on the statement of owner's equity goes on the balance sheet as the new figure for capital.

Note: Financial statements do not show debits or credits. The inside column is used for subtotaling.

BLUEPRINT: PREPARING FINANCIAL STATEMENTS FROM A TRIAL BALANCE

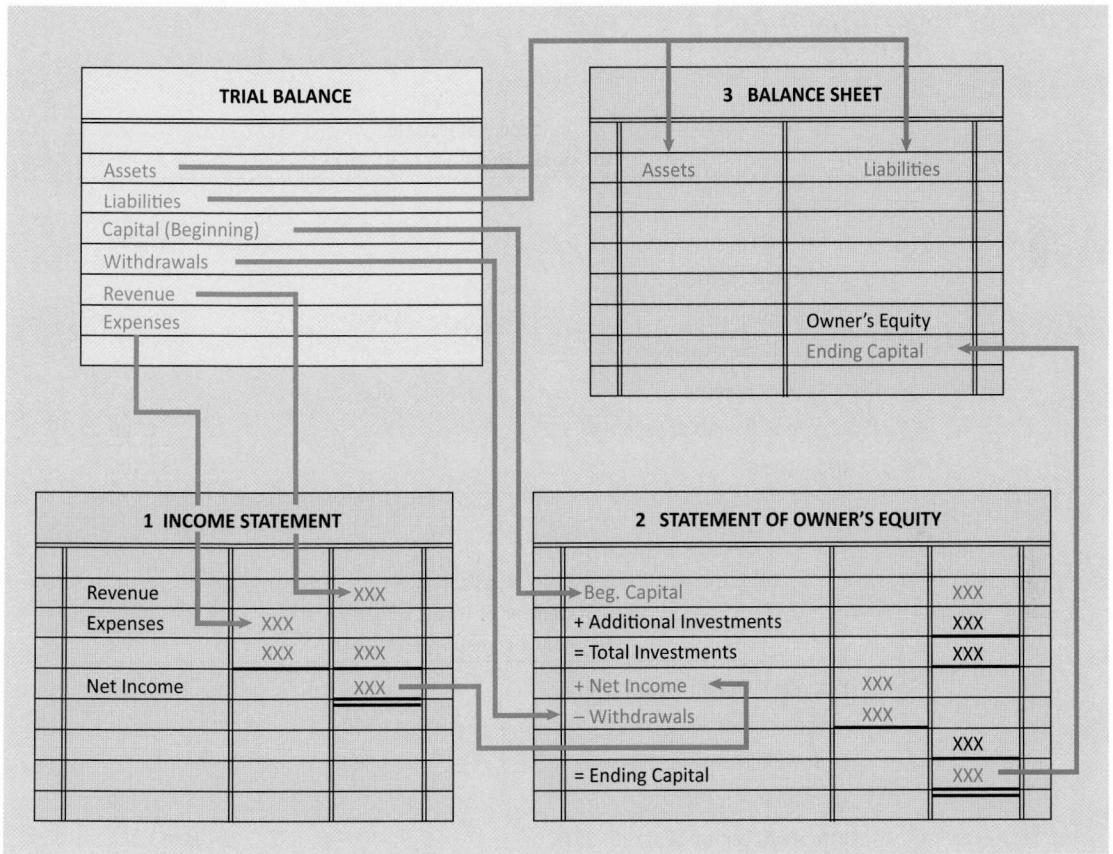

 **TRY IT!**   **Solutions**   MyAccountingLab

Learning Unit 2-1

	Cash		
Dr.		Cr.	
4/4	7,000	300	4/6
4/24	6,000	900	4/18
	13,000	1,200	
BAL	11,800		

Learning Unit 2-2

Acct. Affected	Cat.	Inc./Dec.	Rules	T Account
				Cash 111
Cash	Asset	Inc.	Dr.	2,000 Dr.	
				Acc. Rec. 112
Acc. Receivable	Asset	Inc.	Dr.	8,000 Dr.	
				Leg. Fees 411
Legal Fees	Revenue	Inc.	Cr.		10,000 Cr.

Learning Unit 2-3

Ward's Gym
Income Statement
For Month Ended Sept. 30, 201X

Revenue:		
Gym fees		$2,800
Operating Expenses:		
Rent Expense	$700	
Advertising Expense	200	
Salaries Expense	800	
Total Operating Expenses		1,700
Net Income		$1,100

Ward's Gym
Statement of Owner's Equity
For Month Ended Sept. 30, 201X

Pete Ward, Capital Sept. 1, 201X		$2,750
Net Income for Sept.	$1,100	
Less: Withdrawals for Sept.	−500	
Increase in Capital		600
Pete Ward, Capital Sept. 30, 201X		$3,350

Ward's Gym
Balance Sheet
Sept. 30, 201X

Assets		Liabilities and Owner's Equity	
Cash	$ 500	Liabilities	
Accts. Rec.	850	Accts. Payable	$1,000
Gym Equip.	3,000	Owner's Equity	
		P. Ward, Capital	3,350
Total Assets	$4,350	Total Liab. and Owner's Equity	$4,350

ACCOUNTING COACH

The following Coaching Tips are from Learning Units 2-1 to 2-3. Take the Pre-Game Checkup and use the Check Your Score at the bottom of the page to see how you are doing. The Accounting Coach provides tips before each Checkup to help you avoid common accounting errors.

LU 2-1 The T Account and How to Foot and Balance

Pre-Game Tips: Think of "debit" or "credit" as only indicating a position (left or right). To balance an account, total the left (debit) side and the right (credit) side and take the difference between the two totals. This ending balance is placed on the side that is greater. Do not think at this point of "debit" or "credit" as being good or bad. They simply indicate a position, left or right.

Pre-Game Checkup: Answer true or false to the following statements.

1. A number entered on the left side of an account is said to be credited to the account.
2. Debits are always positive.
3. Footings are always a credit balance.
4. "Credit" always means the number should be put on the right side.
5. A ledger does not use debits or credits.

LU 2-2 The Chart of Accounts: Recording Transactions in T Accounts According to Rules of Debits and Credits

Pre-Game Tips: Assets, withdrawals, and expenses will increase on the debit side, while liabilities, capital, and revenues will increase on the credit side. The normal balance of an account is on the side that increases it. The goal of each transaction is for the sum of the left side of the accounting equation to equal the sum of the right side. Compound entries result when three or more accounts affect a transaction.

Pre-Game Checkup: Answer true or false to the following statements.

1. Rules for debit and credit work in the opposite direction for capital and revenue.
2. An increase in an asset is always a debit.
3. Withdrawals increase with a credit.
4. After a transaction is recorded it can have only one debit and one credit.
5. An unpaid bill results in a debit to a liability and a credit to an expense.

LU 2-3 The Trial Balance and Preparation of Financial Statements

Pre-Game Tips: A trial balance is a list of the accounts in the ledger with their ending balances. Each account can only have either a debit or a credit balance. A trial balance will list assets, liabilities, capital, withdrawals, revenue, and expenses. When the financial statements are prepared there are no debits or credits on the financial reports. It is the ending balance of each account that is listed. The inside columns of financial reports are used for subtotaling.

Pre-Game Checkup: Answer true or false to the following statements.

1. Withdrawals are usually a credit balance on the trial balance.
2. A balance sheet will list only debit accounts.
3. The balance sheet is always prepared before the income statement.
4. Subtotaling is only used on the trial balance.
5. The beginning balance of capital is shown on the balance sheet.

CHECK YOUR SCORE: Answers to the Pre-Game Checkup

LU 2-1

1. False—A number entered on the left side of an account is said to be debited to the account.
2. False—Debits are on the left-hand side of the account.
3. False—Whether or not footings are a credit balance depends on which side is larger after balancing.
4. True.
5. False—A ledger does use debits and credits.

LU 2-2

1. False—Rules for debit and credit work in the same direction for capital and revenue.
2. True.
3. False—Withdrawals increase with a debit.
4. False—After a transaction is recorded it can have more than one debit or credit as long as the total of debits equals the total of credits.
5. False—An unpaid bill results in a debit to expense and a credit to liability.

LU 2-3

1. False—Withdrawals are usually a debit balance on the trial balance.
2. False—The balance sheet can list accounts with either a debit or credit balance, but the balance sheet does not show debits or credits.
3. False—The balance sheet is prepared after the income statement.
4. False—Subtotaling is used in preparing financial reports; the trial balance is not a financial report.
5. False—The ending figure for capital is shown on the balance sheet.

Chapter Summary

Here are all the key terms and equations to help you understand the concepts of this chapter and prepare you for your exam. After completing this review, go to MyAccountingLab for more practice opportunities.

MyAccountingLab

Concepts You Should Know	Key Terms
L01 **Explain T Accounts and How to Foot and Balance** 1. A T account is a simplified version of a standard account. 2. A ledger is a group of accounts. 3. A debit is the left-hand position (side) of an account, and a credit is the right-hand position (side). 4. A footing is the total of one side of an account. The ending balance is the difference between the footings.	Account (p. 34) Credit (p. 34) Debit (p. 34) Ending balance (p. 35) Footings (p. 35) Ledger (p. 34) Standard account (p. 34) T account (p. 34)
L02 **Use a Chart of Accounts to Record Transactions in T Accounts According to the Rules of Debits and Credits** 1. A chart of accounts lists the account titles and their numbers for a company. 2. The transaction analysis chart is a teaching device. 3. A compound entry is a transaction involving more than one debit or credit. 4. In double-entry bookkeeping, the recording of each business transaction affects two or more accounts, and the total of debits equals the total of credits.	Chart of accounts (p. 37) Compound entry (p. 38) Double-entry bookkeeping (p. 38) Normal balance of an account (p. 36)
L03 **Prepare a Trial Balance and the Financial Statements** 1. A trial balance is a list of the ending balances of all accounts, listed in the same order as the chart of accounts. 2. Any additional investments during the period result in the Capital balance on the trial balance not being the beginning figure. 3. No debit or credit columns are used in the three financial statements. 4. To prepare the financial statements, take the balances of each ledger account to prepare the income statement, statement of owner's equity, and balance sheet.	Trial balance (p. 45)

Discussion Questions and Critical Thinking/Ethical Case

1. Define a ledger.

2. Why is the left-hand side of an account called a debit?

3. Footings are used in balancing all accounts. True or false? Please explain.

4. What is the end product of the accounting process?

5. What do we mean when we say that a transaction analysis chart is a teaching device?

6. What are the five steps of the transaction analysis chart?

7. Computers cannot do debits and credits—agree or disagree and explain why.

8. A trial balance is a formal statement. True or false? Please explain.

9. Why are there no debit or credit columns on financial statements?

10. Compare the financial statements prepared from the expanded accounting equation with those prepared from a trial balance.

11. Meg Ryan, the bookkeeper of Logan Co., was scheduled to leave on a three-week vacation at 5:00 on Friday. She couldn't get the company's trial balance to balance. At 4:30, she decided to put in fictitious figures in her computer to make it balance. Meg told herself she would fix it when she got back from her vacation. Was Meg right or wrong to do this? Why?

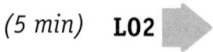

Concept Checks

(5 min) **L01**

The T Account

1. From the following, foot and balance each account.

	Cash 110				M. Meade, Capital 311	
9/5	4,000	800	7/25		9,000	6/9
9/9	10,000				5,000	9/3
					3,000	9/7

(5 min) **L02**

Transaction Analysis

2. Complete the following:

Account	Category	↑	↓	Normal Balance
A. Salaries Payable				
B. Taxable Fees Earned				
C. Accounts Receivable				
D. Sam Slater, Capital				
E. Sam Slater, Withdrawals				
F. Prepaid Advertising				
G. Rent Expense				

Transaction Analysis

LO2 *(5 min)*

3. Record the following transaction in the transaction analysis chart: Provided tutoring fees for $4,000, receiving $1,100 cash with the remainder to be paid next month.

Accounts Affected	Category	↓	↑	Rules of Dr. and Cr.	T Accounts

Trial Balance

LO3 *(5 min)*

4. Rearrange the following titles in the order they would appear on a trial balance:

B. O'Mally, Withdrawals   Hair Salon Fees Earned

Accounts Receivable   Selling Expense

Cash   Salary Expense

B. O'Mally, Capital   Advertising Expense

Office Equipment   Accounts Payable

Trial Balance/Financial Statements

LO3 *(10 min)*

5. From the following trial balance, identify which statement each title will appear on:
- Income statement (IS)
- Statement of owner's equity (OE)
- Balance sheet (BS)

Bradford Co.
Trial Balance
Nov. 30, 201X

		Dr.	Cr.
A. _____	Cash	600	
B. _____	Computer	100	
C. _____	Computer Equipment	1,000	
D. _____	Accounts Payable		800
E. _____	L. Bradford, Capital		200
F. _____	L. Bradford, Withdrawals	500	
G. _____	Legal Fees Earned		1,500
H. _____	Consulting Fees Earned		300
I. _____	Wage Expense	200	
J. _____	Supplies Expense	250	
K. _____	Internet Advertising Expense	150	
	Totals	2,800	2,800

MyAccountingLab   **Exercises**

Set A

(10 min)   **LO2**   **2A-1.**   From the following, prepare a chart of accounts.

Microsoft Surface Tablet	Legal Fees
Salary Expense	L. Janas, Capital
Accounts Payable	Cash
Accounts Receivable	Advertising Expense
Repair Expense	L. Janas, Withdrawals

(5 min)   **LO2**   **2A-2.**   Record the following transaction in the transaction analysis chart: Shawna Portia bought a new piece of computer equipment for $25,000, paying $6,000 down and charging the rest.

(5 min)   **LO2**   **2A-3.**   Complete the following table. For each account listed on the left, fill in what category it belongs to, whether increases and decreases in the account are marked on the debit or credit sides, and on which financial statement the account appears. A sample is provided.

Accounts Affected	Category	↑	↓	Appears on Which Financial Statements
Computer Supplies	Asset	Dr.	Cr.	Balance Sheet
Legal Fees Earned				
P. Roy, Withdrawals				
Accounts Payable				
Salaries Expense				
Auto				

(20 min)   **LO2**   **2A-4.**   Given the following accounts, complete the table by inserting appropriate numbers next to the individual transaction to indicate which account is debited and which account is credited.

1. Cash
2. Accounts Receivable
3. Equipment
4. Accounts Payable
5. B. Barker, Capital
6. B. Barker, Withdrawals
7. Plumbing Fees Earned
8. Salaries Expense
9. Advertising Expense
10. Supplies Expenses

			Rules	
	Transaction		Dr.	Cr.
Example:	A.	Paid salaries expense.	8	1
	B.	Bob paid personal utilities bill from the company checkbook.		
	C.	Advertising bill received but unpaid.		
	D.	Received cash from plumbing fees.		
	E.	Paid supplies expense.		
	F.	Bob invested in additional equipment for the business.		
	G.	Billed customers for plumbing services rendered.		
	H.	Received one-half the balance from transaction G.		
	I.	Bought equipment on account.		

2A-5. From the trial balance of Hugo's Cleaners in Figure 2.5, prepare the following for July:

- Income statement
- Statement of owner's equity
- Balance sheet

LO3 *(20 min)*

FIGURE 2.5

HUGO'S CLEANERS TRIAL BALANCE JULY 31, 201X		
	Dr.	Cr.
Cash	6 0 0 0 0	
Equipment	6 9 2 0 0	
Accounts Payable		3 0 0 0 0
J. Hugo, Capital		8 5 3 0 0
J. Hugo, Withdrawals	1 1 5 0 0	
Cleaning Fees		5 0 4 0 0
Salaries Expense	1 7 5 0 0	
Utilities Expense	7 5 0 0	
Totals	1 6 5 7 0 0	1 6 5 7 0 0

Set B

2B-1. From the following, prepare a chart of accounts.

LO2 *(10 min)*

Apple iPad	Legal Fees Earned
Salary Expense	L. Jones, Capital
Accounts Payable	Cash
Accounts Receivable	Advertising Expense
Rent Expense	L. Jones, Withdrawals

2B-2. Record the following transaction in the transaction analysis chart: Sue Prazier bought a new piece of computer equipment for $22,000, paying $5,000 down and charging the rest.

LO2 *(5 min)*

2B-3. Complete the following table. For each account listed on the left, fill in what category it belongs to, whether increases and decreases in the account are marked on the debit or credit sides, and on which financial statement the account appears. A sample is provided.

LO2 *(5 min)*

Accounts Affected	Category	↓	↑	Appears on Which Financial Statements
Office Supplies	Asset	Dr.	Cr.	Balance Sheet
Rental Fees Earned				
A. Troy, Withdrawals				
Accounts Payable				
Wage Expense				
Computer				

2B-4. Given the following accounts, complete the table by inserting appropriate numbers next to the individual transactions to indicate which account is debited and which account is credited.

LO2 *(20 min)*

1. Cash
2. Accounts Receivable
3. Furniture
4. Accounts Payable

5. B. Martin, Capital
6. B. Martin, Withdrawals
7. Photography Fees Earned
8. Salaries Expense
9. Advertising Expense
10. Supplies Expenses

	Transaction	Rules Dr.	Cr.
Example:	**A.** Paid salaries expense.	8	1
	B. Bill paid personal utilities bill from the company checkbook.		
	C. Advertising bill received but unpaid.		
	D. Received cash from photography fees.		
	E. Paid supplies expense.		
	F. Bill invested in additional furniture for the business.		
	G. Billed customers for photography services rendered.		
	H. Received one-half the balance from transaction G.		
	I. Bought furniture on account.		

(20 min) **LO3** ➤   **2B-5.** From the following trial balance of Helm's Cleaners in Figure 2.6, prepare the following for May:

• Income statement

• Statement of owner's equity

• Balance sheet

FIGURE 2.6

HELM'S CLEANERS TRIAL BALANCE MAY 31, 201X		
	Dr.	**Cr.**
Cash	3 0 0 0 0	
Equipment	9 1 0 0 0	
Accounts Payable		2 9 0 0 0
J. Helm, Capital		8 6 2 0 0
J. Helm, Withdrawals	1 4 0 0 0	
Cleaning Fees		4 2 0 0 0
Salaries Expense	1 2 5 0 0	
Utilities Expense	9 7 0 0	
Totals	1 5 7 2 0 0	1 5 7 2 0 0

MyAccountingLab   **Problems**

Set A

(20 min) **LO2** ➤   **2A-1.** The following transactions occurred in the opening and operation of Brenden's Delivery Service.

A. Brenden Oulette opened the delivery service by investing $21,000 from his personal savings account.

B. Purchased used delivery trucks on account, $6,000.

C. Rent expense due but unpaid, $900.

D. Received cash for delivery, $1,400.

E. Billed a client on account, $370.

F. Brenden withdrew cash for personal use, $750.

Check Figure:
After F:

Cash	
(A) 21,000	750 (F)
(D) 1,400	

Complete a transaction analysis chart for each of the transactions.

The chart of accounts includes Cash; Accounts Receivable; Delivery Trucks; Accounts Payable; Brenden Oulette, Capital; Brenden Oulette, Withdrawals; Delivery Fees Earned; and Rent Expense.

2A-2. Brett Pillows opened a consulting company, and the following transactions resulted:

A. Brett invested $20,000 in the consulting agency.
B. Bought office equipment on account, $8,000.
C. Agency received cash for consulting work that it completed for a client, $2,900.
D. Brett paid a personal bill from the company checkbook, $90.
E. Paid advertising expense for the month, $550.
F. Rent expense for the month due but unpaid, $1,400.
G. Paid $1,000 as partial payment of what was owed from transaction B.

As Brett's accountant, analyze and record the transactions in T account form. Set up the T accounts and label each entry with the letter of the transaction.

LO2 *(20 min)*

Check Figure:
After G:

	Cash	
(A) 20,000		90 (D)
(C) 2,900		550 (E)
		1,000 (G)

Chart of Accounts

Assets	Revenue
Cash 111	Consulting Fees Earned 411
Office Equipment 121	**Expenses**
Liabilities	Advertising Expense 511
Accounts Payable 211	Rent Expense 512
Owner's Equity	
Brett Pillows, Capital 311	
Brett Pillows, Withdrawals 312	

2A-3. From the following T accounts of Bill's Cleaning Service, (a) foot and determine ending balances, and (b) prepare a trial balance in proper form for December 201X.

LO1,3 *(20 min)*

Check Figure:
Trial Balance Total $21,600

	Cash 111				Accounts Payable 211				Cleaning Fees Earned 411	
(A)	12,000	(D)	700	(D)	700	(C)	1,300		(B)	9,000
(G)	2,500	(E)	250							
		(F)	300							
		(H)	350							
		(I)	300							

	Accounts Receivable 112				Bill Jolt, Capital 311				Rent Expense 511	
(B)	9,000	(G)	2,500			(A)	12,000	(F)	300	

	Office Equipment 121				Bill Jolt, Withdrawals 312				Utilities Expense 512	
(C)	1,300			(I)	300			(E)	250	
(H)	350									

2A-4. From the trial balance of Girtie Lillis, Attorney-at-Law given in Figure 2.7 on page 62, prepare (a) an income statement for the month of May, (b) a statement of owner's equity for the month ended May 31, and (c) a balance sheet at May 31, 201X.

LO3 *(40 min)*

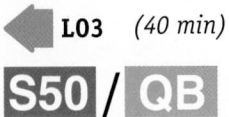

FIGURE 2.7

GIRTIE LILLIS, ATTORNEY-AT-LAW TRIAL BALANCE MAY 31, 201X		
Account	Debit	Credit
Cash	4 0 0 0 0	
Accounts Receivable	1 4 0 0 0	
Office Equipment	1 0 0 0 0	
Accounts Payable		2 9 0 0 0
Salaries Payable		1 0 3 0 0
G. Lillis, Capital		2 7 2 0 0
G. Lillis, Withdrawals	8 0 0 0 0	
Revenue from Legal Fees		1 8 0 0 0 0
Utilities Expense	2 5 0 0 0	
Rent Expense	5 0 0 0 0	
Salaries Expense	5 0 0 0 0	
Totals	8 4 5 0 0 0	8 4 5 0 0 0

Check Figure:
Total Assets $6,400

(60 min)   **LO2,3**

2A-5.   The chart of accounts for Adler's Delivery Service is as follows:

Chart of Accounts

Assets	**Revenue**
Cash 111	Delivery Fees Earned 411
Accounts Receivable 112	**Expenses**
Office Equipment 121	Advertising Expense 511
Delivery Trucks 122	Gas Expense 512
Liabilities	Salaries Expense 513
Accounts Payable 211	Telephone Expense 514
Owner's Equity	
Andrea Adler, Capital 311	
Andrea Adler, Withdrawals 312	

Adler's Delivery Service completed the following transactions during the month of July:

A. Andrea Adler invested $30,000 in the delivery service from her personal savings account.
B. Bought delivery trucks on account, $14,000.
C. Bought office equipment for cash, $1,500.
D. Paid advertising expense, $500.
E. Collected cash for delivery services rendered, $2,400.
F. Paid drivers' salaries, $900.
G. Paid gas expense for trucks, $1,100.
H. Performed delivery services for a customer on account, $900.
I. Telephone expense due but unpaid, $100.
J. Received $600 as partial payment of transaction H.
K. Andrea withdrew cash for personal use, $250.

As Andrea's newly hired accountant, you must perform the following:

1. Set up T accounts using the chart of accounts. Record transactions in the T accounts. (Place the letter of the transaction next to the entry.)
2. Foot the T accounts where appropriate and determine the ending balances.
3. Prepare a trial balance at the end of July.
4. Prepare from the trial balance, in proper form, (a) an income statement for the month of July, (b) a statement of owner's equity, and (c) a balance sheet as of July 31, 201X.

Check Figure:
Total Trial Balance $47,400

Set B

2B-1. The following transactions occurred in the opening and operation of Bob's Delivery Service.

 **L02**   *(20 min)*

  A. Bob O'Brien opened the delivery service by investing $25,000 from his personal savings account.
  B. Purchased used delivery trucks on account, $12,000.
  C. Rent expense due but unpaid, $1,100.
  D. Received cash for delivery, $1,500.
  E. Billed a client on account, $600.
  F. Bob withdrew cash for personal use, $700.

Complete a transaction analysis chart for each of the transactions.

The chart of accounts for the shop includes Cash; Accounts Receivable; Delivery Truck; Accounts Payable; B. O'Brien, Capital; B. O'Brien, Withdrawals; Delivery Fees Earned; and Rent Expense.

Check Figure:
After F:

Cash	
(A) 25,000	700 (F)
(D) 1,500	

2B-2. Bill Palu opened a consulting company, and the following transactions resulted.

L02   *(20 min)*

  A. Bill invested $30,000 in the consulting agency.
  B. Bought office equipment on account, $5,000.
  C. Agency received cash for consulting work that it completed for a client, $1,100.
  D. Bill paid a personal bill from the company checkbook, $115.
  E. Paid advertising expense for the month, $600.
  F. Rent expense for the month due but unpaid, $1,000.
  G. Paid $700 as partial payment of what was owed from transaction B.

As Bill's accountant, analyze and record the transactions in T account form. Set up the T accounts and label each entry with the letter of the transaction.

Check Figure:
After G:

Cash	
(A) 30,000	115 (D)
(C) 1,100	600 (E)
	700 (G)

Chart of Accounts

Assets	**Revenue**
Cash 111	Consulting Fees Earned 411
Office Equipment 121	**Expenses**
Liabilities	Advertising Expense 511
Accounts Payable 211	Rent Expense 512
Owner's Equity	
Bill Palu, Capital 311	
Bill Palu, Withdrawals 312	

2B-3. From the following T accounts of Breck's Cleaning Service, (a) foot and determine the ending balances, and (b) prepare a trial balance in proper form for May 31, 201X.

L01,3   *(20 min)*

Cash 111			
(A)	15,000	(D)	800
(G)	1,000	(E)	200
		(F)	250
		(H)	200
		(I)	1,100

Accounts Receivable 112			
(B)	15,000	(G)	1,000

Office Equipment 121		
(C)	1,900	
(H)	200	

Accounts Payable 211			
(D)	800	(C)	1,900

Breck Jal, Capital 311		
	(A)	15,000

Breck Jal, Withdrawals 312		
(I)	1,100	

Check Figure:
Trial Balance Total $31,100

Cleaning Fees Earned 411		
	(B)	15,000

Rent Expense 511		
(F)	250	

Utilities Expense 512		
(E)	200	

(40 min)   **LO3**

2B-4.   From the trial balance of Gretchen Lyman, Attorney-at-Law, given in Figure 2.8, prepare (a) an income statement for the month of January, (b) a statement of owner's equity for the month ended January 31, and (c) a balance sheet at January 31, 201X.

FIGURE 2.8

Check Figure:
Total Assets $10,100

GRETCHEN LYMAN, ATTORNEY-AT-LAW TRIAL BALANCE JANUARY 31, 201X		
Account	Dr.	Cr.
Cash	7 0 0 0 0 0	
Accounts Receivable	8 0 0 0 0	
Office Equipment	2 3 0 0 0 0	
Accounts Payable		2 9 0 0 0 0
Salaries Payable		9 3 0 0 0
G. Lyman, Capital		5 7 9 5 0 0
G. Lyman, Withdrawals	1 7 5 0 0	
Revenue from Legal Fees		1 3 5 0 0 0
Utilities Expense	3 0 0 0 0	
Rent Expense	3 0 0 0 0	
Salaries Expense	1 0 0 0 0	
Totals	10 9 7 5 0 0	10 9 7 5 0 0

(60 min)   **LO2,3**

2B-5.   The chart of accounts of Aikman's Delivery Service is as follows:

Chart of Accounts	
Assets	**Revenue**
Cash 111	Delivery Fees Earned 411
Accounts Receivable 112	**Expenses**
Office Equipment 121	Advertising Expense 511
Delivery Trucks 122	Gas Expense 512
Liabilities	Salaries Expense 513
Accounts Payable 211	Telephone Expense 514
Owner's Equity	
Andrea Aikman, Capital 311	
Andrea Aikman, Withdrawals 312	

Aikman's Delivery Service completed the following transactions during the month of May:

A. Andrea Aikman invested $20,000 in the delivery service from her personal savings account.

B. Bought delivery trucks on account, $13,000.

C. Bought office equipment for cash, $1,500.

D. Paid advertising expense, $450.

E. Collected cash for delivery services rendered, $2,600.

F. Paid drivers' salaries, $700.

G. Paid gas expense for trucks, $900.

H. Performed delivery services for a customer on account, $1,700.

I. Telephone expense due but unpaid, $500.

J. Received $900 as partial payment of transaction H.

K. Andrea withdrew cash for personal use, $200.

As Andrea's newly hired accountant, you must perform the following:

1. Set up T accounts using the chart of accounts. Record transactions in the T accounts. (Place the letter of the transaction next to the entry.)
2. Foot the T accounts where appropriate and determine the ending balances.
3. Prepare a trial balance at the end of May.
4. Prepare from the trial balance, in proper form, (a) an income statement for the month of May, (b) a statement of owner's equity, and (c) a balance sheet as of May 31, 201X.

Check Figure:
Trial Balance Total $37,800

Financial Report Problem

Reading the Kellogg's Annual Report

 **L02** *(5 min)*

Go to http://investor.kelloggs.com/investor-relations/annual-reports/ to access the Kellogg's 2013 Annual Report and find the balance sheet of Kellogg's. Did Kellogg's Accounts Payable go up or down from 2012 to 2013? What does this change mean? Into what category does Accounts Payable fall by rules of debit and credit? Which side of the T account would make Accounts Payable increase?

ON THE JOB SMITH COMPUTER CENTER

MyAccountingLab

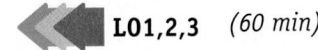 **L01,2,3** *(60 min)*

The Smith Computer Center created its chart of accounts as follows:

Chart of Accounts as of July 1, 201X			
Assets		**Revenue**	
1000	Cash	4000	Service Revenue
1020	Accounts Receivable	**Expenses**	
1030	Supplies	5010	Advertising Expense
1080	Computer Shop Equipment	5020	Rent Expense
1090	Office Equipment	5030	Utilities Expense
Liabilities		5040	Phone Expense
2000	Accounts Payable	5050	Supplies Expense
Owner's Equity		5060	Insurance Expense
3000	Feldman, Capital	5070	Postage Expense
3010	Feldman, Withdrawals		

You will use this chart of accounts to complete the Continuing Problem.
   The following problem continues from Chapter 1.

Assignment

1. Set up T accounts in a ledger and post the ending balances from Chapter 1.
2. Record transactions k through s in the appropriate T accounts.
3. Foot and take the balances of the T accounts where appropriate.
4. Prepare a trial balance at the end of August.
5. From the trial balance, prepare an income statement, statement of owner's equity, and a balance sheet for the two months ending with August 31, 201X.

k. Received the phone bill for the month of July, $80.

l. Paid $450 (check #8099) for insurance for the month.

m. Paid $150 (check #8100) of the amount due from transaction d in Chapter 1.

n. Paid advertising expense for the month, $900 (check #8101).

o. Billed a client (Erin Caffrey) for services rendered, $1,700.

p. Collected $1,300 for services rendered. (Assume cash collection occurred at the same time services were rendered.)

q. Paid the electric bill in full for the month of July (check #8102, transaction h, Chapter 1).

r. Paid cash (check #8103) for $70 in stamps.

s. Purchased $300 worth of supplies from Computers R Us on credit.

Beginning the Accounting Cycle

CHAPTER PREVIEW: THE BIG PICTURE

John Rey is taking aviation science at a community college. His freshman year requires him to take an accounting class. John wonders if airlines like American really use accounting to maintain their records. In fact, American Airlines must follow specific steps in accounting to properly maintain its accounting records over a period of time. These procedures or steps are referred to as the accounting cycle. Once one cycle is completed (usually called a fiscal year), another cycle is begun. Learning the accounting procedures necessary during an accounting cycle will help you understand how businesses like American Airlines maintain consistent accounting records.

Learning Objectives

LO1 Analyze and Record Business Transactions into a Journal

LO2 Posting to the Ledger

LO3 Preparing the Trial Balance

Accounting cycle For each accounting period, the process that begins with the recording of business transactions or procedures into a journal and ends with the completion of a post-closing trial balance.

Accounting period The period of time for which an income statement is prepared.

Calendar year The 12-month period a business chooses for its accounting year. Alternatively known as **fiscal year** and **natural business year**. A fiscal year can be something other than a calendar year.

Interim reports Financial statements that are prepared for a month, quarter, or some other portion of the fiscal year.

Companies like American Airlines have to perform certain accounting procedures. The normal accounting procedures that are performed over a period of time are called the accounting cycle. The accounting cycle takes place in a period of time called an accounting period. An accounting period is the period of time covered by the income statement. Although it can be any time period up to 1 year (e.g., 1 month or 3 months), most businesses use a 1-year accounting period. The year can be either a calendar year (January 1 through December 31) or a fiscal year.

A fiscal year is an accounting period that runs for any 12 consecutive months, so it can be the same as a calendar year. Big Dollar Stores and Aeropostale, Inc., end their accounting periods on January 31. A business can choose any fiscal year that is convenient. For example, some retailers may decide to end their fiscal year when inventories and business activity are at a low point, such as after the Christmas season. This period is called a natural business year. Using a natural business year allows the business to count its year-end inventory when it is easiest to do so.

Businesses would not be able to operate successfully if they only prepared financial reports at the end of their calendar or fiscal year. For more timely information, most businesses prepare interim reports on a monthly, quarterly, or semiannual basis.

In this chapter, as well as in Chapters 4 and 5, we follow Mel Blass's new business, Mel's Computer Repair Service. We follow the normal accounting procedures that the business performs over a period of time. Blass has chosen to use a fiscal period of January 1 to December 31, which also is the calendar year.

LEARNING UNIT 3-1

L01

Analyzing and Recording Business Transactions into a Journal (Steps 1 and 2 of the Accounting Cycle)

The General Journal

Journal A listing of business transactions in chronological order. The journal links on one page the debit and credit parts of transactions. Alternatively known as **general journal**.

Journal entry The transaction (debits and credits) that is recorded into a journal once it is analyzed.

Journalizing The process of recording a transaction into the journal.

Book of original entry Book that records the first formal information about business transactions. Example: a journal.

Book of final entry Book that records information about business transactions from a book of original entry (a journal). Example: a ledger.

Chapter 2 taught us how to analyze and record business transactions into T accounts, or ledger accounts. Recording a debit in an account on one page of the ledger and recording the corresponding credit on a different page of the ledger, however, can make it difficult to find errors. It would be much easier if all the business's transactions were located in the same place. That is the function of the journal or general journal. Transactions are entered in the journal in chronological order (January 1, 8, 15, etc.), and then this recorded information is used to update the ledger accounts. In computerized accounting, a journal may be stored on a flash drive.

We will use a general journal, the simplest form of a journal, to record the transactions of Mel's Computer Repair Service. A transaction [debit(s) + credit(s)] that has been analyzed and recorded in a journal is called a journal entry. The process of recording the journal entry into the journal is called journalizing.

The journal is called the book of original entry because it contains the first formal information about business transactions. The ledger is known as the book of final entry because the information the journal contains will be transferred to the ledger. With computers today, much has changed how entries are recorded in journals and ledgers. For now, we need to focus on the manual aspects; however, at the end of this chapter, there are computer workshops that will show how the manual system is computerized. Each of the journal pages looks like or is similar to the one in Figure 3.1. The pages of the journal are numbered consecutively from page 1. Keep in mind that the journal and the ledger are separate books in a manual accounting system.

Relationship between the Journal and the Chart of Accounts. The accountant must refer to the business's chart of accounts for the account names that are to be used in the journal. Every company has its own "unique" chart of accounts.

The following chart of accounts for Mel's Computer Repair Service lists the accounts used in the business. By the end of Chapter 5, we will have discussed each of these accounts.

MEL'S COMPUTER REPAIR SERVICE GENERAL JOURNAL					
					Page 1
Date	Account Titles and Description	PR	Dr.	Cr.	

FIGURE 3.1
The General Journal

Mel's Computer Repair Service
Chart of Accounts

Assets (100–199)

111 Cash

112 Accounts Receivable

114 Computer Supplies

115 Prepaid Rent

121 Computer Equipment

122 Accumulated Depreciation,
     Computer Equipment

Liabilities (200–299)

211 Accounts Payable

212 Salaries Payable

Owner's Equity (300–399)

311 Mel Blass, Capital

312 Mel Blass, Withdrawals

313 Income Summary

Revenue (400–499)

411 Computer Repair Fees

Expenses (500–599)

511 Office Salaries Expense

512 Advertising Expense

513 Telephone Expense

514 Computer Supplies Expense

515 Rent Expense

516 Depreciation Expense,
     Computer Equipment

Journalizing the Transactions of Mel's Computer Repair Service. Certain formalities must be followed in making journal entries:

- The debit portion of the transaction is always recorded first.
- The credit portion of a transaction is indented ½ inch and placed below the debit portion.
- The explanation of the journal entry follows immediately after the credit and is indented 1 inch from the date column.
- One line space follows each transaction and explanation. This makes the journal easier to read, and there is less chance of mixing transactions.
- Each transaction must affect at least two different accounts.
- Finally, as always, the total amount of debits must equal the total amount of credits. The same format is used for each of the entries in the journal.

Note that we will continue to use transaction analysis charts as a teaching aid in the journalizing process.

May 1, 201X: Mel Blass Began the Business by Investing $10,000 in Cash			
1	**2**	**3**	**4**
Accounts Affected	**Category**	↓ ↑	**Rules of Dr. and Cr.**
Cash	Asset	↑	Dr.
Mel Blass, Capital	Capital	↑	Cr.

FIGURE 3.2
Owner Investment

			MEL'S COMPUTER REPAIR SERVICE GENERAL JOURNAL							
									Page 1	
	Date		Account Titles and Description	PR	Dr.			Cr.		
201X May		1	Cash		10 0 0 0 00					
			Mel Blass, Capital					10 0 0 0 00		
			Initial investment of cash by owner							

COACHING TIP

For now the PR (posting reference) column is blank; we discuss it later.

Let's now look at the structure of this journal entry (Figure 3.2). The entry contains the following information:

1. Year of the journal entry   201X
2. Month of the journal entry   May
3. Day of the journal entry   1
4. Name(s) of accounts debited   Cash
5. Name(s) of accounts credited   Mel Blass, Capital
6. Explanation of transaction   Initial investment by owner
7. Amount of debit(s) $10,000
8. Amount of credit(s) $10,000

May 1: Purchased Computer Equipment from Ben Co. for $6,000, Paying $1,000 and Promising to Pay the Balance Within 30 Days

1	2	3	4
Accounts Affected	Category	↓ ↑	Rules of Dr. and Cr.
Computer Equipment	Asset	↑	Dr.
Cash	Asset	↓	Cr.
Accounts Payable	Liability	↑	Cr.

Compound journal entry A journal entry that affects more than two accounts.

This transaction affects three accounts. When a journal entry has more than two accounts, it is called a compound journal entry.

In this entry (Figure 3.3), only the day is entered in the date column because the year and month were entered at the top of the page from the first transaction. This information doesn't need to be repeated until a new page is needed or a change of months occurs.

FIGURE 3.3
Purchase of Equipment

		1	Computer Equipment		6 0 0 0 00					
			Cash					1 0 0 0 00		
			Accounts Payable					5 0 0 0 00		
			Purchase of computer equipment from Ben Co.							

May 1: Rented Office Space, Paying $1,200 in Advance for the First Three Months			
1 **Accounts Affected**	**2** **Category**	**3** ↓↑	**4** **Rules of Dr. and Cr.**
Prepaid Rent	Asset	↑	Dr.
Cash	Asset	↓	Cr.

In this transaction (Figure 3.4) Blass gains an asset called prepaid rent and gives up an asset, cash. The prepaid rent does not become an expense until it expires.

COACHING TIP

Rent paid in advance is an asset.

	1	Prepaid Rent		1 2 0 0 00		
		Cash			1 2 0 0 00	
		Rent paid in advance—(3 months)				

FIGURE 3.4
Paid Rent in Advance

May 3: Purchased Computer Supplies from Norris Co. on Account, $600			
1 **Accounts Affected**	**2** **Category**	**3** ↓↑	**4** **Rules of Dr. and Cr.**
Computer Supplies	Asset	↑	Dr.
Accounts Payable	Liability	↑	Cr.

Remember, computer supplies are an asset when they are purchased. Once they are used up or consumed in the operation of business, they become an expense (Figure 3.5).

COACHING TIP

Computer Supplies become an expense when used up.

	3	Computer Supplies		6 0 0 00		
		Accounts Payable			6 0 0 00	
		Purchase of computer supplies on account				
		from Norris				

FIGURE 3.5
Purchased Supplies on Account

May 7: Completed Computer Repairs for a Client and Immediately Collected $3,000			
1 **Accounts Affected**	**2** **Category**	**3** ↓↑	**4** **Rules of Dr. and Cr.**
Cash	Asset	↑	Dr.
Computer Repair Fees	Revenue	↑	Cr.

Revenue is earned and cash is received (Figure 3.6).

	7	Cash		3 0 0 0 00		
		Computer Repair Fees			3 0 0 0 00	
		Cash received for services rendered				

FIGURE 3.6
Services Rendered

May 13: Paid Office Salaries, $650

1 Accounts Affected	2 Category	3 ↓↑	4 Rules of Dr. and Cr.
Office Salaries Expense	Expense	↑	Dr.
Cash	Asset	↓	Cr.

Salaries expenses are increasing and cash is going down (see Figure 3.7).

FIGURE 3.7
Paid Salaries

	13	Office Salaries Expense		6 5 0 00	
		Cash			6 5 0 00
		Payment of office salaries			

COACHING TIP

Remember, advertising expenses are recorded when they are incurred, no matter when they are paid.

May 18: Advertising Bill from Al's News Co. Comes in But Is Not Paid, $250

1 Accounts Affected	2 Category	3 ↓↑	4 Rules of Dr. and Cr.
Advertising Expense	Expense	↑	Dr.
Accounts Payable	Liability	↑	Cr.

Here an expense increases although no cash was yet paid (see Figure 3.8).

FIGURE 3.8
Received Advertising Bill

	18	Advertising Expense		2 5 0 00	
		Accounts Payable			2 5 0 00
		Bill in but not paid from Al's News			

COACHING TIP

Keep in mind that as withdrawals increase, owner's equity decreases.

May 20: Mel Blass Wrote a Check on the Bank Account of the Business to Pay His Home Mortgage Payment of $625

1 Accounts Affected	2 Category	3 ↓↑	4 Rules of Dr. and Cr.
Mel Blass, Withdrawals	Withdrawals	↑	Dr.
Cash	Asset	↓	Cr.

Mel is gaining a withdrawal while the business is losing cash (see Figure 3.9).

FIGURE 3.9
Personal Withdrawal

	20	Mel Blass, Withdrawals		6 2 5 00	
		Cash			6 2 5 00
		Personal withdrawal of cash			

May 22: Billed Morris Company for a Complete Repair of All Its Computers, $5,000

1 Accounts Affected	2 Category	3 ↓ ↑	4 Rules of Dr. and Cr.
Accounts Receivable	Asset	↑	Dr.
Computer Repair Fees	Revenue	↑	Cr.

Note the revenue is earned although cash was not received (see Figure 3.10).

	22	Accounts Receivable		5 0 0 0 00	
		Computer Repair Fees			5 0 0 0 00
		Billed Morris Co. for fees earned			

COACHING TIP

Reminder: Computer repair fees, a revenue, is recorded when it is earned, no matter when the cash is actually received.

FIGURE 3.10
Fees Earned

May 27: Paid Office Salaries, $650

1 Accounts Affected	2 Category	3 ↓ ↑	4 Rules of Dr. and Cr.
Office Salaries Expense	Expense	↑	Dr.
Cash	Asset	↓	Cr.

Salaries expense is increasing while the cash in the business is decreasing (see Figure 3.11).

MEL'S COMPUTER REPAIR SERVICE GENERAL JOURNAL						
						Page 2
Date		Account Titles and Description	PR	Dr.	Cr.	
201X May	27*	Office Salaries Expense		6 5 0 00		
		Cash			6 5 0 00	
		Payment of office salaries				

*Note that this is a new page, so the year and month are repeated.

FIGURE 3.11
Paid Salaries

May 28: Paid Half the Amount Owed for Computer Equipment Purchased May 1 from Ben Co., $2,500

1 Accounts Affected	2 Category	3 ↓ ↑	4 Rules of Dr. and Cr.
Accounts Payable	Liability	↓	Dr.
Cash	Asset	↓	Cr.

A liability is being reduced by the payment of cash (see Figure 3.12).

FIGURE 3.12
Partial Payment

	28	Accounts Payable		2 5 0 0 00	
		Cash			2 5 0 0 00
		Paid half the amount owed Ben Co.			

May 29: Received and Paid Telephone Bill, $220

1	2	3	4
Accounts Affected	**Category**	↓ ↑	**Rules of Dr. and Cr.**
Telephone Expense	Expense	↑	Dr.
Cash	Asset	↓	Cr.

The company expense for telephone is increasing and is being paid with cash (see Figure 3.13).

FIGURE 3.13
Paid Telephone Bill

	29	Telephone Expense		2 2 0 00	
		Cash			2 2 0 00
		Paid telephone bill			

This concludes the journal transactions of Mel's Computer Repair Service for the month of May.

▶ **TRY IT!**   **Learning Unit 3-1**

Given the following partial chart of accounts:

   Cash (110), Accounts Receivable (111), Supplies (112), and Accounts Payable (210)

Complete a transaction analysis chart and journal entry from the following transaction:

   June 30, 201X Logan Co. purchased supplies for $600, paying $100 down and the balance due next month.

The solution is shown after the Blueprint at the end of the chapter.

LEARNING UNIT 3-2

LO2 ▶

Posting to the Ledger (Step 3 of the Accounting Cycle)

The general journal serves a particular purpose: It puts every transaction the business does in one place. It cannot do certain things, though. For example, if you were asked to find the balance of the Cash account from the general journal, you would have to go through the entire journal and look for only the cash entries. Then you would have to add up the debits and credits for the Cash account and determine the difference between the two.

What we really need to do to find the balances of accounts is to transfer the information from the journal to the ledger. This process is called posting. In the ledger we accumulate an ending balance for each account so that we can prepare financial statements.

In Chapter 2 we used the T account form to make our ledger entries. T accounts are simple, but they are not used in the real business world; they are only used for demonstration purposes. In practice, accountants often use a four-column account form that includes a column for the business's running balance. Figure 3.14 shows a standard four-column account. We use this format in the text from now on.

Posting The transferring, copying, or recording of information from a journal to a ledger.

Four-column account
A running balance account that records debits and credits and has a column for an ending balance (debit or credit). It replaces the standard two-column account we used earlier.

Accounts Payable				Dr.		Cr.		Balance Dr.		Cr.		Account No. 211
Date		Explanation	Post. Ref.	Dr.		Cr.		Dr.		Cr.		
201X May	1		GJ1			5 0 0 0 00				5 0 0 0 00		
	3		GJ1			6 0 0 00				5 6 0 0 00		
	18		GJ1			2 5 0 00				5 8 5 0 00		
	28		GJ2	2 5 0 0 00						3 3 5 0 00		

FIGURE 3.14
Four-Column Account

COACHING TIP

$5,000 Cr. + $600 Cr. = $5,600 Cr.

Posting

Now let's look at how to post the journal entries of Mel's Computer Repair Service from its journal. The diagram in Figure 3.15 (page 76) shows how to post the cash line from the journal to the ledger. The steps in the posting process are numbered and illustrated in the figure.

STEP 1: In the Cash account in the ledger, record the date (May 1, 201X).

STEP 2: Record the page number of the journal "GJ1" in the posting reference (PR) column of the Cash account.

STEP 3: Transfer the dollar amount of the debit portion of the entry to the ledger. Calculate the new balance of the account. To keep a running balance in each account, as you would in your personal checkbook, take the present balance in the account on the previous line and add or subtract the transaction as necessary to arrive at your new balance.

STEP 4: Record the account number of Cash (111) in the posting reference (PR) column of the journal. This listing is known as cross-referencing.

The same sequence of steps occurs for each line in the journal. In a manual system like Blass's, the debits and credits in the journal may be posted in the order they were recorded, or all the debits may be posted first and then all the credits. If Blass used a computer with accounting software, the program menu would post at the press of a button.

Cross-referencing Adding to the PR column of the journal the account number of the ledger account that was updated from the journal.

FIGURE 3.15 How to Post from Journal to Ledger

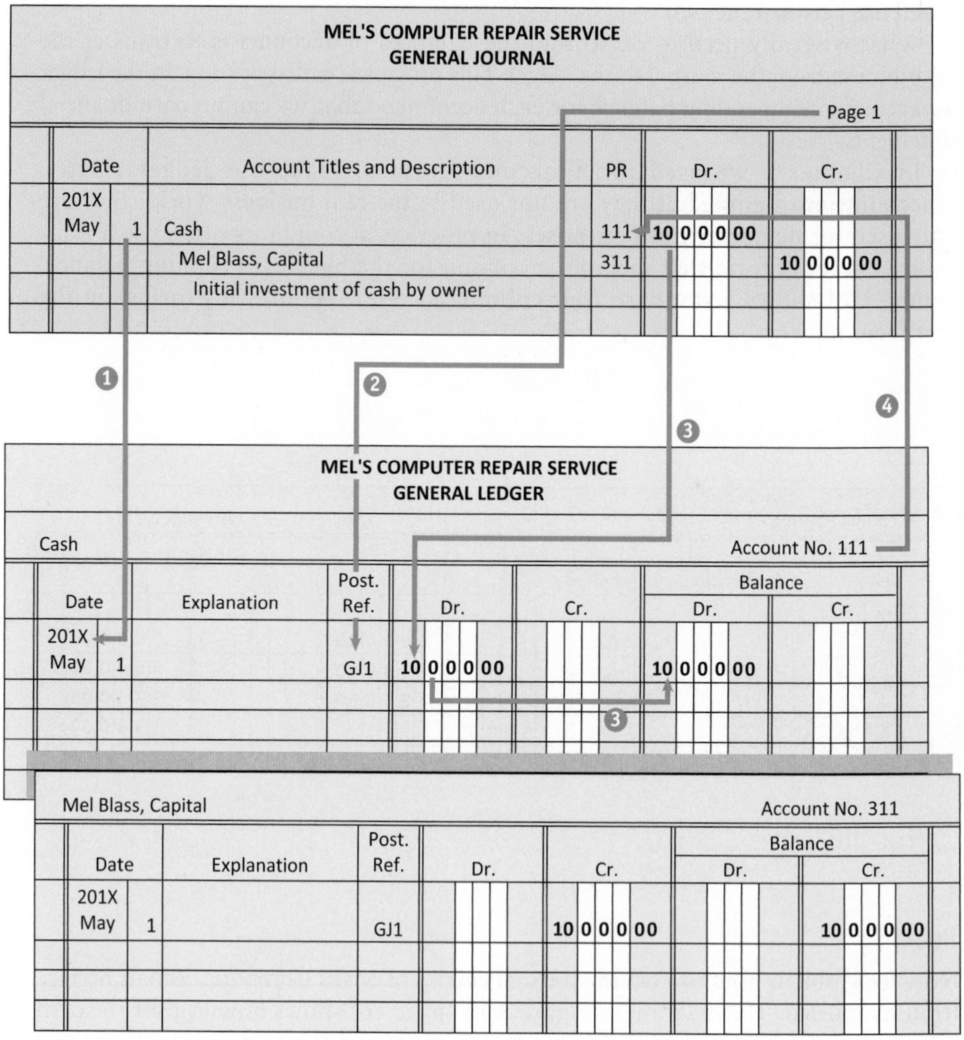

Using Posting References. The posting references are helpful. In the journal, the PR column tells us which journal entries have or have not been posted and also to which accounts they were posted. In the ledger, the posting reference leads us back to the original journal entry in its entirety, so we can see why the debit or credit was recorded and what other accounts were affected. (It leads us back to the original journal entry by identifying the journal and the page in the journal from which the information came.) Figure 3.16 shows the completed journal and ledger for Mel's Computer Repair Service after postings:

FIGURE 3.16
Posting from Journal to the Ledger Using PR Columns

MEL'S COMPUTER REPAIR SERVICE
GENERAL JOURNAL

Page 1

Date		Account Titles and Description	PR	Dr.	Cr.
201X May	1	Cash	111	10 0 0 0 00	
		Mel Blass, Capital	311		10 0 0 0 00
		Initial investment of cash by owner			
	1	Computer Equipment	121	6 0 0 0 00	
		Cash	111		1 0 0 0 00
		Accounts Payable	211		5 0 0 0 00
		Purchase of equip. from Ben Co.			
	1	Prepaid Rent	115	1 2 0 0 00	
		Cash	111		1 2 0 0 00
		Rent paid in advance (3 months)			
	3	Computer Supplies	114	6 0 0 00	
		Accounts Payable	211		6 0 0 00
		Purchase of supplies on acct. from Norris			
	7	Cash	111	3 0 0 0 00	
		Computer Repair Fees	411		3 0 0 0 00
		Cash received from services rendered			
	13	Office Salaries Expense	511	6 5 0 00	
		Cash	111		6 5 0 00
		Payment of office salaries			
	18	Advertising Expense	512	2 5 0 00	
		Accounts Payable	211		2 5 0 00
		Bill received but not paid from Al's News			
	20	Mel Blass, Withdrawals	312	6 2 5 00	
		Cash	111		6 2 5 00
		Personal withdrawal of cash			
	22	Accounts Receivable	112	5 0 0 0 00	
		Computer Repair Fees	411		5 0 0 0 00
		Billed Morris Co. for fees earned			

(continued on page 78)

FIGURE 3.16 *(continued)*

MEL'S COMPUTER REPAIR SERVICE
GENERAL JOURNAL

Page 2

Date		Account Titles and Description	PR	Dr.	Cr.
201X May	27	Office Salaries Expense	511	6 5 0 00	
		Cash	111		6 5 0 00
		Payment of office salaries			
	28	Accounts Payable	211	2 5 0 0 00	
		Cash	111		2 5 0 0 00
		Paid half the amount owed Ben Co.			
	29	Telephone Expense	513	2 2 0 00	
		Cash	111		2 2 0 00
		Paid telephone bill			

COACHING TIP

Posting is done from journal (green) to ledger (blue).

MEL'S COMPUTER REPAIR SERVICE
PARTIAL GENERAL LEDGER

Cash   Account No. 111

Date		Explanation	Post. Ref.	Dr.	Cr.	Balance Dr.	Cr.
201X May	1		GJ1	10 0 0 0 00		10 0 0 0 00	
	1		GJ1		1 0 0 0 00	9 0 0 0 00	
	1		GJ1		1 2 0 0 00	7 8 0 0 00	
	7		GJ1	3 0 0 0 00		10 8 0 0 00	
	13		GJ1		6 5 0 00	10 1 5 0 00	
	20		GJ1		6 2 5 00	9 5 2 5 00	
	27		GJ2		6 5 0 00	8 8 7 5 00	
	28		GJ2		2 5 0 0 00	6 3 7 5 00	
	29		GJ2		2 2 0 00	6 1 5 5 00	

Accounts Receivable   Account No. 112

Date		Explanation	Post. Ref.	Dr.	Cr.	Balance Dr.	Cr.
201X May	22		GJ1	5 0 0 0 00		5 0 0 0 00	

FIGURE 3.16 (continued)

Computer Supplies — Account No. 114

Date		Explanation	Post. Ref.	Dr.	Cr.	Balance Dr.	Balance Cr.
201X May	3		GJ1	6 0 0 00		6 0 0 00	

Prepaid Rent — Account No. 115

Date		Explanation	Post. Ref.	Dr.	Cr.	Balance Dr.	Balance Cr.
201X May	1		GJ1	1 2 0 0 00		1 2 0 0 00	

Computer Equipment — Account No. 121

Date		Explanation	Post. Ref.	Dr.	Cr.	Balance Dr.	Balance Cr.
201X May	1		GJ1	6 0 0 0 00		6 0 0 0 00	

Accounts Payable — Account No. 211

Date		Explanation	Post. Ref.	Dr.	Cr.	Balance Dr.	Balance Cr.
201X May	1		GJ1		5 0 0 0 00		5 0 0 0 00
	3		GJ1		6 0 0 00		5 6 0 0 00
	18		GJ1		2 5 0 00		5 8 5 0 00
	28		GJ2	2 5 0 0 00			3 3 5 0 00

Mel Blass, Capital — Account No. 311

Date		Explanation	Post. Ref.	Dr.	Cr.	Balance Dr.	Balance Cr.
201X May	1		GJ1		10 0 0 0 00		10 0 0 0 00

Mel Blass, Withdrawals — Account No. 312

Date		Explanation	Post. Ref.	Dr.	Cr.	Balance Dr.	Balance Cr.
201X May	20		GJ1	6 2 5 00		6 2 5 00	

Computer Repair Fees — Account No. 411

Date		Explanation	Post. Ref.	Dr.	Cr.	Balance Dr.	Balance Cr.
201X May	7		GJ1		3 0 0 0 00		3 0 0 0 00
	22		GJ1		5 0 0 0 00		8 0 0 0 00

(continued on page 80)

FIGURE 3.16
(continued)

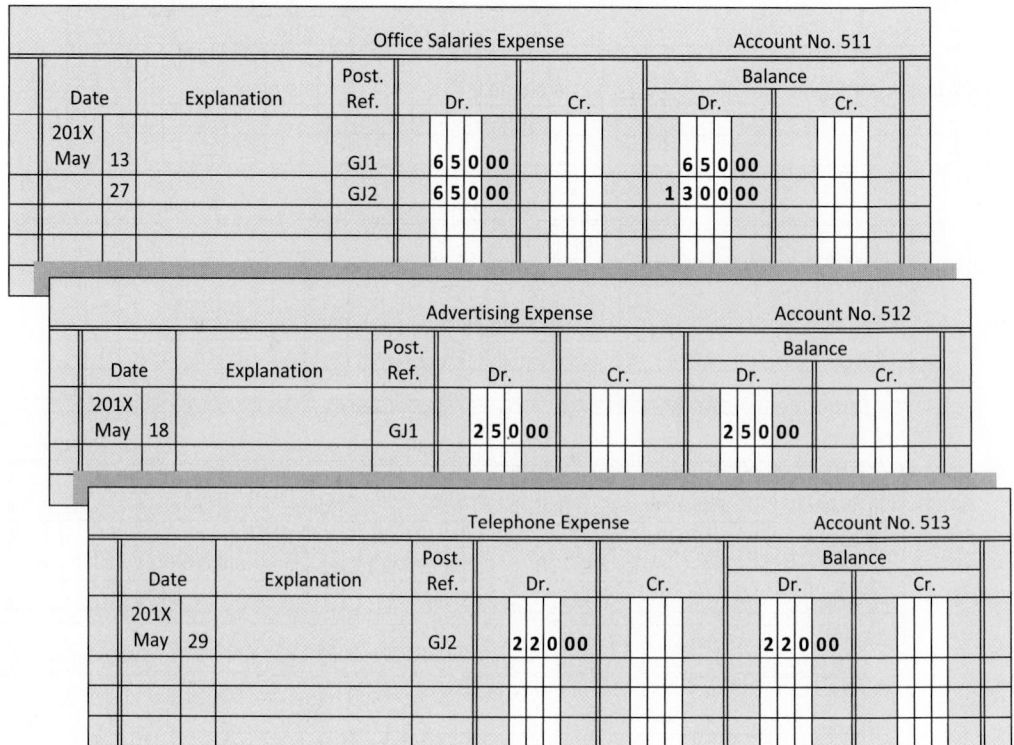

Office Salaries Expense							Account No. 511	
Date	Explanation	Post. Ref.	Dr.	Cr.	Balance			
					Dr.		Cr.	
201X May 13		GJ1	6 5 0 00		6 5 0 00			
27		GJ2	6 5 0 00		1 3 0 0 00			

Advertising Expense							Account No. 512	
Date	Explanation	Post. Ref.	Dr.	Cr.	Balance			
					Dr.		Cr.	
201X May 18		GJ1	2 5 0 00		2 5 0 00			

Telephone Expense							Account No. 513	
Date	Explanation	Post. Ref.	Dr.	Cr.	Balance			
					Dr.		Cr.	
201X May 29		GJ2	2 2 0 00		2 2 0 00			

▶ TRY IT!

Learning Unit 3-2

From the following general journal and partial ledger of Joan's Salon, post from the journal to the ledger T accounts. Be sure to cross-reference.

Joan's Salon

General Journal   p. 3

Date	Account Titles/Description	PR	Dr.	Cr.
201X June 4	Cash		600	
	Accounts Receivable		200	
	Salon Fees Earned			800

Partial Ledger: Cash (111); Accounts Receivable (112); Salon Fees Earned (410)

The solution is shown after the Blueprint at the end of the chapter.

LEARNING UNIT 3-3

L03 ▶

Preparing the Trial Balance (Step 4 of the Accounting Cycle)

Trial balance An informal listing of the ledger accounts and their balances in the ledger to aid in proving the equality of debits and credits.

- The list of the individual accounts with their balances taken from the ledger is called a trial balance.

The trial balance shown in Figure 3.17 was developed from the ledger accounts of Mel's Computer Repair Service that were posted and balanced in Figure 3.16. If the information is journalized or posted incorrectly, the trial balance will not be correct.

A trial balance has two separate columns for accounts with debit or credit balances. When preparing a trial balance the following chart will be helpful:

TRIAL BALANCE

Debits	Credits
Assets	*Liabilities*
Expenses	*Revenue*
Withdrawals	*Capital*

The trial balance will not show everything:

- The capital figure on the trial balance may not be the beginning capital figure. For instance, if Mel Blass had made additional investments during the period, the additional investment would have been journalized and posted to the Capital account. The only way to tell if the capital balance on the trial balance is the original balance is to check the ledger Capital account to see whether any additional investments were made. This confirmation of beginning capital will be important when we make financial reports.
- Even careful cross-referencing does not guarantee that transactions have been properly recorded. For example, the following errors would remain undetected: (1) a transaction that may have been omitted in the journalizing process, (2) a transaction incorrectly analyzed and recorded in the journal, and (3) a journal entry journalized or posted twice.

COACHING TIP

The totals of a trial balance can balance and yet be incorrect.

FIGURE 3.17 Trial Balance

MEL'S COMPUTER REPAIR SERVICE
TRIAL BALANCE
MAY 31, 201X

	Dr.	Cr.
Cash	6 1 5 5 00	
Accounts Receivable	5 0 0 0 00	
Computer Supplies	6 0 0 00	
Prepaid Rent	1 2 0 0 00	
Computer Equipment	6 0 0 0 00	
Accounts Payable		3 3 5 0 00
Mel Blass, Capital		10 0 0 0 00
Mel Blass, Withdrawals	6 2 5 00	
Computer Repair Fees		8 0 0 0 00
Office Salaries Expense	1 3 0 0 00	
Advertising Expense	2 5 0 00	
Telephone Expense	2 2 0 00	
Totals	21 3 5 0 00	21 3 5 0 00

The trial balance lists the accounts in the same order as in the ledger. The $6,155 figure of cash came from the ledger.

What to Do if a Trial Balance Doesn't Balance

The trial balance of Mel's Computer Repair Service shows that the total of debits is equal to the total of credits. What happens, however, if the trial balance is in balance but the correct amount is not recorded in each ledger account? Accuracy in the journalizing and posting process will help ensure that no errors are made.

Even if you find an error, the first rule is "don't panic." Everyone makes mistakes, and accepted ways of correcting them are available. Once an entry has been made in ink, correcting an error in it must always show that the entry has been changed and who changed it. Sometimes the change has to be explained.

Some Common Mistakes

If the trial balance does not balance, the cause could be something relatively simple. Here are some common errors and how they can be fixed:

- If the difference (the amount you are off) is 10, 100, 1,000, and so forth, it is probably a mathematical error in addition.
- If the difference is equal to an individual account balance in the ledger, the amount could have been omitted. It is also possible the figure was not posted from the general journal.
- Divide the difference by two, then check to see whether a debit should have been a credit, or vice versa, in the ledger or trial balance. Example: \$150 difference ÷ 2 = \$75 means you may have placed \$75 as a debit to an account instead of a credit, or vice versa.
- If the difference is evenly divisible by nine, a slide or transposition may have occurred. A slide is an error resulting from adding or deleting zeros in writing numbers. For example, \$4,175.00 may have been copied as \$41.75. A transposition is the accidental rearrangement of digits of a number. For example, \$4,175 might have been accidentally written as \$4,157.
- Compare the balances in the trial balance with the ledger accounts to check for copying errors.
- Recompute balances in each ledger account.
- Trace all postings from journal to ledger.

Slide The error that results in adding or deleting zeros in the writing of a number. Example: 79,200 → 7,920.

Transposition The accidental rearrangement of digits of a number. Example: 152 → 125.

If you cannot find the error after taking all these steps, take a coffee break. Then start all over again.

Making a Correction Before Posting

Before posting, manual error correction is straightforward. Simply draw a line through the incorrect entry, write the correct information above the line, and write your initials near the change. It is important to remember we are looking at a manual system. When a company is using a computerized system it is quite easy to make corrections that the software has built in. Understanding a manual system gives you an appreciation of what computers can do today.

Correcting an Error in an Account Title. Figure 3.18 shows an error and its correction in an account title.

FIGURE 3.18
Account Error

1	Computer Equipment		6000 00	
	Cash			1000 00
	Accounts Payable amp ~~Accounts Receivable~~			5000 00
	Purchase of equipment from Ben Co.			

Correcting a Numerical Error. Numbers are handled the same way as account titles, as the next change from 520 to 250 in Figure 3.19 shows.

FIGURE 3.19
Number Error

18	Advertising Expense		250 00	
	Accounts Payable			amp 250 00 ~~520 00~~
	Bill from Al's News			

Correcting an Entry Error. If a number has been entered in the wrong column, a straight line is drawn through it. The number is then written in the correct column, as shown in Figure 3.20.

				Dr.	Cr.
	1	Computer Equipment		6 0 0 0 00	
		Cash			1 0 0 0 00
		Accounts Payable	amp 5 0 0 0 00	5 0 0 0 00	
		Purchase of equip. from Ben Co.			

FIGURE 3.20
Correcting Entry

Making a Correction After Posting

It is also possible to manually correct an amount that is correctly entered in the journal but posted incorrectly to the ledger of the proper account. The first step is to draw a line through the error and write the correct figure above it. The next step is changing the running balance to reflect the corrected posting. Here, too, a line is drawn through the balance and the corrected balance is written above it. Both changes must be initialed, as shown in Figure 3.21.

			Computer Repair Fees				Account No. 411	
			Post.				Balance	
Date		Explanation	Ref.	Dr.	Cr.	Dr.	Cr.	
201X								
May	7		GJ1		2 5 0 0 00		2 5 0 0 00	
	22		GJ1		4 1 0 0 00 1 0 0 0 00 amp		6 6 0 0 00 2 6 0 0 00 amp	

FIGURE 3.21
Correction After Posting

Correcting an Entry Posted to the Wrong Account

Drawing a line through an error and writing the correction above it is possible when a mistake has occurred within the proper account, but when an error involves a posting to the wrong account, the journal must include a correction accompanied by an explanation. In addition, the correct information must be posted to the appropriate accounts in the ledger.

Suppose, for example, that as a result of tracing postings from journal entries to ledgers you find that a $180 telephone bill was incorrectly debited as an advertising expense. The following illustration shows how this correction is done.

> STEP 1: The journal entry is corrected and the correction is explained (Figure 3.22):

		GENERAL JOURNAL			Page 3	
Date		Account Titles and Description	PR	Dr.	Cr.	
201X						
May	29	Telephone Expense	513	1 8 0 00		
		Advertising Expense	512		1 8 0 00	
		To correct error in which				
		Advertising Exp. was debited				
		for charges to Telephone Exp.				

FIGURE 3.22
Corrected Entry for Telephone

STEP 2: The Advertising Expense ledger account is corrected (Figure 3.23):

FIGURE 3.23
Ledger Update for Advertising

Date		Explanation	Post. Ref.	Dr.	Cr.	Balance Dr.	Balance Cr.
							Advertising Expense — Account No. 512
201X May	18		GJ1	1 7 5 00		1 7 5 00	
	23		GJ1	1 8 0 00		3 5 5 00	
	29	Correcting entry	GJ3		1 8 0 00	1 7 5 00	

STEP 3: The Telephone Expense ledger is corrected (Figure 3.24):

FIGURE 3.24
Ledger Update for Telephone

Date		Explanation	Post. Ref.	Dr.	Cr.	Balance Dr.	Balance Cr.
							Telephone Expense — Account No. 513
201X May	29		GJ3	1 8 0 00		1 8 0 00	

▶ **TRY IT!**   **Learning Unit 3-3**

Given the following ledger accounts for Morse Cleaners, prepare a trial balance as of January 31, 201X.

```
                    Cash                    110
Dr.                           Cr.
1/1/1X 5,000 GJ1              800/1/3/1X GJ1
1/1/1X 1,200 GJ2             600 1/5/1X GJ1
                            100 1/15/1X GJ2
                             50 1/18/1X GJ2
                            200 1/18/1X GJ2

                  Prepaid Rent               111
Dr.                           Cr.
1/3/1X 800 GJ1

               Cleaning Equipment            112
Dr.                           Cr.
1/5/1X   600 GJ1
1/10/1X 900 GJ2

                Accounts Payable             210
Dr.                           Cr.
                             900 1/10/1X GJ2

                J. Morse, Capital            310
Dr.                           Cr.
                             5,000 1/1/1X GJ1
```

J. Morse, Withdrawals	311
Dr.	Cr.
1/15/1X 100 GJ2	

Cleaning Fees	410
Dr.	Cr.
	1,200 1/1/1X GJ2

Advertising Expense	510
Dr.	Cr.
1/18/1X 50 GJ2	

Salaries Expense	520
Dr.	Cr.
1/18/1X 200 GJ2	

DEMONSTRATION SUMMARY PROBLEM

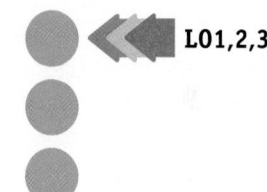

L01,2,3

In March, Abby's Employment Agency had the following transactions:

201X		
Mar.	1	Abby Todd invested $5,000 cash in the new employment agency.
	4	Bought equipment for cash, $200.
	5	Earned employment fee commission, $200, but payment from Blue Co. will not be received until June.
	6	Paid wages expense, $300.
	7	Abby paid her home utility bill from the company checkbook, $75.
	9	Placed Rick Wool at VCR Corporation, receiving $1,200 cash.
	15	Paid cash for supplies, $200.
	28	Telephone bill received but not paid, $180.
	29	Advertising bill received but not paid, $400.

The chart of accounts includes Cash, 111; Accounts Receivable, 112; Supplies, 131; Equipment, 141; Accounts Payable, 211; A. Todd, Capital, 311; A. Todd, Withdrawals, 321; Employment Fees Earned, 411; Wage Expense, 511; Telephone Expense, 521; and Advertising Expense, 531.

Requirements

Your tasks are to do the following:

1. Journalize business transactions in the General Journal (all page 1).
2. Set up a ledger based on the chart of accounts.
3. Post journal entries.
4. Prepare a trial balance for March 31.

Solutions

Requirements 1, 2, 3

Set up ledger based on chart of accounts. Journalize (all page 1) and post journal entries. (See Figures 3.25 and 3.26 on pages 86 and 87.)

FIGURE 3.25
Journal Entries and Posting
References

ABBY'S EMPLOYMENT AGENCY						Page 1

Date			Account Titles and Description	PR	Dr.	Cr.
201X Mar.	1		Cash	111	5 0 0 0 00	
			A. Todd, Capital	311		5 0 0 0 00
			Owner investment			
	4		Equipment	141	2 0 0 00	
			Cash	111		2 0 0 00
			Bought equipment for cash			
	5		Accounts Receivable	112	2 0 0 00	
			Employment Fees Earned	411		2 0 0 00
			Fees on account from Blue Co.			
	6		Wage Expense	511	3 0 0 00	
			Cash	111		3 0 0 00
			Paid wages			
	7		A. Todd, Withdrawals	321	7 5 00	
			Cash	111		7 5 00
			Personal withdrawals			
	9		Cash	111	1 2 0 0 00	
			Employment Fees Earned	411		1 2 0 0 00
			Cash fees			
	15		Supplies	131	2 0 0 00	
			Cash	111		2 0 0 00
			Bought supplies for cash			
	28		Telephone Expense	521	1 8 0 00	
			Accounts Payable	211		1 8 0 00
			Telephone bill owed			
	29		Advertising Expense	531	4 0 0 00	
			Accounts Payable	211		4 0 0 00
			Advertising bill received			

FIGURE 3.26
General Ledger

Cash   111

Date		PR	Dr.	Cr.	Balance Dr.	Balance Cr.
201X Mar.	1	GJ1	5,000		5,000	
	4	GJ1		200	4,800	
	6	GJ1		300	4,500	
	7	GJ1		75	4,425	
	9	GJ1	1,200		5,625	
	15	GJ1		200	5,425	

Accounts Receivable   112

Date		PR	Dr.	Cr.	Balance Dr.	Balance Cr.
201X Mar.	5	GJ1	200		200	

Supplies   131

Date		PR	Dr.	Cr.	Balance Dr.	Balance Cr.
201X Mar.	15	GJ1	200		200	

Equipment   141

Date		PR	Dr.	Cr.	Balance Dr.	Balance Cr.
201X Mar.	4	GJ1	200		200	

Accounts Payable   211

Date		PR	Dr.	Cr.	Balance Dr.	Balance Cr.
201X Mar.	28	GJ1		180		180
	29	GJ1		400		580

A. Todd, Capital   311

Date		PR	Dr.	Cr.	Balance Dr.	Balance Cr.
201X Mar.	1	GJ1		5,000		5,000

A. Todd, Withdrawals   321

Date		PR	Dr.	Cr.	Balance Dr.	Balance Cr.
201X Mar.	7	GJ1	75		75	

Employment Fees Earned   411

Date		PR	Dr.	Cr.	Balance Dr.	Balance Cr.
201X Mar.	5	GJ1		200		200
	9	GJ1		1,200		1,400

Wage Expense   511

Date		PR	Dr.	Cr.	Balance Dr.	Balance Cr.
201X Mar.	6	GJ1	300		300	

Telephone Expense   521

Date		PR	Dr.	Cr.	Balance Dr.	Balance Cr.
201X Mar.	28	GJ1	180		180	

Advertising Expense   531

Date		PR	Dr.	Cr.	Balance Dr.	Balance Cr.
201X Mar.	29	GJ1	400		400	

Tips to Journalizing

1. When journalizing, the PR column is not filled in.
2. Write the name of the debit against the date column. Indent credits and list them below debits. Be sure total debits for each transaction equal total credits.
3. Skip a line between each transaction.

COACHING TIP

This analysis is what should be going through your head before determining debit or credit.

The Analysis of the Journal Entries

Mar.	1	Cash	Asset	↑	Dr.	$5,000
		A. Todd, Capital	Capital	↑	Cr.	$5,000
	4	Equipment	Asset	↑	Dr.	$ 200
		Cash	Asset	↓	Cr.	$ 200
	5	Accts. Receivable	Asset	↑	Dr.	$ 200
		Empl. Fees Earned	Revenue	↑	Cr.	$ 200
	6	Wage Expense	Expense	↑	Dr.	$ 300
		Cash	Asset	↓	Cr.	$ 300
	7	A. Todd, Withdrawals	Withdrawal	↑	Dr.	$ 75
		Cash	Asset	↓	Cr.	$ 75
	9	Cash	Asset	↑	Dr.	$1,200
		Empl. Fees Earned	Revenue	↑	Cr.	$1,200
	15	Supplies	Asset	↑	Dr.	$ 200
		Cash	Asset	↓	Cr.	$ 200
	28	Telephone Expense	Expense	↑	Dr.	$ 180
		Accounts Payable	Liability	↑	Cr.	$ 180
	29	Advertising Expense	Expense	↑	Dr.	$ 400
		Accounts Payable	Liability	↑	Cr.	$ 400

Tips for the General Ledger

The PR column in the ledger Cash account tells you from which page journal information came. After the ledger Cash account is posted, account number 111 is put in the PR column of the journal for cross-referencing.

Note how we keep a running balance in the cash account. A $5,000 debit balance and a $200 credit entry result in a new debit balance of $4,800.

Requirement 4

Preparing a Trial Balance from the Ledger. See Figure 3.27.

FIGURE 3.27

ABBY'S EMPLOYMENT AGENCY TRIAL BALANCE MARCH 31, 201X	Dr.	Cr.
Cash	5 4 2 5 00	
Accounts Receivable	2 0 0 00	
Supplies	2 0 0 00	
Equipment	2 0 0 00	
Accounts Payable		5 8 0 00
A. Todd, Capital		5 0 0 0 00
A. Todd, Withdrawals	7 5 00	
Employment Fees Earned		1 4 0 0 00
Wage Expense	3 0 0 00	
Telephone Expense	1 8 0 00	
Advertising Expense	4 0 0 00	
Totals	6 9 8 0 00	6 9 8 0 00

Solution to Preparing a Trial Balance

The trial balance lists the ending balances of the accounts in the order in which they appear in the ledger. The total of 6,980 on the left equals 6,980 on the right in Figure 3.27.

BLUEPRINT OF FIRST FOUR STEPS OF ACCOUNTING CYCLE

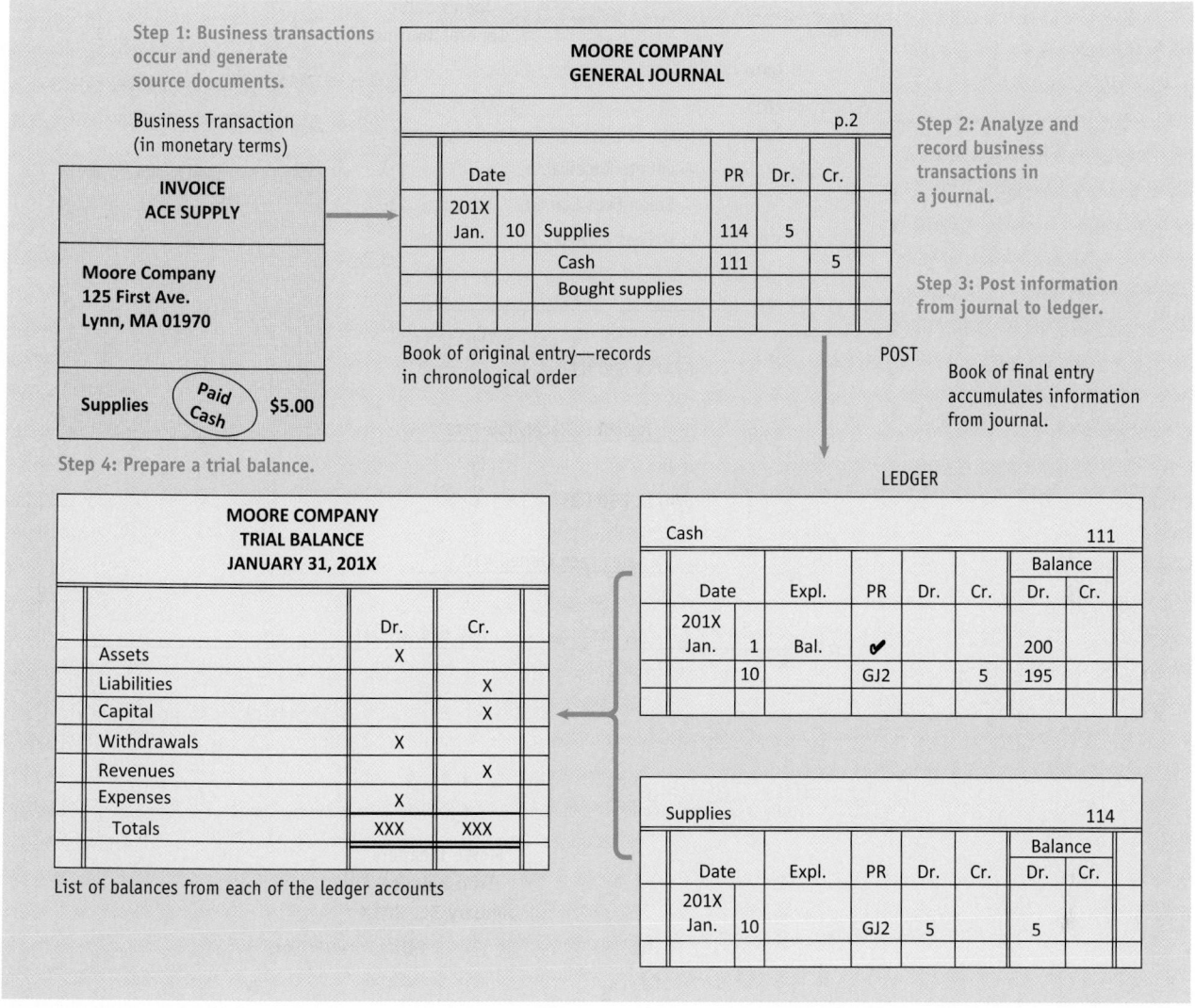

Solutions   MyAccountingLab

TRY IT!   Solutions   MyAccountingLab

Learning Unit 3-1

Accounts Affected	Category	↓ ↑	Rule
Supplies	Asset	↑	Dr. $600
Accounts Payable	Liability	↑	Cr. $500
Cash	Asset	↓	Cr. $100

Date	Account Title and Description	PR	Dr.	Cr.
201X June 30				
	Supplies		600	
	Accounts Payable			500
	Cash			100
	Bought supplies			

Learning Unit 3-2

Joan's Salon
General Journal   p. 3

Date		PR	Dr.	Cr.
201X				
June 4	Cash	111	600	
	Accounts Receivable	112	200	
	Salon Fees Earned	410		800
	Fees earned			

Cash 111

Dr.	Cr.
6/4/1X 600 GJ3	

Accounts Receivable 112

Dr.	Cr.
6/4/1X 200 GJ3	

Sales Fees Earned 410

Dr.	Cr.
	800 6/4/1X GJ3

Learning Unit 3-3

Morse Cleaners
Trial Balance
January 31, 201X

	Dr.	Cr.
Cash	4,450	
Prepaid Rent	800	
Cleaning Equipment	1,500	
Accounts Payable		900
J. Morse, Capital		5,000
J. Morse, Withdrawals	100	
Cleaning Fees		1,200
Advertising Expense	50	
Salaries Expense	200	
Totals	7,100	7,100

ACCOUNTING COACH

The following Coaching Tips are from Learning Units 3-1 to 3-3. Take the Pre-Game Checkup and use the Check Your Score at the bottom of the page to see how you are doing. The Accounting Coach provides tips before each Checkup to help you avoid common accounting errors.

LU 3-1 Analyzing and Recording Business Transactions into a Journal (Steps 1 and 2 of the Accounting Cycle)

Pre-Game Tips: When journalizing transactions be sure to use the Chart of Accounts. It provides the specific titles you will use for either debit(s) or credit(s). You will not use the Chart of Accounts for the explanations in the journal. In the journal, the debit portion of the transaction is listed first, followed by the credit portion. Remember that these titles come from the Chart of Accounts. The total of all debits must equal the total of all credits for each individual transaction.

Pre-Game Checkup: Answer true or false to the following statements.

1. The ledger is the book of original entry.
2. Compound journal entries must have no more than three credits.
3. Billing a company for services on account would result in a debit to cash.
4. When you journalize, the PR column must be completed.
5. Rent paid in advance is an expense.

LU 3-2 Posting to the Ledger (Step 3 of the Accounting Cycle)

Pre-Game Tips: Posting is transferring information from the journal to the ledger. The ledger accounts keep a running balance of each account, while the journal does not. Cross-referencing helps to fill in the PR column of the journal to show the account number that was posted from that line. With computer software, today's posting could be just a click away.

Pre-Game Checkup: Answer true or false to the following statements.

1. Posting can only be done manually.
2. Posting means transferring information from the ledger to the journal.
3. Cross-referencing means the PR column in the ledger is up to date.
4. Posting can only be done once a month.
5. Posting results in information being accumulated in the journal.

LU 3-3 Preparing the Trial Balance (Step 4 of the Accounting Cycle)

Pre-Game Tips: The trial balance is listed in the same order as the general ledger. Only one balance is shown for each account in the trial balance. Keep in mind that the trial balance could be in balance and still be incorrect due to posting twice, missing transactions, or analyzing them incorrectly.

Pre-Game Checkup: Answer true or false to the following statements.

1. The trial balance is in the same order as the journal.
2. A trial balance can have two balances for some accounts.
3. Slides and transpositions can help locate errors in the trial balance.
4. If a journal entry is posted, no corrections can be made.
5. In the trial balance, account titles that have credit balances are indented.

CHECK YOUR SCORE: Answers to the Pre-Game Checkup

LU 3-1
1. False—The ledger is the book of final entry.
2. False—Compound journal entries must have more than two accounts.
3. False—Billing a company for services on account would result in a debit to accounts receivable.
4. False—When you post, the PR column is completed.
5. False—Rent paid in advance is an asset.

LU 3-2
1. False—Posting can be done by computer.
2. False—Posting means transferring information from the journal to the ledger.

3. False—Cross-referencing means the PR column is updated in the journal.
4. False—Posting can be done at various times.
5. False—Posting results in information being accumulated in the ledger.

LU 3-3
1. False—The trial balance is in the same order as the ledger.
2. False—A trial balance can have only one balance per title.
3. True
4. False—If a journal entry is posted, corrections can still be made.
5. False—All account titles are listed with no indentations.

Chapter Summary

MyAccountingLab   Here are all the key terms and equations to help you understand the concepts of this chapter and prepare you for your exam. After completing this review, go to MyAccountingLab for more practice opportunities.

Concepts You Should Know	Key Terms

L01

Analyze and Record Business Transactions into a Journal

1. The accounting cycle is a sequence of accounting procedures that are usually performed during an accounting period.

2. An accounting period is the time period (up to 1 year) for which the income statement is prepared.

3. A calendar year is from January 1 to December 31. The fiscal year is any 12-month period.

4. Interim statements are statements that are usually prepared for a portion of the business's calendar or fiscal year.

5. A general journal is a book that records transactions in chronological order. It is the book of original entry.

6. Journalizing is the process of recording journal entries.

7. The chart of accounts provides the specific titles of accounts to be entered in the journal.

8. When journalizing, the posting reference (PR) column is left blank.

9. A compound journal entry occurs when more than two accounts are affected in the journalizing process of a business transaction.

Key Terms:

Accounting cycle (p. 68)
Accounting period (p. 68)
Book of final entry (p. 68)
Book of original entry (p. 68)
Calendar year (p. 68)
Compound journal entry (p. 70)
Fiscal year (p. 68)
General journal (p. 68)
Interim reports (p. 68)
Journal (p. 68)
Journal entry (p. 68)
Journalizing (p. 68)
Natural business year (p. 68)

L02

Posting to the Ledger

1. The ledger is a collection of accounts in which information is accumulated from the postings of the journal. The ledger is the book of final entry.

2. Posting is the process of transferring information from the journal to the ledger.

3. The journal and ledger contain the same information but in a different form.

4. The four-column account aids in keeping a running balance of an account.

5. The normal balance of an account will be located on the side that increases it according to the rules of debit and credit.

6. The mechanical process of posting requires care in transferring to the appropriate account the dates, posting references, and amounts.

Key Terms:

Cross-referencing (p. 75)
Four-column account (p. 75)
Posting (p. 75)

L03

Preparing the Trial Balance

1. A trial balance can balance but be incorrect.

2. If a trial balance doesn't balance, check for errors in addition, omission of postings, slides, transpositions, copying errors, and so on.

Key Terms:

Slide (p. 82)
Transposition (p. 82)
Trial balance (p. 80)

Discussion Questions and Critical Thinking/Ethical Case

1. Not all businesses have or need an accounting cycle. Agree or disagree and defend your position.

2. An accounting period is based on the balance sheet. Agree or disagree and defend your position.

3. Compare and contrast a calendar year versus a fiscal year.

4. What are interim statements?

5. With computers today, ledgers are not needed in today's accounting system. Agree or disagree and defend your position.

6. How do transactions get "linked" in a general journal?

7. What is the relationship of the chart of accounts to the general journal?

8. What is a compound journal entry?

9. Posting means updating the journal. Agree or disagree? Please comment.

10. The side that decreases an account is the normal balance. True or false?

11. The PR column of a general journal is the last item to be filled in during the manual posting process. Agree or disagree?

12. Discuss the concept of cross-referencing.

13. What is the difference between a transposition and a slide?

14. Pete Rose, the accountant of Rich Co., would like to buy a new software package for his general ledger. He couldn't do it because all funds were frozen for the rest of the fiscal period. Pete called his friend at Flynn Industries and asked whether he could copy its software. Comment on why it is or is not okay for Pete to make such a request.

Concept Checks

MyAccountingLab

General Journal

◀ **L01** (5 min)

1. Complete the following from the general journal of Munro Co. (see Figure 3.28):

   a. Year of journal entry _____
   b. Month of journal entry _____
   c. Day of journal entry _____
   d. Name(s) of accounts debited _____
   e. Name(s) of accounts credited _____
   f. Explanation of transaction _____
   g. Amount of debit(s) _____
   h. Amount of credit(s) _____
   i. Page of journal _____

FIGURE 3.28
General Journal

MUNRO COMPANY
GENERAL JOURNAL

Page 1

Date		Account Titles and Description	PR	Dr.	Cr.
201X Mar.	2	Cash		400 00	
		Equipment		19 000 00	
		B. Munro, Capital			19 400 00
		Initial Investment by Owner			

(5 min) **LO2**

General Journal

2.   Provide the explanation for each of the general journal entries in Figure 3.29.

FIGURE 3.29
Journal Entries

			GENERAL JOURNAL							Page 4	
	Date		Account Titles and Descriptions	PR		Dr.			Cr.		
201X Nov.	10		Cash		30	0 0 0	00				
			Office Equipment			7 0 0	00				
			J. Walsh, Capital					30	7 0 0	00	
			(A)								
	16		Cash			1 2 5	00				
			Accounts Receivable			1 5 0	00				
			Consulting Fees Earned						2 7 5	00	
			(B)								
	18		Salaries Expense			2 0 0	00				
			Salaries Payable						2 0 0	00	
			(C)								

(5 min) **LO2**

Posting and Balancing

3.   Balance this four-column account. What function does the PR column serve? When will Account 111 be used in the journalizing and posting process?

	Cash					Acct. 111	
						Balance	
Date	Explanation	PR	Dr.	Cr.		Dr.	Cr.
201X Mar. 6		GJ 1	29				
10		GJ 1	90				
15		GJ 2		7			
18		GJ 3	75				

(15 min) **LO3**

The Trial Balance

4.   The following trial balance (Figure 3.30) was prepared *incorrectly*.

   a.   Rearrange the accounts in proper order.

FIGURE 3.30

KENNEDY CO. TRIAL BALANCE JULY 31, 201X					
Account		Dr.		Cr.	
D. Kennedy, Capital		8 8	00		
Equipment		1 1 2	00		
Rent Expense				1 2	00
Advertising Expense				7	00
Accounts Payable				4 3	00
Taxi Fees		1 8	00		
Cash		1 3	00		
D. Kennedy, Withdrawals				5	00
Totals		2 3 1	00	6 7	00

b. Calculate the total of the trial balance. (Small numbers are used intentionally so that you can do the calculations in your head.) Assume each account has a normal balance.

Correcting Entry

LO3 *(5 min)*

5. On June 1, 201X, a telephone expense for $250 was debited to Repair Expense. On June 10, 201X, this error was found. Prepare the corrected journal entry. When would a correcting entry *not* be needed?

Exercises

MyAccountingLab

Set A

3A-1. Prepare journal entries for the following transactions that occurred during April:

LO1 *(10 min)*

201X		
April	1	Jamie Moore invested $110,000 cash and $12,000 of equipment into her new business.
	3	Purchased building for $70,000 on account.
	12	Purchased a truck from Leominster Co. for $12,000 cash.
	18	Bought supplies from Gregoire Co. for $700 on account.

3A-2. Record the following into the general journal of Remy's Auto Shop.

LO1 *(10 min)*

201X		
May	1	Remy Tarsia invested $150,000 cash in the auto shop.
	5	Paid $6,000 for auto equipment.
	8	Bought auto equipment from Littleton Co. for $4,000 on account.
	14	Received $1,700 for repair fees earned.
	18	Billed McVey Co. $1,500 for services rendered.
	20	Remy withdrew $100 for personal use.

3A-3. Post the journal entries in Figure 3.31 to the ledger of Kramer Company. The partial ledger of Kramer Company is Cash, 111; Equipment, 121; Accounts Payable, 211; and A. Kramer, Capital, 311. Please use four-column accounts in the posting process.

LO2 *(10 min)*

				PR	Dr.	Cr.
			Page 4			
Date				PR	Dr.	Cr.
201X Feb.	6	Cash			12 0 0 0 00	
		A. Kramer, Capital				12 0 0 0 00
		Cash investment				
	14	Equipment			8 0 0 0 00	
		Cash				5 0 0 0 00
		Accounts Payable				3 0 0 0 00
		Purchase of equipment				

FIGURE 3.31
Journal Entries

3A-4. From the following transactions for Lucas Company for the month of May, (a) prepare journal entries (assume that it is page 1 of the journal), (b) post journal entries to the ledger (use a four-column account), and (c) prepare a trial balance.

LO1,2,3 *(20 min)*

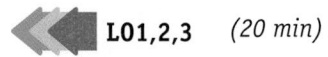

201X		
May	1	Jenna Lucas invested $8,000 in the business.
	4	Bought equipment from Ovak Co. for $1,300 on account.
	15	Billed Sister Co. for services rendered, $2,000.
	18	Received $7,000 cash for services rendered.
	24	Paid salaries expense, $1,000.
	28	Jenna withdrew $200 for personal use.

A partial chart of accounts includes Cash, 111; Accounts Receivable, 112; Equipment, 121; Accounts Payable, 211; J. Lucas, Capital, 311; J. Lucas, Withdrawals, 312; Fees Earned, 411; and Salaries Expense, 511.

(15 min) **LO3** ▶ **3A-5.** You have been hired to correct the trial balance in Figure 3.32 that has been recorded improperly from the ledger to the trial balance.

FIGURE 3.32
Incorrect Trial Balance

SALT LAKE CO. TRIAL BALANCE OCTOBER 31, 201X		
Account	Dr.	Cr.
Accounts Payable	3 9 0 0 00	
A. Salt Lake, Capital		12 2 5 0 00
A. Salt Lake, Withdrawals		9 5 0 00
Services Earned		8 0 0 0 00
Concessions Earned	2 5 0 0 00	
Rent Expense	4 0 0 00	
Salaries Expense	2 2 0 0 00	
Miscellaneous Expense		1 9 0 0 00
Cash	20 0 0 0 00	
Accounts Receivable		1 2 0 0 00
Totals	29 0 0 0 00	24 3 0 0 00

(10 min) **LO3** ▶ **3A-6.** On February 6, 201X, Mark Sullivan made the journal entry in Figure 3.33 to record the purchase on account of office equipment priced at $1,200. This journal entry had not yet been posted when the error was discovered. Make the appropriate correction.

FIGURE 3.33
Recording Error

GENERAL JOURNAL					
Date		Account Titles and Description	PR	Dr.	Cr.
201X Feb.	6	Office Equipment		8 0 0 00	
		Accounts Payable			8 0 0 00
		Purchase of office equip. on account			

Set B

3B-1. Prepare journal entries for the following transactions that occurred during April: 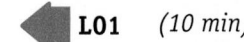 **L01** *(10 min)*

201X	
Apr. 1	Jan Dimon invested $100,000 cash and $18,000 of equipment into her new business.
3	Purchased building for $40,000 on account.
12	Purchased a truck from Leominster Co. for $11,000 cash.
18	Bought supplies from Lee Co. for $500 on account.

3B-2. Record the following into the general journal of Rick's Auto Shop.  **L01** *(10 min)*

201X	
Apr. 1	Rick Savareses invested $80,000 cash in the auto shop.
5	Paid $15,000 for auto equipment.
8	Bought auto equipment from Laverty Co. for $5,000 on account.
14	Received $1,300 for repair fees earned.
18	Billed Boutlier Co. $750 for services rendered.
20	Rick withdrew $500 for personal use.

3B-3. Post the journal entries in Figure 3.34 to the ledger of Kingston Company. **L02** *(10 min)*
The partial ledger of Kingston Company is Cash, 111; Equipment, 121;
Accounts Payable, 211; and A. Kingston, Capital, 311. Please use four-
column accounts in the posting process.

FIGURE 3.34

Page 4

Date			PR	Dr.	Cr.
201X					
Nov.	6	Cash		52 0 0 0 00	
		A. Kingston, Capital			52 0 0 0 00
		Cash investment			
	14	Equipment		3 0 0 0 00	
		Cash			1 0 0 0 00
		Accounts Payable			2 0 0 0 00
		Purchase of equipment			

3B-4. From the following transactions for Lowe Company for the month of 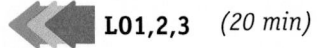 **L01,2,3** *(20 min)*
December, (a) prepare journal entries (assume that it is page 1 of the
journal), (b) post journal entries to the ledger (use a four-column account),
and (c) prepare a trial balance.

201X		
Dec.	1	Jen Lowe invested $52,000 in the business.
	4	Bought equipment from Ham Co. for $2,000 on account.
	15	Billed Kin Co. for services rendered, $14,000.
	18	Received $4,000 cash for services rendered.
	24	Paid salary expense, $1,800.
	28	Jen withdrew $1,000 for personal use.

A partial chart of accounts includes Cash, 111; Accounts Receivable, 112; Equipment, 121; Accounts Payable, 211; J. Lowe, Capital, 311; J. Lowe, Withdrawals, 312; Fees Earned, 411; and Salaries Expense, 511.

(15 min) **LO3**

3B-5. You have been hired to correct the trial balance in Figure 3.35 that has been recorded improperly from the ledger to the trial balance.

FIGURE 3.35

SUNG CO.
TRIAL BALANCE
August 31, 201X

	Dr.	Cr.
Accounts Payable	5 2 0 0 00	
A. Sung, Capital		4 7 5 0 00
A. Sung, Withdrawals		5 5 0 00
Services Earned		6 6 0 0 00
Concessions Earned	1 4 0 0 00	
Rent Expense	8 0 0 00	
Salaries Expense	1 8 0 0 00	
Miscellaneous Expense		1 1 0 0 00
Cash	10 0 0 0 00	
Accounts Receivable		3 7 0 0 00
Totals	19 2 0 0 00	16 7 0 0 00

(10 min) **LO3**

3B-6. On February 6, 201X, Morris Sanford made the journal entry in Figure 3.36 to record the purchase on account of office equipment priced at $1,000. This journal entry had not yet been posted when the error was discovered. Make the appropriate correction.

FIGURE 3.36

GENERAL JOURNAL

Date		Account Titles and Description	PR	Dr.	Cr.
201X Feb.	6	Office Equipment		9 00	
		Accounts Payable			9 00
		Purchase of office equipment on account			

Problems

Set A

3A-1.   Jason Lang operates Jason's Cleaning Service. As the bookkeeper, you have been requested to journalize the following transactions:

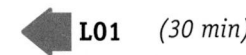 **LO1**   *(30 min)*

201X		
Oct. 1	Paid 2 months' rent in advance, $9,000.	
6	Purchased cleaning equipment on account from Brian's Supply House, $7,000.	
12	Purchased cleaning supplies from Lawrence's Wholesale for $600 cash.	
14	Received $1,200 cash from cleaning fees earned.	
20	Jason withdrew $500 for personal use.	
21	Advertising bill received from *First One News* but unpaid, $450.	
25	Paid electrical expense, $70.	
28	Paid salaries expense, $1,000.	
29	Performed cleaning work for $2,300, but payment will not be received until December.	
30	Paid Brian's Supply House half the amount owed from October 6 transaction.	

Check Figure:
October 21
Dr. Advertising Expense $450
Cr. Accounts Payable $450

The chart of accounts for Jason's Cleaning Service is as follows:

Chart of Accounts			
Assets		**Owner's Equity**	
111	Cash	311	Jason Lang, Capital
112	Accounts Receivable	312	Jason Lang, Withdrawals
114	Prepaid Rent	**Revenue**	
116	Cleaning Supplies	411	Cleaning Fees Earned
120	Cleaning Equipment	**Expenses**	
121	Office Equipment	511	Advertising Expense
Liabilities		512	Electrical Expense
211	Accounts Payable	514	Salaries Expense

3A-2.   On June 1, 201X, Brenda Rennicke opened Brenda's Art Studio. The following transactions occurred in June:

LO1,2,3   *(45 min)*

S50 / QB

201X	
June 1	Brenda Rennicke invested $52,000 in the art studio.
1	Paid 3 months' rent in advance, $2,000.
3	Purchased $2,000 of equipment from Martin Co. on account.
5	Received $10,000 cash for art-training workshop for teachers.
8	Purchased art supplies for $500 cash.
9	Billed Arthur Co. $2,500 for group art lesson for its employees.
10	Paid salaries of assistants, $1,300.
15	Brenda withdrew $200 for personal use.
28	Paid electric bill, $80.
29	Paid telephone bill for June, $220.

Check Figure:
Trial Balance
Total $66,500

Your tasks are to do the following:

a. Set up the ledger based on the following chart of accounts using four-column accounts.
b. Journalize (journal is page 1) and post the June journal entries.
c. Prepare a trial balance as of June 30, 201X.

The chart of accounts for Brenda's Art Studio is as follows:

Chart of Accounts			
Assets		**Owner's Equity**	
111	Cash	311	B. Rennicke, Capital
112	Accounts Receivable	312	B. Rennicke, Withdrawals
114	Prepaid Rent	**Revenue**	
121	Art Supplies	411	Art Fees Earned
131	Equipment	**Expenses**	
Liabilities		511	Electrical Expense
211	Accounts Payable	521	Salaries Expense
		531	Telephone Expense

(45 min)   **LO1,2,3**

3A-3. The following transactions occurred in June 201X for A. One's Placement Agency:

Check Figure:
Trial Balance
Total $16,750

201X	
June 1	A. One invested $9,000 cash in the placement agency.
1	Bought equipment from Tinker Co. for $1,500 on account.
3	Earned placement fees of $1,400, but payment will not be received until July.
5	A. One withdrew $600 for personal use.
7	Paid wages expense, $300.
9	Placed a client on a local TV show, receiving $4,000 cash.
15	Bought supplies from Cinder Co. for $350 on account.
28	Paid telephone bill for June, $220.
29	Advertising bill from Shawl Co. received but not paid, $500.

The chart of accounts for A. One Placement Agency is as follows:

Chart of Accounts			
Assets		**Owner's Equity**	
111	Cash	311	A. One, Capital
112	Accounts Receivable	312	A. One, Withdrawals
131	Supplies	**Revenue**	
141	Equipment	411	Placement Fees Earned
Liabilities		**Expenses**	
211	Accounts Payable	511	Wage Expense
		521	Telephone Expense
		531	Advertising Expense

Your tasks are to do the following:

a. Set up the ledger based on the chart of accounts using four-column accounts.

b. Journalize (page 1) and post the June journal entries.

c. Prepare a trial balance as of June 30, 201X.

Set B

3B-1. Jimmy Cook operates Jimmy's Cleaning Service. As the bookkeeper, you have been requested to journalize the following transactions:

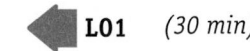 **L01** *(30 min)*

201X		
Mar.	1	Paid 2 months' rent in advance, $2,000.
	6	Purchased cleaning equipment from Ryce's Supply House for $5,000 on account.
	12	Purchased cleaning supplies from Lexington's Wholesale for $900 cash.
	14	Received $1,600 cash from cleaning fees earned.
	20	Jimmy withdrew $100 for personal use.
	21	Advertising bill received from *Minute News* but unpaid, $600.
	25	Paid electrical expense, $100.
	28	Paid salaries expense, $300.
	29	Performed cleaning work for $2,500, but payment will not be received until May.
	30	Paid Ryce's Supply House half the amount owed from the March 6 transaction.

Check Figure:
March 21
Dr. Advertising expense $600
 Cr. Accounts payable $600

The chart of accounts for Jimmy's Cleaning Service is as follows:

Chart of Accounts			
Assets		**Owner's Equity**	
111	Cash	311	Jimmy Cook, Capital
112	Accounts Receivable	312	Jimmy Cook, Withdrawals
114	Prepaid Rent	**Revenue**	
116	Cleaning Supplies	411	Cleaning Fees Earned
120	Cleaning Equipment	**Expenses**	
121	Office Equipment	511	Advertising Expense
Liabilities		512	Electrical Expense
211	Accounts Payable	514	Salaries Expense

3B-2. On April 1, 201X, Beth Orth opened Beth's Art Studio. The following transactions occurred in April.

 **L01,2,3** *(45 min)*

201X		
Apr.	1	Beth Orth invested $15,000 in the art studio.
	1	Paid 2 months' rent in advance, $1,600.
	3	Purchased equipment from Martin Co. for $1,300 on account.
	5	Received $3,000 cash for art-training workshop for teachers.
	8	Purchased art supplies for $350 cash.
	9	Billed Harry Co. $3,300 for group art lessons for its employees.
	10	Paid salaries of assistants, $700.
	15	Beth withdrew $1,000 for personal use.
	28	Paid electric bill, $50.
	29	Paid telephone bill for April, $130.

Check Figure:
Total Trial Balance $22,600

Your tasks are to do the following:

a. Set up a ledger based on the following chart of accounts using four-column accounts.
b. Journalize (journal is page 1) and post the April journal entries.
c. Prepare a trial balance as of April 30, 201X.

The chart of accounts for Beth's Art Studio is as follows:

Chart of Accounts

Assets		Owner's Equity	
111	Cash	311	Beth Orth, Capital
112	Accounts Receivable	312	Beth Orth, Withdrawals
114	Prepaid Rent	**Revenue**	
121	Art Supplies	411	Art Fees Earned
131	Equipment	**Expenses**	
Liabilities		511	Electrical Expense
211	Accounts Payable	521	Salaries Expense
		531	Telephone Expense

(45 min) **LO1,2,3**   **3B-3.**   The following transactions occurred in April 201X for A. French's Placement Agency:

201X	
Apr. 1	A. French invested $12,000 cash in the placement agency.
1	Bought equipment from Tiger Co. for $2,100 on account.
3	Earned placement fees of $1,800, but payment will not be received until May.
5	A. French withdrew $600 for personal use.
7	Paid wages expense, $400.
9	Placed a client on a local TV show, receiving $3,000 cash.
15	Bought supplies from Howdi Co. for $600 on account.
28	Paid telephone bill for April, $200.
29	Advertising bill from Shaker Co. received but not paid, $130.

Check Figure:
Total Trial Balance $19,630

The chart of accounts for A. French Placement Agency is as follows:

Chart of Accounts

Assets		Owner's Equity	
111	Cash	311	A. French, Capital
112	Accounts Receivable	312	A. French, Withdrawals
131	Supplies	**Revenue**	
141	Equipment	411	Placement Fees Earned
Liabilities		**Expenses**	
211	Accounts Payable	511	Wage Expense
		521	Telephone Expense
		531	Advertising Expense

Your task is to do the following:

a. Set up a ledger based on the chart of accounts using four-column accounts.
b. Journalize (page 1) and post the April journal entries.
c. Prepare a trial balance at April 30, 201X.

Financial Report Problem

Reading the Kellogg's Annual Report

Go to http://investor.kelloggs.com/investor-relations/annual-reports/ to access Kellogg's 2013 Annual Report. Find the statement of earnings. Sales are the revenue for a merchandise company. How much did Kellogg's sales increase or decrease from 2012 to 2013? What inward flows could result from these net sales?

 **LO3**   (5 min)

ON THE JOB SMITH COMPUTER CENTER

MyAccountingLab

Thad's computer center's business is picking up, so he has decided to expand his bookkeeping system to a general journal/ledger system. The balances from August have been forwarded to the ledger accounts.

LO1,2,3   (45 min)

Assignment

1. Use the chart of accounts in Chapter 2 to record the following transactions in Figures 3.37 through 3.47.

Smith Computer Center
385 N. Escondido Blvd.
Escondido CA 92025

8104

September 1,--201X------

Pay
To the
Order of—*Chapin Corp.* ------------------------- $ 1500.00 --------

One thousand five hundred and 00/100

First Union Bank
322 Glen Ave.
Escondido, CA 92025
memo *Prepaid Rent—Aug. Sept. Oct.**
0611 062 78 72

-------*Thad Feldman* --------

FIGURE 3.37
Prepaid Rent

*One check is written for 3 months' rent on September 1. That included August rent. For this problem, consider it all prepaid.

FIGURE 3.38 Service Revenue

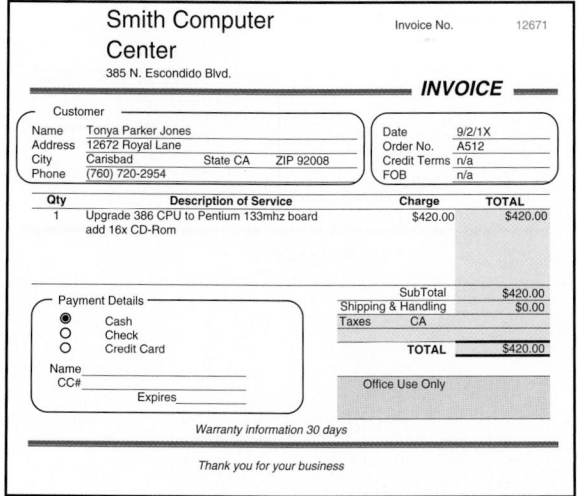

FIGURE 3.39 Service Revenue

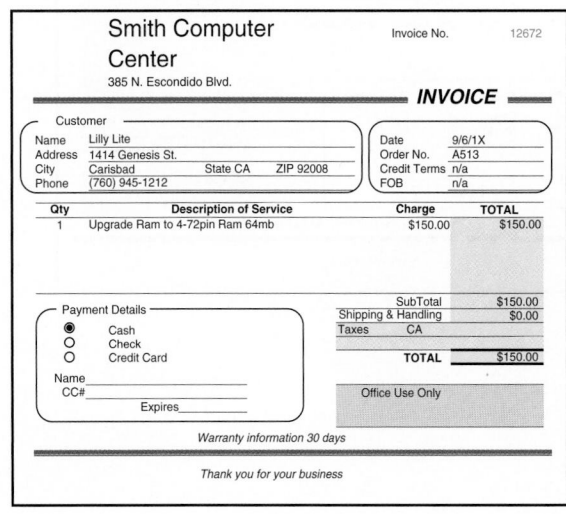

FIGURE 3.40 Phone Bill

Smith Computer Center   8105
385 N. Escondido Blvd.
Escondido CA 92025   *September 8, 201X*

Pay
To the
Order of— *Pacific Bell* ----------------------------- $ *80.00* --------
   Eighty and 00/100

First Union Bank
322 Glen Ave.
Escondido, CA 92025
memo *August phone bill transaction (6) Chpt. 2*   ------*Thad Feldman* ------
0611 062 78 72

Refer back to Chapter 2, transaction k.

FIGURE 3.41 Caffrey Collection

Erin Caffrey   251
1919 Sierra St.
Escondido CA 92025   *September 12, 201X*

Pay
To the
Order of— *Smith Computer Center* ----------------------- $ *1700.00* -----
   One thousand seven hundred dollars and 00/100

Bank First
322 Cardiff Ave.
Escondido, CA 92025
memo *Computer Fixed. Transaction (o) Chpt. 2*   ------ *Erin Caffrey* ------
0611 062 78 72

Refer back to Chapter 2, transaction o.

FIGURE 3.42 Paid Computers R Us

Smith Computer Center   8106
385 N. Escondido Blvd.
Escondido CA 92025   *September 15, 201X*

Pay
To the
Order of— *Computers R Us* ----------------------- $ *300.00* --------
   Three hundred dollars and 00/100

First Union Bank
322 Glen Ave.
Escondido, CA 92025
memo *Account due from transaction (s) Chpt. 2*   ------*Thad Feldman* ------
0611 062 78 72

Refer back to Chapter 2, transaction s.

FIGURE 3.43 Purchased Computer Equipment

Smith Computer Center   8107
385 N. Escondido Blvd.
Escondido CA 92025   *September 17, 201X*

Pay
To the
Order of— *A-Tech. Inc.* ----------------------- $ *2,100.00* --------
   Two thousand one hundred dollars and 00/100

First Union Bank
322 Glen Ave.
Escondido, CA 92025
   Purchase order 200
memo *Computer Equipment-Bench Workstations*   ------*Thad Feldman* ------
0611 062 78 72

FIGURE 3.44 Received Phone Bill

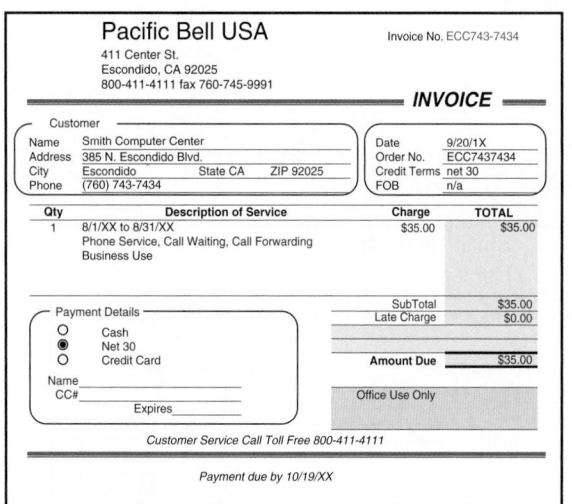

FIGURE 3.45 Received Electric Bill

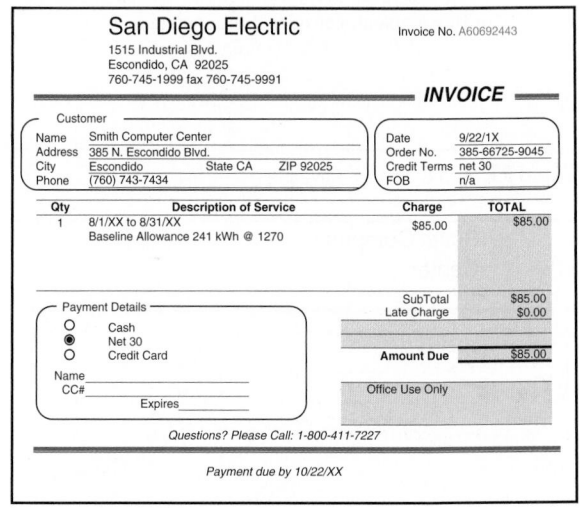

FIGURE 3.46 Service Revenue

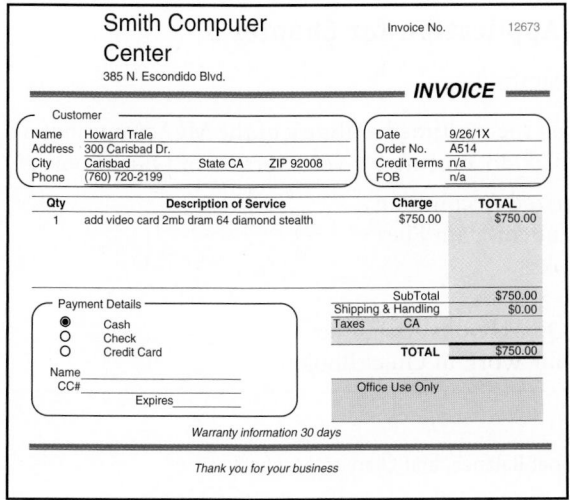

FIGURE 3.47 Service Revenue

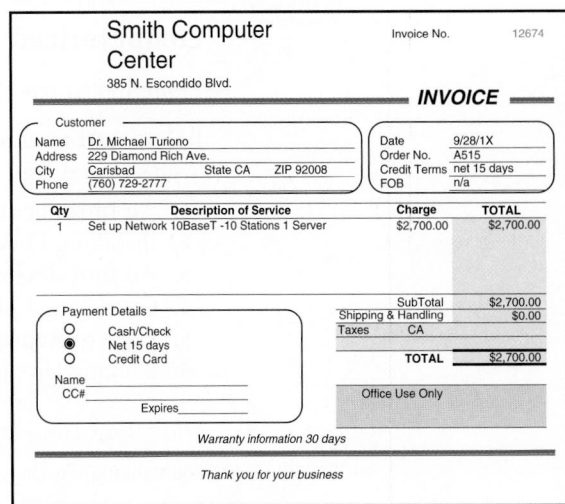

2. Post all journal entries to the general ledger accounts (the Prepaid Rent Account #1025 has been added to the chart of accounts).

3. Prepare a trial balance for September 30, 201X.

4. Prepare the financial statements for the 3 months ended September 30, 201X.

SAGE 50 COMPUTER WORKSHOP

S50

Computerized Accounting Application for Chapter 3

Preparing to use Sage 50 Complete Accounting

Before starting this assignment, visit the multimedia library of the MyAccountingLab Web site and read the following PDF documents for your version of Sage 50.

1. An Introduction to Computerized Accounting
2. Installing Sage 50 and Student Data Files
3. An Introduction to Sage 50
4. Correcting Sage 50 Transactions
5. How to Repeat or Restart a Sage 50 Assignment
6. Backing Up and Restoring Your Work in Sage 50

Workshop 1:

Journalizing, Posting, General Ledger, Trial Balance, and Chart of Accounts

In this workshop, you will enter, post, and edit journal entries for the Atlas Company using Sage 50. You will also print the general journal report, trial balance, and chart of accounts.

Instructions and data files for completing this assignment are in the multimedia library of the MyAccountingLab Web site. Open the *Workshop 1 Atlas Company* PDF document for your version of Sage 50 and download the *Atlas Company* data file for your version of Sage 50.

QUICKBOOKS COMPUTER WORKSHOP

Computerized Accounting Application for Chapter 3

Preparing to use QuickBooks Accountant

Before starting this assignment, visit the multimedia library of the MyAccountingLab Web site and read the following PDF documents for your version of QuickBooks.

1. An Introduction to Computerized Accounting
2. Installing QuickBooks and Student Data Files
3. An Introduction to QuickBooks
4. Correcting QuickBooks Transactions
5. How to Repeat or Restart a QuickBooks Assignment
6. Backing Up and Restoring Your Work in QuickBooks

Workshop 1:

Journalizing, Posting, General Ledger, Trial Balance, and Chart of Accounts

In this workshop, you will enter, post, and edit journal entries for the Atlas Company using QuickBooks. You will also print the general journal report, trial balance, and chart of accounts.

Instructions and data files for completing this assignment are in the multimedia library of the MyAccountingLab Web site. Open the *Workshop 1 Atlas Company* PDF document for your version of QuickBooks and download the *Atlas Company* data file for your version of QuickBooks.

The Accounting Cycle Continued

CHAPTER PREVIEW: THE BIG PICTURE

New cars have more advanced technology than ever before. Jill Rice loves her new Ford Explorer, which can park itself. Designers at Ford Motors first sketched the concept of parallel parking using software and then considered how this new feature could be manufactured. While accountants do not design cars, they do use a sketch pad called a worksheet to make changes and adjustments to the trial balance and financial statements. Today, whether in the accounting department at Ford Motors or a small business, these "design sheets" or worksheets are "sketched" by accounting software. Laying out a worksheet will provide you with a tool to aid you in understanding the "design"—the financial statements generated by your accounting software.

Learning Objectives

LO1   Explain Adjustments and How to Record Them on a Worksheet

LO2   Complete the Worksheet

LO3   Prepare Financial Statements from the Worksheet

Each year, Ford Motors completes an accounting cycle. Figure 4.1 shows the first four steps of the manual accounting cycle that were completed for Mel's Computer Repair Service in the previous chapter. This chapter continues the cycle with Steps 5–6: the preparation of a worksheet and the three financial statements.

LEARNING UNIT 4-1

LO1

Explaining Adjustments and How to Record Them on a Worksheet

Worksheet A columnar device used by accountants to aid them in completing the accounting cycle—often just referred to as "spreadsheet." It is not a formal report.

An accountant uses a worksheet to organize and check data before preparing the financial statements necessary to complete the accounting cycle. When an accounting software package is used, a worksheet is not needed. Most worksheets are completed using Microsoft Excel. The most important function of the worksheet is to allow the accountant to find and correct errors before financial statements are prepared. In a way, the worksheet acts as the accountant's scratch pad. No one sees the worksheet once the financial statements are prepared. A sample partial worksheet is shown in Figure 4.2.

The accounts listed on the far left of the worksheet are taken from the ledger. The rest of the worksheet has five sections: the trial balance, adjustments, adjusted trial balance, income statement, and balance sheet. Each of these sections is divided into debit and credit columns.

The Trial Balance Section

We discussed how to prepare a trial balance in Chapter 2. Some companies prepare a separate trial balance; others, such as Mel's Computer Repair Service, prepare the trial balance directly on the worksheet. A trial balance is taken on every account listed in the ledger that has a balance. Additional titles from the ledger are added as they are needed. (We show how to add account titles later.)

The Adjustments Section

Chapters 1–3 discussed transactions that occurred with outside suppliers and companies. In a business, also inside transactions occur during the accounting cycle.

FIGURE 4.1

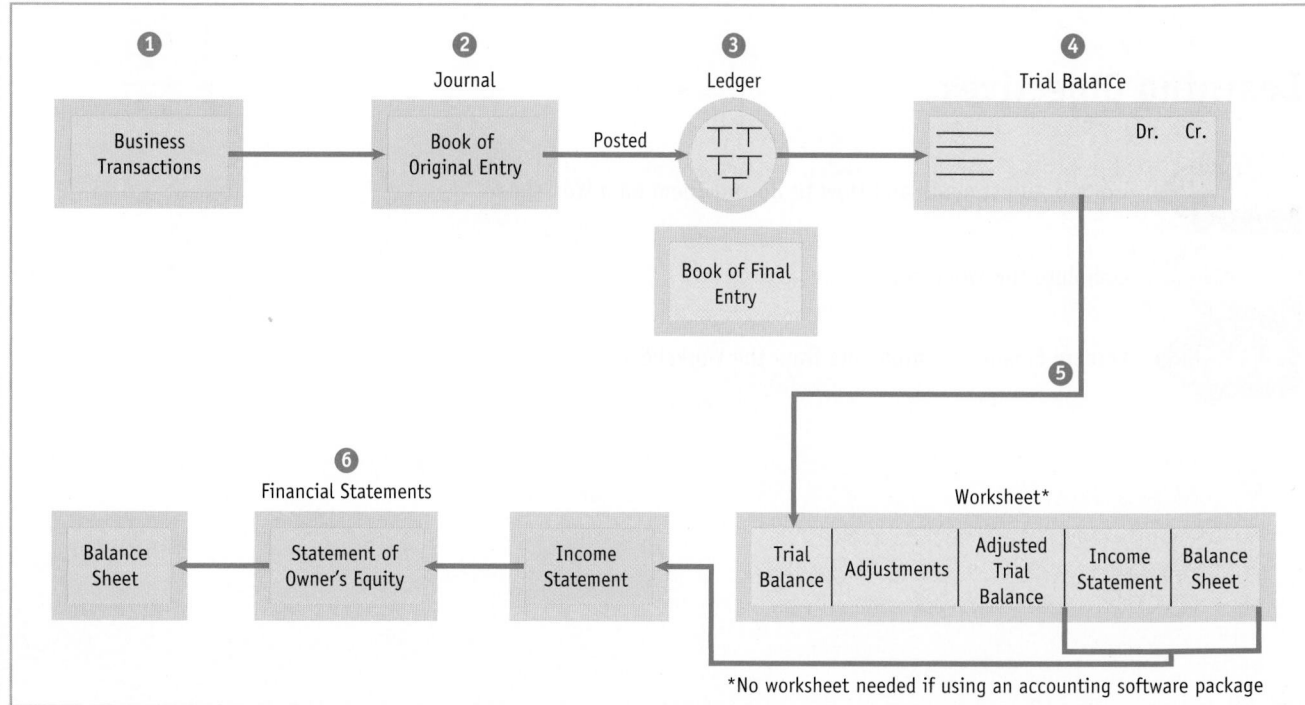

*No worksheet needed if using an accounting software package

FIGURE 4.2 Sample Worksheet

	Trial Balance		Adjustments		Adjusted Trial Balance		Income Statement	
Account Titles	Dr.	Cr.	Dr.	Cr.	Dr.	Cr.	Dr.	Cr.
Cash	6155 00							
Accounts Receivable	5000 00							
Computer Supplies	600 00							
Prepaid Rent	1200 00							
Computer Equipment	6000 00							
Accounts Payable		3350 00						
Mel Blass, Capital		10000 00						
Mel Blass, Withdrawals	625 00							
Computer Repair Fees		8000 00						
Office Salaries Expense	1300 00							
Advertising Expense	250 00							
Telephone Expense	220 00							
Totals	21350 00	21350 00						

MEL'S COMPUTER REPAIR SERVICE
WORKSHEET
FOR MONTH ENDING MAY 31, 201X

These transactions must be recorded, too. At the end of the worksheet process, the accountant will have all of the business's accounts up-to-date and ready to be used to prepare the formal financial statements. The Sarbanes-Oxley Act specifically states the need to have accurate financial statements. By analyzing each of Mel's accounts on the worksheet, the accountant will be able to identify specific accounts that must be adjusted to bring them up-to-date. The accountant for Mel's Computer Repair Service needs to adjust the following accounts:

a. Computer Supplies
b. Prepaid Rent
c. Computer Equipment
d. Office Salaries Expense

Let's look at how to analyze and adjust each of these accounts.

A. Adjusting the Computer Supplies Account. On May 31, the accountant found out that the company had only $100 worth of computer supplies on hand. When the company had originally purchased $600 of computer supplies, they were considered an asset. As the supplies were used up, they became an expense.

- Computer supplies available: $600 on trial balance.
- Computer supplies left or on hand as of May 31: $100 will end up on adjusted trial balance.
- Computer supplies used up in the operation of the business for the month of May: $500 is shown in the adjustments column.

As a result, the asset Computer Supplies is too high on the trial balance (it should be $100, not $600). At the same time, if we don't show the additional expense of supplies used, the company's *net income* will be too high.

If Blass's accountant does not adjust the trial balance to reflect the change, the company's net income will be too high on the income statement and both sides (Assets and Owner's Equity) of the balance sheet will be too high.

COACHING TIP

Worksheets can be completed on Excel spreadsheets.

Adjusting The process of calculating the latest up-to-date balance of each account at the end of an accounting period.

Now let's look at the adjustment for computer supplies in terms of the transaction analysis chart.

Will go on income statement

Accounts Affected	Category	↓↑	Rules
Computer Supplies Expense	Expense	↑	Dr.
Computer Supplies	Asset	↓	Cr.

Will go on balance sheet

Computer Supplies Exp. 514	Computer Supplies 114
500	600 | 500
This amount is supplies used up.	100 |

↑
This amount is supplies on hand.

The Computer Supplies Expense account comes from the chart of accounts in Chapter 3. Because it is not listed in the account titles, it must be listed below the trial balance. Let's see how we enter this adjustment in the worksheet in Figure 4.3.

Place $500 in the debit column of the adjustments section on the same line as Computer Supplies Expense. Place $500 in the credit column of the adjustments section on the same line as Computer Supplies. The numbers in the adjustment column show what is used, *not* what is on hand.

COACHING TIP

The adjustment for supplies deals with the amount of supplies *used up*.

FIGURE 4.3

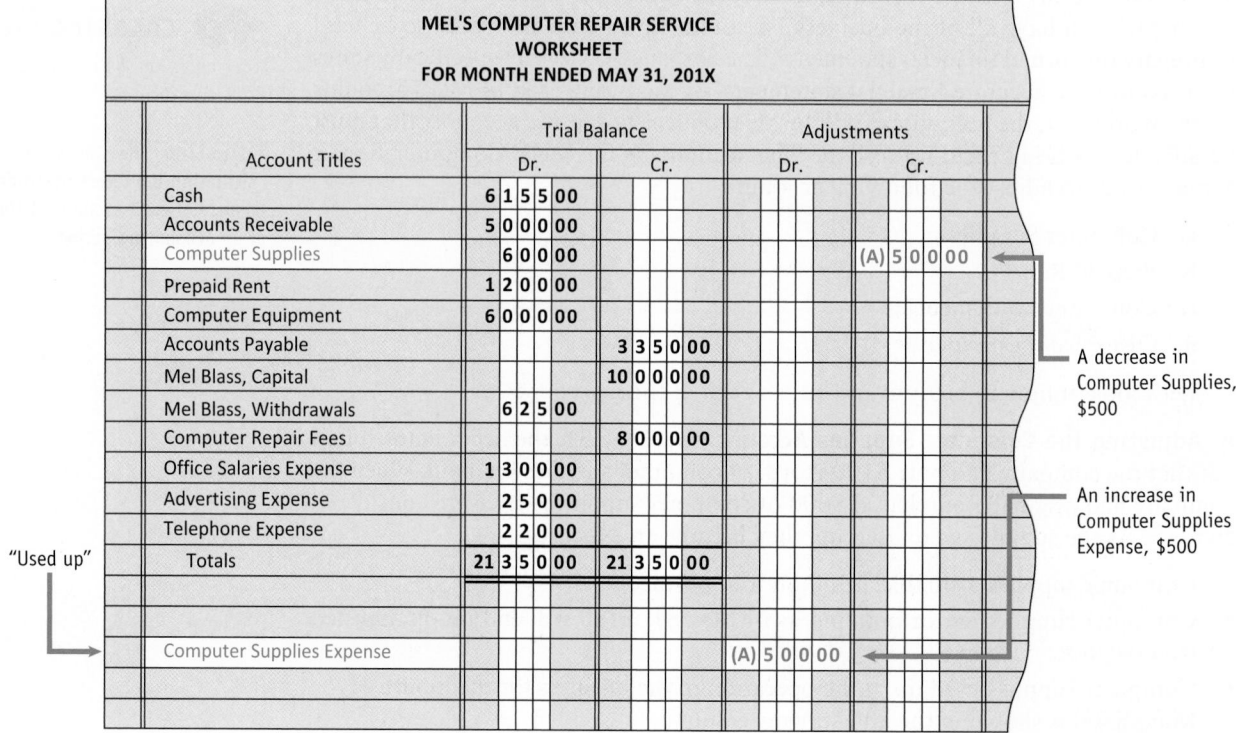

Note: Amount "used up" for computer supplies, $500, goes in adjustments section.

B. Adjusting the Prepaid Rent Account. Back on May 1, Mel's Computer Repair Service paid three months' rent in advance. The accountant realized that the rent expense would be $400 per month ($1,200 ÷ 3 months = $400).

Remember, when rent is paid in advance, it is considered an asset called *prepaid rent*. When the asset, prepaid rent, begins to expire or be used up, it becomes an expense. Now it is May 31, and one month's prepaid rent has become an expense.

How is this type of rent handled? Should the account be $1,200, or is only $800 of prepaid rent left as of May 31? What do we need to do to bring Prepaid Rent to the "true" balance? The answer is that we must increase Rent Expense by $400 and decrease Prepaid Rent by $400 (so that there is only $800 left; see Figure 4.4).

Without this adjustment, the expenses for Mel's Computer Repair Service for May will be too low, and the asset prepaid rent will be too high. If unadjusted amounts were used in the formal reports, the net income shown on the income statement would be too high, and both sides (Assets and Owner's Equity) would be too high on the balance sheet. In terms of our transaction analysis chart, the adjustment would look like this:

Will go on income statement

Accounts Affected	Category	↓↑	Rules	
Rent Expense	Expense	↑	Dr.	
Prepaid Rent	Asset	↓	Cr.	

Will go on balance sheet

Rent Expense 515		Prepaid Rent 115	
400		1200	400
		800	

Like the Computer Supplies Expense account, the Rent Expense account comes from the chart of accounts in Chapter 3.

Figure 4.4 shows how to enter an adjustment to Prepaid Rent.

FIGURE 4.4

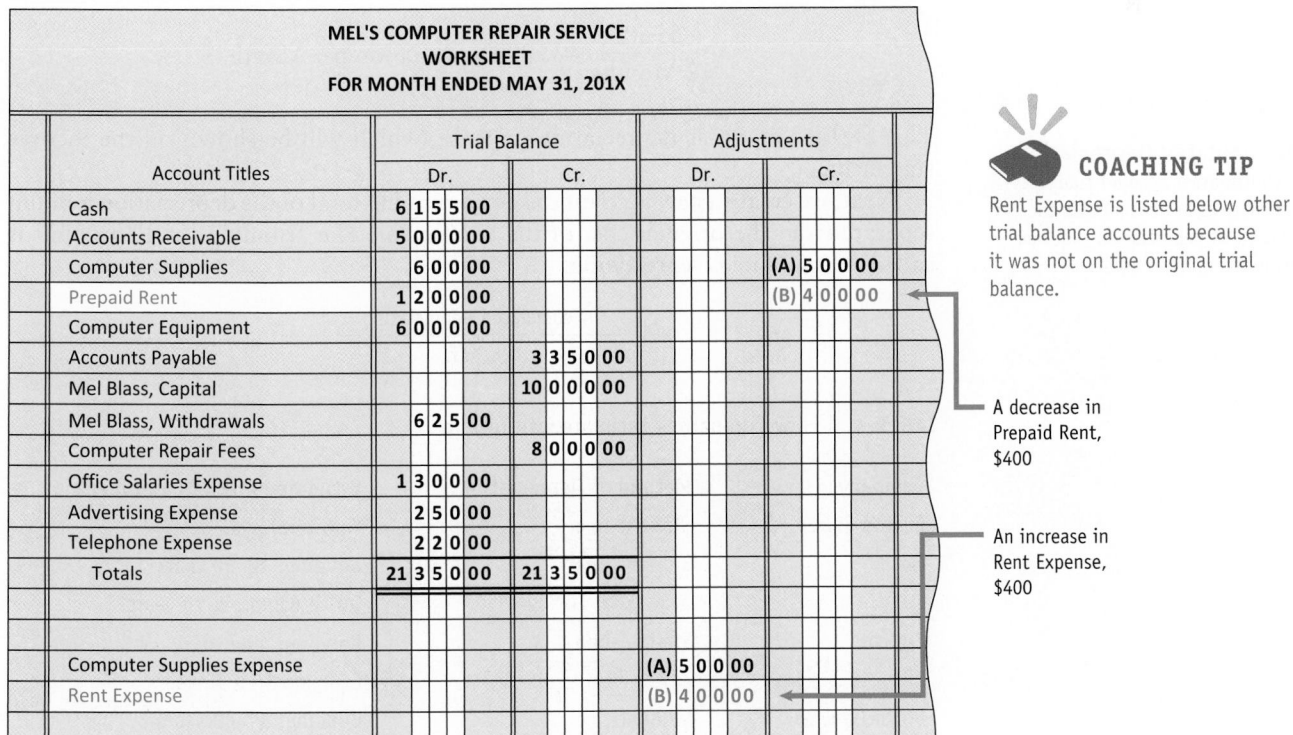

MEL'S COMPUTER REPAIR SERVICE
WORKSHEET
FOR MONTH ENDED MAY 31, 201X

Account Titles	Trial Balance Dr.	Trial Balance Cr.	Adjustments Dr.	Adjustments Cr.
Cash	6 1 5 5 00			
Accounts Receivable	5 0 0 0 00			
Computer Supplies	6 0 0 00			(A) 5 0 0 00
Prepaid Rent	1 2 0 0 00			(B) 4 0 0 00
Computer Equipment	6 0 0 0 00			
Accounts Payable		3 3 5 0 00		
Mel Blass, Capital		10 0 0 0 00		
Mel Blass, Withdrawals	6 2 5 00			
Computer Repair Fees		8 0 0 0 00		
Office Salaries Expense	1 3 0 0 00			
Advertising Expense	2 5 0 00			
Telephone Expense	2 2 0 00			
Totals	21 3 5 0 00	21 3 5 0 00		
Computer Supplies Expense			(A) 5 0 0 00	
Rent Expense			(B) 4 0 0 00	

COACHING TIP

Rent Expense is listed below other trial balance accounts because it was not on the original trial balance.

A decrease in Prepaid Rent, $400

An increase in Rent Expense, $400

C. Adjusting the Computer Equipment Account for Depreciation. The life of the asset affects how it is adjusted. The two accounts we just discussed, Computer Supplies and Prepaid Rent, involve things that are used up relatively quickly. Computer Equipment is expected to last much longer. Computer Equipment is expected to help produce revenue over a longer period. For that reason accountants treat it differently. The balance sheet reports the historical cost, or original cost, of the equipment. The original cost is also reflected in the ledger. The adjustment shows how the cost of the equipment is allocated (spread) over its expected useful life. This spreading is called depreciation. To depreciate the equipment, we have to figure out how much its cost goes down each month. Then we have to keep a running total of how that depreciation mounts up over time. The Internal Revenue Service (IRS) issues guidelines, tables, and formulas to estimate the amount of depreciation. The IRS tax guidelines are used for tax purposes and do not have to be used in financial reporting. Different methods can be used to calculate depreciation. We will use the simplest method—straight-line depreciation—to calculate the depreciation of Mel's Computer Repair Service's equipment. Under the straight-line method, equal amounts are taken over successive periods of time. Table 4.1 shows how some companies estimate the lives of equipment using the straight-line method.

The calculation of depreciation for the year for Mel's Computer Repair Service is as follows:

$$\frac{\text{Cost of Equipment} - \text{Residual Value}}{\text{Estimated Years of Usefulness}} = \text{Depreciation per Year}$$

According to the IRS, computer equipment has an expected life of five years. At the end of that time, the property's value is called its "residual value." Think of residual value as the estimated value of the equipment at the end of the fifth year. For Blass, the equipment has an estimated residual value of $1,200.

$$\frac{\$6,000 - \$1,200}{5 \text{ Years}} = \frac{\$4,800}{5} = \$960 \text{ Depreciation per Year}$$

Our trial balance is for one month, so we must determine the adjustment for that month:

$$\frac{\$960}{12 \text{ Months}} = \$80 \text{ Depreciation per Month}$$

This $80 is known as depreciation expense, which will be shown on the income statement.

Next, we create a new account to keep a running total of the depreciation amount separate from the original cost of the equipment. The "running total" account is called Accumulated Depreciation.

Accumulated Depreciation	
Dr.	Cr.

TABLE 4.1 How Companies Estimate Useful Life

Company	Method of Depreciation	Estimated Life of Equipment
Claire's Stores	Straight-line	Furniture: 3–25 years
Merck	Straight-line	Building: 10–50 years
		Office Equip.: 3–15 years
Big Lots	Straight-line	Building: 40 years
		Equipment: 3–15 years
Dollar General	Straight-line	Building: 39–40 years
		Furniture: 3–10 years

Historical cost The actual cost of an asset at time of purchase.

Depreciation The allocation (spreading) of the cost of an asset (such as an auto or equipment) over its expected useful life.

COACHING TIP

Original cost of $6,000 for computer equipment remains *unchanged* after adjustments.

Residual value Estimated value of an asset after all the allowable depreciation has been taken.

Accumulated Depreciation A contra-asset account that summarizes or accumulates the amount of depreciation that has been taken on an asset.

Accumulated Depreciation is a contra-asset account found on the balance sheet. A credit will increase it.

The Accumulated Depreciation account shows the relationship between the original cost of the equipment and the amount of depreciation that has been taken or accumulated over a period of time. This *contra-asset* account has the opposite balance of an asset such as equipment. Accumulated Depreciation will summarize, accumulate, or build up the amount of depreciation that is taken on the computer equipment over its estimated useful life.

Figure 4.5 shows how this calculation of depreciation would look on a partial balance sheet of Mel's Computer Repair Service.

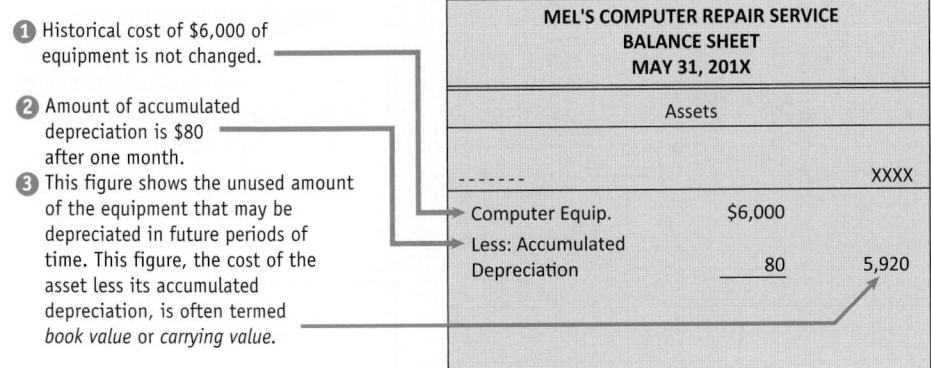

FIGURE 4.5

Let's summarize the key points before going on to mark the adjustment on the worksheet:

1. Depreciation Expense goes on the income statement, which results in
   - an increase in total expenses,
   - a decrease in net income, and, therefore,
   - less to be paid in taxes.
2. Accumulated Depreciation is a contra-asset account found on the balance sheet next to its related equipment account. Accumulated depreciation increases with a credit.
3. The original cost of equipment is not reduced; it stays the same until the equipment is sold or removed.
4. Each month the amount in the Accumulated Depreciation account grows larger while the cost of the equipment remains the same.

Now, let's analyze the adjustment on the transaction analysis chart:

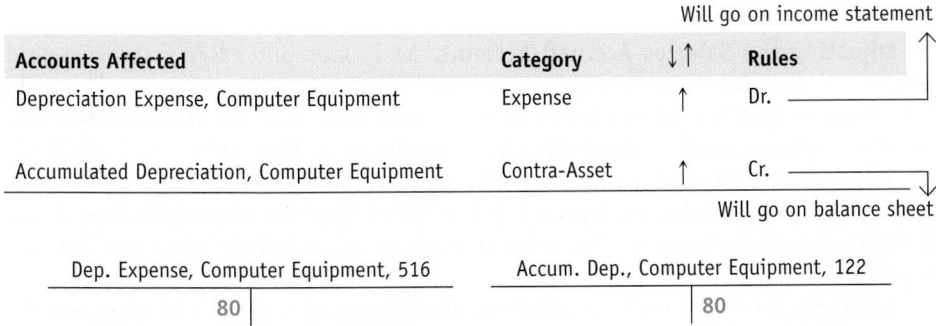

Remember, the original cost of the equipment never changes. The Equipment account is not included among the affected accounts because the original cost of equipment remains the same. As the accumulated depreciation increases (as a credit), the equipment's book value decreases.

Figure 4.6 (page 114) shows how we enter the adjustment for depreciation of computer equipment.

Book value Cost of equipment less accumulated depreciation.

FIGURE 4.6

Account Titles	Trial Balance				Adjustments			
	Dr.		Cr.		Dr.		Cr.	
Cash	6 1 5 5 00							
Accounts Receivable	5 0 0 0 00							
Computer Supplies	6 0 0 00						(A) 5 0 0 00	
Prepaid Rent	1 2 0 0 00						(B) 4 0 0 00	
Computer Equipment	6 0 0 0 00							
Accounts Payable			3 3 5 0 00					
Mel Blass, Capital			10 0 0 0 00					
Mel Blass, Withdrawals	6 2 5 00							
Computer Repair Fees			8 0 0 0 00					
Office Salaries Expense	1 3 0 0 00							
Advertising Expense	2 5 0 00							
Telephone Expense	2 2 0 00							
Totals	21 3 5 0 00		21 3 5 0 00					
Computer Supplies Expense					(A) 5 0 0 00			
Rent Expense					(B) 4 0 0 00			
Depreciation Exp., Computer Equip.					(C) 8 0 00			
Accum. Deprec., Computer Equip.							(C) 8 0 00	

**MEL'S COMPUTER REPAIR SERVICE
WORKSHEET
FOR MONTH ENDED MAY 31, 201X**

> **COACHING TIP**
> Note that the original cost of the equipment on the worksheet has *not* been changed ($6,000).

An increase in Depreciation Expense, Computer Equipment

An increase in Accumulated Depreciation, Computer Equipment

Because it is a new business, neither account had a previous balance. Therefore, neither is listed in the account titles of the trial balance. We need to list both accounts below Rent Expense in the account titles section. On the worksheet, put $80 in the debit column of the adjustments section on the same line as Depreciation Expense, Computer Equipment, and put $80 in the credit column of the adjustments section on the same line as Accumulated Depreciation, Computer Equipment.

Next month, on June 30, $80 would be entered under Depreciation Expense, Computer Equipment and Accumulated Depreciation, Computer Equipment would show a balance of $160. Remember, in May, Blass's was a new company so no previous depreciation had been taken.

Now let's look at the last adjustment for Mel's Computer Repair Service.

D. Adjusting the Salaries Accrued Account. Mel's Computer Repair Service paid $1,300 in office salaries expense (see the trial balance of any previous worksheet in this chapter). The last salary checks for the month were paid on May 27. How can we update this account to show the salary expense as of May 31?

John Murray worked for Blass on May 28, 29, 30, and 31 (see Figure 4.7). His next paycheck is not due until June 3. John earned $350 for these four days. Is the $350 an expense to Blass in May when it was earned, or in June when it is due and is paid?

Think back to Chapter 1, in which we first discussed revenue and expenses. We noted then that revenue is recorded when it is earned and expenses are recorded when they are incurred, not when they are actually paid. This principle will be discussed further in a later chapter. For now, it is enough to remember that we record revenue and expenses when they occur because we want to match earned revenue with the expenses that resulted in earning those revenues. In this case, by working those 4 days,

> **COACHING TIP**
> Note that accounts listed below the trial balance are always *increasing*.

> **COACHING TIP**
> An expense can be incurred without being paid as long as it helped create earned revenue for a period of time.

May						
Sunday	Monday	Tuesday	Wednesday	Thursday	Friday	Saturday
						1
2	3	4	5	6	7	8
9	10	11	12	13	14	15
16	17	18	19	20	21	22
23	24	25	26	27	28	29
30	31					

FIGURE 4.7

John Murray created some revenue for Blass in May. Therefore, the office salaries expense must be shown in May—the month the revenue was earned.

The results are as follows:

- Office Salaries Expense is increased by $350. This unpaid and unrecorded expense for salaries for which payment is not yet due is called accrued salaries payable. In effect, we now show the true expense for salaries ($1,650 instead of $1,300):

Office Salaries Expense	
1,300	
350	
1,650	

Accrued salaries payable Salaries that are earned by employees but unpaid and unrecorded during the period (and thus need to be recorded by an adjustment) and will not come due for payment until the next accounting period.

- Salaries Payable is also increased by $350. Blass created a liability called salaries payable, which means that the firm owes money for salaries. When the firm pays John Murray, it will reduce its liability salaries payable as well as decrease its cash.

In terms of the transaction analysis chart, the following would be done:

Will go on income statement

Accounts Affected	Category	↓↑	Rules
Office Salaries Expense	Expense	↑	Dr.
Salaries Payable	Liability	↑	Cr.

Will go on balance sheet

Office Salaries Exp. 511		Salaries Payable 212	
1,300			350
350			

How the adjustment for accrued salaries is entered in the worksheet is shown in Figure 4.8, page 116.

The account Office Salaries Expense is already listed in the account titles, so $350 is placed in the debit column of the adjustments section on the same line as Office Salaries Expense. However, because Salaries Payable is not listed in the account titles, it is added below the trial balance after Accumulated Depreciation, Computer Equipment. The amount of $350 is also placed in the credit column of the adjustments section on the same line as Salaries Payable.

Now that we have finished all the adjustments that we intended to make, we total the adjustments section, as shown in Figure 4.9, page 116.

Now let's check your progress.

FIGURE 4.8

MEL'S COMPUTER REPAIR SERVICE
WORKSHEET
FOR MONTH ENDED MAY 31, 201X

Account Titles	Trial Balance Dr.	Trial Balance Cr.	Adjustments Dr.	Adjustments Cr.
Cash	6 1 5 5 00			
Accounts Receivable	5 0 0 0 00			
Computer Supplies	6 0 0 00			(A) 5 0 0 00
Prepaid Rent	1 2 0 0 00			(B) 4 0 0 00
Computer Equipment	6 0 0 0 00			
Accounts Payable		3 3 5 0 00		
Mel Blass, Capital		10 0 0 0 00		
Mel Blass, Withdrawals	6 2 5 00			
Computer Repair Fees		8 0 0 0 00		
Office Salaries Expense	1 3 0 0 00		(D) 3 5 0 00	
Advertising Expense	2 5 0 00			
Telephone Expense	2 2 0 00			
Totals	21 3 5 0 00	21 3 5 0 00		
Computer Supplies Expense			(A) 5 0 0 00	
Rent Expense			(B) 4 0 0 00	
Depreciation Exp., Computer Equip.			(C) 8 0 00	
Accum. Deprec., Computer Equip.				(C) 8 0 00
Salaries Payable				(D) 3 5 0 00

An increase in Office Salaries Expense, $350

An increase in Salaries Payable, $350

FIGURE 4.9
The Adjustments Section of a Worksheet

MEL'S COMPUTER REPAIR SERVICE
WORKSHEET
FOR MONTH ENDED MAY 31, 201X

Account Titles	Trial Balance Dr.	Trial Balance Cr.	Adjustments Dr.	Adjustments Cr.
Cash	6 1 5 5 00			
Accounts Receivable	5 0 0 0 00			
Computer Supplies	6 0 0 00			(A) 5 0 0 00
Prepaid Rent	1 2 0 0 00			(B) 4 0 0 00
Computer Equipment	6 0 0 0 00			
Accounts Payable		3 3 5 0 00		
Mel Blass, Capital		10 0 0 0 00		
Mel Blass, Withdrawals	6 2 5 00			
Computer Repair Fees		8 0 0 0 00		
Office Salaries Expense	1 3 0 0 00		(D) 3 5 0 00	
Advertising Expense	2 5 0 00			
Telephone Expense	2 2 0 00			
Totals	21 3 5 0 00	21 3 5 0 00		
Computer Supplies Expense			(A) 5 0 0 00	
Rent Expense			(B) 4 0 0 00	
Depreciation Exp., Computer Equip.			(C) 8 0 00	
Accum. Deprec., Computer Equip.				(C) 8 0 00
Salaries Payable				(D) 3 5 0 00
Totals			1 3 3 0 00	1 3 3 0 00

 **TRY IT!**   Learning Unit 4-1

Given the following, prepare a transaction analysis boxes to record the adjustments for computer supplies and computer equipment:

Beginning Computer Supplies $6,000
Computer Supplies on hand at end of period $4,000
Cost of Computer Equipment $15,000
Beginning balance in Accumulated Depreciation, Computer Equipment $300
Depreciation to be taken for this period $150

The Worksheet (Step 5 of the Accounting Cycle)

 LEARNING UNIT 4-2

L02

The Adjusted Trial Balance

The adjusted trial balance is the next section on the worksheet. To fill it out we must summarize the information in the trial balance and adjustments sections, as shown in Figure 4.10 on page 118.

Note that when the numbers are brought across from the trial balance to the adjusted trial balance, two debits will be added together and two credits will be added together. If the numbers include a debit and a credit, take the difference between the two and place it on the side that is larger.

Now that we have completed the adjustments and adjusted trial balance sections of the worksheet, it is time to move on to the income statement and the balance sheet sections. Before we tackle the statements, look at the chart shown in Table 4.2, page 119. This table should be used as a reference to help you in filling out the next two sections of the worksheet.

Keep in mind that the numbers from the adjusted trial balance are carried over to one of the last four columns of the worksheet before the bottom section is completed.

The Income Statement Section

As shown in Figure 4.11 on page 119, the income statement section lists only revenue and expenses from the adjusted trial balance. Note that Accumulated Depreciation and Salaries Payable do not go on the income statement. Accumulated Depreciation is a contra-asset found on the balance sheet. Salaries Payable is a liability found on the balance sheet.

The revenue ($8,000) and all the individual expenses are listed in the income statement section. The revenue is placed in the credit column of the income statement section because it has a credit balance. The expenses have debit balances so they are placed in the debit column of the income statement section. The following steps must be taken after the debits and credits are placed in the correct columns:

STEP 1: Total the debits and credits.

STEP 2: Calculate the difference between the debit and credit columns and place the difference on the smaller side.

STEP 3: Total the columns.

The worksheet in Figure 4.11 shows that the label Net Income is added in the account titles column on the same line as $4,900. When the figures result in a net income, it will be placed in the debit column of the income statement section of the worksheet. A net loss is placed in the credit column. The $8,000 total indicates that the two columns are in balance.

The Balance Sheet Section

To fill out the balance sheet section of the worksheet, the following are carried over from the adjusted trial balance section: assets, contra-assets, liabilities, capital, and withdrawals. Because the beginning figure for Capital* is used on the worksheet, Net Income is brought over to the credit column of the balance sheet so both columns balance.

*We assume no additional investments during the period.

 COACHING TIP

The difference between $3,100 Dr. and $8,000 Cr. indicates Net Income of $4,900. The $4,900 is placed in the debit column to balance both columns to $8,000. Actually, the credit side is larger by $4,900.

 **COACHING TIP**

Remember: The ending figure for Capital is not on the worksheet.

FIGURE 4.10 The Adjusted Trial Balance Section of the Worksheet

MEL'S COMPUTER REPAIR SERVICE
WORKSHEET
FOR MONTH ENDED MAY 31, 201X

Account Titles	Trial Balance Dr.	Trial Balance Cr.	Adjustments Dr.	Adjustments Cr.	Adjusted Trial Balance Dr.	Adjusted Trial Balance Cr.
Cash	6 1 5 5 00				6 1 5 5 00	
Accounts Receivable	5 0 0 0 00				5 0 0 0 00	
Computer Supplies	6 0 0 00			(A) 5 0 0 00	1 0 0 00	
Prepaid Rent	1 2 0 0 00			(B) 4 0 0 00	8 0 0 00	
Computer Equipment	6 0 0 0 00				6 0 0 0 00	
Accounts Payable		3 3 5 0 00				3 3 5 0 00
Mel Blass, Capital		10 0 0 0 00				10 0 0 0 00
Mel Blass, Withdrawals	6 2 5 00				6 2 5 00	
Computer Repair Fees		8 0 0 0 00				8 0 0 0 00
Office Salaries Expense	1 3 0 0 00		(D) 3 5 0 00		1 6 5 0 00	
Advertising Expense	2 5 0 00				2 5 0 00	
Telephone Expense	2 2 0 00				2 2 0 00	
Totals	21 3 5 0 00	21 3 5 0 00				
Computer Supplies Expense			(A) 5 0 0 00		5 0 0 00	
Rent Expense			(B) 4 0 0 00		4 0 0 00	
Depreciation Exp., Computer Equip.			(C) 8 0 00		8 0 00	
Accum. Deprec., Computer Equip.				(C) 8 0 00		8 0 00
Salaries Payable				(D) 3 5 0 00		3 5 0 00
			1 3 3 0 00	1 3 3 0 00	21 7 8 0 00	21 7 8 0 00

If no adjustment is made, just carry over amount from trial balance on same side.

Supplies were $600, but we used up $500, leaving us with a $100 balance (on hand) in Supplies. *Note:* If the account lists both a debit and a credit, take the *difference* between the two and place it on the side that is larger.

Note: Equipment is *not* adjusted here.

Two debits are added together. If there were two credits, they also would be added together.

Carry these amounts over to adjusted trial balance in the same positions.

Note: The total of the left (debit) must equal the total of the right (credit) ($21,780).

TABLE 4.2 Normal Balances and Account Categories

Account Titles	Category	Normal Balance on Adjusted Trial Balance	Income Statement		Balance Sheet	
			Dr.	Cr.	Dr.	Cr.
Cash	Asset	Dr.			X	
Accounts Receivable	Asset	Dr.			X	
Computer Supplies	Asset	Dr.			X	
Prepaid Rent	Asset	Dr.			X	
Computer Equipment	Asset	Dr.			X	
Accounts Payable	Liability	Cr.				X
Mel Blass, Capital	Capital	Cr.				X
Mel Blass, Withdrawals	Withdrawal	Dr.			X	
Computer Repair Fees	Revenue	Cr.		X		
Office Salaries Exp.	Expense	Dr.	X			
Advertising Expense	Expense	Dr.	X			
Telephone Expense	Expense	Dr.	X			
Computer Supplies Exp.	Expense	Dr.	X			
Rent Expense	Expense	Dr.	X			
Dep. Exp., Computer Equip.	Expense	Dr.	X			
Acc. Dep., Computer. Equip.	Contra-Asset	Cr.				X
Salaries Payable	Liability	Cr.				X

FIGURE 4.11 The Income Statement Section of the Worksheet

MEL'S COMPUTER REPAIR SERVICE
WORKSHEET
FOR MONTH ENDED MAY 31, 201X

Account Titles	Adjusted Trial Balance Dr.	Adjusted Trial Balance Cr.	Income Statement Dr.	Income Statement Cr.
Cash	6 1 5 5 00			
Accounts Receivable	5 0 0 0 00			
Computer Supplies	1 0 0 00			
Prepaid Rent	8 0 0 00			
Computer Equipment	6 0 0 0 00			
Accounts Payable		3 3 5 0 00		
Mel Blass, Capital		10 0 0 0 00		
Mel Blass, Withdrawals	6 2 5 00			
Computer Repair Fees		8 0 0 0 00		8 0 0 0 00
Office Salaries Expense	1 6 5 0 00		1 6 5 0 00	
Advertising Expense	2 5 0 00		2 5 0 00	
Telephone Expense	2 2 0 00		2 2 0 00	
Computer Supplies Expense	5 0 0 00		5 0 0 00	
Rent Expense	4 0 0 00		4 0 0 00	
Depreciation Exp., Computer Equip.	8 0 00		8 0 00	
Accum. Deprec., Computer Equip.		8 0 00		
Salaries Payable		3 5 0 00		
Totals	21 7 8 0 00	21 7 8 0 00	3 1 0 0 00	8 0 0 0 00
Net Income			4 9 0 0 00	
Totals			8 0 0 0 00	8 0 0 0 00

$8,000
−3,100
$4,900

Let's now look at the completed worksheet in Figure 4.12 to see how the balance sheet section is completed. Note how the Net Income of $4,900 is brought over to the credit column of the balance sheet section. The figure for Capital is also in the credit column while the figure for Withdrawals is in the debit column. By placing Net Income in the credit column, both sides total $18,680. If a net loss were to occur, it would be placed in the debit column of the balance sheet section.

Now that we have completed the worksheet, it's time to check your progress.

 **TRY IT!**   Learning Unit 4-2

Given the following trial balance and adjustment data, complete a partial worksheet up to the adjusted trial balance:

Logan's Car Detailing
Trial Balance
June 30, 201X

	Dr.	Cr.
Cash	2,000	
Detailing Supplies	400	
Prepaid Rent	800	
Detailing Equipment	1,400	
Accounts Payable		900
B. Logan, Capital		3,600
B. Logan, Withdrawals	200	
Detailing Fees		1,200
Salaries Expense	600	
Advertising Expense	300	
Totals	5,700	5,700

Adjustment Data

A. $50 of supplies on hand
B. One-fourth of prepaid rent expired
C. Depreciation on detailing equipment $200
D. Accrued Salaries $300

LEARNING UNIT 4-3

L03

The Financial Statements from the Worksheet (Step 6 of the Accounting Cycle)

The formal financial statements can be prepared from the worksheet completed in Learning Unit 4-2. Before beginning, we must check that the entries on the worksheet are correct and in balance. To ensure the accuracy of the figures, we double-check that (1) all entries are recorded in the appropriate column, (2) the correct amounts are entered in the proper places, (3) the addition is correct across the columns (i.e., from the trial balance to the adjusted trial balance to the financial statements), and (4) the columns are added correctly.

Preparing the Income Statement

The first statement to be prepared for Mel's Computer Repair Service is the income statement. When preparing the income statement it is important to remember the following:

1. Every figure on the formal statement is on the worksheet. Figure 4.13 on page 122 shows where each of these figures goes on the income statement.
2. No debit or credit columns appear on the formal statement.

FIGURE 4.12

Original cost of $6,000 is *not* adjusted

"Used up" "On hand"

MEL'S COMPUTER REPAIR SERVICE
WORKSHEET
FOR MONTH ENDED MAY 31, 201X

Account Titles	Trial Balance Dr.	Trial Balance Cr.	Adjustments Dr.	Adjustments Cr.	Adjusted Trial Balance Dr.	Adjusted Trial Balance Cr.	Income Statement Dr.	Income Statement Cr.	Balance Sheet Dr.	Balance Sheet Cr.
Cash	6 1 5 5 00				6 1 5 5 00				6 1 5 5 00	
Accounts Receivable	5 0 0 0 00				5 0 0 0 00				5 0 0 0 00	
Computer Supplies	6 0 0 0 00			(A) 5 0 0 0 00	1 0 0 0 00				1 0 0 0 00	
Prepaid Rent	1 2 0 0 00			(B) 4 0 0 00	8 0 0 00				8 0 0 00	
Computer Equipment	6 0 0 0 00				6 0 0 0 00				6 0 0 0 00	
Accounts Payable		3 3 5 0 00				3 3 5 0 00				3 3 5 0 00
Mel Blass, Capital		10 0 0 0 00				10 0 0 0 00				10 0 0 0 00
Mel Blass, Withdrawals	6 2 5 00				6 2 5 00				6 2 5 00	
Computer Repair Fees		8 0 0 0 00				8 0 0 0 00		8 0 0 0 00		
Office Salaries Expense	1 3 0 0 00		(D) 3 5 0 00		1 6 5 0 00		1 6 5 0 00			
Advertising Expense	2 5 0 00				2 5 0 00		2 5 0 00			
Telephone Expense	2 2 0 00				2 2 0 00		2 2 0 00			
Totals	21 3 5 0 00	21 3 5 0 00								
Computer Supplies Expense			(A) 5 0 0 0 00		5 0 0 0 00		5 0 0 0 00			
Rent Expense			(B) 4 0 0 00		4 0 0 00		4 0 0 00			
Depreciation Exp., Computer Equip.			(C) 8 0 00		8 0 00		8 0 00			
Accum. Deprec., Computer Equip.				(C) 8 0 00		8 0 00				8 0 00
Salaries Payable				(D) 3 5 0 00		3 5 0 00				3 5 0 00
Totals			1 3 3 0 00	1 3 3 0 00	21 7 8 0 00	21 7 8 0 00	3 1 0 0 00	8 0 0 0 00	18 6 8 0 00	13 7 8 0 00
Net Income							4 9 0 0 00			4 9 0 0 00
Totals							8 0 0 0 00	8 0 0 0 00	18 6 8 0 00	18 6 8 0 00

contra-asset

121

FIGURE 4.13 From Worksheet to Income Statement

MEL'S COMPUTER REPAIR SERVICE
INCOME STATEMENT
FOR MONTH ENDED MAY 31, 201X

Revenue:		
Computer Repair Fees		$8 0 0 0 00
Operating Expenses:		
Office Salaries Expense	$1 6 5 0 00	
Advertising Expense	2 5 0 00	
Telephone Expense	2 2 0 00	
Computer Supplies Expense	5 0 0 00	
Rent Expense	4 0 0 00	
Depreciation Expense, Computer Equipment	8 0 00	
Total Operating Expenses		3 1 0 0 00
Net Income		$4 9 0 0 00

Worksheet (partial):

Account Titles	Income Statement Dr.	Income Statement Cr.
Cash		
Accounts Receivable		
Computer Supplies		
Prepaid Rent		
Computer Equipment		
Accounts Payable		
Mel Blass, Capital		
Mel Blass, Withdrawals		
Computer Repair Fees		8 0 0 0 00
Office Salaries Expense	1 6 5 0 00	
Advertising Expense	2 5 0 00	
Telephone Expense	2 2 0 00	
Computer Supplies Expense	5 0 0 00	
Rent Expense	4 0 0 00	
Depreciation Expense, Computer Equip.	8 0 00	
Accum. Deprec., Computer Equip.		
Salaries Payable		
Totals	3 1 0 0 00	8 0 0 0 00
Net Income	4 9 0 0 00	
Totals	8 0 0 0 00	8 0 0 0 00

FIGURE 4.14 Completing a Statement of Owner's Equity

MEL'S COMPUTER REPAIR SERVICE
STATEMENT OF OWNER'S EQUITY
FOR MONTH ENDED MAY 31, 201X

Mel Blass, Capital, May 1, 201X		$10 0 0 0 00
Net Income for May	$4 9 0 0 00	
Less Withdrawals for May	− 6 2 5 00	
Increase in Capital		4 2 7 5 00
Mel Blass, Capital, May 31, 201X		$14 2 7 5 00

→ Balance Sheet Cr. column on worksheet

→ From income statement, Net Income on worksheet (or from formal report just prepared)

→ Balance Sheet Dr. column on worksheet

→ This figure is not on the worksheet. It is calculated here and used to prepare the balance sheet. Note that no additional investments were made during May.

3. The inside column on financial statements is used for subtotaling.
4. Withdrawals do not go on the income statement; they go on the statement of owner's equity.

Take a moment to look at the income statement in Figure 4.13. Note where items go from the income statement section of the worksheet onto the formal statement.

Preparing the Statement of Owner's Equity

Figure 4.14 is the statement of owner's equity for Blass. The figure shows where the information comes from on the worksheet. It is important to remember that if additional investments were made, the figure on the worksheet for Capital would not be the beginning figure for Capital in the Statement of Owner's Equity. Checking the ledger account for Capital will tell you whether the amount is correct. Note how Net Income and Withdrawals aid in calculating the new figure for Capital.

Preparing the Balance Sheet

In preparing the balance sheet (Figure 4.15, page 124), remember that the balance sheet section totals on the worksheet ($18,680) do *not* match the totals on the formal balance sheet ($17,975). This information is grouped differently on the formal statement. First, in the formal report Accumulated Depreciation, Computer Equipment ($80) is subtracted from Computer Equipment, reducing the balance. Second, Withdrawals ($625) are subtracted from Owner's Equity, reducing the balance further. These two reductions (−$80 − $625 = −$705) represent the difference between the worksheet total and the total on the formal report of the balance sheet ($17,975 − $18,680 = −$705). Figure 4.15 shows how to prepare the balance sheet from the worksheet.

 **TRY IT!** Learning Unit 4-3

From the last four columns of this partial worksheet for Lee's Nails, complete the three financial statements:

Lee's Nails
Partial Worksheet
For Month Ended September 30, 201X

	Income Statement		Balance Sheet	
	Dr.	Cr.	Dr.	Cr.
Cash			5,000	
Accounts Receivable			2,000	
Nail Supplies			400	
Salon Equipment			1,000	
Accounts Payable				1,500
P. Lee, Capital				6,100
P. Lee, Withdrawals			200	
Nail Fees		2,500		
Advertising Expense	200			
Rent Expense	600			
Salaries Expense	700			
Nail Supplies Expense	100			
Depreciation Expense, Salon Equip.	200			
Accumulated Depreciation, Salon Equip.				200
Salaries Payable				100
Totals	1,800	2,500	8,600	7,900
Net Income	700			700
Totals	2,500	2,500	8,600	8,600

FIGURE 4.15 From Worksheet to Balance Sheet

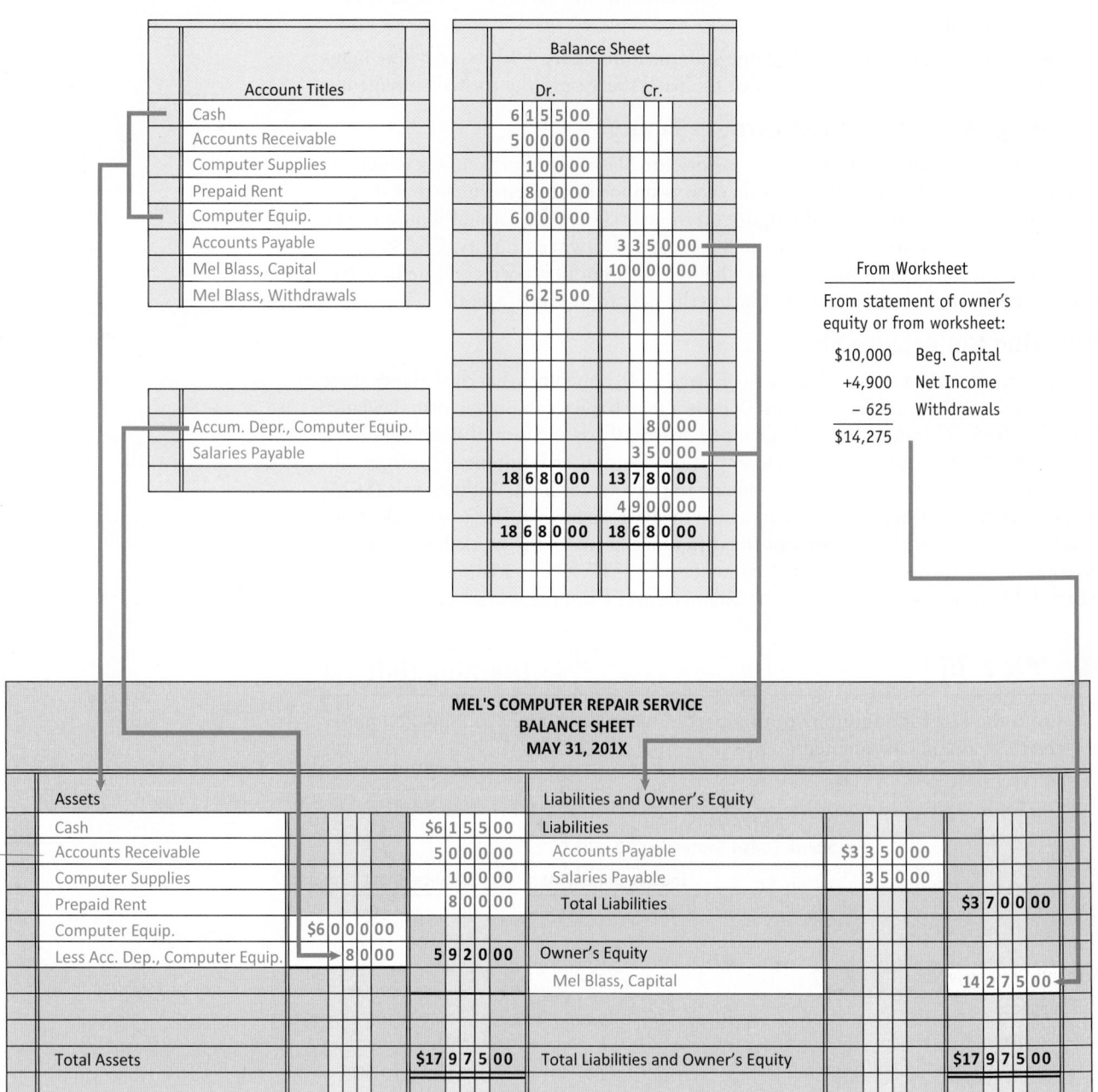

DEMONSTRATION SUMMARY PROBLEM

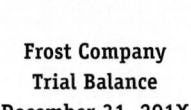 **L01,2,3**

From the following trial balance and adjustment data, complete (1) a worksheet and (2) the three financial statements (numbers are intentionally small so you may concentrate on the theory).

Frost Company
Trial Balance
December 31, 201X

	Dr.	Cr.
Cash	14	
Accounts Receivable	4	
Prepaid Insurance	5	
Plumbing Supplies	3	
Plumbing Equipment	7	
Accumulated Depreciation, Plumbing Equipment		5
Accounts Payable		1
J. Frost, Capital		12
J. Frost, Withdrawals	3	
Plumbing Fees		27
Rent Expense	4	
Salaries Expense	5	
Totals	45	45

Adjustment Data

a. Insurance Expired, $3.

b. Plumbing Supplies on hand, $1.

c. Depreciation Expense, Plumbing Equipment, $1.

d. Salaries owed but not paid to employees, $2.

Requirements

1. Prepare a worksheet
2. Prepare financial statements for month of December

Solutions

Requirement 1

Preparing a worksheet

Tips for Adjustments

a.

Insurance Expense	Expense	↑	Dr.	$3
Prepaid Insurance	Asset	↓	Cr.	$3
			Expired means used up.	

b.

Plumbing Supplies Expense	Expense	↑	Dr.	$2
Plumbing Supplies	Asset	↓	Cr.	$2
			$3 − 1 = $2 *used up*	

(continued on page 127)

FIGURE 4.16 Solution to Worksheet

Original cost not adjusted   "Used up"   "On hand"

FROST COMPANY
WORKSHEET
FOR MONTH ENDED DECEMBER 31, 201X

Account Titles	Trial Balance Dr.	Trial Balance Cr.	Adjustments Dr.	Adjustments Cr.	Adjusted Trial Balance Dr.	Adjusted Trial Balance Cr.	Income Statement Dr.	Income Statement Cr.	Balance Sheet Dr.	Balance Sheet Cr.
Cash	1400				1400				1400	
Accounts Receivable	400				400				400	
Prepaid Insurance	500			(A) 300	200				200	
Plumbing Supplies	300			(B) 200	100				100	
Plumbing Equipment	700				700				700	
Accum. Depr., Plumb. Equip.		500		(C) 100		600				600
Accounts Payable		100				100				100
J. Frost, Capital		1200				1200				1200
J. Frost, Withdrawals	300				300				300	
Plumbing Fees		2700				2700		2700		
Rent Expense	400				400		400			
Salaries Expense	500		(D) 200		700		700			
Totals	4500	4500								
Insurance Expense			(A) 300		300		300			
Plumbing Supplies Expense			(B) 200		200		200			
Depr. Exp. Plumb. Equip.			(C) 100		100		100			
Salaries Payable				(D) 200		200				200
Totals			800	800	4800	4800	1700	2700	3100	2100
Net Income							1000			1000
Totals							2700	2700	3100	3100

c.

Depreciation Expense, Plumbing Equipment	Expense	↑	Dr.	$1
Accumulated Depreciation, Plumbing Equipment	Contra-Asset	↑	Cr.	$1

The original cost of equipment of $7 is not "touched."

d.

Salaries Expense	Expense	↑	Dr.	$2
Salaries Payable	Liability	↑	Cr.	$2

The last four columns of the worksheet (Figure 4.16) are prepared from the Adjusted Trial Balance.

Capital of $12 is the old figure. Net income of $10 (revenue – expenses) is brought over to the same side as Capital on the balance sheet Cr. column to balance columns. This is done because the worksheet contains the old figure for Capital.

Requirement 2

Preparing financial statements

Tips for Preparing Financial Statements from a Worksheet

The inside columns of the three financial statements are used for subtotaling. No debits or credits appear on the formal statements.

	Statements
Income Statement	From Income Statement columns of worksheet for revenue and expenses.
Statement of Owner's Equity	Beginning figure for Capital from Balance Sheet worksheet Cr. column. Net Income from income statement. Withdrawals figure from Balance Sheet worksheet Dr. column.
Balance Sheet	Assets from Balance Sheet worksheet Dr. column. Liabilities and Accumulated Depreciation from Balance Sheet worksheet Cr. Column. New figure for Capital from statement of owner's equity.

Note how Plumbing Equipment $7 and Accumulated Depreciation $6 are rearranged on the formal balance sheet. The Total Assets of $22 is not on the worksheet. Remember, no debits or credits appear on formal statements (see Figure 4.17, page 128).

FIGURE 4.17

FROST COMPANY
INCOME STATEMENT
FOR MONTH ENDED DECEMBER 31, 201X

Revenue:		
Plumbing Fees		$27
Operating Expenses:		
Rent Expense	$4	
Salaries Expense	7	
Insurance Expense	3	
Plumbing Supplies Expense	2	
Depreciation Expense, Plumbing Equipment	1	
Total Operating Expenses		17
Net Income		$10

FROST COMPANY
STATEMENT OF OWNER'S EQUITY
FOR MONTH ENDED DECEMBER 31, 201X

J. Frost, Capital, Dec. 1, 201X		$12
Net Income for December	$10	
Less: Withdrawals for December	−3	
Increase in Capital		7
J. Frost, Capital, Dec. 31, 201X		$19

FROST COMPANY
BALANCE SHEET
DECEMBER 31, 201X

Assets			Liabilities and Owner's Equity		
Cash		$14	Liabilities		
Accounts Receivable		4	Accounts Payable	$1	
Prepaid Insurance		2	Salaries Payable	2	
Plumbing Supplies		1	Total Liabilities		$3
Plumbing Equipment	$7				
Less: Accumulated Dep.	6	1	Owner's Equity		
			J. Frost, Capital		19
			Total Liabilities and		
Total Assets		$22	Owner's Equity		$22

BLUEPRINT OF STEPS 5 AND 6 OF THE ACCOUNTING CYCLE

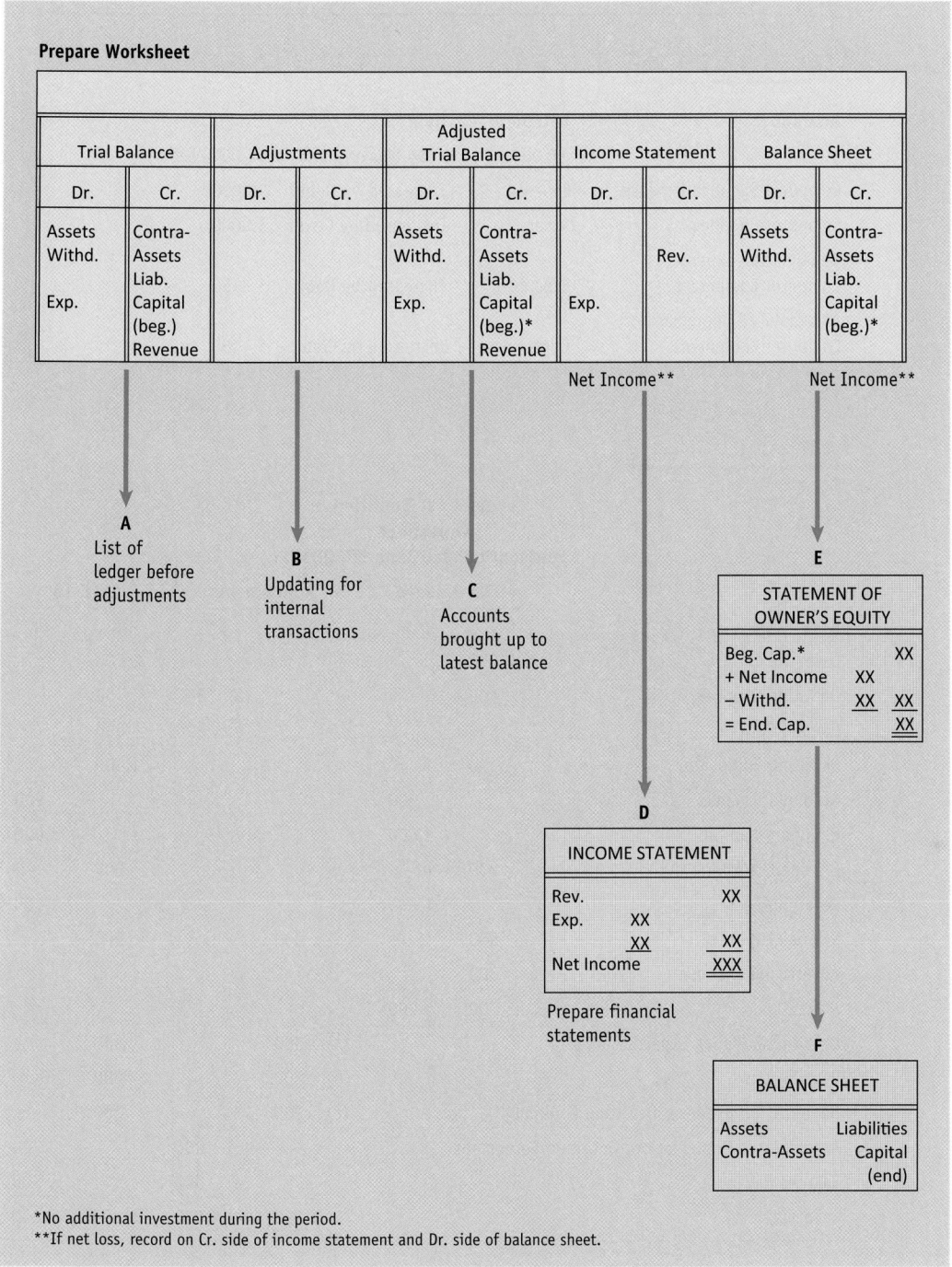

Prepare Worksheet

	Trial Balance		Adjustments		Adjusted Trial Balance		Income Statement		Balance Sheet	
	Dr.	Cr.	Dr.	Cr.	Dr.	Cr.	Dr.	Cr.	Dr.	Cr.
	Assets Withd. Exp.	Contra-Assets Liab. Capital (beg.) Revenue			Assets Withd. Exp.	Contra-Assets Liab. Capital (beg.)* Revenue	Exp.	Rev.	Assets Withd.	Contra-Assets Liab. Capital (beg.)*

Net Income**   Net Income**

A
List of ledger before adjustments

B
Updating for internal transactions

C
Accounts brought up to latest balance

E

STATEMENT OF OWNER'S EQUITY

Beg. Cap.*		XX
+ Net Income	XX	
− Withd.	XX	XX
= End. Cap.		XX

D

INCOME STATEMENT

Rev.		XX
Exp.	XX	
	XX	XX
Net Income		XXX

Prepare financial statements

F

BALANCE SHEET

Assets	Liabilities
Contra-Assets	Capital (end)

*No additional investment during the period.
**If net loss, record on Cr. side of income statement and Dr. side of balance sheet.

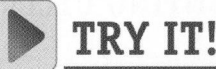

Learning Unit 4-1

Account	Category	Rule	
	$6,000	— $4,000 on hand = $2,000 used up	
Computer Supplies Expense	Expense	Increased by Debit	$2,000
Computer Supplies	Asset	Decreased by Credit	$2,000
Depreciation Expense, Computer Equipment	Expense	Increased by Debit	$ 150
Accumulated Depreciation, Computer Equipment	Contra-asset	Increased by Credit	$ 150

Learning Unit 4-2

Logan's Car Detailing
Worksheet
For Month Ended June 30, 201X.

Acct Titles	Trial Balance Dr.	Trial Balance Cr.	Adjustments Dr.		Adjustments Cr.		Adj. TB Dr.	Adj. TB Cr.
Cash	2,000						2,000	
Detailing Supplies	400				(a)	350	50	
Prepaid Rent	800				(b)	200	600	
Detailing Equipment	1,400						1,400	
Accounts Payable		900						900
B. Logan, Capital		3,600						3,600
B. Logan, Withdrawals	200						200	
Detailing Fees		1,200						1,200
Salaries Expense	600		(d)	300			900	
Advertising Expense	300						300	
Totals	5,700	5,700						
Detailing Supplies Expense			(a)	350			350	
Rent Expense			(b)	200			200	
Depreciation Expense, Detailing Equipment			(c)	200			200	
Accumulated Depreciation, Detailing Equipment					(c)	200		200
Salaries Payable					(d)	300		300
Totals				1,050		1,050	6,200	6,200

Learning Unit 4-3

Lee's Nails
Income Statement
For Month Ended September 30, 201X

Revenue:		
Nail Fees		$2,500
Operating Expenses:		
Advertising Expense	$ 200	
Rent Expense	600	
Salaries Expense	700	
Nail Supplies Expense	100	
Depreciation Expense, Salon Equip.	200	
Total Operating Expenses		1,800
Net Income		$ 700

Lee's Nails
Statement of Owner's Equity
For Month Ended September 30, 201X

P. Lee, Capital, September 1, 201X		$6,100
Net Income for September	$700	
Less: Withdrawals for September	−200	
Increase in Capital		500
P. Lee, Capital, September 30, 201X		$6,600

Lee's Nails
Balance Sheet
September 30, 201X

Assets			Liabilities and Owner's Equity		
Cash		$5,000	Liabilities		
Acc. Rec.		2,000	Accounts Payable	$1,500	
Nail Supplies		400	Salaries Payable	100	
Salon Equip.	$1,000		Total Liabilities		$1,600
Less: Acc. Dep.	200	800	Owner's Equity		
			P. Lee, Capital		6,600
Total Assets		$8,200	Total Liabilities and Owner's Equity		$8,200

ACCOUNTING COACH

The following Coaching Tips are from Learning Units 4-1, 4-2, and 4-3. Take the Pre-Game Checkup and use the Check Your Score at the bottom of the page to see how you are doing. The Accounting Coach provides tips before each Checkup to help you avoid common accounting errors.

LU 4-1 Explaining Adjustments and How to Record Them on a Worksheet

Pre-Game Tips: When preparing adjustments on a worksheet, the accounts listed below the trial balance will always be increasing. In the adjustment for supplies, the adjustment is the amount of supplies used—not what is on hand. Keep in mind that for the adjustment for depreciation the original cost of the asset is not touched. The adjustment is an increase in Depreciation Expense and an increase in Accumulated Depreciation. Depreciation Expense goes on the income statement as an expense, and accumulated depreciation goes on the balance sheet as a contra-asset account. Keep in mind that the original cost of the asset and accumulated depreciation are both listed on the balance sheet.

Pre-Game Checkup: Answer true or false to the following statements.

1. Prepaid Rent is a liability.
2. Accumulated Depreciation is a contra-liability.
3. The adjustment for supplies is the amount of supplies on hand.
4. The normal balance of Accumulated Depreciation is a debit.
5. The historical cost of equipment is not adjusted.

LU 4-2 The Worksheet (Step 5 of the Accounting Cycle)

Pre-Game Tips: The income statement columns record revenues and expenses. Net income will be recorded at the bottom of the balance sheet section on the same side as capital since old capital is on the worksheet. Withdrawals go in the debit column of the balance sheet section of the worksheet. Accumulated depreciation is a contra-asset in the credit column of the balance sheet. Depreciation Expense goes in the debit column of the income statement.

Pre-Game Checkup: Answer true or false to the following statements.

1. Net loss is the result of revenues greater than expenses.
2. Accumulated Depreciation is never adjusted.
3. Assets do not go in the income statement column on a worksheet.
4. A net loss would go in the debit column of the balance sheet on a worksheet.
5. Withdrawals go in the credit column of the balance sheet on a worksheet.

LU 4-3 The Financial Statements from the Worksheet (Step 6 of the Accounting Cycle)

Pre-Game Tips: The worksheet uses debits and credits; however, when the three formal financial statements are prepared they do not use debits and credits. The worksheet uses the beginning figure for Capital (no additional investment during the month), but when the financial statements are complete the formal balance sheet will list the figure for ending Capital from the statement of owner's equity.

Pre-Game Checkup: Answer true or false to the following statements.

1. Subtotaling is not used in preparing the formal financial statements from a worksheet.
2. Withdrawals are listed on the income statement.
3. Accumulated Depreciation is added to the cost of the asset on the balance sheet.
4. Debits are the inside column on the formal reports.
5. Totals on the formal balance sheet will match totals on the worksheet.

CHECK YOUR SCORE: Answers to the Pre-Game Checkup

LU 4-1
1. False—Prepaid Rent is an asset.
2. False—Accumulated Depreciation is a contra-asset.
3. False—The adjustment for Supplies is the amount of supplies used up.
4. False—The normal balance of Accumulated Depreciation is a credit.
5. True.

LU 4-2
1. False—Revenues are less than expenses.
2. False—Accumulated Depreciation is usually adjusted by an increase to the Accumulated Account.
3. True

4. True
5. False—Withdrawals go in the debit column.

LU 4-3
1. False—Subtotaling *is* used in preparing the formal financial statements from a worksheet.
2. False—Withdrawals are listed on the statement of owner's equity.
3. False—Accumulated depreciation is subtracted from the cost of the asset on the balance sheet.
4. False—There are no debits or credits on financial statements.
5. False—Totals on formal reports do not match totals on the worksheet since there are no debits and credits on financial reports and subtotaling is used.

Chapter Summary

Here are all the key terms and equations to help you understand the concepts of this chapter and prepare you for your exam. After completing this review, go to MyAccountingLab for more practice opportunities.

MyAccountingLab

Concepts You Should Know	Key Terms
L01 ► **Explain Adjustments and How to Record Them on a Worksheet** 1. The worksheet is not a formal statement. 2. Adjustments update certain accounts so that they will reflect their latest balance before financial statements are prepared. 3. Adjustments will affect both the income statement and the balance sheet. 4. The original cost of a piece of equipment is not adjusted; historical cost is not lost. 5. Depreciation is the process of spreading the original cost of the asset over its expected useful life. 6. Accumulated depreciation is a contra-asset on the balance sheet.	Accrued salaries payable (p. 115) Accumulated Depreciation (p. 112) Adjusting (p. 109) Book value (p. 113) Depreciation (p. 112) Historical cost (p. 112) Residual value (p. 112) Worksheet (p. 108)
L02 ► **Complete the Worksheet** 1. Accounts listed below the account titles on the trial balance of the worksheet are increasing. Supplies adjustment is amount used up. Rent adjustment is amount expired. Original cost of equipment is not adjusted. 2. Revenue and expenses go on income statement sections of the worksheet. 3. Assets, contra-assets, liabilities, capital, and withdrawals go on balance sheet sections of the worksheet.	
L03 ► **Prepare Financial Statements from the Worksheet** 1. The formal statements prepared from a worksheet do not have debit or credit columns. 2. Revenue and expenses go on the income statement. 3. Beginning capital plus net income less withdrawals (or, beginning capital minus net loss less withdrawals) go on the statement of owner's equity. 4. Assets, contra-assets, liabilities, and the new figure for capital go on the balance sheet.	

Discussion Questions and Critical Thinking/Ethical Case

1. With computer software, the need for worksheets has been completely eliminated. Agree or disagree and explain your answer.

2. What is the purpose of adjusting accounts?

3. What is the relationship of internal transactions to the adjusting process?

4. Explain how an adjustment can affect both the income statement and balance sheet. Please give an example.

5. Why do we need the Accumulated Depreciation account?

6. Depreciation expense goes on the balance sheet. True or false. Why?

7. Each month Accumulated Depreciation grows while Equipment goes up. Agree or disagree? Defend your position.

8. Define the term *accrued salaries*.

9. Why don't the formal financial statements contain debit or credit columns?

10. Explain how the financial statements are prepared from the worksheet.

11. Alice Hawkins, president of Realon Co., went to a conference on tax planning. One of the speakers at the seminar advised the audience to put off showing expenses until next year because doing so would allow them to take advantage of a new tax law. When Alice returned to the office, she called in her accountant, Lynn O'Riley. She told Lynn to forget about making any adjustments for salaries in the old year so more expenses could be shown in the new year. Lynn told her that putting off these expenses would not follow generally accepted accounting procedures. Alice said she should do it anyway. You make the call. Write your specific recommendations to Lynn.

MyAccountingLab

Concept Check

(5 min) **LO1** ▶ **Adjustment for Supplies**

1. *Before Adjustment*

Office Supplies	Office Supplies Expense
1,100	

Given: At year end, an inventory of Office Supplies showed $400.

a. How much is the adjustment for Office Supplies?
b. Complete a transaction analysis box for this adjustment.
c. What will the balance of Office Supplies be on the adjusted trial balance?

(10 min) **LO1** ▶ **Adjustment for Prepaid Rent**

2. *Before Adjustment*

Prepaid Rent	Rent Expense
900	

Given: At year end, rent expired is $300.

a. How much is the adjustment for Prepaid Rent?
b. Complete a transaction analysis box for this adjustment.
c. What will be the balance of Prepaid Rent on the adjusted trial balance?

Adjustment for Depreciation

L01 *(10 min)*

3. *Before Adjustment*

Equip.	Acc. Dep., Equip.	Dep. Exp., Equip.
9,800	1,500	

Given: At year end, depreciation on Equipment is $1,700.

a. Which of these three T accounts is not affected?
b. Which account is a contra-asset?
c. Complete a transaction analysis box for this adjustment.
d. What will be the balance of these three accounts on the adjusted trial balance?

Adjustment for Accrued Salaries

L01 *(10 min)*

4. *Before Adjustment*

Salaries Expense	Salaries Payable
1,000	

Given: Accrued Salaries, $125.

a. Complete a transaction analysis box for this adjustment.
b. What will be the balance of these two accounts on the adjusted trial balance?

Worksheet

L02 *(15 min)*

5. From the following adjusted trial balance titles of a worksheet, identify in which column each account will be listed on the last four columns of the worksheet:

(ID) Income Statement Dr. Column

(IC) Income Statement Cr. Column

(BD) Balance Sheet Dr. Column

(BC) Balance Sheet Cr. Column

	Adjusted Trial Balance		Income Statement	Balance Sheet
A. Ex: Legal Fees Earned	~~~~~	~~~~~	IC	_____
B. Accts. Payable	~~~~~	~~~~~	_____	_____
C. Cash	~~~~~	~~~~~	_____	_____
D. Prepaid Advertising	~~~~~	~~~~~	_____	_____
E. Salaries Payable	~~~~~	~~~~~	_____	_____
F. Dep. Expense	~~~~~	~~~~~	_____	_____
G. V., Capital	~~~~~	~~~~~	_____	_____
H. V., Withdrawals	~~~~~	~~~~~	_____	_____
I. Computer Supplies	~~~~~	~~~~~	_____	_____
J. Rent Expense	~~~~~	~~~~~	_____	_____
K. Supplies Payable	~~~~~	~~~~~	_____	_____
L. Advertising Expense	~~~~~	~~~~~	_____	_____
M. Accum. Depreciation	~~~~~	~~~~~	_____	_____
N. Wages Payable	~~~~~	~~~~~	_____	_____

(15 min) **L02,3**

6. From the following balance sheet (Figure 4.18, which was made from the worksheet and other financial statements), explain why the lettered numbers were not found on the worksheet. *Hint:* No debits or credits appear on the formal financial statements.

FIGURE 4.18

LAZE CO. BALANCE SHEET DECEMBER 31, 201X					
Assets			**Liabilities and Owner's Equity**		
Cash		$6	Liabilities		
Acc. Receivable		2	Accounts Payable	$2	
Supplies		2	Salaries Payable	1	
Equipment	$10		Total Liabilities		$3 (B)
Less: Acc. Dep.	4	6 (A)	Owner's Equity		
			J. Laze, Capital		13
			Total Liabilities and		
Total Assets		$16	**Owner's Equity**		$16

MyAccountingLab

Exercises

Set A

(5 min) **L03**

4A-1. Complete the following table.

Account	Category	Normal Balance	Which Financial Statement(s) Found
Accumulated Depreciation, Office Equipment			
Prepaid Rent			
Office Equipment			
Depreciation Expense, Office Equipment			
B. Reel, Capital			
B. Reel, Withdrawals			
Wages Payable			

(10 min) **L01**

4A-2. Use transaction analysis charts to analyze the following adjustments:

   a. Depreciation on equipment, $700.
   b. Rent expired, $400.

(10 min) **L01**

4A-3. From the following adjustment data, calculate the adjustment amount and record appropriate debits or credits:

   a. Supplies purchased, $800.
       Supplies on hand, $500.
   b. Store equipment, $14,000.
       Accumulated depreciation, store equipment, before adjustment, $1,000.
       Depreciation expense, store equipment, $400.

(20 min) **L01,2**

4A-4. From the following trial balance (Figure 4.19) and adjustment data, complete a worksheet for J. Revere as of January 31, 201X:

   a. Depreciation expense, store equipment, $6.
   b. Insurance expired, $3.
   c. Store supplies on hand, $5.
   d. Wages owed, but not paid for (they are an expense in the old year), $8.

FIGURE 4.19

Account Titles	Dr.	Cr.
J. REVERE		
TRIAL BALANCE		
JANUARY 31, 201X		
Cash	4 00	
Accounts Receivable	10 00	
Prepaid Insurance	7 00	
Store Supplies	10 00	
Store Equipment	20 00	
Accumulated Depreciation, Store Equipment		6 00
Accounts Payable		12 00
J. Revere, Capital		6 00
J. Revere, Withdrawals	3 00	
Revenue from Clients		46 00
Rent Expense	9 00	
Wage Expense	7 00	
Totals	70 00	70 00

4A-5. From the completed worksheet in Exercise 4A-4, prepare **LO3** *(20 min)*

  a. an income statement for January.
  b. a statement of owner's equity for January.
  c. a balance sheet as of January 31, 201X.

Set B

4B-1. Complete the following table. **LO3** *(5 min)*

Account	Category	Normal Balance	Which Financial Statement(s) Found
Accounts Payable			
Prepaid Insurance			
Computer Equipment			
Depreciation Expense, Computer Equipment			
B. Free, Capital			
B. Free, Withdrawals			
Salaries Payable			
Accumulated Depreciation, Computer Equipment			

4B-2. Use transaction analysis charts to analyze the following adjustments: **LO1** *(5 min)*
  a. Depreciation on equipment, $700.
  b. Rent expired, $300.

4B-3. From the following adjustment data, calculate the adjustment amount and record appropriate debits or credits: **LO1** *(10 min)*

  a. Supplies purchased, $1,000.
    Supplies on hand, $50.
  b. Store equipment, $10,000.
    Accumulated depreciation, store equipment, before adjustment, $1,100.
    Depreciation expense, store equipment, $300.

(20 min)   **LO1,2**   **4B-4.** From the following trial balance (Figure 4.20) and adjustment data, complete a worksheet for J. Tutle as of March 31, 201X:

  a. Depreciation expense, store equipment, $1.
  b. Insurance expired, $1.
  c. Store supplies on hand, $7.
  d. Wages owed but not paid for (they are an expense in the old year), $2.

FIGURE 4.20

J. TUTLE TRIAL BALANCE MARCH 31, 201X		
Account Titles	Dr.	Cr.
Cash	2 2 00	
Accounts Receivable	8 00	
Prepaid Insurance	8 00	
Store Supplies	1 0 00	
Store Equipment	1 1 00	
Accumulated Depreciation, Store Equipment		9 00
Accounts Payable		1 1 00
J. Tutle, Capital		2 6 00
J. Tutle, Withdrawals	1 0 00	
Revenue from Clients		2 9 00
Rent Expense	3 00	
Wage Expense	3 00	
Totals	7 5 00	7 5 00

(20 min)   **LO3** ▶   **4B-5.** From the completed worksheet in Exercise 4B-4, prepare

  a. an income statement for March
  b. a statement of owner's equity for March.
  c. a balance sheet as of March 31, 201X.

MyAccountingLab   **Problems**

(15 min)   **LO1** ▶   **Set A**

4A-1. Use the following adjustment data on August 31 to complete a partial worksheet up to the adjusted trial balance (see Figure 4.21).

  a. Fitness supplies on hand, $3,900.
  b. Depreciation taken on fitness equipment, $800.

FIGURE 4.21

Check Figure:
Total of Adjusted Trial Balance
$37,750

JACK'S FITNESS CENTER TRIAL BALANCE AUGUST 31, 201X		
Account Titles	Dr.	Cr.
Cash in Bank	9 0 0 0 00	
Accounts Receivable	5 5 0 0 00	
Fitness Supplies	5 9 0 0 00	
Fitness Equipment	13 2 0 0 00	
Accumulated Depreciation, Fitness Equipment		4 3 0 0 00
J. Wrights, Capital		23 7 5 0 00
J. Wrights, Withdrawals	3 0 0 0 00	
Fitness Fees		8 9 0 0 00
Rent Expense	3 0 0 00	
Advertising Expense	5 0 00	
Totals	36 9 5 0 00	36 9 5 0 00

4A-2. Update the trial balance for Lemmings's Landscaping Service (Figure 4.22) for August 31, 201X.

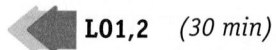 **LO1,2** *(30 min)*

Adjustment Data to Update the Trial Balance

a. Rent expired, $700.
b. Landscaping supplies on hand (remaining), $325.
c. Depreciation expense, landscaping equipment, $300.
d. Wages earned by workers but not paid or due until September, $250.

FIGURE 4.22

LEMMINGS'S LANDSCAPING SERVICE TRIAL BALANCE AUGUST 31, 201X		
Account Titles	Dr.	Cr.
Cash in Bank	5 5 0 0 00	
Accounts Receivable	9 0 0 00	
Prepaid Rent	8 0 0 00	
Landscaping Supplies	1 1 9 5 00	
Landscaping Equipment	1 4 0 0 00	
Accumulated Depreciation, Landscaping Equipment		8 6 0 00
Accounts Payable		8 3 6 00
A. Lemmings, Capital		5 6 1 4 00
Landscaping Revenue		4 7 0 0 00
Heat Expense	4 7 5 00	
Advertising Expense	3 0 0 00	
Wage Expense	1 4 4 0 00	
Totals	12 0 1 0 00	12 0 1 0 00

Check Figure:
Total of Adjusted Trial Balance
$12,560

Your task is to prepare a worksheet for Lemmings's Landscaping Service for the month of August.

4A-3. Update the trial balance for Kent's Moving Co. (Figure 4.23 on page 140) for December 31, 201X.

 **LO1,2,3** *(60 min)*

Adjustment Data to Update Trial Balance

a. Insurance expired, $200.
b. Moving supplies on hand, $1,100.
c. Depreciation on moving truck, $450.
d. Wages earned but unpaid, $275.

Your task is to:

1. Complete a worksheet for Kent's Moving Co. for the month of December.
2. Prepare an income statement for December, a statement of owner's equity for December, and a balance sheet as of December 31, 201X.

FIGURE 4.23

Check Figure:
Net Income $2,734

KENT'S MOVING CO. TRIAL BALANCE DECEMBER 31, 201X		
Account Titles	Dr.	Cr.
Cash	5 0 0 0 00	
Prepaid Insurance	2 2 0 0 00	
Moving Supplies	1 6 0 0 00	
Moving Truck	14 0 0 0 00	
Accumulated Depreciation, Moving Truck		7 0 0 0 00
Accounts Payable		2 5 0 0 00
K. Hull, Capital		10 1 4 1 00
K. Hull, Withdrawals	1 0 0 0 00	
Revenue from Moving		9 0 0 0 00
Wage Expense	3 8 4 1 00	
Rent Expense	6 0 0 00	
Advertising Expense	4 0 0 00	
Totals	28 6 4 1 00	28 6 4 1 00

(60 min)   **L01,2,3**

S50 / QB

4A-4. The trial balance for Damon's Repair Service appears in Figure 4.24.

Adjustment Data to Update Trial Balance

a. Insurance expired, $600.
b. Repair supplies on hand, $2,400.
c. Depreciation on repair equipment, $600.
d. Wages earned but unpaid, $200.

Your task is to:

1. Complete a worksheet for Damon's Repair Service for the month of April.
2. Prepare an income statement for April, a statement of owner's equity for April, and a balance sheet as of April 30, 201X.

FIGURE 4.24

Check Figure:
Net Income $3,180

DAMON'S REPAIR SERVICE TRIAL BALANCE APRIL 30, 201X		
Account Titles	Dr.	Cr.
Cash	3 0 0 0 00	
Prepaid Insurance	5 1 0 0 00	
Repair Supplies	4 5 0 0 00	
Repair Equipment	4 5 0 0 00	
Accumulated Depreciation, Repair Equipment		1 4 0 0 00
Accounts Payable		4 8 5 0 00
D. Heines, Capital		4 1 7 0 00
Revenue from Repairs		9 5 0 0 00
Wages Expense	1 8 0 0 00	
Rent Expense	7 0 0 00	
Advertising Expense	3 2 0 00	
Totals	19 9 2 0 00	19 9 2 0 00

Set B

(15 min)   **L01**

4B-1. Use the following adjustment data on December 31 to complete a partial worksheet up to the adjusted trial balance (see Figure 4.25).

a. Fitness supplies on hand, $600.
b. Depreciation taken on fitness equipment, $900.

FIGURE 4.25

JANA'S FITNESS CENTER TRIAL BALANCE DECEMBER 31, 201X		
Account Titles	Dr.	Cr.
Cash in Bank	7 0 0 0 00	
Accounts Receivable	5 8 0 0 00	
Fitness Supplies	5 6 0 0 00	
Fitness Equipment	7 7 0 0 00	
Accumulated Depreciation, Fitness Equipment		6 3 0 0 00
J. Wacker, Capital		11 3 5 0 00
J. Wacker, Withdrawals	1 7 5 0 00	
Fitness Fees		10 9 0 0 00
Rent Expense	5 0 0 00	
Advertising Expense	2 0 0 00	
Totals	28 5 5 0 00	28 5 5 0 00

Check Figure:
Total of Adjusted Trial Balance
$29,450

4B-2. Update the trial balance for Lajoie's Landscaping Service (Figure 4.26) for January 31, 201X.

L01,2   *(30 min)*

Adjustment Data to Update the Trial Balance

   a. Rent expired, $300.
   b. Landscaping supplies on hand (remaining), $350.
   c. Depreciation expense, landscaping equipment, $400.
   d. Wages earned by workers but not paid or due until February, $700.

FIGURE 4.26

LAJOIE'S LANDSCAPING SERVICE TRIAL BALANCE JANUARY 31, 201X		
Account Titles	Dr.	Cr.
Cash in Bank	3 1 0 0 00	
Accounts Receivable	3 0 0 00	
Prepaid Rent	1 4 0 0 00	
Landscaping Supplies	7 4 2 00	
Landscaping Equipment	2 4 0 0 00	
Accumulated Depreciation, Landscaping Equipment		8 6 0 00
Accounts Payable		9 3 8 00
A. Lajoie, Capital		1 8 4 4 00
Landscaping Revenue		6 2 0 0 00
Heat Expense	5 0 0 00	
Advertising Expense	8 0 00	
Wage Expense	1 3 2 0 00	
Totals	9 8 4 2 00	9 8 4 2 00

Check Figure:
Total of Adjusted Trial Balance
$10,942

Your task is to prepare a worksheet for Lajoie's Landscaping Service for the month of January.

4B-3. Update the trial balance for Kyle's Moving Co. (Figure 4.27 on page 142) for October 31, 201X.

L01,2,3   *(60 min)*

S50 / QB

Adjustment Data to Update Trial Balance

   a. Insurance expired, $600.
   b. Moving supplies on hand, $800.
   c. Depreciation on moving truck, $500.
   d. Wages earned but unpaid, $350.

Your task is to:

1. Complete a worksheet for Kyle's Moving Co. for the month of October.
2. Prepare an income statement for October, a statement of owner's equity for October, and a balance sheet as of October 31, 201X.

FIGURE 4.27

	KYLE'S MOVING CO.			
	TRIAL BALANCE			
	OCTOBER 31, 201X			
Account Titles	Dr.		Cr.	
Cash	8 0 0 0 00			
Prepaid Insurance	2 1 0 0 00			
Moving Supplies	1 5 0 0 00			
Moving Truck	15 0 0 0 00			
Accumulated Depreciation, Moving Truck			4 0 0 0 00	
Accounts Payable			2 6 7 0 00	
K. Hull, Capital			16 5 7 1 00	
K. Hull, Withdrawals	1 0 0 0 00			
Revenue from Moving			8 8 0 0 00	
Wages Expense	3 3 8 0 00			
Rent Expense	5 5 0 00			
Advertising Expense	5 1 1 00			
Totals	32 0 4 1 00		32 0 4 1 00	

Check Figure:
Net Income $2,209

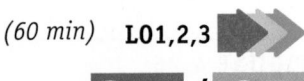

(60 min)   **LO1,2,3**

4B-4. The trial balance for Don's Repair Service appears in Figure 4.28.

Adjustment Data to Update Trial Balance

a. Insurance expired, $400.
b. Repair supplies on hand, $2,900.
c. Depreciation on repair equipment, $350.
d. Wages earned but unpaid, $300.

Your task is to:

1. Complete a worksheet for Don's Repair Service for the month of September.
2. Prepare an income statement for September, a statement of owner's equity for September, and a balance sheet as of September 30, 201X.

FIGURE 4.28

	DON'S REPAIR SERVICE			
	TRIAL BALANCE			
	SEPTEMBER 30, 201X			
Account Titles	Dr.		Cr.	
Cash	4 0 0 0 00			
Prepaid Insurance	3 7 0 0 00			
Repair Supplies	5 0 0 0 00			
Repair Equipment	5 0 0 0 00			
Accumulated Depreciation, Repair Equipment			1 5 0 0 00	
Accounts Payable			5 1 7 0 00	
D. Hilton, Capital			3 9 1 0 00	
Revenue from Repairs			9 5 0 0 00	
Wages Expense	1 7 0 0 00			
Rent Expense	3 6 0 00			
Advertising Expense	3 2 0 00			
Totals	20 0 8 0 00		20 0 8 0 00	

Check Figure:
Net Income $3,970

Financial Report Problem

LO1 *(20 min)*

Reading the Kellogg's Annual Report

Go to http://investor.kelloggs.com/investor-relations/annual-reports/ to access the Kellogg's 2013 Annual Report, and look at how Kellogg's depreciates its equipment. How is the equipment recorded?

ON THE JOB SMITH COMPUTER CENTER

MyAccountingLab

LO1,2,3 *(45 min)*

At the end of September, Thad took a complete inventory of his supplies and found the following:

3 dozen $\frac{1}{4}$" screws at a cost of $5.00 a dozen

6 dozen $\frac{1}{2}$" screws at a cost of $10.00 a dozen

5 cartons of computer inventory paper at a cost of $8 a carton

7 feet of coaxial cable at a cost of $11.00 per foot

After speaking to his accountant, he found that a reasonable depreciation amount for each of his long-term assets is as follows:

Computer purchased July 5, 201X	Depreciation $50 a month
Office equipment purchased July 17, 201X	Depreciation $55 a month
Computer workstations purchased Sept. 17, 201X	Depreciation $35 a month

Thad uses the straight-line method of depreciation and declares no salvage value for any of the assets. If any long-term asset is purchased in the first 15 days of the month, he will charge depreciation for the full month. If an asset is purchased on the 16th of the month, or later, he will not charge depreciation in the month it was purchased.

August and September's rent has now expired.

Assignment

Use your trial balance from the completed problem in Chapter 3 and the adjusting information given here to complete the worksheet for the three months ended September 30, 201X. From the worksheets, prepare the financial statements.

SAGE 50 COMPUTER WORKSHOP

S50

Computerized Accounting Application for Chapter 4

Refresher on using Sage 50 Complete Accounting

Before starting this assignment, you may want to refresh your memory by reading the following PDF documents found in the multimedia library on the MyAccountingLab Web site. Remember to choose the PDF document for your version of Sage 50.

1. An Introduction to Sage 50
2. Correcting Sage 50 Transactions
3. How to Repeat or Restart a Sage 50 Assignment
4. Backing Up and Restoring Your Work in Sage 50

You also should have completed Workshop 1 for the Atlas Company in Chapter 3.

Workshop 2:

Compound Journal Entries, Adjusting Entries, and Financial Reports

In this workshop, you will post compound journal entries and adjusting journal entries for Zell Company using Sage 50. You will also print the general journal report, trial balance, income statement, and balance sheet.

Instructions and the data file for completing this assignment are in the multimedia library of the MyAccountingLab Web site. Open the *Workshop 2 Zell Company* PDF document for your version of Sage 50 and download the *Zell Company* data file for your version of Sage 50.

QUICKBOOKS COMPUTER WORKSHOP

QB

Computerized Accounting Application for Chapter 4

Refresher on using QuickBooks Accountant

Before starting this assignment, you may want to refresh your memory by reading the following PDF documents found in the multimedia library on the MyAccountingLab Web site. Remember to choose the PDF document for your version of QuickBooks.

1. An Introduction to Computerized Accounting
2. Installing QuickBooks Pro and Student Data Files
3. An Introduction to QuickBooks
4. Correcting QuickBooks Transactions
5. How to Repeat or Restart a QuickBooks Assignment
6. Backing Up and Restoring Your Work in QuickBooks. You also should have completed Workshop 1 for the Atlas Company in Chapter 3.

Workshop 2:

Compound Journal Entries, Adjusting Entries, and Financial Reports

In this workshop you will post compound journal entries and adjusting journal entries for Zell Company using Quickbooks. You will also print the general journal report, trial balance, income statement, and balance sheet.

Instructions and the data file for completing this assignment are in the multimedia library of the MyAccountingLab Web site. Open the *Workshop 2 Zell Company* PDF document for your version of Quickbooks and download the *Zell Company* data file for your version of Quickbooks.

CHAPTER 5

The Accounting Cycle Completed

CHAPTER PREVIEW: THE BIG PICTURE

On April 15, Matty Kaminsky sent in his Federal Income Tax forms; he was very happy that he met the deadline. The same concept holds true in accounting for companies as well. For example, Disney must report to investors and government regulators how operations performed during its accounting cycle. When one accounting cycle is closed, the next one begins. This period of time is called the fiscal year. Many companies end their fiscal years in March, July, or October. Other companies, like retailers, end on December 31 so holiday sales can be included in the final results. No matter when companies end their fiscal years, the accounting cycle must be completed and financial reports prepared so that companies can report to the appropriate governmental authorities, such as the Securities and Exchange Commission and the Internal Revenue Service, investors, and creditors.

Learning Objectives

LO1 Journalize and Post Adjusting Entries

LO2 Journalize and Post Closing Entries

LO3 Prepare a Post-Closing Trial Balance

Each accounting cycle completed by Disney will end with the preparation of a post-closing trial balance. In Chapters 3 and 4 we completed these steps of the manual accounting cycle for Mel's Computer Repair Service:

STEP 1: Business transactions occurred and generated source documents.

STEP 2: Business transactions were analyzed and recorded in a journal.

STEP 3: Information was posted or transferred from journal to ledger.

STEP 4: A trial balance was prepared.

STEP 5: A worksheet was completed.

STEP 6: Financial statements were prepared.

This chapter covers the following steps to complete Blass's accounting cycle for the month of May:

STEP 7: Journalizing and posting adjusting entries.

STEP 8: Journalizing and posting closing entries.

STEP 9: Preparing a post-closing trial balance.

Adjusting Entries (Step 7 of the Accounting Cycle)

Recording Journal Entries from the Worksheet

The information in the worksheet is up-to-date. The financial reports prepared from that information can give the business's management and other interested parties a good idea of where the business stands as of a particular date. However, the worksheet is only an informal report. The information concerning the adjustments has not been placed into the journal or posted to the ledger accounts yet, which means that the books are not up-to-date and ready for the next accounting cycle to begin. For example, the ledger shows $1,200 of Prepaid Rent, but the balance sheet we prepared in Chapter 4 shows an $800 balance. Essentially, the worksheet is a tool for preparing financial statements. Now we must use the adjustment columns of the worksheet as a basis for bringing the ledger up-to-date. To update the ledger, we use adjusting journal entries (see Figures 5.1 and 5.2). Again, the updating must be done before the next accounting period starts. For Mel's Computer Repair Service, the next period begins on June 1.

Figure 5.2 shows the adjusting journal entries for Mel's taken from the adjustments section of the worksheet. Once the adjusting journal entries are posted to the ledger, the accounts making up the financial statements that were prepared from the worksheet will equal the updated ledger. (Keep in mind that we are using the same journal and ledger as in the previous chapters.) Let's look at some simplified T accounts to show how Mel's ledger looked before and after the adjustments (A–D) were posted.

Adjusting journal entries Journal entries that are needed in order to update specific ledger accounts to reflect correct balances at the end of an accounting period.

Adjustment (A)

Before Posting:	Computer Supplies 114	Computer Supplies Expense 514
	600	
After Posting:	Computer Supplies 114	Computer Supplies Expense 514
	600 | 500	500 |

Adjustment (B)

Before Posting:	Prepaid Rent 115	Rent Expense 515
	1,200	
After Posting:	Prepaid Rent 115	Rent Expense 515
	1,200 | 400	400 |

Account Titles	Trial Balance		Adjustments	
	Dr.	Cr.	Dr.	Cr.
Cash	6 1 5 5 00			
Accounts Receivable	5 0 0 0 00			
Computer Supplies	6 0 0 00			(A) 5 0 0 00
Prepaid Rent	1 2 0 0 00			(B) 4 0 0 00
Computer Equipment	6 0 0 0 00			
Accounts Payable		3 3 5 0 00		
Mel Blass, Capital		10 0 0 0 00		
Mel Blass, Withdrawals	6 2 5 00			
Computer Repair Fees		8 0 0 0 00		
Office Salaries Expense	1 3 0 0 00		(D) 3 5 0 00	
Advertising Expense	2 5 0 00			
Telephone Expense	2 2 0 00			
Totals	21 3 5 0 00	21 3 5 0 00		
Computer Supplies Expense			(A) 5 0 0 00	
Rent Expense			(B) 4 0 0 00	
Depreciation Exp., Computer Equip.			(C) 8 0 00	
Accum. Deprec., Computer Equip.				(C) 8 0 00
Salaries Payable				(D) 3 5 0 00
Totals			1 3 3 0 00	1 3 3 0 00

FIGURE 5.1
Adjustments A–D in the Adjustments Section of the Worksheet Must Be Recorded in the Journal and Posted to the Ledger

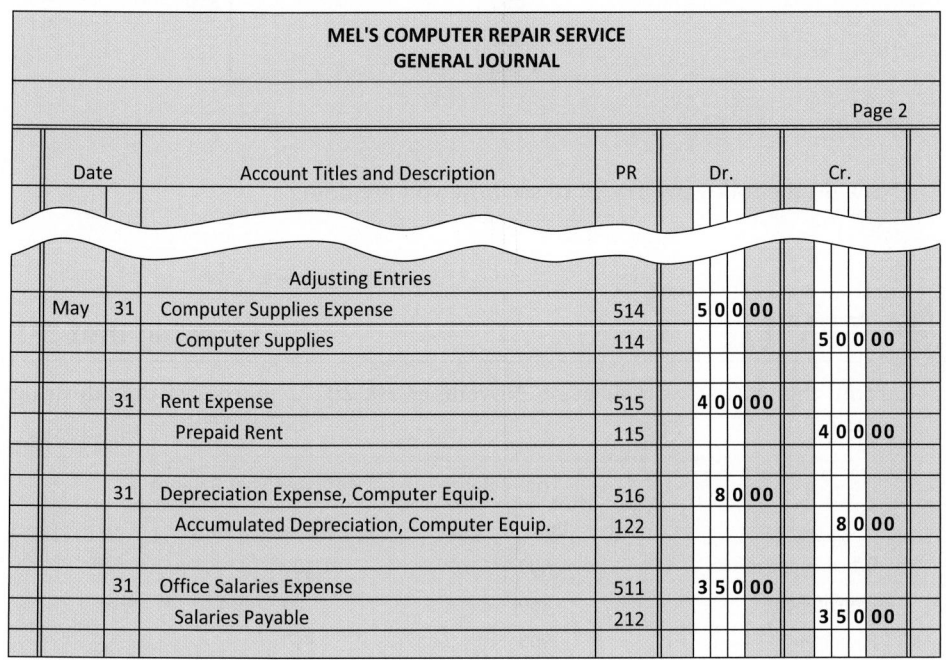

MEL'S COMPUTER REPAIR SERVICE
GENERAL JOURNAL

Page 2

Date		Account Titles and Description	PR	Dr.	Cr.
		Adjusting Entries			
May	31	Computer Supplies Expense	514	5 0 0 00	
		Computer Supplies	114		5 0 0 00
	31	Rent Expense	515	4 0 0 00	
		Prepaid Rent	115		4 0 0 00
	31	Depreciation Expense, Computer Equip.	516	8 0 00	
		Accumulated Depreciation, Computer Equip.	122		8 0 00
	31	Office Salaries Expense	511	3 5 0 00	
		Salaries Payable	212		3 5 0 00

FIGURE 5.2
Journalizing and Posting Adjustments from the Adjustments Section of the Worksheet

COACHING TIP

Each adjustment affects both the income statement and balance sheet.

Adjustment (C)

Before Posting:

Computer Equipment 121	Depreciation Expense, Computer Equipment 516	Accumulated Depreciation, Computer Equipment 122
6,000		

(continued on page 148)

After Posting:

Computer Equipment 121	Depreciation Expense, Computer Equipment 516	Accumulated Depreciation, Computer Equipment 122
6,000	80	80

The first adjustment in (C) shows the same balances for Depreciation Expense, Computer Equipment and Accumulated Depreciation, Computer Equipment. However, in subsequent adjustments the Accumulated Depreciation balance will keep getting larger, but the debit to Depreciation Expense and the credit to Accumulated Depreciation will stay the same. We will see why in a moment.

Adjustment (D)

Before Posting:

Office Salaries Expense 511	Salaries Payable 212
650	
650	

After Posting:

Office Salaries Expense 511	Salaries Payable 212
650	350
650	
350	

Now do the following Try It! to see how you are doing.

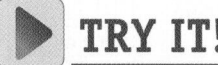 **TRY IT!**   Learning Unit 5-1

From this partial worksheet on November 30, 201X, journalize the adjusting entries:

	Trial Balance		Adjusted Trial Balance	
	Dr.	Cr.	Dr.	Cr.
Office Supplies	1,500		1,200	
Prepaid Rent	260		60	
Equipment	900		900	
Salaries Expense	400		600	
Office Supplies Expense	300		600	
Rent Expense	200		400	
Dep. Expense, Equip.	100		200	
Acc. Depreciation, Equip.		100		200
Salaries Payable				200

Why does Equipment remain at $900 on the adjusted trial balance?

Closing Entries (Step 8 of the Accounting Cycle)

To make recording of the next period's transactions easier, a mechanical step, called *closing*, is taken by Mel's accountant. Closing is intended to end—or close off—the revenue, expense, and withdrawal accounts at the end of the accounting period. The information needed to complete closing entries will be found in the income statement and balance sheet sections of the worksheet.

To make it easier to understand this process, we first look at the difference between temporary (nominal) accounts and permanent (real) accounts.

Here is the expanded accounting equation we used in an earlier chapter:

$$\text{Assets} = \text{Liabilities} + \text{Capital} - \text{Withdrawals} + \text{Revenues} - \text{Expenses}$$

Three of the items in that equation—Assets, Liabilities, and Capital—are known as real or permanent accounts because their balances are carried over from one accounting period to another. The other three items—Withdrawals, Revenues, and Expenses—are called nominal or temporary accounts because their balances are not carried over from one accounting period to another. Instead, their "balances" are reset at zero at the beginning of each accounting period by closing their balances at the end of the prior period. This process allows us to accumulate new data about revenue, expenses, and withdrawals in the new accounting period. The process of closing summarizes the effects of the temporary accounts on Capital for that period using closing journal entries. When the closing process is complete, the accounting equation will be reduced to

$$\text{Assets} = \text{Liabilities} + \text{Ending Capital}$$

If you look back to Chapter 4, you will see that we already calculated the new capital on the balance sheet to be $14,275 for Mel's Computer Repair Service. Before the mechanical closing procedures are journalized and posted, Mel's Capital account in the ledger is only $10,000 (see Chapter 3). Let's now look at how to journalize and post closing entries.

How to Journalize Closing Entries

Four steps are needed in journalizing closing entries:

STEP 1: Clear to zero the revenue balance and transfer it to Income Summary. Income Summary is a temporary account in the ledger needed for closing. At the end of the closing process, Income Summary will no longer hold a balance.

$$\text{Revenue} \rightarrow \text{Income Summary}$$

STEP 2: Clear to zero the individual expense balances and transfer them to Income Summary.

$$\text{Expenses} \rightarrow \text{Income Summary}$$

STEP 3: Clear to zero the balance in Income Summary and transfer it to Capital.

$$\text{Income Summary} \rightarrow \text{Capital}$$

STEP 4: Clear to zero the balance in Withdrawals and transfer it to Capital.

$$\text{Withdrawals} \rightarrow \text{Capital}$$

Figure 5.3 on page 150 is a visual representation of these four steps. Keep in mind that this information must first be journalized and then posted to the appropriate ledger accounts. The worksheet presented in Figure 5.4 on page 150 contains all the figures we will need for the closing process.

Permanent (real) accounts Accounts whose balances are carried over to the next accounting period. Examples: Assets, Liabilities, Capital.

Temporary (nominal) accounts Accounts whose balances at the end of an accounting period are not carried over to the next accounting period.

Closing journal entries Journal entries that are prepared to (a) reset all temporary accounts to a zero balance and (b) update Capital to a new balance.

 COACHING TIP

Think of the goals of closing like sweeping a room. First, you sweep or clear all revenue and expenses into a dustpan (Income Summary), and then you place the balance into a barrel (like Capital).

Income Summary A temporary account in the ledger that summarizes revenue and expenses and transfers the balance (net income or net loss) to Capital. This account does not have a normal balance (i.e., it could have a debit or a credit balance).

 COACHING TIP

After all closing entries are journalized and posted to the ledger, all temporary accounts have a zero balance in the ledger. Closing is a step-by-step process.

FIGURE 5.3

Four Steps in Journalizing Closing Entries (All numbers can be found on the worksheet in Figure 5.4.)

COACHING TIP

Don't forget two goals of closing:

1. Clear all temporary accounts in ledger.
2. Update Capital to a new balance that reflects a summary of all the temporary accounts.

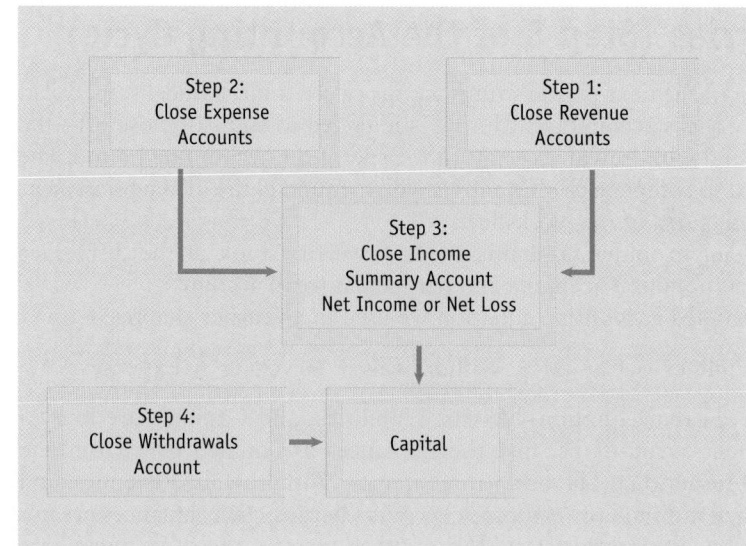

FIGURE 5.4

Closing Figures on the Worksheet

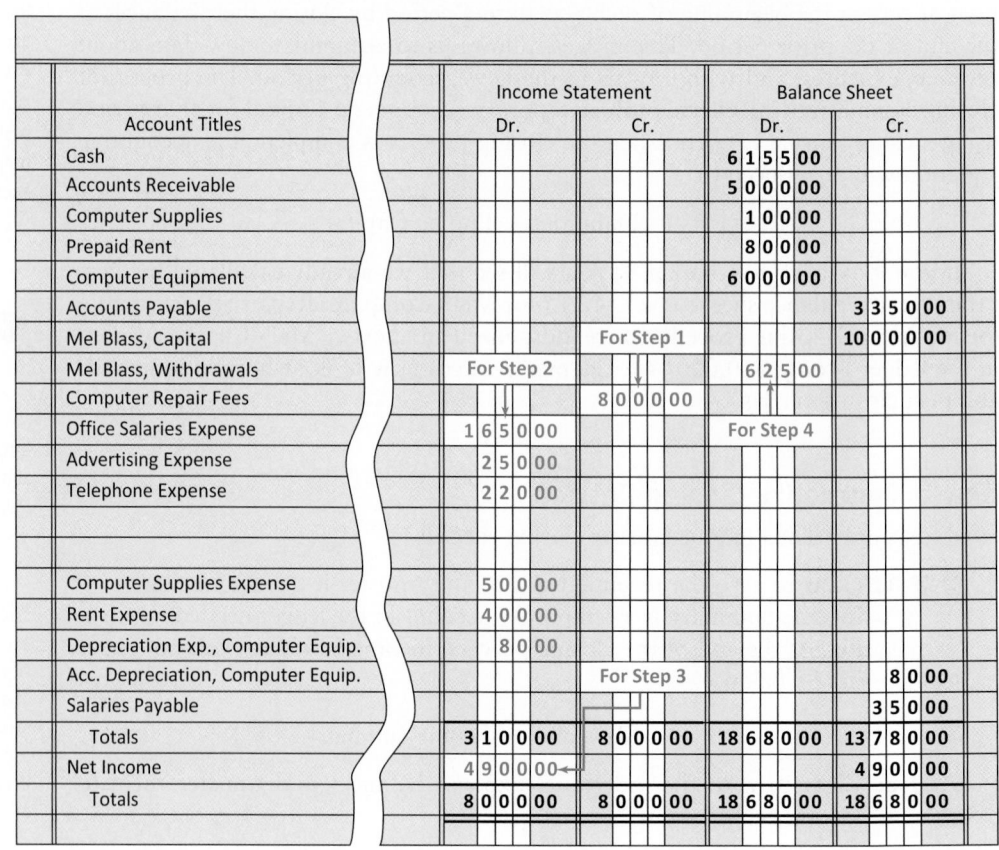

Account Titles	Income Statement		Balance Sheet	
	Dr.	Cr.	Dr.	Cr.
Cash			6 1 5 5 00	
Accounts Receivable			5 0 0 0 00	
Computer Supplies			1 0 0 00	
Prepaid Rent			8 0 0 00	
Computer Equipment			6 0 0 0 00	
Accounts Payable				3 3 5 0 00
Mel Blass, Capital		For Step 1		10 0 0 0 00
Mel Blass, Withdrawals	For Step 2		6 2 5 00	
Computer Repair Fees		8 0 0 0 00		
Office Salaries Expense	1 6 5 0 00		For Step 4	
Advertising Expense	2 5 0 00			
Telephone Expense	2 2 0 00			
Computer Supplies Expense	5 0 0 00			
Rent Expense	4 0 0 00			
Depreciation Exp., Computer Equip.	8 0 00			
Acc. Depreciation, Computer Equip.		For Step 3		8 0 00
Salaries Payable				3 5 0 00
Totals	3 1 0 0 00	8 0 0 0 00	18 6 8 0 00	13 7 8 0 00
Net Income	4 9 0 0 00			4 9 0 0 00
Totals	8 0 0 0 00	8 0 0 0 00	18 6 8 0 00	18 6 8 0 00

COACHING TIP

All numbers used in the closing process can be found on the worksheet.

Step 1: Clear Revenue Balance and Transfer to Income Summary. Here is what is in the ledger before closing entries are journalized and posted:

Computer Repair Fees 411	Income Summary 313
8,000	

The income statement section on the worksheet in Figure 5.4 shows that Computer Repair Fees has a credit balance of $8,000. To close or clear this balance to zero, a debit of $8,000 is needed. But if we add an amount to the debit side, we must also add a credit—so we add $8,000 on the credit side of the Income Summary.

Figure 5.5 is the journalized closing entry for Step 1.

May	31	Computer Repair Fees	411	8 0 0 0 00	
		Income Summary	313		8 0 0 0 00

FIGURE 5.5
Closing Revenue to Income Summary

After the first step of closing entries is journalized and posted, the Computer Repair Fees and Income Summary ledger accounts should look like the following:

Computer Repair Fees 411	
8,000	**8,000**
Closing	**Revenue**

Income Summary 313
8,000
Revenue

Note that the revenue balance is cleared to zero and transferred to Income Summary, a temporary account also located in the ledger.

Step 2: Clear Individual Expense Balances and Transfer the Total to Income Summary. The ledger for each expense account is shown here before closing entries are journalized and posted. Each expense is listed on the worksheet in the debit column of the income statement section in Figure 5.4.

COACHING TIP
Remember, the worksheet is a tool. The accountant realizes that the information about the total of the expenses will be transferred to the Income Summary account.

Office Salaries Expense 511	
650	
650	
350	

Advertising Expense 512	
250	

Telephone Expense 513	
220	

Computer Supplies Expense 514	
500	

Depreciation Expense, Computer Equipment 516	
80	

Rent Expense 515	
400	

The income statement section of the worksheet lists all the expenses as debits. If we want to reduce each expense to zero, each one must be credited.

Figure 5.6 is the journalized closing entry for Step 2.

	31	Income Summary	313	3 1 0 0 00	
		Office Salaries Expense	511		1 6 5 0 00
		Advertising Expense	512		2 5 0 00
		Telephone Expense	513		2 2 0 00
		Computer Supplies Expense	514		5 0 0 00
		Rent Expense	515		4 0 0 00
		Depreciation Expense, Computer Equip.	516		8 0 00

FIGURE 5.6
Closing Each Expense Account
Balance to Income Summary

COACHING TIP
The $3,100 is the total of all expense account balances.

Individual expenses and Income Summary accounts should look like the following after closing entries are journalized and posted:

Office Salaries Expense 511		
650	Closing	1,650
650		
350		

Advertising Expense 512		
250	Closing	250

Telephone Expense 513		
220	Closing	220

Computer Supplies Expense 514		
500	Closing	500

Rent Expense 515		
400	Closing	400

Depreciation Expense, Computer Equipment 516		
80	Closing	80

Income Summary 313			
	Expenses	Revenue	
Step 2	3,100	8,000	Step 1

Step 3: Clear Balance in Income Summary (Net Income) and Transfer It to Capital. The Income Summary and Mel Blass, Capital accounts look this way before Step 3:

Income Summary 313			Mel Blass, Capital 311	
3,100	8,000			10,000
	4,900			

Note that the ending balance of Income Summary is $4,900. (Revenues minus Expenses, or $8,000 Cr. − $3,100 Dr. = $4,900 Cr.) We must clear that amount from the Income Summary account and transfer it to the Mel Blass, Capital account.

In order to transfer the Credit Balance of $4,900 from Income Summary to Capital, it will be necessary to debit Income Summary for $4,900 and credit or increase Capital of Mel Blass for $4,900.

Figure 5.7 is the journalized closing entry for Step 3:

FIGURE 5.7
Closing Net Income for Mel Blass, Capital

	31	Income Summary	313	4 9 0 0 00	
		Mel Blass, Capital	311		4 9 0 0 00

The Income Summary and Mel Blass, Capital accounts will look like the following in the ledger after the closing entries of Step 3 are journalized and posted:

	Income Summary 313			Mel Blass, Capital 311	
Total of Expenses →	3,100	8,000	← Revenue		10,000
Debit to close → account	4,900	4,900	← Net Income		4,900 ← Net Income

Step 4: Clear the Withdrawals Balance and Transfer It to Capital. Next, we must close the Withdrawals account. The Mel Blass, Withdrawals and Mel Blass, Capital accounts currently look like this:

Mel Blass, Withdrawals 312		Mel Blass, Capital 311	
625			10,000
			4,900

COACHING TIP

At the end of these three steps, the Income Summary has a zero balance. If we had a net loss, the end result would be to decrease Capital. The entry would be debit Capital and credit Income Summary for the loss.

To bring the Withdrawals account to a zero balance and summarize its effect on Capital, we must credit Withdrawals and debit Capital.

Remember, withdrawals are a nonbusiness expense and thus are not transferred to Income Summary. The closing entry is journalized, as shown in Figure 5.8.

	31	Mel Blass, Capital	311	6 2 5 00	
		Mel Blass, Withdrawals	312		6 2 5 00

FIGURE 5.8
Closing Withdrawal to Mel Blass, Capital

At this point the Mel Blass, Withdrawals and Mel Blass, Capital accounts would look this way in the ledger:

Mel Blass, Withdrawals 312

625	Closing 625

Mel Blass, Capital 311

→ 625	10,000 ←
Withdrawals	Beg. Balance
	4,900 ←
	Net Income

COACHING TIP

Note that the $10,000 is a beginning balance because no additional investments were made during the period.

Now let's look at a summary of the closing entries in Figure 5.9.

		General Journal					Page 2			
	Date	Account Titles and Description	PR	Dr.			Cr.			
		Closing Entries								
201X										
May	31	Computer Repair Fees	411	8 0 0 0 00						
		Income Summary	313				8 0 0 0 00			← Step 1
	31	Income Summary	313	3 1 0 0 00						
		Office Salaries Expense	511				1 6 5 0 00			
		Advertising Expense	512				2 5 0 00			
		Telephone Expense	513				2 2 0 00			← Step 2
		Computer Supplies Expense	514				5 0 0 00			
		Rent Expense	515				4 0 0 00			
		Depreciation Expense, Computer Equip.	516				8 0 00			
	31	Income Summary	313	4 9 0 0 00						
		Mel Blass, Capital	311				4 9 0 0 00			← Step 3
	31	Mel Blass, Capital	311	6 2 5 00						
		Mel Blass, Withdrawals	312				6 2 5 00			← Step 4

FIGURE 5.9
Four Closing Entries

Figure 5.10 on pages 154–157 shows the complete ledger for Mel's Computer Repair Service after posting adjusting and closing entries.

Note how "adjusting" or "closing" is written in the explanation column of individual accounts, as, for example, in the one for Computer Supplies. If the goals of closing have been achieved, only permanent accounts will have balances carried to the next accounting period. All temporary accounts should have zero balances.

FIGURE 5.10
Complete Ledger

MEL'S COMPUTER REPAIR SERVICE
GENERAL LEDGER

Cash   Account No. 111

Date		Explanation	Post. Ref.	Dr.	Cr.	Balance Dr.	Balance Cr.
201X May	1		GJ1	10 00 00 0		10 00 00 0	
	1		GJ1		1 00 00 0	9 00 00 0	
	1		GJ1		1 20 00 0	7 80 00 0	
	7		GJ1	3 00 00 0		10 80 00 0	
	13		GJ1		6 50 00	10 15 00 0	
	20		GJ1		6 25 00	9 52 50 0	
	27		GJ2		6 50 00	8 87 50 0	
	28		GJ2		2 50 00 0	6 37 50 0	
	29		GJ2		2 20 00	6 15 50 0	

Accounts Receivable   Account No. 112

Date		Explanation	Post. Ref.	Dr.	Cr.	Balance Dr.	Balance Cr.
201X May	22		GJ1	5 00 00 0		5 00 00 0	

Computer Supplies   Account No. 114

Date		Explanation	Post. Ref.	Dr.	Cr.	Balance Dr.	Balance Cr.
201X May	3		GJ1	6 00 00		6 00 00	
	31	Adjusting	GJ2		5 00 00	1 00 00	

FIGURE 5.10 (continued)

Prepaid Rent   Account No. 115

Date		Explanation	Post. Ref.	Dr.	Cr.	Balance Dr.	Balance Cr.
201X May	1		GJ1	1 2 0 0 00		1 2 0 0 00	
	31	Adjusting	GJ2		4 0 0 00	8 0 0 00	

Computer Equipment   Account No. 121

Date		Explanation	Post. Ref.	Dr.	Cr.	Balance Dr.	Balance Cr.
201X May	1		GJ1	6 0 0 0 00		6 0 0 0 00	

Accumulated Depreciation, Computer Equipment   Account No. 122

Date		Explanation	Post. Ref.	Dr.	Cr.	Balance Dr.	Balance Cr.
201X May	31	Adjusting	GJ2		8 0 00		8 0 00

Accounts Payable   Account No. 211

Date		Explanation	Post. Ref.	Dr.	Cr.	Balance Dr.	Balance Cr.
201X May	1		GJ1		5 0 0 0 00		5 0 0 0 00
	3		GJ1		6 0 0 00		5 6 0 0 00
	18		GJ1		2 5 0 00		5 8 5 0 00
	28		GJ2	2 5 0 0 00			3 3 5 0 00

Salaries Payable   Account No. 212

Date		Explanation	Post. Ref.	Dr.	Cr.	Balance Dr.	Balance Cr.
201X May	31	Adjusting	GJ2		3 5 0 00		3 5 0 00

Mel Blass, Capital   Account No. 311

Date		Explanation	Post. Ref.	Dr.	Cr.	Balance Dr.	Balance Cr.
201X May	1		GJ1		10 0 0 0 00		10 0 0 0 00
	31	Closing (Net Income)	GJ2		4 9 0 0 00		14 9 0 0 00
	31	Closing (Withdrawals)	GJ2	6 2 5 00			14 2 7 5 00

Note how this amount is same ending balance as Figure 4.14 (p. 122).

(continued on next page)

FIGURE 5.10 *(continued)*

Mel Blass, Withdrawals   Account No. 312

Date		Explanation	Post. Ref.	Dr.	Cr.	Balance Dr.	Balance Cr.
201X May	20		GJ1	6 2 5 00		6 2 5 00	
	31	Closing	GJ2		6 2 5 00	—	—

Income Summary   Account No. 313

Date		Explanation	Post. Ref.	Dr.	Cr.	Balance Dr.	Balance Cr.
201X May	31	Closing (Revenue)	GJ2		8 0 0 0 00		8 0 0 0 00
	31	Closing (Expenses)	GJ2	3 1 0 0 00			4 9 0 0 00
	31	Closing (Net Income)	GJ2	4 9 0 0 00		—	—

Computer Repair Fees   Account No. 411

Date		Explanation	Post. Ref.	Dr.	Cr.	Balance Dr.	Balance Cr.
201X May	7		GJ1		3 0 0 0 00		3 0 0 0 00
	22		GJ1		5 0 0 0 00		8 0 0 0 00
	31	Closing	GJ2	8 0 0 0 00		—	—

Office Salaries Expense   Account No. 511

Date		Explanation	Post. Ref.	Dr.	Cr.	Balance Dr.	Balance Cr.
201X May	13		GJ1	6 5 0 00		6 5 0 00	
	27		GJ2	6 5 0 00		1 3 0 0 00	
	31	Adjusting	GJ2	3 5 0 00		1 6 5 0 00	
	31	Closing	GJ2		1 6 5 0 00	—	—

Advertising Expense   Account No. 512

Date		Explanation	Post. Ref.	Dr.	Cr.	Balance Dr.	Balance Cr.
201X May	18		GJ1	2 5 0 00		2 5 0 00	
	31	Closing	GJ2		2 5 0 00	—	—

FIGURE 5.10 *(continued)*

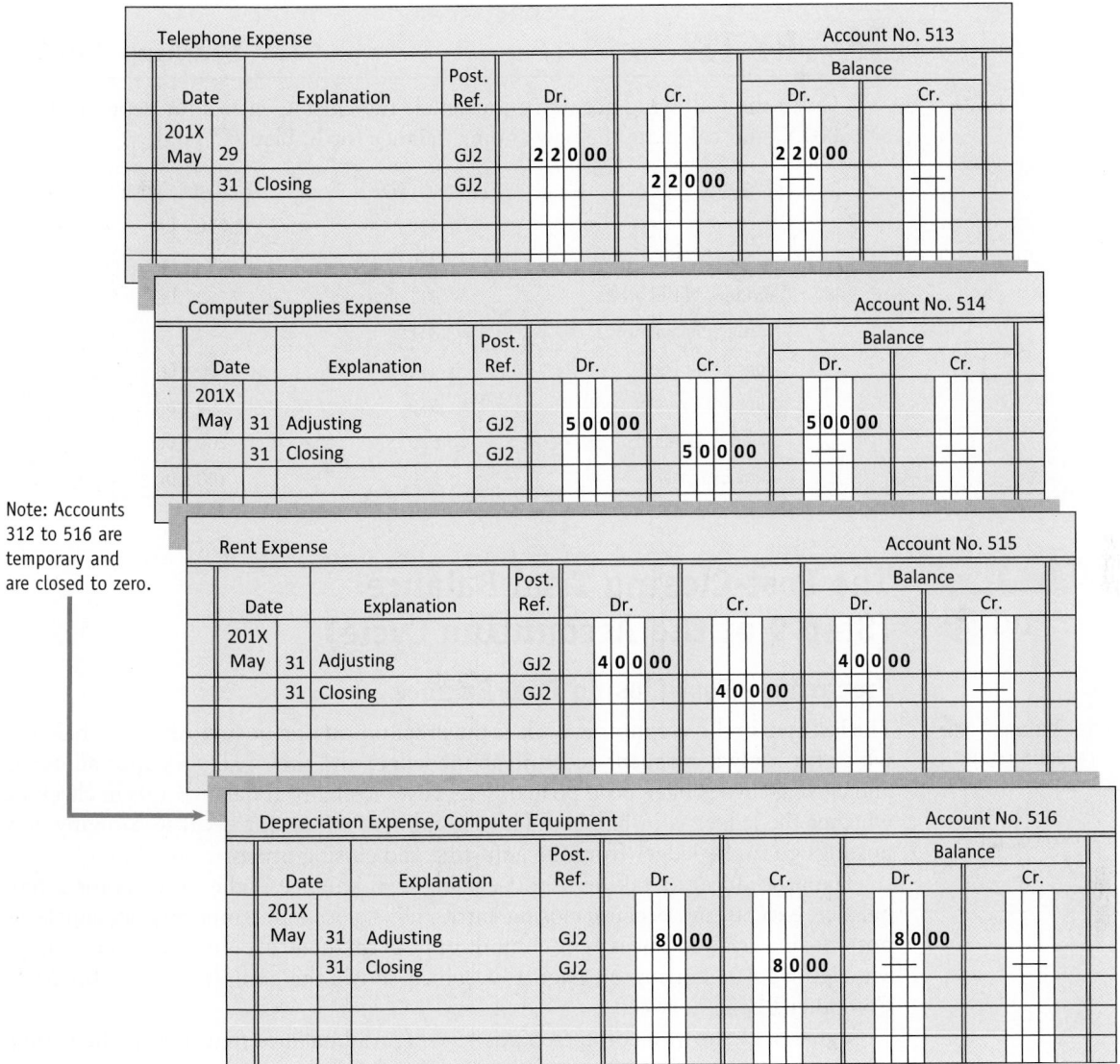

Note: Accounts 312 to 516 are temporary and are closed to zero.

Telephone Expense   Account No. 513

Date		Explanation	Post. Ref.	Dr.	Cr.	Balance Dr.	Balance Cr.
201X May	29		GJ2	2 2 0 00		2 2 0 00	
	31	Closing	GJ2		2 2 0 00	—	—

Computer Supplies Expense   Account No. 514

Date		Explanation	Post. Ref.	Dr.	Cr.	Balance Dr.	Balance Cr.
201X May	31	Adjusting	GJ2	5 0 0 00		5 0 0 00	
	31	Closing	GJ2		5 0 0 00	—	—

Rent Expense   Account No. 515

Date		Explanation	Post. Ref.	Dr.	Cr.	Balance Dr.	Balance Cr.
201X May	31	Adjusting	GJ2	4 0 0 00		4 0 0 00	
	31	Closing	GJ2		4 0 0 00	—	—

Depreciation Expense, Computer Equipment   Account No. 516

Date		Explanation	Post. Ref.	Dr.	Cr.	Balance Dr.	Balance Cr.
201X May	31	Adjusting	GJ2	8 0 00		8 0 00	
	31	Closing	GJ2		8 0 00	—	—

Insight into Closing in a Computerized System

In a computerized system, the closing entries are done in seconds because the software automatically closes the books. The end results are permanent accounts that have balances. At the end of this chapter is a Mini Practice Set for a fictional company called Sousa Realty that allows you to use Sage 50 or QuickBooks to see how fast a computer can journal and post. (Check with your instructor to see if this Mini Practice Set will be covered in your course.)

Now you can check your progress with a Try It!

 **TRY IT!**   Learning Unit 5-2

Given the following accounts, journalize the closing entries for September 30, 201X, and calculate the new ending balance for B. Blew, Capital.

Account	Acct. No.	Ending Balance	
Cash	110	2,000	Dr.
B. Blew, Capital	310	200	Cr.
B. Blew, Withdrawals	311	50	Dr.
Income Summary	312	—	
Consulting Fees	410	600	Cr.
Supplies Expense	510	50	Dr.
Salaries Expense	520	200	Dr.
Rent Expense	530	100	Dr.

LEARNING UNIT 5-3

L03

The Post-Closing Trial Balance (Step 9 of the Accounting Cycle)

Preparing a Post-Closing Trial Balance

Post-closing trial balance The final step in the accounting cycle that lists only permanent accounts in the ledger and their balances after adjusting and closing entries have been posted.

The last step in the accounting cycle is the preparation of a post-closing trial balance, which lists only permanent accounts in the ledger and their balances after adjusting and closing entries have been posted. This post-closing trial balance aids in checking whether the ledger is in balance. This checking is important because so many new postings go to the ledger from the adjusting and closing process.

The procedure for taking a post-closing trial balance is the same as for a trial balance, except that, because closing entries have closed all temporary accounts, the post-closing trial balances will contain only permanent accounts (balance sheet). See Figure 5.10, starting on page 154, which shows the complete ledger for Mel's Computer Repair Service.

Figure 5.11 shows a completed post-closing trial balance that reflects the permanent accounts. Now let's review the accounting cycle.

FIGURE 5.11
Post-Closing Trial Balance for Mel's Computer Repair Service

MEL'S COMPUTER REPAIR SERVICE POST-CLOSING TRIAL BALANCE MAY 31, 201X	Dr.	Cr.
Cash	6 1 5 5 00	
Accounts Receivable	5 0 0 0 00	
Computer Supplies	1 0 0 00	
Prepaid Rent	8 0 0 00	
Computer Equipment	6 0 0 0 00	
Accumulated Depreciation, Computer Equip.		8 0 00
Accounts Payable		3 3 5 0 00
Salaries Payable		3 5 0 00
Mel Blass, Capital		14 2 7 5 00
Totals	18 0 5 5 00	18 0 5 5 00

The Accounting Cycle Reviewed

Table 5.1 lists the steps we completed in the manual accounting cycle for Mel's Computer Repair Service for the month of May.

TABLE 5.1 Steps of the Manual Accounting Cycle

Steps	Explanation
1. Collect source documents from business transactions as they occur.	Cash register tape, sales tickets, bills, checks, payroll cards
2. Analyze and record business transactions in a journal.	Called journalizing
3. Post or transfer information from journal to ledger.	Copying the debits and credits of the journal entries into the ledger accounts
4. Prepare a trial balance.	Summarizing each individual ledger account and listing those accounts to test for mathematical accuracy in recording transactions
5. Prepare a worksheet.	A multicolumn form that summarizes accounting information to complete the accounting cycle
6. Prepare financial statements.	Income statement, statement of owner's equity, and balance sheet
7. Journalize and post adjusting entries.	Using figures in the adjustment columns of the worksheet
8. Journalize and post closing entries.	Using figures in the income statement and balance sheet sections of the worksheet
9. Prepare a post-closing trial balance.	Proving the mathematical accuracy of the adjusting and closing process of the accounting cycle

COACHING TIP

Remember: No worksheet is needed when using accounting software.

Insight. Most companies journalize and post adjusting and closing entries only at the end of their fiscal year. A company that prepares interim statements may complete only the first six steps of the cycle. Worksheets allow the preparation of interim reports without the formal adjusting and closing of the books. In this case, footnotes on the interim report will indicate the extent to which adjusting and closing entries were completed.

Now do the following Try It! to check your progress.

COACHING TIP

An amusement park works on a daily cycle. Each day when the park closes, the employees clean and restock it to get ready for the next "cycle" of customers. This is similar to the yearly accounting cycle.

 **TRY IT!**   Learning Unit 5-3

From the following accounts, list those that will not be found on the Post-Closing Trial Balance. Please explain your answers.

Cash; Accounts Receivable; Office Supplies; Prepaid Rent; iPad Equipment; Accumulated Depreciation, iPad Equipment; Accounts Payable; Salaries Payable; B. Boy, Capital; B. Boy, Withdrawals; Income Summary; Computer Fees; Software Fees; Rent Expense; Salaries Expense; Office Supplies Expense; and Depreciation Expense, iPad Equipment.

DEMONSTRATION SUMMARY PROBLEM

Requirements

1. Journalize transactions and post to ledger.
2. Prepare a worksheet.
3. Prepare financial statements.
4. Journalize adjusting and closing entries and prepare a post-closing trial balance.

COACHING TIP

Note: Accounts 312 to 515 are temporary accounts.

Assets	Owner's Equity
111 Cash	311 R. Kern, Capital
112 Accounts Receivable	312 R. Kern, Withdrawals
114 Prepaid Rent	313 Income Summary
115 Office Supplies	**Revenue**
121 Office Equipment	411 Fees Earned
122 Accumulated Depreciation, Office Equipment	**Expenses**
Liabilities	511 Salaries Expense
211 Accounts Payable	512 Advertising Expense
212 Salaries Payable	513 Rent Expense
	514 Office Supplies Expense
	515 Depreciation Expense, Office Equipment

We will use unusually small numbers to simplify calculation and emphasize the theory.

201X			
Jan.	1	Rolo Kern invested $1,200 cash and $100 of office equipment to open Rolo Co.
	1	Paid rent for 3 months in advance, $300.
	4	Purchased office equipment on account, $50.
	6	Bought office supplies for cash, $40.
	8	Collected $400 for services rendered.
	12	Rolo paid his home electric bill from the company checkbook, $20.
	14	Provided $100 worth of services to clients who will not pay until next month.
	16	Paid salaries, $60.
	18	Advertising bill received for $70 but will not be paid until next month.

Adjustment Data on January 31

A. Supplies on hand, $6.
B. Rent expired, $100.
C. Depreciation, Office Equipment, $20.
D. Salaries accrued, $50.

Solutions

Requirement 1

Journalize transactions and post to ledger (see Figure 5.12).

General Journal							Page 1	
Date		Account Titles and Description	PR	Dr.			Cr.	
201X Jan	1	Cash	111	1 2 0 0 00				
		Office Equipment	121	1 0 0 00				
		R. Kern, Capital	311			1 3 0 0 00		
		Initial Investment						
	1	Prepaid Rent	114	3 0 0 00				
		Cash	111			3 0 0 00		
		Rent Paid in Advance—3 months						
	4	Office Equipment	121	5 0 00				
		Accounts Payable	211			5 0 00		
		Purchased Equipment on Account						
	6	Office Supplies	115	4 0 00				
		Cash	111			4 0 00		
		Supplies purchased for cash						
	8	Cash	111	4 0 0 00				
		Fees Earned	411			4 0 0 00		
		Services rendered						
	12	R. Kern, Withdrawals	312	2 0 00				
		Cash	111			2 0 00		
		Personal payment of a bill						
	14	Accounts Receivable	112	1 0 0 00				
		Fees Earned	411			1 0 0 00		
		Services rendered on account						
	16	Salaries Expense	511	6 0 00				
		Cash	111			6 0 00		
		Paid salaries						
	18	Advertising Expense	512	7 0 00				
		Accounts Payable	211			7 0 00		
		Advertising bill, but not paid						

FIGURE 5.12
Journal Entries for Rolo Company

Tips to Journalizing and Posting Transactions

Jan.	1	Cash	Asset	↑	Dr.	$1,200
		Office Equipment	Asset	↑	Dr.	$ 100
		R. Kern, Capital	Capital	↑	Cr.	$1,300
	1	Prepaid Rent	Asset	↑	Dr.	$ 300
		Cash	Asset	↓	Cr.	$ 300
	4	Office Equipment	Asset	↑	Dr.	$ 50
		Accounts Payable	Liability	↑	Cr.	$ 50
	6	Office Supplies	Asset	↑	Dr.	$ 40
		Cash	Asset	↓	Cr.	$ 40

(continued on page 162)

8	Cash	Asset	↑	Dr.	$ 400
	Fees Earned	Revenue	↑	Cr.	$ 400
12	R. Kern, Withdrawals	Withdrawals	↑	Dr.	$ 20
	Cash	Asset	↓	Cr.	$ 20
14	Accounts Receivable	Asset	↑	Dr.	$ 100
	Fees Earned	Revenue	↑	Cr.	$ 100
16	Salaries Expense	Expense	↑	Dr.	$ 60
	Cash	Asset	↓	Cr.	$ 60
18	Advertising Expense	Expense	↑	Dr.	$ 70
	Accounts Payable	Liability	↑	Cr.	$ 70

Note: All account titles come from the chart of accounts. When journalizing, the PR column of the general journal is blank. It is in the posting process that we update the ledger. The PR column in the ledger accounts tells us from what journal page the information came. After the title in the ledger is posted to, we fill in the PR column of the journal, telling us to what account number the information was transferred.

Requirement 2

Prepare a worksheet (Figure 5.13).

Tips to the Trial Balance and Completion of the Worksheet

After the posting process is complete from the journal to the ledger, we take the ending balance in each account and prepare a trial balance on the worksheet (see Figure 5.13). If a title has no balance, it is not listed on the trial balance. New titles on the worksheet will be added as needed.

Adjustments

COACHING TIP

Supplies on hand of $6 is not the adjustment. You need to calculate amount used up. Do not touch original cost of equipment.

Office Supplies Expense	Expense	↑	Dr.	$ 34	($40 – $6)
Office Supplies	Asset	↓	Cr.	$ 34	
Rent Expense	Expense	↑	Dr.	$100	
Prepaid Rent	Asset	↓	Cr.	$100	
Depr. Exp., Office Equip.	Expense	↑	Dr.	$ 20	
Accum. Dep., Office Equip.	Contra-Asset	↑	Cr.	$ 20	
Salaries Expense	Expense	↑	Dr.	$ 50	
Salaries Payable	Liability	↑	Cr.	$ 50	

Note: This information on the worksheet has *not* been updated in the ledger. (Updating happens when we journalize and post adjustments at the end of the cycle.)

Note that the last four columns of the worksheet come from numbers on the adjusted trial balance.

On the worksheet we copy the Net Income of $166 to the Balance Sheet credit column in order to make it balance, because the Capital figure there is the old one, hence the net income has not yet been included.

FIGURE 5.13 Completed Worksheet for Rolo Company

Supplies used up

Supplies on hand

ROLO CO.
WORKSHEET
FOR MONTH ENDED JANUARY 31, 201X

Account Titles	Trial Balance Dr.	Trial Balance Cr.	Adjustments Dr.	Adjustments Cr.	Adjusted Trial Balance Dr.	Adjusted Trial Balance Cr.	Income Statement Dr.	Income Statement Cr.	Balance Sheet Dr.	Balance Sheet Cr.
Cash	118000				118000				118000	
Accounts Receivable	10000				10000				10000	
Prepaid Rent	30000			(B) 10000	20000				20000	
Office Supplies	4000			(A) 3400	600				600	
Office Equipment	15000				15000				15000	
Accounts Payable		12000				12000				12000
R. Kern, Capital		130000				130000				130000
R. Kern, Withdrawals	2000				2000				2000	
Fees Earned		50000				50000		50000		
Salaries Expense	6000		(D) 5000		11000		11000			
Advertising Expense	7000				7000		7000			
Totals	192000	192000								
Office Supplies Expense			(A) 3400		3400		3400			
Rent Expense			(B) 10000		10000		10000			
Depr. Exp., Office Equip.			(C) 2000		2000		2000			
Acc. Dep., Office Equip.				(C) 2000		2000				2000
Salaries Payable				(D) 5000		5000				5000
Totals			20400	20400	199000	199000	33400	50000	165600	149000
Net Income							16600			16600
Totals							50000	50000	165600	165600

163

Requirement 3

Prepare the financial statements (see Figures 5.14, 5.15, and 5.16).

FIGURE 5.14
Income Statement for Rolo Company

ROLO CO. INCOME STATEMENT FOR MONTH ENDED JANUARY 31, 201X			
Revenue:			
Fees Earned			$5000 00
Operating Expenses			
Salaries Expense	$1100 00		
Advertising Expense	700 00		
Office Supplies Expense	340 00		
Rent Expense	1000 00		
Depreciation Expense, Office Equipment	200 00		
Total Operating Expenses		3340 00	
Net Income		$1660 00	

FIGURE 5.15
Statement of Owner's Equity for Rolo Company

ROLO CO. STATEMENT OF OWNER'S EQUITY FOR MONTH ENDED JANUARY 31, 201X			
R. Kern, Capital, January 1, 201X			$13000 00*
Net Income for January	$1660 00		
Less: Withdrawals for January	−200 00		
Increase in Capital		1460 00	
R. Kern, Capital, January 31, 201X		$14460 00	

*This capital is made up of zero beginning investment plus investment of Kern on January 1.

FIGURE 5.16 Balance Sheet for Rolo Company

ROLO CO. BALANCE SHEET JANUARY 31, 201X						
Assets			Liabilities & Owner's Equity			
Cash		$11800 00	Liabilities			
Accounts Receivable		100 00	Accounts Payable	$120 00		
Prepaid Rent		200 00	Salaries Payable	50 00		
Office Supplies		6 00	Total Liabilities		$170 00	
Office Equipment	$150 00		Owner's Equity			
Less: Accum. Depr.	20 00	130 00	R. Kern, Capital		14460 00	
			Total Liabilities &			
Total Assets		$16160 00	Owner's Equity		$16160 00	

Tips to Preparing the Financial Statements

The statements are prepared from the worksheet. (Many of the ledger accounts are not up-to-date.) The income statement (Figure 5.14) lists revenue and expenses. The Net Income figure of $166 is used to update the statement of owner's equity. The statement of owner's equity (Figure 5.15) calculates a new figure for Capital, $1,446 (Beginning Capital + Investments + Net Income – Withdrawals). This new figure is then listed on the balance sheet (Figure 5.16) (Assets, Liabilities, and a new figure for Capital).

Requirement 4

Journalize and post adjusting and closing entries and prepare a post-closing trial balance (Figure 5.17).

FIGURE 5.17 Adjusting and Closing Entries Journalized and Posted

	Date		Account Titles and Description	PR	Dr.	Cr.
General Journal						Page 2
			ADJUSTING ENTRIES			
	Jan.	31	Office Supplies Expense	514	3 4 00	
			Office Supplies	115		3 4 00
		31	Rent Expense	513	1 0 0 00	
			Prepaid Rent	114		1 0 0 00
		31	Depr. Expense, Office Equipment	515	2 0 00	
			Accum. Depr., Office Equip.	122		2 0 00
		31	Salaries Expense	511	5 0 00	
			Salaries Payable	212		5 0 00
			CLOSING ENTRIES			
Step 1		31	Fees Earned	411	5 0 0 00	
			Income Summary	313		5 0 0 00
Step 2		31	Income Summary	313	3 3 4 00	
			Salaries Expense	511		1 1 0 00
			Advertising Expense	512		7 0 00
			Office Supplies Expense	514		3 4 00
			Rent Expense	513		1 0 0 00
			Depr. Expense, Office Equip.	515		2 0 00
Step 3		31	Income Summary	313	1 6 6 00	
			R. Kern, Capital	311		1 6 6 00
Step 4		31	R. Kern, Capital	311	2 0 00	
			R. Kern, Withdrawals	312		2 0 00

Closing { Step 1, Step 2, Step 3, Step 4 }

Tips to Journalizing and Posting Adjusting and Closing Entries

Adjustments

The adjustments from the worksheet are journalized (same journal as transactions) and posted to the ledger. Now ledger accounts will be brought up-to-date. Remember, we have already prepared the financial statements from the worksheet. Our goal now is to get the ledger up-to-date.

Closing

Note that Income Summary is a temporary account located in the ledger.

Goals

1. Wipe out all temporary accounts in the ledger to zero balances.
2. Get a new figure for Capital in the ledger.

Steps in the Closing Process

STEP 1: Close revenue accounts to Income Summary.

STEP 2: Close expense accounts to Income Summary.

STEP 3: Close balance of Income Summary to Capital. (This amount really is the Net Income and equal to the figure on the worksheet.)

STEP 4: Close balance of Withdrawals to Capital.

All the journal closing entries are posted. (No new calculations are needed because all figures are on the worksheet.) The result in the ledger is that all temporary accounts have a zero balance (Figure 5.18).

FIGURE 5.18 General Ledger for Rolo Company

GENERAL LEDGER

Cash 111

Date	PR	Dr.	Cr.	Balance Dr.	Balance Cr.
1/1	GJ1	1,200		1,200	
1/1	GJ1		300	900	
1/6	GJ1		40	860	
1/8	GJ1	400		1,260	
1/12	GJ1		20	1,240	
1/16	GJ1		60	1,180	

Accounts Receivable 112

Date	PR	Dr.	Cr.	Balance Dr.	Balance Cr.
1/14	GJ1	100		100	

Accumulated Depreciation, Office Equipment 122

Date	PR	Dr.	Cr.	Balance Dr.	Balance Cr.
1/31 Adj.	GJ2		20		20

Accounts Payable 211

Date	PR	Dr.	Cr.	Balance Dr.	Balance Cr.
1/4	GJ1		50		50
1/18	GJ1		70		120

Salaries Payable 212

Date	PR	Dr.	Cr.	Balance Dr.	Balance Cr.
1/31 Adj.	GJ2		50		50

FIGURE 5.18 *(continued)*

Prepaid Rent 114

Date	PR	Dr.	Cr.	Balance Dr.	Cr.
1/1	GJ1	300		300	
1/31 Adj.	GJ2		100	200	

Office Supplies 115

Date	PR	Dr.	Cr.	Balance Dr.	Cr.
1/6	GJ1	40		40	
1/31 Adj	GJ2		34	6	

Office Equipment 121

Date	PR	Dr.	Cr.	Balance Dr.	Cr.
1/1	GJ1	100		100	
1/4	GJ1	50		150	

Fees Earned 411

Date	PR	Dr.	Cr.	Balance Dr.	Cr.
1/8	GJ1		400		400
1/14	GJ1		100		500
1/31 Clos.	GJ2	500		—	—

Salaries Expense 511

Date	PR	Dr.	Cr.	Balance Dr.	Cr.
1/16	GJ1	60		60	
1/31 Adj.	GJ2	50		110	
1/31 Clos.	GJ2		110	—	

Advertising Expense 512

Date	PR	Dr.	Cr.	Balance Dr.	Cr.
1/18	GJ1	70		70	
1/31 Clos.	GJ2		70	—	

R. Kern, Capital 311

Date	PR	Dr.	Cr.	Balance Dr.	Cr.
1/1	GJ1		1,300		1,300
1/31 Clos.	GJ2		166		1,466
1/31 Clos.	GJ2	20			1,446

R. Kern, Withdrawals 312

Date	PR	Dr.	Cr.	Balance Dr.	Cr.
1/12	GJ1	20		20	
1/31 Clos.	GJ2		20	—	

Income Summary 313

Date	PR	Dr.	Cr.	Balance Dr.	Cr.
1/31 Clos.	GJ2		500		500
1/31 Clos.	GJ2	334			166
1/31 Clos.	GJ2	166		—	

Rent Expense 513

Date	PR	Dr.	Cr.	Balance Dr.	Cr.
1/31 Adj.	GJ2	100		100	
1/31 Clos.	GJ2		100	—	

Office Supplies Expense 514

Date	PR	Dr.	Cr.	Balance Dr.	Cr.
1/31 Adj.	GJ2	34		34	
1/31 Clos.	GJ2		34	—	

Depreciation Expense, Office Equipment 515

Date	PR	Dr.	Cr.	Balance Dr.	Cr.
1/31 Adj.	GJ2	20		20	
1/31 Clos.	GJ2		20	—	

Tips for the Post-Closing Trial Balance

The post-closing trial balance is a list of the ledger *after* adjusting and closing entries have been completed. Note that the figure for Capital, $1,446, is the new figure (see Figure 5.19).

FIGURE 5.19

Post-Closing Trial Balance for Rolo Company

COACHING TIP

The post-closing trial balance contains all permanent accounts.

ROLO CO. POST-CLOSING TRIAL BALANCE JANUARY 31, 201X	Dr.	Cr.
Cash	1 1 8 0 00	
Accounts Receivable	1 0 0 00	
Prepaid Rent	2 0 0 00	
Office Supplies	6 00	
Office Equipment	1 5 0 00	
Accum. Dep., Office Equipment		2 0 00
Accounts Payable		1 2 0 00
Salaries Payable		5 0 00
R. Kern, Capital		1 4 4 6 00
Totals	1 6 3 6 00	1 6 3 6 00

Beginning Capital	$1,300*
+ Net Income	166
– Withdrawals	20
= Ending Capital	$1,446

*Beginning capital zero plus $1,300 investment

The post-closing trial balance is made up of permanent accounts only. Next accounting period we will enter new amounts in the Revenues, Expenses, and Withdrawal accounts.

BLUEPRINT OF CLOSING PROCESS FROM THE WORKSHEET

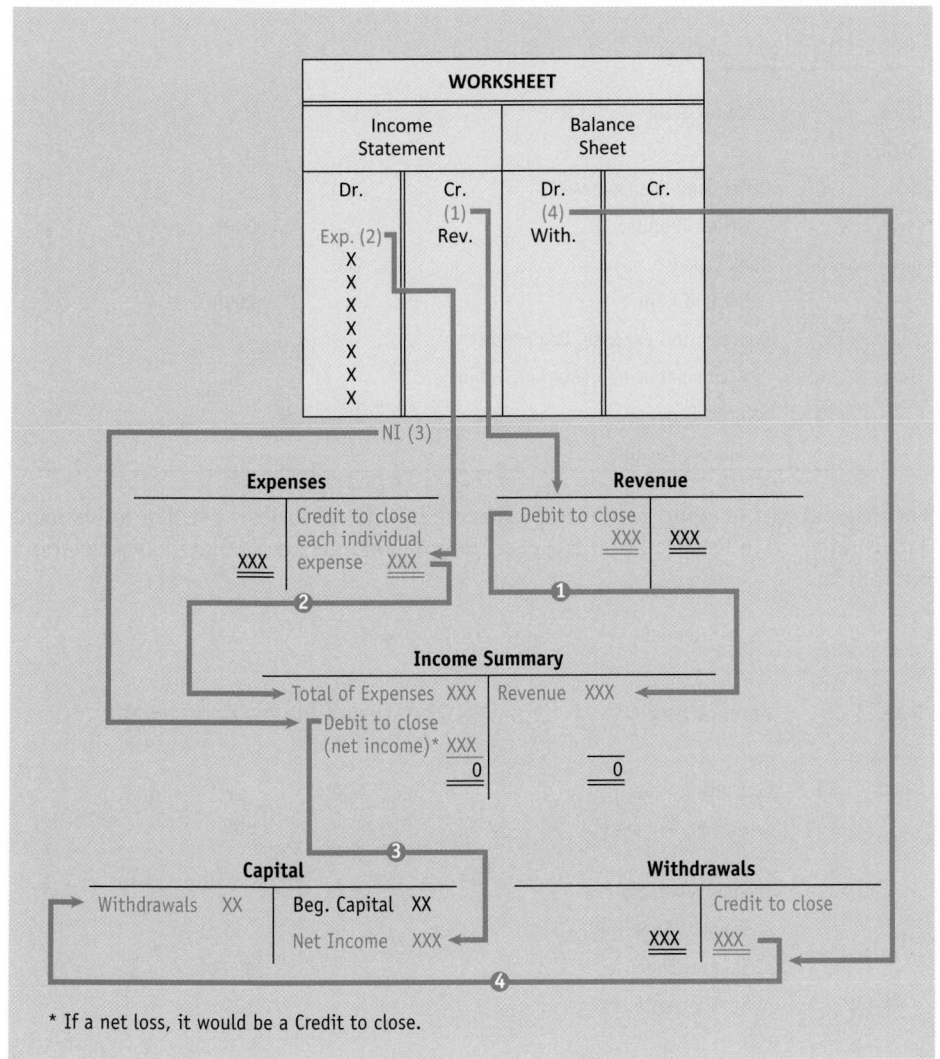

* If a net loss, it would be a Credit to close.

The Closing Steps

1. Close revenue ($) balance to Income Summary.
2. Close each *individual* expense and transfer *total* of all expenses to Income Summary.
3. Transfer balance in Income Summary (net income or net loss) to Capital.
4. Close Withdrawals to Capital.

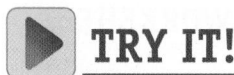

Learning Unit 5-1

Date		Account Title	Dr.	Cr.
201X				
Nov.	30	Office Supplies Expense	300	
		Office Supplies		300
	30	Rent Expense	200	
		Prepaid Rent		200
	30	Depreciation Expense, Equipment	100	
		Accumulated Depreciation, Equipment		100
	30	Salaries Expense	200	
		Salaries Payable		200

The original cost of equipment is not adjusted. It is the historical cost. The adjustment data is reflected in Depreciation Expense, Equipment and Accumulated Depreciation, Equipment.

Learning Unit 5-2

Date		Account Title	Dr.	Cr.
201X				
Sept.	30	Consulting Fees	600	
		Income Summary		600
	30	Income Summary	350	
		Supplies Expense		50
		Salaries Expense		200
		Rent Expense		100
	30	Income Summary	250	
		B. Blew, Capital		250
	30	B. Blew, Capital	50	
		B. Blew, Withdrawals		50

B. Blew, Capital, Beg.		$200
Plus Net Income	$250	
Less Withdrawals	−50	
Increase in Capital		200
B. Blew, Capital, End.		$400

Learning Unit 5-3

B. Boy, Withdrawals; Income Summary; Computer Fees; Software Fees; Rent Expense; Salaries Expense; Office Supplies Expense; Depreciation Expense, iPad Equipment.

All temporary accounts are closed to a zero balance when closing entries are journalized and posted.

ACCOUNTING COACH

The following Coaching Tips are from Learning Units 5-1 to 5-3. Take the Pre-Game Checkup and use the Check Your Score at the bottom of the page to see how you are doing. The Accounting Coach provides tips before each Checkup to help you avoid common accounting errors.

LU 5-1 Adjusting Entries (Step 7 of the Accounting Cycle)

Pre-Game Tips: All adjustments can be journalized and posted from the adjustments section of the worksheet. Remember that all accounts listed below the original trial balance are increasing. The adjustment for supplies is the amount used up. The adjustment for rent is the amount of rent that has expired. The adjustment for depreciation does not affect the original cost of the asset. The adjustment for salaries shows a new expense creating a liability because it is not yet paid.

Pre-Game Checkup: Answer true or false to the following statements.

1. After the adjustment is posted, the Supplies ledger account shows the amount on hand.
2. After posting, Accumulated Depreciation has a debit balance.
3. Adjustments on a worksheet do not have to be journalized and posted.
4. After the adjustment is posted, Prepaid Rent shows the amount expired.
5. Depreciation Expense is a contra-asset.

LU 5-2 Closing Entries (Step 8 of the Accounting Cycle)

Pre-Game Tips: The goal of closing is to update the ledger for the next accounting cycle. All temporary accounts need to be cleared, and a new figure for capital results. In the process, Income Summary is a temporary account that is used to close revenues and expenses to Capital. Withdrawals will be closed directly to Capital since it is not a business expense. When the closing process is complete, all temporary accounts will be closed. All information needed to do the closing can be found in the income statement and balance sheet sections of the worksheet.

Pre-Game Checkup: Answer true or false to the following statements.

1. Income Summary is a permanent account.
2. Income Summary is found on the worksheet.
3. Expenses are permanent accounts.
4. The balance in Income Summary is closed to the Cash account.
5. Income Summary has a normal debit balance.

LU 5-3 The Post-Closing Trial Balance (Step 9 of the Accounting Cycle)

Pre-Game Tips: The post-closing trial balance lists the accounts of the ledger after all closing entries have been posted. Only permanent accounts remain, and all temporary accounts now have a zero balance. The account "Income Summary" is used only in the closing process and thus never ends up on the post-closing trial balance.

Pre-Game Checkup: Answer true or false to the following statements.

1. Income Summary is listed on the post-closing trial balance.
2. Interim reports are always prepared each month.
3. Capital on the post-closing trial balance is the beginning balance for the next accounting cycle.
4. Accumulated Depreciation is a temporary account.
5. Supplies on the post-closing trial balance represent the amount of supplies used up.

CHECK YOUR SCORE: Answers to the Pre-Game Checkup

LU 5-1
1. True
2. False—After posting, Accumulated Depreciation has a credit balance.
3. False—Adjustments on a worksheet have to be journalized and posted.
4. False—After the adjustment is posted, Prepaid Rent shows the amount that has not expired yet.
5. False—Depreciation Expense is an expense.

LU 5-2
1. False—Income Summary is a temporary account.
2. False—Income Summary is not found on the worksheet.
3. False—Expenses are temporary accounts.
4. False—The balance in Income Summary is closed to Capital.
5. False—Income Summary has no normal balance.

LU 5-3

1. False—Income Summary is a temporary account and thus not listed on the post-closing trial balance since it is closed.
2. False—Interim reports are only optional and there is no set requirement for when or how often they are prepared.

3. True
4. False—Accumulated Depreciation is a permanent account.
5. False—Supplies on the post-closing trial balance represent the amount of supplies on hand.

Chapter Summary

MyAccountingLab   Here are all the key terms and equations to help you understand the concepts of this chapter and prepare you for your exam. After completing this review, go to MyAccountingLab for more practice opportunities.

Concepts You Should Know	Key Terms
L01 ▶ **Journalize and Post Adjusting Entries** 1. After formal financial statements have been prepared, the ledger has still not been brought up-to-date. 2. Information for journalizing adjusting entries comes from the adjustments section of the worksheet.	Adjusting journal entries (p. 146)
L02 ▶ **Journalize and Post Closing Entries** 1. Closing is a mechanical process that aids the accountant in recording transactions for the next period. 2. Assets, Liabilities, and Capital are permanent (real) accounts; their balances are carried over from one accounting period to another. Withdrawals, Revenue, and Expenses are temporary (nominal) accounts; their balances are not carried over from one accounting period to another. 3. Income Summary is a temporary account in the general ledger and does not have a normal balance. It will summarize revenue and expenses and transfer the balance to Capital. Withdrawals do not go into Income Summary. 4. All information for closing can be obtained from the worksheet or ledger. 5. When closing is complete, all temporary accounts in the ledger will have a zero balance, and all this information will be updated in the Capital account.	Closing journal entries (p. 149) Income Summary (p. 149) Permanent (real) accounts (p. 149) Temporary (nominal) accounts (p. 149)
L03 ▶ **Prepare a Post-Closing Trial Balance** 1. Closing entries are usually done only at year-end. Interim reports can be prepared from worksheets that are prepared monthly, quarterly, or at some other regular interval. 2. The post-closing trial balance is prepared from the ledger accounts after the adjusting and closing entries have been posted. 3. The accounts on the post-closing trial balance are all permanent titles.	Post-closing trial balance (p. 158)

Discussion Questions and Critical Thinking/Ethical Case

1. When a worksheet is completed, what balances are found in the general ledger?

2. Why must adjusting entries be journalized even though the formal statements have already been prepared?

3. "Closing slows down the recording of next year's transactions." Defend or reject this statement with supporting evidence.

4. What is the difference between temporary and permanent accounts?

5. How has computer software affected use of closing entries?

6. List the four steps of closing.

7. What is the purpose of Income Summary and where is it located?

8. How can a worksheet aid the closing process?

9. What accounts are usually listed on a post-closing trial balance?

10. Closing entries are always prepared once a month. Agree or disagree? Why?

11. Burton Fish is the purchasing agent for Lyle Co. One of his suppliers, Grant Co., offers Burton a free vacation to Spain if he buys at least 50% of Lyle's supplies from Grant Co. Burton, who is angry because Lyle Co. has not given him a raise in over a year, is considering the offer. Write your recommendation to Burton.

Concept Checks

MyAccountingLab

Journalizing and Posting Adjusting Entries

◀ **LO1**   *(5 min)*

1. Post the following adjusting entries that came from the adjustments section of the following worksheet to the T accounts and be sure to cross-reference back to the journal. (See Figure 5.20 on page 174.)

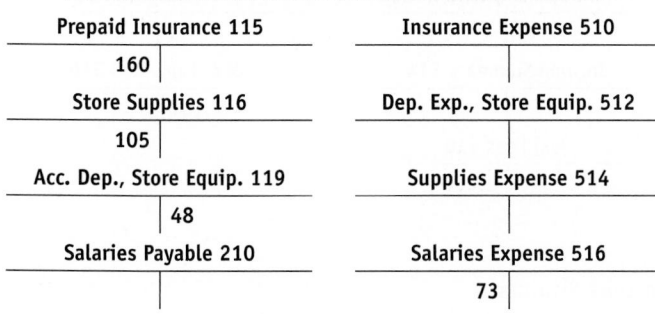

LEDGER ACCOUNTS BEFORE ADJUSTING ENTRIES POSTED

Prepaid Insurance 115	Insurance Expense 510
160	
Store Supplies 116	**Dep. Exp., Store Equip. 512**
105	
Acc. Dep., Store Equip. 119	**Supplies Expense 514**
48	
Salaries Payable 210	**Salaries Expense 516**
	73

FIGURE 5.20
Journalized Adjusting Entries

	General Journal				Page 3
Date	Account Titles and Description	PR	Dr.	Cr.	
Jan. 31	Insurance Expense		7 5 00		
	Prepaid Insurance			7 5 00	
31	Supplies Expense		4 6 00		
	Store Supplies			4 6 00	
31	Depr. Exp., Store Equipment		1 0 6 00		
	Accum. Depr., Store Equipment			1 0 6 00	
31	Salaries Expense		7 8 00		
	Salaries Payable			7 8 00	

(10 min)   **LO2**   ▶   **Steps of Closing and Journalizing Closing Entries**

2.   Explain the four steps of the closing process given the following:

May 31 ending balance, before closing	
Fees Earned	$ 200
Rent Expense	350
Advertising Expense	60
T. Molanaro, Capital	3,000
T. Molanaro, Withdrawals	45

(15 min)   **LO2**   ▶   **Journalizing Closing Entries**

3.   From the following accounts, journalize the closing entries (assume December 31).

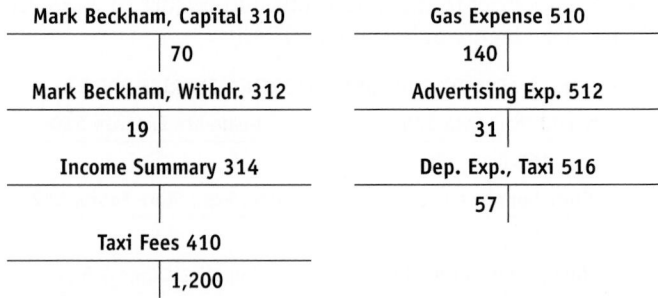

Mark Beckham, Capital 310 | 70

Mark Beckham, Withdr. 312 | 19

Income Summary 314

Taxi Fees 410 | 1,200

Gas Expense 510 | 140

Advertising Exp. 512 | 31

Dep. Exp., Taxi 516 | 57

(10 min)   **LO2**   ▶   **Posting to Income Summary**

4.   Draw a T account of Income Summary and post to it all entries from Question 3 that affect it. Is Income Summary a temporary or permanent account?

(10 min)   **LO2**   ▶   **Posting to Capital**

5.   Draw a T account for Mark Beckham, Capital, and post to it all entries from Question 3 that affect it. What is the final balance of the Capital account?

Exercises

Set A

5A-1. From the adjustments section of a worksheet (see Figure 5.21), prepare adjusting journal entries for the end of December.

L01   *(15 min)*

FIGURE 5.21
Adjustments on Worksheet

	Adjustments	
	Dr.	Cr.
Prepaid Rent		(A) 1 3 0 0 00
Office Supplies		(B) 4 5 0 00
Accumulated Depreciation, Equipment		(C) 3 7 5 00
Salaries Payable		(D) 6 0 0 00
Rent Expense	(A) 1 3 0 0 00	
Office Supplies Expense	(B) 4 5 0 00	
Depreciation Expense, Equipment	(C) 3 7 5 00	
Salaries Expense	(D) 6 0 0 00	
Totals	2 7 2 5 00	2 7 2 5 00

5A-2. Complete the following table by placing an X in the correct column.

L01,2   *(10 min)*

	Temporary	Permanent	Will Be Closed
Ex. Accounts Receivable		X	
1. Income Summary			
2. Jan Ralls, Capital			
3. Rent Expense			
4. Jan Ralls, Withdrawals			
5. Fees Earned			
6. Accounts Payable			
7. Cash			

5A-3. From the following T accounts, journalize the four closing entries on October 31, 201X.

L02   *(15 min)*

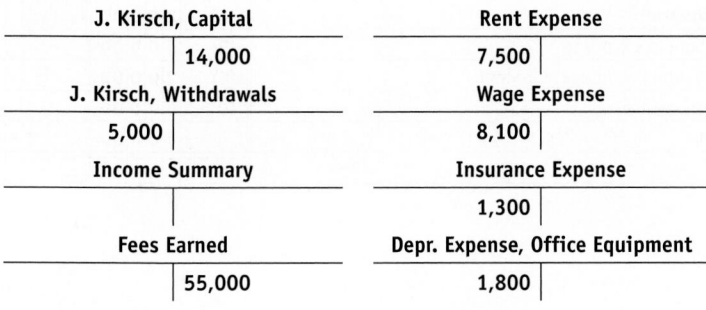

J. Kirsch, Capital		Rent Expense	
	14,000	7,500	
J. Kirsch, Withdrawals		**Wage Expense**	
5,000		8,100	
Income Summary		**Insurance Expense**	
		1,300	
Fees Earned		**Depr. Expense, Office Equipment**	
	55,000	1,800	

(20 min) **LO2** ▶

5A-4.   From the following posted T accounts, reconstruct the closing journal entries for August 31, 201X.

M. Fahy, Capital		Insurance Expense	
Withdrawals 100	7,000 (Aug. 1)	275	Closing 275
	375 Net Income		

M. Fahy, Withdrawals		Wage Expense	
100	Closing 100	400	Closing 400

Income Summary		Rent Expense	
Expenses 2,925	Revenue 3,300	1,800	Closing 1,800
Closing 375	Balance 375		

Salon Fees		Depreciation Expense, Equipment	
Closing 3,300	3,300	450	Closing 450

(20 min) **LO3** ▶

5A-5.   From the following accounts (not in order), prepare a post-closing trial balance for Wurley Co. on March 31, 201X. *Note:* These balances are *before* closing.

Accounts Receivable	$24,700	P. Wurley, Capital	$25,320
Legal Supplies	10,400	P. Wurley, Withdrawals	1,000
Office Equipment	34,000	Legal Fees Earned	21,000
Repair Expense	1,740	Accounts Payable	47,000
Salaries Expense	1,480	Cash	20,000

Set B

(15 min) **LO1** ▶

5B-1.   From the adjustments section of a worksheet presented in Figure 5.22, prepare adjusting journal entries for the end of October.

FIGURE 5.22
Adjustments on Worksheet

	Adjustments	
	Dr.	Cr.
Prepaid Rent		(A) 1 2 0 0 00
Office Supplies		(B) 4 0 0 00
Accumulated Depreciation, Equipment		(C) 2 0 0 00
Salaries Payable		(D) 2 0 0 0 00
Rent Expense	(A) 1 2 0 0 00	
Office Supplies Expense	(B) 4 0 0 00	
Depreciation Expense, Equipment	(C) 2 0 0 00	
Salaries Expense	(D) 2 0 0 0 00	
Totals	3 8 0 0 00	3 8 0 0 00

5B-2. Complete the following table by placing an X in the correct column.  **LO1,2** *(10 min)*

	Temporary	Permanent	Will Be Closed
Ex. Accounts Receivable		X	
1. Income Summary			
2. Jen Rich, Capital			
3. Salary Expense			
4. Jen Rich, Withdrawals			
5. Fees Earned			
6. Accounts Payable			
7. Cash			

5B-3. From the following T accounts, journalize the four closing entries on July 31, 201X. **LO2** *(15 min)*

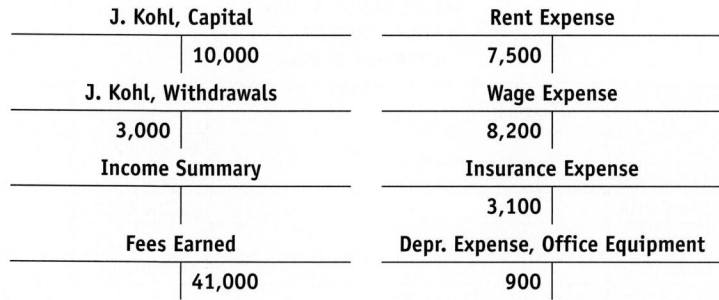

J. Kohl, Capital	
	10,000

J. Kohl, Withdrawals	
3,000	

Income Summary	

Fees Earned	
	41,000

Rent Expense	
7,500	

Wage Expense	
8,200	

Insurance Expense	
3,100	

Depr. Expense, Office Equipment	
900	

5B-4. From the following posted T accounts, reconstruct the closing journal entries for March 31, 201X. **LO2** *(20 min)*

M. Faulks, Capital	
Withdrawals 1,700	8,000 (Mar. 1)
	4,200 Net Income

M. Faulks, Withdrawals	
1,700	Closing 1,700

Income Summary	
Expenses 1,100	Revenue 5,300
Closing 4,200	Balance 4,200

Salon Fees	
Closing 5,300	5,300

Insurance Expense	
300	Closing 300

Wage Expense	
100	Closing 100

Rent Expense	
200	Closing 200

Depreciation Expense, Equipment	
500	Closing 500

(20 min)   **LO3** ➤   **5B-5.**   From the following accounts (not in order), prepare a post-closing trial balance for Washington Company on December 31, 201X. *Note:* These balances are *before* closing.

Accounts Receivable	$25,525	P. Washington, Capital	$74,785
Legal Supplies	8,200	P. Washington, Withdrawals	4,000
Office Equipment	66,000	Legal Fees Earned	21,000
Repair Expense	3,050	Accounts Payable	38,000
Salaries Expense	1,010	Cash	26,000

MyAccountingLab

Problems

Set A

(40 min)   **LO1,2** ➤   **5A-1.**   Consider the data in Figure 5.23 for Drew's Dance Studio:

FIGURE 5.23
Trial Balance for Drew's Dance Studio

DREW'S DANCE STUDIO TRIAL BALANCE NOVEMBER 30, 201X		
Account Titles	Dr.	Cr.
Cash	50 0 0 0 00	
Accounts Receivable	11 0 0 0 00	
Prepaid Insurance	1 2 0 0 00	
Dance Supplies	1 5 0 0 00	
Dance Equipment	14 0 0 0 00	
Accumulated Depreciation, Dance Equipment		8 0 0 0 00
Accounts Payable		14 0 0 0 00
D. Desmond, Capital		34 5 0 0 00
D. Desmond, Withdrawals	2 0 0 0 00	
Dance Fees Earned		23 8 0 0 00
Salaries Expense	1 3 0 0 00	
Telephone Expense	4 0 0 00	
Advertising Expense	7 0 0 00	
Totals	80 3 0 0 00	80 3 0 0 00

Check Figure:
Net Income $18,100

Adjustment Data

a. Insurance expired, $400.
b. Dance supplies on hand, $800.
c. Depreciation on dance equipment, $1,500.
d. Salaries earned by employees but not to be paid until December, $700.

Your task is to do the following:

1. Prepare a worksheet.
2. Journalize adjusting and closing entries.

5A-2. Enter the beginning balance in each account in your working papers from the Trial Balance columns of the worksheet (Figure 5.24 on page 180). From that worksheet, (1) journalize and post adjusting and closing entries and (2) prepare from the ledger a post-closing trial balance for the month of December.

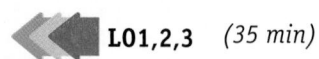

LO1,2,3 *(35 min)*

Check Figure:
Post-Closing Trial Balance $4,576

5A-3. As the bookkeeper of Pat's Plowing, you have been asked to complete the entire accounting cycle for Pat from the following information.

LO1,2,3 *(150 min)*

S50 / QB

201X

Jan.	1	Pat invested $16,000 cash and $10,200 worth of snow equipment into the plowing company.
	1	Paid rent 6 months in advance for garage space, $2,400.
	4	Purchased office equipment from Lang Corp. for $12,000 on account.
	6	Purchased snow supplies for $300 cash.
	8	Collected $8,000 from plowing local shopping centers.
	12	Pat Munro withdrew $8,000 from the business for personal use.
	20	Plowed Hayfield parking lots, payment not to be received until March, $5,000.
	26	Paid salaries to employees, $2,200.
	28	Paid Lang Corp. one-half amount owed for office equipment.
	29	Advertising bill received from Taft Co. but will not be paid until March, $800.
	30	Paid telephone bill, $140.

Use the following chart of accounts.

Chart of Accounts

Assets	Owner's Equity
111 Cash	311 P. Munro, Capital
112 Accounts Receivable	312 P. Munro, Withdrawals
114 Prepaid Rent	313 Income Summary
115 Snow Supplies	**Revenue**
121 Office Equipment	411 Plowing Fees
122 Accumulated Depreciation, Office Equipment	**Expenses**
123 Snow Equipment	511 Salaries Expense
124 Accumulated Depreciation, Snow Equipment	512 Advertising Expense
Liabilities	513 Telephone Expense
211 Accounts Payable	514 Rent Expense
212 Salaries Payable	515 Snow Supplies Expense
	516 Depreciation Expense, Office Equipment
	517 Depreciation Expense, Snow Equipment

FIGURE 5.24 Worksheet for Parkhouse's Cleaning Service

PARKHOUSE'S CLEANING SERVICE
WORKSHEET
FOR MONTH ENDED DECEMBER 31, 201X

Account Titles	Trial Balance Dr.	Trial Balance Cr.	Adjustments Dr.	Adjustments Cr.	Adjusted Trial Balance Dr.	Adjusted Trial Balance Cr.	Income Statement Dr.	Income Statement Cr.	Balance Sheet Dr.	Balance Sheet Cr.
Cash	400 00				400 00				400 00	
Prepaid Insurance	1450 00			(A) 390 00	1060 00				1060 00	
Cleaning Supplies	466 00			(B) 390 00	76 00				76 00	
Auto	3040 00				3040 00				3040 00	
Accum. Depr., Auto		540 00		(C) 450 00		990 00				990 00
Accounts Payable		590 00				590 00				590 00
B. Parkhouse, Capital		181 00				181 00				181 00
B. Parkhouse, Withdrawals	1150 00				1150 00				1150 00	
Cleaning Fees		6900 00				6900 00		6900 00		
Salaries Expense	1050 00		(D) 360 00		1410 00		1410 00			
Telephone Expense	235 00				235 00		235 00			
Advertising Expense	260 00				260 00		260 00			
Gas Expense	160 00				160 00		160 00			
Totals	8211 00	8211 00								
Insurance Expense			(A) 390 00		390 00		390 00			
Cleaning Supplies Expense			(B) 390 00		390 00		390 00			
Depr. Expense, Auto			(C) 450 00		450 00		450 00			
Salaries Payable				(D) 360 00		360 00				360 00
Totals			1590 00	1590 00	9021 00	9021 00	3295 00	6900 00	5726 00	2121 00
Net Income							3605 00			3605 00
Totals							6900 00	6900 00	5726 00	5726 00

Adjustment Data

a. Snow supplies on hand, $100.
b. Rent expired, $400.
c. Depreciation on office equipment, $200:
   ($12,000/5 yr. = $2,400/12 mo. = $200).
d. Depreciation on snow equipment, $170:
   ($10,200/5 yr. = $2,040/12 mo. = $170).
e. Accrued salaries, $150.

Check Figure:
Net Income $8,740

Set B

5B-1.   Consider the data in Figure 5.25 for Deb's Dance Studio:

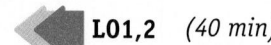 **L01,2**   *(40 min)*

FIGURE 5.25
Trial Balance for Deb's Dance Studio

Account Titles	Dr.	Cr.
DEB'S DANCE STUDIO **TRIAL BALANCE** **APRIL 30, 201X**		
Cash	62 0 0 0 00	
Accounts Receivable	3 0 0 0 00	
Prepaid Insurance	7 0 0 00	
Dance Supplies	2 0 0 0 00	
Dance Equipment	19 0 0 0 00	
Accumulated Depreciation, Dance Equipment		5 7 0 0 00
Accounts Payable		20 0 0 0 00
D. Draper, Capital		46 1 0 0 00
D. Draper, Withdrawals	7 0 0 00	
Dance Fees Earned		18 7 0 0 00
Salaries Expense	1 6 0 0 00	
Telephone Expense	1 1 0 0 00	
Advertising Expense	4 0 0 00	
Totals	90 5 0 0 00	90 5 0 0 00

Check Figure:
Net Income $11,700

Adjustment Data

a. Insurance expired, $500.
b. Dance supplies on hand, $400.
c. Depreciation on dance equipment, $1,200.
d. Salaries earned by employees but not due to be paid until May, $600.

Your task is to do the following:

1. Prepare a worksheet.
2. Journalize adjusting and closing entries.

5B-2.   Enter the beginning balance in each account in your working papers from the Trial Balance columns of the worksheet (Figure 5.26 on page 182). From the worksheet, (1) journalize and post adjusting and closing entries and (2) prepare from the ledger a post-closing trial balance at the end of July.

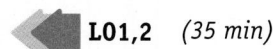 **L01,2**   *(35 min)*

Check Figure:
Post-Closing Trial Balance $4,672

FIGURE 5.26 Worksheet for Potter's Cleaning Service

POTTER'S CLEANING SERVICE
WORKSHEET
FOR MONTH ENDED JULY 31, 201X

Account Titles	Trial Balance Dr.	Trial Balance Cr.	Adjustments Dr.	Adjustments Cr.	Adjusted Trial Balance Dr.	Adjusted Trial Balance Cr.	Income Statement Dr.	Income Statement Cr.	Balance Sheet Dr.	Balance Sheet Cr.
Cash	1 3 0 0 00				1 3 0 0 00				1 3 0 0 00	
Prepaid Insurance	6 1 0 00			(A) 2 1 0 00	4 0 0 00				4 0 0 00	
Cleaning Supplies	1 7 6 00			(B) 4 4 00	1 3 2 00				1 3 2 00	
Auto	2 8 4 0 00				2 8 4 0 00				2 8 4 0 00	
Accumulated Depreciation, Auto		6 1 0 00		(C) 4 5 0 00		1 0 6 0 00				1 0 6 0 00
Accounts Payable		3 8 4 00				3 8 4 00				3 8 4 00
B. Potter, Capital		7 5 8 00				7 5 8 00				7 5 8 00
B. Potter, Withdrawals	5 5 0 00				5 5 0 00				5 5 0 00	
Cleaning Fees		5 2 9 0 00				5 2 9 0 00		5 2 9 0 00		
Salaries Expense	1 0 5 0 00		(D) 1 9 0 00		1 2 4 0 00		1 2 4 0 00			
Telephone Expense	1 1 0 00				1 1 0 00		1 1 0 00			
Advertising Expense	1 9 6 00				1 9 6 00		1 9 6 00			
Gas Expense	2 1 0 00				2 1 0 00		2 1 0 00			
Totals	7 0 4 2 00	7 0 4 2 00								
Insurance Expense			(A) 2 1 0 00		2 1 0 00		2 1 0 00			
Cleaning Supplies Expense			(B) 4 4 00		4 4 00		4 4 00			
Depreciation Expense, Auto			(C) 4 5 0 00		4 5 0 00		4 5 0 00			
Salaries Payable				(D) 1 9 0 00		1 9 0 00				1 9 0 00
Totals			8 9 4 00	8 9 4 00	7 6 8 2 00	7 6 8 2 00	2 4 6 0 00	5 2 9 0 00	5 2 2 2 00	2 3 9 2 00
Net Income							2 8 3 0 00			2 8 3 0 00
Totals							5 2 9 0 00	5 2 9 0 00	5 2 2 2 00	5 2 2 2 00

5B-3. As the bookkeeper of Palmer's Plowing, you have been asked to complete the entire accounting cycle for Palmer from the following information.

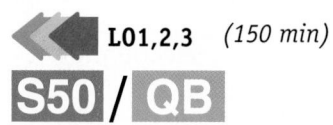

L01,2,3 (150 min)

201X

Jan.	1	Palmer invested $9,000 cash and $9,000 worth of snow equipment into the plowing company.
	1	Paid 5 months' rent in advance for garage space, $4,000.
	4	Purchased office equipment from Lewis Corp. for $9,600 on account.
	6	Purchased snow supplies for $600 cash.
	8	Collected $11,000 from plowing local shopping centers.
	12	Palmer Mao withdrew $8,000 from the business for personal use.
	20	Plowed Riverton Co. parking lots, payment not to be received until March, $8,000.
	26	Paid salaries to employees, $2,100.
	28	Paid Lewis Corp. one-half amount owed for office equipment.
	29	Advertising bill received from Taft Co. but will not be paid until March, $300.
	30	Paid telephone bill, $180.

Check Figure:
Net Income $14,470

Use the following chart of accounts.

Chart of Accounts

Assets	Owner's Equity
111 Cash	311 P. Mao, Capital
112 Accounts Receivable	312 P. Mao, Withdrawals
114 Prepaid Rent	313 Income Summary
115 Snow Supplies	**Revenue**
121 Office Equipment	411 Plowing Fees
122 Accumulated Depreciation, Office Equipment	**Expenses**
123 Snow Equipment	511 Salaries Expense
124 Accumulated Depreciation, Snow Equipment	512 Advertising Expense
Liabilities	513 Telephone Expense
211 Accounts Payable	514 Rent Expense
212 Salaries Payable	515 Snow Supplies Expense
	516 Depreciation Expense, Office Equipment
	517 Depreciation Expense, Snow Equipment

Adjustment Data

a. Snow supplies on hand, $100.
b. Rent expired, $800.
c. Depreciation on office equipment, $160:
   ($9,600/5 yr = $1,920/12 mo. = $160).
d. Depreciation on snow equipment, $150:
   ($9,000/5 yr = $1,800/12 mo. = $150).
e. Accrued salaries, $340.

Financial Report Problem

L03 (15 min)

Reading the Kellogg's Annual Report

Go to http://investor.kelloggs.com/investor-relations/annual-reports/ to access the Kellogg's 2013 Annual Report and find out what the fiscal year is for Kellogg's Company.

ON THE JOB SMITH COMPUTER CENTER

(60 min)   **LO1,2,3**

Thad decided to end the Smith Computer Center's first year as of September 30, 201X. Following is an updated chart of accounts.

Assets	Revenue
1000 Cash	4000 Service Revenue
1020 Accounts Receivable	**Expenses**
1025 Prepaid Rent	5010 Advertising Expense
1030 Supplies	5020 Rent Expense
1080 Computer Shop Equip.	5030 Utilities Expense
1081 Accum. Depr., C.S. Equip.	5040 Phone Expense
1090 Office Equipment	5050 Supplies Expense
1091 Accum. Depr., Office Equip.	5060 Insurance Expense
Liabilities	5070 Postage Expense
2000 Accounts Payable	5080 Depr. Exp., C.S. Equip.
Owner's Equity	5090 Depr. Exp., Office Equip.
3000 T. Feldman, Capital	
3010 T. Feldman, Withdrawals	
3020 Income Summary	

Assignment

1. Journalize the adjusting entries from Chapter 4.

2. Post the adjusting entries to the ledger.

3. Journalize the closing entries.

4. Post the closing entries to the ledger.

5. Prepare a post-closing trial balance.

Mini Practice Set

Sousa Realty

Est. Time: 5 hours

Reviewing the Accounting Cycle Twice

This comprehensive review problem requires you to complete the accounting cycle for Sousa Realty twice. This practice set allows you to review Chapters 1–5 while reinforcing the relationships between all parts of the accounting cycle. By completing two cycles, you will see how the ending September balances in the ledger are used to accumulate data in October.

First, look at the chart of accounts for Sousa Realty.

Sousa Realty
Chart of Accounts

Assets	**Revenue**
111 Cash	411 Commissions Earned
112 Accounts Receivable	**Expenses**
114 Prepaid Rent	511 Rent Expense
115 Office Supplies	512 Salaries Expense
121 Office Equipment	513 Gas Expense
122 Accumulated Depreciation, Office Equipment	514 Repairs Expense
123 Automobile	515 Telephone Expense
124 Accumulated Depreciation, Automobile	516 Advertising Expense
Liabilities	517 Office Supplies Expense
211 Accounts Payable	518 Depreciation Expense, Office Equipment
212 Salaries Payable	519 Depreciation Expense, Automobile
Owner's Equity	524 Miscellaneous Expense
311 James Sousa, Capital	
312 James Sousa, Withdrawals	
313 Income Summary	

On September 1, 201X, James Sousa opened a real estate office called Sousa Realty. The following transactions were completed for the month of September:

201X

September 1 James Sousa invested $12,000 cash in the real estate agency along with $5,000 of office equipment.

Sept.   1   Rented and paid 5 months' rent in advance to Murray Property Management, $1,000.

SOUSA REALTY (213) 478-3584   0001

8200 SUNSET BOULEVARD
LOS ANGELES, CA 90028   *September 1   201X*

PAY TO THE
ORDER OF   *Murray Property Mgmt Co.* $ *1,000 $\frac{XX}{100}$*

~~~ *One Thousand and $\frac{XX}{100}$* ~~~~~~~ DOLLARS

BAY BANK
Box 1739 Terminal Annex
Los Angeles, CA 90052

MEMO   *Rent Sept.-Jan. 201X*   *James Sousa*

Sept.   1   Bought an automobile on account from Hyundai North, $19,000.

Hyundai North   1 Salem St.
Los Angeles, CA 90052
(213) 639-1917

INVOICE

INVOICE NO. 1113
DATE: September 1/1X
TERMS: Net 90

To: SOUSA REALTY
8200 Sunset Blvd.
Los Angeles, CA 90028

QUANTITY		DESCRIPTION	UNIT PRICE	AMOUNT
1	ONLY	4-Door Automatic	$19,000.00	$19,000.00

Make all checks payable to Hyundai North	SUBTOTAL	19,000.00
	FREIGHT	
	TAX	
	TOTAL DUE	$19,000.00

THANK YOU FOR YOUR BUSINESS!

Sept.   4   Purchased office supplies from Paper Company, for cash, $600.

Paper Company

INVOICE

1 Ferncroft Rd.
Los Angeles, CA 90052
Phone (213) 631-0288

DATE: September 4/1X
NUMBER: D198795
TERMS: Cash

SOLD TO:
Sousa Realty
8200 Sunset Blvd.
Los Angeles, CA 90028

SHIPPED TO:
Sousa Realty
8200 Sunset Blvd.
Los Angeles, CA 90028

DATE	DESCRIPTION	UNIT PRICE	AMOUNT
Sept. 4/1X	Office supplies PAYMENT RECEIVED - - CHK #0002 - THANK YOU		$600.00
		Subtotal	600.00
		Total	$600.00

Business Number: 115555559

PLEASE PAY THE ABOVE

THANK YOU FOR YOUR BUSINESS

SOUSA REALTY (213) 478-3584   0002

8200 SUNSET BOULEVARD
LOS ANGELES, CA 90028   *September 4*   *201X*

PAY TO THE
ORDER OF *Paper Company* $ *600* $\frac{XX}{100}$

Six Hundred and $\frac{XX}{100}$ ———————————— DOLLARS

BAY BANK
Box 1739 Terminal Annex
Los Angeles, CA 90052

MEMO *Office supplies*   *James Sousa*

Sept.   5   Purchased additional office supplies from Paper Company, on account, $250.

Paper Company   INVOICE

1 Ferncroft Rd.   DATE: Sept. 5/1X
Los Angeles, CA 90052   NUMBER: D198825
Phone (213) 631-0288   TERMS: net 60

SOLD TO:	SHIPPED TO:
Sousa Realty 8200 Sunset Blvd. Los Angeles, CA 90028	Sousa Realty 8200 Sunset Blvd. Los Angeles, CA 90028

DATE	DESCRIPTION	UNIT PRICE	AMOUNT
Sept. 5/1X	Office supplies		$250.00
		Subtotal	250.00
		Total	$250.00

Business Number: 115555559

THANK YOU FOR YOUR BUSINESS

PLEASE PAY
THE ABOVE

Sept.   6   Sold a house to Brendan Hue and collected a $11,000 commission.

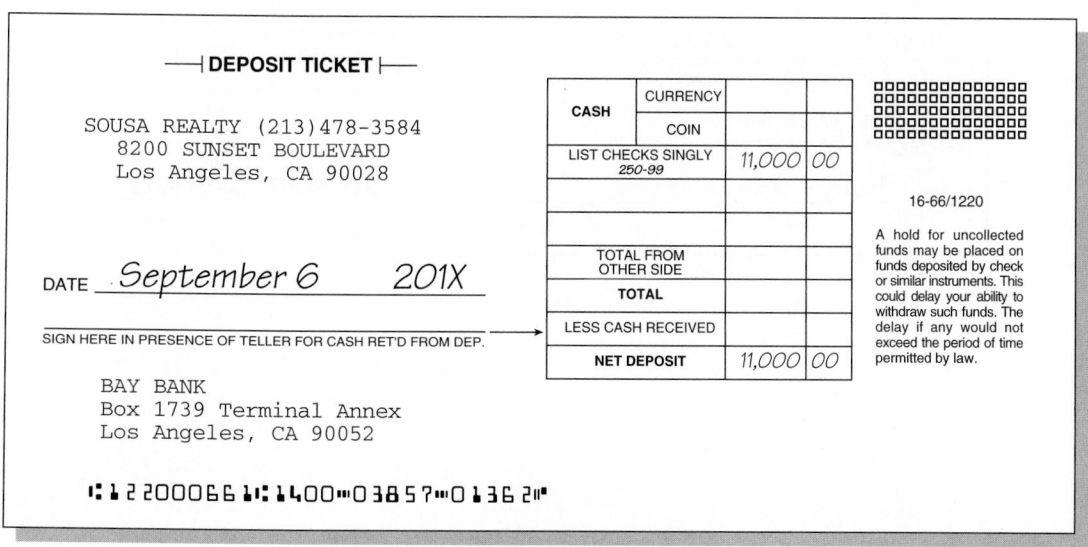

—| DEPOSIT TICKET |—

SOUSA REALTY (213)478-3584
8200 SUNSET BOULEVARD
Los Angeles, CA 90028

DATE *September 6*   *201X*

SIGN HERE IN PRESENCE OF TELLER FOR CASH RET'D FROM DEP.

BAY BANK
Box 1739 Terminal Annex
Los Angeles, CA 90052

CASH	CURRENCY		
	COIN		
LIST CHECKS SINGLY 250-99		11,000	00
TOTAL FROM OTHER SIDE			
TOTAL			
LESS CASH RECEIVED			
NET DEPOSIT		11,000	00

16-66/1220

A hold for uncollected
funds may be placed on
funds deposited by check
or similar instruments. This
could delay your ability to
withdraw such funds. The
delay if any would not
exceed the period of time
permitted by law.

⑈⑈2 2000 66 ⑈⑈: ⑈400 ⑈ 0 3 85 7 ⑈ 0 ⑈36 2 ⑈

SOUSA REALTY					
COMMISSION REPORT				*Date:*	September 6, 201X
Name:	Brendan Hue				
Date:	*Sales Description*	*Sales No.*	*Commission Amount*		
Sept. 6/1X	*Home at 66 Sullivan St.*	*A1001*	*$11,000.00*	*Paid in full.*	
C001			*Remarks:*		

Sept.   8   Paid gas bill to Haffner Gas Co., $45.

SOUSA REALTY (213) 478-3584   0003

8200 SUNSET BOULEVARD
LOS ANGELES, CA 90028   *September 8   201X*

PAY TO THE
ORDER OF   *Haffner Gas Co.* $ *45 XX/100*

Forty-Five and XX/100 ———————————— DOLLARS

BAY BANK
Box 1739 Terminal Annex
Los Angeles, CA 90052

MEMO   *Gas Bill – Sept. 6*   *James Sousa*

Sept.   15   Paid Rosie Petrillo, office secretary, $300.

SOUSA REALTY (213) 478-3584   0004

8200 SUNSET BOULEVARD
LOS ANGELES, CA 90028   *September 15   201X*

PAY TO THE
ORDER OF   *Rosie Petrillo* $ *300 XX/100*

Three Hundred and XX/100 ———————————— DOLLARS

BAY BANK
Box 1739 Terminal Annex
Los Angeles, CA 90052

MEMO   *Salary – Sept. 1–15*   *James Sousa*

Sept.   17   Sold a building lot to Tropic Developers and earned a commission, $10,000; payment to be received on October 8.

SOUSA REALTY				
COMMISSION REPORT			**Date:** September 17, 201X	
Name: Tropic Developers				
Date:	**Sales Description**	**Sales No.**	**Commission Amount**	
Sept. 17/1X	Lot at 8 Ridge Rd.	A1002	$10,000.00	
C002		**Remarks:** Payment due October 8, 201X		

Sept.   20   James Sousa withdrew $4,000 from the business to pay personal expenses.

SOUSA REALTY (213) 478-3584   0005

8200 SUNSET BOULEVARD
LOS ANGELES, CA 90028   *September 20   201X*

PAY TO THE ORDER OF   *James Sousa* $ *4,000 XX/100*

Four Thousand and XX/100 ———————— DOLLARS

BAY BANK
Box 1739 Terminal Annex
Los Angeles, CA 90052

MEMO *Withdrawal*   *James Sousa*

Sept.   21   Sold a house to Suzanne Horngam and collected a $7,000 commission.

┤ **DEPOSIT TICKET** ├

SOUSA REALTY (213)478-3584
8200 SUNSET BOULEVARD
Los Angeles, CA 90028

CASH	CURRENCY		
	COIN		
LIST CHECKS SINGLY 270-88		7,000	00
TOTAL FROM OTHER SIDE			
TOTAL			
LESS CASH RECEIVED			
NET DEPOSIT		7,000	00

DATE *September 21   201X*

SIGN HERE IN PRESENCE OF TELLER FOR CASH RET'D FROM DEP.

BAY BANK
Box 1739 Terminal Annex
Los Angeles, CA 90052

16-66/1220

A hold for uncollected funds may be placed on funds deposited by check or similar instruments. This could delay your ability to withdraw such funds. The delay if any would not exceed the period of time permitted by law.

⑆122000066⑈1400⑉03857⑉0136 2⑈

SOUSA REALTY COMMISSION REPORT				_Date:_ September 21, 201X	
Name:	Suzanne Horngam				
Date:	_Sales Description_	_Sales No._	_Commission Amount_		
Sept. 21/1X	_Home at 666 Jersey St._	_A1003_	_$7,000.00_	_Paid in full._	
C003			_Remarks:_		

Sept. 22   Paid gas bill, $80, to Haffner Gas Co.

SOUSA REALTY (213) 478-3584	0006
8200 SUNSET BOULEVARD LOS ANGELES, CA 90028	_September 22 201X_

PAY TO THE ORDER OF _Haffner Gas Co._ _____ $ ☐ _80 XX/100_

Eighty and XX/100 ～～～～～～～～～～ ____ DOLLARS

BAY BANK
Box 1739 Terminal Annex
Los Angeles, CA 90052

MEMO _Gas Bill—Sept. 22_ ____   _James Sousa_

Sept. 24   Paid Hyundai North $800 to repair automobile.

Hyundai North

1 Salem St.
Los Angeles, CA 90052
(213) 639-1917

INVOICE

INVOICE NO. 1184

DATE: September 24/1X

TERMS: Cash

To: SOUSA REALTY
8200 Sunset Blvd.
Los Angeles, CA 90028

Ship To: Pickup

QUANTITY	DESCRIPTION		UNIT PRICE	AMOUNT
1	ONLY	Air conditioning repair		$ 800.00

Make all checks payable to Hyundai North

PAYMENT RECEIVED - Check #0007

SUBTOTAL	800.00
FREIGHT	
TAX	
TOTAL DUE	$ 800.00

THANK YOU FOR YOUR BUSINESS!

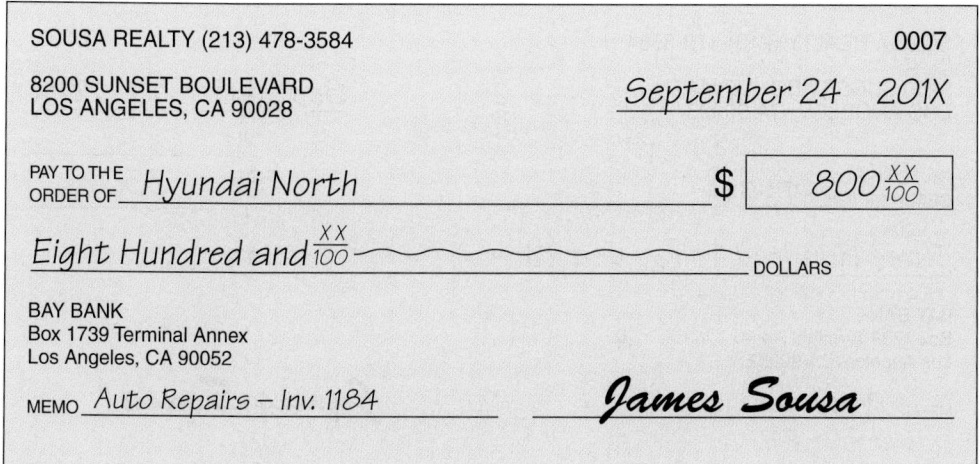

SOUSA REALTY (213) 478-3584   0007

8200 SUNSET BOULEVARD
LOS ANGELES, CA 90028   *September 24   201X*

PAY TO THE
ORDER OF *Hyundai North* $ *800 XX/100*

Eight Hundred and XX/100 ———————————— DOLLARS

BAY BANK
Box 1739 Terminal Annex
Los Angeles, CA 90052

MEMO *Auto Repairs – Inv. 1184*   *James Sousa*

Sept.   30   Paid Rosie Petrillo, office secretary, $300.

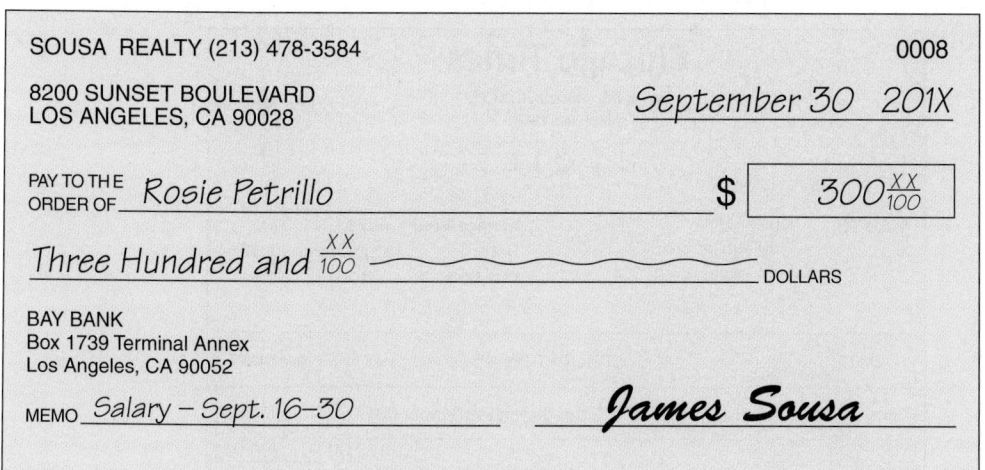

SOUSA REALTY (213) 478-3584   0008

8200 SUNSET BOULEVARD
LOS ANGELES, CA 90028   *September 30   201X*

PAY TO THE
ORDER OF *Rosie Petrillo* $ *300 XX/100*

Three Hundred and XX/100 ———————————— DOLLARS

BAY BANK
Box 1739 Terminal Annex
Los Angeles, CA 90052

MEMO *Salary – Sept. 16–30*   *James Sousa*

Sept.   30   Paid Comcast September telephone bill, $330.

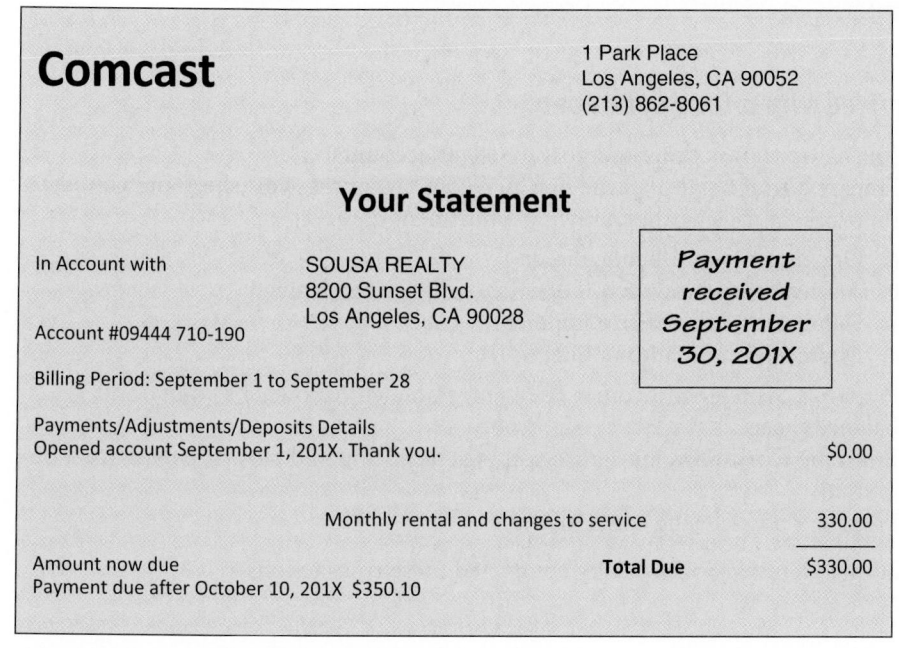

Comcast

1 Park Place
Los Angeles, CA 90052
(213) 862-8061

Your Statement

In Account with   SOUSA REALTY
                           8200 Sunset Blvd.   *Payment
                           Los Angeles, CA 90028   received
Account #09444 710-190   September
                                                       30, 201X*

Billing Period: September 1 to September 28

Payments/Adjustments/Deposits Details
Opened account September 1, 201X. Thank you. $0.00

                    Monthly rental and changes to service   330.00
                                                                      _____
Amount now due   **Total Due** $330.00
Payment due after October 10, 201X $350.10

```
SOUSA REALTY (213) 478-3584                                    0009

8200 SUNSET BOULEVARD                         September 30  201X
LOS ANGELES, CA 90028


PAY TO THE
ORDER OF  Comcast                              $        330 XX/100

Three Hundred Thirty and  XX/100 ~~~~~~~~~~~~~~~~~ DOLLARS

BAY BANK
Box 1739 Terminal Annex
Los Angeles, CA 90052

MEMO  September Phone Bill                      James Sousa
```

Sept. 30 Received advertising bill for September, $900, from *Chicago Times*. The bill is to be paid on October 2.

Chicago Times

1 Long Rd., Chicago, IL 60527
(630) 744-1000

I N V O I C E

SOLD TO:	Sousa Realty	Invoice No.:	4879
	8200 Sunset Blvd.	Date:	September 30, 201X
	Los Angeles, CA 90028	Due Date:	October 2, 201X

DATE	DESCRIPTION		AMOUNT
Sept. 26/1X	Advertising in Chicago Times during September 201X		$900.00
		SUBTOTAL	900.00
Business Number 944122338		TOTAL	$900.00

MAKE ALL CHECKS PAYABLE TO CHICAGO TIMES

Required Work for September

1. Journalize transactions and post to ledger accounts.
2. Prepare a trial balance in the first two columns of the worksheet and complete the worksheet using the following adjustment data:
   a. One month's rent had expired.
   b. An inventory shows $100 of office supplies remaining.
   c. Depreciation on office equipment, $160.
   d. Depreciation on automobile, $210.
3. Prepare a September income statement, statement of owner's equity, and balance sheet.
4. From the worksheet, journalize and post adjusting and closing entries (p. 3 of journal).
5. Prepare a post-closing trial balance.

During October, Sousa Realty completed these transactions:

Check Figure:
September Post-Closing Trial Balance
$57,445

Oct. 1 Purchased additional office supplies on account from Paper Co., $850.

Paper Company **INVOICE**

1 Ferncroft Rd.
Los Angeles, CA 90052
Phone (213) 631-0288

DATE: Oct. 1/1X
NUMBER: D1996035
TERMS: Net 60

SOLD TO:

Sousa Realty
8200 Sunset Blvd.
Los Angeles, CA 90028

SHIPPED TO:

Sousa Realty
8200 Sunset Blvd.
Los Angeles, CA 90028

DATE	DESCRIPTION	UNIT PRICE	AMOUNT
Oct. 1/1X	Office supplies		$850.00
		Subtotal	850.00
		Total	$850.00

Business Number: 115555559

THANK YOU FOR YOUR BUSINESS

PLEASE PAY
THE ABOVE

Oct. 2 Paid *Chicago Times* advertising bill for September, $900.

SOUSA REALTY (213) 478-3584 0010

8200 SUNSET BOULEVARD
LOS ANGELES, CA 90028

October 2 *201X*

PAY TO THE
ORDER OF *Chicago Times* $ 900 $\frac{XX}{100}$

Nine Hundred and $\frac{XX}{100}$ DOLLARS

BAY BANK
Box 1739 Terminal Annex
Los Angeles, CA 90052

MEMO *Invoice # 4879* *James Sousa*

⑆122000661⑆1400⑉03857⑉0136 2⑈0010

Oct. 3 Sold a house to Helen Baker and collected a commission of $7,300.

SOUSA REALTY					
COMMISSION REPORT			*Date:*	October 3, 201X	
Name:	Helen Baker				
Date:	*Sales Description*	*Sales No.*	*Commission Amount*		
Oct. 3/1X	Home at 800 Rose Ave.	A1004	$7,300.00	*Paid in full.*	
C004		*Remarks:*			

—| **DEPOSIT TICKET** |—

SOUSA REALTY (213)478-3584
8200 SUNSET BOULEVARD
Los Angeles, CA 90028

DATE _October 3   201X_

SIGN HERE IN PRESENCE OF TELLER FOR CASH RET'D FROM DEP.

BAY BANK
Box 1739 Terminal Annex
Los Angeles, CA 90052

⑆12200066⑆1⑈1400⑉03857⑉0136 2⑈

CASH	CURRENCY		
	COIN		
LIST CHECKS SINGLY 278-92	7,300	00	
TOTAL FROM OTHER SIDE			
TOTAL			
LESS CASH RECEIVED			
NET DEPOSIT	7,300	00	

16-66/1220

A hold for uncollected funds may be placed on funds deposited by check or similar instruments. This could delay your ability to withdraw such funds. The delay if any would not exceed the period of time permitted by law.

Oct.   6   Paid gas bill to Haffner Gas Co., $29.

SOUSA REALTY (213) 478-3584   0011

8200 SUNSET BOULEVARD   _October 6   201X_
LOS ANGELES, CA 90028

PAY TO THE
ORDER OF ___Haffner Gas Co._____ $ 29 $\frac{XX}{100}$

Twenty-nine and $\frac{XX}{100}$ _____ DOLLARS

BAY BANK
Box 1739 Terminal Annex
Los Angeles, CA 90052

MEMO ___Gas Bill – October 6___   ___James Sousa___

Oct.   8   Collected commission from Tropic Developers for sale of building lot on September 17, $10,000.

—| **DEPOSIT TICKET** |—

SOUSA REALTY (213)478-3584
8200 SUNSET BOULEVARD
Los Angeles, CA 90028

DATE _October 8   201X_

SIGN HERE IN PRESENCE OF TELLER FOR CASH RET'D FROM DEP.

BAY BANK
Box 1739 Terminal Annex
Los Angeles, CA 90052

⑆12200066⑆1⑈1400⑉03857⑉0136 2⑈

CASH	CURRENCY		
	COIN		
LIST CHECKS SINGLY 228-114	10,000	00	
TOTAL FROM OTHER SIDE			
TOTAL			
LESS CASH RECEIVED			
NET DEPOSIT	10,000	00	

16-66/1220

A hold for uncollected funds may be placed on funds deposited by check or similar instruments. This could delay your ability to withdraw such funds. The delay if any would not exceed the period of time permitted by law.

Oct.   12   Paid $530 to Long Realtors Assoc. to send employees to realtors' workshop.

SOUSA REALTY (213) 478-3584	0012

SOUSA REALTY (213) 478-3584   0012

8200 SUNSET BOULEVARD
LOS ANGELES, CA 90028   *October 12   201X*

PAY TO THE
ORDER OF   *Long Realtors Assoc.* $ *530 XX/100*

Five Hundred Thirty and XX/100 ~~~~~~~~~~~~~~~~ DOLLARS

BAY BANK
Box 1739 Terminal Annex
Los Angeles, CA 90052

MEMO *Workshop Registration*   *James Sousa*

Oct.   15   Paid Rosie Petrillo, office secretary, $300.

SOUSA REALTY (213) 478-3584   0013

8200 SUNSET BOULEVARD
LOS ANGELES, CA 90028   *October 15   201X*

PAY TO THE
ORDER OF   *Rosie Petrillo* $ *300 XX/100*

Three Hundred and XX/100 ~~~~~~~~~~~~~~~~ DOLLARS

BAY BANK
Box 1739 Terminal Annex
Los Angeles, CA 90052

MEMO *Salary October 1–15*   *James Sousa*

Oct.   17   Sold a house to Gary Schneider and earned a commission of $2,900. Commission to be received on November 10.

SOUSA REALTY COMMISSION REPORT				**Date:** October 17, 201X	
Name:	Gary Schneider				
Date:	**Sales Description**	**Sales No.**	**Commission Amount**		
Oct. 17/1X	Home at RR2, Site 3	A1010	$2,900.00		
C005		**Remarks:** Payment due November 10, 201X			

Oct.   18   Sold a building lot to Lombardi Builders and collected a commission of $4,500.

⊣ DEPOSIT TICKET ⊢

SOUSA REALTY (213)478-3584
8200 SUNSET BOULEVARD
Los Angeles, CA 90028

DATE _____ October 18 _____ 201X _____

SIGN HERE IN PRESENCE OF TELLER FOR CASH RET'D FROM DEP.

BAY BANK
Box 1739 Terminal Annex
Los Angeles, CA 90052

⑃122000661⑃1400″03857″0136 2″

CASH	CURRENCY		
	COIN		
LIST CHECKS SINGLY 269-10		4,500	00
TOTAL FROM OTHER SIDE			
TOTAL			
LESS CASH RECEIVED			
NET DEPOSIT		4,500	00

16-66/1220

A hold for uncollected funds may be placed on funds deposited by check or similar instruments. This could delay your ability to withdraw such funds. The delay if any would not exceed the period of time permitted by law.

SOUSA REALTY COMMISSION REPORT				*Date:*	October 18, 201X
Name: Lombardi Builders					
Date:	*Sales Description*	*Sales No.*	*Commission Amount*		
Oct. 18/1X	Building lot at 5004 King St. E	A1005	$4,500.00	Paid in full.	
C006		*Remarks:*			

Oct.   22   Sent a check to Heritage Charities for $65 to help sponsor a local road race to aid the poor. (This amount is not to be considered an advertising expense; it is a business expense and is posted to Miscellaneous Expense.)

SOUSA REALTY (213) 478-3584   0014

8200 SUNSET BOULEVARD
LOS ANGELES, CA 90028   *October 22   201X*

PAY TO THE
ORDER OF *Heritage Charities* $ 65 $\frac{XX}{100}$

Sixty-Five and $\frac{XX}{100}$ _____ DOLLARS

BAY BANK
Box 1739 Terminal Annex
Los Angeles, CA 90052

MEMO *Aid to Poor*   *James Sousa*

⑃122000661⑃1400″03857″0136 2″0014

Oct.   24   Paid Hyundai North $620 for repairs to automobile due to accident.

Hyundai North	1 Salem St. Los Angeles, CA 90052 (213) 639-1917	**INVOICE**

INVOICE NO. 2119

DATE: October 24/1X

TERMS: Cash

To: SOUSA REALTY
       8200 Sunset Blvd.
       Los Angeles, CA 90028

QUANTITY	DESCRIPTION	UNIT PRICE	AMOUNT
	Accident Repairs		$ 620.00

Make all checks payable to Hyundai North	SUBTOTAL	620.00
PAYMENT RECEIVED - Check #0015	FREIGHT	
	TAX	
	TOTAL DUE	$ 620.00

SOUSA REALTY (213) 478-3584		0015

8200 SUNSET BOULEVARD
LOS ANGELES, CA 90028

October 24   201X

PAY TO THE ORDER OF *Hyundai North* $ 620 $\frac{XX}{100}$

Six Hundred Twenty and $\frac{XX}{100}$ —————————— DOLLARS

BAY BANK
Box 1739 Terminal Annex
Los Angeles, CA 90052

MEMO *Auto Repairs – Inv. 2119*   *James Sousa*

Oct.   28   James Sousa withdrew $2,200 from the business to pay personal expenses.

SOUSA REALTY (213) 478-3584		0016

8200 SUNSET BOULEVARD
LOS ANGELES, CA 90028

October 28   201X

PAY TO THE ORDER OF *James Sousa* $ 2,200 $\frac{XX}{100}$

Two Thousand Two Hundred and $\frac{XX}{100}$ —————— DOLLARS

BAY BANK
Box 1739 Terminal Annex
Los Angeles, CA 90052

MEMO *Withdrawal*   *James Sousa*

Oct.   30   Paid Rosie Petrillo, office secretary, $300.

SOUSA REALTY (213) 478-3584		0017
8200 SUNSET BOULEVARD LOS ANGELES, CA 90028		*October 30 201X*
PAY TO THE ORDER OF *Rosie Petrillo*	$	*300 XX/100*
Three Hundred and XX/100		DOLLARS
BAY BANK Box 1739 Terminal Annex Los Angeles, CA 90052		
MEMO *Salary – October 16–31*		*James Sousa*

Oct.   30   Paid Comcast telephone bill, $480.

Comcast

1 Park Place
Los Angeles, CA 90052
(213) 862-8061

Your Statement

In Account with

SOUSA REALTY
8200 Sunset Blvd.
Los Angeles, CA 90028

Payment received October 30, 201X

Account #09444 710-190

Billing Period: October 1 to October 28

Payments/Adjustments/Deposits Details		$330.00
Payment Received October 2. Thank you.		−$330.00
	Monthly rental and changes to service	$480.00
Amount now due	**Total Due**	$480.00

Payment due after November 10, 201X $519.15

SOUSA REALTY (213) 478-3584		0018
8200 SUNSET BOULEVARD LOS ANGELES, CA 90028		*October 30 201X*
PAY TO THE ORDER OF *Comcast*	$	*480 XX/100*
Four Hundred Eighty and XX/100		DOLLARS
BAY BANK Box 1739 Terminal Annex Los Angeles, CA 90052		
MEMO *October Phone Bill*		*James Sousa*

Oct. 30 Advertising bill from *Chicago Times* for October, $1,300. The bill is to be paid on November 2.

Chicago Times
1 Long Rd. Chicago, IL 60527
(630) 744-1000
I N V O I C E

SOLD TO: Sousa Realty
8200 Sunset Blvd.
Los Angeles, CA 90028

Invoice No.: 5400
Date: October 30, 201X
Due Date: November 2, 201X

DATE	DESCRIPTION		AMOUNT
Oct. 30/1X	Advertising in Chicago Times during October 201X		$1,300.00
		SUBTOTAL	1,300.00
Business Number 944122338		TOTAL	$1,300.00

MAKE ALL CHECKS PAYABLE TO CHICAGO TIMES

Required Work for October

1. Journalize transactions in a general journal (p. 4) and post to ledger accounts.
2. Prepare a trial balance in the first two columns of a blank, fold-out worksheet located at the end of your textbook and complete the worksheet using the following adjustment data:

   a. One month's rent had expired. Paid 5 months' rent in advance on September 1, $1,000
   b. An inventory shows $130 of office supplies remaining.
   c. Depreciation on office equipment, $160.
   d. Depreciation on automobile, $210.

3. Prepare an October income statement, statement of owner's equity, and balance sheet.
4. From the worksheet, journalize and post adjusting and closing entries (p. 6 of journal).
5. Prepare a post-closing trial balance.

Check Figure:
Post-Closing Trial Balance end of October $66,551

SAGE 50 COMPUTER WORKSHOP

S50

Computerized Accounting Application for Chapter 5

Refresher on using Sage 50 Complete Accounting

Before starting this assignment, you may want to refresh your memory by reading the following PDF documents in the multimedia library of the MyAccountingLab Web site. Remember to choose the PDF document for your version of Sage 50.

1. An Introduction to Sage 50
2. Correcting Sage 50 Transactions
3. How to Repeat or Restart a Sage 50 Assignment
4. Backing Up and Restoring Your Work in Sage 50

   You also should have completed the following workshops:

1. Workshop 1 Atlas Company from Chapter 3
2. Workshop 2 Zell Company from Chapter 4

Workshop 3:

Accounting Cycle Mini Practice Set

In this workshop, you will complete the September and October accounting cycles for Sousa Realty using Sage 50. Tasks include posting journal entries and adjusting journal entries, printing reports and financial statements, and closing the accounting period.

Instructions and the data file for completing this assignment are in the multimedia library of the MyAccountingLab Web site. Open the **Workshop 3 Sousa Realty** PDF document for your version of Sage 50 and download the **Sousa Realty** data file for your version of Sage 50.

QUICKBOOKS COMPUTER WORKSHOP

QB

Computerized Accounting Application for Chapter 5

Refresher on using QuickBooks Accountant

Before starting this assignment, you may want to refresh your memory by reading the following PDF documents in the multimedia library of the MyAccountingLab Web site. Remember to choose the PDF document for your version of QuickBooks.

1. An Introduction to QuickBooks
2. Correcting QuickBooks Transactions
3. How to Repeat or Restart a QuickBooks Assignment
4. Backing Up and Restoring Your Work in QuickBooks

You also should have completed the following workshops:

1. Workshop 1 Atlas Company from Chapter 3
2. Workshop 2 Zell Company from Chapter 4

Workshop 3:

Accounting Cycle Mini Practice Set

In this workshop, you will complete the September and October accounting cycles for Sousa Realty using QuickBooks. Tasks include posting journal entries and adjusting journal entries, printing reports and financial statements, and closing the accounting period.

Instructions and the data file for completing this assignment are in the multimedia library of the MyAccountingLab Web site. Open the **Workshop 3 Sousa Realty** PDF document for your version of QuickBooks and download the **Sousa Realty** data file for your version of QuickBooks.

Banking Procedures and Control of Cash

CHAPTER
6

CHAPTER PREVIEW: THE BIG PICTURE

A.J. Foss does all his banking with his smartphone. He believes mobile banking is the best way to bank. With his downloaded app, he can send money, check his balance before a large purchase, and make a deposit. In this chapter, we look at banking procedures, the reconciliation of bank statements with company accounting records, and the control of cash. Maintaining accurate records of transactions, rather than just relying on bank-prepared statements, is important to the control of cash, and shows the importance of accounting in business.

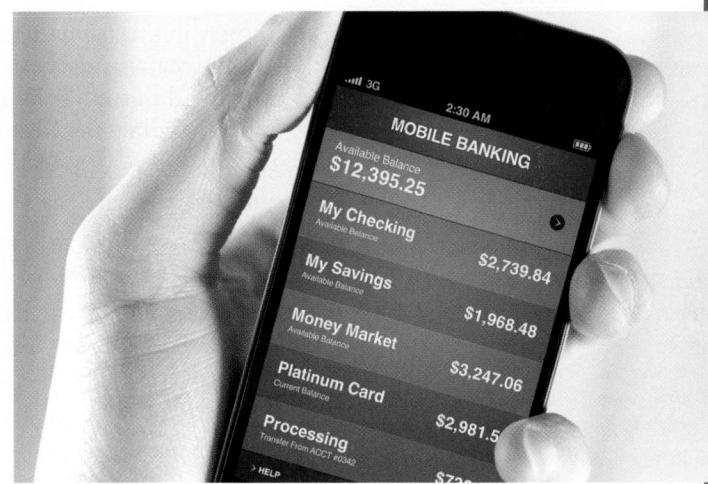

Learning Objectives

LO1 Explain Banking Procedures and Checking Accounts

LO2 Explain Bank Reconciliation

LO3 Explain Petty Cash and Change Funds

Banking Procedures and Checking Accounts

LO1

Internal control system
Procedures and methods to control a firm's assets as well as monitor its operations.

Today, your smartphone, a tool that can be used for both personal and business banking, is part of a growing trend in mobile banking. Before we look at specific trends in banking it is important to understand the manual system of banking. First, we turn our attention to Becca's Jewelry Store, a merchandising company that earns revenue by selling goods (or merchandise) to customers. When Becca's business began to increase, she became concerned that she was not monitoring the business's cash closely. She understood that a business with good internal control systems safeguards cash. Cash is the asset that is most easily stolen, lost, or mishandled. Therefore, it is important to protect all cash receipts and to control cash payments so that payments are made only for authorized business purposes.

After studying the situation carefully, Becca began a series of procedures that were to be followed by all company employees. The new company policies that Becca's Jewelry Store put into place are as follows:

1. Responsibilities and duties of employees will be divided. For example, the person receiving the cash, whether at the register or by opening the mail, will not record this information into the accounting records. The accountant will not be handling the cash receipts.

2. All cash receipts of Becca's Jewelry Store will be deposited into the bank the same day they arrive.

3. All cash payments will be made by check (except petty cash, which is discussed later in this chapter).

4. Employees will be rotated. This change allows workers to become acquainted with the work of others as well as to prepare for a possible changeover of jobs.

5. Becca Baker will sign all checks after receiving authorization to pay from the departments concerned.

6. At time of payment, all supporting invoices or documents will be stamped "paid." The stamp will show when the invoice or document is paid as well as the number of the check used.

7. All checks will be prenumbered. Periodically, the number of the checks that were issued and the numbers of the blank check forms remaining will be verified to make sure that all check numbers are accounted for. This change will control the use of checks and make it difficult to use a check fraudulently without it being revealed at some point.

8. Monthly bank statements will be sent to and reconciled by someone other than the employees who handle, record, or deposit the cash.

Becca knew that a checking account is one of the most useful and common banking services available, but she had many questions and decisions to make. She wanted to know about account options, monthly service charges, check-printing charges, minimum balance requirements, interest paid on the account, availability of automatic teller machines (ATMs), line of credit, and debit cards. Before Becca's Jewelry opened on April 1, 201X, she met with the manager of Sunshine Bank to discuss opening and using a checking account for the company.

Opening a Checking Account

Signature card A form signed by a bank customer that the bank uses to verify signature authenticity on all checks.

COACHING TIP

A signature card is another safeguard.

The bank manager gave Becca a signature card to fill out. The bank uses the signature card to verify the authenticity of the signature on company checks. Because Becca would be signing all the checks for her company, she was the only person who needed to sign the card.

The bank account enabled Becca to implement two basic internal control procedures. First, all revenue sources (cash and checks from cash sales and accounts receivable collections as well as credit card and debit card proceeds) were deposited in the bank account. Second, all withdrawals were to be made by check.

After Becca completed the initial paperwork, she received deposit slips and a set of checks. A deposit slip is a form that is used when making deposits of currency, coins, or checks in a bank or other financial institution. When filling out a deposit slip, you list the total amount of currency, coins, and checks that you are depositing (see Figure 6.1, page 204).

You list each check that you are depositing individually. Also, alongside each check you list its American Bankers Association (ABA) code. The ABA code is found in the upper-right corner of each check, below the check number. In Figure 6.1, the *16* identifies the large city or state in which the bank is located, and the *21* identifies the bank. The *112* is split into two parts: *1* represents the First Federal Reserve District, and *12* is a routing number used by the Federal Reserve Bank. When completing a deposit slip, only the first two numbers are required.

When a deposit is completed, the depositor receives a copy of the deposit slip as a receipt or proof of the transaction. The deposit should also be recorded on the current check stub. The bank manager told Becca that she could give the deposits to a bank teller or she could use an ATM. Often, Becca makes her deposits after business hours when the bank is closed. (Keep in mind that today many people use their smartphones to make deposits. We will be discussing trends in banking later in this chapter.) At those times, the bank will credit Becca's account when the deposit is processed. Becca plans to make all business payments by written check (except petty cash) and deposit all money received (cash and checks) in the bank account.

Check Endorsement

Checks have to be *endorsed* (signed) by the person to whom the check is made out before they can be deposited or cashed. Endorsement is the signing or stamping of one's name on the back left-hand side of the check. This signature means that the payee has transferred the right to deposit or cash the check to someone else (the bank). The bank can then collect the money from the person or company that issued the check.

Three different types of endorsement can be used (see Figure 6.2, page 205). The first is a *blank endorsement*. A blank endorsement does not specify that a particular person or firm must endorse it. It can be further endorsed by someone else. The bank will pay the last person who signs the check. This type of endorsement is not very safe. If the check is lost, the person who finds it can sign it and get the money.

The second type of endorsement is a *full endorsement*. The person or company signing (or stamping) the back of the check indicates the name of the company or the person to whom the check is to be paid. Only the person or company named in the endorsement can transfer the check to someone else.

Restrictive endorsements, the third type of endorsement, are the safest for businesses. Becca's Jewelry Store stamps the back of the check so that it must be deposited in the firm's account. This stamp limits any further use of the check.

Deposit slip A form provided by a bank for use in depositing money or checks into a checking account.

COACHING TIP

When a bank credits your account, it is increasing the balance.

Endorsement *Blank:* Could be further endorsed. *Full:* Restricts further endorsement to only the person or company named. *Restrictive:* Restricts any further endorsement.

COACHING TIP

Endorsements can be made by using a rubber stamp instead of a handwritten signature.

COACHING TIP

The regulations require the endorsement to be within the top $1\frac{1}{2}$ inches to speed up the check-clearing process.

FIGURE 6.1 Deposit Slip

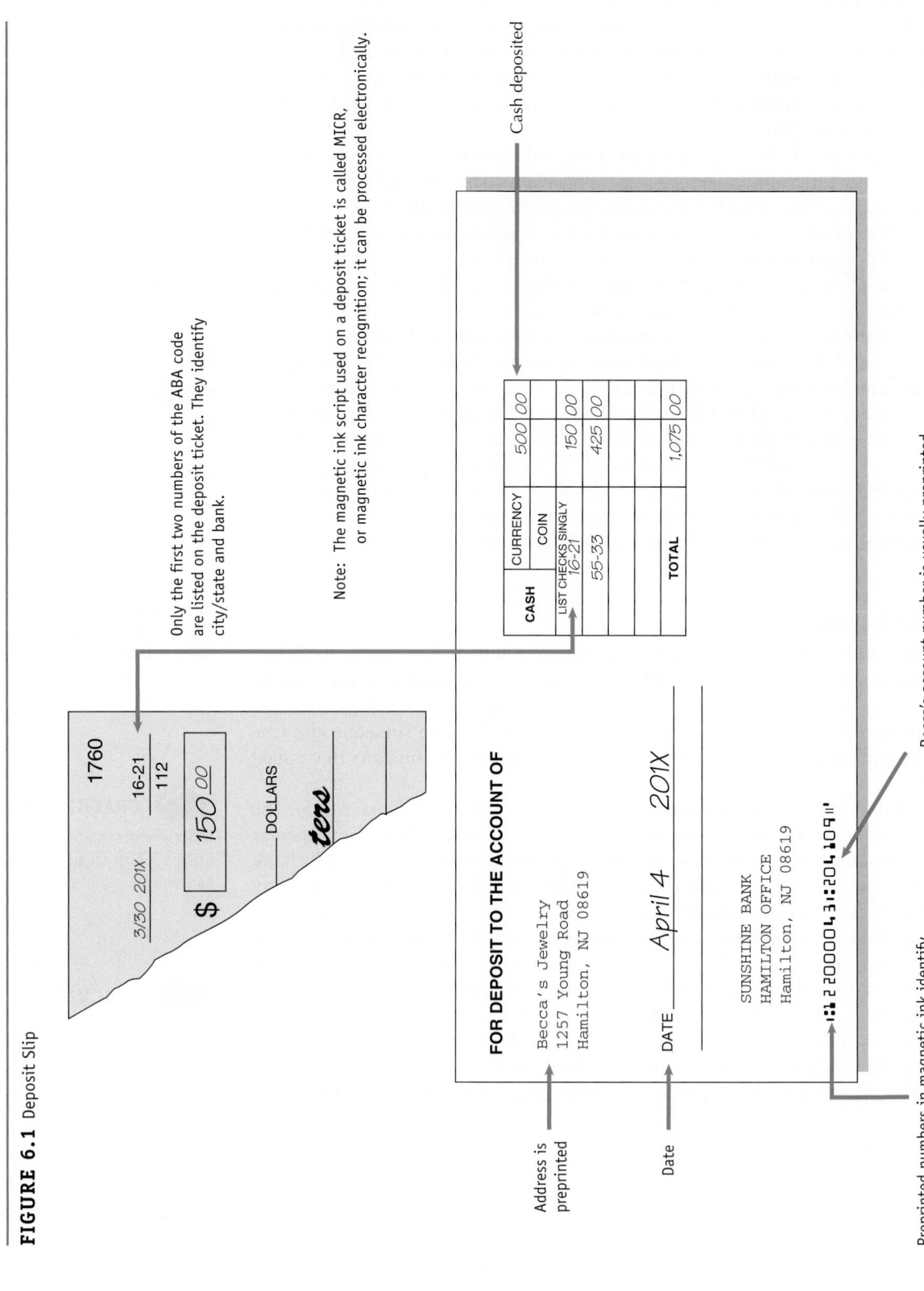

Only the first two numbers of the ABA code are listed on the deposit ticket. They identify city/state and bank.

Note: The magnetic ink script used on a deposit ticket is called MICR, or magnetic ink character recognition; it can be processed electronically.

Cash deposited

1760

16-21
112

$ 150 00

DOLLARS

tens

FOR DEPOSIT TO THE ACCOUNT OF

Becca's Jewelry
1257 Young Road
Hamilton, NJ 08619

DATE _____ April 4 _____ 201X

SUNSHINE BANK
HAMILTON OFFICE
Hamilton, NJ 08619

⑆2 200004 3⑆:204 ⑈09⑆

CASH	CURRENCY	500	00
	COIN		
LIST CHECKS SINGLY 16-21		150	00
55-33		425	00
TOTAL		1,075	00

Address is preprinted

Date

Becca's account number is usually preprinted.

Preprinted numbers in magnetic ink identify bank number and routing and sorting of check.

Types of Check Endorsement

Blank Endorsement

Becca Baker

204109

A signature on the back left side of a check of the person or firm the check is payable to. This check can be *further* endorsed by someone else; the bank will give the money to the last person who signs the check. This type of endorsement is not very safe. If the check is lost, anyone who picks it up can sign it and get the money.

Full Endorsement

Pay to the order of
Sunshine Bank
Becca's Jewelry Store
204109

This type of endorsement is safer than a simple signature, because the person or company signing (or stamping) the back of the check indicates the name of the company or person to whom the check is to be paid. Only the person or company named in the endorsement can transfer the check to someone else.

Restrictive Endorsement

Payable to the order of
Sunshine Bank
for deposit only.
Becca's Jewelry Store
204109

This endorsement is the safest for businesses. Becca's Jewelry Store stamps the back of the check so that it must be deposited in the firm's account. This endorsement limits any further use of the check (it can only be deposited in the specified account).

FIGURE 6.2
Types of Check Endorsement

In the past and to a lesser extent in the present, the primary sources of cash were cash sales and the collection of company accounts receivable. The journal entries to record the collection and deposit of cash in a bank vary only by the source. If the deposit is composed of the proceeds of cash sales, the journal entry is as follows (see Figure 6.3).

Date	Accounts	PR	Dr.	Cr.
	Cash		5 0 0 00	
	Sales			5 0 0 00

FIGURE 6.3
Journal Entry to Record the Deposit of the Proceeds of a Cash Sale

If the deposit is composed of collections of company accounts receivable, the journal entry would be as follows:

Date	Accounts	PR	Dr.	Cr.
	Cash		7 5 0 00	
	Accounts Receivable			7 5 0 00

FIGURE 6.3A
Journal Entry to Record the Collection of a Company's Accounts Receivable

There are two other sources of revenue that have taken on greater importance to businessmen and businesswomen: the credit card and the debit card. There are two categories of credit cards: those issued by financial institutions and those issued by credit card companies. Many of those issued by financial institutions, such as MasterCard, VISA, and Discover, are co-branded by other institutions such as airlines, NFL teams, and colleges and universities. These credit cards offer revolving credit facilities. Other credit cards, such as American Express, are issued by credit card companies. These companies generally extend credit for 30 days at a time.

There are several good reasons for a merchant to accept credit cards in payment for its goods or services. The seller does not have to make a decision as to whether it should grant credit or the amount of the credit to be granted. The seller also avoids the risk that the purchaser cannot or will not pay. Additionally, the seller does not have to maintain an accounts receivable system. Credit cards offer a greater number of repayment plans than do merchants, and this may actually increase sales. A credit card may facilitate purchases over the phone or Internet as cash does not need to change hands at the time of sale, and the seller usually receives payment to the company's bank account within 24 hours from VISA, MasterCard, or Discover. American Express typically takes longer than one day to credit the merchant's bank account, however. With the increase in mobile banking many transactions can be processed instantly. You should check with your local bank to see how long a transaction takes to clear. A drawback of accepting credit cards is that merchants typically must pay a service fee associated with the cost of processing the credit card transaction. The example in Figure 6.4 reflects a 1.5% service charge.

FIGURE 6.4

Journal Entry to Record the Deposit of the Proceeds of Credit Card Sales

Date	Account	PR	Dr.	Cr.
	Cash		9 8 5 00	
	Service Charge Expense		1 5 00	
	Sales			1 0 0 0 00

A debit card is an instrument very similar to the credit card that is used by the buyer to purchase goods and services. Debit cards are issued by banks, savings and loan institutions, and credit unions on behalf of depositors having an account with the institution. In addition, a debit card is not an extension of credit, as the debit card holder cannot spend more than the balance currently in his or her institutional account. As far as the merchant accepting the card is concerned, a debit card, with minor exceptions, is the same as a credit card. Both eliminate the need for the buyer to carry cash or checks to complete a purchase. Within 24 hours the merchant usually receives payment that is reduced by the amount of the service charge fee associated with the debit card transaction. The journal entry to record a debit card transaction is the same as the one shown in Figure 6.4.

The Checkbook

When Becca opened her business's checking account, she received checks. These checks can be used to buy items for the business or to pay bills or salaries.

A check is a written order signed by a drawer (the person who writes the check) instructing a drawee (the person who pays the check) to pay a specific sum of money to the payee (the person to whom the check is payable). Figure 6.5 shows a check issued by Becca's Jewelry Store. Becca Baker is the drawer, Sunshine Bank is the drawee, and Ziegler Wholesalers is the payee.

Look at the check in Figure 6.5. Notice that certain features, such as the company's name and address and the check number, are preprinted. Also notice (1) the line drawn after xx/100, which is to fill up the empty space and ensure that the amount cannot be changed, and (2) the word *and*, which should be used only to differentiate between dollars and cents.

Figure 6.5 includes a check stub. The check stub is used to record transactions, and it is kept for future reference. The information found on the stub includes the

Check A form used to indicate a specific amount of money that is to be paid by the bank to a named person or company.

Drawer Person who writes a check.

Drawee Bank that drawer has an account with.

Payee The person or company to whom the check is payable.

FIGURE 6.5 A Company Check

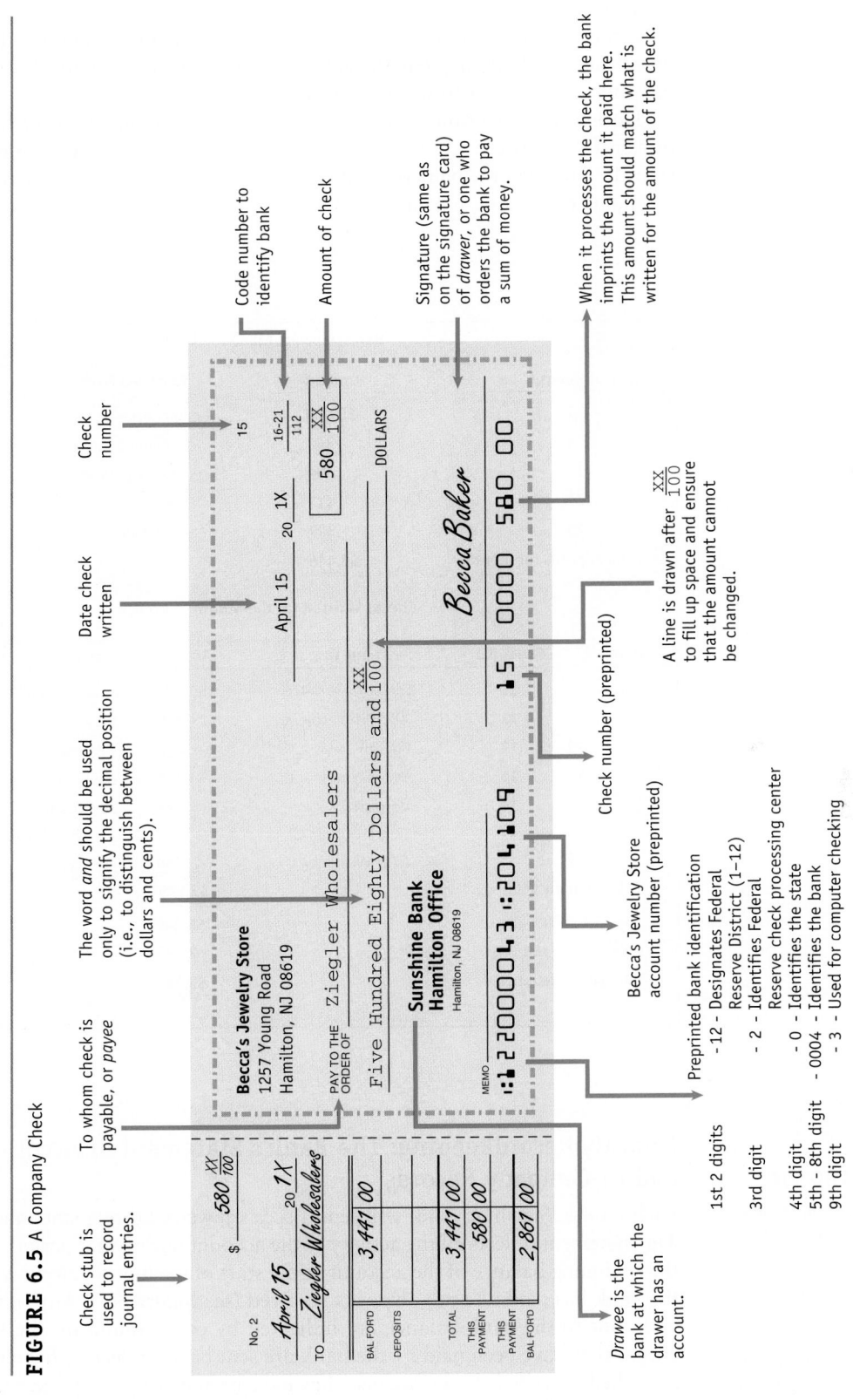

Check stub is used to record journal entries.

To whom check is payable, or *payee*

The word *and* should be used only to signify the decimal position (i.e., to distinguish between dollars and cents).

Date check written

Check number

Code number to identify bank

Amount of check

Signature (same as on the signature card) of *drawer*, or one who orders the bank to pay a sum of money.

When it processes the check, the bank imprints the amount it paid here. This amount should match what is written for the amount of the check.

A line is drawn after $\frac{XX}{100}$ to fill up space and ensure that the amount cannot be changed.

Check number (preprinted)

Becca's Jewelry Store account number (preprinted)

Drawee is the bank at which the drawer has an account.

Preprinted bank identification

1st 2 digits	-12 - Designates Federal Reserve District (1–12)
3rd digit	- 2 - Identifies Federal Reserve check processing center
4th digit	- 0 - Identifies the state
5th - 8th digit	- 0004 - Identifies the bank
9th digit	- 3 - Used for computer checking

No. 2

April 15 20 1X

TO *Ziegler Wholesalers*

$ 580 $\frac{XX}{100}$

BAL FOR'D	3,441	00
DEPOSITS		
TOTAL	3,441	00
THIS PAYMENT	580	00
THIS PAYMENT		
BAL FOR'D	2,861	00

Becca's Jewelry Store
1257 Young Road
Hamilton, NJ 08619

PAY TO THE ORDER OF   *Ziegler Wholesalers*

April 15   20 1X

15
16-21
112

580 $\frac{XX}{100}$

Five Hundred Eighty Dollars and $\frac{XX}{100}$ DOLLARS

Sunshine Bank
Hamilton Office
Hamilton, NJ 08619

MEMO

Becca Baker

⑈2200004⑆⑈204⑈09   ⦙5   0000 580 00

beginning balance of the checkbook ($3,441), the amount of any deposits ($0), the total amount in the account ($3,441), the amount of the check being written ($580), and the ending balance ($2,861). The check stub should be filled out before the check is written.

If the written amount on the check does not match the amount expressed in figures, Sunshine Bank may pay the amount written in words, return the check unpaid, or contact the drawer to see what was meant.

During the same time period, in-company records must be kept for all transactions affecting Becca's Jewelry Store's checkbook balance. Figure 6.6 shows these records. Note that the bank deposits ($6,446) minus the checks written ($2,529) give an ending checkbook balance of $3,917.

FIGURE 6.6

Transactions (In-Company Records) Affecting Checkbook Balance

Bank Deposits Made for April		
Date of Deposit	**Amount**	**Received From**
Apr. 1	$5,000	Becca Baker, Capital
4	340	Jennifer Leung
15	89	Mary Figueroa
27	117	Carl Jones
28	900	Cash Sales
Total deposits for month:	$6,446	

Checks Written for the Month of April				
Date	**Check No.**	**Payment To**	**Amount**	**Description**
Apr. 2	10	Quality Insurance	$ 500	Insurance paid in advance
7	11	ABC Wholesalers	400	Merchandise
9	12	Payroll	800	Salaries
10	13	Times Newspaper	100	Advertising
12	14	Verizon	99	Telephone
15	15	Ziegler Wholesalers	580	Merchandise
15		ATM Withdrawal	50	Postage
Total Amount of Checks Written:			$2,529	
Deposits and Credits			$6,446	
Withdrawals and Fees			−2,529	
Balance in Account			$3,917	

COACHING TIP

Figure 6.7 shows one format for a bank statement. Different banks use different formats.

Cancelled check A check that has been processed by a bank and is no longer negotiable.

Monthly Recordkeeping: The Bank's Statement of Account and In-Company Records

Each month, Sunshine Bank will send Becca's Jewelry Store a statement of account. This statement reflects all the activity in the account during that period. It begins with the beginning balance of the account at the start of the month, along with the checks the bank has paid and any deposits received (see Figure 6.7). Any other charges or additions to the bank balance are indicated by codes found on the statement. All checks that have been paid by the bank are sent back to Becca's Jewelry Store. They are called cancelled checks because they have been processed by the bank and are no longer negotiable. The ending balance in Figure 6.7 is $3,592.

Sunshine Bank

Becca's Jewelry Store
1257 Young Road
Hamilton, NJ 08619

ACCOUNT NUMBER	20 410 9
CLOSING PERIOD	4/30/1X

AMOUNT ENCLOSED $ _____

RETURN THIS PORTION WITH YOUR PAYMENT IF YOU ARE NOT USING OUR AUTOMATIC PAYMENT PLAN   Address Correction on Reverse Side ☐

CHECKING ACCOUNT							
ON	YOUR BALANCE WAS	NO.	WE SUBTRACTED CHECKS TOTALING	LESS SERVICE CHARGE	NO.	WE ADDED DEPOSITS OF	MAKING YOUR PRESENT BALANCE
	0	5	1,949.00	5.00	4	5,546.00	3,592.00

DATE	CHECKS • WITHDRAWALS • PAYMENTS	DEPOSITS • INTEREST • ADVANCES	BALANCE
4/1		5,000.00	5,000.00
4/2	500.00		4,500.00
4/4		340.00	4,840.00
4/7	400.00		4,440.00
4/9	800.00		3,640.00
4/10	100.00		3,540.00
4/12	99.00		3,441.00
4/15		89.00	3,530.00
4/15	50.00 ATM		3,480.00
4/27		117.00	3,597.00
4/30	5.00 SC		3,592.00

FIGURE 6.7
A Bank Statement

Now let's check your progress.

TRY IT!   Learning Unit 6-1

Answer true or false to the following statements.

1. The payee is the person or organization to whom a check is made payable.
2. A check stub is used to record journal entries.
3. Computers today require more internal controls in banking than ever.
4. Restrictive endorsement is the safest for a business.
5. Smartphones have no place in banking.

The Bank Reconciliation Process

The problem is that the ending bank balance of $3,592 does not agree with the amount in Becca's checkbook, $3,917, or the balance in the Cash account in the ledger, $3,917. Such differences are caused partly by the time a bank takes to process a company's transactions. A company records a transaction when it occurs, but a bank cannot record a deposit until it receives that deposit, and it cannot pay a check until the check is presented by the payee. In addition, the bank statement will report fees and transactions that the company did not know about.

LEARNING UNIT 6-2

 LO2

 **COACHING TIP**

Online banking and computer software have made the reconciliation process even easier.

Bank reconciliation The process of reconciling the checkbook balance with the bank balance given on the bank statement.

Bank statement A report sent by a bank to a customer indicating the previous balance, ATM transactions, nonsufficient funds, individual checks processed, individual deposits received, service charges, and ending bank balance.

Becca's accountant has to find out why there is a $325 difference between the balances and how the records can be brought into balance. The process of reconciling the bank balance on the bank statement versus the company's checkbook balance is called a bank reconciliation. Bank reconciliations involve several steps, including calculating the deposits in transit and the outstanding checks. The bank reconciliation is usually done on the back of the bank statement (see Figure 6.8). However, it can also be done by computer software.

FIGURE 6.8
Bank Reconciliation Using Back of the Bank Statement

COACHING TIP

Keep in mind that both the bank and the depositor can make mistakes that will not be discovered until the reconciliation process.

CHECKS OUTSTANDING				
NUMBER	**AMOUNT**		1. Enter balance shown on this statement	3,592 : 00
15	580 : 00			
			2. If you have made deposits since the date of this statement add them to the above balance.	900 : 00
			3. SUBTOTAL	4,492 : 00
			4. Deduct total of checks outstanding	580 : 00
			5. ADJUSTED BALANCE This should agree with your checkbook.	3,912 : 00*
TOTAL OF CHECKS OUTSTANDING	580 : 00			

TO VERIFY YOUR CHECKING BALANCE

1. Sort checks by number or by date issued and compare with your check stubs and prior outstanding list. Make certain all checks paid have been recorded in your checkbook. If any of your checks were not included with this statement, list the numbers and amounts under "CHECKS OUTSTANDING."
2. Deduct the Service Charge as shown on the statement from your checkbook balance.
3. Review copies of charge advices included with this statement and check for proper entry in your checkbook.

IF THE ADJUSTED BALANCE DOES NOT AGREE WITH YOUR CHECKBOOK BALANCE, THE FOLLOWING SUGGESTIONS ARE OFFERED FOR YOUR ASSISTANCE.

- Recheck additions and subtractions in your checkbook and figures to the left.
- Make certain checkbook balances have been carried forward properly.
- Verify deposits recorded on statement against deposits entered in checkbook.
- Compare amount on each checkbook stub.

*Note that the $5 service charge is included

Deposits in transit Deposits that were made by customers of a bank but did not reach, or were not processed by, the bank before the preparation of the bank statement.

Deposits in Transit. In comparing the list of deposits received by the bank with the checkbook, the accountant notices that a deposit made on April 28 for $900 was not on the bank's statement. The accountant realizes that to prepare this statement, the bank only included deposit information about Becca's Jewelry Store up to April 27. This deposit made by Becca was not shown on the monthly bank statement because it arrived at the bank after the cutoff date of April 27. Thus, timing becomes a consideration in the reconciliation process. Deposits not yet added to the bank balance are called deposits in transit. This deposit needs to be added to the bank balance shown on the bank statement. Becca's checkbook is not affected because the deposit has already been added to its balance. The bank has no way of knowing that the deposit is coming until it receives it.

Outstanding checks Checks written by a company or person that were not received or not processed by the bank before the preparation of the bank statement.

Outstanding Checks. The first thing the accountant does when the bank statement is received is put the checks in numerical order (1, 2, 3, etc.). In doing so, the accountant notices that one payment was not made by the bank and check no. 15 was not returned by the bank.

Becca's books showed that this check had been deducted from the checkbook balance. The outstanding check, however, had not yet been presented to the bank for

COACHING TIP

Check no. 15 is outstanding in Figure 6.8.

payment or deducted from the bank balance. When this check does reach the bank, the bank will reduce the amount of Becca's bank balance.

Service Charges. Becca's accountant also notices a bank service charge of $5. Becca's book balance will be lowered by $5.

A journal entry is also needed to bring the ledger accounts of Cash and Service Charge expense up-to-date. Any adjustment to the checkbook balance results in a journal entry. The entry in Figure 6.9 was made to accomplish this step.

Apr.	30	Service Charge Expense			5 00		
		Cash				5 00	
		Bank service charge for April					

FIGURE 6.9
Service Charge Journalized

COACHING TIP

This charge could be recorded as a miscellaneous expense.

NSF (nonsufficient funds) Notation indicating that a check has been written on an account that lacks sufficient funds to back it up.

Debit memorandum Decrease in depositor's balance.

Nonsufficient Funds. While Becca's Jewelry Store did not experience either of the following two transactions, both may occur in the normal course of business. An NSF (nonsufficient funds) check is a check that has been returned because the drawer did not have enough money in its account to pay the check. Accountants are continually on the lookout for NSF checks. An NSF check means that there is less money in the checking account than was thought. Becca will have to (1) lower the checkbook balance and (2) try to collect the amount from the customer. The bank will notify Becca's Jewelry of an NSF check (or other deductions) by a debit memorandum. Think of a <u>de</u>bit memorandum as a <u>de</u>duction from the account holder's balance.

If the bank acts as a collecting agent for Becca's Jewelry, say in collecting notes, it will charge Becca a small fee, and the net amount collected will be added to Becca's bank balance. The bank will send to Becca a credit memorandum verifying the increase in the depositor's balance.

Credit memorandum Increase in depositor's balance.

It is important for Becca to prepare a bank reconciliation when she receives her bank statement every month as part of the cash control procedure. It verifies the amount of cash in her checking account. Another important reason to do a bank reconciliation is that it may uncover irregularities such as employee theft of funds.

Here are step-by-step instructions for preparing a bank reconciliation:

COACHING TIP

Adjustments to the checkbook balance must be journalized and posted. These steps keep the depositor's ledger accounts (especially Cash) up-to-date.

1. **Prepare a list of deposits in transit.** Compare the deposits listed on your bank statement with the bank deposits shown in your checkbook. On your bank reconciliation, list any deposits that have not yet cleared the bank statement. Also, take a look at the bank reconciliation you prepared last month. Did all of last month's deposits in transit clear on this month's bank statement? If not, you should find out what happened. Today, many customers are checking their bank balances online with their tablets or smartphones.

2. **Prepare a list of outstanding checks.** In your checkbook, mark each check that cleared the bank statement this month. On your bank reconciliation, list all the checks in your checkbook that did not clear. Also, take a look at the bank reconciliation you prepared last month. Did any checks outstanding from last month still not clear the bank? If so, be sure they are on your list of outstanding checks this month. If a check is several months old and still has not cleared the bank, you may want to investigate further.

3. **Record any bank charges or credits.** Take a close look at your bank statement. Are all special charges made by the bank recorded in your books? If not, journalize them now as if you had just written a check for that amount. By the same token, any credits made to your account by the bank should be journalized as well. Post the entries to your general ledger.

4. **Compute the cash balance per your books.**

5. **Enter the bank balance on the reconciliation.** At the top of the bank reconciliation statement, enter the ending balance from the bank statement.

6. **Total the deposits in transit.** Add up the deposits in transit and enter the total on the reconciliation. Add the total deposits in transit to the bank balance to arrive at a subtotal.

7. **Total the outstanding checks.** Add up the outstanding checks, and enter the total on the reconciliation.

8. **Compute the balance per the reconciliation.** Subtract the total outstanding checks (see Step 7) from the subtotal in Step 6. The result should equal the balance shown in your general ledger.

Before we look at a more comprehensive bank statement, let's look at trends in banking.

Trends in Banking

Have you ever heard of mobile remote deposit capture (RDC)? By 2015 it is projected that more than 40 million bank customers will take a picture of a check with their smartphone and transfer it to a financial institution for posting and clearing. Customers can download apps to check balances, pay bills, or make deposits.

Today, financial institutions have developed ways to transfer funds electronically, without the use of paper checks. Such systems are called electronic funds transfers (EFTs). Most EFTs are established to save money and avoid theft.

Financial institutions use powerful computer networks to automate millions of daily transactions. Today, banks are able to use computer technology to give you the option of bypassing the time-consuming, paper-based aspects of traditional banking so that you can manage your finances more quickly and efficiently.

The first step toward online banking, automatic teller machines (ATMs), were first installed in banks about 40 years ago. For the first time, customers could make deposits, withdraw money, and obtain account balances without having to stand in line during the times that the bank was open. Today, customers are able to use an ATM in banks, supermarkets, malls, on college campuses, etc., or on their smartphone to complete banking transactions.

The latest development in banking is Internet or online banking. Most of the large banks offer fully secure, fully functional online banking for free or for a small fee. Some smaller banks offer limited access; for instance, you may be able to view your account balance and history but may not be able to initiate transactions online. As more banks are succeeding online and more customers are using their sites, fully functional online banking is becoming as common as ATMs.

With a debit card and personal identification number (PIN), you can use an ATM to withdraw cash, make deposits, or transfer funds between accounts. Some ATMs charge a fee if you are not a member of their ATM network or are making a transaction at a remote location.

Retail purchases can also be made with a debit card. You enter your PIN or sign for the purchase. Some banks that issue debit cards are charging customers a fee for a debit card purchase made with a PIN. Although a debit card looks like a credit card, the money for the purchase is transferred from your bank account to the store's account at the time of the purchase. The purchase will be shown on your bank account statement.

Immediately call the card issuer when you suspect a debit card may be lost or stolen. Most companies have toll-free numbers and a 24-hour service to deal with such emergencies. Although federal law limits your liability for a stolen credit card to $50, your liability for unauthorized use of your ATM or debit card can be much greater—depending on how quickly you report the loss. Also, it is important to

Electronic funds transfer (EFT) An electronic system that transfers funds without the use of paper checks.

ATM (automatic teller machine) Machine that allows for depositing, withdrawal, and advanced banking transactions.

COACHING TIP

Internet banking is expanding rapidly.

remember that when you use a debit card, federal law does not give you the right to stop payment. You must resolve the problem with the seller.

If you don't mind foregoing the teller window and the lobby cookie, a virtual bank or e-bank, such as Virtual Bank or Giant Bank, may save you real money. Virtual banks are banks without bricks. They exist entirely online and offer much of the same range of services and adhere to the same regulations as your corner bank. Virtual banks pass the money that they save on overhead, such as buildings and tellers, along to you in the form of higher yields and lower fees. Banking is available everywhere, all the time.

Advantages of Online Banking. Customers who use online banking services enjoy many advantages. They can do almost everything from the comfort of their own homes at convenient times and without standing in long lines.

- *Convenience:* Unlike your corner bank, online banks never close. They are available 24 hours a day, 7 days a week.
- *Availability:* If you are out of state or even out of the country when a money problem arises, you can log on instantly to your online bank and take care of business, 24/7.
- *Transaction speed:* Online bank sites generally execute and confirm transactions as quickly or even faster than ATM processing speeds.
- *Efficiency:* You can access and manage all of your bank accounts, including IRAs and CDs, from one secure site.
- *Effectiveness:* Many online banking sites now offer sophisticated tools to help you manage all of your assets more effectively. Most of these tools are compatible with money managing programs such as Quicken and Microsoft Money.

Disadvantages of Online Banking. Although online banking has many advantages, it also has some disadvantages.

- *Start-up may take time:* In order to register for your bank's online program, you will probably have to provide some personal identification and sign a form at a branch bank.
- *Learning curve:* Banking sites can be difficult to navigate at first. Plan to invest time to read the tutorials in order to become comfortable in your virtual lobby.
- *Bank site changes:* Even the largest banks periodically upgrade their online programs, adding new features in unfamiliar places. In some cases, you may need to reenter account information.
- *Trust:* For many people, the biggest hurdle to online banking is learning to trust it. Did my transaction go through? Did I push the transfer button once or twice? Best bet: Always print the transaction receipt and keep it with your bank records until it shows up on your personal site or your bank statement.

When problems arise, it is usually much easier to sort them out face to face rather than to use e-mail or the telephone. Perhaps the biggest problem with online banking is security. It is important to keep passwords safe and to be aware of fake e-mails that may arrive in your inbox. These e-mails pretend to be from your bank and attempt to obtain log-in information from you. This kind of fraud is called phishing.

Phishing Fake e-mails that attempt to obtain information about online banking customers.

Fraudulent practices can happen at cash registers when you make a purchase or at restaurants when you pay with a credit card and the waiter is out of your sight. Skimming is the theft of credit card information used in an otherwise legitimate debit card or credit card transaction. Skimming at ATMs can be much more damaging because of the number of accounts and the amount of money that can be quickly accessed. Card-based purchases—online, debit, and credit—are convenient for consumers. For example, tens of thousands of ATMs are swipe-based. The large number of ATMs contributes to the skimming problem. In a way, we've become victims of the convenience we demand.

Here are some tips to help you avoid becoming a skimming victim.

- Keep your PIN safe. Don't give it to anyone.
- Watch out for people who try to "help" you at an ATM.
- Look at the ATM before using it. If it doesn't look right, don't use it.
- If an ATM has any unusual signage, don't use it. No bank would hang a sign that says, "Swipe your ATM here before inserting it in the card reader" or something to that effect.
- If your card is not returned after the transaction or after pressing cancel, immediately contact the institution that issued the card.
- Check your statement to be sure that no unusual withdrawals appear on it.

Check truncation (safekeeping) Procedure whereby checks are not returned to the drawer with the bank statement but are instead kept at the bank for a certain amount of time before being first transferred to microfilm and then destroyed.

Check Truncation (Safekeeping). Some banks do not return cancelled checks to the depositor but instead use a procedure called check truncation or safekeeping. This practice is increasing rapidly. The bank holds a cancelled check for a specific period of time (usually 90 days) and then keeps a microfilm copy handy and destroys the original check. In Texas, for example, some credit unions and savings and loan institutions do not send back checks. Instead, the check date, number, and amount are listed on the bank statement. If the customer needs a copy of a check, the bank will provide the check or a photocopy for a small fee. (Photocopies are accepted as evidence in Internal Revenue Service tax returns and audits.)

Truncation cuts down on the amount of "paper" that is returned to customers and thus provides substantial cost savings. It is estimated that more than 80 million checks are written each day in the United States.

Example of a More Comprehensive Bank Statement. The bank reconciliation of Becca's Jewelry was not as complicated as it is for many companies, even using today's computer technology. Let's look at a reconciliation for Matty's Supermarket (Figures 6.10 and 6.11, on page 216), which is based on the following business transactions:

Matty's checkbook balance		$13,176.84
Bank balance		23,726.04
Leased space to Subway		8,456.00
Leased space to Dunkin' Donuts		3,616.12
Both lease payments are deposited by electronic transfer.		
Matty pays a health insurance payment each month by electronic transfer		1,444.00
Deposits in transit 6/30		6,766.52
Checks outstanding		
Ck #738	$1,144.00	
739	1,277.88	
740	332.00	
741	812.56	
742	1,834.12	
Check #734 was overstated by $1,440 in the company's books.		

FIGURE 6.10
Bank Statement for Matty's
Supermarket

Ranger Bank
1 Left St.
Marblehead, MA 01945

ACCOUNT STATEMENT

Matty's Supermarket
20 Sullivan St.
Lynn, MA 01917

Checking Account: 775800061

Checking Account Summary as of 6/30/1X

Beginning Balance	Total Deposits	Total Withdrawals	Service Charge	Ending Balance
$26,224.48	$17,410.56	$19,852.00	$57.00	$23,726.04

Checking Account Transactions

Deposits	Date	Amount
Deposit	6/05	4,000.00
Deposit	6/05	448.00
Deposit	6/09	778.40
EFT leasing: Dunkin' Donuts	6/18	3,616.12
EFT leasing: Subway	6/27	8,456.00
Interest	6/30	112.04

Charges	Date	Amount
EFT: Blue Cross/Blue Shield	6/21	1,444.00
NSF	6/21	208.00
Service charge: Check printing	6/30	57.00

Checks			Daily Balance			
Number	Date	Amount	Date	Balance	Date	Balance
401	6/07	400.00	5/31	26,224.48	6/18	21,267.00
733	6/13	12,000.00	6/05	30,672.48	6/21	19,615.00
734	6/13	600.00	6/07	30,272.48	6/27	28,071.00
735	6/11	400.00	6/09	31,050.88	6/30	23,726.04
736	6/18	400.00	6/11	30,650.88		
737	6/30	4,400.00	6/13	18,050.88		

FIGURE 6.11
Bank Reconciliation for Matty's
Supermarket

MATTY'S SUPERMARKET Bank Reconciliation as of June 30, 201X				
Checkbook balance			**Bank balance**	
Matty's checkbook balance		$13,176.84	Bank balance	$23,726.04
Add:			Add:	
EFT leasing: Dunkin' Donuts			Deposits in transit, 6/30	6,766.52
	$ 3,616.12			$30,492.56
EFT leasing: Subway				
	8,456.00			
Interest	112.04			
Error: Overstated				
check no. 734	1,440.00	13,624.16		
		$26,801.00		
Deduct:			Deduct:	
Service charge	$ 57.00		Outstanding checks:	
NSF check	208.00		No. 738	$1,144.00
EFT health insurance			No. 739	1,277.88
payment	1,444.00	1,709.00	No. 740	332.00
			No. 741	812.56
			No. 742	1,834.12	5,400.56
Reconciled balance		$25,092.00	Reconciled balance	$25,092.00

Note that in Figure 6.11 each adjustment to Matty's checkbook in the reconciliation process would result in general journal entries in the company's accounting records.

Now let's check your understanding with a Try It!

 **TRY IT!**   Learning Unit 6-2

From the following information, construct a bank reconciliation for P.J. Co. as of March 31, 201X:

Checkbook balance	$2,200
Bank statement balance	1,600
Deposits (in transit)	600
Outstanding checks	85
Bank service charge	20
NSF check	65

(Lois Long's check in payment of an account was returned for insufficient funds.)

LEARNING UNIT 6-3

 L03

The Establishment of Petty Cash and Change Funds

Petty cash fund Fund (source) that allows payment of small amounts without the writing of checks.

Becca realized how time-consuming and expensive it would be to write checks for small amounts to pay for postage, small supplies, and so forth, so she set up a **petty cash fund**. Similarly, she established a *change fund* to make cash transactions more convenient. This unit explains how to manage petty cash and change funds.

Setting Up the Petty Cash Fund

The petty cash fund is an account dedicated to paying small day-to-day expenses. These petty cash expenses are recorded in an auxiliary record and later summarized, journalized, and posted. Becca estimated that the company would need a fund of $60 to cover small expenditures during the month of May. This petty cash was not expected to last longer than one month. She gave one of her employees the responsibility for overseeing the fund. This person is called the *custodian*.

Becca named her office manager, John Sullivan, as custodian. In other companies, the cashier or secretary may be in charge of petty cash. Check no. 6 was drawn to the order of the custodian and cashed to establish the fund. John keeps the petty cash fund in a small tin box in the office safe.

Shown here is the transaction analysis chart for the establishment of a $60 petty cash fund, which would be journalized on May 1, 201X, as shown in Figure 6.12.

Accounts Affected	Category	↓ ↑	Rules
Petty Cash	Asset	↑	Dr.
Cash (checks)	Asset	↓	Cr.

Note that the new asset called Petty Cash, which was created by writing check no. 6, reduced the asset Cash. In reality, the total assets stay the same; what has occurred is a shift from the asset Cash (check no. 6) to a new asset account called Petty Cash.

		GENERAL JOURNAL				Page 1	
Date		Account Title and Description	PR	Dr.		Cr.	
201X May	1	Petty Cash		60 00			
		Cash				60 00	
		Establishment of petty cash.					

FIGURE 6.12
Establishing Petty Cash

The Petty Cash account is not debited or credited again if the size of the fund is not changed. If the $60 fund is used up quickly, the fund should be increased. If the fund is too large, the Petty Cash account should be reduced. We take a closer look at this issue when we discuss the replenishment of petty cash.

Making Payments from the Petty Cash Fund

John Sullivan has the responsibility for filling out a petty cash voucher for each cash payment made from the petty cash fund. The petty cash vouchers are numbered in sequence.

Note that when the voucher (shown in Figure 6.13, page 218) is completed, it will include:

- The voucher number (which will be in sequence)
- The date
- The person or organization to whom the payment was made
- The amount of payment
- The reason for payment (in this case, cleaning)
- The signature of the person who approved the payment
- The signature of the person who received the payment from petty cash
- The account to which the expense will be charged

Petty cash voucher A petty cash form to be completed when money is taken out of petty cash.

FIGURE 6.13
Petty Cash Voucher

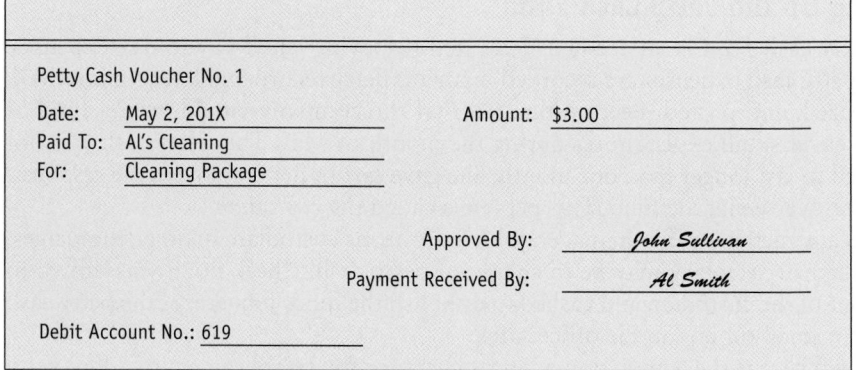

Petty Cash Voucher No. 1

Date: May 2, 201X   Amount: $3.00
Paid To: Al's Cleaning
For: Cleaning Package

                                          Approved By: _John Sullivan_

                                  Payment Received By: _Al Smith_

Debit Account No.: 619

COACHING TIP

The check for $60 is usually drawn to the order of the custodian and is cashed, and the proceeds are turned over to John Sullivan, the custodian.

The completed vouchers are placed in the petty cash box. No matter how many vouchers John Sullivan fills out, the total of the vouchers in the box and the cash on hand should equal the original amount of petty cash with which the fund was established ($60).

Assume that at the end of May the following items are documented by petty cash vouchers in the petty cash box as having been paid by John Sullivan:

201X
May

2	Cleaning package, $3.00
5	Postage stamps, $9.00
8	First-aid supplies, $15.00
9	Delivery expense, $6.00
14	Delivery expense, $15.00
27	Postage stamps, $6.00

Auxiliary petty cash record A supplementary record for summarizing petty cash information.

John records this information in the auxiliary petty cash record shown in Figure 6.14. It is not a required record but it is an aid to John. In other words, it is an auxiliary record that is not essential but that is quite helpful as part of the petty cash system. You may want to think of the auxiliary petty cash record as an optional worksheet. Let's look at how to replenish the petty cash fund.

FIGURE 6.14 Auxiliary Petty Cash Record

									Category of Payments			
							Postage Expense	Delivery Expense	Sundry			
Date		Voucher No.	Description	Receipts	Payments				Account		Amount	
201X May	1		Establishment	60 00								
	2	1	Cleaning		3 00				Cleaning		3 00	
	5	2	Postage		9 00		9 00					
	8	3	First Aid		15 00				Misc.		15 00	
	9	4	Delivery		6 00			6 00				
	14	5	Delivery		15 00			15 00				
	27	6	Postage		6 00		6 00					
			Total	60 00	54 00		15 00	21 00			18 00	

How to Replenish the Petty Cash Fund

No postings are done from the auxiliary record because it is not a journal. At some point the summarized information found in the auxiliary petty cash record is used as a basis for a journal entry in the general journal and eventually posted to appropriate ledger accounts to reflect up-to-date balances.

The $54 of expenses (see Figure 6.14) is recorded in the general journal (Figure 6.15) and a new check, no. 17, for $54 is cashed and returned to John Sullivan. In replenishment, old expenses are updated in the journal and ledger to show where money has gone. The petty cash box now once again reflects $60 cash. The old vouchers that were used are stamped to indicate that they have been processed and the fund replenished.

COACHING TIP

A new check, which is payable to the custodian and is cashed by John, is written in the replenishment process, and the cash is placed in the petty cash box.

FIGURE 6.15 Establishment and Replenishment of Petty Cash Fund

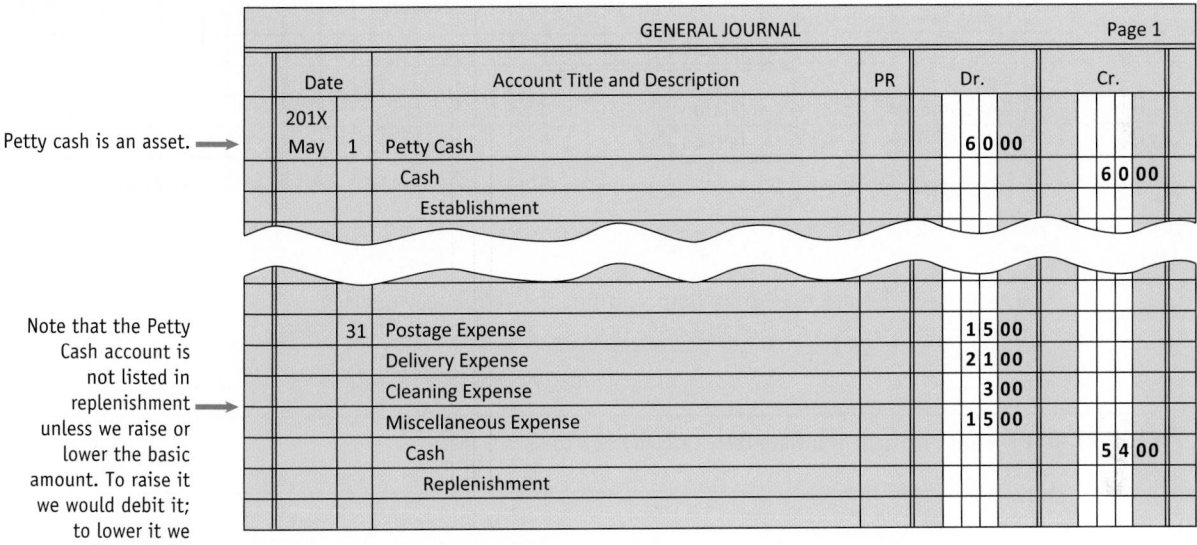

Petty cash is an asset.

Note that the Petty Cash account is not listed in replenishment unless we raise or lower the basic amount. To raise it we would debit it; to lower it we would credit it.

	Date		Account Title and Description	PR	Dr.	Cr.
	201X					
	May	1	Petty Cash		60 00	
			Cash			60 00
			Establishment			
		31	Postage Expense		15 00	
			Delivery Expense		21 00	
			Cleaning Expense		3 00	
			Miscellaneous Expense		15 00	
			Cash			54 00
			Replenishment			

GENERAL JOURNAL — Page 1

Note that in the replenishment process the debits are a summary of the totals (except sundry, because individual items are different) of expenses or other items from the auxiliary petty cash record. Posting these specific expenses will ensure that the expenses will not be understated on the income statement. The credit to Cash allows us to draw a check for $54 to put money back in the petty cash box. The $60 in the box now agrees with the Petty Cash account balance. The end result is that our petty cash box is filled, and we have justified for which accounts the petty cash money was spent. Think of replenishment as a single, summarizing entry.

Remember that if at some point the petty cash fund is to be greater than $60, a check can be written that will increase Petty Cash and decrease Cash. If the Petty Cash account balance is to be reduced, we can credit or reduce Petty Cash. For our present purpose, however, Petty Cash will remain at $60.

The auxiliary petty cash record after replenishment would look as shown in Figure 6.16 on page 220 (keep in mind that no postings are made from the auxiliary).

FIGURE 6.16 Auxiliary Petty Cash Record with Replenishment

								Category of Payments			
							Postage Expense	Delivery Expense	Sundry		
Date		Voucher No.	Description	Receipts	Payments				Account	Amount	
201X May	1		Establishment	60 00							
	2	1	Cleaning		3 00				Cleaning	3 00	
	5	2	Postage		9 00		9 00				
	8	3	First Aid		15 00				Misc.	15 00	
	9	4	Delivery		6 00			6 00			
	14	5	Delivery		15 00			15 00			
	27	6	Postage		6 00		6 00				
			Total	60 00	54 00		15 00	21 00		18 00	
			Ending Balance		6 00						
				60 00	60 00						
			Ending Balance	6 00							
	31		Replenishment	54 00							
	31		Balance (New)	60 00							

Figure 6.17 may help you put the sequence together.

FIGURE 6.17 Which Transactions Involve Petty Cash and How to Record Them

Date		Description	New Check Written	Petty Cash Voucher Prepared	Recorded in Auxiliary Petty Cash Record	
201X May	1	Establishment of petty cash for $60	X		X	} Dr. Petty Cash Cr. Cash
	2	Paid salaries, $2,000	X			
	10	Paid $10 from petty cash for Band-Aids		X	X	} No journal entries
	19	Paid $8 from petty cash for postage		X	X	
	24	Paid light bill, $200	X			
	29	Replenishment of petty cash to $60	X		X	} Dr. individual expenses Cr. Cash

Has nothing to do with petty cash (amounts too great)

In this step the old expenses are listed in the general journal and a new check is written to replenish. All old vouchers are removed from the petty cash box.

Before concluding this unit, let's look at how Becca will handle setting up a change fund and problems with cash shortages and overages.

Setting Up a Change Fund and Insight into Cash Short and Over

If a company such as Becca's Jewelry expects to have many cash transactions occurring, it may be a good idea to establish a change fund. This fund is placed in the cash register drawer and used to make change for customers who pay cash. Becca decides to put $120 in the change fund, made up of various denominations of bills and coins. Let's look at a transaction analysis chart and the journal entry (Figure 6.18) for this sort of transaction.

Change fund Fund made up of various denominations that are used to make change for customers.

COACHING TIP

Beg. change fund
+ Cash register total
= Cash should have on hand
− Counted cash
= Shortage or overage of cash

Accounts Affected	Category	↓ ↑	Rules
Change Fund	Asset	↑	Dr.
Cash	Asset	↓	Cr.

Apr.	1	Change Fund		1 2 0 00		
		Cash			1 2 0 00	
		Establish change fund				

FIGURE 6.18
Change Fund Established

At the close of the business day, Becca will place the amount of the change fund back in the safe in the office. She will prepare the change fund (the same $120) in the appropriate denominations for the next business day. She will deposit in the bank the *remainder* of the cash taken in for the day.

In the next section, we look at how to record errors that are made in making change, called cash short and over.

Cash Short and Over The account that records cash shortages and overages. If the ending balance is a debit, it is recorded on the income statement as a miscellaneous expense; if it is a credit, it is recorded as miscellaneous income.

Cash Short and Over

In a local pizza shop the total cash sales for the day did not match the amount of cash on hand. Errors often happen in making change. To record and summarize the differences in cash, an account called *Cash Short and Over* is used. This account records both overages (too much money) and shortages (not enough money). Let's first look at the account (in T account form).

Cash Short and Over

Dr.	Cr.
shortage	overage

All shortages will be recorded as debits and all overages will be recorded as credits. This account is temporary. If the ending balance of the account is a debit (a shortage), it is considered a miscellaneous expense that would be reported on the income statement. If the balance of the account is a credit (an overage), it is considered as miscellaneous income reported on the income statement. Let's look at how the Cash Short and Over account could be used to record shortages or overages in sales as well as in the petty cash process.

Example 1: Shortages and Overages in Sales. On December 5 a pizza shop rang up cash sales of $560 for the day but only had $530 in cash.

Accounts Affected	Category	↓ ↑	Rules
Cash	Asset	↑	Debit $530
Cash Short and Over	Misc. Exp.	↑	Debit $30
Sales	Revenue	↑	Credit $560

The journal entry would be as shown in Figure 6.19.

FIGURE 6.19
Cash Shortage

Dec.	5	Cash		5 3 0 00				
		Cash Short and Over		3 0 00				
		Sales				5 6 0 00		
		Cash shortage						

Note that the shortage of $30 is a debit and would be recorded on the income statement as a miscellaneous expense.

What would the entry look like if the pizza shop showed a $50 overage (i.e., if the cash at the end of the day was $610)?

Accounts Affected	Category	↓ ↑	Rules
Cash	Asset	↑	Debit $610
Cash Short and Over	Miscellaneous Income	↑	Credit $50
Sales	Revenue	↑	Credit $560

The journal entry would be as shown in Figure 6.20.

FIGURE 6.20
Cash Overage

Dec.	5	Cash		6 1 0 00				
		Cash Short and Over				5 0 00		
		Sales				5 6 0 00		
		Cash overage						

Note that the Cash Short and Over account would be reported as miscellaneous income on the income statement. Now let's look at how to use this Cash Short and Over account to record petty cash transactions.

Example 2: Cash Short and Over in Petty Cash. A local computer company established petty cash for $200. On November 30, the petty cash box had $160 in vouchers as well as $32 in coin and currency. What would be the journal entry to replenish petty cash? Assume the vouchers were made up of $90 for postage and $70 for supplies expense.

If you add up the vouchers and cash in the box, cash is short by $8.

COACHING TIP

NOTE: The account Petty Cash is not used since the level in petty cash is not raised or lowered.

Accounts Affected	Category	↓ ↑	Rules
Postage Expense	Expense	↑	Debit $90
Supplies Expense	Expense	↑	Debit $70
Cash Short and Over	Misc. Expense	↑	Debit $8
Cash	Asset	↓	Credit $168

The journal entry is shown in Figure 6.21.

Nov.	30	Postage Expense		9 0 00		
		Supplies Expense		7 0 00		
		Cash Short and Over		8 00		
		Cash			1 6 8 00	

FIGURE 6.21
Petty Cash Replenished with Shortage

In the case of an overage, the Cash Short and Over would be a credit as miscellaneous income.

Now it's time to check your progress.

TRY IT! Learning Unit 6-3

Prepare a general journal entry to establish, replenish, and raise the petty cash level from the following;

On November 1, 201X, a $200 Petty Cash Fund was established. At the end of the month, Petty Cash had a balance of $40 plus the following paid vouchers:

Donations Expense $35; Postage Expense $40; Office Supplies Expense $35; and Miscellaneous Expenses of $50.

On November 30 replenishment of Petty Cash was complete.

On December 2 it was decided that the level of Petty Cash was too low and thus it was raised to a new level of $230.

DEMONSTRATION SUMMARY PROBLEM

Janet Fay, the bookkeeper for Lee Co., received the bank statement for March 31, 201X, from Ryan Federal Bank. She noted the following:

Bank Balance $1,525.60

Checkbook Balance 1,599.60

Checks not clearing bank:

No. 160 $261.10

No. 169   133.60

No. 171   205.80

Janet made a deposit of $1,640.30 that did not show up on the bank statement. A mortgage payment paid by the bank was $1,234.60. An IRS refund check was mailed directly to the bank for $2,200.40.

Also, Janet received a memo indicating the following transactions regarding Petty Cash that needed to be journalized:

201X

March 1 Petty Cash established for $400.

12 Needed to replenish Petty Cash; Petty Cash had a balance of $50 with vouchers for donations of $60, vouchers for Supplies Expense for $70, and Miscellaneous Expenses for $220.

On March 18 the Petty Cash level was raised to $500.

Requirements

Please do the following:

1. Prepare a bank reconciliation for Janet.
2. Prepare three journal entries to record Petty Cash transactions.

Solutions

Requirement 1

Prepare a bank reconciliation for Janet.

Tips for Preparing a Bank Reconciliation

> IRS Refund Check to bank—add to checkbook
> Automatic Mortgage Withdrawal—subtract from checkbook
> Deposits in Transit—add to bank balance
> Outstanding Checks—subtract from bank balance

Lee Co.

Bank Reconciliation as of March 31, 201X

Checkbook Bal.	$1,599.60		Bank Bal.		$1,525.60
Add:			Add:		
IRS Refund Check	2,200.40		Dep. in Transit		1,640.30
	$3,800.00				$3,165.90
Deduct:			Deduct:		
Mortg. Withdrawals	1,234.60		Outstanding checks:		
			No. 160	$261.10	
			No. 169	133.60	
			No. 171	205.80	600.50
Reconciled Balance	$2,565.40		Reconciled Balance		$2,565.40

Requirement 2

Prepare three journal entries to record Petty Cash transactions.

Date		Account Title	Dr.	Cr.
201X				
March	1	Petty Cash	400	
		Cash		400
	12	Donation Expense	60	
		Supplies Expense	70	
		Miscellaneous Expense	220	
		Cash		350
	18	Petty Cash	100	
		Cash		100

Tips for Journaling Petty Cash Transactions

Petty Cash is an asset. It is only debited to establish it or raise or lower its level. Note in Replenishment all old expenses are shown, and a new check is written to bring Petty Cash back to its original level ($400).

When Petty Cash is increased to a new level of $500, $100 is added to the Petty Cash account, and a check is cashed for that amount.

BLUEPRINT: A BANK RECONCILIATION

Checkbook Balance	Bank Balance
+/− EFT (electronic funds transfer)	+ Deposits in transit
+ Interest earned	− Outstanding checks
+ Notes collected	± Bank errors
+ Direct deposits	
− ATM withdrawals	
− Check redeposits	
− NSF check	
− Online fees	
− Automatic withdrawals	
− Overdrafts	
− Service charges	
− Stop payments	
± Book errors*	
+ Credit Memo—adds to balance	
− Debit Memo—deducts from balance	

*If a $60 check is recorded as $50, we must decrease the checkbook balance by $10.

 **TRY IT!**   **Solutions**   MyAccountingLab

Learning Unit 6-1

Only number 5 is false. Smartphones are used heavily in banking today.

Learning Unit 6-2

P.J. Co.
Bank Reconciliation as of March 31, 201X

Checkbook Balance		$2,200	Bank Balance		$1,600
Deduct:			Add:		
NSF Check	65		Deposits in Transit		600
Bank Service Charge	20				$2,200
			Deduct:		
		85	Outstanding Checks		85
Reconciled Balance		$2,115	Reconciled Balance		$2,115

Learning Unit 6-3

Date		Account Title	Dr.	Cr.
201X				
November	1	Petty Cash	200	
		Cash		200
		Established Petty Cash		
	30	Donations Expense	35	
		Postage Expense	40	
		Office Supplies Expense	35	
		Miscellaneous Expense	50	
		Cash		160
		Replenished Petty Cash		
December	2	Petty Cash	30	
		Cash		30
		Increased Petty Cash Level		

ACCOUNTING COACH

The following Coaching Tips are from Learning Units 6-1 through 6-3. Take the Pre-Game Checkup and use the Check Your Score at the bottom of the page to see how you are doing. The Accounting Coach provides tips before each Checkup to help you avoid common accounting errors.

LU 6-1 Banking Procedures and Checking Accounts

Pre-Game Tips: With mobile banking today checks can be processed or deposited via your smart phone. Banks will vary on policies about deposit requirements and minimum balances required to receive free checking or interest. It is still important to know the manual structure of checks, deposits and endorsements as they still are tools used in mobile banking.

Pre-Game Checkup: Answer true or false to the following statements.

1. A credit memo from the bank means that it is decreasing your balance.
2. Restrictive endorsements are not very safe.
3. Blank endorsements are the safest type of endorsement.
4. The drawer is the one receiving a check.
5. The drawee is the bank at which the drawer has an account.

LU 6-2 The Bank Reconciliation Process

Pre-Game Tips: When reconciling a bank statement, timing is a key consideration. Deposits in transit would be added to the bank balance while checks outstanding would be subtracted. Sometimes on the bank statement, interest is shown and must be updated on the checkbook side. If you forget to record a withdrawal from an ATM, you must update your book balance. Keep in mind that any adjustments to the checkbook will require journal entries so the cash ledger account will be correct. Today, online banking is taking over many of the manual tasks, but the accounting theory remains the same.

Pre-Game Checkup: Answer true or false to the following statements.

1. All reconciliations must be done on paper and not on computers.
2. Automatic payment of a mortgage by a bank will increase the checkbook balance.
3. A note collected by a bank will lower the checkbook balance.
4. An IRS refund collected by the bank will decrease your checkbook balance.
5. Reconciliations can only be done once a year.

LU 6-3 The Establishment of Petty Cash and Change Funds

Pre-Game Tips: Petty cash is an asset. When petty cash is replenished to the same level, all of the old expenses are shown and a new check is written. The account Petty Cash is not touched. When a new level of petty cash is desired, the account Petty Cash will be debited to increase it or credited to decrease it. Keep in mind that the account Cash Short and Over is a miscellaneous account found on the income statement. A debit balance on Cash Short and Over means that you have a shortage, and a credit balance means you have an overage.

Pre-Game Checkup: Answer true or false to the following statements.

1. Petty cash is an expense.
2. Increasing the Petty Cash account means that you have to credit it.
3. In the replenishment process, cash is not involved.
4. When petty cash is established, the Petty Cash account is debited.
5. A shortage in the Cash Short and Over account results in a credit balance.

CHECK YOUR SCORE: Answers to the Pre-Game Checkup

LU 6-1
1. False—A credit memo from the bank means that it is increasing your balance.
2. False—Restrictive endorsements are the safest type of endorsement.
3. False—Restrictive endorsements are the safest type of endorsement.
4. False—The payee is to whom a check is payable.
5. True

LU 6-2

1. False—Many reconciliations today are done by computer.
2. False—Automatic payment of a mortgage will decrease the checkbook balance.
3. False—A note will increase the checkbook balance.
4. False—An IRS refund will increase the checkbook balance.
5. False—Reconciliations are usually done monthly.

LU 6-3

1. False—Petty cash is an asset.
2. False—Increasing the Petty Cash account means that you have to debit it.
3. False—In the replenishment process, a new check (cash) needs to be written.
4. True
5. False—A shortage in the Cash Short and Over account results in a debit balance.

Chapter Summary

Here are all the key terms and equations to help you understand the concepts of this chapter and prepare you for your exam. After completing this review, go to MyAccountingLab for more practice opportunities.

MyAccountingLab

Concepts You Should Know	Key Terms

L01

Explain Banking Procedures and Checking Accounts

1. Restrictive endorsement limits any further negotiation of a check.
2. The payee is the person to whom the check is payable. The drawer is the one who orders the bank to pay a sum of money. The drawee is the bank with which the drawer has an account.

Cancelled check (p. 208)
Check (p. 206)
Deposit slip (p. 203)
Drawee (p. 206)
Drawer (p. 206)
Endorsement (p. 203)
Internal control system (p. 202)
Payee (p. 206)
Signature card (p. 202)

L02

Explain Bank Reconciliation

1. The process of reconciling the bank balance with the company's cash balance is called the bank reconciliation.
2. Deposits in transit are added to the bank balance.
3. Checks outstanding are subtracted from the bank balance.
4. NSF means that a check previously deposited has nonsufficient funds to be credited (deposited) to a checking account; therefore, the amount is not included in the bank balance and thus the checking account balance is lowered.
5. When a bank debits your account, it is deducting an amount from your balance. A credit to the account is an increase to your balance.
6. All adjustments to the checkbook balance require journal entries.
7. The Internet has created online banking options.

ATM (automatic teller machine) (p. 212)
Bank reconciliation (p. 210)
Bank statement (p. 210)
Check truncation (safekeeping) (p. 214)
Credit memorandum (p. 211)
Debit memorandum (p. 211)
Deposits in transit (p. 210)
Electronic funds transfer (EFT) (p. 212)
NSF (nonsufficient funds) (p. 211)
Outstanding checks (p. 210)
Phishing (p. 213)

L03

Explain Petty Cash and Change Funds

1. Petty Cash is an asset found on the balance sheet.
2. The auxiliary petty cash record is an auxiliary book; therefore, no postings are done from this record.
3. When a petty cash fund is established, the amount is entered as a debit to Petty Cash and a credit to Cash.
4. At the time of replenishment of the petty cash fund, all expenses are debited (by category) and a credit to Cash (a new check) results. This replenishment, when journalized and posted, updates the ledger from the journal.
5. The only time the Petty Cash account is used is to establish the fund initially or to bring the fund to a higher or lower level.
6. A change fund is an asset that is used to give change to cash customers.
7. Cash Short and Over is an account that is either a miscellaneous expense or miscellaneous income, depending on whether the ending balance is a shortage or overage.

Auxiliary petty cash record (p. 218)
Cash Short and Over (p. 221)
Change fund (p. 221)
Petty cash fund (p. 216)
Petty cash voucher (p. 217)

Discussion Questions and Critical Thinking/Ethical Case

1. Discuss how smartphone apps are making banking more mobile.

2. What is the advantage of having preprinted deposit slips?

3. Explain the difference between a blank endorsement and a restrictive endorsement.

4. Explain the difference between payee, drawer, and drawee.

5. Why should check stubs be filled out first, before the check itself is written?

6. A bank statement is sent twice a month. True or false? Please explain.

7. Explain the end product of a bank reconciliation.

8. Why are outstanding checks subtracted from the bank balance?

9. An NSF check results in a bank issuing the depositor a credit memorandum. Agree or disagree? Please explain your response.

10. Why do adjustments to the checkbook balance in the reconciliation process need to be journalized?

11. What is EFT?

12. What are the major advantages and disadvantages of online banking?

13. What is meant by check truncation or safekeeping?

14. Petty cash is a liability. Agree or disagree? Explain.

15. Explain the relationship of the auxiliary petty cash record to the recording of the cash payment.

16. At the time of replenishment, why are the totals of individual expenses debited?

17. Explain the purpose of a change fund.

18. Explain how Cash Short and Over can be a miscellaneous expense.

19. Sean Nah, the bookkeeper for Revell Co., received a bank statement from Lone Bank. Sean noticed a $250 mistake made by the bank in the company's favor. Sean called his supervisor, who said that as long as it benefits the company, he should not tell the bank about the error. You make the call. Write your specific recommendations to Sean.

MyAccountingLab

Concept Checks

(10 min) **LO2** **Bank Reconciliation**

1. Indicate what effect (#1–4) each situation (#a–f) will have on the bank reconciliation process.

    1. Add to bank balance.
    2. Deduct from bank balance.
    3. Add to checkbook balance.
    4. Deduct from checkbook balance.

        _____ **a.** Check no. 140 was outstanding for $200.
        _____ **b.** $300 deposit in transit.
        _____ **c.** $190 NSF check.

_____ **d.** A check written for $15 was recorded in the company's books as $25.
_____ **e.** Bank collected a $1,000 note less a $50 collection fee.
_____ **f.** $12 bank service charge.

Journal Entries in Reconciliation Process

LO2 *(5 min)*

2. Which of the transactions in Exercise 1 would require a journal entry?

Bank Reconciliation

LO2 *(10 min)*

3. From the following, construct a bank reconciliation for Capital Co. as of September 30, 201X.

Checkbook balance	$1,855.80
Bank statement balance	1975.40
Deposits in transit	271.20
Outstanding checks	461.50
Bank service charge	10.90
NSF check	59.80

Petty Cash

LO3 *(10 min)*

4. Indicate what effects (#1–4) each situation (#a–f) will have. (Note: There might be more than one effect applicable for a situation.)

   1. New check written.
   2. Recorded in general journal.
   3. Petty cash voucher prepared.
   4. Recorded in auxiliary petty cash record.

   _____ **a.** Established petty cash.
   _____ **b.** Paid $1,400 bill.
   _____ **c.** Paid $3 for Band-Aids from petty cash.
   _____ **d.** Paid $4 for stamps from petty cash.
   _____ **e.** Paid electric bill, $270.
   _____ **f.** Replenished petty cash.

Replenishment of Petty Cash

LO3 *(15 min)*

5. Petty cash was originally established for $23. During the month, $5.20 was paid out for thumbtacks and $5.90 for paper cups. During replenishment, the custodian discovered that the balance in petty cash was $7.80. Record, using a general journal entry, the replenishment of petty cash back to $23.

Increasing Petty Cash

LO3 *(10 min)*

6. In Exercise 5, if the custodian decided to raise the level of petty cash to $30.75, what would be the journal entry to replenish? (Use a general journal entry.)

MyAccountingLab   **Exercises**

Set A

(15 min) **LO2**   **6A-1.**   From the following information, construct a bank reconciliation for Bang Co. as of February 28, 201X. Then prepare journal entries if needed.

Checkbook balance	$1,314	Outstanding checks	$654
Bank statement balance	1,050	Bank service charge	65
Deposits (in transit)	800	NSF: Tamara Carter check in payment of account was returned for insufficient funds.	53

(15 min) **LO3**   **6A-2.**   In general journal form, prepare journal entries to establish a petty cash fund on March 1 and replenish it on March 31.

201X		
March	1	A $102 petty cash fund is established.
	31	At the end of the month, $22 cash plus the following paid vouchers exist: donations expense, $18; postage expense, $17; office supplies expense, $25; miscellaneous expense, $20.

(15 min) **LO3**   **6A-3.**   If in Exercise 6A-2 cash on hand is $16, prepare the entry to replenish the petty cash on March 31.

(15 min) **LO3**   **6A-4.**   If in Exercise 6A-2 cash on hand is $28, prepare the entry to replenish the petty cash on March 31.

(15 min) **LO3**   **6A-5.**   At the end of the day the clerk for Ken's Variety Shop noticed an error in the amount of cash he should have. Total cash sales from the sales tape were $1,192, whereas the total cash in the register was $1,152. Ken keeps a $25 change fund in his shop. Prepare an appropriate general journal entry to record the cash sales as well as reveal the cash shortage.

Set B

(15 min) **LO2**   **6B-1.**   From the following information, construct a bank reconciliation for Zoom Co. as of October 31, 201X. Then prepare journal entries if needed.

Checkbook balance	$1,580	Outstanding checks	$638
Bank statement balance	1,000	Bank service charge	70
Deposits (in transit)	1,100	NSF: Mia Kaminsky's check in payment of account was returned for insufficient funds.	48

(15 min) **LO3**   **6B-2.**   In general journal form, prepare journal entries to establish a petty cash fund on March 1 and replenish it on March 31.

201X		
March	1	A $104 petty cash fund is established.
	31	At the end of the month, $21 cash plus the following paid vouchers exist: donations expense, $21; postage expense, $18; office supplies expense, $29; miscellaneous expense, $15.

6B-3. If in Exercise 6B-2 cash on hand is $17, prepare the entry to replenish the petty cash on March 31.

LO3 *(15 min)*

6B-4. If in Exercise 6B-2 cash on hand is $29, prepare the entry to replenish the petty cash on March 31.

LO3 *(15 min)*

6B-5. At the end of the day the clerk for Harold's Variety Shop noticed an error in the amount of cash he should have. Total cash sales from the sales tape were $1,196, whereas the total cash in the register was $1,156. Harold keeps a $29 change fund in his shop. Prepare an appropriate general journal entry to record the cash sales as well as reveal the cash shortage.

LO3 *(15 min)*

Problems

MyAccountingLab

Set A

6A-1. Denim.com received a bank statement from Waldorf Bank indicating a bank balance of $7,900. Based on Denim.com's check stubs, the ending checkbook balance was $8,974. Your task is to prepare a bank reconciliation for Denim.com as of July 31, 201X, from the following information (journalize entries as needed):

LO2 *(20 min)*

Check Figure:
Reconciled Balance $8,710

  a. Checks outstanding: no. 122, $850; no. 130, $640.
  b. Deposits in transit, $2,300.
  c. Denim.com forgot to record a $1,200 equipment purchase made with a debit card.
  d. Bank service charges, $50.
  e. Waldorf Bank collected a note for Denim.com, $1,000, less a $14 collection fee.

6A-2. From the following bank statement, please (1) complete the bank reconciliation for Josh's Deli found on the reverse of the following bank statement and (2) journalize the appropriate entries as needed.

LO2 *(20 min)*

Check Figure:
Reconciled Balance $4,785

  a. A deposit of $2,400 is in transit.
  b. Josh's Deli has an ending checkbook balance of $5,600.
  c. Checks outstanding: no. 111, $550; no. 119, $1,300; no. 121, $280.
  d. Dwight Smith's check for $800 bounced due to lack of sufficient funds.
  e. Bank Service Charge $15.

Bolton National Bank
Rio Mean Branch
Bugna, Texas
Josh's Deli
8811 2nd St.
Bugna, Texas

Old Balance	Checks and Other Withdrawals in Order of Payment		Deposits	Date	New Balance
5,700				2/2	5,700
	100	250		2/3	5,350
	180.00		390.00	2/10	5,560
	540.00		660.00	2/15	5,680
	800.00	NSF	250.00	2/20	5,130
	1,400.00		1,190.00	2/24	4,920
	600.00	15.00 SC	210.00	2/28	4,515

(30 min) **LO3**

Check Figure:
Cash Replenishment $86

6A-3.   The following transactions occurred in April for Exultant Co.:

201X		
Apr.	1	Issued check no. 14 for $150 to establish a petty cash fund.
	5	Paid $20 from petty cash for postage, voucher no. 1.
	8	Paid $25 from petty cash for office supplies, voucher no. 2.
	15	Issued check no. 15 to Upright Corp. for $250 from past purchases on account.
	17	Paid $19 from petty cash for office supplies, voucher no. 3.
	20	Issued check no. 16 to Moore Corp., $725 for past purchases on account.
	24	Paid $10 from petty cash for postage, voucher no. 4.
	26	Paid $12 from petty cash for local church donation, voucher no. 5 (a miscellaneous payment).
	28	Issued check no. 17 to Jeff Kloon to pay for office equipment, $750.
	30	Replenished petty cash, check no. 18. Assume no shortage or overage.

Your tasks are to do the following:
a. Record the appropriate entries in the general journal as well as the auxiliary petty cash record as needed.
b. Replenish the petty cash fund on April 30 (check no. 18).

(40 min) **LO3**

Check Figure:
Cash Replenishment $107

6A-4.   From the following, record the transactions in Rochester's auxiliary petty cash record and general journal as needed:

201X		
Oct.	1	A check was drawn (no. 444) payable to Harold Hauer, petty cashier, to establish a $210 petty cash fund.
	5	Paid $20 for postage stamps, voucher no. 1.
	9	Paid $14 for delivery charges on goods for resale, voucher no. 2.
	12	Paid $8 for donation to a church (miscellaneous expense), voucher no. 3.
	14	Paid $15 for postage stamps, voucher no. 4.
	17	Paid $14 for delivery charges on goods for resale, voucher no. 5.
	27	Purchased computer supplies from petty cash for $12, voucher no. 6.
	28	Paid $13 for postage, voucher no. 7.
	29	Drew check no. 628 to replenish petty cash and a $11 shortage.

Set B

(20 min) **LO2**

Check Figure:
Reconciled Balance $8,090

6B-1.   Work.com received a bank statement from Waldorf Bank indicating a bank balance of $7,800. Based on Work.com's check stubs, the ending checkbook balance was $8,320. Your task is to prepare a bank reconciliation for Work.com as of July 31, 201X, from the following information (journalize as needed):
a. Checks outstanding: no. 122, $830; no. 130, $680.
b. Deposits in transit, $1,800.
c. Work.com forgot to record a $1,220 equipment purchase made with a debit card.
d. Bank service charges, $45.
e. Waldorf Bank collected a note for Work.com, $1,050, less a $15 collection fee.

6B-2. From the following statement, please (1) complete the bank reconciliation for Jackie's Deli found on the reverse of the following bank statement and (2) journalize the appropriate entries as needed.

a. A deposit of $2,500 is in transit.

b. Jackie's Deli has an ending checkbook balance of $5,990.

c. Checks outstanding: no. 111, $750; no. 119, $1,450; no. 121, $370.

d. Dwight Smith's check for $1,400 bounced due to lack of sufficient funds.

e. Bank service charges, $45.

LO2 *(20 min)*

S50 / **QB**

Check Figure:
Reconciled Balance $4,545

Mattapoisett National Bank
Rio Mean Branch
Bugna, Texas
Jackie's Deli
8811 2nd St.
Bugna, Texas

Old Balance	Checks and Other Withdrawals in Order of Payment		Deposits	Date	New Balance
6,300				2/2	6,300
	140.00	260.00		2/3	5,900
	120.00		310.00	2/10	6,090
	610.00		580.00	2/15	6,060
	1,400.00	NSF	260.00	2/20	4,920
	1,150.00		1,240.00	2/24	5,010
	520.00	45.00 SC	170.00	2/28	4,615

6B-3. The following transactions occurred in April for Jolly Co.:

LO3 *(30 min)*

S50 / **QB**

Check Figure:
Cash Replenishment $77

201X		
Apr.	1	Issued check no. 14 for $120 to establish a petty cash fund.
	5	Paid $10 from petty cash for postage, voucher no. 1.
	8	Paid $19 from petty cash for office supplies, voucher no. 2.
	15	Issued check no. 15 to Upright Corp. for $160 for past purchases on account.
	17	Paid $17 from petty cash for office supplies, voucher no. 3.
	20	Issued check no. 16 to Barret Corp. $675 for past purchases on account.
	24	Paid $19 from petty cash for postage, voucher no. 4.
	26	Paid $12 from petty cash for local church donation, voucher no. 5 (a miscellaneous payment).
	28	Issued check no. 17 to Jay Loon to pay for office equipment, $625.
	30	Replenished petty cash, check no. 18. Assume no shortage or overage.

Your tasks are to do the following:

a. Record the appropriate entries in the general journal as well as the auxiliary petty cash record as needed.

b. Replenish the petty cash fund on April 30 (check no. 18).

(40 min) **LO3**

6B-4. From the following, record the transactions in Kona's auxiliary petty cash record and general journal as needed:

Check Figure:
Cash Replenishment $109

201X		
Oct.	1	A check was drawn (no. 444) payable to Harold Hauer, petty cashier, to establish a $220 petty cash fund.
	5	Paid $29 for postage stamps, voucher no. 1.
	9	Paid $7 for delivery charges on goods for resale, voucher no. 2.
	12	Paid $13 for donation to a church (miscellaneous expense), voucher no. 3.
	14	Paid $5 for postage stamps, voucher no. 4.
	17	Paid $19 for delivery charges on goods for resale, voucher no. 5.
	27	Purchased computer supplies from petty cash for $16, voucher no. 6.
	28	Paid $18 for postage, voucher no. 7.
	29	Drew check no. 618 to replenish petty cash and a $2 shortage.

Financial Report Problem

(15 min) **LO2**

Reading the Kellogg's Annual Report

Go to http://investor.kelloggs.com/investor-relations/annual-reports to access the Kellogg's 2013 Annual Report. How often do you think Kellogg's reconciles its bank statement? What type of security control may be in place? Support your position.

MyAccountingLab

ON THE JOB SMITH COMPUTER CENTER

(60 min) **LO2,3**

The books have been closed for the first year of business for Smith Computer Center. The company ended up with a marginal profit for the first three months in operation. Thad expects faster growth as he enters a busy season.

Following is a list of transactions for the month of October. Petty Cash account #1010 and Miscellaneous Expense account #5100 have been added to the chart of accounts.

Oct.		
	1	Paid rent for November, December, and January, $1,500 (check no. 8108).
	2	Established a petty cash fund for $300.
	4	Collected $4,600 from a cash customer for building five systems.
	5	Collected $2,700, the amount due from Dr. Michael Turiono's invoice no. 12674, customer on account.
	6	Purchased $40 worth of stamps using petty cash voucher no. 101.
	7	Withdrew $900 (check no. 8109) for personal use.
	8	Purchased $25 worth of supplies using petty cash voucher no. 102.
	12	Paid the newspaper carrier $15 using petty cash voucher no. 103.
	16	Paid the amount due on the August phone bill, $35 (check no. 8110). (Recorded on Sept. 20)
	17	Paid the amount due on the August electric bill, $85 (check no. 8111). (Recorded on Sept. 22)
	22	Performed computer services for Phil's Photography; billed the client $5,400 (invoice no. 12675).
	23	Paid $20 for computer paper using petty cash voucher no. 104.
	30	Took $15 out of petty cash for lunch, voucher no. 105.
	31	Replenished the petty cash. Coin and currency in drawer total $185.

Because Thad was so busy trying to close his books, he forgot to reconcile his last three months of bank statements. A list of all deposits and checks written for the past three months (each entry is identified by chapter, transaction date, or transaction letter) and the bank statements for July through September are provided. The statement for October won't arrive until the first week of November.

Assignment

1. Record the transactions in general journal and auxiliary petty cash record.
2. Post the transactions to the general ledger accounts.
3. Prepare a trial balance.
4. Compare the Smith Computer Center's deposits and checks with the bank statements and complete a bank reconciliation as of September 30, 201X.

Smith Computer Center Summary of Deposits and Checks

Chapter	Transaction	Deposits Payor/Payee	Amount
1	a	Thad Feldman	$6,000
1	f	Cash customer	800
1	i	Phil's Photography	1,800
1	g	Cash customer	600
2	p	Cash customer	1,300
3	Sept. 2	Tonya Parker Jones	420
3	Sept. 6	Lilly Life	150
3	Sept. 12	Erin Caffrey	1,700
3	Sept. 26	Howard Trale	750

Chapter	Transaction	Check #	Checks Payor/Payee	Amount
1	b	8095	A-Tech, Inc.	$1,800
1	c	8096	Bertha and Pac Furniture, Inc.	3,300
1	e	8097	Chapin Corp.	500
1	j	8098	Thad Feldman	175
2	l	8099	Insurance Protection, Inc.	450
2	m	8100	The Staple Store	150
2	n	8101	Computer Edge Magazine	900
2	q	8102	San Diego Electric	75
2	r	8103	U.S. Postmaster	70
3	Sept. 1	8104	Chapin Corp.	1,500
3	Sept. 8	8105	Pacific Bell USA	80
3	Sept. 15	8106	Computers R Us	300
3	Sept. 17	8107	A-Tech, Inc.	2,100

Bank Statement

First Union Bank 322 Glen Ave. Escondido, CA 92025

Smith Computer Center			Statement Date: July 22, 201X	
Checks Paid:			Deposits and Credits:	
Date paid	Number	Amount	Date received	Amount
7-4	8095	1,800.00	7-1	6,000.00
7-7	8096	3,300.00	7-10	800.00
7-15	8097	500.00	7-20	1,800.00
			7-21	600.00
Total 3 checks paid for $5,600.00			Total Deposits	$9,200.00
Ending balance on July 22—$3,600.00				

Received statement July 29, 201X.

Bank Statement

First Union Bank 322 Glen Ave. Escondido, CA 92025

Smith Computer Center			Statement Date: August 21, 201X	
Checks Paid:			Deposits and Credits:	
Date paid	Number	Amount	Date received	Amount
8-2	8098	175.00	8-12	1,300.00
8-3	8099	450.00		
8-10	8100	150.00		
8-15	8101	900.00		
8-20	8102	75.00		
Total 5 checks paid for $1,750.00			Total Deposits	$1,300.00
Beginning balance on July 22—$3,600.00			Ending balance on August 21—$3,150.00	

Received statement August 27, 201X.

Bank Statement

First Union Bank 322 Glen Ave. Escondido, CA 92025

Smith Computer Center			Statement Date: September 30, 201X	
Checks Paid:			Deposits and Credits:	
Date paid	Number	Amount	Date received	Amount
9-2	8103	70.00	9-4	420.00
9-6	8104	1,500.00	9-7	150.00
9-12	8105	80.00	9-14	1,700.00
Total 3 checks paid for $1,650.00			Total Deposits	$2,270.00
Beginning balance on August 21			Ending balance on September 30	
$3,150.00			$3,770.00	

Received statement September 30, 201X.

Calculating Pay and Recording Payroll Taxes: The Beginning of the Payroll Process

CHAPTER PREVIEW: THE BIG PICTURE

Wow! You just got your first paycheck from your new job at Target. You expected a check for $500 but are disappointed when you realize the check is for much less. Although your friends warned you about taxes taken out of your pay, you forgot. Where did all of your money go?

Target, like many other companies, has a payroll department that prepares its payroll. Clerks within the payroll department calculate employee earnings and all deductions to be withheld. These deductions include federal and state income tax as well as Social Security and Medicare tax. You realize the company is probably correct, but you want to understand where all the extra money went. Your new mission is to understand the payroll process. In this chapter, you learn how to compute gross pay and all of the taxes and other reductions that lead to net pay.

Learning Objectives

LO1 Calculate Gross Pay, Employee Payroll Tax Deductions for Federal Income Tax Withholding, State Income Tax Withholding, FICA (OASDI, Medicare), and Net Pay

LO2 Prepare a Payroll Register and Maintain an Employee Earnings Record

LO3 Calculate Employer Taxes for FICA (OASDI, Medicare), FUTA, SUTA, and Workers' Compensation Insurance

LO4 Journalize the Payroll Register, Employer Tax Liability, and Workers' Compensation Insurance

Most businesses can't run without employees, so hiring and paying employees are pretty typical business events. The accounting for payroll transactions is really the same whether a business is a small, family-owned gardening business in your town or a nationwide retail department store. Either way, it's important to know how to calculate, pay, record, and report payroll and payroll taxes in this payroll process.

Federal, state, and maybe even local laws regulate the payroll process. A business may be fined substantial penalties and interest for failing to follow these laws properly. The penalties are based on the length of time the correct forms are delinquent. For example, if forms are filed up to 30 days late, the penalty is $30 per form; if filed between March 30 and August 1, the penalty is $60 per form. However, if forms are not correctly filed by August 1 of the calendar year following the tax year, the penalty is $100 per form up to a maximum of $1,500,000. Because of this, there are many companies—such as ADP, Paychex, and Ceridian—that will handle payroll processing and tax reporting for a fee. However, it is often less costly for the business to complete the payroll functions in-house.

In this chapter, we take a close look at the employees of Travelwithus.com to see how a payroll is computed and recorded. Travelwithus.com is a new Internet-based company specializing in cruises and business travel. The company was formed as a corporation. We look at how its payroll is affected by federal, state, and local taxes and how the accountant at Travelwithus.com handles payroll transactions for the company.

Gross Pay, Employee Payroll Tax Deductions for Federal Income Tax Withholding, State Income Tax Withholding, FICA (OASDI, Medicare), and Net Pay

Katherine Kurtz is the accountant for Travelwithus.com who calculates and records each payroll for the company. Several parts of Katherine's job are especially important. First, Katherine must be accurate in everything she does, because any mistake she makes in working with the payroll may affect both the employee and the company. Second, Katherine needs to be on time when working on the company's payroll so that employees get their paychecks as expected and governments receive payroll taxes when due. Third, Katherine must at all times obey the appropriate federal, state, and local laws governing payroll matters. Fourth, because processing payroll involves personal employee information such as pay rates and marital status, Katherine always needs to keep payroll data confidential.

Gross Earnings

It is important to understand there is a federal law governing most employers as to how employee payroll is handled. This law is the Fair Labor Standards Act (FLSA), sometimes referred to as the Federal Wage and Hour Law. An employer must follow the Fair Labor Standards Act if it is involved in interstate commerce, in other words, if it is doing business in more than one state. Most businesses follow this Act because interstate commerce involves the sale or receipt of anything outside of the state border. Child labor laws, the federal minimum wage, and overtime requirements are included within the FLSA.

To begin the payroll process, Katherine must first calculate the earnings for Travelwithus.com's employees. To make the correct calculations, Katherine must know how each employee has been classified for payroll purposes. As a rule, a company will classify every employee either as "hourly" or "salaried." If an employee is an hourly employee, that employee is paid only for the hours he or she worked. Employees classified as salaried employees receive a fixed dollar amount for the time

Fair Labor Standards Act (Federal Wage and Hour Law) A law the majority of employers must follow that contains rules stating the minimum hourly rate of pay and the maximum number of hours a worker will work before being paid time and a half for overtime hours worked. This law also has other rules and regulations that employers must follow for payroll purposes.

Interstate commerce A test that is applied to determine whether an employer must follow the rules of the Fair Labor Standards Act. If an employer communicates or does business with another business in some other state, it is usually considered to be involved in interstate commerce.

period worked. The FLSA identifies the correct treatment of hourly and salaried employees. This means you cannot classify an employee as salaried strictly to avoid overtime pay.

Travelwithus.com classified three of its six employees as hourly. For these three employees, Katherine must compute the hours they worked during a specific time period known as a pay period; the number of hours determines how much each has earned. For payroll purposes, pay periods are defined as daily, weekly, biweekly (every 2 weeks), semimonthly (twice each month), monthly, quarterly, or annually. A pay period can start on any day of the week and must end after the specified period of time has passed. Most companies use weekly, biweekly, semimonthly, or monthly pay periods when calculating their payrolls.

Companies can use different pay periods for different groups of employees. However, Travelwithus.com chose a biweekly pay period for its employees, both salaried and hourly. The biweekly pay period starts on Monday and ends 2 weeks later on a Sunday. All employees actually receive their paychecks on the following Wednesday because it takes Katherine a few days to calculate the payroll.

After determining the pay period, Katherine will calculate the gross earnings for each employee. Gross earnings includes all earnings before any deductions. This includes salaries, regular and overtime hours, bonuses, and commissions. Katherine first completes the hourly employees. She knows that overtime earnings must be computed according to the FLSA. For most employers, this law says that an hourly employee must be paid at least one and a half times his or her regular pay rate for any hours worked in excess of 40 in a workweek. A workweek, according to the law, is a 7-day (or 168-hour) period that can start at any time, but once the starting time for the week is determined, it must stay the same for each week.

It is important to know that some states also have payroll laws that need to be followed in determining pay. For example, California requires employers to pay overtime pay to hourly employees who have worked more than 8 hours in any day, even if they work less than 40 hours total for that week. Employers must follow both sets of laws, and in this case, Travelwithus.com would pay overtime if an employee works more than 8 hours in one day and if an employee works more than 40 hours in one week.

Hourly employees of Travelwithus.com have two workweeks in each biweekly pay period. Travelwithus.com's hourly workweek starts on Monday morning at 12:01 A.M. each week and ends 7 days later on Sunday evening at 12:00 midnight. Thus, Katherine must calculate overtime pay for any employee who worked more than 40 hours in each week of this two-week period.

Stephanie Higuera is one of the three hourly employees working for Travelwithus.com. Travelwithus.com's most recent biweekly pay period began on Monday, October 13, at 12:01 A.M. and ended on Sunday, October 26 at 12:00 midnight. The first week of this period ended on Sunday, October 19, and during this week Stephanie worked 44 hours. During the second week that ended on October 26, Stephanie worked 38 hours.

How much should she be paid? Katherine will answer this question by first calculating both Stephanie's regular hours and her overtime hours. According to federal law, Katherine must look at each week separately. Stephanie worked 44 hours during the first week, which means that she worked 40 regular hours and 4 overtime hours. Because she worked fewer than 40 hours in the second week, all of these hours are regular hours.

Pay or payroll period
A length of time used by an employer to calculate the amount of an employee's earnings. Pay periods can be daily, weekly, biweekly (once every 2 weeks), semimonthly (twice each month), monthly, quarterly, or annually.

Gross earnings (gross pay) All earnings before any deductions.

Workweek A 7-day (168-hour) period used to determine overtime hours for employees. A workweek can begin on any given day, but must end 7 days later.

Week No.	Week Ending	Regular Hours	Overtime Hours	Total Hours
1	October 19	40	4	44
2	October 26	38	0	38
Total		78	4	82

Stephanie earns $11.40 for each hour she works, so Katherine computes Stephanie's pay as follows:

$11.40 *regular rate* × 1.5 = $17.10 *overtime rate*

78 *regular hours* × $11.40 *regular rate* = $889.20 *regular earnings*

4 *overtime hours* × $17.10 *overtime rate* =   68.40 *overtime earnings*

$889.20 *regular earnings* + $68.40 *overtime earnings* = $957.60 *gross earnings*   ◄

Or, Katherine could figure Stephanie's pay this way: SAME

$11.40 *regular rate* × 0.5 = $5.70 *extra pay*
    for each overtime hour

82 *total hours* × $11.40 *regular rate* = $934.80 *earnings at the regular rate*

4 *overtime hours* × $5.70 *extra pay for each*
    overtime hour =   22.80 *extra earnings*

$934.80 *earnings at the regular rate* + $22.80 *extra*
    earnings = $957.60 *gross earnings*   ◄

Notice that either way, Katherine computed exactly the same amount of gross earnings. The advantage of using the first method is that it clearly shows the amount of extra money that Stephanie earned from working those additional overtime hours. The advantage of the second is that it shows the effect of being paid at a higher, overtime rate for those extra hours worked.

After computing all hourly employees, Katherine starts the process with the salaried employees. Julia Regan also works for Travelwithus.com. She qualifies as a salaried employee, and earns $4,875 per month. There are two ways to convert her monthly pay into biweekly pay. First, annualize the monthly pay, then divide by 26 pay periods ($4,875 × 12 = $58,500/26 = $2,250). The second method follows the rule that there are 4 1/3 weeks in the month. Therefore, divide $4,875 by 4 1/3 = $1,125 per week × 2 = $2,250.

Federal Income Tax Withholding

After Katherine determines Stephanie's and Julia's gross earnings, she figures out how much each of them will actually receive in their paychecks after several different taxes have been withheld. These taxes are called payroll taxes and must be paid by the employees. Employees pay these amounts by having them taken out, or withheld, from their paychecks. Their employer then sends them to the Internal Revenue Service (IRS), state governments, and maybe even local governments so they count against the amount of federal, state, and possible local income taxes that the employees will owe for the year.

In this way, Stephanie and Julia pay their taxes on a "pay as you go basis." In other words, when Stephanie and Julia complete their federal income tax returns at the end of the year, they will deduct the amount of income tax withheld during the year from the total amount owed for the year. How and when Travelwithus.com turns these amounts over to the federal, state, and local governments will be discussed in Chapter 8. Katherine computes the amount of taxes to be withheld based on each employee's gross earnings for the pay period.

Katherine starts figuring out how much to withhold from each employee's pay by looking at the W-4 that he or she completed. The IRS Form W-4, Employee's Withholding Allowance Certificate, is completed by every employee and provides information that will be used to determine the amount of federal income tax (FIT) withholdings. Figure 7.1 is Stephanie's W-4 form. Notice that it shows Stephanie's marital status and total number of allowances she claims for federal income tax purposes. Usually, an employee may claim one allowance for himself or herself, one for his or her spouse, and one for each of his or her dependents, such as a child. Employees who want more

Form W-4 (Employee's Withholding Allowance Certificate) A form filled out by employees and used by employers to supply needed information about the number of allowances claimed, marital status, and so forth. The form is used for payroll purposes to determine federal income tax withholding from an employee's paycheck.

Federal income tax (FIT) withholding Amount of federal income tax withheld by the employer from the employee's gross pay; the amount withheld is determined by the employee's gross pay, the pay period, the number of allowances claimed by the employee on the W-4 form, and the marital status indicated on the W-4 form.

Allowances (also called *exemptions*) Certain dollar amounts of a person's income tax that will be considered nontaxable for income tax withholding purposes.

FIGURE 7.1 Completed W-4 Form

Cut here and give Form W-4 to your employer. Keep the top part for your records.

Form **W-4**

Department of the Treasury
Internal Revenue Service

Employee's Withholding Allowance Certificate

▶ **Whether you are entitled to claim a certain number of allowances or exemption from withholding is subject to review by the IRS. Your employer may be required to send a copy of this form to the IRS.**

OMB No. 1545-0074

201X

1 Type or print your first name and middle initial. *Stephanie A.* Last name *Higuera*

2 Your social security number *123 : 45 : 6789*

Home address (number and street or rural route) *104 Inverness Way*

City or town, state, and ZIP code *Southside, MA 01945*

3 ☒ Single ☐ Married ☐ Married, but withhold at higher Single rate.
Note. If married, but legally separated, or spouse is a nonresident alien, check the "Single" box.

4 If your last name differs from that shown on your social security card, check here. You must call 1-800-772-1213 for a new card. ▶ ☐

5 Total number of allowances you are claiming (from line **H** above **or** from the applicable worksheet on page 2) 5 *1*

6 Additional amount, if any, you want withheld from each paycheck 6 $

7 I claim exemption from withholding for 2006, and I certify that I meet **both** of the following conditions for exemption.
• Last year I had a right to a refund of **all** federal income tax withheld because I had **no** tax liability **and**
• This year I expect a refund of **all** federal income tax withheld because I expect to have **no** tax liability.
If you meet both conditions, write "Exempt" here ▶ 7

Under penalties of perjury, I declare that I have examined this certificate and to the best of my knowledge and belief, it is true, correct, and complete.

Employee's signature
(Form is not valid
unless you sign it.) ▶ *Stephanie A. Higuera* Date ▶ *January 3, 201X*

8 Employer's name and address (Employer: Complete lines 8 and 10 only if sending to the IRS.) 9 Office code (optional) 10 Employer identification number (EIN)

For Privacy Act and Paperwork Reduction Act Notice, see page 2. Cat. No. 10220Q Form **W-4** (201X)

withheld from their paychecks can claim fewer allowances than they really have. However, they are not allowed to claim more allowances than they really deserve.

To look up the amount of federal income tax that needs to be withheld from Stephanie's paycheck, Katherine uses Stephanie's marital status and the number of claimed allowances listed on her Form W-4. She also uses Stephanie's gross earnings for the pay period and the length of the pay period. The amount of federal income tax that needs to be withheld is listed in a wage bracket table that can be found in IRS Publication 15 *Employer's Tax Guide*, also called Circular E. Check out one of the tables from

Wage bracket table One of various charts in IRS Circular E that provide information about deductions for federal income tax based on earnings and data supplied on the W-4 form.

Circular E An IRS tax publication of payroll procedures, including tax tables.

the Circular that's shown in Figure 7.2. Notice from the heading "SINGLE Persons—BIWEEKLY Payroll Period" that this table applies to single persons who are paid biweekly. Wage bracket tables are prepared according to marital status and pay period; Circular E has a similar table for married persons who are paid biweekly, as well as tables for single and married persons who are paid daily, weekly, semimonthly, or monthly. Also notice that the table has rows for different ranges of gross pay, starting from lower amounts of pay in the top rows of the table to higher amounts in the bottom rows.

Katherine determines the amount of federal income tax that needs to be withheld from Stephanie's paycheck by first locating the correct table in Publication 15. She finds the table for single persons who are paid biweekly. Then, she locates the row that says "At least $940 but less than $960." Stephanie's gross pay for this pay period is $957.60, so this row applies to her. Katherine traces this row to the column for one withholding allowance, and finds that the amount of withholding tax is $89. Based on Stephanie's gross earnings of $957.60 and her one claimed allowance, Katherine will withhold $89 in federal income taxes from Stephanie's pay.

What if Stephanie had earned $960 instead of $957.60? Would the amount of federal income tax withheld be the same? No, Katherine would have withheld $92. To see this, check out the heading for the columns showing the wages. Notice that it says, "If the wages are—." Katherine will look at the rows of wage ranges, stopping when she sees the line that says, "At least $940 but less than $960." If Stephanie's gross wages are exactly $960—not less than $960—Katherine must go to the next line, which says, "At least $960 but less than $980" and withhold the amount in the column for one withholding allowance, which is $92.

Please note that the Wage Bracket method can be used for employees earning up to $2,100 in a biweekly pay period. So what about Julia? She earned $2,250. In this case, Katherine must use the percentage method for withholding taxes. This method is also found in Publication 15, Circular E. However, we will not cover this method here.

State Income Tax Withholding

State income tax (SIT) withholding Amount of state income tax withheld by the employer from the employee's gross pay.

Most states also charge their residents an income tax based on the amount of money they earn from their employers. In 2014, only Alaska, Florida, Nevada, South Dakota, Texas, Washington, and Wyoming do not. (Technically, New Hampshire and Tennessee also do not have a state income tax; it is only imposed on interest and dividends.) So, in addition to withholding federal income taxes, Katherine may also have to determine amounts for state income tax (SIT) withholding. Fortunately for Katherine, the process for withholding state income tax is much the same as it is for withholding federal income tax. In many states, withholding amounts are based on the same information that is listed in the employee's W-4, although some states do have their own versions of this form that are used instead. Employers use state publications similar to the federal Publication 15 to figure the amount to be withheld for state income taxes. However, because the 43 states can differ significantly in the way they calculate income tax, we keep our discussion simple by assuming that state income tax is a fixed percentage of employee earnings. For our example we use an 8% tax rate. Therefore, Katherine calculates Stephanie's SIT withholding at $76.61 ($957.60 × 8%).

Other Income Tax Withholding

We pointed out previously that employees would have state income taxes withheld from their paychecks if they live in one of the 43 states collecting such a tax. In addition, many cities and counties tax employee earnings. Sometimes the tax will be a percentage of gross earnings much like federal income tax, or it may be a fixed dollar amount that the employer will withhold for every pay period. These cities and counties have their own rules regarding payroll tax deposits and tax reports for this type of withholding tax.

Employee Withholding for FICA Taxes

In addition to withholding federal and, probably, state income tax, Katherine must also compute and withhold Social Security and Medicare taxes from Travelwithus.com employees. A brief history shows that Social Security tax came about with the signing of the Social Security Act in 1935. When this tax was incorporated into the Internal

FIGURE 7.2 Wage Bracket Tables

SINGLE Persons—BIWEEKLY Payroll Period

(For Wages Paid through December 2014)

And the wages are—		And the number of withholding allowances claimed is—										
At least	But less than	0	1	2	3	4	5	6	7	8	9	10
		The amount of income tax to be withheld is—										
$800	$820	$91	$68	$45	$27	$12	$0	$0	$0	$0	$0	$0
820	840	94	71	48	29	14	0	0	0	0	0	0
840	860	97	74	51	31	16	0	0	0	0	0	0
860	880	100	77	54	33	18	2	0	0	0	0	0
880	900	103	80	57	35	20	4	0	0	0	0	0
900	920	106	83	60	38	22	6	0	0	0	0	0
920	940	109	86	63	41	24	8	0	0	0	0	0
940	960	112	89	66	44	26	10	0	0	0	0	0
960	980	115	92	69	47	28	12	0	0	0	0	0
980	1,000	118	95	72	50	30	14	0	0	0	0	0
1,000	1,020	121	98	75	53	32	16	1	0	0	0	0
1,020	1,040	124	101	78	56	34	18	3	0	0	0	0
1,040	1,060	127	104	81	59	36	20	5	0	0	0	0
1,060	1,080	130	107	84	62	39	22	7	0	0	0	0
1,080	1,100	133	110	87	65	42	24	9	0	0	0	0
1,100	1,120	136	113	90	68	45	26	11	0	0	0	0
1,120	1,140	139	116	93	71	48	28	13	0	0	0	0
1,140	1,160	142	119	96	74	51	30	15	0	0	0	0
1,160	1,180	145	122	99	77	54	32	17	2	0	0	0
1,180	1,200	148	125	102	80	57	34	19	4	0	0	0
1,200	1,220	151	128	105	83	60	37	21	6	0	0	0
1,220	1,240	154	131	108	86	63	40	23	8	0	0	0
1,240	1,260	157	134	111	89	66	43	25	10	0	0	0
1,260	1,280	160	137	114	92	69	46	27	12	0	0	0
1,280	1,300	163	140	117	95	72	49	29	14	0	0	0
1,300	1,320	166	143	120	98	75	52	31	16	1	0	0
1,320	1,340	169	146	123	101	78	55	33	18	3	0	0
1,340	1,360	172	149	126	104	81	58	35	20	5	0	0
1,360	1,380	175	152	129	107	84	61	38	22	7	0	0
1,380	1,400	178	155	132	110	87	64	41	24	9	0	0
1,400	1,420	181	158	135	113	90	67	44	26	11	0	0
1,420	1,440	184	161	138	116	93	70	47	28	13	0	0
1,440	1,460	187	164	141	119	96	73	50	30	15	0	0
1,460	1,480	190	167	144	122	99	76	53	32	17	2	0
1,480	1,500	193	170	147	125	102	79	56	34	19	4	0
1,500	1,520	196	173	150	128	105	82	59	37	21	6	0
1,520	1,540	201	176	153	131	108	85	62	40	23	8	0
1,540	1,560	206	179	156	134	111	88	65	43	25	10	0
1,560	1,580	211	182	159	137	114	91	68	46	27	12	0
1,580	1,600	216	185	162	140	117	94	71	49	29	14	0
1,600	1,620	221	188	165	143	120	97	74	52	31	16	0
1,620	1,640	226	191	168	146	123	100	77	55	33	18	2
1,640	1,660	231	194	171	149	126	103	80	58	35	20	4
1,660	1,680	236	199	174	152	129	106	83	61	38	22	6
1,680	1,700	241	204	177	155	132	109	86	64	41	24	8
1,700	1,720	246	209	180	158	135	112	89	67	44	26	10
1,720	1,740	251	214	183	161	138	115	92	70	47	28	12
1,740	1,760	256	219	186	164	141	118	95	73	50	30	14
1,760	1,780	261	224	189	167	144	121	98	76	53	32	16
1,780	1,800	266	229	192	170	147	124	101	79	56	34	18
1,800	1,820	271	234	196	173	150	127	104	82	59	36	20
1,820	1,840	276	239	201	176	153	130	107	85	62	39	22
1,840	1,860	281	244	206	179	156	133	110	88	65	42	24
1,860	1,880	286	249	211	182	159	136	113	91	68	45	26
1,880	1,900	291	254	216	185	162	139	116	94	71	48	28
1,900	1,920	296	259	221	188	165	142	119	97	74	51	30
1,920	1,940	301	264	226	191	168	145	122	100	77	54	32
1,940	1,960	306	269	231	194	171	148	125	103	80	57	34
1,960	1,980	311	274	236	198	174	151	128	106	83	60	37
1,980	2,000	316	279	241	203	177	154	131	109	86	63	40
2,000	2,020	321	284	246	208	180	157	134	112	89	66	43
2,020	2,040	326	289	251	213	183	160	137	115	92	69	46
2,040	2,060	331	294	256	218	186	163	140	118	95	72	49
2,060	2,080	336	299	261	223	189	166	143	121	98	75	52
2,080	2,100	341	304	266	228	192	169	146	124	101	78	55

$2,100 and over   Use Table 2(a) for a **SINGLE person** on page 43. Also see the instructions on page 41.

FICA (Federal Insurance Contributions Act) Part of the Social Security Act of 1935, this law taxes both the employer and employee up to a certain maximum rate and wage base for OASDI tax purposes. It also taxes both the employer and employee for Medicare purposes, but this tax has no wage base maximum.

Revenue Code in 1939, it was renamed the Federal Insurance Contributions Act (FICA). Later, in 1965, Medicare was signed into law as an amendment to the Social Security Act of 1935. Today, the term *FICA* includes both Social Security tax (OASDI, or Old Age, Survivors and Disability Insurance) and Medicare tax.

The government uses the taxes collected to make the following payments:

- Monthly retirement benefits for persons over 62 years old
- Medical benefits for persons over 65 years old
- Benefits for persons who have become disabled
- Benefits for families of deceased workers who were covered by this law

Because each tax is calculated differently, it is important you understand that OASDI and Medicare are separate taxes. OASDI puts a limit on the amount of tax that an employee must pay by setting a maximum annual dollar amount of earnings that can be taxed. This amount is called the wage base. The same is not true of Medicare; all wages earned are subject to the Medicare tax.* The OASDI and Medicare tax rates and the OASDI wage base amount are all set by Congress; the OASDI wage base increases annually based on cost-of-living adjustments. The amounts for 2014 are as follows:

Tax	2014 Tax Rate	2014 Wage Base
OASDI	6.2%	$117,000
Medicare	1.45%	None

COACHING TIP

Unlike OASDI, Medicare does not have a wage base; all gross earnings are subject to taxation.

Calendar year A 1-year period beginning on January 1 and ending on December 31. Employers must use a calendar year for payroll purposes, even if the employer uses a fiscal year for financial statements and for any other reason.

Katherine begins to calculate the amount of Social Security tax that needs to be withheld from Stephanie's pay by looking at Stephanie's current and year-to-date (YTD) gross earnings. She needs to know the amount of earnings from the current pay period so that she can calculate the current amount of taxes. However, she also needs to know the YTD earnings so that she can see whether Stephanie had previously reached the maximum amount of OASDI taxable earnings or if Stephanie will reach it in this pay period. YTD earnings include all gross pay earned and paid to an employee from January 1 to December 31 of any year, also known as a calendar year. Employers must use a calendar year for payroll purposes, even if the employer uses a fiscal year for financial statements or for any other reason. So far in this calendar year, Stephanie has earned a total of $19,471.20. This amount includes the $957.60 that she has earned for the most recent biweekly pay period.

Katherine calculates Stephanie's OASDI and Medicare taxes as follows:

$957.60 gross earnings × 6.2% OASDI tax rate = $59.37 OASDI tax
$957.60 gross earnings × 1.45% Medicare tax rate = $13.89 Medicare tax

Because Stephanie has earned less than the wage base limit of $117,000, all of her earnings for the current pay period are taxable. But what if Stephanie had earned more this year so far? Suppose she had earned $116,640 before this pay period. With her current earnings of $957.60, she would have earned a total of $117,597.60 for the year thus far, which is more than the wage base limit of $117,000. In that case, Katherine would have calculated the amount of OASDI tax to be withheld from Stephanie's pay by first calculating the amount of OASDI taxable earnings for the current period:

Stephanie's YTD earnings before this pay period	$116,640.00
Plus: Stephanie's current earnings	957.60
Stephanie's YTD earnings after this pay period	$117,597.60
Less: 2014 OASDI tax wage base limit	117,000.00
Stephanie's earnings above the limit, and thus, not taxable	$597.60
Stephanie's current earnings	$957.60
Less: Stephanie's earnings above the limit, and thus, not OASDI taxable	597.60
Stephanie's current OASDI taxable earnings	$360.00

*Note to student: Effective January 1, 2013, any employee who earns more than $200,000 in a calendar year is subject to a 0.9% (0.009) additional Medicare withholding tax.

Now Katherine would calculate the amount of OASDI tax as follows:

$360.00 current taxable earnings $\times$ 6.2% OASDI tax rate = $22.32 OASDI tax

Stephanie has now reached the maximum amount of taxable wages (taxable earnings), which means she will no longer pay the OASDI tax for the remainder of the calendar year. What if Stephanie had already earned $117,000 or more before the current pay period? In that case, none of Stephanie's current gross earnings would be subject to the OASDI tax. In other words, Stephanie would already have paid her maximum OASDI tax for the year by paying tax on the money she made up to this $117,000 wage base limit. What about next year? Social Security taxes are calculated on a calendar-year basis, and Stephanie would have to start paying the OASDI tax again until she reached the maximum for that year.

What about the Medicare tax? Would the current amount that Stephanie needs to pay for this tax change too? No, because the Medicare tax does not limit the amount of earnings that can be taxed, all of Stephanie's earnings will be taxable. In other words, even if Stephanie had already earned $117,000 this year, all of her current earnings of $957.60 would be taxable, and she would still have $13.89 withheld from her current paycheck for the Medicare tax.

Taxable earnings Shows amount of earnings subject to a tax. The tax itself is not shown.

Other Withholdings (Voluntary Deductions)

Sometimes employees have additional amounts withheld from their paychecks for various reasons. For example, they may choose to buy medical insurance for themselves and maybe even their spouse and dependents through an insurance plan offered by their employer. Sometimes the employer pays the premium for this insurance coverage, or at least pays for the part of the premium that covers the employee. Even if the employer pays some of the premium, however, it is common for the employee to pay the rest. The employee pays this premium by having it withheld from his or her pay, just as the employee pays income and Social Security taxes by having these amounts withheld by the employer. Travelwithus.com currently offers this opportunity to its employees, and the cost to the hourly employee is $33 for each pay period. Other companies may allow their employees to have funds withheld from their paychecks for union dues, retirement plan contributions, or life insurance premiums.

Medical insurance Health care insurance for which premiums may be paid through a deduction from an employee's paycheck.

Net Pay

Katherine's next step in the payroll accounting process is to calculate the amount of pay that Stephanie will actually receive in her paycheck; this amount is called net pay. At this point, Katherine has computed all of the amounts necessary to determine Stephanie's net pay. Now she simply needs to combine them as follows:

Net pay Gross earnings, less deductions. Net pay, or take-home pay, is what the worker actually takes home.

Gross earnings for the current biweekly pay period:		$957.60
Deductions for employee withholding taxes:		
Federal income tax	$89.00	
State income tax	76.61	
OASDI tax	59.37	
Medicare tax	13.89	
Medical insurance	33.00	
Total deductions		271.87
Net pay		$685.73

TRY IT!   Learning Unit 7-1

1. John Jackson is a salaried employee earning $3,900.00 per month. What is John's weekly salary?

2. Millie Smith is a bookkeeper who is paid $16 per hour on a biweekly basis. Please compute her gross pay if she worked 35 hours in week 1 and 45 hours in week 2. Assume her company falls under the FLSA.

3. Assume Jorge Cantu earns gross pay of $1,500.00 during the current biweekly pay period ending January 26. Calculate Jorge's net pay based on the following assumptions:

   - Jorge claims S-1 on his Form W-4. Use Figure 7.2 to compute federal income tax withholding.
   - The state income tax rate is 4%, with no wage base limit.
   - FICA tax rates are: OASDI = 6.2% on a wage base limit of $117,000; Medicare = 1.45%.

LEARNING UNIT 7-2

L02

Preparing a Payroll Register and Maintaining an Employee Earnings Record

At this point, Katherine Kurtz, the accountant for Travelwithus.com, knows how much each of the three hourly employees earned for the most recent biweekly pay period and how many dollars of taxes need to be withheld from their paychecks. She now needs to enter this information into the accounting records for the company. Two primary records are used in accounting systems to keep track of payroll information for a company. The first of these records is a worksheet, known as a payroll register, which shows all information related to an entire pay period. The second record is called the employee earnings record and is used to keep track of an individual employee's payroll history for an entire calendar year.

The Payroll Register

Payroll register A multicolumn form that is used to record payroll data.

Katherine enters information about the current payroll period for all employees in a payroll register. The register includes each employee's gross earnings, employee withholding taxes, net pay, taxable earnings, cumulative earnings, and the accounts to be charged (Travel Scheduling or Administrative) for the salary and wage expense for that pay period. Figure 7.3 shows the completed payroll register for the payroll covering the biweekly pay period from October 13 through October 26. Remember, however, that the biweekly payroll takes additional processing time. This means that the actual biweekly paychecks will be distributed the Wednesday after the pay period ends, so in this case, the checks are dated and distributed October 29.

The Employee Earnings Record

 COACHING TIP

The Payroll Register is prepared first and provides data for the preparation of the Employee Earnings Record.

Individual employee earnings record An accounting document that summarizes the total amount of wages paid and the deductions for the calendar year. It aids in preparing governmental reports. A new record is prepared for each employee each year.

After Katherine prepares the payroll register for the period, and in order to comply with all applicable employment laws and regulations, she also completes a payroll record known as the individual employee earnings record. This record provides a summary of each employee's earnings, withholding taxes, net pay, and cumulative earnings during each calendar year, as shown in Figure 7.4 (page 250). Katherine uses the information summarized in this record to prepare quarterly and annual payroll tax reports. Thus, the employee earnings record is split into calendar quarters, with each quarter being 13 weeks long. It is important to understand that the wages are listed in the quarter based on the date of pay, not the pay period covered.

TRAVELWITHUS.COM INC
PAYROLL REGISTER

PAY PERIOD: OCTOBER 13–26, 201X PAY DATE: OCTOBER 29, 201X

Employee Name	W-4 Allow	Prior Earnings (YTD)	Salary	Regular Hours	Regular Rate	Regular Amount	Overtime Hours	Overtime Rate	Overtime Amount	Gross Pay	Current Earnings (YTD)
Goldman, Ernie	M-1	100 000 00 00	5 000 00							5 000 00	105 000 00
Higuera, Stephanie	S-1	18 513 60		78	11 40	889 20	4	17 10	68 40	957 60	19 471 20
Kurtz, Katherine	S-3	40 000 00	2 000 00							2 000 00	42 000 00
Regan, Julia	M-2	45 000 00	2 250 00							2 250 00	47 250 00
Sui, Annie	S-0	21 212 00		80	15 15	1 212 00	4	22 73	90 92	1 302 92	34 233 92
Taylor, Harold	S-2	19 043 70		78	12 10	943 80	4	18 15	72 60	1 016 40	20 060 10
Totals		224 678 30	9 250 00	236		3 045 00	12		231 92	12 526 92	237 205 22

TRAVELWITHUS.COM INC
PAYROLL REGISTER

PAY PERIOD: OCTOBER 13–26, 201X PAY DATE: OCTOBER 29, 201X

Employee Name	Taxable Earnings FUTA/SUTA	Taxable Earnings OASDI	FIT	SIT	FICA OASDI	FICA Medicare	Medical Insurance	Net Pay	Check #	Travel Scheduling	Admin.
Goldman, Ernie		5 000 00	812 00	400 00	310 00	72 50	33 00	3 372 50	819	2 500 00	2 500 00
Higuera, Stephanie		957 60	89 00	76 61	59 37	13 89	33 00	685 73	820	957 60	
Kurtz, Katherine		2 000 00	208 00	160 00	124 00	29 00	33 00	1 446 00	821		2 000 00
Regan, Julia		2 250 00	208 00	180 00	139 50	32 62	33 00	1 656 88	822	2 250 00	
Sui, Annie	1 302 92	1 302 92	166 00	104 23	80 78	18 89	33 00	900 02	823	1 302 92	
Taylor, Harold		1 016 40	75 00	81 31	63 02	14 74	33 00	749 33	824	1 016 40	
Totals	1 302 92	12 526 92	1 558 00	1 002 15	776 67	181 64	198 00	8 810 46		8 026 92	4 500 00

FIGURE 7.4 Employee Earnings Record

TRAVELWITHUS.COM INC.
EMPLOYEE EARNINGS RECORD
Stephanie Higuera Social Security No. 123-45-6789

Pay Period	Pay Date	Hours Regular	Hours Overtime	Earnings Regular	Earnings Overtime	Earnings Gross	FIT	SIT	FICA OASDI	FICA Medicare	Medical Insurance	Net Pay	Check No.	YTD Earnings
09/15–09/28	10/1/201X	80	0	912 00	0 00	912 00	83 00	72 96	56 54	13 22	33 00	653 28	790	17 601 60
09/29–10/12	10/15/201X	80	0	912 00	0 00	912 00	83 00	72 96	56 54	13 22	33 00	653 28	806	18 513 60
10/13–10/26	10/29/201X	78	4	889 20	68 40	957 60	89 00	76 61	59 37	13 89	33 00	685 73	820	19 471 20
10/27–11/09	11/12/201X	76	0	866 40	0 00	866 40	77 00	69 31	53 72	12 56	33 00	620 81	825	20 337 60
11/10–11/23	11/26/201X	80	2	912 00	34 20	946 20	89 00	75 70	58 66	13 72	33 00	676 12	839	21 283 80
11/24–12/07	12/10/201X	80	4	912 00	68 40	980 40	95 00	78 43	60 78	14 22	33 00	699 97	844	22 264 20
12/08–12/21	12/24/201X	80	0	912 00	0 00	912 00	83 00	72 96	56 54	13 22	33 00	653 28	858	23 176 20
4th Quarter Totals		554	10	6315 60	171 00	6486 60	599 00	518 93	402 15	94 05	231 00	4641 47		
YTD Totals				22 594 80	581 40	23 176 20	2 248 86	1 854 10	1 436 92	336 05	858 00	16 442 27		

 **TRY IT!**   **Learning Unit 7-2**

Answer true or false to the following statements.

1. The payroll register is used to compute and total all employees' earnings, tax deductions, other authorized deductions, and net pay for a single pay period.

2. The payroll register does not show current YTD earnings.

3. The individual employee earnings record is updated each pay period after the completion of the payroll register.

Employer Taxes for FICA (OASDI, Medicare), FUTA, SUTA, and Workers' Compensation Insurance

LEARNING UNIT 7-3

 L03

Employer Payment for FICA Taxes

As we discussed, employees pay payroll taxes including federal income tax, FICA taxes, probably state income tax, and maybe even a city or county income tax. It surprises some employees to find that their employers pay payroll taxes, too. As a matter of fact, employers pay exactly the same amount of FICA taxes (OASDI and Medicare) for each employee as the employee pays. In addition to paying OASDI and Medicare taxes for each employee, employers also pay unemployment taxes that are used to provide unemployed workers with benefits while they are looking for work.

As Travelwithus.com's accountant, Katherine calculates the amount of FICA taxes that the company must pay as an employer much the same way that she calculated them for each employee. She first determines the amount of current gross earnings for all employees that fall below the wage base limit of $117,000. She looks at the OASDI Taxable Earnings total in the payroll register for the current period. She then multiplies this total by the OASDI tax rate of 6.2% to determine the OASDI tax that Travelwithus.com must pay:

$12,526.92 gross earnings × 6.2% OASDI tax rate = $776.67 OASDI tax

Katherine then calculates Travelwithus.com's Medicare tax by taking the current gross earnings for all employees and multiplying this total by the Medicare tax rate of 1.45%. Remember that the amount of Medicare tax for each employee is not subject to any limit; every dollar that an employee earns is taxed at the Medicare tax rate of 1.45%.

$12,526.92 gross earnings × 1.45% Medicare tax rate = $181.64 Medicare tax

The way Katherine computes these taxes differs in only one way compared to how she computed them for each employee. Because Katherine is now calculating Travelwithus.com's share of these taxes, Katherine uses current gross earnings for the company in total instead of using each employee's current gross earnings as she did when she was determining the amount to withhold from each employee's paycheck. Please note: The employer share of OASDI and Medicare should match, or be within a few cents of, the payroll register totals for the same taxes (see Figure 7.3). Many employers just record matching amounts found on the payroll register, without going through any additional computations.

FUTA and SUTA

In addition to paying its employer share of FICA taxes, Travelwithus.com must also pay unemployment taxes. Unemployment tax, or unemployment insurance as it is sometimes called, was created by the same 1935 law that created Social Security. This federal law requires all 50 states, the District of Columbia, and U.S. territories to run unemployment compensation programs that are approved and monitored by the federal government. Unemployment taxes are paid by employers based on wages

COACHING TIP

Only employers, not employees, must calculate and pay both FUTA and SUTA taxes.

Federal Unemployment Tax Act (FUTA) A tax paid by employers to the federal government. The current rate is 0.6% on the first $7,000 of earnings of each employee after the normal FUTA tax credit is applied.

State Unemployment Tax Act (SUTA) A tax usually paid only by employers to the state for employee unemployment insurance.

paid to employees. Federal Unemployment Tax Act (FUTA) taxes pay the costs of administering the federal and state programs but do not pay benefits to employees. State Unemployment Tax Act (SUTA) taxes pay the benefits to unemployed persons.

Currently, employers pay FUTA tax at a rate of 6.0% on wages earned by each employee up to a wage base limit of $7,000. However, the federal government allows employers to take a tax credit for SUTA tax against this tax, up to a maximum credit of 5.4%.

FUTA tax rate	6.0%
Less: Normal FUTA tax credit	5.4%
Net FUTA tax rate	0.6%

Employers are allowed to take this credit as long as they have paid all amounts that they owe for SUTA taxes and have paid them on time. In other words, the federal law essentially says to employers, "Comply with your state's unemployment tax laws and your total FUTA tax rate will not exceed a maximum of 0.6% to the federal government." Remember that employers alone are responsible for paying FUTA tax; it is never withheld from the earnings of employees.

Katherine calculates FUTA tax by referring to the FUTA Taxable Earnings total in the current payroll register. This column tells her how much, in total, Travelwithus .com's employees have earned this period that falls below the FUTA wage base limit of $7,000. She uses this amount to calculate the FUTA tax by multiplying it by the net FUTA tax rate as follows:

$1,302.92 FUTA taxable earnings × 0.6% FUTA tax rate = $7.82 FUTA tax

Because states run their own unemployment programs, each state may use a different SUTA wage base limit. These amounts are based on the needs of the unemployment funds in each state. In 2014 the wage base limits for states ranged from $7,000 to $41,300. Different states have different SUTA tax rates for the same reason that the wage base limits vary; they are based on the needs of the unemployment funds in each state.

Additionally, the SUTA tax rate can vary from employer to employer within a state. In any state, an employer's SUTA tax rate will be based on how many dollars it contributes to the state unemployment fund and the dollar amount of claims that its employees make against that fund. The rate is tied to the employer's employment history. In other words, employers who rarely lay off their workers will be charged a lower SUTA rate than employers who lay off workers often. In this way, the SUTA tax rate motivates employers to stabilize their workforce.

Travelwithus.com's current SUTA rate is 5.4% and the wage base limit for the state in which it is located is $7,000. Katherine calculates Travelwithus.com's SUTA tax similar to the way she calculated its FUTA tax. She first looks at the SUTA Taxable Earnings total in the current payroll register to see how much, in total, Travelwithus.com's employees earned this period below the SUTA wage base limit of $7,000. She then calculates the SUTA tax by multiplying this amount by the SUTA tax rate as follows:

$1,302.92 SUTA taxable earnings × 5.4% SUTA tax rate = $70.36

Workers' Compensation Insurance

Workers' compensation insurance Insurance purchased by most employers to protect their employees against losses due to injury or death while on the job.

Workers' compensation insurance insures employees against losses they may incur due to work caused injury or death while on the job. Most employers purchase this insurance through an insurance broker or state agency. In most states, this cost is paid completely by the employer, not the employee.

Travelwithus.com's premium for this insurance is based on its total estimated gross payroll, and the rate is calculated for each $100 of weekly payroll.

By estimating payroll before the beginning of the year, the insurance company can determine the amount of the premium to charge Travelwithus.com. If actual payroll for the year turns out to differ from estimated payroll, then the insurance company will either credit Travelwithus.com for any overpayment or bill it for any underpayment. The experience or merit rating for Travelwithus.com is based on the type of work that its employees perform as well as the amount and extent of any on-the-job injuries that its employees experience. The rate is based on physical difficulty of jobs within various industries and the history/cost of prior employee accident claims submitted. Dangerous jobs and large numbers of claims filed result in a higher rate.

Travelwithus.com has two groups of employees: travel schedulers and administrative. It estimated that it would have $50,000 of gross payroll for its schedulers in the next year, and its rate is $1.80 for every $100 of this payroll. The company also estimated that it will incur $190,000 of payroll for managers, and its rate for this group is $.22 for every $100 of payroll. Travelwithus.com then calculated its premium as follows:

Workers' compensation premium for schedulers:	$50,000/$100 = 500	500 × $1.80 =	$ 900.00
Workers' compensation premium for managers:	$190,000/$100 = 1,900	1,900 × $.22 =	418.00
Total workers' compensation premium =			**$1,318.00**

Suppose, however, that at the end of the year, Travelwithus.com's scheduler payroll totaled $57,977.14 and its manager payroll totaled $220,648.16. The actual premiums for the year would be calculated in the following manner:

Workers' compensation premium for schedulers:	$57,977.14/$100 = 580	580 × $1.80 =	$1,044.00
Workers' compensation premium for managers:	$220,648.16/$100 = 2,206	2,206 × $.22 =	485.32
Total workers' compensation premium =			**$1,529.32**

Travelwithus.com would then owe an additional amount of premium:

Workers' compensation premium based on actual gross payroll	$1,529.32
Workers' compensation premium based on estimated gross payroll	1,318.00
Additional workers' compensation premium owed =	**$ 211.32**

 TRY IT!   **Learning Unit 7-3**

Compute the employer's payroll tax expense based on the following totals found on a completed payroll register dated November 15.

- Gross pay = $40,500.00
- Taxable earnings for FUTA/SUTA = $1,460.00
- Taxable earnings for OASDI = $36,000.00
- Deductions: FIT = $6,330.00; SIT = $1,620.00; FICA OASDI = $2,232.00; FICA Medicare = $587.25
- Other information: FUTA rate = 0.6%; SUTA rate = 2.7%

Experience or merit rating A rate assigned by an insurance company to determine the cost of insurance coverage. This rate is based on the physical difficulty of jobs within various industries and the history/cost of prior employee accident claims submitted.

 COACHING TIP

Workers' compensation insurance is based on the type of work each employee performs (more hazardous jobs have higher rates) and the extent of any previous on-the-job injuries.

The Payroll Register, Employer Tax Liability, and Workers' Compensation Insurance

At this point in the payroll process, Katherine Kurtz, the accountant for Travelwithus.com, has calculated gross earnings, deductions for employee withholding taxes, and net pay for each of Travelwithus.com's employees. She entered these amounts into two accounting records for Travelwithus.com called the payroll register and the employee earnings record. She also computed the amount of payroll taxes that Travelwithus.com must pay as an employer. Now Katherine must record these payroll amounts in the accounts of Travelwithus.com by making journal entries and posting these entries to accounts in the general ledger. By entering these amounts into Travelwithus.com's accounting system, Travelwithus.com's financial statements will include these payroll transactions.

Recording Payroll

Before we discuss how payroll transactions are recorded, let's first review the accounts that we will be using and the rules for increasing and decreasing these account types:

Accounts Affected	Category	↑ ↓	Rules	Financial Statement
Travel Scheduling Expense	Expense	↑	Dr.	Income Statement
Administrative Expense	Expense	↑	Dr.	Income Statement
Payroll Tax Expense	Expense	↑	Dr.	Income Statement
Workers' Compensation Expense	Expense	↑	Dr.	Income Statement
Insurance Expense	Expense	↑	Dr.	Income Statement
Payroll Cash	Asset	↑	Dr.	Balance Sheet
Prepaid Workers' Compensation Insurance	Asset	↑	Dr.	Balance Sheet
FICA OASDI Payable	Liability	↑	Cr.	Balance Sheet
FICA Medicare Payable	Liability	↑	Cr.	Balance Sheet
FIT Payable	Liability	↑	Cr.	Balance Sheet
SIT Payable	Liability	↑	Cr.	Balance Sheet
FUTA Payable	Liability	↑	Cr.	Balance Sheet
SUTA Payable	Liability	↑	Cr.	Balance Sheet
Medical Insurance Payable	Liability	↑	Cr.	Balance Sheet
Wages and Salaries Payable	Liability	↑	Cr.	Balance Sheet

Katherine needs to record the expense of wages and salaries. The information needed to make these journal entries comes from the payroll register. Figure 7.3 shows the payroll register for the current payroll period. Katherine locates this register and uses totals from it to make the following journal entry:

			GENERAL JOURNAL				
	Date			PR	Dr.	Cr.	
	201X						
	Oct.	26	Travel Scheduling Expense		8 0 2 6 92		
			Administrative Expense		4 5 0 0 00		
			FIT Payable			1 5 5 8 00	
			SIT Payable			1 0 0 2 15	
			FICA OASDI Payable			7 7 6 67	
			FICA Medicare Payable			1 8 1 64	
			Medical Insurance Payable			1 9 8 00	
			Wages and Salaries Payable			8 8 1 0 46	
			To record payroll for the pay period				
			ending October 26, 201X				

A couple of things may be surprising about the journal entry. First, notice that the gross earnings, not the net pay, are recorded as expenses for the two different departments in which the employees worked. This total amount of earnings is the real expense to Travelwithus.com. Employees will actually only receive the lower, net pay; the difference relates to deductions that are made for FICA, FIT, and state income taxes, and one other deduction authorized by the employee.

Also notice that the amounts of taxes withheld are recorded in "Payable" accounts, which means that they are liabilities of Travelwithus.com. How can Travelwithus.com be liable for these taxes if the taxes are paid by employees? The answer is that Travelwithus.com collects these amounts by withholding them from the paychecks of its employees and then turns them over to the federal and, in this case, state government. In other words, Travelwithus.com is the intermediary in this process. Until it does pay these amounts to the governments, Travelwithus.com owes these taxes. The same is true of the medical insurance premiums that the employees pay; the company collects them and then pays them to the insurance company.

Recording Payroll Tax Expense

Katherine's next task is to record the employer payroll taxes for Travelwithus.com. The entry to record the taxes for the current hourly payroll follows:

		GENERAL JOURNAL				
Date			PR	Dr.	Cr.	
201X						
Oct.	26	Payroll Tax Expense		1036 49		
		FICA OASDI Payable			776 67	
		FICA Medicare Payable			181 64	
		FUTA Payable			7 82	
		SUTA Payable			70 36	
		To record payroll tax expense				
		for pay period ending October 26, 201X				

Notice that FICA OASDI, FICA Medicare, FUTA, and SUTA were recorded in separate liability accounts because they are different taxes and, except for the FICA taxes, are paid to different government agencies. Also note that the amount of all of these taxes are added together and recorded as one amount for Travelwithus.com's **payroll tax expense**. These amounts are an expense to Travelwithus.com because they represent the cost of the payroll taxes that it must pay as an employer.

Payroll tax expense The cost to employers that includes the total of the employer's FICA OASDI, FICA Medicare, FUTA, and SUTA taxes. Remember, the employer matches the employee contributions for OASDI and Medicare.

Recording Workers' Compensation Expense

The original purchase of the annual workers' compensation policy at the beginning of the year is journalized as follows:

		GENERAL JOURNAL				
Date			PR	Dr.	Cr.	
201X						
Jan.	1	Prepaid Workers' Compensation Insurance		1318 00		
		Cash			1318 00	
		To record prepaid insurance				

When preparing end-of-month adjusting entries during the year, Travelwithus.com expenses 1/12 of the policy. This is computed as $1,318.00/12 = $109.83. Because of rounding, the last month's adjustment is $109.87.

GENERAL JOURNAL				
Date		PR	Dr.	Cr.
201X				
Jan. 31	Workers' Compensation Expense		1 0 9 83	
	Prepaid Workers' Compensation Insurance			1 0 9 83
	To adjust prepaid insurance			

At the end of the previous unit, we computed the additional cost for workers' compensation insurance. This additional liability came from underestimating the original annual payroll cost. We determined that an additional $211.32 was owed. The following journal entry records this additional liability:

GENERAL JOURNAL				
Date		PR	Dr.	Cr.
201X				
Dec. 31	Workers' Compensation Expense		2 1 1 32	
	Accounts Payable			2 1 1 32
	To record additional insurance premium due			

 TRY IT!   **Learning Unit 7-4**

Use the information given in the previous Try It! (Learning Unit 7-3) to complete the following:

1. Journalize the information from a completed payroll register dated November 15.
   - Gross pay = $40,500.00
   - Taxable earnings for FUTA/SUTA = $1,460.00
   - Taxable earnings for OASDI = $36,000.00
   - Deductions: FIT = $6,330.00; SIT = $1,620.00; FICA OASDI = $2,232.00; FICA Medicare = $587.25

2. Journalize the employer's payroll tax expense based on the above information as well as: FUTA rate = 0.6%; SUTA rate = 2.7%

LO1,3,4

DEMONSTRATION SUMMARY PROBLEM

Davidson Company pays their employees biweekly and is required to follow the FLSA. The FICA-OASDI rate is 6.2% on earnings up to $117,000 per year; the FICA-Medicare rate is 1.45% on all earnings; the SIT rate = 4%; medical insurance = $35.00 per employee; FUTA rate is 0.6%; and SUTA rate is 3.2%. Both unemployment taxes are computed on earnings up to $7,000.00 per year. The salaried employee is charged to Administrative Expense, and hourly employees are charged to Sales Expense. The following information is available for Davidson Company's three employees:

Pay Period: 17 February-March 2, 201X;			Pay Date: March 5, 201X		
Employee Name	W-4 Allow	Prior YTD Earnings	Salary or Rate of Pay	Hours Week 1	Hours Week 2
Jennie Davis	S-1	$6,000.00	$3,250.00 per month		
Michelle Foy	S-3	$3,966.00	$12.00 per hour	41	39
Charles Leon	S-2	$4,900.00	$14.00 per hour	45	43

Requirements:

Use the above information to:

1. Complete the two week payroll register (the first check number is 141).

2. Journalize the payroll register.

3. Journalize the employer's payroll tax expense.

Solutions

Requirement 1

Complete the payroll register.

Jennie's biweekly salary is computed as follows: $3,250 × 12/26 = $1,500.

Michelle earned 40 regular hours in week 1 and 39 regular hours in week 2. Michelle receives 1 hour of overtime for week 1 because she worked more than 40 hours that week. The overtime rate is computed at her regular rate of $12 × 1.5 = $18.

Charles worked more than 40 hours each week. Therefore, Charles earned 80 regular hours with the remaining 8 hours at his overtime rate of $14 × 1.5 = $21.

Gross Pay = the sum of the Salary + Regular Pay + Overtime Pay.

Current Earnings YTD = Prior Earnings YTD + Gross Pay

FUTA/SUTA Taxable: Jennie is the only employee who went over the $7,000 wage base. Her FUTA/SUTA taxable income is $1,500 salary − $500 in excess of wage base = $1,000.

OASDI wages: No employee has earned more than the wage base of $117,000. Therefore OASDI wages = Gross Pay.

FIT: Use the biweekly tax chart (Figure 7.2)

SIT = Gross Pay × 4%

Net pay = Gross Pay less deductions for FIT, SIT, FICA-OASDI, FICA-Medicare, and insurance.

Total Admin. Expense + Total Sales Expense = Total Gross Pay.

Verify totals: Foot and crossfoot each column and row.

Additional accuracy checks recommended: Total Gross Pay × 4% should equal or be within pennies of the column total for SIT deductions; Total OASDI wages × 6.2% should equal or be within pennies of the column total for OASDI deductions; Total Gross Pay × 1.45% should equal or be within pennies of the column total for Medicare deductions.

Davidson Company

Payroll Register

Pay Period: February 17 - March 2, 201X   Pay Date: March 5, 201X

Employee Name	W-4 Allow	Prior Earnings YTD	Salary	Regular Hours	Regular Rate	Regular Amount	Overtime Hours	Overtime Rate	Overtime Amount	Gross Pay	Current Earnings YTD
Jennie Davis	S-1	6,000.00	1,500.00							1,500.00	7,500.00
Michelle Foy	S-3	3,966.00		79.00	12.00	948.00	1.00	18.00	18.00	966.00	4,932.00
Charles Leon	S-2	4,900.00		80.00	14.00	1,120.00	8.00	21.00	168.00	1,288.00	6,188.00
		14,866.00	1,500.00	159.00		2,068.00	9.00		186.00	3,754.00	18,620.00

Davidson Company

Payroll Register

Pay Period: February 17 - March 2, 201X   Pay Date: March 5, 201X

Employee Name	Taxable Earnings		Deductions					Net Pay	Check #	Expense Account	
	FUTA/SUTA	OASDI	FIT	SIT	FICA OASDI	FICA Medicare	Medical Insurance			Admin.	Sales
Jennie Davis	1,000.00	1,500.00	173.00	60.00	93.00	21.75	35.00	1,117.25	141	1,500.00	
Michelle Foy	966.00	966.00	47.00	38.64	59.89	14.01	35.00	771.46	142		966.00
Charles Leon	1,288.00	1,288.00	117.00	51.52	79.86	18.68	35.00	985.94	143		1,288.00
	3,254.00	3,754.00	337.00	150.16	232.75	54.44	105.00	2,874.65		1,500.00	2,254.00

Requirement 2

Journalize the payroll register.

Use the payroll register second page totals to journalize the payroll. Remember to list the debits (expenses) first when journalizing.

GENERAL JOURNAL						
Date		Account	PR	Dr.	Cr.	
201X						
Mar.	2	Administrative Expense		1 5 0 0 00		
		Sales Expense		2 2 5 4 00		
		FIT Payable			3 3 7 00	
		SIT Payable			1 5 0 16	
		FICA OASDI Payable			2 3 2 75	
		FICA Medicare Payable			5 4 44	
		Medical Insurance Payable			1 0 5 00	
		Wages and Salaries Payable			2 8 7 4 65	
		To record payroll for the pay period ending March 2, 201X				

Requirement 3

Journalize the employer's payroll tax expense.

GENERAL JOURNAL						
Date		Account	PR	Dr.	Cr.	
201X						
Mar.	2	Payroll Tax Expense		4 1 0 84		
		FICA OASDI Payable			2 3 2 75	
		FICA Medicare Payable			5 4 44	
		FUTA Payable			1 9 52	
		SUTA Payable			1 0 4 13	
		To record payroll tax expense for pay period ending March 2, 201X				

BLUEPRINT FOR RECORDING TRANSACTIONS IN A PAYROLL REGISTER

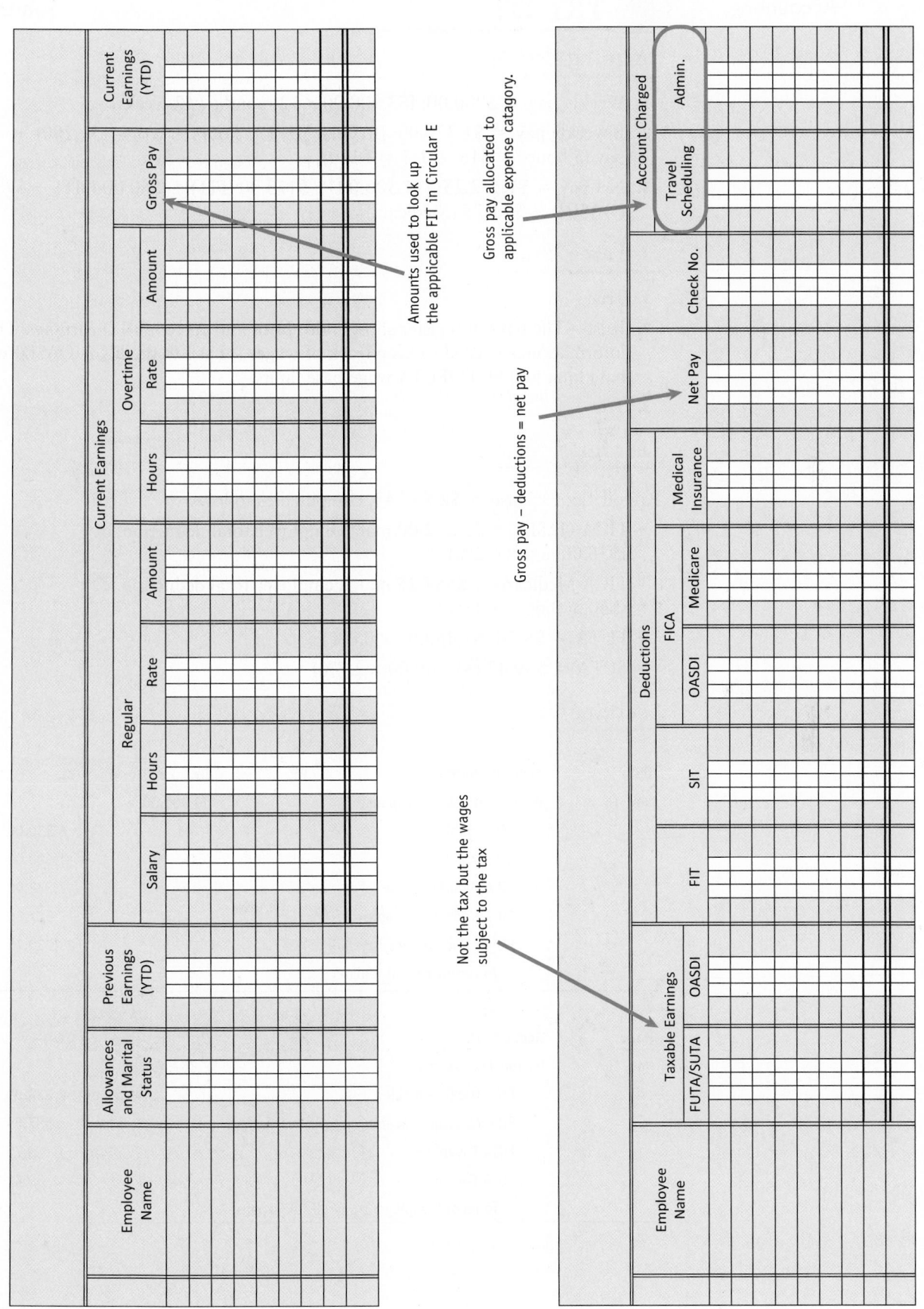

Amounts used to look up
the applicable FIT in Circular E

Gross pay allocated to
applicable expense catagory.

Gross pay – deductions = net pay

Not the tax but the wages
subject to the tax

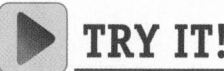 **TRY IT!**   Solutions

Learning Unit 7-1

1. Weekly pay = $900.00: [$3,900.00 × 12 months / 52 weeks]
2. Biweekly pay = $1,320.00: [Regular pay (75 hours × $16 = $1,200) + OT pay (5 hours × $16 × 1.5 = $120)]
3. Net pay = $1,152.25: [$1,500.00 − $173.00 (FIT) − $60.00 (SIT) − $93.00 (OASDI) − $21.75 (Medicare)]

Learning Unit 7-2

1. True
2. False—The payroll register shows both prior and current YTD earnings. This information is needed to keep track of wages subject to the FICA-OASDI wage base limit and SUTA/FUTA wage base limits.
3. True

Learning Unit 7-3

Payroll Tax Expense = $2,867.43, computed as follows:
- FICA OASDI = $2,232.00 match employee total deduction, or ($36,000.00 × 6.2%)
- FICA Medicare = $587.25 match employee total deduction, or ($40,500.00 × 1.45%)
- FUTA = $8.76 ($1,460.00 × 0.6%)
- SUTA = $39.42 ($1,460.00 × 2.7%)

Learning Unit 7-4

Date	Account Name	PR	Dr.	Cr.
Nov. 15	Wages and Salaries Expense		40,500.00	
	FIT Payable			6,330.00
	SIT Payable			1,620.00
	FICA OASDI Payable			2,232.00
	FICA Medicare Payable			587.25
	Wages and Salaries Payable			29,730.75
	To record payroll register			

Date	Account Name	PR	Dr.	Cr.
Nov. 15	Payroll Tax Expense		2,867.43	
	FICA OASDI Payable			2,232.00
	FICA Medicare Payable			587.25
	FUTA Payable			8.76
	SUTA Payable			39.42
	To record employer's payroll tax expense			

ACCOUNTING COACH

The following Coaching Tips are from Learning Units 7-1 through 7-4. Take the Pre-Game Checkup and use the Check Your Score to see how you are doing. The Accounting Coach provides tips before each Checkup to help you avoid common accounting errors.

LU 7-1 Gross Pay, Employee Payroll Tax Deductions for Federal Income Tax Withholding, State Income Tax Withholding, FICA (OASDI, Medicare), and Net Pay

Pre-Game Tips: The maximum amount of FICA (OASDI) tax is capped by a wage base of $117,000, while the FICA (Medicare) tax has no limit on the amount that may be collected.

Pre-Game Checkup: Answer true or false to the following statements.

1. A pay period is always defined as a 2-week period.
2. The Fair Labor Standards Act states that an employee must be paid overtime pay if he or she works over 40 hours in a work week.
3. An employee may claim fewer allowances on his or her IRS Form-W4, Employee's Withholding Allowance Certificate than he or she really has.
4. Withholding of FICA taxes (OASDI and Medicare) are limited to the amount due on all earnings below $117,000 (the wage base) in 2014.
5. Gross pay is the amount the employee receives in his or her paycheck.

LU 7-2 Preparing a Payroll Register and Maintaining an Employee Earnings Record

Pre-Game Tips: Following the calculation of gross and net pay, records must be maintained on both a pay period and individual employee basis to ensure that appropriate reports are prepared timely and accurately.

Pre-Game Checkup: Answer true or false to the following statements.

1. The employee earnings record shows gross earnings, deductions, net pay, and taxable earnings for only a single payroll period.
2. The individual employee earnings record is used to update the payroll register.
3. The taxable earnings columns of the payroll register do not show the amount of tax owed.
4. Only the employee earnings record indicates the employee's marital status and the number of allowances claimed.
5. The payroll register shows gross earnings, deductions, net pay, and taxable earnings for a payroll period.

LU 7-3 Employer Taxes for FICA (OASDI, Medicare), FUTA, SUTA, and Workers' Compensation Insurance

Pre-Game Tips: Not only must employees pay a variety of payroll taxes, but their employers must also pay a number of payroll taxes.

Pre-Game Checkup: Answer true or false to the following statements.

1. Employers must pay FICA (OASDI and Medicare) equal to 1½ times the employee payment.
2. Only employers, not employees, must calculate and pay both FUTA and SUTA taxes.
3. FUTA and SUTA taxes are calculated on a wage base of $117,000.
4. Workers' compensation insurance is paid by the employer to insure that each employee is fairly compensated.
5. Workers' compensation insurance has a single rate for each employee of a firm, much like FICA.

LU 7-4 The Payroll Register, Employer Tax Liability, and Workers' Compensation Insurance

Pre-Game Tips: The FICA (OASDI and Medicare) payable accounts contain both the employee deductions and the matching amount from the employer.

Pre-Game Checkup: Answer true or false to the following statements.

1. The payroll register is the source of the data used to journalize the payroll in the general journal.
2. The FICA (OASDI and Medicare) payable accounts reflect the tax liability of only the employer.
3. Deductions for payroll withholding taxes represent a liability of the employees until the taxes are paid by the employer.
4. Workers' compensation insurance is paid by the employer to ensure that employees are compensated if they lose their job.
5. The year-end computation for annual workers' compensation shows additional money is owed. You will record the amount with a debit to Workers' Compensation Expense and a credit to Accounts Payable.

CHECK YOUR SCORE: Answers to the Pre-Game Checkup

LU 7-1

1. False—Pay periods are defined as daily, weekly, biweekly, semi-monthly, monthly, quarterly, or annually.
2. True
3. True
4. False—(OASDI) tax is limited by a wage base of $117,000. (Medicare) tax does not have a wage base limit; therefore, all wages earned are subject to the Medicare tax.
5. False—Gross pay is the amount calculated as earned by the employee before employee withholdings such as FIT, SIT, and FICA (OASDI and Medicare). After these deductions from gross pay, the employee receives his or her net pay.

LU 7-2

1. False—The employee earnings record shows gross earnings, deductions, and net pay for the employee for each calendar quarter and the entire calendar year.
2. False—The payroll register is used to update the employee earnings record.
3. True—They show the amount of earnings to be taxed for unemployment taxes and Social Security (OASDI).
4. False—The employee's marital status and the number of allowances are found on the payroll register.
5. True

LU 7-3

1. False—The employer pays exactly the same amount of FICA taxes (OASDI and Medicare) as do its employees.
2. True

3. False—In this text, both FUTA and SUTA are calculated on a wage base of $7,000 for each employee.
4. False—Workers' compensation insurance is paid by the employer to insure employees against work-related death or injury.
5. False—The rate paid by the employer is based on the type of work each employee performs (more hazardous jobs have higher rates) and the extent of any previous on-the-job injuries or deaths.

LU 7-4

1. True
2. False—The FICA (OASDI and Medicare) payable accounts accumulate FICA taxes from both the employees and the employer.
3. False—The employee's liability for FICA (OASDI and Medicare) cease the moment the employer deducts the taxes from the employee's gross pay. Those taxes then become the responsibility of the employer.
4. False—Workers' compensation insurance premiums are paid by the employer to insure the employee against work-related injury or death.
5. True

Chapter Summary

Here are all the key terms and equations to help you understand the concepts of this chapter and prepare you for your exam. After completing this review, go to MyAccountingLab for more practice opportunities.

MyAccountingLab

Concepts You Should Know	Key Terms
LO1 **Calculate Gross Pay, Employee Payroll Tax Deductions for Federal Income Tax Withholding, State Income Tax Withholding, FICA (OASDI, Medicare), and Net Pay** 1. The Fair Labor Standards Act states that hourly workers will receive a minimum of one and a half times their regular hourly rate of pay for all hours they work over 40 hours during a workweek. 2. Salaried employees are employees who are classified as salaried according to the provisions of the Fair Labor Standards Act. 3. For the rules of the Fair Labor Standards Act to apply to an employer, the employer must be involved in interstate commerce. 4. Employees and employers pay equal amounts of FICA tax. FICA tax is made up of two taxes: OASDI and Medicare. The OASDI tax is based on a tax rate and wage base amount that is set for each calendar year. 5. Gross earnings minus deductions equal net pay. 6. Federal income tax withholding amounts are listed in tax tables found in IRS Circular E, Employer's Tax Guide, also known as Publication 15.	Allowances (also called exemptions) (p. 242) Calendar year (p. 246) Circular E (p. 243) Fair Labor Standards Act (Federal Wage and Hour Law) (p. 240) Federal income tax (FIT) withholding (p. 242) FICA (Federal Insurance Contributions Act) (p. 246) Form W-4 (Employee's Withholding Allowance Certificate) (p. 242) Gross earnings (gross pay) (p. 241) Interstate commerce (p. 240) Medical insurance (p. 247) Net pay (p. 247) Pay or payroll period (p. 241) State income tax (SIT) withholding (p. 244) Taxable earnings (p. 247) Wage bracket table (p. 243) Workweek (p. 241)
LO2 **Prepare a Payroll Register and Maintain an Employee Earnings Record** 1. The two primary accounting records used to keep track of payroll amounts are the payroll register and employee earnings record. The payroll register shows gross earnings, deductions, net pay, and taxable earnings for a payroll period. 2. The taxable earnings columns of the payroll register do not show the tax. They show the amount of earnings to be taxed for unemployment taxes and OASDI. 3. The employee earnings record shows the gross earnings, deductions, and net pay for an employee for an entire calendar year. 4. The individual employee earnings records are updated soon after the payroll register is prepared.	Payroll register (p. 248) Individual employee earnings record (p. 248)

L03  **Calculate Employer Taxes for FICA (OASDI, Medicare), FUTA, SUTA, and Workers' Compensation Insurance**

1. The payroll tax expense for an employer is made up of FICA OASDI, FICA Medicare, FUTA, and SUTA.

2. The OASDI tax rate for 2014 is 6.2%, and the wage base limit for this year is $117,000.

3. Medicare has no wage base limit, so an employee and employer will pay this tax on all of an employee's earnings during the calendar year, at a rate of 1.45% for 2014.

4. The maximum amount of credit given for state unemployment taxes paid against the FUTA tax is 5.4%. This figure is known as the normal FUTA tax credit. The normal FUTA tax credit typically results in employers paying 0.6% for FUTA tax.

5. Employers pay workers' compensation insurance premiums based on estimated payroll. At the end of the year, estimated payroll is compared to actual payroll, and the employer either pays any additional premium or receives a credit for any overpayment of premium.

Experience or merit rating (p. 253)

Federal Unemployment Tax Act (FUTA) (p. 252)

State Unemployment Tax Act (SUTA) (p. 252)

Workers' compensation insurance (p. 252)

L04  **Journalize the Payroll Register, Employer Tax Liability, and Workers' Compensation Insurance**

1. The payroll register provides the data for journalizing the payroll in the general journal.

2. Deductions for payroll withholding taxes represent liabilities of the employer until paid.

3. The Accounts Charged columns in the payroll register indicate which accounts will be debited to record the total wages and salaries expense when a journal entry is prepared.

Payroll tax expense (p. 255)

Discussion Questions and Critical Thinking/Ethical Case

1. What is the purpose of the Fair Labor Standards Act (also called the Federal Wage and Hour Law)?

2. Explain how to calculate overtime pay.

3. Explain how a W-4 form, called the Employee's Withholding Allowance Certificate, is used to determine Federal Income Tax (FIT) withheld.

4. The more allowances an employee claims on a W-4 form, the more take-home pay the employee gets with each paycheck. Agree or disagree?

5. Explain how federal and state income tax withholdings are determined.

6. Explain why a business should prepare a payroll register before employees are paid.

7. The taxable earnings column of a payroll register records the amount of tax due. Agree or disagree?

8. Define and state the purpose of FICA taxes.

9. Explain how to calculate OASDI and Medicare taxes.

10. The employer doesn't have to contribute to FICA. Agree or disagree? Please explain.

11. What purpose does the individual employee earnings record serve?

12. Please draw a diagram showing how the following items relate to each other: (a) weekly payroll, (b) payroll register, (c) individual employee earnings record, and (d) general journal entries for payroll.

13. If you earned $130,000 this year, you would pay more OASDI and Medicare than your partner who earned $75,000. Do you agree or disagree? Please provide calculations to support your answer.

14. Explain how an employer can receive a credit against the FUTA tax due.

15. Explain what an experience or merit rating is and how it affects the amount paid by an employer for state unemployment insurance.

16. Who pays workers' compensation insurance, the employee or the employer? What types of benefits does this insurance provide? How are premiums calculated?

17. An employee for Repairs to Go, Inc., works different numbers of hours each week depending on the needs of the business. To simplify the accounting, the bookkeeper for Repairs to Go classifies this employee as a salaried person. Is this practice appropriate? Please explain.

18. What taxes are recorded when recording Payroll Tax Expense?

19. What is a calendar year?

20. An employer must always use a calendar year for payroll purposes. Agree or disagree and explain your answer.

MyAccountingLab   ## Concept Check

(10 min) **LO1** ▶   **Calculating Gross Earnings**

1.   Calculate the total wages earned (assume an overtime rate of time and a half over 40 hours).

Employee	Hourly Rate	No. of Hours Worked
Adam Williams	$17	34
Arnold Smith	14	53

(15 min) **LO1** ▶   **FIT and FICA**

2.   Ben Stein, single, claiming one exemption, has cumulative earnings before this biweekly pay period of $116,200. If he is paid $1,980 this period, what will his deductions be for FIT and FICA (OASDI and Medicare)? The FICA tax rate for Social Security is 6.2% on $117,000, and Medicare is 1.45% on all earnings.

(15 min) **LO1** ▶   **Net Pay**

3.   From Exercise 2, calculate Ben's net pay. The state income tax rate is 5%, and health insurance is $35.

(10 min) **LO2** ▶   **Payroll Register**

4.   Match the following:
   1. Total gross pay
   2. A deduction
   3. Net pay
        a. _____ Office Salary Expense
        b. _____ FICA OASDI
        c. _____ FICA Medicare
        d. _____ Federal Income Tax
        e. _____ Medical Insurance
        f. _____ Wages and Salaries Payable

(10 min) **LO2,3** ▶   **Employer and Employee Taxes**

5.   Identify which of the following taxes are paid by the employee (EE) and which are paid by the employer (ER):
        a. _____ FICA Medicare
        b. _____ FIT
        c. _____ FUTA
        d. _____ SUTA

(10 min) **LO4** ▶   **Account Classifications**

6.   Complete the following table. Indicate whether a debit or credit results in an increase to the account balance.

Accounts Affected	Category	↑↓	Rules
a. Payroll Tax Expense			
b. FICA OASDI Payable			
c. SIT Payable			
d. SUTA Payable			
e. Prepaid Workers' Compensation Insurance			

Exercises

MyAccountingLab

Set A

7A-1. **a.** Calculate the total wages earned for each hourly employee assuming an overtime rate of time and a half over 40 hours.

L01   *(15 min)*

Employee	Hourly Rate	No. of Hours Worked
Paula Anderson	$10	37
Olivia Turner	13	41
Kellen Gates	18	45

b. Calculate the total biweekly earnings of these newly hired salaried employees.

	Monthly Salary
John Smith	$4,000
Jane Doe	$5,000

7A-2. Compute the net pay for each employee using the federal income tax withholding table in Figure 7.2. Assume that FICA OASDI tax is 6.2% on a wage base limit of $117,000, Medicare is 1.45% on all earnings, the payroll is paid biweekly, and no state income tax applies.

L01   *(20 min)*

Employee	Status	Allowances	Cumulative Pay	Biweekly Pay
Xu Daoning	Single	2	$59,000	$1,650
William Pierce	Single	0	61,500	1,630

7A-3. From the following information, calculate the payroll tax expense for Driving Company for the payroll of April 9:

L03   *(20 min)*

Employee	Cumulative Earnings Before Weekly Payroll	Gross Pay for the Week
O. Barns	$3,600	$925
C. Hart	6,600	600
Q. Roberts	7,500	330

The FICA tax rate for OASDI is 6.2% on the first $117,000 earned, and Medicare is 1.45% on all earnings. Federal unemployment tax is 0.6% on the first $7,000 earned by each employee. The SUTA tax rate for Driving Company is 5.8% on the first $7,000 of employee earnings for state unemployment purposes.

(15 min)   **LO3**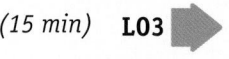

7A-4. Refer to Exercise 7A-3 and assume that the state changed Driving Company's SUTA tax rate to 4.6%. What effect would this change have on the total payroll tax expense?

(15 min)   **LO3**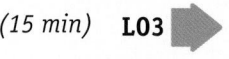

7A-5. Refer to Exercise 7A-3. If Q. Roberts earned $2,100 for the week instead of $330, what effect would this change have on the total payroll tax expense?

(20 min)   **LO3,4**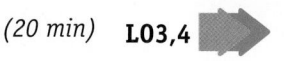

7A-6. The total wage expense for Edgar Co. was $166,000. Of this total, $26,000 was above the OASDI wage base limit and not subject to this tax. All earnings are subject to Medicare tax, and $55,000 was above the federal and state unemployment wage base limits and not subject to unemployment taxes. Please calculate and journalize the total payroll tax expense for Edgar Co. given the following rates and wage base limits:

  a. FICA tax rate: OASDI, 6.2% with a wage base limit of $117,000; Medicare, 1.45% with no wage base limit

  b. State unemployment tax rate: 5.7% with a wage base limit of $7,000

  c. Federal unemployment tax rate (after credit): 0.6% with a wage base limit of $7,000

(20 min)   **LO3,4**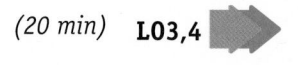

7A-7. At the end of the first quarter of 201X, you are asked to determine the FUTA tax liability for Aim Company. The FUTA tax rate is 0.6% on the first $7,000 each employee earns during the year (assuming 13 weeks for the first quarter) and each employee earned the same gross weekly pay for all 13 weeks).

Employee	Gross Pay Per Week
W. Duncan	$690
S. Ivan	780
V. North	560
H. Young	430

(10 min)   **LO3**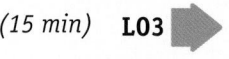

7A-8. From the following data, estimate the annual premium for workers' compensation insurance:

Type of Work	Estimated Payroll	Rate per $100
Office	$32,000	$0.22
Repairs	77,000	1.78

Set B

(15 min)   **LO1**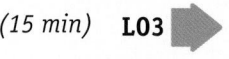

7B-1. **a.** Calculate the total wages earned for each employee assuming an overtime rate of time and a half over 40 hours.

Employee	Hourly Rate	No. of Hours Worked
Marie Norris	$11	35
Heidi Rodes	13	50
Norman Duncan	16	47

b. Calculate the total biweekly earnings of these newly hired salaried employees.

	Monthly Salary
George Day	$4,400
Min Lee	$5,600

7B-2. Compute the net pay for each employee using the federal income tax withholding table in Figure 7.2. Assume that FICA OASDI tax is 6.2% on a wage base limit of $117,000; Medicare is 1.45% on all earnings, the payroll is paid biweekly, and no state income tax applies.

L01 *(20 min)*

Employee	Status	Allowances	Cumulative Pay	Biweekly Pay
Alvin Pang	Single	2	$61,500	$1,680
David Parker	Single	0	63,300	1,600

7B-3. From the following information, calculate the payroll tax expense for New Company for the payroll of April 9:

L03 *(20 min)*

Employee	Cumulative Earnings Before Weekly Payroll	Gross Pay for the Week
I. Benson	$3,300	$800
K. Larry	6,200	625
Q. Roberts	7,600	290

The FICA tax rate for OASDI is 6.2% on the first $117,000 earned, and Medicare is 1.45% on all earnings. Federal unemployment tax is 0.6% on the first $7,000 earned by each employee. The SUTA tax rate for New is 5.9% on the first $7,000 of earnings for state unemployment purposes.

7B-4. Refer to Exercise 7B-3 and assume that the state changed New's SUTA tax rate to 3.8%. What effect would this change have on the total payroll tax expense?

L03 *(15 min)*

7B-5. Refer to Exercise 7B-3. If Q. Roberts earned $3,100 for the week instead of $290, what effect would this change have on the total payroll tax expense?

L03 *(15 min)*

7B-6. The total wage expense for Orange Co. was $158,000. Of this total, $32,000 was above the OASDI wage base limit and not subject to this tax. All earnings are subject to Medicare tax, and $60,000 was above the federal and state unemployment wage base limits and not subject to unemployment taxes. Please calculate and journalize the total payroll tax expense for Orange Co. given the following rates and wage base limits:

L03,4 *(20 min)*

a. FICA tax rate: OASDI, 6.2% with a wage base limit of $117,000; Medicare, 1.45% with no wage base limit.

b. State unemployment tax rate 6.0% with a wage base limit of $7,000.

c. Federal unemployment tax rate (after credit): 0.6% with a wage base limit of $7,000.

7B-7. At the end of the first quarter of 201X, you are asked to determine the FUTA tax liability for Gray Company. The FUTA tax rate is 0.6% on the first $7,000 each employee earns during the year (assuming 13 weeks for the first quarter and each employee earned the same gross weekly pay for all 13 weeks).

L03,4 *(20 min)*

Employee	Gross Pay Per Week
O. Barn	$650
Z. Grande	790
J. Mathison	580
E. Walsh	460

(10 min) **LO3**

7B-8. From the following data, estimate the annual premium for worker's compensation insurance:

Type of Work	Estimated Payroll	Rate per $100
Office	$29,000	$0.23
Repairs	78,000	1.62

MyAccountingLab

Problems

Set A

(20 min) **LO1**

7A-1. From the following information, please complete the chart for gross earnings for the week. (Assume an overtime rate of time and a half over 40 hours.)

Check Figure:
Dmitri Wittman: $980.00 Gross
Earnings

Employee	Hourly Rate	No. of Hours Worked	Gross Earnings
Jade Martina	$ 9	50	
Lauren McBride	15	39	
Natala Polino	16	40	
Dmitri Wittman	20	46	

(30 min) **LO1**

7A-2. April Company has five salaried employees. Your task is to use the following information to prepare a payroll register to calculate net pay for each employee:

Employee	Allowance and Marital Status	Cumulative Earnings Before This Payroll	Biweekly Salary	Department
Bristow, Helen	S-0	$ 42,000	$1,600	Customer Service
Fein, Kristen	S-1	33,000	1,250	Office
Kent, Hailey	S-1	56,500	1,050	Office
Barr, Brent	S-3	115,420	2,080	Customer Service
Alden, Liam	S-3	28,000	810	Customer Service

Assume the following:
1. FICA OASDI is 6.2% on $117,000; FICA Medicare is 1.45% on all earnings.
2. Each employee contributes $25 biweekly for medical insurance.
3. State income tax is 3% of gross pay.
4. FIT is calculated from Figure 7.2.

Check Figure:
Total Net Pay $5,258.85

(40 min) **LO1,2**

7A-3. The bookkeeper of Triad Co. gathered the following data from individual employee earnings records and daily time cards. Your task is to complete a payroll register on October 13.

Employee	Allowance and Marital Status	Cumulative Earnings Before This Payroll	M	T	W	T	F	Hourly Rate of Pay	FIT
Rock, Patrick	M-1	$15,400	7	7	11	8	6	$22	$75
King, Diana	S-0	16,500	10	12	5	11	2	19	101
Dean, Rowland	M-3	61,000	10	9	9	6	9	15	27
Snow, John	S-1	18,000	12	6	6	9	9	27	182

Assume the following:

1. FICA OASDI is 6.2% on $117,000; FICA Medicare is 1.45% on all earnings.
2. Federal income tax has been calculated from a weekly table for you.
3. Each employee contributes $28 weekly for health insurance.
4. Overtime is paid at a rate of time and a half over 40 hours.
5. Rock and Dean work in the office; the other employees work in sales.

Check Figure:
Total Net Pay $2,685.84

7A-4. You gathered the following data from time cards and individual employee earnings records. Your tasks are as follows:

1. On December 5, 201X, prepare a payroll register for this biweekly payroll.
2. Calculate the employer taxes of FICA OASDI, FICA Medicare, FUTA, and SUTA.
3. Journalize the Payroll Register and the Employer's tax liability.

L01,2,3,4 *(40 min)*

S50 / QB

Employee	Allowance and Marital Status	Cumulative Earnings Before This Payroll	Biweekly Salary	Check No.	Department
Avery, Joanna	S-3	$37,600	$1,540	30	Production
Garth, Natashia	S-1	48,200	2,040	31	Office
Martinez, Joan	S-2	64,500	2,090	32	Production
Seward, Peter	S-1	4,800	880	33	Office

Assume the following:

1. FICA OASDI is 6.2% on $117,000; FICA Medicare is 1.45% on all earnings.
2. Federal income tax is calculated from Figure 7.2.
3. State income tax is 7% of gross pay.
4. Union dues are $17 biweekly.
5. The SUTA rate is 5.0% and the FUTA rate is 0.6% on earnings up to $7,000.

Check Figure:
Total Net Pay $4,748.42

Set B

7B-1. From the following information, please complete the chart for gross earnings for the week. (Assume an overtime rate of time and a half over 40 hours.)

L01 *(20 min)*

Employee	Hourly Rate	No. of Hours Worked	Gross Earnings
Jag Valleria	$ 8	49	
Lara Harrison	16	45	
Natalie Whittier	18	47	
Dmitri Jacobson	15	52	

Check Figure:
Dmitri Jacobson Gross Pay $870

7B-2. Autumn Company has five salaried employees. Your task is to use the following information to prepare a payroll register to calculate net pay for each employee:

L01 *(30 min)*

Employee	Allowance and Marital Status	Cumulative Earnings Before This Payroll	Biweekly Salary	Department
Burby, Dylan	S-0	$39,000	$1,300	Customer Service
Huntington, Marc	S-1	37,000	900	Office
Stanwood, Alison	S-1	57,400	1,150	Office
Athol, Audrey	S-2	115,710	1,790	Customer Service
Bellamont, Lionel	S-3	34,000	1,010	Customer Service

Check Figure:
Total Net Pay $4,440.01

Assume the following:

1. FICA OASDI is 6.2% on $117,000; FICA Medicare is 1.45% on all earnings.
2. Each employee contributes $70 biweekly for medical insurance.
3. State income tax is 5% of gross pay.
4. FIT is calculated from Figure 7.2.

(40 min) **LO1,2** ▶

7B-3. The bookkeeper of Triad Co. gathered the following data from individual employee earnings records and daily time cards. Your task is to complete a payroll register on August 8.

Employee	Allowance and Marital Status	Cumulative Earnings Before This Payroll	Daily Time					Hourly Rate of Pay	FIT
			M	T	W	T	F		
Cruz, Pam	M-1	$25,600	10	6	9	7	6	$30	$119
Pitt, Don	S-0	17,000	6	8	13	11	4	20	126
Pope, Ria	M-3	59,000	6	6	16	11	7	22	85
Snow, Jane	S-1	18,500	12	7	5	10	9	25	169

Assume the following:

1. FICA OASDI is 6.2% on $117,000; FICA Medicare is 1.45% on all earnings.
2. Federal income tax has been calculated from a weekly table for you.
3. Each employee contributes $28 weekly for health insurance.
4. Overtime is paid at a rate of time and a half over 40 hours.
5. Cruz and Pope work in the office; the other employees work in sales.

Check Figure:
Total Net Pay $3,258.92

(40 min) **LO1,2,3,4** ▶▶▶

7B-4. You gathered the following data from time cards and individual employee earnings records. Your tasks are as follows:

1. On December 5, 201X, prepare a payroll register for this biweekly payroll.
2. Calculate the employer taxes of FICA OASDI, FICA Medicare, FUTA, and SUTA.
3. Journalize the Payroll Register & Employer's tax liability.

Employee	Allowance and Marital Status	Cumulative Earnings Before This Payroll	Biweekly Salary	Check No.	Department
Ackery, John	S-3	$37,600	$1,500	30	Production
Geary, Nicki	S-1	48,400	1,990	31	Office
Martin, Jeff	S-2	65,200	2,060	32	Production
Sherard, Paul	S-1	4,300	860	33	Office

Check Figure:
Total Net Pay $4,613.83

Assume the following:

1. FICA OASDI is 6.2% on $117,000; FICA Medicare is 1.45% on all earnings.
2. Federal income tax is calculated from Figure 7.2.
3. State income tax is 8% of gross pay.
4. Union dues are $12 biweekly.
5. The SUTA rate is 5.4%, and the FUTA rate is 0.6% on earnings up to $7,000.

Financial Report Problem

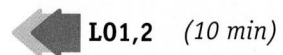

LO1,2 *(10 min)*

Reading the Kellogg's Annual Report

Go to http://investor.kelloggs.com/investor-relations/annual-reports to access the Kellogg's 2013 Annual Report. Look at Notes to Consolidated Financial Statements and use information from Note 17 page 68 to calculate how much Advertising Expense has increased from 2012 to 2013.

ON THE JOB SMITH COMPUTER CENTER

MyAccountingLab

During the month of November, the following transactions occurred.

Assignment

LO1 *(60 min)*

1. Record the following transactions in the general journal and post them to the general ledger.

2. Prepare a trial balance as of November 30, 201X.

Assume the following transactions:

Nov.	1	Billed Worldwide Professionals $7,400, invoice no. 12676, for services rendered.
	3	Billed All Star Sports, Inc. $4,400, invoice no. 12677, for services rendered.
	5	Purchased new shop benches for $1,800 on account from Quality Office Furniture.
	9	Received the phone bill, $170.
	12	Collected $725 of the amount due from Phil's Photography.
	18	Collected $900 of the amount due from Phil's Photography.
	20	Purchased a fax machine for the office from A-Tech, Inc., on credit, $550.00.

Paying the Payroll, Depositing Payroll Taxes, and Filing the Required Quarterly and Annual Tax Forms: The Conclusion of the Payroll Process

CHAPTER
8

CHAPTER PREVIEW: THE BIG PICTURE

Every month or every 2 weeks you might receive a paycheck. When reviewing all the deductions, did you ever wonder what they were for? Your employer must report these deductions in order to meet its state and federal reporting requirements. For example, Google must take taxes out of its employees' paychecks and report the amounts to the federal and state authorities. By law, Google will have to make periodic payroll deposits of these taxes along with some matching requirements like Social Security. Google and other companies also are required by law to contribute to unemployment programs. This chapter focuses on the payroll reporting responsibilities of the employer. For both small and large businesses the payroll process is an inseparable part of the accounting process.

Learning Objectives

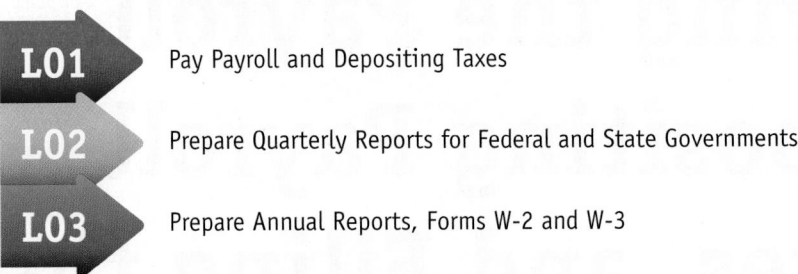

L01   Pay Payroll and Depositing Taxes

L02   Prepare Quarterly Reports for Federal and State Governments

L03   Prepare Annual Reports, Forms W-2 and W-3

Google has many thousands of employees. With the aid of computers, the accounting department of Google must monitor as well as complete in a timely manner its employer tax responsibilities. In Chapter 7 we learned how to calculate gross earnings, employee withholding taxes, net pay, and employer payroll taxes. We now look at how businesses pay, record, and report these amounts. The journal entries necessary to record all of the payroll transactions for Travelwithus.com appear in the next section.

LEARNING UNIT 8-1

L01

Payroll and Depositing Taxes

Transferring Funds to the Payroll Account and Distributing the Paychecks

Katherine must write and distribute paychecks to the employees of Travelwithus .com. Like most companies, Travelwithus.com uses a special checking account for paying its payroll. This account is called Cash – Payroll Checking and only paychecks are written from this account. A company with a substantial number of employees might want to use an extra account just for payroll for a number of reasons. First, having a separate account just for paychecks provides much better internal control over the funds deposited to pay employees. Also, because only payroll checks are written from this account, it is easier to reconcile it to the bank statement each month and determine whether someone has not cashed his or her paycheck for some reason. Finally, the business can still manage its cash effectively even with this extra bank account; the business simply deposits the total net pay amount in this account and thus has enough money to pay every paycheck without leaving extra in the account that could be used for other purposes. The following journal entry illustrates the transfer of funds from the general bank account to the payroll bank account. This transfer is made sometime between the completion of the payroll register and the date the checks are distributed.

GENERAL JOURNAL				
Date		PR	Dr.	Cr.
201X				
Oct. 26	Cash – Payroll Checking		8 8 1 0 46	
	Cash – Regular Checking			8 8 1 0 46
	To record transfer between two accounts			

The following journal entry illustrates the distribution of the payroll dated October 29.

GENERAL JOURNAL				
Date		PR	Dr.	Cr.
201X				
Oct. 29	Wages & Salaries Payable		8 8 1 0 46	
	Cash – Payroll Checking			8 8 1 0 46
	To record distribution of paychecks			

COACHING TIP:
Many companies now pay their employees electronically. The pay stub information is available for each employee through their confidential, online payroll records.

The paychecks that Travelwithus.com gives to its employees are, like the paychecks of most companies, attached to pay stubs that show the employee's gross earnings, deductions for employee withholding taxes, and net pay. Figure 8.1 illustrates Stephanie Higuera's current paycheck and stub:

Travelwithus.com Inc.

Employee	Social Security	Check	Net Pay	Pay Date	Marital Status	Allowances
Stephanie Higuera	123-45-6789	820	$685.73	October 29, 201X	S	1

Earnings	Current			Deductions		
	Pay Rate	Hours	Earnings	Item	Current	YTD
Regular Earnings	11.40	78	889.20	FIT	$89.00	2,067.00
Overtime Earnings	17.10	4	68.40	SIT	76.61	1,557.70
Current Gross Earnings			957.60	OASDI	59.37	1,207.21
				Medicare	13.89	282.33
				Medical insurance	33.00	693.00
				Total	$271.87	5,807.24

FIGURE 8.1
Stephanie Higuera's Paycheck and Stub

Travelwithus.com Inc.
504 Washington Blvd.
Salem, MA 01970

11-325/1210

No. 820

October 29, 201X

PAY TO THE ORDER OF Stephanie Higuera $685.73

Six hundred eighty-five and 73/100 _____ DOLLARS

BC | Bank of Commerce

MEMO Oct 13–26 payroll   *Julia Regan*

Depositing Payroll Taxes

As we discussed in Chapter 7, both employers and employees pay payroll taxes. Employers continue recording the various tax liabilities until it is time to remit to the tax authorities. Any payment obligations for state or local taxes are specific to that taxing unit. Because these tax authorities have various rules, we omit discussion of the topic in this text. Therefore, we focus only on the federal requirements for depositing and reporting payroll taxes. Let's now discuss how Travelwithus.com carries out these responsibilities.

For Travelwithus.com, the process began when the business opened. When opening a business, every employer must get a federal identification number. This number is also called an employer identification number (EIN) and is like a Social Security number for businesses in the sense that it identifies businesses to the government. To get an EIN, an employer fills out Form SS-4, much like individuals fill out Form SS-5 to get a Social Security number. Travelwithus.com will use its EIN, 58-1213479, when remitting or reporting any business tax.

Employer identification number (EIN) A number assigned by the IRS that is used by an employer when recording and paying payroll and income taxes.

Form SS-4 The form filled out by an employer to get an EIN. The form is sent to the IRS, which assigns the number to the business.

Form 941 taxes Another term used to describe FIT, OASDI, and Medicare. This name comes from the form used to report these taxes.

COACHING TIP:

Remember, payrolls are entered on the register based on the date the check is actually given to the employee.

After the paychecks have been released, the company needs to evaluate the need of remitting to the IRS the federal taxes owed. The rules on how and when to remit the tax payments are lengthy and are covered in more detail later. However, because Travelwithus.com is a new employer this year, the company is allowed to deposit the taxes monthly. As a monthly depositor, all FIT and FICA taxes withheld and matched during the month (also referred to as Form 941 taxes) will be electronically transferred to the IRS on or before the 15th day of the following month.

The Worksheet Summary of Payroll Registers (see Figure 8.4 on page 281) contains all payroll detail for the fourth quarter. This worksheet helps Katherine compute the 941 tax deposit needed for each month within that quarter. For now, let's focus on the month of October.

To compute the tax deposit, Katherine will add the total October federal income tax and twice the FICA taxes. Why do we pay twice the total FICA? Remember, in the previous chapter, the employer had to match the employee FICA deductions. To illustrate her computation, look at the October totals for each federal tax category found on the worksheet summary:

FIT	FICA × 2	Total Deposit
$4,548.00	($2,307.07 + $539.56) × 2	$10,241.26

Because Travelwithus.com is a monthly depositor, the total deposit for the three October pay dates must be paid to the IRS on or before November 15. If that date is a Saturday, Sunday, or bank holiday, the due date is extended to the next banking day. Additionally, the IRS requires that businesses submit all tax payments electronically if they owe more than $2,500.00 in a calendar quarter.

Let's also view the general ledger accounts for the October Form 941 taxes. You can see the postings to the individual accounts for FIT, FICA-OASDI, and FICA-Medicare. This will also clarify how to journalize the deposit needed.

FIT Payable		
10/1	1,495.00
10/15	1,495.00
10/29	1,558.00
	4,548.00

FICA-OASDI Payable		
10/1	765.20
10/1	765.20
10/15	765.20
10/15	765.20
10/29	776.67
10/29	776.67
	4,614.14

FICA-Medicare Payable		
10/1	178.96
10/1	178.96
10/15	178.96
10/15	178.96
10/29	181.64
10/29	181.64
	1,079.12

GENERAL JOURNAL					
		PR	Dr.	Cr.	
FIT Payable			4 5 4 8 00		
FICA OASDI Payable			4 6 1 4 14		
FICA Medicare Payable			1 0 7 9 12		
Cash-Regular Checking				10 2 4 1 26	

Look-back period A period of time used to determine whether a business should make its Form 941 tax deposits on a monthly or semiweekly basis. The IRS defines this period as July 1 through June 30 of the year prior to the year in which Form 941 tax deposits will be made.

General Rules for Determining a Depositor Classification

As mentioned earlier, the rules for depositing payroll taxes are lengthy. Let's start by discussing the look-back period. The IRS determines a company's tax depositor classification by reviewing the taxes paid during the look-back period. This period of time is a 12-month period that starts July 1 two years earlier. If a company's payroll tax liability was less than $50,000 in that 12-month period, the company is considered a monthly depositor. However, if the company owes more than $50,000 during that time frame, the company is considered a semiweekly depositor.

As a new company this year, Travelwithus.com does not have a 12-month tax paying history. Therefore, they are considered a monthly depositor. You should read all of the exact rules and exceptions that are found in Publication 15 online at www .IRS.gov. Figure 8.2 provides general information about the look-back period.

Monthly depositor A business classified as a monthly depositor will make its payroll tax deposits only once each month for the amount of Form 941 taxes due from the prior month.

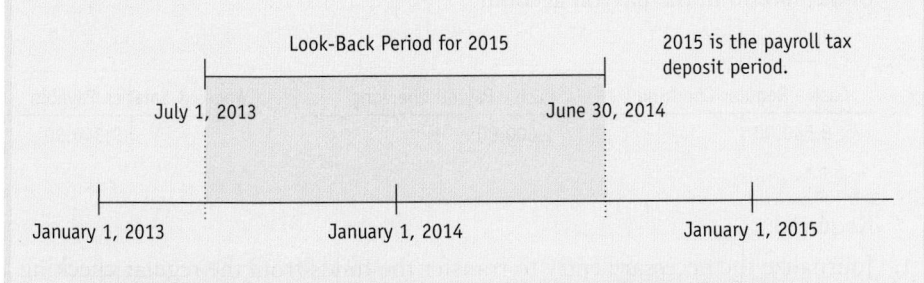

FIGURE 8.2
Look-Back Illustration

General Rules for Depositing Payroll Taxes

Once the classification is determined, Katherine knows when she must deposit the 941 taxes collected. In addition to the two primary classifications (see 1 and 2 below), there are two other rules that may apply (see 3 and 4 below).

1. **Monthly Depositor Classification:** Deposit payroll taxes collected by the 15th day of the month following the payroll month. Example: Any pay date that falls in January must have taxes deposited by February 15.

2. **Semiweekly Depositor Classification:** If your pay date falls on Saturday, Sunday, Monday, or Tuesday, the company must deposit taxes on the third banking day after Tuesday (usually Friday). If your pay date falls on Wednesday, Thursday, or Friday, the company must deposit taxes on the third banking day after Friday (usually the following Wednesday). See Figure 8.3.

3. **One-Day Rule:** If the payroll tax liability for either classification above exceeds $100,000 at any time during the quarter, the company must deposit all taxes by the close of the next business day (also known as the 24-hour rule). Normally, this rule applies to very large employers such as ExxonMobil or Walmart.

4. **Deposits Not Required:** If the company is very small, and the tax liability is less than $2,500 for the quarter, the taxes can be sent with the 941 quarterly report.

Semiweekly depositor A business classified as a semiweekly depositor may have to make its payroll tax deposits up to twice in one week, depending on when payroll is paid.

Banking day A banking day is any day that a bank is open to the public for business. Generally, a banking day will end at 2:00 or 3:00 P.M. local time. Banking business transacted after this time is usually considered to be the next day's business. Saturdays, Sundays, and federal holidays are usually not considered banking days.

	Sat	Sun	Mon	Tues	Wed	Thurs	Fri	Sat	Sun	Mon	Tues	Wed
If payday is												
Then deposit is due												

FIGURE 8.3
Semiweekly Deposit Rules Illustration

Tax Deposit Exceptions

1. If the deposit date falls on a Saturday, Sunday, or legal holiday, the deposit date is extended to the next business day.

2. Semiweekly depositors only: If a legal holiday falls on any of the three banking days referenced, the company gets one additional day to deposit. Example: The pay date is on a Thursday. The following Monday is a federal holiday. The deposit, which is normally due on Wednesday, can be made on Thursday.

COACHING TIP:

Regardless of how often a company pays payroll, they are classified as either a monthly or semiweekly tax depositor.

TRY IT!

The following T accounts reflect a partial list of general ledger account balances for B & K Company after recording the payroll register for the pay period ending March 3, 201X. It is now March 5, 201X, and Mr. Brent, the company owner, needs to transfer money from the regular account to the payroll account so that the paychecks can be released. Mr. Brent wants to maintain a minimum of $1,000.00 in the payroll account.

Cash - Regular Checking		Cash - Payroll Checking		Wages & Salaries Payable	
8,540.00		1,000.00			3,346.00

Required:

1. Journalize the necessary entry to transfer the funds from the regular checking account to the payroll checking account.

2. Journalize the entry needed to reflect the release and payment of the paychecks.

3. Post entries 1 and 2 into the T accounts and compute the balance of each account after posting.

LEARNING UNIT 8-2

LO2

COACHING TIP:

Remember, 941 taxes include FIT and FICA (both employee and employer).

Form 941, Employer's Quarterly Federal Tax Return A tax report that a business will complete after the end of each calendar quarter indicating the total FICA (OASDI and Medicare) taxes owed plus the amount of FIT withheld from employees' pay for the quarter. If federal tax deposits have been made correctly and on time, the total amount deposited should equal the amount due on Form 941. Any difference results in a payment due or a refund.

Calendar quarter A three-month, 13-week time period. Four calendar quarters occur during a calendar year that runs from January 1 through December 31. The first quarter is January through March, the second is April through June, the third is July through September, and the fourth is October through December.

Quarterly Reports for Federal and State Governments

Form 941

The IRS requires all employers to periodically report all tax liability incurred for FIT and FICA as well as all deposits made toward payment of those taxes. This is done by filing a quarterly tax report on a Form 941, Employer's Quarterly Federal Tax Return. The reporting periods are calendar quarters ending on March 31, June 30, September 30, and December 31. The filing date for any of the reports is the last day of the month following the quarter. This gives the company time to gather and verify the information before needing to file Form 941. In order to find Form 941 and see the instructions for reporting and filing, go to www.irs.gov and click on Forms and Publications.

Katherine Kurtz, the accountant for Travelwithus.com, used the worksheet in Figure 8.4 to prepare Form 941 for the last quarter of the year. See the completed Form 941, Figure 8.5 (pages 282–283).

The top section of Travelwithus.com's fourth quarter Form 941 in Figure 8.5 identifies the taxpayer, Travelwithus.com, and lists its address, the date that the quarter ended, and its EIN. For Part 1, compare the data found on Form 941 to the Worksheet (Figure 8.4).

Part 1:

- Line 1 asks for the number of employees on one specific date during the quarter.
- Line 2 requires the total gross pay for the quarter.
- Line 3 lists the total quarterly Federal Income Tax (FIT) withheld from all employees.

FIGURE 8.6 *(continued)*

850212

Name *(not your trade name)*	Employer identification number (EIN)
Travelwithus.com, Inc.	58-1213479

Part 5: Report your FUTA tax liability by quarter only if line 12 is more than $500. If not, go to Part 6.

16 Report the amount of your FUTA tax liability for each quarter; do NOT enter the amount you deposited. If you had no liability for a quarter, leave the line blank.

16a 1st quarter (January 1 – March 31) . . . . **16a** ☐ .

16b 2nd quarter (April 1 – June 30) . . . . **16b** ☐ .

16c 3rd quarter (July 1 – September 30) . . . . **16c** ☐ .

16d 4th quarter (October 1 – December 31) . . . . **16d** ☐ .

17 Total tax liability for the year (lines 16a + 16b + 16c + 16d = line 17) **17** ☐ .   Total must equal line 12.

Part 6: May we speak with your third-party designee?

Do you want to allow an employee, a paid tax preparer, or another person to discuss this return with the IRS? See the instructions for details.

☐ **Yes.**   Designee's name and phone number ☐   ☐

Select a 5-digit Personal Identification Number (PIN) to use when talking to IRS ☐ ☐ ☐ ☐ ☐

☒ **No.**

Part 7: Sign here. You MUST complete both pages of this form and SIGN it.

Under penalties of perjury, I declare that I have examined this return, including accompanying schedules and statements, and to the best of my knowledge and belief, it is true, correct, and complete, and that no part of any payment made to a state unemployment fund claimed as a credit was, or is to be, deducted from the payments made to employees. Declaration of preparer (other than taxpayer) is based on all information of which preparer has any knowledge.

✗ **Sign your name here**   *Katherine Kurtz*

Print your name here   Katherine Kurtz

Print your title here   Controller

Date   01/31/1Y

Best daytime phone   (978)555-4040

Paid Preparer Use Only   Check if you are self-employed . ☐

Preparer's name	PTIN
Preparer's signature	Date / /
Firm's name (or yours if self-employed)	EIN
Address	Phone
City State	ZIP code

FIGURE 8.7 Stephanie Higuera's W-2 Form

22222	Void ☐	**a** Employee's social security number 123-45-6789	For Official Use Only ▶ OMB No. 1545-0008		

b Employer identification number (EIN) 58-1213479		**1** Wages, tips, other compensation 23,176.20	**2** Federal income tax withheld 2,248.86

c Employer's name, address, and ZIP code Travelwithus.com, Inc. 10 Lovett Road Salem, MA 01970	**3** Social security wages 23,176.20	**4** Social security tax withheld 1,436.92
	5 Medicare wages and tips 23,176.20	**6** Medicare tax withheld 336.05
	7 Social security tips	**8** Allocated tips

d Control number	**9**	**10** Dependent care benefits

e Employee's first name and initial	Last name	Suff.	**11** Nonqualified plans	**12a** See instructions for box 12
Stephanie A.	Higuera			
			13 Statutory employee ☐ Retirement plan ☐ Third-party sick pay ☐	**12b**
1014 Inverness Way Southside, MA 01945			**14** Other	**12c**
				12d

f Employee's address and ZIP code					

15 State Employer's state ID number MA | 621-8966-4	**16** State wages, tips, etc. 23,176.20	**17** State income tax 1,854.10	**18** Local wages, tips, etc.	**19** Local income tax	**20** Locality name

Form **W-2** Wage and Tax Statement   **201X**

Copy A For Social Security Administration — Send this entire page with
Form W-3 to the Social Security Administration; photocopies are **not** acceptable.

Department of the Treasury—Internal Revenue Service
For Privacy Act and Paperwork Reduction
Act Notice, see the separate instructions.
Cat. No. 10134D

Do Not Cut, Fold, or Staple Forms on This Page

**Form W-3, Transmittal of
Wage and Tax Statements**
A form completed by the employer
to verify the number of W-2s and
amounts withheld as shown on
them. This form is sent to the
Social Security Administration data
processing center along with copies
of each employee's W-2 forms.

COACHING TIP:

Remember that the employee
completes a W-4 when hired. The
employer completes the W-2 form
after year end.

Preparing Form W-3: Transmittal of Income and Tax Statements

The IRS also requires Travelwithus.com to prepare its Form W-3, Transmittal of Wage
and Tax Statements. Employers such as Travelwithus.com send this form to the Social
Security Administration along with Copy A of the W-2s for all employees. Form W-3
(see Figure 8.8) reports the total amounts of wages, tips, and compensation paid to
employees, the total OASDI and Medicare taxes withheld, and some other information. Figure 8.9 provides the information for Figure 8.8.

The Social Security Administration, under a special agreement with the IRS, makes
all information found on individual W-2 forms electronically available to the IRS so
that it can check the accuracy of the employer's 941 forms and individual employees'
federal income tax returns.

Employers not using tax software or a tax preparation service can create
forms W-2 and W-3 electronically by using Business Services Online found at
http://www.socialsecurity.gov. This is a free service and easy to use.

Other Annual Reporting Requirements

If an employer hires independent contractors, the company is required to prepare
and distribute Form 1099 to each contractor that was paid $600 or more during
the calendar year. These forms are submitted to the IRS with a recap Form 1096.
Travelwithus.com did not use independent contractors during the year. Therefore,
there are no forms to file or exhibit.

FIGURE 8.8 Travelwithus.com's W-3 Form

DO NOT STAPLE

a Control number		For Official Use Only ▶ OMB No. 1545-0008	

| b Kind of Payer (Check one) | 941 [X] CT-1 [ ] | Military [ ] Hshld. emp. [ ] | 943 [ ] Medicare govt. emp. [ ] | 944 [ ] | Kind of Employer (Check one) | None apply [ ] State/local non-501c [ ] | 501c non-govt. [ ] State/local 501c [ ] Federal govt. [ ] | Third-party sick pay (Check if applicable) [ ] |

c Total number of Forms W-2	d Establishment number	1 Wages, tips, other compensation	2 Federal income tax withheld
6		323,647.70	39,605.00

e Employer identification number (EIN) 58-1213479

3 Social security wages 315,647.70
4 Social security tax withheld 19,570.16

f Employer's name

Travelwithus.com, Inc.

5 Medicare wages and tips 323,647.70
6 Medicare tax withheld 4,692.89

7 Social security tips
8 Allocated tips

**10 Lovett Road
Salem, MA 01970**

9
10 Dependent care benefits

11 Nonqualified plans
12a Deferred compensation

g Employer's address and ZIP code

h Other EIN used this year

13 For third-party sick pay use only
12b

15 State MA Employer's state ID number 621-8966-4

14 Income tax withheld by payer of third-party sick pay

16 State wages, tips, etc. 323,647.70
17 State income tax 25,891.81
18 Local wages, tips, etc.
19 Local income tax

Employer's contact person **Katherine Kurtz**

Employer's telephone number **978-555-4040**

For Official Use Only

Employer's fax number

Employer's email address **kkurtz@travelwithus.com**

Under penalties of perjury, I declare that I have examined this return and accompanying documents and, to the best of my knowledge and belief, they are true, correct, and complete.

Signature ▶ Title ▶ **Controller** Date ▶ **2/28/201Y**

Form **W-3** **Transmittal of Wage and Tax Statements** **201X** Department of the Treasury Internal Revenue Service

Send this entire page with the entire Copy A page of Form(s) W-2 to the Social Security Administration (SSA). Photocopies are not acceptable. Do not send Form W-3 if you filed electronically with the SSA. **Do not** send any payment (cash, checks, money orders, etc.) with Forms W-2 and W-3.

FIGURE 8.9 Travelwithus.com's Employee YTD Earnings Summary

TRAVELWITHUS.COM INC.
Employee YTD Earnings Summary
201X

Employee Name		Gross Earnings YTD	OASDI Taxable Earnings	FIT	SIT	FICA OASDI	FICA Medicare	FUTA Taxable	FUTA Rate 0.60%
Goldman, Ernie		125 000 00	117 000 00	21 112 00	10 000 00	7 254 00	1 812 50	7 000 00	42 00
Higuera, Stephanie		23 176 20	23 176 20	2 248 86	1 854 10	1 436 92	336 05	7 000 00	42 00
Kurtz, Katherine		65 000 00	65 000 00	6 406 00	5 200 00	4 030 00	942 50	7 000 00	42 00
Regan, Julia		76 250 00	76 250 00	6 910 00	6 100 00	4 727 50	1 105 63	7 000 00	42 00
Sui, Annie		10 095 80	10 095 80	876 00	807 66	625 94	146 39	7 000 00	42 00
Taylor, Harold		24 125 70	24 125 70	2 052 14	1 930 05	1 495 80	349 82	7 000 00	42 00
Total YTD	per W-3	323 647 70	315 647 70	39 605 00	25 891 81	19 570 16	4 692 89	42 000 00	252 00

 **TRY IT!**   **Learning Unit 8-3**

Answer true or false to the following statements.

1. A Form W-2 is sent annually to each employee on or before December 31 of the pay year.

2. Form W-3 is a re-cap of all W-2s and is submitted to the Social Security Administration.

3. FUTA tax Form 940 is submitted and paid annually.

L01,2,3    # DEMONSTRATION SUMMARY PROBLEM

House of Colors, owned by Jordan Lewis, is a growing company providing interior design services. The company is located at 123 Pine Street, Concord, MA 01742. House of Colors is classified as a monthly tax depositor, and their EIN # is 22-2222222. They currently have four employees who are paid monthly on the last day of the month. In the current year, all employees earned in excess of the FUTA wage limit; however, only one earned in excess of the OASDI wage limit. The following is a Worksheet Summary of the fourth-quarter payroll activity for House of Colors.

House of Colors
Worksheet Summary of Monthly Payroll Registers
4th Quarter, 201X

Pay Period Ending and Pay Date	Total Gross Earnings	OASDI Taxable Earnings	FIT	SIT	FICA		Medical Insurance	Net Pay
					OASDI	Medicare		
YTD @ September 30	147,600.00	147,600.00	18,980.00	7,380.00	9,151.20	2,140.20	2,700.00	107,248.60
10/31/1X	17,517.40	17,517.40	2,180.00	875.87	1,086.08	254.00	300.00	12,821.45
11/30/1X	17,229.17	17,029.17	2,010.00	861.46	1,055.81	249.82	300.00	12,752.08
12/31/1X	18,686.00	8,686.00	2,416.00	934.30	538.53	270.95	300.00	14,226.22
4th Qtr. Total	53,432.57	43,232.57	6,606.00	2,671.63	2,680.42	774.77	900.00	39,799.75
YTD Total	201,032.57	190,832.57	25,586.00	10,051.63	11,831.62	2,914.97	3,600.00	147,048.35

Requirements

1. Compute the payroll tax deposit for each month. When is the general due date for each deposit?

2. Prepare a Form 941 for the fourth quarter.

3. Prepare a Form 940.

4. Find the general due date for filing Forms 941 and 940.

Solutions

Requirement 1

Compute the payroll tax deposit for each month.

Using the Worksheet Summary above, compute each month's tax deposit by adding the total FIT + twice the OASDI + twice the Medicare. Why twice? Remember, the employer is required to match the employee deduction for OASDI and Medicare. See the computation schedule below. Because the company is a monthly depositor, the general deposit due date is the 15th day of the following month.

Computations

Month of Pay	FIT	+ 2(OASDI	+ Medicare)
October 201X	$2,180.00 + 2($1,086.08	+ $254.00)
November 201X	$2,010.00 + 2($1,055.81	+ $249.82)
December 201X	$2,416.00 + 2($ 538.53	+ $270.95)

Solution

Month of Pay	Amount of Deposit	Deposit Due Date
October 201X	$4,860.16	November 15, 201X
November 201X	$4,621.26	December 15, 201X
December 201X	$4,034.96	January 15, 201Y

Requirement 2

Prepare a Form 941 for the fourth quarter.

Tips for Computing a Basic Form 941

COACHING TIP:

When operating as a sole proprietorship, the owner's name is listed as NAME, with company name listed as TRADE NAME.

STEP 1: Complete the employer information at the top of page 1. This includes the company name, address, EIN, and quarter.

STEP 2: Complete necessary lines 1-6 of Part 1 using the information given. If a line is not used, leave it blank. Lines 2, 3, 5a (column 1), and 5b (column 1) are found on the 4th Qtr. Total line of the Worksheet Summary of Monthly Payroll Registers.

STEP 3: Complete page 2 of the form. In Part 2, House of Colors marks the monthly depositor box, then lists the liability per individual month. Use the amounts computed in Requirement 1. The total liability for the quarter is recorded here and on page 1, line 10.

STEP 4: Compare page 1, lines 6 and 10. If these amounts differ by only a few cents, record the pennies on line 7, so that line 6 plus/minus line 7 will equal line 10. Record all deposits made on line 11. Lines 10 and 11 should equal, if all deposits were accurately made.

STEP 5: The owner will sign and date page 2, Part 5. Mail by due date.

Solution of completed 941 for House of Colors (see pages 292–293).

Requirement 3

Prepare a Form 940.

Tips for Computing a Basic Form 940

STEP 1: Complete the employer information at the top of page 1. This includes the company name, address, EIN, and quarter.

STEP 2: Complete Part 1.

STEP 3: Complete Part 2 by recording the total YTD earnings for all employees on line 3. The problem stated that all four employees earned in excess of the FUTA wage limit of $7,000.00. Therefore, line 7 = $28,000.00 (4 × $7,000). The difference between lines 3 and 7 is the amount of compensation in excess of the FUTA limit and is recorded on lines 5 and 6. Line 8 records the FUTA owed, the result of line 7 × 0.6% ($28,000.00 × 0.6% = $168.00). Because this amount is less than $500.00, a check can be sent with the report.

STEP 4: Complete Parts 3 and 4.

STEP 5: Complete page 2. The owner will sign and date page 2, Part 7. Mail by due date.

Completed solution form 940 for House of Colors (see pages 294–295).

Form **941 for 201X:** **Employer's QUARTERLY Federal Tax Return**   950114
(Rev. January 2014)   Department of the Treasury — Internal Revenue Service

OMB No. 1545-0029

Employer identification number (EIN) | 2 | 2 | – | 2 | 2 | 2 | 2 | 2 | 2 | 2

Name *(not your trade name)* Jordan Lewis

Trade name *(if any)* House of Colors

Address 123 Pine Street
Number   Street   Suite or room number

Concord   MA   01742
City   State   ZIP code

Foreign country name   Foreign province/county   Foreign postal code

Report for this Quarter of 201X
(Check one.)

☐ **1:** January, February, March

☐ **2:** April, May, June

☐ **3:** July, August, September

☒ **4:** October, November, December

Instructions and prior year forms are
available at *www.irs.gov/form941.*

Read the separate instructions before you complete Form 941. Type or print within the boxes.

Part 1: Answer these questions for this quarter.

1	Number of employees who received wages, tips, or other compensation for the pay period including: *Mar. 12* (Quarter 1), *June 12* (Quarter 2), *Sept. 12* (Quarter 3), or *Dec. 12* (Quarter 4)	**1**	4
2	Wages, tips, and other compensation	**2**	53432 . 57
3	Federal income tax withheld from wages, tips, and other compensation	**3**	6606 . 00
4	If no wages, tips, and other compensation are subject to social security or Medicare tax	☐ Check and go to line 6.	

		Column 1		**Column 2**	
5a	Taxable social security wages . .	43232 . 57	× .124 =	5360 . 84	
5b	Taxable social security tips . . .	.	× .124 =	.	
5c	Taxable Medicare wages & tips. .	53432 . 57	× .029 =	1549 . 54	
5d	Taxable wages & tips subject to Additional Medicare Tax withholding	.	× .009 =	.	

5e	Add Column 2 from lines 5a, 5b, 5c, and 5d	**5e**	6910 . 38
5f	Section 3121(q) Notice and Demand—Tax due on unreported tips (see instructions) . .	**5f**	.
6	Total taxes before adjustments. Add lines 3, 5e, and 5f	**6**	13516 . 38
7	Current quarter's adjustment for fractions of cents	**7**	.
8	Current quarter's adjustment for sick pay	**8**	.
9	Current quarter's adjustments for tips and group-term life insurance	**9**	.
10	Total taxes after adjustments. Combine lines 6 through 9	**10**	13516 . 38
11	Total deposits for this quarter, including overpayment applied from a prior quarter and overpayments applied from Form 941-X, 941-X (PR), 944-X, 944-X (PR), or 944-X (SP) filed in the current quarter	**11**	13516 . 38
12	Balance due. If line 10 is more than line 11, enter the difference and see instructions . . .	**12**	.
13	Overpayment. If line 11 is more than line 10, enter the difference	.	Check one: ☐ Apply to next return. ☐ Send a refund.

▶ **You MUST complete both pages of Form 941 and SIGN it.**   Next ▶

For Privacy Act and Paperwork Reduction Act Notice, see the back of the Payment Voucher.   Cat. No. 17001Z   Form **941** (Rev. 1-2014)

950214

Name *(not your trade name)*	Employer identification number (EIN)
Jordan Lewis	22-2222222

Part 2: Tell us about your deposit schedule and tax liability for this quarter.

If you are unsure about whether you are a monthly schedule depositor or a semiweekly schedule depositor, see Pub. 15 (Circular E), section 11.

14 Check one: ☐ Line 10 on this return is less than $2,500 or line 10 on the return for the prior quarter was less than $2,500, and you did not incur a $100,000 next-day deposit obligation during the current quarter. If line 10 for the prior quarter was less than $2,500 but line 10 on this return is $100,000 or more, you must provide a record of your federal tax liability. If you are a monthly schedule depositor, complete the deposit schedule below; if you are a semiweekly schedule depositor, attach Schedule B (Form 941). Go to Part 3.

☒ **You were a monthly schedule depositor for the entire quarter.** Enter your tax liability for each month and total liability for the quarter, then go to Part 3.

Tax liability:	Month 1	4860. 16
	Month 2	4621. 26
	Month 3	4034. 96
Total liability for quarter		13516. 38	Total must equal line 10.

☐ **You were a semiweekly schedule depositor for any part of this quarter.** Complete Schedule B (Form 941), Report of Tax Liability for Semiweekly Schedule Depositors, and attach it to Form 941.

Part 3: Tell us about your business. If a question does NOT apply to your business, leave it blank.

15 If your business has closed or you stopped paying wages . . . . ☐ Check here, and

enter the final date you paid wages   [/   /   ].

16 If you are a seasonal employer and you do not have to file a return for every quarter of the year . . ☐ Check here.

Part 4: May we speak with your third-party designee?

Do you want to allow an employee, a paid tax preparer, or another person to discuss this return with the IRS? See the instructions for details.

☐ Yes. Designee's name and phone number [   ] [   ]

Select a 5-digit Personal Identification Number (PIN) to use when talking to the IRS. ☐ ☐ ☐ ☐ ☐

☒ No.

Part 5: Sign here. You MUST complete both pages of Form 941 and SIGN it.

Under penalties of perjury, I declare that I have examined this return, including accompanying schedules and statements, and to the best of my knowledge and belief, it is true, correct, and complete. Declaration of preparer (other than taxpayer) is based on all information of which preparer has any knowledge.

✗

Sign your name here	*Jordan Lewis*	Print your name here	Jordan Lewis
		Print your title here	owner
Date	01/31/1Y	Best daytime phone	

Paid Preparer Use Only

Check if you are self-employed . . . ☐

Preparer's name		PTIN	
Preparer's signature		Date	/ /
Firm's name (or yours if self-employed)		EIN	
Address		Phone	
City		State	ZIP code	

Form **940 for 201X:** **Employer's Annual Federal Unemployment (FUTA) Tax Return**   850113

Department of the Treasury — Internal Revenue Service

OMB No. 1545-0028

Employer identification number (EIN)   2 2 – 2 2 2 2 2 2 2

Name *(not your trade name)*   Jordan Lewis

Trade name *(if any)*   House of Colors

Address   123 Pine Street

Number   Street   Suite or room number

Concord   MA   01742

City   State   ZIP code

Foreign country name   Foreign province/county   Foreign postal code

Type of Return
(Check all that apply.)

☐ **a.** Amended

☐ **b.** Successor employer

☐ **c.** No payments to employees in 201X

☐ **d.** Final: Business closed or stopped paying wages

Instructions and prior-year forms are available at *www.irs.gov/form940.*

Read the separate instructions before you complete this form. Please type or print within the boxes.

Part 1:   Tell us about your return. If any line does NOT apply, leave it blank.

1a   If you had to pay state unemployment tax in one state only, enter the state abbreviation .   **1a**   M   A

1b   If you had to pay state unemployment tax in more than one state, you are a multi-state employer .   **1b** ☐   Check here. Complete Schedule A (Form 940).

2   If you paid wages in a state that is subject to **CREDIT REDUCTION** .   **2** ☐   Check here. Complete Schedule A (Form 940).

Part 2:   Determine your FUTA tax before adjustments for 201X. If any line does NOT apply, leave it blank.

3   Total payments to all employees .   **3**   201032 . 57

4   Payments exempt from FUTA tax .   **4**   .

Check all that apply: **4a** ☐ Fringe benefits   **4c** ☐ Retirement/Pension   **4e** ☐ Other
4b ☐ Group-term life insurance   **4d** ☐ Dependent care

5   Total of payments made to each employee in excess of $7,000 .   **5**   173032 . 57

6   Subtotal (line 4 + line 5 = line 6) .   **6**   173032 . 57

7   Total taxable FUTA wages (line 3 – line 6 = line 7) (see instructions) .   **7**   28000 . 00

8   FUTA tax before adjustments (line 7 x .006 = line 8) .   **8**   168 . 00

Part 3:   Determine your adjustments. If any line does NOT apply, leave it blank.

9   If ALL of the taxable FUTA wages you paid were excluded from state unemployment tax, multiply line 7 by .054 (line 7 × .054 = line 9). Go to line 12 .   **9**   .

10   If SOME of the taxable FUTA wages you paid were excluded from state unemployment tax, OR you paid ANY state unemployment tax late (after the due date for filing Form 940), complete the worksheet in the instructions. Enter the amount from line 7 of the worksheet .   **10**   .

11   If credit reduction applies, enter the total from Schedule A (Form 940) .   **11**   .

Part 4:   Determine your FUTA tax and balance due or overpayment for 2013. If any line does NOT apply, leave it blank.

12   Total FUTA tax after adjustments (lines 8 + 9 + 10 + 11 = line 12) .   **12**   168 . 00

13   FUTA tax deposited for the year, including any overpayment applied from a prior year .   **13**   .

14   Balance due (If line 12 is more than line 13, enter the excess on line 14.)
• If line 14 is more than $500, you must deposit your tax.
• If line 14 is $500 or less, you may pay with this return. (see instructions) .   **14**   168 . 00

15   Overpayment (If line 13 is more than line 12, enter the excess on line 15 and check a box below.) .   **15**   .

▶ You **MUST** complete both pages of this form and **SIGN** it.   Check one: ☐ Apply to next return. ☐ Send a refund.

Next ▶

850212

Name *(not your trade name)*	Employer identification number (EIN)
Jordan Lewis	22-2222222

Part 5:   Report your FUTA tax liability by quarter only if line 12 is more than $500. If not, go to Part 6.

16   Report the amount of your FUTA tax liability for each quarter; do NOT enter the amount you deposited. If you had no liability for a quarter, leave the line blank.

16a   **1st quarter** (January 1 – March 31) . . . .   **16a** [.]

16b   **2nd quarter** (April 1 – June 30) . . . .   **16b** [.]

16c   **3rd quarter** (July 1 – September 30) . . . .   **16c** [.]

16d   **4th quarter** (October 1 – December 31) . . . .   **16d** [.]

17   **Total tax liability for the year** (lines 16a + 16b + 16c + 16d = line 17)   **17** [.]   **Total must equal line 12.**

Part 6:   May we speak with your third-party designee?

Do you want to allow an employee, a paid tax preparer, or another person to discuss this return with the IRS? See the instructions for details.

[ ] **Yes.**   Designee's name and phone number

   Select a 5-digit Personal Identification Number (PIN) to use when talking to IRS   [ ][ ][ ][ ][ ]

[X] **No.**

Part 7:   Sign here. You MUST complete both pages of this form and SIGN it.

Under penalties of perjury, I declare that I have examined this return, including accompanying schedules and statements, and to the best of my knowledge and belief, it is true, correct, and complete, and that no part of any payment made to a state unemployment fund claimed as a credit was, or is to be, deducted from the payments made to employees. Declaration of preparer (other than taxpayer) is based on all information of which preparer has any knowledge.

X Sign your name here   *Jordan Lewis*

Print your name here   Jordan Lewis

Print your title here   owner

Date   01/31/1Y

Best daytime phone

Paid Preparer Use Only   Check if you are self-employed   [ ]

Preparer's name		PTIN	
Preparer's signature		Date	/ /
Firm's name (or yours if self-employed)		EIN	
Address		Phone	
City	State	ZIP code	

Form **940** (2013)

Requirement 4

Find the general due date for filing Forms 941 and 940.

    The general due date for filing Form 941 (Quarterly Report) is the last day of the month following the calendar quarter. The general due date for filing Form 940 (Annual Report) is the last day of the month following the calendar year. In this specific case, both reports should be filed by January 31, 201Y.

BLUEPRINT: FORM 941 TAX DEPOSIT RULES

Ten Frequently Asked Questions and Answers About Depositing OASDI, Medicare, and FIT to the Government

Here is a summary of questions and answers to help you understand the payroll tax deposit rules for Form 941 taxes:

1. **What are Form 941 taxes?** The term *Form 941 taxes* is used to describe the amount of FIT, OASDI, and Medicare paid by employees and the amount of OASDI and Medicare taxes that are matched and paid by an employer. The total of these taxes is known as Form 941 taxes because it is reported on Form 941 each quarter.

2. **When does an employer deposit Form 941 taxes?** How often an employer deposits Form 941 taxes depends on how the employer is classified for this purpose. The IRS usually classifies an employer as either a monthly or semiweekly depositor based on the amount of Form 941 taxes paid during a time period known as a look-back period.

3. **When is a look-back period?** A look-back period is a fiscal year that begins on July 1, two years earlier, and ends on June 30 of the year before the calendar year when the deposits will be made. For example, for the 2015 calendar year, an employer's look-back period will begin on July 1, 2013, and end on June 30, 2014.

4. **What is the dollar amount used to classify an employer for Form 941 tax deposits?** The key dollar amount used to determine whether an employer is a monthly or semiweekly depositor is $50,000 in Form 941 taxes. Two rules apply here:

   a. If the total amount deposited in Form 941 taxes is less than $50,000 during the look-back period, the employer is considered a monthly tax depositor.

   b. If the total amount deposited in Form 941 taxes is $50,000 or more during the look-back period, the employer is considered a semiweekly tax depositor.

5. **How do employers deposit Form 941 taxes?** Unless an employer pays Form 941 taxes of less than $2,500 per quarter the employer must utilize the Electronic Federal Tax Payment System (EFTPS) to deposit the Form 941 taxes. If the amount of Form 941 taxes owed is less than $2,500 per quarter, payment may be made by check at the time of the submission of the Form 941.

6. **When do monthly depositors make their deposits?** A monthly depositor will figure the total amount of Form 941 taxes owed in a calendar month and then pay this amount by the 15th of the next month. If an employer owes $3,125 in Form 941 taxes for the month of June, it will deposit this same amount no later than July 15 of the same year.

7. **When do semiweekly depositors make their deposits?** The rules for making deposits are a little more complicated for a semiweekly depositor. When a tax deposit is due depends on when the employees are paid. To keep the rules consistent, the IRS has taken a calendar week and divided it into two payday time periods.

Two deposit rules apply to these two time periods. We can call these rules the Wednesday and Friday rules.

a. Wednesday rule: If employees are paid during the Wednesday through Friday of week 1 period, the tax deposit will be due on Wednesday of week 2.

b. Friday rule: If employees are paid anytime from Saturday of week 1 through Tuesday of week 2, the tax deposit will be due on Friday of week 2.

c. Exception to the rules: If an employer owes more than $100,000 Form 941 tax at any time during the pay period, the money must be deposited within 24 hours. If an employer owes less than $2,500 in a calendar quarter, the money can be submitted with Form 941.

8. What is a banking day? The term *banking day* refers to any day that banks are open to the public for business. Saturdays, Sundays, and legal holidays are not banking days.

9. How do legal holidays affect payroll tax deposits? If a legal holiday occurs after the last day of a payday time period, the employer will get one extra day to make its Form 941 tax deposit as follows:

a. For monthly depositors: If the 15th of the month is a Saturday, Sunday, or legal holiday, the deposit will be due and payable on the next banking day.

b. For semiweekly depositors: A deposit due on Wednesday will be due on Thursday of the same week, and a Friday deposit will be due on Monday of the following week. Remember that the employer will always have three banking days after the last day of either payday time period to make its payroll tax deposit.

10. What happens if an employer is late with its Form 941 tax deposit? If a Form 941 tax deposit is not made the day it should be deposited, the employer may be assessed a fine for lateness and may even be charged interest, depending on how late the deposit is.

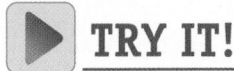

Learning Unit 8-1

1.

GENERAL JOURNAL				
	PR	Dr.		Cr.
Cash – Payroll Checking		3 3 4 6 00		
Cash – Regular Checking				3 3 4 6 00
To transfer money to the payroll account				

2.

GENERAL JOURNAL				
	PR	Dr.		Cr.
Wages & Salaries Payable		3 3 4 6 00		
Cash – Payroll Checking				3 3 4 6 00
To record release of paychecks dated Mar. 5				

3.

Cash - Regular Checking		Cash - Payroll Checking		Salaries & Wages Payable	
8,540.00		1,000.00			3,346.00
	3,346.00(1)	(1)3,346.00	3,346.00(2)	(2)3,346.00	
5,194.00		1,000.00			0.00

Learning Unit 8-2

1. True
2. The rate of 0.124 is twice the employee rate of 6.2% because the employer must match the employee FICA OASDI tax withheld.
3. This adjustment comes from rounding differences when computing individual payroll register tax to the total tax for the quarter.
4. No. Only semiweekly depositors are required to submit Form 941, Schedule B.

Learning Unit 8-3

1. False. Forms W-2 are distributed to each employee no later than January 31.
2. True
3. False. If the FUTA tax liability is equal to or greater than $500.00 at the end of any quarter, the FUTA tax must be electronically submitted to the IRS by the last day of the month following the quarter. However, Form 940 is an annual report filed by the last day of month following the year.

ACCOUNTING COACH

The following Coaching Tips are from Learning Units 8-1 through 8-3. Take the Pre-Game Checkup and use the Check Your Score at the bottom of the page to see how you are doing. The Accounting Coach provides tips before each Checkup to help you avoid common accounting errors.

LU 8-1 Payroll and Depositing Taxes

Pre-Game Tips: Federal Form 941 reports the FIT, OASDI, and Medicare taxes withheld from employees, as well as reports the OASDI and Medicare taxes due from the employer.

Pre-Game Checkup: Answer true or false to the following statements.

1. If an employer owed less than $50,000 in total taxes during the look-back period, it would be classified as a quarterly depositor.
2. The majority of businesses normally make their payroll tax deposits to pay their Form 941 taxes either monthly or semiweekly.
3. FIT, OASDI, Medicare, and FUTA taxes are known as Form 941 taxes.
4. Regardless of the amount of taxes owed, an employer must pay its Form 941 taxes using Electronic Federal Payment System (EFTPS).
5. Very few companies use a special checking account for paying their payroll.

LU 8-2 Quarterly Reports for Federal and State Governments

Pre-Game Tips: Form 941 is filed quarterly. This form is used by the IRS to reconcile payroll tax liability to the tax deposits made.

Pre-Game Checkup: Answer true or false to the following statements.

1. If the amount of FUTA tax is less than $500 during a given quarter, no deposit is required

until the FUTA tax liability reaches $500 or until the year ends.
2. Form 941 is prepared monthly.
3. Form 941 reports OASDI taxable earnings.
4. Line 7 of Form 941 is used to adjust for small differences between line 6 and line 10.
5. Line 6 of Form 941 is the total of lines 1–5f.

LU 8-3 Annual Reports, Forms W-2 and W-3

Pre-Game Tips: At the end of a calendar year, a company prepares a form W-2 for each employee. This form records the gross earnings of and taxes withheld by the employee during the year.

Pre-Game Checkup: Answer true or false to the following statements.

1. Generally, the Employer's Annual Federal Unemployment (FUTA) Tax Return, Form 940 is not due until January 31.
2. Form W-2s must be distributed to employees no later than February 10.
3. Small employers can electronically file W-2s and W-3s using the Business Services Office found on the Social Security Web site.
4. Employers send Form W-2s and Form W-3s to the Social Security Administration so employees' individual federal income tax returns may be checked.
5. FUTA taxes owed at the end of the year are always paid electronically.

CHECK YOUR SCORE: Answers to the Pre-Game Checkup

LU 8-1
1. False—If an employer owed less than $50,000 in total taxes during the look-back period, it would be classified as a monthly depositor.
2. True
3. False—FIT, OASDI, and Medicare taxes are known as Form 941 taxes. FUTA is not a Form 941 tax; it is paid using a Form 940, FUTA Tax Return.
4. False—An employer is required to use EFTPS only if the employer owes more than $2,500 in a quarter.
5. False—Almost all large companies establish a special account for paying their payroll. It strengthens cash control, simplifies check reconciliation, and reduces the likelihood of an overdraft.

LU 8-2
1. True
2. False—Form 941 is prepared quarterly.
3. True—OASDI taxable earnings are reported on line 5a, column 1.
4. True
5. False—Line 6 is the total of lines 3, 5e, and 5f.

LU 8-3
1. True
2. False—Form W-2s must be distributed to employees by January 31.
3. True
4. True
5. False—FUTA taxes owed at the end of the year are usually paid electronically, but can be paid by check if the amount owed is less than $500.00.

Chapter Summary

MyAccountingLab

Here are all the key terms and equations to help you understand the concepts of this chapter and prepare you for your exam. After completing this review, go to MyAccountingLab for more practice opportunities.

Concepts You Should Know	Key Terms

L01 ▶

Pay Payroll and Deposit Taxes

1. Transferring money into a special payroll account results in debiting Cash – Payroll Checking and crediting Cash – Regular Checking.

2. Distributing paychecks to employees using a special account results in debiting Wages & Salaries Payable and crediting Cash – Payroll Checking.

3. The look-back period covers a 12-month time frame that begins in the third quarter of year 201A and ends in the second quarter of year 201B. The amount of 941 taxes deposited during this time determines the employer tax depositor classification to be used in January of year 201C.

4. There are two tax depositor classifications: monthly or semiweekly.

5. A new company that does not have a full look-back period starts out as a monthly tax depositor.

6. Tax depositors classified as monthly will remit electronically, all 941 taxes withheld and matched during any month by the 15th day of the following month.

7. Tax depositors classified as semiweekly will remit electronically, all 941 taxes withheld and matched by the third banking day of the end of the semiweekly period in which the pay date occurred. If the pay date falls within the Saturday through Tuesday period, the deposit is due Friday (the third banking day from Tuesday). If the pay date falls within the Wednesday through Friday period, the deposit is due on Wednesday of the following week.

8. One exception to the above tax deposit rule is known as the 24-hour rule. This rule states that any depositor that owes $100,000.00 or more at any time must make the full deposit by the next banking day.

9. Another exception is that if an employer owes less than $2,500 in a quarter, the employer can remit taxes when filing the quarterly 941 report.

Key Terms

Banking day (p. 279)

Employer identification number (EIN) (p. 277)

Form SS-4 (p. 277)

Form 941 taxes (p. 278)

Look-back period (p. 278)

Monthly depositor (p. 279)

Semiweekly depositor (p. 279)

L02   ### Prepare Quarterly Reports for Federal and State Governments

1. Federal Form 941 is prepared and filed no later than 1 month after the calendar quarter ends. It reports the amount of FIT, FICA-OASDI, and FICA-Medicare tax withheld from employees and the OASDI and Medicare taxes matched by the employer for the calendar quarter.

2. FIT, OASDI, and Medicare taxes are known as Form 941 taxes.

3. State and local income taxes are usually filed and paid quarterly.

4. Although the FUTA report (Form 940) is filed annually, the employer is required to deposit FUTA taxes quarterly by the last day of the month following the quarter if the amount of the FUTA liability is $500.00 or more.

5. SUTA is for state unemployment. States will have different rates, depending on their unemployment history.

Calendar quarter (p. 280)

Form 941, Employer's Quarterly Federal Tax Return (p. 280)

L03   ### Prepare Annual Reports, Forms W-2 and W-3

1. Form 940 is the annual report for reporting federal unemployment taxes. The report is filed by January 31 of the following year.

2. Information to prepare W-2 forms can be obtained from the individual employee earnings records. These forms must be distributed to each employee by January 31.

3. Form W-3 is used by the Social Security Administration to verify that taxes have been withheld as reported on individual employee W-2 forms. This form must be filed with the SSA by the end of February.

Form 940, Employer's Annual Federal Unemployment Tax Return (p. 285)

Form W-2, Wage and Tax Statement (p. 285)

Form W-3, Transmittal of Wage and Tax Statements (p. 288)

Discussion Questions and Critical Thinking/Ethical Case

1. Why might a company have a separate cash account for payroll?

2. How do you transfer money into the payroll cash account?

3. What account is debited when recording the distribution of the payroll checks to the employees?

4. What is a look-back period?

5. How is an employer classified as a monthly or semiweekly depositor for Form 941 tax purposes?

6. How are Form 941 taxes paid to the Treasury Department?

7. How often is Form 941 completed?

8. Under what circumstance(s) does the amount on line 14 of Form 941 match the amount found on line 10?

9. Bill Smith leaves his job on July 9. He requests a copy of his W-2 form when he leaves. His boss tells him to wait until January of next year. Please discuss whether Bill's boss is correct in making this statement.

10. Why would one employer prepare a Form 940 completing Part 1, line 1a, but another would prepare a Form 940 Part 1, line 1b?

11. Employer A has a FUTA tax liability of $67.49 on March 31 of the current year. When does the employer have to make the deposit for this liability?

12. Employer B has a FUTA tax liability of $553.24 on January 31 of the current year. When does the employer have to make the deposit for this liability?

13. Who completes Form W-2? Form W-3? When is each form completed?

14. Discuss ways an employer can prepare and submit forms W-2 and W-3 online.

15. Happy Carpet Cleaning, Inc., collects FIT, OASDI, and Medicare from its employees by withholding these taxes from its employees' pay. However, Happy does not pay these amounts to the federal government until the end of the calendar year so that it can maximize its cash during the year. Because it will be paying these amounts to the government, it believes that this practice does not affect its employees. Please comment on this practice.

MyAccountingLab

Concept Check

(10 min)   **LO1**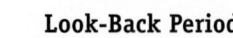

Look-Back Periods

1.   Label the following look-back periods for 200C by months.

A	B	C	D
	200A		200B

(15 min)   **LO1**

Monthly versus Semiweekly Depositor

2.   In December 200B, Glenda tries to find out whether she is a monthly or semiweekly depositor for FICA (OASDI and Medicare) and federal income tax for 200C. Please advise based on the following taxes owed:

200A	Quarter 3	$37,000
	Quarter 4	12,000
200B	Quarter 1	3,400
	Quarter 2	10,900

Monthly versus Semiweekly Depositor

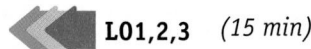 **L01** *(15 min)*

3. In December 200B, Glenda is trying to find out whether she is a monthly or semiweekly depositor for FICA (OASDI and Medicare) and federal income tax for 200C. Please advise based on the following taxes owed:

200A	Quarter 3	$17,000
	Quarter 4	12,000
200B	Quarter 1	3,400
	Quarter 2	10,900

Paying the Tax

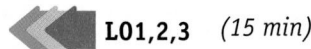 **L01** *(15 min)*

4. Complete the following table:

Depositor	4-Quarter Look-Back Period Tax Liability	Payroll Paid	Tax Paid by
Monthly	$28,000	November	a.
Semiweekly	$66,000	On Wednesday	b.
		On Thursday	c.
		On Friday	d.
		On Saturday	e.
		On Sunday	f.
		On Monday	g.

Payroll Account

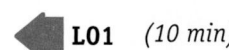 **L01,2,3** *(15 min)*

5. Indicate which of the following items apply to the following account titles.
   1. An asset
   2. A liability
   3. An expense
   4. Appears on the income statement
   5. Appears on the balance sheet
      _____ **a.** FICA OASDI Payable
      _____ **b.** Office Salaries Expense
      _____ **c.** Federal Income Tax Payable
      _____ **d.** FICA Medicare Payable
      _____ **e.** Wages and Salaries Payable

Exercises

MyAccountingLab

Set A

8A-1. Blanca Company uses a special payroll account to pay employees. The gross amount of the payroll this week is $5,000; the net amount is $4,125. Journalize the transfer of funds to the payroll account and the distribution of paychecks to the employees.

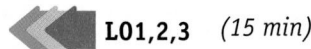 **L01** *(10 min)*

8A-2. Based on the following payroll tax depositor classifications, determine the 941 tax deposit due date for each taxpayer:

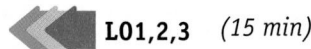 **L01** *(15 min)*

   a. Monthly depositor, owing $1,500 tax for the first quarter. _____
   b. Monthly depositor, owing $5,000 tax for the month of July. _____
   c. Monthly depositor, owing $110,000 tax as of Tuesday. _____
   d. Semiweekly depositor, owing $110,000 tax as of Tuesday. _____
   e. Semiweekly depositor, owing $20,000 tax as of Friday. _____

(20 min)   **LO2**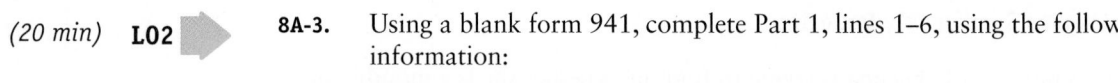

8A-3. Using a blank form 941, complete Part 1, lines 1–6, using the following information:

Total employees during the first quarter	3
Total wages during the first quarter, none came from tips	$26,050.66
Federal income tax withheld	$ 2,050.00

(20 min)   **LO1**

8A-4. At the end of October 201X, the total amount of OASDI, $530, and Medicare, $210, was withheld as tax deductions from the employees of Training, Inc. Federal income tax of $2,970 was also deducted from their paychecks. Training is classified as a monthly depositor of Form 941 taxes. Indicate when this payroll tax deposit is due and provide a general journal entry to record the payment.

(20 min)   **LO3**

8A-5. Mocha Company has four employees, and each employee earned $50,000 for the calendar year. Using a blank Form 940, complete Part 2, lines 3–8, to answer the following questions:

Total annual payroll for the year	?
Payments made in excess of $7,000 FUTA limit	?
Total FUTA liability before any adjustments	?

(10 min)   **LO1**

8A-6. Lauren's Grocery Store made the following Form 941 payroll tax deposits during the look-back period of July 1, 201A, through June 30, 201B:

Quarter Ended	Amount Paid in 941 Taxes
September 30, 201A	$15,781.57
December 31, 201A	13,894.72
March 31, 201B	13,601.11
June 30, 201B	14,019.42

Should Lauren's Grocery Store make Form 941 tax deposits monthly or semiweekly for 201C?

(15 min)   **LO1**

8A-7. If Lauren's Grocery Store downsized its operation during the second quarter of 201B and, as a result, paid only $6,121.54 in Form 941 taxes for the quarter that ended on June 30, 201B, should Lauren's Grocery Store make its Form 941 payroll tax deposits monthly or semiweekly for 201C?

(15 min)   **LO2,3**

8A-8. Assuming a semiweekly depositor, from the following T accounts, record: (a) the July 3 payment for FICA (OASDI and Medicare) and federal income taxes, (b) the July 31 payment of SUTA tax, and (c) the July 31 deposit of any FUTA tax that may be required.

FICA OASDI Payable 203		FICA Medicare Payable 204	
	June 30 410 (EE)		June 30 130 (EE)
	410 (ER)		130 (ER)

FIT Payable 205		FUTA Payable 206	
	June 30 3,005		June 30 139

SUTA Payable 207	
	June 30 616

Set B

(10 min)   **LO1**

8B-1. Taylor Company uses a special payroll account to pay employees. The gross amount of the payroll this week is $6,600; the net amount is $5,425. Journalize the transfer of funds to the payroll account and the distribution of paychecks to the employees.

8B-2. Based on the following payroll tax depositor classifications, determine the 941 tax deposit due date for each taxpayer: **LO1** *(15 min)*

   a. Monthly depositor, owing $1,850 tax for the third quarter. _____

   b. Monthly depositor, owing $4,100 tax for the month of May. _____

   c. Monthly depositor, owing $121,000 tax as of Thursday. _____

   d. Semiweekly depositor, owing $121,000 tax as of Friday. _____

   e. Semiweekly depositor, owing $32,000 tax as of Friday. _____

8B-3. Using a blank Form 941, complete Part 1, lines 1–6, using the following information: **LO2** *(20 min)*

Total employees during the first quarter	3
Total wages during the first quarter, none came from tips	$33,050.00
Federal income tax withheld	$ 3,750.00

8B-4. At the end of August 201X, the total amount of OASDI, $570, and Medicare, $230, was withheld as tax deductions from the employees of ABC, Inc. Federal income tax of $2,960 was also deducted from their paychecks. ABC is classified as a monthly depositor of Form 941 taxes. Indicate when this payroll tax deposit is due and provide a general journal entry to record the payment.   **LO1** *(20 min)*

8B-5. Walkwood Company has six employees, and each employee earned $45,600 for the calendar year. Using a blank Form 940, complete Part 2, lines 3–8, to answer the following questions: **LO3** *(20 min)*

Total annual payroll for the year	?
Payments made in excess of $7,000 FUTA limit	?
Total FUTA liability before any adjustments	?

8B-6. Joan's Grocery Store made the following Form 941 payroll tax deposits during the look-back period of July 1, 201A, through June 30, 201B: **LO1** *(10 min)*

Quarter Ended	Amount Paid in 941 Taxes
September 30, 201A	$15,784.01
December 31, 201A	13,893.56
March 31, 201B	13,600.33
June 30, 201B	14,021.21

Should Joan's Grocery Store make Form 941 tax deposits monthly or semiweekly for 201C?

8B-7. If Joan's Grocery Store downsized its operation during the second quarter of 201B and, as a result, paid only $6,119.83 in Form 941 taxes for the quarter that ended on June 30, 201B, should Joan's Grocery Store make Form 941 tax deposits monthly or semiweekly for 201C?   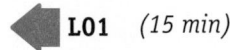 **LO1** *(15 min)*

8B-8. Assuming a semiweekly depositor, from the following T accounts, record: (a) the July 3 payment for FICA (OASDI and Medicare) and federal income taxes, (b) the July 31 payment of SUTA tax, and (c) the July 31 deposit of any FUTA tax that may be required.    **LO2,3** *(15 min)*

FICA OASDI Payable 203		FICA Medicare Payable 204	
	June 30 400 (EE)		June 30 190 (EE)
	400 (ER)		190 (ER)

FIT Payable 205		FUTA Payable 206	
	June 30 3,002		June 30 145

SUTA Payable 207	
	June 30 610

MyAccountingLab

Problems

Set A

(50 min) **LO1,2**

8A-1.   The following is the monthly payroll of White Company, owned by Dana White. Employees are paid on the last day of each month.

JANUARY

Employee	Monthly Earnings	YTD Earnings	FICA OASDI	FICA Medicare	Federal Income Tax
Steven Koy	$1,970	$1,970	$122.14	$ 28.57	$ 258.00
Juanita Lane	3,160	3,160	195.92	45.82	355.00
Alison Pickens	3,820	3,820	236.84	55.39	494.00
	$8,950	$8,950	$554.90	$129.78	$1,107.00

FEBRUARY

Employee	Monthly Earnings	YTD Earnings	FICA OASDI	FICA Medicare	Federal Income Tax
Steven Koy	$2,090	$4,060	$129.58	$30.31	$306.00
Juanita Lane	3,400	6,560	210.80	49.30	331.00
Alison Pickens	3,900	7,720	241.80	56.55	420.00
	$9,390	$18,340	$582.18	$136.16	$1,057.00

MARCH

Check Figure:
Deposit of SUTA Tax $1,149.12

Employee	Monthly Earnings	YTD Earnings	FICA OASDI	FICA Medicare	Federal Income Tax
Steven Koy	$2,100	$6,160	$130.20	$30.45	$578.00
Juanita Lane	2,500	9,060	155.00	36.25	554.00
Alison Pickens	4,110	11,830	254.82	59.60	549.00
	$8,710	$27,050	$540.02	$126.30	$1,681.00

White Company is located at 2 Square Street, Marblehead, Massachusetts 01945. Its EIN is 29-3458822. The FICA tax rate for Social Security is 6.2% on up to $117,000 in earnings during the year, and Medicare is 1.45% on all earnings. The SUTA tax rate is 5.7% on the first $7,000. The FUTA tax rate is 0.6% on the first $7,000 of earnings. White Company is classified as a monthly depositor for Form 941 taxes.

Your tasks are to do the following:

1. Journalize the entries to record the employer's payroll tax expense for each pay period in the general journal.
2. Journalize entries for the payment of each tax liability in the general journal.

8A-2. John Andrews, the accountant for White Company, must complete Form 941 for the first quarter of the current year. John gathered the needed data as presented in Problem 8A-1. Suddenly called away to an urgent budget meeting, John requested that you assist him by preparing the Form 941 for the first quarter. Please note that the difference in the tax liability, a few cents, should be adjusted on line 7; this difference is due to the rounding of FICA tax amounts.

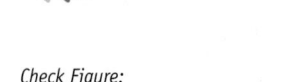 **LO1,2** *(50 min)*

Check Figure:
Total Liability for Quarter $7,983.68

8A-3. The following is the monthly payroll for the last three months of the year for Allen's Sporting Goods Shop, 2 Boat Road, Lynn, Massachusetts 01945. The shop is a sole proprietorship owned and operated by Bill Allen. The EIN for Allen's Sporting Goods Shop is 28-9311893.

Allen's are paid once each month on the last day of the month. Karen Becker is the only employee who has contributed the maximum into Social Security. None of the other employees will reach the Social Security wage base limit by the end of the year. Assume the rate for Social Security to be 6.2% with a wage base maximum of $117,000, and the rate for Medicare to be 1.45% on all earnings. Allen's is classified as a monthly depositor for Form 941 payroll tax deposit purposes.

Your tasks are to do the following:

1. Compute the December OASDI tax for Karen Becker.
2. Journalize the entries to record the employer's payroll tax expense for each period in the general journal. SUTA rate: 5.7%; FUTA rate: 0.6%.
3. Journalize the payment of each tax liability in the general journal.
4. Complete Form 941 for the fourth quarter of the current year.

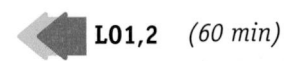 **LO1,2** *(60 min)*

Check Figure:
Dec. 31 Payroll Tax Expense $792.57

OCTOBER

Employee	Monthly Earnings	YTD Earnings	FICA OASDI	FICA Medicare	Federal Income Tax
Karen Becker	$ 2,800	$112,500	$173.60	$ 40.60	$ 526.00
Beth Orange	3,420	39,650	212.04	49.59	422.00
Sean Peters	3,860	43,950	239.32	55.97	532.00
	$10,080	$196,100	$624.96	$146.16	$1,480.00

NOVEMBER

Employee	Monthly Earnings	YTD Earnings	FICA OASDI	FICA Medicare	Federal Income Tax
Karen Becker	$ 2,860	$115,360	$177.32	$ 41.47	$ 597.00
Beth Orange	3,880	43,530	240.56	56.26	463.00
Sean Peters	3,720	47,670	230.64	53.94	555.00
	$10,460	$206,560	$648.52	$151.67	$1,615.00

DECEMBER

Employee	Monthly Earnings	YTD Earnings	FICA OASDI	FICA Medicare	Federal Income Tax
Karen Becker	$ 4,280	$119,640	$101.68	$ 62.06	$ 865.00
Beth Orange	3,880	47,410	240.56	56.26	477.00
Sean Peters	4,340	52,010	269.08	62.93	699.00
	$12,500	$219,060	$611.32	$181.25	$2,041.00

(20 min) **LO3** ▶

Check Figure:
Total Exempt Payments $198,060.00

8A-4. Using the information from Problem 8A-3, please complete Form 940 for Allen's Sporting Goods for the current year. Additional information needed to complete the form is as follows:

   a. State reporting number: 025-319-2
   b. No FUTA tax deposits were made for this year.
   c. Allen's three employees for the year all earned over $7,000.

Set B

(50 min) **LO1,2** ▶

Check Figure:
Deposit of SUTA tax $1,143.99

8B-1. The following is the monthly payroll of White Company, owned by Dale White. Employees are paid on the last day of each month.

JANUARY

Employee	Monthly Earnings	YTD Earnings	FICA OASDI	FICA Medicare	Federal Income Tax
Saul Hantona	$1,960	$1,960	$121.52	$28.42	$258.00
Jade Alaymo	3,180	3,180	197.16	46.11	351.00
Ariana Santana	3,790	3,790	234.98	54.96	504.00
	$8,930	$8,930	$553.66	$129.49	$1,113.00

FEBRUARY

Employee	Monthly Earnings	YTD Earnings	FICA OASDI	FICA Medicare	Federal Income Tax
Saul Hantona	$2,060	$4,020	$127.72	$29.87	$300.00
Jade Alaymo	3,310	6,490	205.22	48.00	333.00
Ariana Santana	3,825	7,615	237.15	55.46	430.00
	$9,195	$18,125	$570.09	$133.33	$1,063.00

MARCH

Employee	Monthly Earnings	YTD Earnings	FICA OASDI	FICA Medicare	Federal Income Tax
Saul Hantona	$2,050	$6,070	$127.10	$29.73	$578.00
Jade Alaymo	2,525	9,015	156.55	36.61	556.00
Ariana Santana	4,120	11,735	255.44	59.74	543.00
	$8,695	$26,820	$539.09	$126.08	$1,677.00

White Company is located at 2 Square Street, Marblehead, Massachusetts 01945. Its EIN is 29-3458822. The FICA tax rate for Social Security is 6.2% on up to $117,000 in earnings during the year, and Medicare is 1.45% on all earnings. The SUTA tax rate is 5.7% on the first $7,000 of earnings. The FUTA tax rate is 0.6% on the first $7,000 of earnings. White Company is classified as a monthly depositor for Form 941 taxes.

Your tasks are to do the following:

1. Journalize the entries to record the employer's payroll tax expense for each pay period in the general journal.
2. Journalize entries for the payment of each tax liability in the general journal.

8B-2. John Andrews, the accountant for White Company, must complete Form 941 for the first quarter of the current year. John gathered the needed data as presented in Problem 8B-1. Suddenly called away to an urgent budget meeting, John requested that you assist him by preparing Form 941 for the first quarter. Please note that the difference in the tax liability, a few cents, should be adjusted on line 7; this difference is due to the rounding of FICA tax amounts.

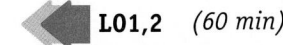

L01,2 *(50 min)*

Check Figure:
Liability for Quarter $7,956.48

8B-3. The following is the monthly payroll for the last three months of the year for Turner's Sporting Goods Shop, 2 Boat Road, Lynn, Massachusetts 01945. The shop is a sole proprietorship owned and operated by Bill Turner. The EIN for Turner's Sporting Goods Shop is 28-9311893.

The employees at Turner's are paid once each month on the last day of the month. Amber Bixby is the only employee who has contributed the maximum into Social Security. None of the other employees will reach the Social Security wage base limit by the end of the year. Assume the rate for Social Security to be 6.2% with a wage base maximum of $117,000, and the rate for Medicare to be 1.45% on all earnings. Turner's is classified as a monthly depositor for Form 941 payroll tax deposit purposes.

Your tasks are to do the following:

1. Compute the December OASDI tax for Amber Bixby.
2. Journalize the entries to record the employer's payroll tax expense for each period in the general journal. SUTA rate: 5.7%; FUTA rate: 0.6%.
3. Journalize the payment of each tax liability in the general journal.
4. Complete Form 941 for the fourth quarter of the current year.

L01,2 *(60 min)*

Check Figure:
Dec. 31 Payroll Tax Expense $677.86

OCTOBER

Employee	Monthly Earnings	YTD Earnings	FICA OASDI	FICA Medicare	Federal Income Tax
Amber Bixby	$ 2,860	$117,000	$177.32	$ 41.47	$ 534.00
Ashley King	3,480	39,350	215.76	50.46	423.00
Gina Vale	3,760	44,250	233.12	54.52	533.00
	$10,100	$200,600	$626.20	$146.45	$1,490.00

NOVEMBER

Employee	Monthly Earnings	YTD Earnings	FICA OASDI	FICA Medicare	Federal Income Tax
Amber Bixby	$ 2,860	$119,860	$ 0.00	$ 41.47	$ 601.00
Ashley King	3,880	43,230	240.56	56.26	465.00
Gina Vale	3,760	48,010	233.12	54.52	563.00
	$10,500	$211,100	$473.68	$152.25	$1,629.00

DECEMBER

Employee	Monthly Earnings	YTD Earnings	FICA OASDI	FICA Medicare	Federal Income Tax
Amber Bixby	$ 4,120	$123,980	$ 0.00	$ 59.74	$ 868.00
Ashley King	3,700	46,930	229.40	53.65	476.00
Gina Vale	4,380	52,390	271.56	63.51	702.00
	$12,200	$223,300	$500.96	$176.90	$2,046.00

(20 min) **LO3** ▶

8B-4. Using the information from Problem 8B-3, please complete Form 940 for Turner's Sporting Goods for the current year. Additional information needed to complete the form is as follows:

Check Figure:
Line 4 Total Exempt Payments
$202,300

  a. State reporting number: 025-319-2
  b. No FUTA tax deposits were made for this year.
  c. Turner's three employees for the year all earned over $7,000.

Financial Report Problem

(20 min) **LO1** ▶

Reading the Kellogg's Annual Report

Go to http://investor.kelloggs.com/investor-relations/annual-reports to access the Kellogg's 2013 Annual Report. Go to Notes to Consolidated Financial Statements and find Note 8: Pension Benefits. How much did Kellogg's spend to fund the 401(k) plans and similar saving plans?

MyAccountingLab

ON THE JOB SMITH COMPUTER CENTER

LO1,2,3 ▶▶▶

In preparing for next year, on December 1, Thad Feldman hired two hourly employees to assist with some troubleshooting and repair work.
  More information:

  Dec. 7   Paid employee wages: Lance Kumm, 38 hours, and Anthony Hall, 42 hours.

  Dec. 14   Paid employee wages: Lance Kumm, 25 hours, and Anthony Hall, 36 hours.

  Dec. 21   Paid employee wages: Lance Kumm, 26 hours, and Anthony Hall, 35 hours.

  a. The following accounts have been added to the chart of accounts: Wages Payable #2010, FICA OASDI Payable #2020, FICA Medicare Payable #2030, FIT Payable #2040, State Income Tax Payable #2050, FUTA Tax Payable #2060, SUTA Tax Payable #2070, Wages Expense #5110, and Payroll Tax Expense #5120.

  b. Assume FICA OASDI is taxed at 6.2% up to $117,000 in earnings, and Medicare is taxed at 1.45% on all earnings.

  c. State income tax is 2% of gross pay.

  d. None of the employees has federal income tax taken out of his or her pay.

  e. Each employee earns $10 an hour and is paid $1\frac{1}{2}$ times salary for hours worked in excess of 40 weekly.

As December comes to an end, Thad Feldman wants to take care of his payroll obligations. He will complete Form 941 for the fourth quarter of the current year and Form 940 for federal unemployment taxes. Thad will make the necessary deposits and payments associated with his payroll.

Assignment

1. Prepare the payroll register for the three pay periods.

2. Using the payroll registers, record the December payrolls and the payment of the payrolls in the general journal and post them to the general ledger.

3. Using the payroll registers, record payroll tax expense for the fourth quarter in the general journal. Use December 31 as the date of the journal entry to record the payroll tax expense for the entire quarter. The FUTA tax ceiling is $7,000, and the SUTA tax ceiling is $7,000 in cumulative wages for each employee. The Smith Computer Center's FUTA rate is 0.6% and the SUTA rate is 2.5%. Post the entry to the general ledger.

4. Record the payment of each tax liability in the general journal and post each entry to the general ledger. Smith Computer Center is classified as a monthly depositor. The company wishes to pay all payroll taxes on December 31 even if no deposits are required.

5. Prepare Form 941 for the fourth quarter. Smith Computer Center's employer identification number is 35-4132588.

6. Complete Form 940 for Smith Computer Center. The state reporting number is 025-025-2.

Hint: Sometimes the amount of Social Security taxes paid by the employee for the quarter will not equal the employee's tax liability because of rounding. Any difference should be reported on line 7 of Form 941.

SAGE 50 COMPUTER WORKSHOP

S50

Computerized Accounting Application for Chapter 8

Refresher on using Sage 50 Complete Accounting

Before starting this assignment, you may want to refresh your memory by reading the following PDF documents in the multimedia library of the MyAccountingLab Web site. Remember to choose the PDF document for your version of Sage 50.

1. An Introduction to Sage 50
2. Correcting Sage 50 Transactions
3. How to Repeat or Restart a Sage 50 Assignment
4. Backing Up and Restoring Your Work in Sage 50

You also should have completed the following workshops:

1. Workshop 1 Atlas Company from Chapter 3
2. Workshop 2 Zell Company from Chapter 4
3. Workshop 3 Sousa Realty from Chapter 5

Workshop 4:

Payroll Mini Practice Set

In this workshop, you will prepare January, February, and March payroll for Pete's Market using Sage 50. Tasks include entering payroll data, producing paychecks, and remitting payroll taxes. You will also print payroll reports.

Instructions and the data file for completing this assignment are in the multimedia library of the MyAccountingLab Web site. Open the **Workshop 4 Pete's Market** PDF document for your version of Sage 50 and download the **Pete's Market** data file for your version of Sage 50.

QUICKBOOKS COMPUTER WORKSHOP

QB

Computerized Accounting Application for Chapter 8

Refresher on using QuickBooks Accountant

Before starting this assignment, you may want to refresh your memory by reading the following PDF documents in the multimedia library of the MyAccountingLab Web site. Remember to choose the PDF document for your version of QuickBooks.

1. An Introduction to QuickBooks
2. Correcting QuickBooks Transactions
3. How to Repeat or Restart a QuickBooks Assignment
4. Backing Up and Restoring Your Work in QuickBooks

   You also should have completed the following workshops:

1. Workshop 1 Atlas Company from Chapter 3
2. Workshop 2 Zell Company from Chapter 4
3. Workshop 3 Sousa Realty from Chapter 5

Workshop 4:

Payroll Mini Practice Set

In this workshop, you will prepare January, February, and March payroll for Pete's Market using QuickBooks. Tasks include entering payroll data, producing paychecks, and remitting payroll taxes. You will also print payroll reports.

Instructions and the data file for completing this assignment are in the multimedia library of the MyAccountingLab Web site. Open the *Workshop 4 Pete's Market* PDF document for your version of QuickBooks and download the *Pete's Market* data file for your version of QuickBooks.

Sales and Cash Receipts

CHAPTER PREVIEW: THE BIG PICTURE

Angela Rose loves to shop online; however, she still likes to go to shopping at her local retail shops. She gets very upset if a certain item has been advertised as a weekly special and is out of stock. One of her biggest complaints is that at a register a sale item may ring up at full price. Home Depot, like other companies, uses the accounting process to gather information about all sales made, whether cash or credit. Individual customer accounts are updated continually. Home Depot must monitor its inventory in order to ensure enough stock so that it does not run out of an item and miss a sale opportunity. In this chapter, in addition to accounting for returns and discounts, we focus on how credit terms and sales tax may affect how we record the return.

Learning Objectives

LO1   Explain and Journalize Entries for Sales, Sales Discounts, and Sales Returns and Allowances

LO2   Record to Subsidiary Ledgers and Post to General Ledger Sales Transactions and Returns

LO3   Record and Post Cash Receipt Transactions and Prepare a Schedule of Accounts Receivable

Let's first look at Chou's Toy Shop to get an overview of merchandise terms and journal entries.

Chou's Toy Shop: Entries for Sales, Sales Discounts, and Sales Returns and Allowances

Retailers Merchants who buy goods from wholesalers for resale to customers.

Merchandise Goods brought into a store for resale to customers.

Chou's Toy Shop, owned by Chou Li, is a retailer. It buys toys, games, bikes, and similar items from manufacturers and wholesalers and resells these goods (or merchandise) to its customers. The shelving, display cases, and so forth are called "fixtures" or "equipment." These items are not for resale.

Gross Sales

Each cash or charge sale made at Chou's Toy Shop is rung up at the register. Suppose the shop had $3,000 in sales on July 18. Of that amount, $1,800 was cash sales and $1,200 was charges. The account that recorded those sales would be

	Sales	
Dr.	**Cr.**	
	3,000 ◄———	Revenue account with a credit balance

This account is a revenue account with a credit balance and will be found on the income statement. Figure 9.1 shows the journal entry for the day. *Note:* We talk about sales tax later. Let's look at a transaction analysis chart of this transaction before we journalize.

Accounts Affected	Category	↑ ↓	Rules	T Account Update
Cash	Asset	↑	Dr.	**Cash**
				1,800 |
Accounts Receivable	Asset	↑	Dr.	**Accounts Receivable**
				1,200 |
Sales	Revenue	↑	Cr.	**Sales**
				| 3,000

FIGURE 9.1
Recording Cash and Charge Sales for the Day

	July	18	Cash		1 8 0 0 00	
			Accounts Receivable		1 2 0 0 00	
			Sales			3 0 0 0 00
			Sales for July 18			

Sales Returns and Allowances

Sales Returns and Allowances (SRA) account A contra-revenue account that records price adjustments and allowances granted on merchandise that is defective and has been returned.

It would be great for Chou if all the customers were completely satisfied, but that rarely is the case. On July 19, Michelle Reese brought back a doll she bought on account for $50. She told Chou that the doll was defective and that she wanted either a price reduction or a new doll. They agreed on a $10 price reduction. Michelle now owes Chou $40. The account called Sales Returns and Allowances (SRA) would record this information.

Sales Returns and Allowances

	Dr.	Cr.
Contra-revenue account with a debit balance ——►	10	

This account is a contra-revenue account with a debit balance. It will be reported on the income statement. Figure 9.2 shows how the journal entry would look. Let's first look at a transaction analysis chart of this transaction before we journalize.

Accounts Affected	Category	↑↓	Rules	T Account Update
Sales Returns and Allowances	Contra-revenue	↑	Dr.	**Sales Ret. & Allow.**
				Dr. / Cr.
				10
Accounts Receivable, Michelle Reese	Asset	↓	Cr.	**Accounts Receivable**
				Dr. / Cr.
				1,200 / 10

	July	19	Sales Returns and Allowances		10 00		
			Accounts Receivable, Michelle Reese			10 00	
			Issued credit memorandum				

FIGURE 9.2
Issuing a Credit Memorandum in the General Journal

Look at how the sales returns and allowances increase.

Sales Discount

Chou gives a 2% sales discount to credit customers who pay their invoice early. He wants his customers to know about this policy, so he posted the following sign at the cash register:

Sales discount Amount a customer is allowed to deduct from the bill total for paying a bill during the discount period.

Sales Discount Policies

2/10, n/30	*2% discount is allowed off price of bill if paid within the first 10 days or full amount is due within 30 days.*
n/10, EOM	*No discount. Full amount of bill is due within 10 days after the end of the month.*

Note that the discount period is the time when a discount is granted. The discount period is less time than the credit period, which is the length of time allowed to pay the amount owed on the invoice.

If Michelle pays her $40 bill early, she will get an $0.80 discount. This information is recorded in the Sales Discount account as follows:

Discount period A period shorter than the credit period when a discount is available to encourage early payment of bills.

Credit period Length of time allowed for payment of goods sold on account.

Sales Discount account A contra-revenue account that records cash discounts granted to customers for payments made within a specific period of time.

Sales Discount

	Dr.	Cr.
Contra-revenue account with a debit balance ——►	0.80	

Michelle's discount is calculated as follows:

$$2\% \times \$40 = \$0.80$$

Michelle pays her bill on July 24. She is entitled to the discount because she paid her bill within 10 days. Figure 9.3 shows how Chou would record this payment on his books. Let's first look at a transaction analysis chart before we journalize.

Accounts Affected	Category	↑↓	Rules	T Account Update
Cash	Asset	↑	Dr.	**Cash**
				Dr. 1,800 / 39.20 — Cr.
Sales Discount	Contra-revenue	↑	Dr.	**Sales Discount**
				Dr. 0.80 — Cr.
Accounts Receivable	Asset	↓	Cr.	**Accounts Receivable**
				Dr. 1,200 — Cr. 10 / 40

COACHING TIP

Gross Sales
— Sales discount
— SRA
= Net sales

FIGURE 9.3
Recording Sales Discount

	July	24	Cash			3 9 20		
			Sales Discount			80		
			Accounts Receivable, Michelle Reese				4 0 00
			Payment from Sale on Account				

Net sales Gross sales less sales returns and allowances less sales discounts.

Gross sales The revenue earned from sale of merchandise to customers.

Sales Tax Payable account An account in the general ledger that accumulates the amount of sales tax owed. It has a credit balance.

Although Michelle pays $39.20, her Accounts Receivable is credited for the full amount, $40.

In the examples so far we have not shown any transactions with sales tax. Note that the actual or **net sales** for Chou would be **gross sales** less sales returns and allowances less any sales discounts. Let's look at how Chou would record his monthly sales if the sales tax were charged.

Sales Tax Payable

None of the preceding examples shows state sales tax. Still, like it or not, Chou must collect that tax from his customers and send it to the state. Sales tax represents a liability to Chou. The amount Chou must pay to the state is recorded in the Sales Tax Payable account.

Assume the state Chou's is located in charges a 5% sales tax. Remember that Chou's sales on July 18 were $3,000. Chou must figure out the sales tax on the purchases. For this purpose, let's assume only two sales were made on that date: the cash sale ($1,800) and the charge sale ($1,200).

The sales tax on the cash purchase is calculated as follows:

$$\$1,800 \times 0.05 = \$90 \text{ Tax}$$
$$\$1,800 + \$90 \text{ tax} = \$1,890 \text{ Cash}$$

Here is how the sales tax on the charge sale is computed:

$$\$1,200 \times 0.05 = \$60 \text{ Tax} + \$1,200 \text{ Charge} = \$1,260 \text{ Accounts Receivable}$$

It would be recorded as shown in Figure 9.4. Let's first look at a transaction analysis chart of this transaction before we journalize.

Accounts Affected	Category	↑↓	Rules	T Account Update
Cash	Asset	↑	Dr.	**Cash**
				Dr. | Cr. 1,890 |
Accounts Receivable	Asset	↑	Dr.	**Accounts Receivable**
				Dr. | Cr. 1,260 |
Sales Tax Payable	Liability	↑	Cr.	**Sales Tax Payable**
				Dr. | Cr. | 90 | 60
Sales	Revenue	↑	Cr.	**Sales**
				Dr. | Cr. | 3,000

July	18	Cash			1 8 9 0 00				
		Accounts Receivable			1 2 6 0 00				
		Sales Tax Payable					1 5 0 00
		Sales					3 0 0 0 00
		July 18 Sales					

FIGURE 9.4
Sales with Sales Tax

In Learning Unit 9-2, we look in detail at Art's Wholesale Company. Now it's time to check your progress.

 **TRY IT!** Learning Unit 9-1

Complete the following table.

Account	Category	Rules of Debit/Credit		Financial Statement
		Increase	Decrease	
Cash				
Accounts Receivable				
Sales Tax Payable				
Sales				
Sales Discounts				
Sales Returns and Allowances				

Subsidiary Ledgers and General Ledger Sales Transactions and Returns

 LEARNING UNIT 9-2

L02

Art's Wholesale Clothing Company, as a **wholesaler**, buys merchandise from suppliers and sells the items to retailers, who in turn sell it to individual consumers.

Wholesalers Merchants who buy goods from suppliers and manufacturers for sale to retailers.

The following transactions occurred in April for Art's Wholesale Clothing Company:

201X		
Apr.	3	Sold on account merchandise to Hal's Clothing, $800; invoice no. 1; terms 2/10, n/30.
	6	Sold on account merchandise to Bevan's Company, $1,600; invoice no. 2; terms 2/10, n/30.
	12	Credit memo #1 to Bevan's Company for returned merchandise, $600.
	18	Sold on account merchandise to Roe Company, $2,000; invoice no. 3; terms 2/10, n/30.
	24	Sold on account merchandise to Roe Company, $500; invoice no. 4; terms 2/10, n/30.
	28	Sold on account merchandise to Mel's Department Store, $900; invoice no. 5; terms 2/10, n/30.
	29	Sold on account merchandise to Mel's Department Store, $700; invoice no. 6; terms 2/10, n/30.

Sales invoice A bill sent to customer(s) reflecting a credit sale.

FIGURE 9.5
Sales Invoice

Let's look closer at the April 3 transaction of Art selling to Hal's Clothing. Figure 9.5 shows the actual bill or the sales invoice for this sale:

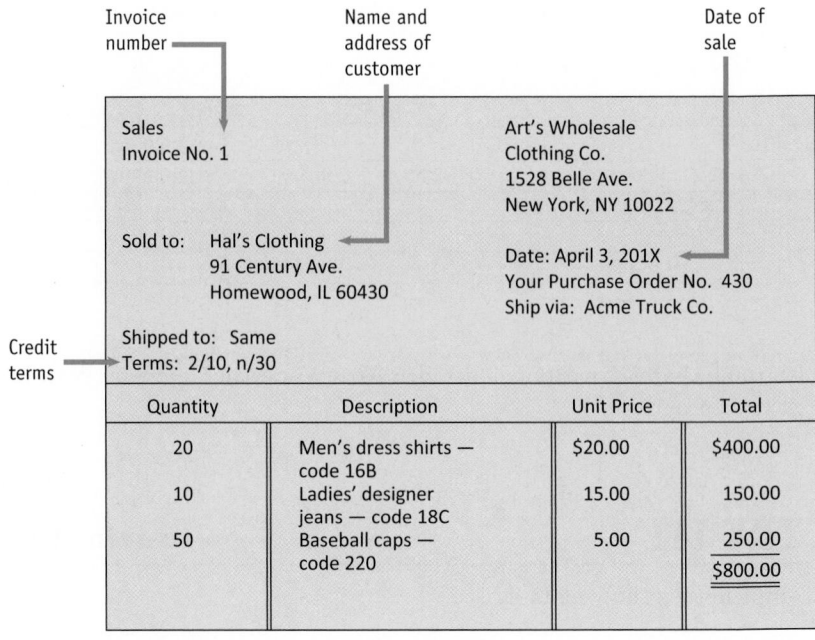

April 3   Sold on account merchandise to Hal's Clothing, $800; terms 2/10, n/30.

Here is an analysis of the transaction by the transaction analysis chart.

Accounts Affected	Category	↑↓	Rules	Amount
Accounts Receivable, Hal's Clothing	Asset	↑	Dr.	$800
Sales	Revenue	↑	Cr.	$800

The general journal is shown in Figure 9.6.

FIGURE 9.6
Merchandise Sold and Accounts Receivable

ART'S WHOLESALE CLOTHING COMPANY GENERAL JOURNAL					
					Page 2
Date		Account Titles and Description	PR	Dr.	Cr.
201X					
Apr.	3	Accounts Receivable, Hal's Clothing		8 0 0 00	
		Sales			8 0 0 00
		Sale on account to Hal's			

Accounts Receivable Subsidiary Ledgers

So far in this text, the only title we have used for recording amounts owed to the seller has been Accounts Receivable. Art could have replaced the Accounts Receivable title in the general ledger with the following list of customers who owe him money:

- Accounts Receivable, Bevans Company
- Accounts Receivable, Hal's Clothing
- Accounts Receivable, Mel's Department Store
- Accounts Receivable, Roe Company

As you can see, this system would not be manageable if Art had 1,000 credit customers. To solve this problem, Art sets up a separate accounts receivable subsidiary ledger. Such a special ledger, often simply called a subsidiary ledger, contains a single type of account, such as credit customers. An account is opened for each customer, and the accounts are arranged alphabetically. Keep in mind that with computer software available today, the accounts can be stored on the computer's hard drive and continually updated.

The diagram in Figure 9.7 shows how the accounts receivable subsidiary ledger fits in with the general ledger. To clarify the difference in updating the general ledger versus the subsidiary ledger, we will *post* to the general ledger and *record* to the subsidiary ledger. The word *post* refers to information that is moved from the journal to the general ledger; the word *record* refers to information that is transferred from the journal into the individual customer's account in the subsidiary ledger.

Accounts receivable subsidiary ledger A book or file that contains the individual records, in alphabetical order, of amounts owed by various credit customers.

Subsidiary ledger A ledger that contains accounts of a single type. Example: The accounts receivable subsidiary ledger records all credit customers.

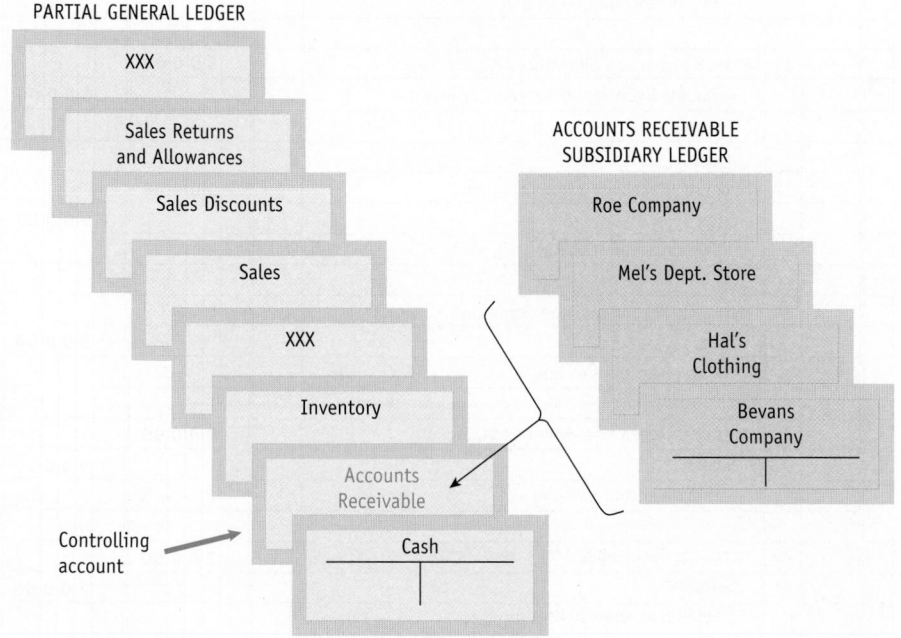

FIGURE 9.7
Partial General Ledger of Art's Wholesale Clothing Company and Accounts Receivable Subsidiary Ledger

 **COACHING TIP**

Proving: At the end of the month, the sum of the accounts in the accounts receivable subsidiary ledger will equal the ending balance in Accounts Receivable, the controlling account in the general ledger.

The accounts receivable subsidiary ledger, or any other subsidiary ledger in a manual system, can be in the form of a hardcopy book or file setup. The accounts receivable subsidiary ledger is organized alphabetically based on customers' names and addresses; new customers can be added and inactive customers deleted. Keep in mind that with the use of computers, many companies now use software such as QuickBooks and Sage 50 that updates customer accounts stored on the computer's hard drive. With the click of a key, the subsidiary ledger can be updated and easily printed out. At the end of Chapter 10, the computer workshops show you how a computerized system works to record transactions and update customer and vendor accounts for a merchandise company.

When using an accounts receivable subsidiary ledger, the account title Accounts Receivable in the general ledger is called the controlling account—Accounts Receivable because it summarizes or controls the accounts receivable subsidiary ledger. At the end of the month the total of the individual accounts in the accounts receivable ledger will equal the ending balance in Accounts Receivable in the general ledger.

Figure 9.8 shows how the general journal looks for Art before posting to the general ledger and recording to the subsidiary ledger this month's sales transactions on account.

Controlling account— Accounts Receivable The Accounts Receivable account in the general ledger, after postings are complete, shows a firm the total amount of money owed to it. This figure is broken down in the accounts receivable subsidiary ledger, where it indicates specifically who owes the money.

FIGURE 9.8
Before Posting and Recording Sales Transactions

		ART'S WHOLESALE CLOTHING COMPANY GENERAL JOURNAL							Page 2				
Date		Account Titles and Description	PR	Dr.					Cr.				
201X													
Apr.	3	Accounts Receivable, Hal's Clothing		8	0	0	00						
		Sales							8	0	0	00	
		Sale on account to Hal's											
	6	Accounts Receivable, Bevan's Company		1	6	0	0	00					
		Sales							1	6	0	0	00
		Sale on account to Bevan's											
	12	Sales Returns and Allowances		6	0	0	00						
		Accounts Receivable, Bevan's Company							6	0	0	00	
		Issued credit memo no. 1											
	18	Accounts Receivable, Roe Company		2	0	0	0	00					
		Sales							2	0	0	0	00
		Sale on account to Roe											
	24	Accounts Receivable, Roe Company		5	0	0	00						
		Sales							5	0	0	00	
		Sale on account to Roe											
	28	Accounts Receivable, Mel's Dept. Store		9	0	0	00						
		Sales							9	0	0	00	
		Sale on account to Mel's											
	29	Accounts Receivable, Mel's Dept. Store		7	0	0	00						
		Sales							7	0	0	00	
		Sale on account to Mel's											

Posting and Recording Sales Transactions. Before we post to the general ledger and record to the subsidiary ledger, consider the following T accounts, which show what each title would look like.

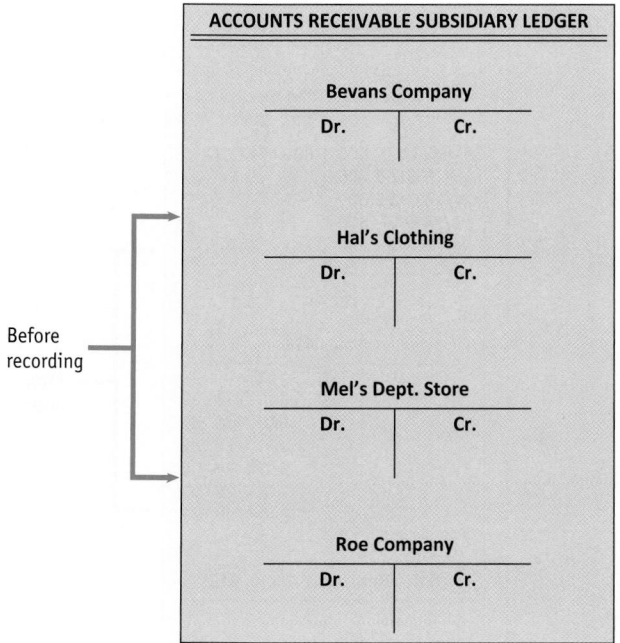

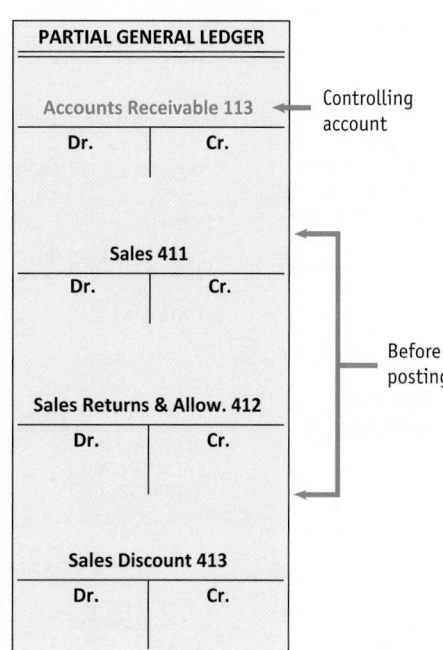

Figure 9.9 shows how the April 3 transaction is posted and recorded.

For this transaction we *post* to the general ledger Accounts Receivable and Sales accounts. Note how the account numbers of 113 and 411 are entered into the PR column of the general journal. We must also *record* to Hal's Clothing in the accounts receivable subsidiary ledger. The amount is placed on the debit side because Hal owed Art the money. When the subsidiary ledger is updated, a (✔) is placed in the PR column of the general journal. The continuation of Figure 9.9 on the following page shows how the accounts receivable subsidiary ledger and partial general ledger would look after postings.

		GENERAL JOURNAL			Page 2	
	Date	Account Titles and Description	PR	Dr.	Cr.	
	201X					
	Apr. 3	Accounts Receivable, Hal's Clothing	113 ✔	8 0 0 00		
		Sales	411		8 0 0 00	
		Sale on account to Hal's				

FIGURE 9.9
Transaction for April 3 Posted and Recorded

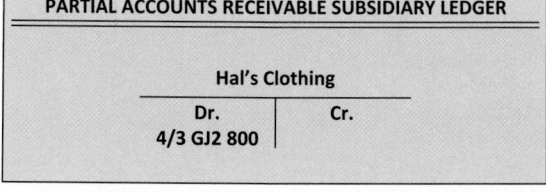

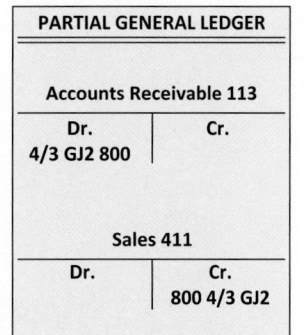

(continued on page 326)

FIGURE 9.9 (continued)

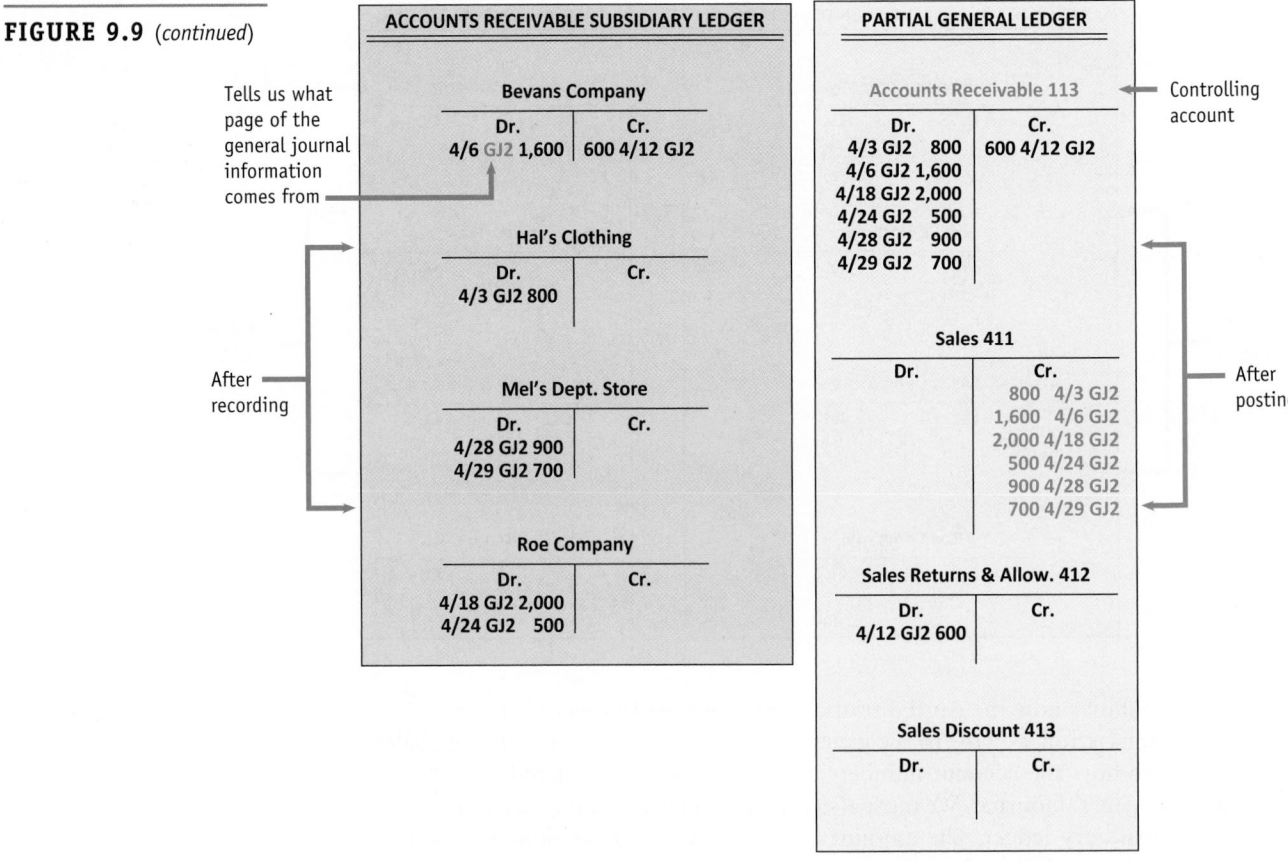

The Credit Memorandum

Credit memorandum A piece of paper sent by the seller to a customer who has returned merchandise previously purchased on credit. The credit memorandum indicates to the customer that the seller is reducing the amount owed by the customer.

Companies usually handle sales returns and allowances by means of a credit memorandum. Credit memoranda inform customers that the amount of the goods returned or the amount allowed for damaged goods has been subtracted (credited) from the customer's ongoing account with the company.

A sample credit memorandum from Art's Wholesale Clothing Company appears in Figure 9.10. It shows that on April 12, Credit Memorandum No. 1 was issued to Bevans Company for defective merchandise that had been returned.

FIGURE 9.10

Sample Credit Memorandum from Art's Wholesale Clothing Company

> Art's Wholesale
> Clothing Co.
> 1528 Belle Ave.
> New York, NY 10022
>
> Credit
> Memorandum No. 1
> Date: April 12, 201X
> Credit to Bevans Company
>   110 Aster Rd.
>   Cincinnati, Ohio 45227
> We credit your account as follows:
> *Merchandise returned 60 model 8 B men's dress gloves—$600*

Let's look at a transaction analysis chart before we journalize, record, and post this transaction.

Accounts Affected	Category	↑ ↓	Rules
Sales Returns and Allowances	Contra-revenue account	↑	Dr.
Accounts Receivable, Bevans Co.	Asset	↓	Cr.

Journalizing, Recording, and Posting the Credit Memorandum

The credit memorandum results in two postings to the general ledger and one recording to the accounts receivable subsidiary ledger (see Figure 9.11).

COACHING TIP

Remember: Sales discounts are not taken on returns.

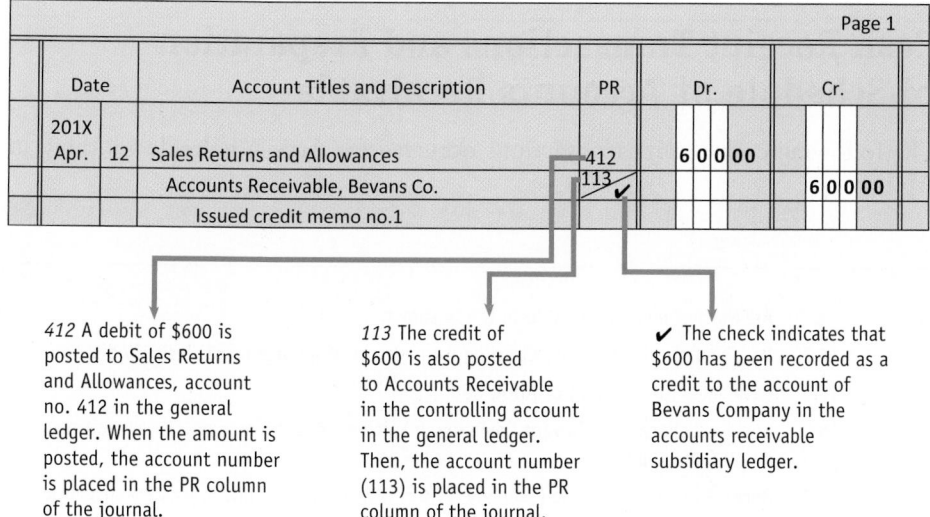

FIGURE 9.11
Postings and Recording for the Credit Memorandum into the Subsidiary and General Ledgers

412 A debit of $600 is posted to Sales Returns and Allowances, account no. 412 in the general ledger. When the amount is posted, the account number is placed in the PR column of the journal.

113 The credit of $600 is also posted to Accounts Receivable in the controlling account in the general ledger. Then, the account number (113) is placed in the PR column of the journal.

✔ The check indicates that $600 has been recorded as a credit to the account of Bevans Company in the accounts receivable subsidiary ledger.

Note that in the PR column next to Accounts Receivable, Bevans Co., a diagonal line separates account number 113 above and a ✔ below. This notation shows that the amount of $600 has been credited to Accounts Receivable in the controlling account in the general ledger *and* credited to the account of Bevans Company in the accounts receivable subsidiary ledger. Keep in mind that with computer software available today, information about returns, for example, is easily updated in the accounting software, and customer accounts are immediately updated in the appropriate ledgers. Now it's time to check your progress.

▶ TRY IT!   Learning Unit 9-2

Given the following, journalize and post these two transactions (the journal is page 6):

201X			
June	5	Sold merchandise on account to Leser Co., $500; terms 2/10, n/30.	
	7	Issued credit memorandum no. 1 to Leser Co. for $100 of returned goods.	

(continued on page 324)

Partial General Ledger				

Accounts Receivable 151			Sales 310	
Dr.	Cr.		Dr.	Cr.
Bal. 900				

Sales Returns and Allowance 312	
Dr.	Cr.

Accounts Receivable Subsidiary Ledger				

Bloom Co.			Leser Co.	
Dr.	Cr.		Dr.	Cr.
Bal. 900				

Cash Receipt Transactions and Preparation of Schedule of Accounts Receivable

The following cash receipt transactions occurred for Art's Wholesale Clothing in April:

201X		
Apr.	1	Art Newner invested $8,000 in the business.
	4	Received check from Hal's Clothing for payment of invoice no. 1, less 2% discount.
	15	Cash sales for first half of April, $900.
	16	Received check from Bevans Company in settlement of invoice no. 2, less returns and 2% discount.
	22	Received check from Roe Company for payment of invoice no. 3, less 2% discount.
	27	Sold store equipment, $500.
	30	Cash sales for second half of April, $1,200.

Figure 9.12 provides a closer look at how the April 4 transaction would be journalized. Let's first look at the transaction analysis chart before showing the journalized transaction.

COACHING TIP

Hal's Clothing is located in the accounts receivable subsidiary ledger.

Accounts Affected	Category	↑ ↓	Rules	T Account Update			
Cash	Asset	↑	Dr.	**Cash**			
					Dr. 784	Cr.	
Sales Discount	Contra-revenue	↑	Dr.	**Sales Discount**			
					Dr. 16	Cr.	
Accounts Receivable, Hal's Clothing	Asset	↓	Cr.	**Acc. Rec.**		**Hal's Clothing**	
				Dr. 800	Cr. 800	Dr. 800	Cr. 800

Apr.	4	Cash			7 8 4 00					
		Sales Discount			1 6 00					
		Accounts Receivable, Hal's Clothing						8 0 0 00	

FIGURE 9.12
Recording Sales Discount in General Journal

Figure 9.13 shows the complete set of April cash receipts transactions for Art's Wholesale journalized for the month, followed by a complete posting to the general ledger and recordings to the accounts receivable subsidiary ledger. (Remember from the past unit that we posted all the sales on account information.)

GENERAL JOURNAL — Page 2

Date		Account Titles and Description	PR	Dr.	Cr.
201X					
Apr.	1	Cash	111	8 0 0 0 00	
		Art Newner, Capital	311		8 0 0 0 00
		Owner Investment			
	4	Cash	111	7 8 4 00	
		Sales Discount	413	1 6 00	
		Accounts Receivable, Hal's Clothing	113 ✔		8 0 0 00
		Hal's paid invoice no. 1			
	15	Cash	111	9 0 0 00	
		Sales	411		9 0 0 00
		Cash sales for first half of April			
	16	Cash	111	9 8 0 00	
		Sales Discount	413	2 0 00	
		Accounts Receivable, Bevan's Company	113 ✔		1 0 0 0 00
		Bevan paid invoice no. 2			
	22	Cash	111	1 9 6 0 00	
		Sales Discount	413	4 0 00	
		Accounts Receivable, Roe Co.	113 ✔		2 0 0 0 00
		Roe paid invoice no. 3			
	27	Cash	111	5 0 0 00	
		Store Equipment	121		5 0 0 00
		Sold store equipment			
	30	Cash	111	1 2 0 0 00	
		Sales	411		1 2 0 0 00
		Cash sales for second half of April			

FIGURE 9.13
Journalized Cash Receipts Transactions

(continued on page 326)

FIGURE 9.13 (*continued*)

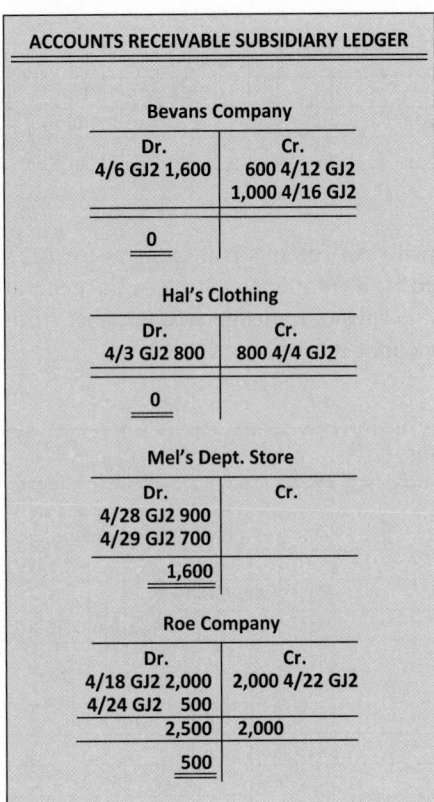

ACCOUNTS RECEIVABLE SUBSIDIARY LEDGER

Bevans Company

Dr.	Cr.
4/6 GJ2 1,600	600 4/12 GJ2
	1,000 4/16 GJ2
0	

Hal's Clothing

Dr.	Cr.
4/3 GJ2 800	800 4/4 GJ2
0	

Mel's Dept. Store

Dr.	Cr.
4/28 GJ2 900	
4/29 GJ2 700	
1,600	

Roe Company

Dr.	Cr.
4/18 GJ2 2,000	2,000 4/22 GJ2
4/24 GJ2 500	
2,500	2,000
500	

PARTIAL GENERAL LEDGER

Cash 111

Dr.	Cr.
4/1 GJ2 8,000	
4/4 GJ2 784	
4/15 GJ2 900	
4/16 GJ2 980	
4/22 GJ2 1,960	
4/27 GJ2 500	
4/30 GJ2 1,200	
14,324	

Accounts Receivable 113 ← Controlling account

Dr.	Cr.
4/3 GJ2 800	800 4/4 GJ2
4/6 GJ2 1,600	600 4/12 GJ2
4/18 GJ2 2,000	1,000 4/16 GJ2
4/24 GJ2 500	2,000 4/22 GJ2
4/28 GJ2 900	4,400
4/29 GJ2 700	
6,500	
Bal. 2,100	

Store Equipment 121

Dr.	Cr.
4/1 Bal. 24,000	500 4/27 GJ2
23,500	

Art Newner, Capital 311

Dr.	Cr.
	8,000 4/1 GJ2
	8,000

Sales 411

Dr.	Cr.
	800 4/3 GJ2
	1,600 4/6 GJ2
	900 4/15 GJ2
	2,000 4/18 GJ2
	500 4/24 GJ2
	900 4/28 GJ2
	700 4/29 GJ2
	1,200 4/30 GJ2
	8,600

Sales Returns & Allow. 412

Dr.	Cr.
4/12 GJ2 600	
600	

Sales Discount 413

Dr.	Cr.
4/4 GJ2 16	
4/16 GJ2 20	
4/22 GJ2 40	
76	

Schedule of Accounts Receivable

The schedule of accounts receivable is an alphabetical list of the companies that have an outstanding balance in the accounts receivable subsidiary ledger. This total should be equal to the balance of the Accounts Receivable controlling account in the general ledger at the end of the month.

Let's examine the schedule of accounts receivable for Art's Wholesale Clothing Company in Figure 9.14.

COACHING TIP

Schedule of Accounts Receivable is listed in alphabetical order.

ART'S WHOLESALE CLOTHING COMPANY SCHEDULE OF ACCOUNTS RECEIVABLE APRIL 30, 201X	
Mel's Dept. Store	$1 6 0 0 00
Roe Company	5 0 0 00
Total Accounts Receivable	$2 1 0 0 00

FIGURE 9.14
Schedule of Accounts Receivable

The balance of the controlling account, Accounts Receivable ($2,100), in the general ledger does indeed equal the sum of the individual customer balances in the accounts receivable ledger ($2,100) as shown in the schedule of accounts receivable. The schedule of accounts receivable can help forecast potential cash inflows as well as possible credit and collection decisions. Remember, if computer software is used, you would just click from a menu to prepare a new schedule and all information is stored on the computer's hard drive. Now it's time to check your progress.

Schedule of accounts receivable A list of the customers, in alphabetical order, that have an outstanding balance in the accounts receivable subsidiary ledger. This total should be equal to the balance of the Accounts Receivable controlling account in the general ledger at the end of the month.

TRY IT!

Learning Unit 9-3

Given the following, journalize, record, post, and prepare a schedule of accounts receivable at the end of April for King Co. (The journal is page 8).

Partial General Ledger

Cash 110

Dr.	Cr.
Bal. 1,000	

Accounts Receivable 120		Sales 410		Sales Discounts 420	
Dr.	Cr.	Dr.	Cr.	Dr.	Cr.
Bal. 600					

Accounts Receivable Subsidiary Ledger

Blue Co.		Pete Long Co.	
Dr.	Cr.	Dr.	Cr.
Bal. 400		Bal. 200	

201X

April   9   Received check from Blue Co. for balance due less 2% discount.
        12   Cash sale collected, $500.

L01,2,3

DEMONSTRATION SUMMARY PROBLEM

Mia Kim owns Kim's Running Shop.

Requirements

From the following information:

1. Journalize the transactions (page 6 of journal).
2. Record to accounts receivable subsidiary ledger and post to general ledger as needed. Also, determine the ending balance in each account on June 30.
3. Prepare a schedule of accounts receivable for June 30, 201X.

Partial General Ledger

Cash 110		Accounts Receivable 120	
Dr.	Cr.	Dr.	Cr.
Bal. 4,000		Bal. 1,400	

Display Equipment 130		M. Kim, Capital 310	
Dr.	Cr.	Dr.	Cr.
Bal. 900			Bal. 8,000

Sales 410		Sales Discounts 420	
Dr.	Cr.	Dr.	Cr.
	Bal. 2,000		

Sales Returns and Allowances 440	
Dr.	Cr.

Accounts Receivable Subsidiary Ledger

Roger Flynn		Bob Jey	
Dr.	Cr.	Dr.	Cr.
Bal. 200		Bal. 400	

Joe Lantz		Valerie Tog	
Dr.	Cr.	Dr.	Cr.
Bal. 800			

201X

June   1   Mia Kim invested an additional $3,000 into the running shop.

       3   Sold $200 of merchandise on account to Bob Jey, sales ticket no. 60; terms 2/10, n/30.

       4   Sold $100 of merchandise on account to Roger Flynn, sales ticket no. 61; terms 2/10, n/30.

       9   Sold $150 of merchandise on account to Joe Lantz, sales ticket no. 62; terms 2/10, n/30.

    10   Received cash from Bob Jey in payment of June 3 transaction, sales ticket no. 60, less discount.

    20   Sold $90 of merchandise on account to Valerie Tog, sales ticket no. 63; terms 2/10, n/30.

    22   Received cash payment from Roger Flynn in payment of June 4 transaction, sales ticket no. 61.

    23   Collected cash sales, $900.

    24   Issued credit memorandum no. 1 to Valerie Tog, $50.

    30   Sold display equipment for $400 (Beware, the cost is $400).

Solutions

Requirements 1, 2, 3

Kim's Running Shop

General Journal Page 6

Date	Accounts	PR	Dr.	Cr.
201X				
June 1	Cash	110	3,000	
	Mia Kim, Capital	310		3,000
3	Accounts Receivable, Bob Jey	120/✓	200	
	Sales	410		200
4	Accounts Receivable, Roger Flynn	120/✓	100	
	Sales	410		100
9	Accounts Receivable, Joe Lantz	120/✓	150	
	Sales	410		150
10	Cash	110	196	
	Sales Discount	420	4	
	Accounts Receivable, Bob Jey	120/✓		200
20	Accounts Receivable, Valerie Tog	120/✓	90	
	Sales	410		90
22	Cash	110	100	
	Accounts Receivable, Roger Flynn	120/✓		100
23	Cash	110	900	
	Sales	410		900
24	Sales Returns and Allowances	440	50	
	Accounts Receivable, Valerie Tog	120/✓		50
30	Cash	110	400	
	Display Equipment	130		400

Tips for Journalizing Transactions and Posting to the Accounts Receivable Subsidiary Ledger and General Ledger

Account	Category	Normal Balance
Cash	Asset	Debit
Accounts Receivable	Asset	Debit
Sales	Revenue	Credit
Sales Discount	Contra-Revenue	Debit
Sales Returns and Allowances	Contra-Revenue	Debit

Partial General Ledger

Cash 110

Dr.	Cr.
Bal. 4,000	
6/1 GJ6 3,000	
6/10 GJ6 196	
6/22 GJ6 100	
6/23 GJ6 900	
6/30 GJ6 400	
Balance 8,596	

Accounts Receivable 120

Dr.	Cr.
Bal. 1,400	200 6/10 GJ6
6/3 GJ6 200	100 6/22 GJ6
6/4 GJ6 100	50 6/24 GJ6
6/9 GJ6 150	
6/20 GJ6 90	
Balance 1,590	

Display Equipment 130

Dr.	Cr.
Bal. 900	400 6/30 GJ6
Balance 500	

Mia Kim, Capital 310

Dr.	Cr.
	8,000 Bal.
	3,000 6/1 GJ6
	Balance 11,000

Sales 410

Dr.	Cr.
	2,000 Bal.
	200 6/3 GJ6
	100 6/4 GJ6
	150 6/9 GJ6
	90 6/20 GJ6
	900 6/23 GJ6
	Balance 3,440

Sales Discount 420

Dr.	Cr.
6/10 GJ6 4	
Balance 4	

Sales Returns and Allowances 440

Dr.	Cr.
6/24 GJ6 50	
Balance 50	

Accounts Receivable Subsidiary Ledger

Roger Flynn

Dr.	Cr.
Bal. 200	100 6/22 GJ6
6/4 GJ6 100	
Balance 200	

Bob Jey

Dr.	Cr.
Bal. 400	200 6/10 GJ6
6/3 GJ6 200	
Balance 400	

Valerie Tog

Dr.	Cr.
6/20 GJ6 90	50 6/24 GJ6
Balance 40	

Joe Lantz

Dr.	Cr.
Bal 800	
6/9 GJ6 150	
Balance 950	

Tips for Preparing a Schedule of Accounts Receivable

The normal balance of the account receivable subsidiary ledger accounts is a debit. After postings are complete both to the general ledger and the subsidiary ledger, the balance in Accounts Receivable in the general ledger should equal the total of all ending balances in the subsidiary ledger.

Kim's Running Shop
Schedule of Accounts Receivable
June 30, 201X

Roger Flynn	$ 200
Bob Jey	400
Joe Lantz	950
Valerie Tog	40
Total Accounts Receivable	$1,590

These amounts for Flynn, Jey, Lantz, and Tog came from the ending balances in the subsidiary ledger. Note this is the ending balance in Accounts Receivable in the general ledger.

BLUEPRINT: TRANSFERRING INFORMATION FROM THE GENERAL JOURNAL

Post → General Ledger (account #)
Record → Subsidiary Ledger (✓)

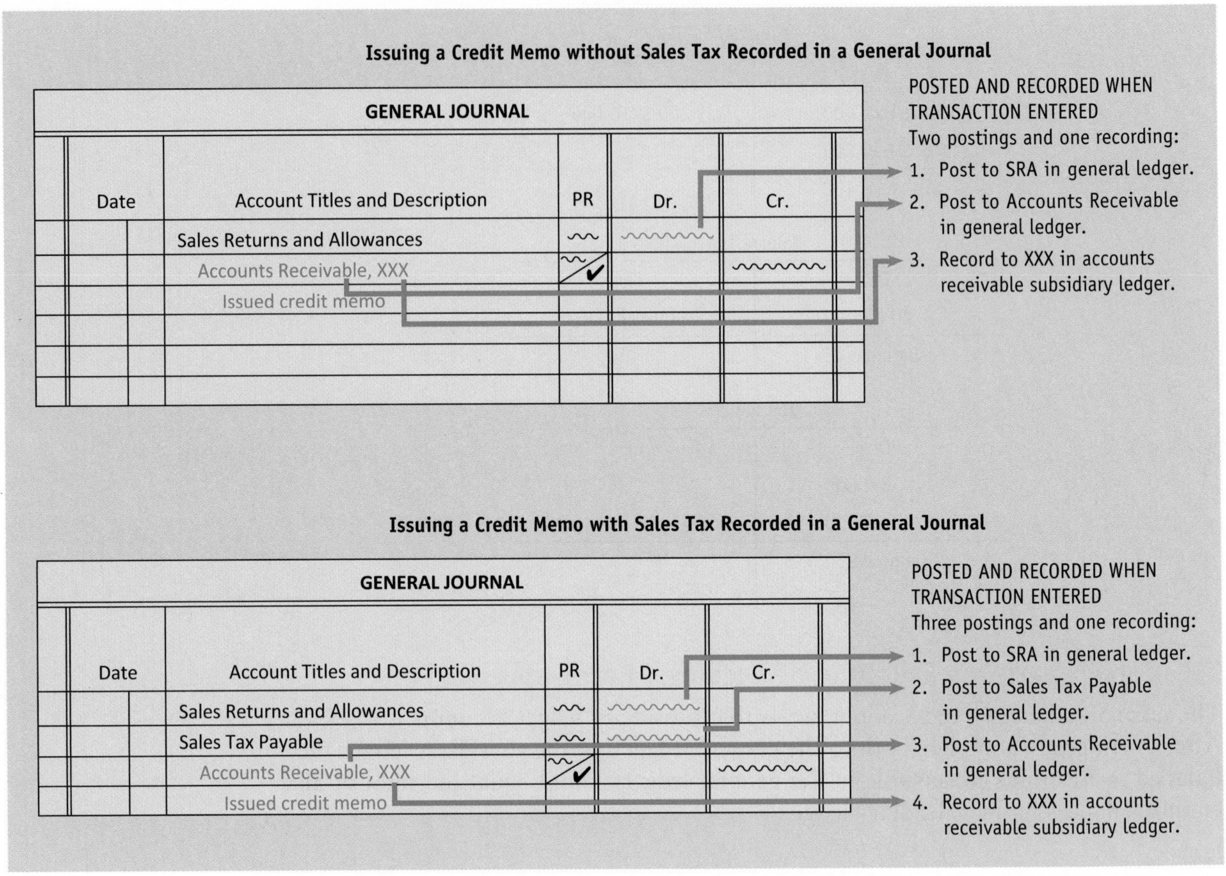

Issuing a Credit Memo without Sales Tax Recorded in a General Journal

		GENERAL JOURNAL			
Date		Account Titles and Description	PR	Dr.	Cr.
		Sales Returns and Allowances	∼	∼∼∼	
		Accounts Receivable, XXX	∼✓		∼∼∼
		Issued credit memo			

POSTED AND RECORDED WHEN TRANSACTION ENTERED
Two postings and one recording:

1. Post to SRA in general ledger.
2. Post to Accounts Receivable in general ledger.
3. Record to XXX in accounts receivable subsidiary ledger.

Issuing a Credit Memo with Sales Tax Recorded in a General Journal

		GENERAL JOURNAL			
Date		Account Titles and Description	PR	Dr.	Cr.
		Sales Returns and Allowances	∼	∼∼∼	
		Sales Tax Payable	∼	∼∼∼	
		Accounts Receivable, XXX	∼✓		∼∼∼
		Issued credit memo			

POSTED AND RECORDED WHEN TRANSACTION ENTERED
Three postings and one recording:

1. Post to SRA in general ledger.
2. Post to Sales Tax Payable in general ledger.
3. Post to Accounts Receivable in general ledger.
4. Record to XXX in accounts receivable subsidiary ledger.

MyAccountingLab    **TRY IT!**   **Solutions**

Learning Unit 9-1

Account	Category	Inc.	Dec.	Financial Statement
Cash	Asset	Dr.	Cr.	BS
Accounts Rec.	Asset	Dr.	Cr.	BS
Sales Tax Pay.	Liability	Cr.	Dr.	BS
Sales	Revenue	Cr.	Dr.	IS
Sales Discounts	Contra-Revenue	Dr.	Cr.	IS
Sales Returns and Allowances	Contra-Revenue	Dr.	Cr.	IS

Learning Unit 9-2

		General Journal			p. 6
Date		Account	PR	Dr.	Cr.
201X					
June	5	Accounts Receivable, Leser Co.	151/✓	500	
		Sales	310		500
		Sale on Account to Leser Co.			
	7	Sales Returns and Allowances	312	100	
		Accounts Receivable, Leser Co.	151/✓		100
		Issued Credit to Leser Co.			

Partial General Ledger

Accounts Receivable 151

Dr.	Cr.
Bal. 900	100 6/7 GJ6
6/5 GJ6 500	

Sales 310

Dr.	Cr.
	500 6/5 GJ6

Sales Returns and Allowances 312

Dr.	Cr.
6/7 GJ6 100	

Accounts Receivable Subsidary Ledger

Bloom Co.		Leser Co.	
Dr.	Cr.	Dr.	Cr.
Bal. 900		6/5 GJ6 500	100 6/7 GJ6

Learning Unit 9-3

King Co.

		General Journal			p. 8
Date		Account	PR	Dr.	Cr.
201X					
April	9	Cash	110	392	
		Sales Discount	420	8	
		Accounts Receivable, Blue Co.	120/✓		400
		Received Cash from Blue Co.			
	12	Cash	110	500	
		Sales	410		500
		Cash Sale			

King Co.
Partial General Ledger

Cash 110	
Dr.	Cr.
Bal. 1,000	
4/9 GJ8 392	
4/12 GJ8 500	

Accounts Receivable 120	
Dr.	Cr.
Bal. 600	400 4/9 GJ8

Sales 120	
Dr.	Cr.
	500 4/12 GJ8

Sales Discount 420	
Dr.	Cr.
4/9 GJ8 8	

Accounts Receivable Subsidiary Ledger	
Blue Co.	
Dr.	Cr.
Bal. 400	400 GJ8 4/9
Bal. 0	

Pete Long Co.	
Dr.	Cr.
Bal. 200	

Schedule of Accounts Receivable April 30, 201X	
Pete Long Co.	$200
Total Accounts Receivable	$200

ACCOUNTING COACH

The following Coaching Tips are from Learning Units 9-1 to 9-3. Take the Pre-Game Checkup and use the Check Your Score to see how you are doing. The Accounting Coach provides tips before each Checkup to help you avoid common accounting errors.

LU 9-1 Chou's Toy Shop: Entries for Sales, Sales Discounts, and Sales Returns and Allowances

Pre-Game Tips: Sales is a revenue account, while Sales Returns and Allowances and Sales Discounts are contra-revenue accounts. Sales Returns and Allowances and Sales Discounts have their normal balances on the debit side. Gross sales less sales returns and allowances, less sales discounts will equal net sales.

Pre-Game Checkup: Answer true or false to the following statements.

1. Net sales and gross sales are the same.
2. Sales Tax Payable is an asset.
3. Sales Discounts is a revenue account with a debit balance.
4. Sales Returns and Allowances increase with a debit.
5. Sales Discounts increase with a credit.

LU 9-2 Subsidiary Ledgers and General Ledger Sales Transactions and Returns

Pre-Game Tips: The controlling account, Accounts Receivable, in the general ledger will equal the sum of Accounts Receivable in the subsidiary ledger at the end of the month. If a credit memorandum is issued, Sales Returns and Allowances will increase with a debit, and an Accounts Receivable controlling account, as well as the specific subsidiary ledger, will be reduced. The normal balance of each account in the subsidiary ledger is a debit balance.

Pre-Game Checkup: Answer true or false to the following statements.

1. The controlling account is located in the subsidiary ledger.
2. A checkmark in the posting reference column means the controlling account has been updated.

3. A credit memorandum only affects the controlling account.
4. Sales discounts are always taken on returns.
5. Subsidiary ledgers can be listed alphabetically.

LU 9-3 Cash Receipt Transactions and Preparation of Schedule of Accounts Receivable

Pre-Game Tips: When all postings are done the sum of the accounts in the subsidiary ledger should equal the ending balance in the controlling account. It is the schedule of accounts receivable that lists each customer with its ending balance. This total in the schedule of accounts receivable is the one that matches the ending balance in the controlling account. There are no debits or credits on the schedule of accounts receivable.

Pre-Game Checkup: Answer true or false to the following statements.

1. The schedule of accounts receivable lists debits first.
2. The normal balance of an Accounts Receivable account is a credit.
3. The controlling account does not match the total of the schedule of accounts receivable at the end of the month.
4. Sales Discounts is a contra-asset.
5. The schedule of accounts receivable shows what we owe vendors.

CHECK YOUR SCORE: Answers to the Pre-Game Checkup

LU 9-1
1. False—Net sales is gross sales less returns and allowances and any discounts.
2. False—Sales Tax Payable is a liability.
3. False—Sales Discounts is a contra-revenue account with a debit balance.
4. True
5. False—Sales Discounts increase with a debit.

LU 9-2
1. False—The controlling account is located in the general ledger.
2. False—A checkmark in the posting reference column means the subsidiary ledger has been updated.
3. False—Credit memorandum affects both the controlling account and the subsidiary ledger.
4. False—Sales discounts are never taken on returns.
5. True

LU 9-3
1. False—There are no debits on the schedule of accounts receivable.
2. False—The normal balance of an Accounts Receivable account is a debit.
3. False—The controlling account does match the total of the schedule of accounts receivable at the end of the month.
4. False—Sales Discounts is a contra-revenue account.
5. False—The schedule of accounts receivable shows the amount customers owe the seller.

Chapter Summary

Here are all the key terms and equations to help you understand the concepts of this chapter and prepare you for your exam. After completing this review, go to MyAccountingLab for more practice opportunities.

MyAccountingLab

Concepts You Should Know	Key Terms
L01 **Explain and Journalize Entries for Sales, Sales Discounts, and Sales Returns and Allowances** 1. Sales Returns and Allowances and Sales Discount are contra-revenue accounts. 2. Net Sales = Gross Sales − Sales Returns and Allowances − Sales Discounts. 3. Sales Tax Payable is a liability account. 4. When a credit memorandum is issued, the result is that Sales Returns and Allowances increases and Accounts Receivable decreases.	Credit period (p. 315) Discount period (p. 315) Gross sales (p. 316) Merchandise (p. 314) Net sales (p. 316) Retailers (p. 314) Sales discount (p. 315) Sales Discount account (p. 315) Sales Returns and Allowances (SRA) account (p. 314) Sales Tax Payable account (p. 316)
L02 **Record to Subsidiary Ledgers and Post to General Ledger Sales Transactions and Returns** 1. When we record an entry into the general journal, all parts of the transaction will be posted to the general ledger. Debits and credits to Accounts Receivable will also be recorded in the Accounts Receivable subsidiary ledger. 2. Sales result in an inflow of cash and/or accounts receivable. All cash receipt transactions result in an inward flow of cash. 3. The normal balance of the accounts receivable subsidiary ledger is a debit. 4. A ✓ in the PR of the general journal means that the subsidiary ledger has been updated. 5. The accounts receivable subsidiary ledger is not in the same book as Accounts Receivable, the controlling account in the general ledger in a manual system	Accounts receivable subsidiary ledger (p. 319) Controlling account—Accounts Receivable (p. 320) Credit memorandum (p. 322) Sales invoice (p. 318) Subsidiary ledger (p. 319) Wholesalers (p. 317)
L03 **Record and Post Cash Receipt Transactions and Prepare a Schedule of Accounts Receivable** 1. The schedule of accounts receivable is an alphabetical list of customers with an outstanding balance. 2. At the end of the month, the total of all customers' ending balances in the accounts receivable subsidiary ledger should be equal to the ending balance in Accounts Receivable, the controlling account in the general ledger.	Schedule of accounts receivable (p. 327)

Discussion Questions and Critical Thinking/Ethical Case

1. Explain the purpose of a contra-revenue account.

2. What is the normal balance of Sales Discount?

3. Give two examples of contra-revenue accounts.

4. What is the difference between a discount period and a credit period?

5. Explain the terms:

    a. 2/10, n/30

    b. n/10, EOM

6. What category is Sales Discount in?

7. Compare and contrast the Controlling Account—Accounts Receivable to the accounts receivable subsidiary ledger.

8. Why is the accounts receivable subsidiary ledger organized in alphabetical order?

9. When is a (✓) used?

10. What is an invoice? What purpose does it serve?

11. Why is sales tax a liability to the business?

12. Sales discounts are taken on sales tax. Agree or disagree? Explain why.

13. When a seller issues a credit memorandum (assume no sales tax), what accounts will be affected?

14. Amy Jak is the National Sales Manager of Land.com. To get sales up to the projection for the old year, Amy asked the accountant to put the first 2 weeks' sales in January back into December. Amy told the accountant that this secret would only be between them. Should Amy move the new sales into the old sales year? You make the call. Write down your specific recommendations to Amy.

MyAccountingLab

Concept Checks

(5 min) **LO1** ▶ **Overview**

1. Complete the following table for Sales, Sales Returns and Allowances, and Sales Discounts.

Accounts Affected	Category	Rules to Increase Account	Temporary or Permanent

(5 min) **LO1** ▶ **Calculating Net Sales**

2. Given the following, calculate net sales:

Gross Sales	$44
Sales Returns and Allowances	7
Sales Discounts	5

General Journal

 **L01,2,3**   *(10 min)*

3. Match the following activities to the three business transactions (more than one number can be used).

   1. Record to the accounts receivable subsidiary ledger.
   2. Journalize the transaction.
   3. Post to the general ledger.

      a. _____ Sold merchandise on account to Clo Co., invoice no. 1, $90.
      b. _____ Sold merchandise on account to Flynn Co., invoice no. 2, $1,500.
      c. _____ Issued credit memorandum no. 1 to Flynn Co. for defective merchandise, $50.

Credit Memorandum

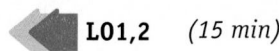 **L02**   *(10 min)*

4. Complete the transactional analysis box for the following transaction: Issued credit memorandum to Pike.com for defective merchandise, $190.

Journalize Transactions

L01,2   *(15 min)*

5. Journalize the following transactions:

   a. Sold merchandise on account to Troy Co., invoice no. 10, $50.
   b. Received check from Brown Co., $300, less 3% discount.
   c. Cash sales, $104.
   d. Issued credit memorandum no. 2 to Troy Co. for defective merchandise, $18.

6. From the following, prepare a schedule of accounts receivable for Lucky Co. for May 31, 201X.

L03   *(15 min)*

Accounts Receivable Subsidiary Ledger					General Ledger				
Jarad Co.					**Accounts Receivable**				
	Dr.	Cr.				Dr.	Cr.		
5/6 GJ1	104				5/31 GJ1	147	12	5/31 GJ1	
Katz Co.									
	Dr.	Cr.							
5/20 GJ1	33	12	5/27 GJ1						
Turtle Co.									
	Dr.	Cr.							
5/9 GJ1	10								

Exercises

Set A

(10 min) **LO2** ▶

9A-1. From the general journal in Figure 9.15, record to the accounts receivable subsidiary ledger and post to the general ledger accounts as appropriate.

FIGURE 9.15
General Journal for September 18 and 19 and Blank Accounts Receivable Subsidiary Ledger

	General Journal					
Date	Account Titles and Explanations	PR	Dr.		Cr.	
201X						
Sept. 18	Accounts Receivable, Twilight Co.		6 4 0 00			
	Sales				6 4 0 00	
	Sold merchandise to Twilight Co.					
19	Accounts Receivable, Falcon Co.		8 5 0 00			
	Sales				8 5 0 00	
	Sold merchandise to Falcon Co.					

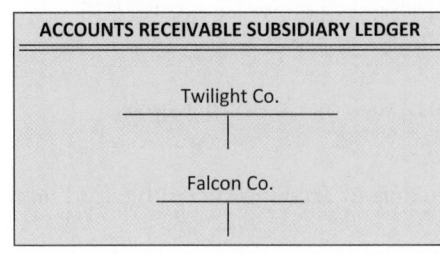

ACCOUNTS RECEIVABLE SUBSIDIARY LEDGER

Twilight Co.

Falcon Co.

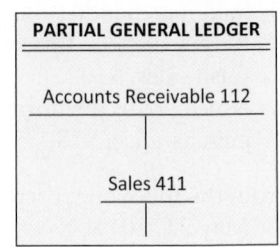

PARTIAL GENERAL LEDGER

Accounts Receivable 112

Sales 411

(10 min) **LO1,2**

9A-2. Journalize, record, and post when appropriate the following transactions in the general journal (all sales carry terms of 5/10, n/30):

201X
Dec. 16   Sold merchandise on account to Cart Co., invoice no. 1, $980.

18   Sold merchandise on account to French Co., invoice no. 2, $2,100.

20   Issued credit memorandum no. 1 to French Co. for defective merchandise, $700.

Use the following account numbers: Accounts Receivable, 112; Sales, 411; Sales Returns and Allowances, 412; Sales Discounts 413.

(10 min) **LO2** ▶

9A-3. From Exercise 9A-2, journalize the receipt of a check from Cart Co. for payment of invoice no. 1 on December 24.

(20 min) **LO2,3**

9A-4. From the following transactions for Ava Co., journalize, record, post, and prepare a schedule of accounts receivable when appropriate. You will have to set up your own accounts receivable subsidiary ledger and partial general ledger as needed. All sales terms are 1/10, n/30.

201X
Oct. 1   Ava Roberts invested $3,300 in the business.

1   Sold merchandise on account to Charleston Co., invoice no. 1, $950.

2   Sold merchandise on account to William Co., invoice no. 2, $960.

3   Cash sale, $220.

8   Issued credit memorandum no. 1 to Charleston Co. for defective merchandise, $350.

10   Received check from Charleston Co. for invoice no. 1, less returns and discount.

15   Cash sale, $440.

18   Sold merchandise on account to Charleston Co., invoice no. 3, $850.

9A-5. From the following facts calculate what Mike Hall paid Lakeville Co. for the purchase of a dining room set. Sale terms are 5/10, n/30.

 **L01** *(10 min)*

 a. Sales ticket price before tax, $11,000, dated April 5.
 b. Sales tax, 10%.
 c. Returned one defective chair for credit of $1,400 on April 8.
 d. Paid bill on April 13.

Set B

9B-1. From the general journal in Figure 9.16, record to the accounts receivable subsidiary ledger and post to the general ledger accounts as appropriate.

 **L02** *(10 min)*

FIGURE 9.16 General Journal for May 18 and 19 and Blank Accounts Receivable Subsidiary Ledger

Date	Account Titles and Explanations	PR	Dr.	Cr.
201X				
May 18	Accounts Receivable, Henry Co.		590 00	
	Sales			590 00
	Sold merchandise to Henry Co.			
19	Accounts Receivable, Lincoln Co.		890 00	
	Sales			890 00
	Sold merchandise to Lincoln Co.			

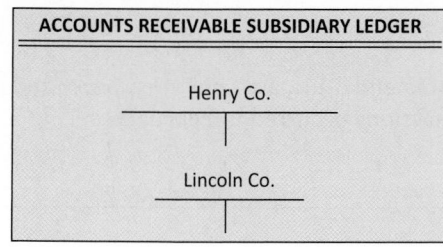
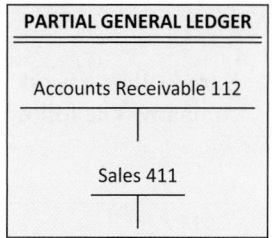

9B-2. Journalize, record, and post when appropriate the following transactions in the general journal (all sales carry terms of 5/10, n/30):

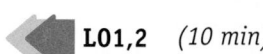 **L01,2** *(10 min)*

201X
Aug. 16 Sold merchandise on account to Ralph Co., invoice no. 1, $940.
     18 Sold merchandise on account to Market Co., invoice no. 2, $1,800.
     20 Issued credit memorandum no. 1 to Market Co. for defective merchandise, $720.

Use the following account numbers: Accounts Receivable, 112; Sales, 411; Sales Returns and Allowances, 412; Sales Discounts, 413.

9B-3. From Exercise 9B-2, journalize the receipt of a check from Ralph Co. for payment of invoice no. 1 on August 24.

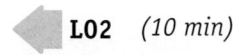 **L02** *(10 min)*

9B-4. From the following transactions for Autumn Co., journalize, record, post, and prepare a schedule of accounts receivable when appropriate.

L02,3 *(20 min)*

You will have to set up your own accounts receivable subsidiary ledger and partial general ledger as needed. All sales terms are 3/10, n/30.

201X		
Aug.	1	Andrew Rodgers invested $3,200 in the business.
	1	Sold merchandise on account to Clearview Co., invoice no. 1, $650.
	2	Sold merchandise on account to Nathan Co., invoice no. 2, $950.
	3	Cash sale, $200.
	8	Issued credit memorandum no. 1 to Clearview Co. for defective merchandise, $250.
	10	Received check from Clearview Co. for invoice no. 1, less returns and discount.
	15	Cash sale, $400.
	18	Sold merchandise on account to Clearview Co., invoice no. 3, $550.

(10 min)   **LO1**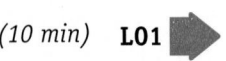

9B-5. From the following facts calculate what Becky Blain paid Rice Co. for the purchase of a dining room set. Sales terms are 1/10, n/30.

   a. Sales ticket price before tax, $10,000, dated April 5.
   b. Sales tax 5%.
   c. Returned one defective chair for credit of $800 on April 8.
   d. Paid bill on April 13.

MyAccountingLab

Problems

Set A

(40 min)   **LO1,2**

9A-1. Kate Collins has opened Fontina and Stuff, a wholesale grocery and cheese company. The following transactions occurred in February:

201X		
Feb.	1	Sold grocery merchandise to Fran Co. on account, $850, invoice no. 1.
	4	Sold cheese merchandise to Groom Co. on account, $1,100, invoice no. 2.
	8	Sold grocery merchandise to Dutch Co. on account, $1,100, invoice no. 3.
	10	Issued credit memorandum no. 1 to Fran Co. for $160 of grocery merchandise returned due to spoilage.
	15	Sold cheese merchandise to Groom Co. on account, $250, invoice no. 4.
	19	Sold grocery merchandise to Dutch Co. on account, $650, invoice no. 5.
	25	Sold cheese merchandise to Fran Co. on account, $700, invoice no. 6.

Check Figure:
Schedule of accounts
receivable $4,490

Required

   1. Journalize the transactions.
   2. Record to the accounts receivable subsidiary ledger and post to the general ledger as appropriate.
   3. Prepare a schedule of accounts receivable for the end of February.

(50 min)   **LO1,2,3**

9A-2. The following transactions of Jeff's Auto Supply occurred in February (Balances as of February 1 are given for general ledger and accounts receivable ledger accounts: Dick, $1,100 Dr.; Metcalf, $200 Dr.; Black,

$100 Dr.; Accounts Receivable, $1,400 Dr.; Sales Tax Payable, $1,100 Cr. Be sure to enter these balances in your working papers before beginning.):

201X		
Feb.	1	Sold auto parts merchandise to R. Dick on account, $800, invoice no. 10, plus 10% sales tax.
	5	Sold auto parts merchandise to J. Metcalf on account, $800, invoice no. 11, plus 10% sales tax.
	8	Sold auto parts merchandise to Lance Black on account, $6,000, invoice no. 12, plus 10% sales tax.
	10	Issued credit memorandum no. 12 to R. Dick for $700 for defective auto parts merchandise returned from Feb. 1 transaction. (Be careful to record the reduction in Sales Tax Payable as well.)
	12	Sold auto parts merchandise to J. Metcalf on account, $400, invoice no. 13, plus 10% sales tax.

Check Figure:
Schedule of accounts
receivable $9,430

Required

1. Journalize the transactions.
2. Record to the accounts receivable subsidiary ledger and post to the general ledger as appropriate.
3. Prepare a schedule of accounts receivable for the end of February.

9A-3. Jared Payne owns Payne's Sneaker Shop. (Balances as of March 1 are provided for the accounts receivable and general ledger accounts as follows: Durant, $250 Dr.; Lanham, $550 Dr.; Pry, $800 Dr.; Zamara, $550 Dr.; Cash, $15,500 Dr.; Accounts Receivable, $2,150 Dr.; Sneaker Rack Equipment, $1,150 Dr.; Jared Payne, Capital $35,000 Cr.; Sales, $2,100 Cr. Be sure to put beginning balances in your working papers.) The following transactions occurred in March:

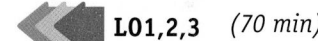 **LO1,2,3** *(70 min)*

201X		
March	1	Jared Payne invested an additional $10,500 in the sneaker store.
	3	Sold $700 of merchandise on account to B. Durant, sales ticket no. 50; terms 4/10, n/30.
	4	Sold $500 of merchandise on account to Ron Lanham, sales ticket no. 51; terms 4/10, n/30.
	9	Sold $200 of merchandise on account to Jim Zamara, sales ticket no. 52; terms 4/10, n/30.
	10	Received cash from B. Durant in payment of March 3 transaction, sales ticket no. 50, less discount.
	20	Sold $3,000 of merchandise on account to Penny Pry, sales ticket no. 53; terms 4/10, n/30.
	22	Received cash payment from Ron Lanham in payment of March 4 transaction, sales ticket no. 51.
	23	Collected cash sales, $3,400.
	24	Issued credit memorandum no. 1 to Penny Pry for $2,000 of merchandise returned from March 20 sales on account.
	26	Received cash from Penny Pry in payment of March 20, sales ticket no. 53. (Don't forget about the credit memo and discount.)
	28	Collected cash sales, $6,200.
	30	Sold sneaker rack equipment for $150 cash. (Beware, sold at cost.)
	30	Sold merchandise priced at $3,400, on account to Ron Lanham, sales ticket no. 54; terms 4/10, n/30.
	31	Issued credit memorandum no. 2 to Ron Lanham for $595 of merchandise returned from March 30 transaction, sales ticket no. 54.

Check Figure:
Schedule of accounts
receivable $5,155

Required

1. Journalize the transactions.
2. Record to the accounts receivable subsidiary ledger and post to the general ledger as needed.
3. Prepare a schedule of accounts receivable for the end of March.

(75 min)   **LO1,2,3**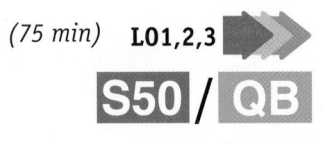

9A-4.   Chevy Canton opened Chevy's Cosmetic Market on May 1. A 16% sales tax is calculated and added to all cosmetic sales. Chevy offers no sales discounts. The following transactions occurred in May:

201X		
May	1	Chevy Canton invested $9,500 in the Cosmetic Market from his personal savings account.
	5	From the cash register tapes, lipstick cash sales were $4,600, plus sales tax.
	5	From the cash register tapes, eye shadow cash sales were $1,900, plus sales tax.
	8	Sold lipstick on account to Lois Kozak Co., $550, sales ticket no. 1, plus sales tax.
	9	Sold eye shadow on account to Ann Marie Maxwell Co., $1,600, sales ticket no. 2, plus sales tax.
	15	Issued credit memorandum no. 1 to Lois Kozak Co. for $250 for lipstick returned. (Be sure to reduce Sales Tax Payable for Chevy.)
	19	Ann Marie Maxwell Co. paid half the amount owed from sales ticket no. 2, dated May 9.
	21	Sold lipstick on account to David Parnell Co., $400, sales ticket no. 3, plus sales tax.
	24	Sold eye shadow on account to Everette Tennis Co., $550, sales ticket no. 4, plus sales tax.
	25	Issued credit memorandum no. 2 to David Parnell Co. for $200 for lipstick returned from sales ticket no. 3, dated May 21.
	29	Cash sales taken from the cash register tape showed the following: 1. Lipstick: $1,200 + $192 sales tax collected. 2. Eye shadow: $2,400 + $384 sales tax collected.
	29	Sold lipstick on account to Ann Marie Maxwell Co., $550, sales ticket no. 5, plus sales tax.
	31	Received payment from Ann Marie Maxwell Co. of sales ticket no. 5, dated May 29.

Check Figure:
Schedule of accounts
receivable $2,146

Required

1. Journalize, record, and post as appropriate.
2. Prepare a schedule of accounts receivable for the end of May.

Set B

(40 min)   **LO1,2**

9B-1.   Sandra Hills has opened Macchiato and More, a wholesale grocery and coffee company. The following transactions occurred in June:

201X		
June	1	Sold grocery merchandise to Fran Co. on account, $700, invoice no. 1.
	4	Sold coffee merchandise to Groom Co. on account, $650, invoice no. 2.
	8	Sold grocery merchandise to Dutch Co. on account, $750, invoice no. 3.
	10	Issued credit memorandum no. 1 to Fran Co. for $170 of grocery merchandise returned due to spoilage.
	15	Sold coffee merchandise to Groom Co. on account, $700, invoice no. 4.
	19	Sold grocery merchandise to Dutch Co. on account, $700, invoice no. 5.
	25	Sold coffee merchandise to Fran Co. on account, $400, invoice no. 6.

Check Figure:
Schedule of accounts
receivable $3,730

Required

1. Journalize the transactions.
2. Record to the accounts receivable subsidiary ledger and post to the general ledger as appropriate.
3. Prepare a schedule of accounts receivable for the end of June.

9B-2. The following transactions of Jack's Auto Supply occurred in January (Balances as of January 1 are given for general ledger and accounts receivable ledger accounts: Nonack, $1,400 Dr.; Seth, $50 Dr.; Corner, $200 Dr.; Accounts Receivable, $1,650 Dr.; Sales Tax Payable, $1,000 Cr. Be sure to enter these balances in your working papers before beginning.):

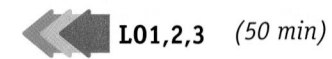 **LO1,2,3** *(50 min)*

201X		
January	1	Sold auto parts merchandise to R. Nonack on account, $700, invoice no. 70, plus 2% sales tax.
	5	Sold auto parts merchandise to J. Seth on account, $600, invoice no. 71, plus 2% sales tax.
	8	Sold auto parts merchandise to Lance Corner on account, $11,000, invoice no. 72, plus 2% sales tax.
	10	Issued credit memorandum no. 12 to R. Nonack for $950 for defective auto parts merchandise returned from January 1 transaction. (Be careful to record the reduction in Sales Tax Payable as well.)
	12	Sold auto parts merchandise to J. Seth on account, $600, invoice no. 73, plus 2% sales tax.

Check Figure:
Schedule of accounts
receivable $13,839

Required

1. Journalize the transactions.
2. Record to the accounts receivable subsidiary ledger and post to the general ledger as appropriate.
3. Prepare a schedule of accounts receivable for the end of January.

9B-3. Max Peney owns Peney's Sneaker Shop. (Balances as of August 1 are provided for the accounts receivable and general ledger accounts as follows: Donovan, $375 Dr.; Littler, $900 Dr.; Pry, $750 Dr.; Zamora, $350 Dr.; Cash, $16,500 Dr.; Accounts Receivable, $2,375 Dr.; Sneaker Rack Equipment, $1,000 Dr.; Max Peney, Capital, $42,000 Cr.; Sales, $2,400 Cr. Be sure to put them in your working papers.) The following transactions occurred in August:

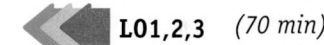 **LO1,2,3** *(70 min)*

201X		
August	1	Max Peney invested an additional $13,500 in the sneaker store.
	3	Sold $600 of merchandise on account to B. Donovan, sales ticket no. 70; terms 4/10, n/30.
	4	Sold $400 of merchandise on account to Ron Littler, sales ticket no. 71; terms 4/10, n/30.
	9	Sold $100 of merchandise on account to Jim Zamora, sales ticket no. 72; terms 4/10, n/30.
	10	Received cash from B. Donovan in payment of August 3 transaction, sales ticket no. 70, less discount.
	20	Sold $4,000 of merchandise on account to Page Pry, sales ticket no. 73; terms 4/10, n/30.
	22	Received cash payment from Ron Littler in payment of August 4 transaction, sales ticket no. 71.
	23	Collected cash sales, $3,000.

24	Issued credit memorandum no. 1 to Page Pry for $2,100 of merchandise returned from August 20 sales on account.
26	Received cash from Page Pry in payment of August 20 sales ticket no. 73. (Don't forget about the credit memo and discount.)
28	Collected cash sales, $6,600.
30	Sold sneaker rack equipment for $650 cash. (Beware, sold at cost.)
30	Sold merchandise priced at $4,400 on account to Ron Littler, sales ticket no. 74, terms 4/10, n/30.
31	Issued credit memorandum no. 2 to Ron Littler for $770 of merchandise returned from August 30 transaction, sales ticket no. 74.

Check Figure:
Schedule of accounts
receivable $6,105

Required

1. Journalize the transactions.
2. Record to the accounts receivable subsidiary ledger and post to the general ledger as needed.
3. Prepare a schedule of accounts receivable for the end of August.

(75 min) **L01,2,3**

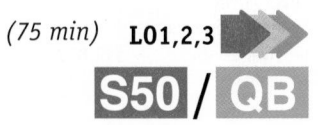

9B-4. Al Franklin opened Al's Cosmetic Market on December 1. An 8% sales tax is calculated and added to all cosmetic sales. Al offers no sales discounts. The following transactions occurred in December:

201X

Dec.	1	Al Franklin invested $6,000 in the Cosmetic Market from his personal savings account.
	5	From the cash register tapes, lipstick cash sales were $5,100, plus sales tax.
	5	From the cash register tapes, eye shadow cash sales were $1,700, plus sales tax.
	8	Sold lipstick on account to Alexander Kozlosky Co., $200, sales ticket no. 1, plus sales tax.
	9	Sold eye shadow on account to Douglas Sabin Co., $800, sales ticket no. 2, plus sales tax.
	15	Issued credit memorandum no. 1 to Alexander Kozlosky Co. for $100 for lipstick returned. (Be sure to reduce Sales Tax Payable for Al.)
	19	Douglas Sabin Co. paid half the amount owed from sales ticket no. 2, dated December 9.
	21	Sold lipstick on account to John Tobin Co., $350, sales ticket no. 3, plus sales tax.
	24	Sold eye shadow on account to Edward Wease Co., $1,000, sales ticket no. 4, plus sales tax.
	25	Issued credit memorandum no. 2 to John Tobin Co. for $250 for lipstick returned from sales ticket no. 3, dated December 21.
	29	Cash sales taken from the cash register tape showed the following: 1. Lipstick: $900 + $72 sales tax collected. 2. Eye shadow: $2,900 + $232 sales tax collected.
	29	Sold lipstick on account to Douglas Sabin Co., $300, sales ticket no. 5, plus sales tax.
	31	Received payment from Douglas Sabin Co. of sales ticket no. 5, dated December 29.

Check Figure:
Schedule of accounts
receivable $1,728

Required

1. Journalize, record, and post as appropriate.
2. Prepare a schedule of accounts receivable for the end of December.

Financial Report Problem

Reading the Kellogg's Annual Report

◀ LO1   (15 min)

Go to http://investor.kelloggs.com/investor-relations/annual-reports to access the Kellogg's 2013 Annual Report and see how Kellogg's records revenue. You will find this information in Note 1.

MyAccountingLab

ON THE JOB SMITH COMPUTER CENTER

To assist you in recording these transactions for the month of January, at the end of this problem is the schedule of accounts receivable as of December 31 and an updated chart of accounts with the current balance listed for each account.

Assignment

1. Journalize the transactions.

2. Record in the accounts receivable subsidiary ledger and post to the general ledger as appropriate. A partial subsidiary ledger is included in the working papers that accompany this text.

   The following accounts have been added to the chart of accounts: Sales #4010, Sales Returns and Allowances #4020, and Sales Discounts #4030.

3. Prepare a schedule of accounts receivable as of January 31, 201X.

   The January transactions are as follows:

Jan.	1	Sold $780 worth of merchandise to Phil's Photography on credit, sales invoice no. 5000; terms 3/10, n/30.
	10	Sold $3,600 worth of merchandise on account to Dr. Michael Turiono, sales invoice no. 5001; terms 3/10, n/30.
	11	Received $2,800 from All Star Sports, Inc., toward payment of its balance; no discount allowed.
	12	Collected $2,800 cash sales.
	19	Sold $4,500 worth of merchandise on account to Worldwide Professionals, sales invoice no. 5002; terms 2/10, n/30.
	20	Collected balance in full from Dr. Michael Turiono, invoice no. 5001.
	29	Issued credit memorandum to Phil's Photography for $460 worth of merchandise returned, invoice no. 5000.
	29	Collected full payment from Worldwide Professionals, invoice no. 5002.

Schedule of Accounts Receivable Smith Computer Center December 31, 201X	
Phil's Photography	$ 3,775.00
Worldwide Professionals	7,400.00
All Star Sports, Inc.	4,400.00
Total Amount Due	$15,575.00

Chart of Accounts and Current Balances as of 12/31/1X

Account #	Account Name	Debit Balance	Credit Balance
1000	Cash	$ 5,861.76	
1010	Petty Cash	300.00	
1020	Accounts Receivable	15,575.00	
1021	Merchandise Inventory	0	
1025	Prepaid Rent	2,000.00	
1030	Supplies	192.00	
1080	Computer Shop Equipment	5,700.00	
1081	Accumulated Dep., C.S. Equip.		$ 150.00
1090	Office Equipment	3,850.00	
1091	Accumulated Dep., Office Equip.		110.00
2000	Accounts Payable		2,570.00
2010	Wages Payable		0
2020	FICA—OASDI Payable		0
2030	FICA—Medicare Payable		0
2040	FIT Payable		0
2050	SIT Payable		0
2060	FUTA Payable		0
2070	SUTA Payable		0
3000	Feldman, Capital		12,282.00
3010	Feldman, Withdrawals	915.00	
3020	Income Summary		0
4000	Service Revenue		21,800.00
4010	Sales		0
4020	Sales Returns and Allowances	0	
4030	Sales Discounts	0	
5010	Advertising Expense	0	
5020	Rent Expense	0	
5030	Utilities Expense	0	
5040	Phone Expense	170.00	
5050	Supplies Expense	45.00	
5060	Insurance Expense	0	
5070	Postage Expense	40.00	
5080	Dep. Exp., C.S. Equipment	0	
5090	Dep. Exp., Office Equipment	0	
5100	Miscellaneous Expense	15.00	
5110	Wage Expense	2,030.00	
5120	Payroll Tax Expense	218.24	
5130	Interest Expense	0	
5140	Bad Debt Expense	0	
6000	Purchases	0	
6010	Purchases Returns and Allowances		0
6020	Purchases Discounts		0
6030	Freight In	0	

Purchases and Cash Payments

CHAPTER PREVIEW: THE BIG PICTURE

Joy Flynn heads to Best Buy to purchase a new XBox One. The advertisement says there are limited quantities so she asks the salesperson if the model is in stock. The salesperson goes to the computer and searches the inventory. Yes, there is one left in stock. Joy buys it, and now that item is reported temporarily out of stock. In this chapter, you learn how inventory is accounted for (be it manually or by computer) when purchased by a company and sold to a buyer.

Learning Objectives

LO1 Explain and Journalize Purchases Transactions, Including Freight

LO2 Journalize and Record Transactions to the Accounts Payable Subsidiary Ledger and Post to the General Ledger Along with a Debit Memorandum

LO3 Journalize, Record, and Post Cash Payments Transactions and Prepare a Schedule of Accounts Payable

LO4 Explain and Journalize Transactions for a Perpetual Inventory System

L01 ▶

Purchases Transactions, Including Freight

Purchases

Purchases Merchandise for resale. It is a cost.

When you go into your local Target, do you ever wonder how a store records all of the merchandise it purchases from a company like Sony? First, let us look at Chou's Toy Shop. Chou brings merchandise into his toy store for resale to customers. The account that records the cost of this merchandise is called Purchases. Suppose Chou buys $4,000 worth of Barbie dolls on account from Mattel Manufacturing on July 6. The Purchases account records all merchandise bought for resale.

	Purchases	
	Dr.	Cr.
Purchases is a cost.		
The rules work the same as an expense.	4,000	

This account has a debit balance and is classified as a cost. Purchases represent costs that are directly related to bringing merchandise into the store for resale to customers. The July 6 entry would be analyzed and journalized as in Figure 10.1.

COACHING TIP

If Chou's purchased a new display case for the store, it would not show up in the Purchases account. The case is considered equipment that is not for resale to customers.

Accounts Affected	Category	↑↓	Rules	T Account Update			
Purchases	Cost	↑	Dr.	**Purchases**			
				Dr.	Cr.		
				4,000			
Accounts Payable, Mattel	Liability	↑	Cr.	**Acc. Payable**		**Mattel**	
				Dr.	Cr.	Dr.	Cr.
					4,000		4,000

FIGURE 10.1
Purchased Merchandise on Account

	Jul.	6	Purchases		4 0 0 0 00		
			Accounts Payable, Mattel			4 0 0 0 00	
			Purchases on account				

Keep in mind that we would have to record to Mattel in the accounts payable subsidiary ledger. We talk about the subsidiary ledger in Learning Unit 10-2.

Purchases Returns and Allowances

Purchases Returns and Allowances A contra-cost account in the ledger that records the amount of defective or unacceptable merchandise returned to suppliers and/or price reductions given for defective items.

Chou noticed that some of the dolls he received were defective, and he notified the manufacturer of the defects. On July 9, Mattel issued a credit memorandum indicating that Chou would get a $500 reduction from the original selling price. Chou then agreed to keep the dolls. The account that records a decrease to a buyer's cost is a contra-cost account called Purchases Returns and Allowances. The account lowers the cost of purchases.

Purchases Returns and Allowances	
Dr.	Cr.
	500 ◀——— **Normal balance is a credit.**

Let's analyze this reduction to cost and prepare a general journal entry (Figure 10.2).

Accounts Affected	Category	↑↓	Rules	T Account Update			
Accounts Payable, Mattel	Liability	↓	Dr.	**Acc. Payable**		**Mattel**	
				Dr. | Cr.		Dr. | Cr.	
				500 | 4,000		500 | 4,000	
Purchases Returns and Allowances	Contra-cost	↑	Cr.	**Purchases Ret. & Allow.**			
				Dr. | Cr.			
				| 500			

When posted to general ledger accounts as well as recorded to Mattel in the accounts payable subsidiary ledger, Chou owes $500 less.

Jul.	9	Accounts Payable, Mattel				5 0 0 00							
		Purchases Returns and Allowances									5 0 0 00		
		Received credit memorandum											

FIGURE 10.2
Credit Memorandum Received

Purchases Discount. Now let's look at the analysis and journal entry when Chou pays Mattel. Mattel offers a 2% cash discount if the invoice is paid within 10 days. To take advantage of this cash discount, Chou sent a check to Mattel on July 15. The discount is taken after the allowance.

$4,000

− 500 allowance

$3,500 × 0.02 = $70 purchases discount

The account that records this discount is called Purchases Discount. It, too, is a contra-cost account because it lowers the cost of purchases.

Purchases Discount

Dr. | Cr.

| 70 ◄——— **Normal balance is a credit.**

Let's analyze and prepare a general journal entry (Figure 10.3).

> **COACHING TIP**
>
> *Remember:* For Chou it is a purchases discount, whereas for Mattel it is a sales discount.
>
> **Purchases Discount**
> A contra-cost account in the general ledger that records discounts offered by vendors of merchandise for prompt payment of purchases by buyers.

> **COACHING TIP**
>
> *Remember:* Purchases are debits; purchases discounts are credits.

FIGURE 10.3
Purchase Discount Journalized

Jul.	15	Accounts Payable, Mattel				3 5 0 0 00							
		Purchases Discount								7 0 00		
		Cash								3 4 3 0 00		
		Paid Mattel balance owed										

Accounts Affected	Category	↑↓	Rules	T Account Update			
Accounts Payable, Mattel	Liability	↓	Dr.	**Acc. Payable**		**Mattel**	
				Dr. | Cr.		Dr. | Cr.	
				500 | 4,000		500 | 4,000	
				3,500 |		3,500 |	
Purchases Discount	Contra-cost	↑	Cr.	**Purchases Discount**			
				Dr. | Cr.			
				| 70			
Cash	Asset	↓	Cr.	**Cash**			
				Dr. | Cr.			
				| 3,430			

After the journal entry is posted and recorded to Mattel, the result will show that Chou saved $70 and reduced what he owed to Mattel. The actual—or net—cost of his purchase is $3,430, calculated as follows:

Purchases	$4,000
− Purchases Returns and Allowances	500
− Purchases Discounts	70
= Net Purchases	$3,430

Freight charges are not taken into consideration in calculating net purchases. Still, they are important. If the seller is responsible for paying the shipping cost until the goods reach their destination, the freight charges are F.O.B. destination. (F.O.B. stands for "free on board" the carrier.) For example, if a seller located in Boston sold goods F.O.B. destination to a buyer in New York, the seller would have to pay the cost of shipping the goods to the buyer.

F.O.B. destination *Seller* pays or is responsible for the cost of freight to purchaser's location or destination.

If the buyer is responsible for paying the shipping costs, the freight charges are F.O.B. shipping point. In this situation, the seller will sometimes prepay the freight charges as a matter of convenience and will add it to the invoice of the purchaser, as in the following example:

F.O.B. shipping point *Purchaser* pays or is responsible for the shipping costs from seller's shipping point to purchaser's location.

Bill amount ($800 + $80 prepaid freight)	$880
Less: 5% cash discount (0.05 × $800)	40
Amount to be paid by buyer	$840

Purchases discounts are not taken on freight. The discount is based on the purchase price.

If the seller ships goods F.O.B. shipping point, legal ownership (title) passes to the buyer *when the goods are shipped.* If goods are shipped by the seller F.O.B. destination, title will change *when goods have reached their destination.* (See Exhibit 10.1.)

EXHIBIT 10.1

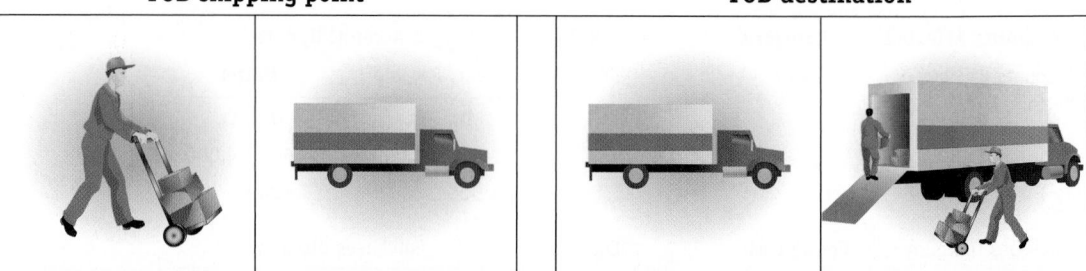

FOB shipping point	FOB destination
FOB shipping point: Title changes hands at the shipping point, and buyer owns the goods while they are in transit. So, the buyer pays the shipping costs.	**FOB destination:** Title changes hands at the destination point, and seller owns the goods while they are in transit. So, the seller, not the buyer, pays the shipping costs.

Now let's check your progress.

 **TRY IT!**   Learning Unit 10-1

Complete the following chart:

Account	Category	Rules of Debit/Credit		Financial Statement
		Inc.	**Dec.**	
Cash				
Accounts Payable				
Purchases				
Purchases Discounts				
Purchases Returns and Allowances				

Journalizing and Recording Transactions to the Accounts Payable Subsidiary Ledger and Posting to the General Ledger Along with a Debit Memorandum

LEARNING UNIT 10-2

 L02

201X		
Apr.	3	Purchased merchandise on account, $5,000, and freight, $50, from Abby Blake Co.; terms 2/10, n/60.
	4	Purchased equipment on account, $4,000, from Joe Francis Co. No discount.
	6	Purchased merchandise on account, $800, from Thorpe Co.; terms 1/10, n/30.
	7	Purchased merchandise on account, $980, from John Sullivan Co.; terms n/10, EOM.
	9	Art's issued debit memo #1, $200, to Thorpe for defective merchandise.
	12	Purchased merchandise on account, $600, from Abby Blake Co.; terms 1/10, n/30.
	25	Purchased $500 of supplies on account from John Sullivan Co.

Let's look at the steps Art's Wholesale Clothing Company took when it ordered goods from Abby Blake Company on April 3.

Step 1: Prepare a Purchase Requisition at Art's Wholesale Clothing Company. The inventory clerk notes a low inventory level of ladies' jackets for resale, so the clerk sends a purchase requisition to the purchasing department. A duplicate copy is sent to the accounting department. A third copy remains with the department that initiated the request to be used as a check on the purchasing department.

Step 2: Purchasing Department of Art's Wholesale Clothing Company Prepares a Purchase Order. After checking various price lists and suppliers' catalogs, the purchasing department fills out a form called a purchase order. This form gives Abby Blake Company the authority to ship the ladies' jackets ordered by Art's Wholesale Clothing Company (see Figure 10.4, page 354).

Purchase requisition A form used within a business by the requesting department asking the purchasing department of the business to buy specific goods.

Purchase order A form used in business to place an order for the buying of goods from a seller.

FIGURE 10.4
Purchase Order

```
                 PURCHASE ORDER NO. 1
             ART'S WHOLESALE CLOTHING COMPANY
                     1528 BELLE AVE.
                    NEW YORK, NY 10022
```

Purchased From:	Abby Blake Company 12 Foster Road Englewood Cliffs, NJ 07632	Date: April 1, 201X Shipped VIA: Freight Truck Terms: 2/10, n/60 FOB: Englewood Cliffs

Quantity	Description	Unit Price	Total
100	Ladies' Jackets Code 14–0	$50	$5,000

Art's Wholesale
By: Bill Joy

Purchase order number must appear on all invoices.

Step 3: Sales Invoice Prepared by Abby Blake Company. Abby Blake Company receives the purchase order and prepares a sales invoice. The sales invoice for the seller is the purchase invoice for the buyer. A sales invoice is shown in Figure 10.5.

Purchase invoice The seller's sales invoice, which is sent to the purchaser.

FIGURE 10.5
Sales Invoice

```
                   SALES INVOICE NO. 228
                    ABBY BLAKE COMPANY
                     12 FOSTER ROAD
                 ENGLEWOOD, CLIFFS, NJ 07632
```

Sold To:	Art's Wholesale Clothing Co. 1528 Belle Ave. New York, NY 10022	Date: April 3, 201X Shipped VIA: Freight Truck Terms: 2/10, n/60 Your Order No: 1 FOB: Englewood Cliffs

Quantity	Description	Unit Price	Total
100	Ladies' Jackets Code 14–0 Freight	$50	$5,000 50 $5,050

The invoice shows that the goods will be shipped F.O.B. Englewood Cliffs. Thus, Art's Wholesale Clothing Company is responsible for paying the shipping costs.

The sales invoice also shows a freight charge. Thus, Abby Blake prepaid the shipping costs as a matter of convenience. Art's will repay the freight charges when it pays the invoice.

Step 4: Receiving the Goods. When goods are received, Art's Wholesale inspects the shipment and completes a receiving report. The receiving report verifies that the exact merchandise that was ordered was received in good condition.

Receiving report A business form used to notify the appropriate people of the ordered goods received along with the quantities and specific condition of the goods.

Invoice approval form Used by the accounting department in checking the invoice and finally approving it for recording and payment.

Step 5: Verifying the Numbers. Before the invoice is approved for recording and payment, the accounting department must check the purchase order, invoice, and receiving report to make sure that all are in agreement and that no steps have been omitted. The form used for checking and approval is an invoice approval form (see Figure 10.6).

```
┌─────────────────────────────────────────────────┐
│              INVOICE APPROVAL FORM                │
│            Art's Wholesale Clothing Co.           │
├─────────────────────────────────┬───────────────┤
│ Purchase Order #                │ _____   │
│ Requisition check               │ _____   │
│ Purchase Order check            │ _____   │
│ Receiving Report check          │ _____   │
│ Invoice check                   │ _____   │
│ Approved for Payment            │ _____   │
└─────────────────────────────────┴───────────────┘
```

FIGURE 10.6
Invoice Approval Form

Keep in mind that Art's Wholesale Clothing Company does not record this purchase until the *invoice is approved for recording and payment*. Abby Blake Company records this transaction in its records when the sales invoice is prepared, however.

Let's look closer at the April 3 transaction.

201X		
Apr.	3	Purchased merchandise on account, $5,000, plus freight, $50, from Abby Blake Co.

THE ANALYSIS

Accounts Affected	Category	↑↓	Rules of Dr. and Cr.
Purchases	Cost	↑	Dr. $5,000
Freight-In	Cost	↑	Dr. $50
Accounts Payable, Abby Blake Co.	Liability	↑	Cr. $5,050

COACHING TIP

	Buyer		Seller	
Purchases	Dr. Cost	Sale	Cr.	Revenue
PRA	Cr. Contra-cost	SRA	Dr.	Contra-revenue
PD	Cr. Contra-cost	SD	Dr.	Contra-revenue

Figure 10.7 shows how the general journal would look.

									Page 2		
Apr.	3	Purchases			5 0 0 0 00						
		Freight-In			5 0 00						
		Accounts Payable, Abby Blake Co.						5 0 5 0 00			
		Purchased merchandise on account									
		From Abby Blake									

FIGURE 10.7
Merchandise Purchase, Plus Freight Cost

Accounts Payable Subsidiary Ledger

In the last chapter we saw the accounts receivable subsidiary ledger. It listed customers owing Art's money from sales on account. Now we look at Art's, the buyer, and an accounts payable subsidiary ledger. See Figure 10.8 (page 356).

Note that the normal balance is a credit for Accounts Payable and its subsidiary ledger, whereas in the last chapter Accounts Receivable had a debit normal balance.

Accounts Payable is the controlling account in the ledger and at the end of the month the sum of the individual amounts owed to the creditors should equal the balance in Accounts Payable at the end of the month.

Figure 10.9 (page 356) shows how the general journal looks for Art's before posting and recording this month's purchases on account.

Accounts payable subsidiary ledger A book or file that contains, in alphabetical order, the name of the creditor and amount owed from purchases on account.

FIGURE 10.8

Partial General Ledger of Art's Wholesale Clothing Company and Accounts Payable Subsidiary Ledger

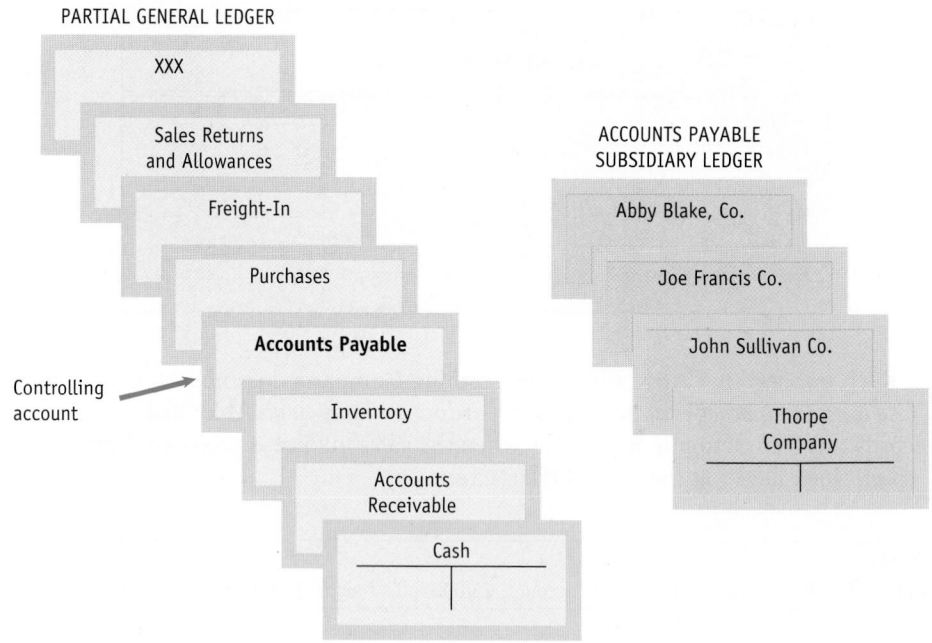

FIGURE 10.9

General Journal Before Posting and Recording

		GENERAL JOURNAL											Page 2			
Date		Account Titles and Description	PR			Dr.							Cr.			
201X																
Apr.	3	Purchases			5	0	0	0	00							
		Freight-In					5	0	00							
		Accounts Payable, Abby Blake Co.									5	0	5	0	00	
		Purchased merchandise on account, Blake														
	4	Equipment			4	0	0	0	00							
		Accounts Payable, Joe Francis									4	0	0	0	00	
		Purchased equipment on account, Francis														
	6	Purchases				8	0	0	00							
		Accounts Payable, Thorpe Company										8	0	0	00	
		Purchased merchandise on account, Thorpe														
	7	Purchases				9	8	0	00							
		Accounts Payable, John Sullivan Co.										9	8	0	00	
		Purchased merchandise on account, Sullivan														
	9	Accounts Payable, Thorpe Company				2	0	0	00							
		Purchases Returns and Allowances										2	0	0	00	
		Debit memo no. 1														
	12	Purchases				6	0	0	00							
		Accounts Payable, Abby Blake Co.										6	0	0	00	
		Purchased merchandise on account, Blake														
	25	Supplies				5	0	0	00							
		Accounts Payable, John Sullivan Co.										5	0	0	00	
		Purchased supplies on account, Sullivan														

Posting and Recording Purchases Transactions. Before we post to the general ledger and record to the subsidiary ledger, let's first examine the T accounts and what each one would look like.

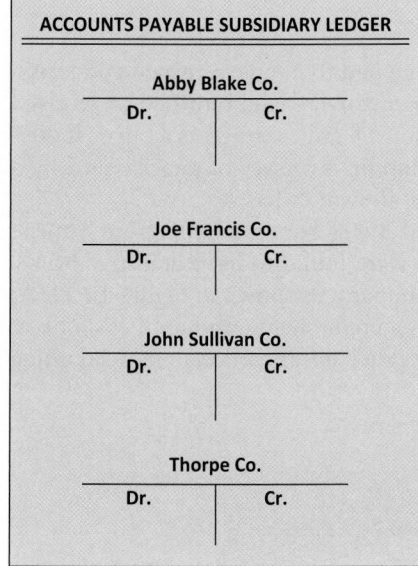

Now let's look at how to post and record the April 3 transaction.

For this transaction we post to the general ledger accounts Purchases, Freight-In, and Accounts Payable. Note how the account numbers 511, 514, and 211 are entered into the PR column of the general journal. We must also *record* to Abby Blake Co. in the accounts payable subsidiary ledger. Note that it is placed on the credit side because we owe Abby the money. When the subsidiary ledger is updated, a (✔) is placed in the PR column of the general journal. Figure 10.10 shows how the accounts

	GENERAL JOURNAL				Page 2	
Date	Account Titles and Description	PR	Dr.		Cr.	
201X						
Apr. 3	Purchases	511	5 0 0 0 00			
	Freight-In	514	5 0 00			
	Accounts Payable, Abby Blake Co.	211 ✔			5 0 5 0 00	
	Purchased merchandise on account, Blake					

FIGURE 10.10
Posting and Recording the April 3 Transaction

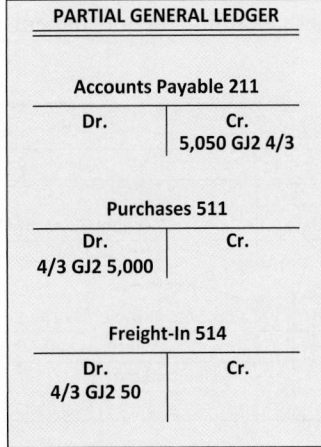

payable subsidiary ledger and the partial general ledger would look after posting and recording.

Before concluding this unit, let's take a closer look at the April 9 transaction when Art's issues a debit memorandum to Thorpe Company. We analyze the transaction and show how to post and record it.

Debit Memorandum

In Chapter 9, Art's Wholesale Clothing Company had to handle returned goods as a seller. It did so by issuing credit memoranda to customers who returned or received an allowance on the price. In this chapter, Art's must handle returns as a buyer. It does so by using debit memoranda. A debit memorandum is a piece of paper issued by a customer to a seller. It indicates that a return or allowance has occurred.

On April 6, Art's Wholesale had purchased men's hats for $800 from Thorpe Company. On April 9, 20 hats valued at $200 were found to have defective brims. Art's issued a debit memorandum to Thorpe Company, as shown in Figure 10.11. At some point in the future, Thorpe will issue Art's a credit memorandum. Let's look at how Art's Wholesale Clothing Company handles such a transaction in its accounting records.

Debit memorandum A memo issued by a purchaser to a seller, indicating that some Purchases Returns and Allowances have occurred and therefore the purchaser now owes less money on account.

FIGURE 10.11
Debit Memorandum

DEBIT MEMORANDUM	No. 1

Art's Wholesale
Clothing Company
1528 Belle Ave.
New York, NY 10022

TO: Thorpe Comany   April 9, 201X
   3 Access Road
   Beverly, MA 01915

WE DEBIT your account as follows:

Quantity		Unit Cost	Total
20	Men's Hats Code 827 – defective brims	$10	$200

Journalizing and Posting the Debit Memo.   First, let's look at a transactional analysis chart.

Accounts Affected	Category	↑↓	Rules
Accounts Payable	Liability	↓	Dr.
Purchases Returns and Allowances	Contra-cost	↑	Cr.

Next, let's examine the journal entry for the debit memorandum (Figure 10.12).

COACHING TIP

Result of debit memo: debits or reduces Accounts Payable. On seller's books, accounts affected would include Sales Returns and Allowances and Accounts Receivable.

FIGURE 10.12
Debit Memorandum Journalized and Posted

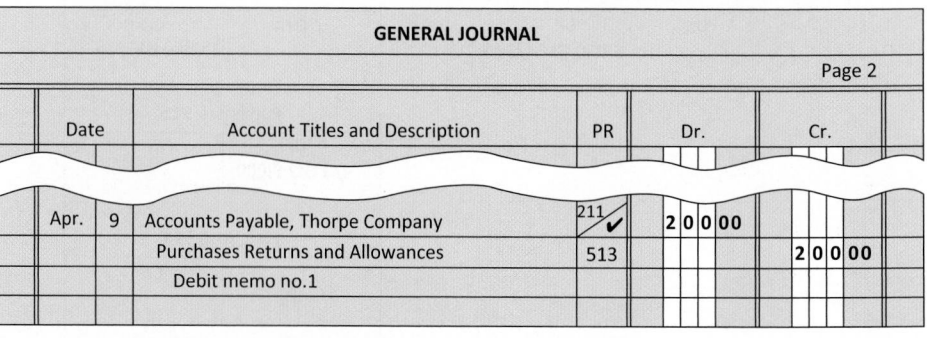

	GENERAL JOURNAL				
					Page 2
Date	Account Titles and Description	PR	Dr.	Cr.	
Apr. 9	Accounts Payable, Thorpe Company	211 ✓	2 0 0 00		
	Purchases Returns and Allowances	513		2 0 0 00	
	Debit memo no.1				

The two postings and one recording are the following:

1. 211: Post to Accounts Payable as a debit in the general ledger (account no. 211). When done, place in the PR column the account number, 211, above the diagonal on the same line as Accounts Payable in the journal.

2. ✓: Record to Thorpe Co. in the accounts payable subsidiary ledger to show that Art's doesn't owe Thorpe as much money. When done, place a ✓ in the journal in the PR column below the diagonal line on the same line as Accounts Payable in the journal. Remember, this check is for a manual system only. In a computerized system, both the general ledger and the subsidiary ledger are updated automatically when you click on "post."

3. 513: Post to Purchases Returns and Allowances as a credit in the general ledger (account no. 513). When done, place the account number, 513, in the PR column of the journal on the same line as Purchases Returns and Allowances. (If equipment was returned that was not merchandise for resale, we would credit Equipment and not Purchases Returns and Allowances.)

COACHING TIP

PURCHASES RETURNS AND ALLOWANCES

Dr.	Cr.
−	+

The following are the completed accounts payable subsidiary ledger and general ledger for Art's:

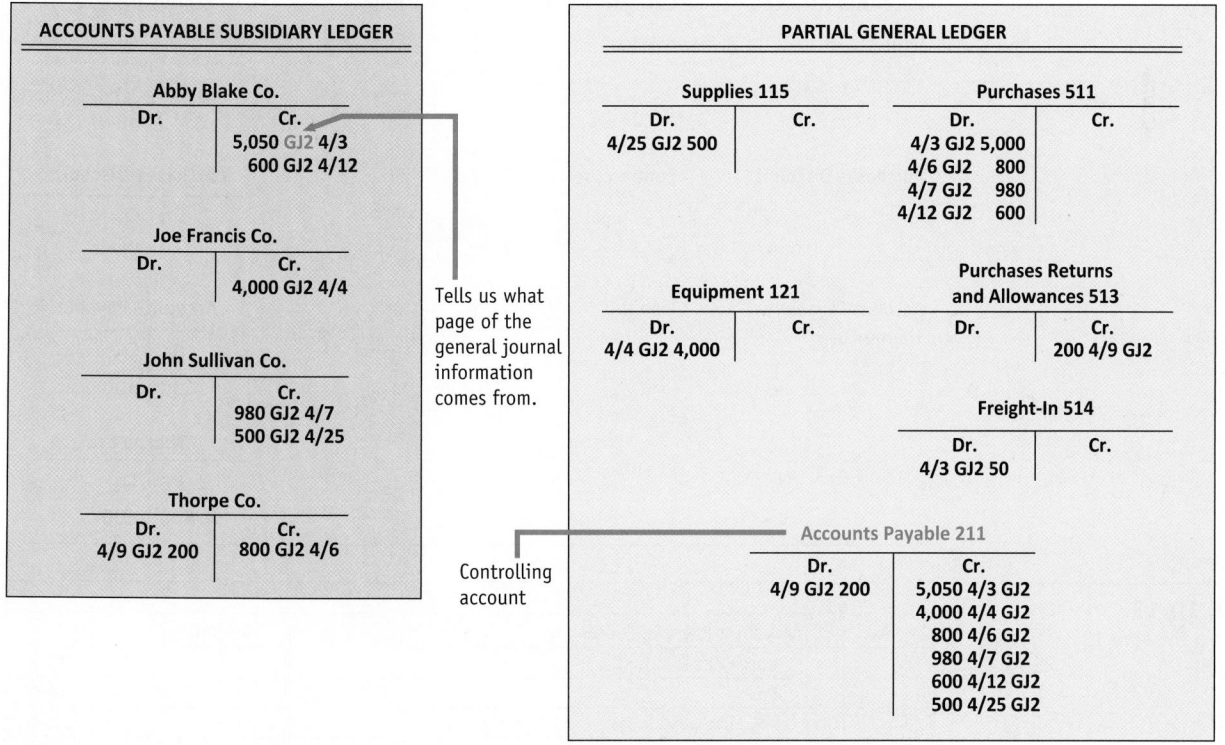

Now let's check your progress.

 TRY IT!   **Learning Unit 10-2**

Journalize, record, and post the following transactions for Moore Co. for July 201X (journal record is page 2). The partial ledger should include: Cash 110 balance of $8,000; Equipment 140; Accounts Payable 210; Purchases 500; Purchases Returns and Allowances 510; Freight-In 514.

Beam Co. is located in the Accounts Payable Subsidiary Ledger

July 5	Purchased merchandise on account, $400, and freight, $25, from Beam Co.; invoice no. 1; Terms 1/10, n/30	
7	Purchased equipment on account, $700, from Beam Co., invoice no. 2, no discount.	
22	Issued debit memorandum no. 1, $100, to Beam Co. for merchandise returned from invoice no. 1	

Cash Payments Transactions and Schedules of Accounts Payable

The following cash payment transactions occurred for Art's Wholesale Clothing Company in April.

201X		
Apr.	2	Issued check no. 1 to Pete Blum for insurance paid in advance, $900.
	7	Issued check no. 2 to Joe Francis Company in payment of its April 4 invoice no. 388.
	9	Issued check no. 3 to Rick Flo Co. for merchandise purchased for cash, $800.
	12	Issued check no. 4 to Thorpe Company in payment of its April 6 invoice no. 414, less the return and 1% discount.
	28	Issued check no. 5, $700, for salaries paid.

Figure 10.13 provides a closer look at how the April 12 transaction would be journalized.

Accounts Affected	Category	↑↓	Rules	T Account Update
Cash	Asset	↓	Cr.	**Cash** Dr. | Cr. | 594
Purchases Discount	Contra-cost	↑	Cr.	**Purchases Discount** Dr. | Cr. | 6
Account Payable, Thorpe Co.	Liability	↓	Dr.	**Accounts Payable** Dr. | Cr. 600 | 600 **Thorpe Co.** Dr. | Cr. 600 | 600

FIGURE 10.13
Journalizing the April 12 Transaction

Apr.	12	Accounts Payable, Thorpe Co.		6 0 0 00		
		Purchases Discount				6 00
		Cash				5 9 4 00
		Paid invoice no. 414				

Figure 10.14 shows the complete set of cash payments transactions journalized for the month, followed by a complete posting to the general ledger and recordings to the accounts payable subsidiary ledger (remember from the past unit that we posted all the purchases on account).

Now let's prove that the sum of the accounts payable subsidiary ledger at the end of the month is equal to the controlling account, Accounts Payable, at the end of April for Art's Wholesale Clothing Company.

To do so, creditors with an ending balance in Art's accounts payable subsidiary ledger must be listed in the schedule of accounts payable (see Figure 10.15). At the end of the month, the total owed ($7,130) in Accounts Payable, the controlling account in the general ledger, should equal the sum owed the individual creditors that are listed on the schedule of accounts payable. If it doesn't, the journalizing, posting, and recording must be checked to ensure that they are complete. Also, the balances of each title should be checked.

Controlling account The account in the general ledger that summarizes or controls a subsidiary ledger. Example: The Accounts Payable account in the general ledger is the controlling account for the accounts payable subsidiary ledger. After postings are complete, it shows the total amount owed from purchases made on account.

\multicolumn{2}{c}{GENERAL JOURNAL}		Page 2		

Date		Account Titles and Description	PR	Dr.	Cr.
201X					
Apr.	2	Prepaid Insurance	116	9 0 0 00	
		Cash	111		9 0 0 00
		Paid for insurance in advance			
	7	Accounts Payable, Joe Francis Co.	211 ✔	4 0 0 0 00	
		Cash	111		4 0 0 0 00
		Paid invoice no. 388			
	9	Purchases	511	8 0 0 00	
		Cash	111		8 0 0 00
		Cash Purchases			
	12	Accounts Payable, Thorpe Co.	211 ✔	6 0 0 00	
		Purchases Discount	512		6 00
		Cash	111		5 9 4 00
		Paid invoice no. 414			
	28	Salaries Expense	611	7 0 0 00	
		Cash	111		7 0 0 00
		Paid salaries			

FIGURE 10.14
Cash Payments Transactions Journalized for the Month and Posting to the General Journal

(continued on next page)

FIGURE 10.14 *(continued)*

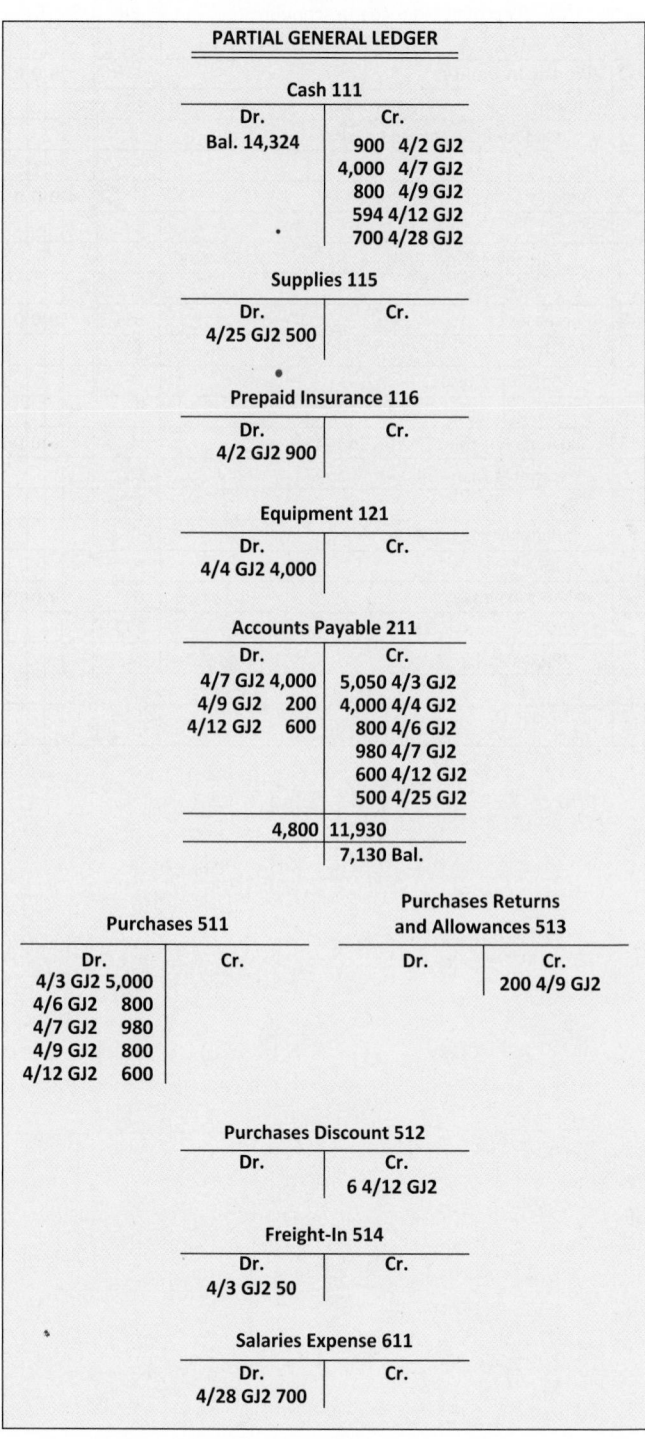

ACCOUNTS PAYABLE SUBSIDIARY LEDGER

Abby Blake Co.

Dr.	Cr.
	5,050 4/3 GJ2
	600 4/12 GJ2
	5,650 Bal.

Joe Francis Co.

Dr.	Cr.
4/7 GJ2 4,000	4,000 4/4 GJ2
	0 Bal.

John Sullivan Co.

Dr.	Cr.
	980 4/7 GJ2
	500 4/25 GJ2
	1,480 Bal.

Thorpe Co.

Dr.	Cr.
4/9 GJ2 200	800 4/6 GJ2
4/12 GJ2 600	
	0 Bal.

PARTIAL GENERAL LEDGER

Cash 111

Dr.	Cr.
Bal. 14,324	900 4/2 GJ2
	4,000 4/7 GJ2
	800 4/9 GJ2
	594 4/12 GJ2
	700 4/28 GJ2

Supplies 115

Dr.	Cr.
4/25 GJ2 500	

Prepaid Insurance 116

Dr.	Cr.
4/2 GJ2 900	

Equipment 121

Dr.	Cr.
4/4 GJ2 4,000	

Accounts Payable 211

Dr.	Cr.
4/7 GJ2 4,000	5,050 4/3 GJ2
4/9 GJ2 200	4,000 4/4 GJ2
4/12 GJ2 600	800 4/6 GJ2
	980 4/7 GJ2
	600 4/12 GJ2
	500 4/25 GJ2
4,800	11,930
	7,130 Bal.

Purchases 511

Dr.	Cr.
4/3 GJ2 5,000	
4/6 GJ2 800	
4/7 GJ2 980	
4/9 GJ2 800	
4/12 GJ2 600	

Purchases Returns and Allowances 513

Dr.	Cr.
	200 4/9 GJ2

Purchases Discount 512

Dr.	Cr.
	6 4/12 GJ2

Freight-In 514

Dr.	Cr.
4/3 GJ2 50	

Salaries Expense 611

Dr.	Cr.
4/28 GJ2 700	

FIGURE 10.15
Schedule of Accounts Payable

ART'S WHOLESALE CLOTHING COMPANY SCHEDULE OF ACCOUNTS PAYABLE APRIL 30, 201X		
Abby Blake Co.		$ 5 6 5 0 00
John Sullivan Co.		1 4 8 0 00
Total Accounts Payable		$ 7 1 3 0 00

Now let's check your progress.

 **TRY IT!**   Learning Unit 10-3

From the following, prepare a Schedule of Accounts Payable for Digital Co. for September 30, 201X:

Accounts Payable 210			L. Von Co.	
Dr.	Cr.		Dr.	Cr.
	100 9/5 GJ4			100 9/5 GJ4
	200 9/7 GJ5		**Xon Co.**	
	300 9/15 GJ6		Dr.	Cr.
	800 9/18 GJ6			300 9/15 GJ6

J. Bee Co.			Zero Co.	
Dr.	Cr.		Dr.	Cr.
	800 9/18 GJ6			200 9/7 GJ5

Journalizing Transactions for a Perpetual Inventory System

LEARNING UNIT 10-4

L04

Introduction to the Merchandise Cycle

In this learning unit we will focus on recording transactions using a perpetual inventory system. This is an inventory system that continually monitors its levels of inventory. The previous units were based on a periodic inventory system. This means that at the end of each accounting period the cost of unsold goods is calculated. There is no continual tracking of inventory.

Let's use Walmart as an example as both the buyer and seller. We know that Walmart must buy inventory from suppliers to sell to you, the customer. This inventory is called merchandise inventory. It is an asset sold to you for cash or accounts receivable and represents *sales revenue* or sales for Walmart.

What did it cost Walmart to bring the inventory into the store? The cost of goods sold is the total cost of merchandise inventory brought into the store and sold. These costs do not include any operating expenses such as heat, advertising, and salaries. To find Walmart's profit before operating expenses, we take the sales revenue less cost of goods sold. Figure 10.16 is called *gross profit on sales*.

Perpetual inventory system An inventory system that keeps *continual track* of each type of inventory by recording units on hand at the beginning of each accounting period, units sold, and the current balance after each sale or purchase.

Periodic inventory system An inventory system that, at the *end* of each accounting period, calculates the cost of the unsold goods on hand by taking the cost of each unit times the number of units of each product on hand.

 | Walmart Sales Revenue | − | Cost of Goods Sold | = | Gross Profit on Sales |

FIGURE 10.16
Calculating Gross Profit on Sales

For example, if Walmart sells a TV for $500 that cost $300 to bring into the store, its gross profit is $200. To find its net income or net loss, Walmart would subtract its operating expenses. Figure 10.17 (page 364) shows how a merchandiser calculates its net income or net loss.

FIGURE 10.17

Introduction to Perpetual Inventory for a Merchandise Company

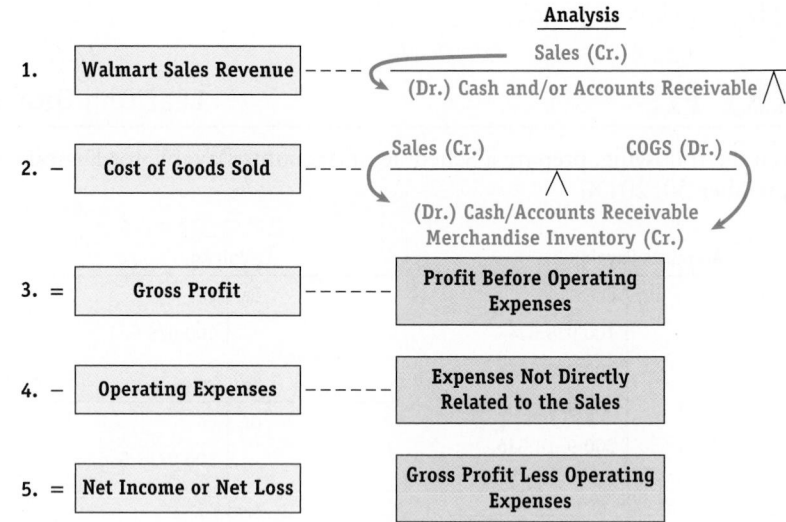

Merchandise Inventory An asset and perpetual inventory system account that records purchases of merchandise. Discounts and returns are recorded in this account for the buyer.

Cost of goods sold In a perpetual inventory system, an account that records the cost of merchandise inventory used to make the sale.

Note: In step 1 the sales provide an inflow of cash or accounts receivable. Step 2 shows that when the inventory is sold, it is recognized as a cost (cost of goods sold). By subtracting cost of goods sold from sales, we arrive at the gross profit in step 3. Step 4 shows that operating expenses subtracted from gross profit result in a net income or net loss in step 5.

What Inventory System Walmart Uses

When you pay at Walmart you see the use of bar codes and optical scanners. Walmart keeps detailed records of the inventory it brings into the store and what inventory is sold. With this method, Walmart keeps track of what it costs to make the sale (cost of goods sold) by matching revenues and costs (see Figure 10.18).

FIGURE 10.18

Matching Revenues and Costs

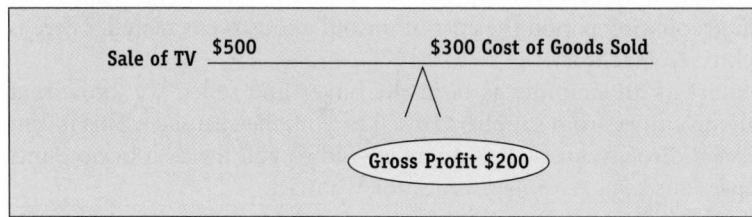

More and more companies, large or small, are using the perpetual inventory system due to increasing computerization. Walmart knows that using the perpetual inventory system will help control stocks of inventory as well as lost or stolen goods.

Recording Merchandise Transactions

Now let's look at Walmart as both a buyer and a seller. Let's first focus on Walmart the buyer.

Walmart: The Buyer. When Walmart brings merchandise inventory into the stores from suppliers it is recorded in the *Merchandise Inventory account*. Think of this account as purchases of merchandise—for cash or on account—that is for resale to customers. Each order is documented by an invoice for Walmart. Keep in mind that Merchandise Inventory is the cost of bringing the merchandise into the store, not the price at which the merchandise will be sold to customers. Let's assume that on July 9 Walmart bought flat-screen TVs from Sony Corp. for $7,000 on account with terms 2/10, n/30. Walmart would record the purchase as shown in Figure 10.19.

Analysis:	Merchandise Inventory	A	↑	Dr.	$7,000
	Accounts Payable	L	↑	Cr.	$7,000

FIGURE 10.19
Purchase of Inventory on Account

Journal Entry:		Jul.	9	Merchandise Inventory		7 0 0 0 00		
				Accounts Payable/Sony			7 0 0 0 00	
				Purchased inventory on account				
				from Sony 2/10, n/30				

Keep in mind that not all purchases will go to Merchandise Inventory. Walmart will buy supplies, equipment, and so forth that are not for resale to customers. These amounts will be debited to the specific account such as equipment and not merchandise inventory. For example, if Walmart bought $5,000 of shelving equipment on account for its store on November 9, the transaction would be recorded as in Figure 10.20.

Analysis:	Shelving Equipment	A	↑	Dr.	$5,000
	Accounts Payable	L	↑	Cr.	$5,000

FIGURE 10.20
Purchase of Equipment on Account

Journal Entry:		Nov.	9	Shelving Equipment		5 0 0 0 00		
				Accounts Payable/Moore Co.			5 0 0 0 00	
				Purchased equipment on account				

What happens if Walmart finds a defective TV among its purchase from Sony?

Recording Purchases Returns and Allowances. Because on July 14 Walmart noticed a damaged TV in the shipment, it issues a debit memorandum. This document notifies Sony, the supplier, that Walmart is reducing what is owed Sony by $600, the cost of the TV (to bring it into the store) and that the TV is being returned. On Walmart's books, the analysis and journal entry in Figure 10.21 results.

Analysis:	Accounts Payable	L	↓	Dr.	$600
	Merchandise Inventory	A	↓	Cr.	$600

FIGURE 10.21
Recording a Debit Memorandum

Journal Entry:		Jul.	14	Accounts Payable/Sony		6 0 0 00		
				Merchandise Inventory			6 0 0 00	
				To record debit memo no. 10				

Note that the cost of merchandise inventory has been reduced by $600 due to the return. In the perpetual inventory system there is no Purchases Returns and Allowances account. The reduction in cost from the return is recorded *directly* into the Merchandise Inventory account. Let's now look at how Walmart would record any cash discounts it receives due to payment of the Sony bill within the discount period.

Recording Purchase Discounts. Let's assume that Walmart pays Sony within the first 10 days. Keep in mind that we take no discounts on returned goods (the $600 return). The amount of purchase discount will be recorded as a reduction to the cost of merchandise inventory. Figure 10.22 (page 366) shows the analysis and journal entry on July 16. A discount lowers the cost of inventory.

FIGURE 10.22
Recording a Purchase Discount

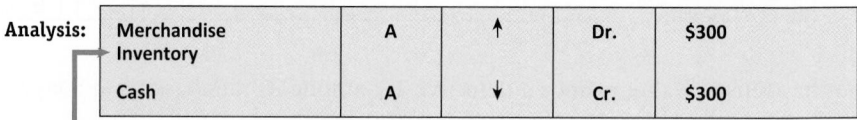

Analysis:					
Accounts Payable	L	↓	Dr.	$6,400
Cash	A	↓	Cr.	$6,272
Merchandise Inventory	A	↓	Cr.	$ 128

($7,000 – $600 Return)

Journal Entry:		Jul.	16	Accounts Payable/Sony		6 4 0 0 00		
				Cash			6 2 7 2 00	
				Merchandise Inventory			1 2 8 00	

2% × $6,400

Keep in mind that had Walmart missed the discount period, it would have debited $6,400 to Accounts Payable and credited Cash for $6,400. Merchandise Inventory would not be reduced.

Recording Cost of Freight. The cost of freight ($300) is to be paid by Walmart. When the purchaser is responsible for cost of freight, it is added to the cost of merchandise inventory. If the cost of freight is paid by the seller, it could be recorded in an operating expense account called Freight-Out. Figure 10.23 is the analysis and journal entry for freight on July 10.

FIGURE 10.23
Recording Cost of Freight

Analysis:					
Merchandise Inventory	A	↑	Dr.	$300
Cash	A	↓	Cr.	$300

Freight Cost added to Merchandise Inventory

Journal Entry:		Jul.	10	Merchandise Inventory		3 0 0 00		
				Cash			3 0 0 00	
				Payment of freight				

Walmart: The Seller. Now let's look at Walmart as the *seller* of merchandise.

Recording Sales at Walmart. Sales revenues are earned at Walmart when the goods are transferred to the buyer. The earned revenue can be for cash and/or credit. Let's look at the following example of the sale of a TV at Walmart for $950 on credit to customer Jones on August 10, which cost Walmart $600. Keep in mind when using the perpetual inventory system that at the time of the earned sale Walmart will do the following:

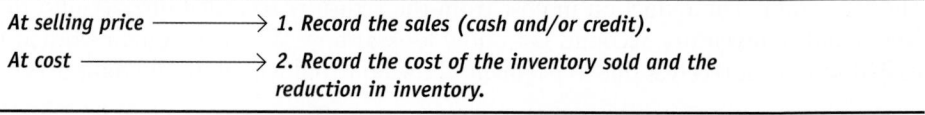

At selling price ───────→ *1. Record the sales (cash and/or credit).*

At cost ───────→ *2. Record the cost of the inventory sold and the reduction in inventory.*

First, let's analyze the transaction in Figure 10.24. Note that we will have two entries, one to record the sale and one to show a new cost and less inventory on hand.

Selling < Price	Accounts Receivable	Asset	↑	Dr.	$950
	Sales	Revenue	↑	Cr.	$950
Cost to < Make sale	Cost of Goods Sold	Cost	↑	Dr.	$600
	Merchandise Inventory	Asset	↓	Cr.	$600

FIGURE 10.24
Recording Sales and Cost of Goods Sold

Journal Entries:

Aug.	10	Account Receivable/Jones	9 5 0 00			
		Sales		9 5 0 00		
		Charge Sales				
	10	Cost of Goods Sold	6 0 0 00			
		Merchandise Inventory		6 0 0 00		
		To record cost of				
		merchandise sold on account				

Be sure to go back to steps 1 and 2 of Figure 10.17. These two steps reinforce the preceding journal entries. Remember that if the sale were a cash sale, we would have debited Cash instead of Accounts Receivable. Note also that the Sales account only records sales of goods held for resale.

How Walmart Records Sales Returns Allowances and Sales Discounts. Keep in mind that we are now looking at how the *seller* of merchandise records a transaction giving the customer a credit due to an allowance or a return of goods from a previous sale. Usually, the seller will issue a *credit memorandum*, a document informing the customer of the adjustment due to the return or allowance. For example, let's look at a customer, Smith Co., who returned a $950 TV on August 15 that had been purchased on account at Walmart. On Walmart's books, the analysis and journal entry in Figure 10.25 resulted.

The first entry records the return at the original selling price using the contra-revenue account Sales Returns and Allowances. The second entry records putting the inventory back in Walmart's books at cost and reducing its Cost of Goods Sold because the inventory was not sold. Remember that we only record the Cost of Goods Sold when the sale has been earned. Keep in mind that if the customer kept the TV but at a reduced price, no entry affecting Merchandise Inventory and Cost of Goods Sold would be needed.

The Analysis: at Selling Price	Sales Returns and Allowances	Contra-Revenue	↑	Dr.	$950
	Accounts Receivable	Asset	↓	Cr.	$950
At Cost	Merchandise Inventory	Asset	↑	Dr.	$600
	Costs of Goods Sold	Cost	↓	Cr.	$600

FIGURE 10.25
Return of Goods

Journal Entries:

Aug.	15	Sales Returns and Allowances	9 5 0 00			
		Accounts Receivable/Smith Co.*		9 5 0 00		
		Returned goods				
	15	Merchandise Inventory	6 0 0 00			
		Cost of Goods Sold		6 0 0 00		

*If it were a *cash* customer, cash would be credited.

Let's assume a customer, Smith Co., on August 25 gets a 2% discount for paying for a $950 TV early. The analysis and entry in Figure 10.26 would result on the seller's books.

FIGURE 10.26
Recording Sales Discount

The Analysis:

Account	Type		Dr/Cr	Amount
Cash	Asset	↑	Dr.	$931
Sales Discount	Contra-Revenue	↑	Dr.	$ 19
Accounts Receivable	Asset	↓	Cr.	$950

Journal Entry:

Aug.	25	Cash			9 3 1	00						
		Sales Discount			1 9	00						
		Accounts Receivable/Smith Co.							9 5 0	00		

Now let's summarize (Figure 10.27) all the entries for both the buyer and the seller (in this case, Walmart).

FIGURE 10.27 Entries for Both the Buyer and the Seller

	Walmart the Buyer			Walmart the Seller	
Bought Inventory for Resale on Account	Merchandise Inventory → At Accounts Payable Cost		Sold Inventory on Account	Accounts Receivable ──────→ At Sales Selling Price Cost of Goods Sold ─────→ At Merchandise Inventory Cost	
Issued a Debit Memo for Merchandise Returned	Accounts Payable ──────→ At Merchandise Inventory Cost		Issued a Credit Memo for Returned Merchandise	Sales Returns and Allowances → At Accounts Receivable Selling Price Merchandise Inventory ──────→ At Cost of Goods Sold Cost	
Recorded a Purchase Discount	Accounts Payable Cash Merchandise Inventory		Recorded a Sales Discount	Cash Sales Discount Accounts Receivable	

Amount of discount ─┘

Figure 10.28 shows a comparison of Perpetual and Periodic Systems.

FIGURE 10.28 Comparison of Perpetual and Periodic Systems

Transaction	Perpetual System			Periodic System		
(A) Sold merchandise that cost $8,000 on account for $20,000.	Accts. Receivable	20 0 0 0 00		Accts. Receivable	20 0 0 0 00	
	Sales		20 0 0 0 00	Sales		20 0 0 0 00
	Cost of Goods Sold	8 0 0 0 00				
	Merch. Inventory		8 0 0 0 00			
(B) Purchased $900 of merchandise on account.	Merch. Inventory	9 0 0 00		Purchases	9 0 0 00	
	Accts. Payable		9 0 0 00	Accts. Payable		9 0 0 00
(C) Paid $50 freight charges.	Merch. Inventory	5 0 00		Freight-In	5 0 00	
	Cash		5 0 00	Cash		5 0 00
(D) Cash customer returned $200 of merchandise. Cost of merchandise was $100.	Sales Ret. & Allow.	2 0 0 00		Sales Ret. & Allow.	2 0 0 00	
	Cash*		2 0 0 00	Cash*		2 0 0 00
	Merch. Inventory	1 0 0 00				
	Cost of Goods Sold		1 0 0 00			
(E) Returned $400 of merchandise previously bought on account because of defects.	Accts. Payable	4 0 0 00		Accts. Payable	4 0 0 00	
	Merch. Inventory		4 0 0 00	Pur. Ret. & Allow.		4 0 0 00

*or Accounts Receivable if made to charge customers

Now let's check your progress.

 TRY IT! Learning Unit 10-4

Journalize the following transactions in July 201X for Elgin Co. using a perpetual inventory system. Partial charts of accounts include Cash 110; Accounts Receivable 112; Merchandise Inventory 120; Accounts Payable 210; A. Elgin, Capital 310; Sales 410; Sales Returns and Allowances 411; Sales Discounts 412; Cost of Goods Sold 510. Omit explanations.

July	8	Sold merchandise costing $5,000 on account for $9,000.
	14	Purchased $1,200 of merchandise on account.
	18	Paid freight charges $100.
	22	A charge customer returned $300 of merchandise. Cost of merchandise was $100.
	30	Returned $500 of merchandise previously bought on account because of defects.

DEMONSTRATION SUMMARY PROBLEM

The following transactions occurred in November 201X for Dale's Electronics Shop. It uses the periodic system.

Nov.	9	Purchased $700 of merchandise from Matty Co., invoice no. 398, dated Nov. 10; terms 2/10, n/60.
	10	Purchased $1,200 of merchandise on account from Mia Co., invoice no. 399, dated Nov. 11; terms 2/10, n/60.
	15	Purchased $600 of electronic supplies on account from Hope Co., invoice no. 410, dated Nov. 16; terms 2/10, n/60.
	17	Issued debit memorandum no.7 to Matty Co. for merchandise returned, $200, from invoice no. 398.
	18	Purchased $600 of electronic equipment on account from Sam Co., invoice no. 411, dated Nov 19; terms 2/10, n/60.

Selected accounts are listed below:

Partial General Ledger
Electronic Supplies 112
Electronic Equipment 120
Accounts Payable 210
Purchases 510
Purch. Ret. + Allow. 512

Accounts Payable Subsidiary Ledger
Hope Co.; Matty Co.; Mia Co.; Sam Co.

Requirements

1. Journalize (p. 2), post, and record the transactions for a periodic system.
2. Prepare a Schedule of Accounts Payable.
3. Journalize the same transactions assuming Dale uses the perpetual system.

Solutions

Requirement 1

Dale's Electronic Shop
General Journal   Page 2

Date		Account Titles and Description	PR	Dr.	Cr.
201X					
Nov.	9	Purchases	510	700	
		Accounts Payable, Matty Co.	210/✓		700
		Invoice no. 398			
	10	Purchases	510	1,200	
		Accounts Payable, Mia Co.	210/✓		1,200
		Invoice no. 399			

Date	Account Titles and Description	PR	Dr.	Cr.
15	Electronic Supplies	112	600	
	Accounts Payable, Hope Co.	210/✓		600
	Invoice no. 410			
17	Accounts Payable, Matty Co.	210/✓	200	
	Purchases Returns and Allowances	512		200
	Debit Memorandum no. 7			
18	Electronic Equipment	120	600	
	Accounts Payable, Sam Co.	210/✓		600
	Invoice no. 411			

Tips for Journalizing, Posting, and Recording the Transactions for a Periodic System

Purchases has a normal balance of a debit while Purchases Returns and Allowances has a normal balance of a credit. Note in the Nov. 17 transaction, Dale's Electronics owes less and its amount of Purchases Returns and Allowances has increased. Each time Accounts Payable is affected, the accounts payable subsidiary ledger is updated.

Partial General Ledger

Electronic Supplies 112

Dr.	Cr.
11/15 GJ2 600	

Electronic Equipment 120

Dr.	Cr.
11/18 GJ2 600	

Accounts Payable 210

Dr.	Cr.
11/17 GJ2 200	700 11/9 GJ2
	1,200 11/10 GJ2
	600 11/15 GJ2
	600 11/18 GJ2
	Balance 2,900

Purchases 510

Dr.	Cr.
11/9 GJ2 700	
11/10 GJ2 1,200	
Balance 1,900	

Purchases Returns and Allowances 512

Dr.	Cr.
	200 11/17 GJ2

Accounts Payable Subsidiary Ledger

Hope Co.

Dr.	Cr.
	600 11/15 GJ2

Matty Co.

Dr.	Cr.
11/17 GJ2 200	700 11/9 GJ2
	Balance 500

Mia Co.

Dr.	Cr.
	1,200 11/10 GJ2

Sam Co.

Dr.	Cr.
	600 11/18 GJ2

Requirement 2

Dale's Electronic Shop
Schedule of Accounts Payable
November 30, 201X

Hope Co.	$ 600
Matty Co.	500
Mia Co.	1,200
Sam Co.	600
Total Accounts Payable	$2,900

Tip for Preparing a Schedule of Accounts Payable

Note that the sum of the accounts payable subsidiary ledger of $2,900 is the ending balance in Accounts Payable in the general ledger.

Requirement 3

Date	Account titles	PR	Dr.	Cr.
201X				
Nov. 9	Merchandise Inventory		700	
	Accounts Payable, Matty Co.			700
10	Merchandise Inventory		1,200	
	Accounts Payable, Mia Co.			1,200
15	Electronic Supplies		600	
	Accounts Payable, Hope Co.			600
17	Accounts Payable, Matty Co.		200	
	Merchandise Inventory			200
18	Electronic Equipment		600	
	Accounts Payable, Sam Co.			600

Tips for Journalizing the Same Transactions Using the Perpetual System

In a perpetual system, purchases are recorded as merchandise inventory. Note in transactions dated Nov. 15 and Nov. 18 that the debit was not to merchandise inventory because they were not for resale. Note in transaction dated Nov. 17 that the return lowers the amount in merchandise inventory. If Dale had sold some goods, then accounts receivable would increase as well as sales. At the same time, Dale's cost of goods sold account would increase and the merchandise inventory account would decrease.

BLUEPRINT: PERIODIC VERSUS PERPETUAL ACCOUNTS USED FOR JOURNAL ENTRIES

Periodic		Perpetual
Purchases	→	Merchandise Inventory
Purchase Discounts	→	Merchandise Inventory
Sales/Accounts Receivable	→	Sales/Accounts Receivable Cost of Goods Sold/Merchandise Inventory
Freight-In	→	Merchandise Inventory
Sales Discounts	→	Sales Discounts
Sales Returns and Allowances	→	Sales Returns and Allowances

TRY IT!

Solutions   MyAccountingLab

Learning Unit 10-1

Account	Category	Rules of Debit/Credit Inc.	Rules of Debit/Credit Dec.	Financial Statement
Cash	Asset	Dr.	Cr.	Balance Sheet
Accounts Payable	Liabilities	Cr.	Dr.	Balance Sheet
Purchases	Cost	Dr.	Cr.	Income Statement
Purchases Discounts	Contra-cost	Cr.	Dr.	Income Statement
Purchases Returns and Allowances	Contra-cost	Cr.	Dr.	Income Statement

Learning Unit 10-2

	Moore Co.			p. 2
Date	Account Titles and Description	PR	Dr.	Cr.
201X				
July 5	Purchases	500	400	
	Freight-in	514	25	
	Accounts Payable, Beam Co.	210/✓		425
	Bought merchandise on account from Beam			
7	Equipment	140	700	
	Accounts Payable, Beam Co.	210/✓		700
	Purchase of equipment on account			
22	Accounts Payable, Beam Co.	210/✓	100	
	Purchases Returns and Allowances	510		100
	Debit memorandum no. 1			

Partial General Ledger

Cash 110	
Dr.	Cr.
Bal. 8,000	

Purchases 500	
Dr.	Cr.
7/5 GJ2 400	

Equipment 140	
Dr.	Cr.
7/7 GJ2 700	

Purchases Returns and Allow. 510	
Dr.	Cr.
	100 7/22 GJ2

Accounts Payable 210	
Dr.	Cr.
7/22 GJ2 100	425 7/5 GJ2
	700 7/7 GJ2

Freight-In 514	
Dr.	Cr.
7/5 GJ2 25	

Partial Accounts Payable Subsidiary Ledger

Beam Co.	
Dr.	Cr.
7/22 GJ2 100	425 7/5 GJ2
	700 7/7 GJ2

Learning Unit 10-3

Digital Co.
Schedule of Accounts Payable
September 30, 201X

J. Bee Co.	$ 800
L. Von Co.	100
Xon Co.	300
Zero Co.	200
Total Accounts Payable	$1,400

Learning Unit 10-4

Date	Accounts	PR	Dr.	Cr.
201X				
July 8	Accounts Receivable		9,000	
	Sales			9,000
	Cost of Goods Sold		5,000	
	Merchandise Inventory			5,000
14	Merchandise Inventory		1,200	
	Accounts Payable			1,200
18	Merchandise Inventory		100	
	Cash			100
22	Sales Returns and Allowances		300	
	Accounts Receivable			300
	Merchandise Inventory		100	
	Cost of Goods Sold			100
30	Accounts Payable		500	
	Merchandise Inventory			500

ACCOUNTING COACH

The following Coaching Tips are from Learning Units 10-1 to 10-4. Take the Pre-Game Checkup and use the Check Your Score on page 376 to see how you are doing. The Accounting Coach provides tips before each Checkup to help you avoid common accounting errors.

LU 10-1 Purchases Transactions, Including Freight

Pre-Game Tips: Merchandise for resale to customers is called a purchase. The Purchases account is a cost that will be shown on the income statement. This cost works just like expenses but is directly related to bringing the goods for resale into the store. Purchases Returns and Allowances and Purchases Discounts are contra-cost accounts that will be reported on the income statement. If shipping terms are F.O.B. destination, the seller will pay the cost of freight.

Pre-Game Checkup: Answer true or false to the following statements.

1. The normal balance of Purchases is a debit.
2. Purchases Discounts is a cost.
3. F.O.B. shipping point means that the seller of the goods is responsible for covering the shipping costs.
4. An increase in Purchases Returns and Allowances is a credit.
5. A credit memorandum received will result in an increase in Accounts Payable.

LU 10-2 Journalizing and Recording Transactions to the Accounts Payable Subsidiary Ledger and Posting to the General Ledger Along with a Debit Memorandum

Pre-Game Tips: The accounts payable subsidiary ledger lists the amounts owed to each vendor. It is just the opposite of the accounts receivable subsidiary ledger. The normal balance of the accounts payable subsidiary ledger is a credit. The controlling account, Accounts Payable, is located in the general ledger. The cost of freight is recorded in the Freight-In account, which represents a cost of freight. It has a debit balance. A debit memorandum means the buyer does not owe as much and thus Accounts Payable is reduced and a purchases returns and allowances results. The debit memorandum also reduces what is owed to the vendor in the subsidiary ledger.

Pre-Game Checkup: Answer true or false to the following statements.

1. Purchases Returns and Allowances is increased by a debit.
2. Freight-In is a cost that will be shown on the income statement.
3. The controlling account, Accounts Payable, is located in the subsidiary ledger.
4. The normal balance of each vendor in the accounts payable subsidiary ledger is a credit.
5. Debit memorandums are issued by the seller.

LU 10-3 Cash Payments Transactions and Schedules of Accounts Payable

Pre-Game Tips: When a cash payment is made within the discount period from a charge purchase the result is a debit to Accounts Payable and the Subsidiary account and a credit to Purchases Discounts and Cash. Remember that Purchases Discounts is a contra-cost account with a normal credit balance. At the end of the month the total from the schedule of accounts payable should equal the ending balance in Accounts Payable, the controlling account.

Pre-Game Checkup: Answer true or false to the following statements.

1. Purchases Discounts is a contra-revenue account.
2. The schedule of accounts payable is listed by debits and credits.
3. An increase in Purchases Discounts is made by debiting the account.
4. Purchases Discounts are shown on the balance sheet.
5. The normal balance of each vendor in the accounts payable subsidiary ledger is a debit.

LU 10-4 Journalizing Transactions for a Perpetual Inventory System

Pre-Game Tips: In a perpetual inventory system, all purchases of inventory are recorded in an asset account called Merchandise Inventory. The cost of selling inventory is recorded in the Cost of Goods Sold account. When a sale is made, the company gets cash and/or accounts receivable and a sale is shown. At the same time, the company records the Cost of Goods Sold along with a reduction in Merchandise Inventory since it is sold. Returns to the seller will increase the Merchandise Inventory account. If a seller pays for the cost of freight, it is a selling expense for the seller.

Pre-Game Checkup: Answer true or false to the following statements.

1. In the perpetual system there are no Purchases, Purchases Discounts, or Purchases Returns and Allowances accounts.
2. The Sales Discount account is not used in a perpetual accounting system.
3. Cost of freight results in a decrease to Merchandise Inventory.
4. Sales plus cost of goods sold equals gross profit.
5. Perpetual systems do not record cash sales.

CHECK YOUR SCORE: Answers to the Pre-Game Checkup

LU 10-1
1. True
2. False—Purchases Discounts is a contra-cost.
3. False—F.O.B. shipping point means that the buyer of the goods is responsible for covering the shipping costs.
4. True
5. False—A credit memorandum received by the purchaser will result in a decrease in Accounts Payable.

LU 10-2
1. False—Purchases Returns and Allowances is increased by a credit.
2. True
3. False—The controlling account, Accounts Payable, is located in the general ledger.
4. True
5. False—Debit memorandums are issued by the buyer.

LU 10-3
1. False—Purchases Discounts is a contra-cost account.
2. False—The schedule of accounts payable contains no debits or credits.

3. False—An increase in Purchases Discounts is made by crediting the account.
4. False—Purchases Discounts are shown on the income statement.
5. False—The normal balance of each vendor in the accounts payable subsidiary ledger is a credit.

LU 10-4
1. True
2. False—The Sales Discount account is used in a perpetual accounting system.
3. False—Cost of freight results in an increase to Merchandise Inventory because it increases the cost of the inventory.
4. False—Sales minus cost of goods sold equals gross profit.
5. False—Perpetual systems record both cash and charge sales.

Chapter Summary

Here are all the key terms and equations to help you understand the concepts of this chapter and prepare you for your exam. After completing this review, go to MyAccountingLab for more practice opportunities.

MyAccountingLab

Concepts You Should Know	Key Terms
L01 **Explain and Journalize Purchases Transactions, Including Freight** 1. Purchases are merchandise for resale. The Purchases account is a cost. 2. Purchases Returns and Allowances and Purchases Discounts are contra-costs. 3. F.O.B. shipping point means that the purchaser of the goods is responsible for covering the shipping costs. 4. Purchases discounts are not taken on freight.	F.O.B. destination (p. 352) F.O.B. shipping point (p. 352) Purchases (p. 350) Purchases Discount (p. 351) Purchases Returns and Allowances (p. 350)

L02 **Journalize and Record Transactions to the Accounts Payable Subsidiary Ledger and Post to the General Ledger Along with a Debit Memorandum**
 	
 1. The steps for buying merchandise from a company may include the following:
 	
   a. The requesting department prepares a purchase requisition.
 	
   b. The purchasing department prepares a purchase order.
 	
   c. The seller receives the order and prepares a sales invoice (a purchase invoice from the buyer).
 	
   d. The buyer receives the goods and prepares a receiving report.
 	
   e. The accounting department verifies and approves the invoice for payment.
 	
 2. The accounts payable subsidiary ledger, organized in alphabetical order, is not in the same book as Accounts Payable, the controlling account in the general ledger.
 	
 3. A debit memorandum (issued by the buyer) indicates that the amount owed from a previous purchase is being reduced because some goods were defective or not up to a specific standard and thus were returned or an allowance requested.
 	
 4. All payments of cash (check) are recorded in the general journal.
	Accounts payable subsidiary ledger (p. 355)
	
	 Debit memorandum (p. 358)
	
	 Invoice approval form (p. 354)
	
	 Purchase invoice (p. 354)
	
	 Purchase order (p. 353)
	
	 Purchase requisition (p. 353)
	
	 Receiving report (p. 354)

Journalize, Record, and Post Cash Payments Transactions and Prepare a Schedule of Accounts Payable

1. The schedule of accounts payable is a list of ending amounts owed to individual creditors.

2. At the end of the month, the total amount on the schedule should equal the ending balance in Accounts Payable, the controlling account in the general ledger.

Controlling account (p. 360)

Explain and Journalize Transactions for a Perpetual Inventory System

1. In a perpetual inventory system, whenever a sale is recognized, the cost of goods sold and merchandise inventory must be updated.

2. Purchases discounts or returns are reflected directly in the Merchandise Inventory account (a credit) for a perpetual inventory system.

Cost of goods sold (p. 364)

Merchandise inventory (p. 364)

Periodic inventory system (p. 363)

Perpetual inventory system (p. 363)

Discussion Questions and Critical Thinking/Ethical Case

1. Explain how net purchases is calculated.

2. What is the normal balance of Purchases Discount?

3. What is a contra-cost?

4. Explain the difference between F.O.B. shipping point and F.O.B. destination.

5. F.O.B. destination means that title to the goods will switch to the buyer when goods are shipped. Do you agree or disagree? Why?

6. What is the normal balance of each creditor in the accounts payable subsidiary ledger?

7. Why could the balance of the controlling account, Accounts Payable, equal the sum of the accounts payable subsidiary ledger during the month?

8. What is the relationship between a purchase requisition and a purchase order?

9. What purpose could a typical invoice approval form serve?

10. Explain the difference between merchandise and equipment.

11. Why would the purchaser issue a debit memorandum?

12. Explain why a trade discount is not a cash discount.

13. What new account is used in a perpetual system compared to the periodic system?

14. What is the normal balance of cost of goods sold?

15. How are discounts recorded in a perpetual system?

16. Spring Co. bought merchandise from All Co. with terms 2/10, n/30. Joanne Ring, the bookkeeper, forgot to pay the bill within the first 10 days. She went to Mel Ryan, the head accountant, who told her to backdate the check so that it looked like the bill was paid within the discount period. Joanne told Mel that she thought they could get away with it. Should Joanne and Mel backdate the check to take advantage of the discount? You make the call. Write down your specific recommendations to Joanne.

Concept Checks

MyAccountingLab

Questions 1–6 are based on a periodic inventory system.
Questions 7–10 are based on a perpetual inventory system.

Accounts for Purchase Activities

◀ **LO1,2** *(10 min)*

1. Complete the following table:

To the Seller		To the Buyer
Sales	↔	a. _____
Sales returns and allowances	↔	b. _____
Sales discount	↔	c. _____
Credit memorandum	↔	d. _____
Schedule of accounts receivable	↔	e. _____
Accounts receivable subsidiary ledger	↔	f. _____

(5 min) **LO1**

Accounts

2. Complete the following table:

Account	Category	↑↓	Temporary or Permanent
Purchases			
Purchases Returns and Allowances			
Purchases Discount			

(5 min) **LO1**

Calculating Net Purchases

3. Calculate Net Purchases from the following: Purchases, $27; Purchases Returns and Allowances, $9; Purchases Discounts, $5.

(10 min) **LO2**

General Journal, Recording, and Posting

4. Match the following to the three business transactions (more than one number can be used).

    1. Recorded to the accounts payable subsidiary ledger.
    2. Recorded to the general journal.
    3. Posted to the general ledger.

        _____ a. Bought merchandise on account from Strong.com, invoice no. 12, $160.

        _____ b. Bought equipment on account from Lee Co., invoice no. 13, $150.

        _____ c. Issued debit memo no. 1 to Strong.com for merchandise returned, $60, from invoice no. 12.

(15 min) **LO2,3**

Journalizing Transactions

5. Journalize the following transactions:
    a. Issued credit memo no. 2, $43, to Lenny Co.
    b. Cash sales, $183.
    c. Received check from Dolly Co., $45, less 2% discount.
    d. Bought merchandise on account from Joseph Co., $31, invoice no. 20; terms 3/10, n/30.
    e. Cash purchase of merchandise, $16.
    f. Issued debit memo to Joseph Co., $9, for merchandise returned from invoice no. 20.

(10 min) **LO3**

Schedule of Accounts Payable

6. From the following prepare a schedule of Accounts Payable for Ronson.com for May 31, 201X:

Accounts Payable Subsidiary Ledger

Roy Co.

	Dr.	Cr.	
		65	5/7 GJ1

Beland Co.

	Dr.	Cr.	
5/25 GJ1	12	53	5/20 GJ1

General Ledger

Accounts Payable

	Dr.	Cr.	
5/31 GJ1	12	118	5/31 GJ1

Perpetual Inventory

L04 *(15 min)*

7. Draw a seesaw similar to the one shown in Figure 10.18 and show a sale of $1,000 that cost the store $450. Be sure to label all the accounts.

Perpetual Inventory Discount

L04 *(10 min)*

8. Balder Co. paid $200 to Pedro Co. and received a $20 purchases discount. Journalize the entry.

Perpetual Inventory Return

L04 *(10 min)*

9. Porter Morse returned $275 (selling price) of merchandise to Labrie Co. The cost of the merchandise to Labrie Co. is $100. What would be the journal entry on the books of both the buyer and seller?

Perpetual Inventory Freight

L04 *(10 min)*

10. Capris Co. paid the cost of freight, $70. Journalize the transaction. Assume that Capris Co. is the buyer.

Exercises

MyAccountingLab

Set A

10A-1. From the general journal in Figure 10.29, record to the accounts payable subsidiary ledger and post to general ledger accounts as appropriate.

L02 *(15 min)*

		GENERAL JOURNAL			Page 2	
Date		Account Titles and Description	PR	Dr.	Cr.	
201X						
Jun.	3	Purchases		9 4 0 00		
		Accounts Payable, Cortland.com			9 4 0 00	
		Purchased merchandise on account				
	4	Purchases		6 2 0 00		
		Accounts Payable, Harold.com			6 2 0 00	
		Purchased merchandise on account				
	8	Equipment		1 9 0 00		
		Accounts Payable, Nickel.com			1 9 0 00	
		Bought equipment on account				

FIGURE 10.29
General Journal Showing Purchases from Cortland.com, Harold.com, and Nickel.com

Partial Accounts Payable Subsidiary Ledger

Cortland.com

Dr.	Cr.

Harold.com

Dr.	Cr.

Nickel.com

Dr.	Cr.

Partial General Ledger

Equipment 120

Dr.	Cr.

Accounts Payable 210

Dr.	Cr.

Purchases 510

Dr.	Cr.

(15 min) **LO2** ➡ **10A-2.** On October 10, 201X, Carrol Co. issued debit memorandum no. 1 for $440 to Roger Co. for merchandise returned from invoice no. 312. Your task is to journalize, record, and post this transaction as appropriate. Use the periodic inventory system.

(20 min) **LO3** ➡ **10A-3.** Journalize, record, and post when appropriate the following transactions into the general journal (p. 2) for Jacob's Clothing. All purchases discounts are 7/10, n/30. Assume the periodic inventory system. If using working papers, be sure to put in beginning balances.

201X

Apr.   1   Issued check no. 20 to A. Jordan Company in payment of its March 28 invoice no. 522.

    8   Issued check no. 21 to Farrow Advertising in payment of its advertising bill, $101, no discount.

   15   Issued check no. 22 to B. Thomas in payment of his March 25 invoice no. 488.

Accounts Payable Subsidiary Ledger

Name	Balance	Invoice No.
A. Jordan	$500	522
B. Thomas	200	488
J. Wright	400	562
B. Campbell	100	821

Partial General Ledger

Account	Balance
Cash 110	$3,100
Accounts Payable 210	1,200
Purchases Discount 511	
Advertising Expense 610	

(10 min) **LO3** ➡ **10A-4.** From Exercise 10A-3, prepare a schedule of accounts payable and verify that the total of the schedule equals the amount in the controlling account.

(10 min) **LO1** ➡ **10A-5.** Record the following transaction in a transaction analysis chart for the buyer: Bought merchandise for $9,400 on account. Shipping terms were F.O.B. destination. The cost of shipping was $470. Assume the periodic inventory system.

(10 min) **LO1** ➡ **10A-6.** Mark Smith bought merchandise with a list price of $4,300. Mark was entitled to a 31% trade discount as well as a 5% cash discount. What was Mark's actual cost of buying this merchandise after the cash discount?

(15 min) **LO4** ➡ **10A-7.** Journalize the following transactions. Assume a perpetual inventory system.

201X

Apr.   8   Purchased merchandise on account from Bachand Supplies, $19,000; terms 3/10, n/30.

   15   Sold merchandise on account, $3,500; terms 3/10, n/30. The cost of merchandise was $2,000.

   20   Received credit from Bachand Supplies for merchandise returned, $150.

(15 min) **LO4** ➡ **10A-8.** Journalize the following transactions. Assume the perpetual inventory system.

201X

Dec.   4   Sold merchandise for $450 cash. The cost of merchandise was $350.

    9   Purchased merchandise from Ree Co. on account, $3,300, F.O.B. shipping point (buyer pays freight); terms 2/10, n/30. Freight to be paid on December 20.

   20   Paid freight on December 9 purchase, $110.

10A-9. Journalize the following transactions. Assume the perpetual inventory system. **L04** *(15 min)*

201X		
Apr.	5	Sold merchandise for $1,350 cash. The cost of the merchandise was $725.
	16	Made refunds to cash customers for defective merchandise, $50. The cost of defective merchandise was $10.

10A-10. Journalize the following transactions. Assume a perpetual inventory system. **L04** *(15 min)*

201X		
Jul.	8	Sold merchandise on account, $630, to Ring Co.; terms 3/10, n/30. Cost of merchandise was $390.
	12	Purchased office equipment on account from MEC Co., $1,600.
	13	Made refunds to cash customers, $200, for defective merchandise. The cost of defective merchandise was $25.

Set B

10B-1. From the general journal in Figure 10.30, record to the accounts payable subsidiary ledger and post to the general ledger accounts as appropriate. **L02** *(15 min)*

		GENERAL JOURNAL					Page 2
Date		Account Titles and Description	PR	Dr.		Cr.	
201X							
Jun.	3	Purchases		9 3 0 00			
		Accounts Payable, Eve.com				9 3 0 00	
		Purchased merchandise on account					
	4	Purchases		6 1 0 00			
		Accounts Payable, Jack.com				6 1 0 00	
		Purchased merchandise on account					
	8	Equipment		2 2 0 00			
		Accounts Payable, Noel.com				2 2 0 00	
		Bought equipment on account					

FIGURE 10.30
General Journal Showing Purchases from Eve.com, Jack.com, and Noel.com

Partial Accounts Payable Subsidiary Ledger

Eve.com

Dr.	Cr.

Jack.com

Dr.	Cr.

Noel.com

Dr.	Cr.

Partial General Ledger

Equipment 120

Dr.	Cr.

Accounts Payable 210

Dr.	Cr.

Purchases 510

Dr.	Cr.

10B-2. On December 10, 201X, Brown Co. issued debit memorandum no. 1 for $430 to Line Co. for merchandise returned from invoice no. 312. Your task is to journalize, record, and post this transaction as appropriate. Use the periodic inventory system. **L02** *(15 min)*

(20 min)   **LO3**   **10B-3.** Journalize, record, and post when appropriate the following transactions into the general journal (p. 2) for Cody's Clothing. All purchases discounts are 1/10, n/30. Assume the periodic inventory system. If using working papers, be sure to put in beginning balances.

201X		
Apr.	1	Issued check no. 20 to A. Jae Company in payment of its March 28 invoice no. 522.
	8	Issued check no. 21 to Flanders Advertising in payment of its advertising bill, $96, no discount.
	15	Issued check no. 22 to B. Miller in payment of its March 25 invoice no. 488.

Accounts Payable Subsidiary Ledger

Name	Balance	Invoice No.
A. Jae	$1,400	522
B. Miller	800	488
J. Hall	1,100	562
B. Parker	250	821

Partial General Ledger

Account	Balance
Cash 110	$3,600
Accounts Payable 210	3,550
Purchases Discount 511	
Advertising Expense 610	

(10 min)   **LO3**   **10B-4.** From Exercise 10B-3, prepare a schedule of accounts payable and verify that the total of the schedule equals the amount in the controlling account.

(10 min)   **LO1**   **10B-5.** Record the following transaction in a transaction analysis chart for the buyer: Bought merchandise for $8,900 on account. Shipping terms were F.O.B. destination. The cost of shipping was $510. Assume the periodic inventory system.

(10 min)   **LO1**   **10B-6.** Steve Wilson bought merchandise with a list price of $3,700. Steve was entitled to a 32% trade discount as well as a 5% cash discount. What was Steve's actual cost of buying this merchandise after the cash discount?

(15 min)   **LO4**   **10B-7.** Journalize the following transactions. Assume a perpetual inventory system.

201X		
Apr.	8	Purchased merchandise on account from Tustin Supplies, $12,000; terms 2/10, n/30.
	15	Sold merchandise on account, $7,000; terms 4/10, n/30. The cost of merchandise was $5,500.
	20	Received credit from Tustin Supplies for merchandise returned, $140.

(15 min)   **LO4**   **10B-8.** Journalize the following transactions. Assume the perpetual inventory system.

201X		
July	4	Sold merchandise for $500 cash. The cost of merchandise was $150.
	9	Purchased merchandise from Rare Co. on account, $2,500, F.O.B. shipping point (buyer pays freight); terms 3/10, n/30. Freight to be paid on July 20.
	20	Paid freight on July 9 purchase, $100.

10B-9. Journalize the following transactions. Assume the perpetual inventory system.

 **LO4** *(15 min)*

201X		
Apr.	5	Sold merchandise for $1,250 cash. The cost of the merchandise was $850.
	16	Made refunds to cash customers for defective merchandise, $70. The cost of defective merchandise was $25.

10B-10. Journalize the following transactions. Assume a perpetual inventory system.

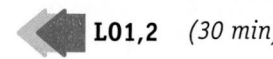 **LO4** *(15 min)*

201X		
Jul.	8	Sold merchandise on account, $620, to Ring Co.; terms 2/10, n/30. Cost of merchandise was $350.
	12	Purchased office equipment on account from TRE Co., $1,900.
	13	Made refunds to cash customers, $250, for defective merchandise. The cost of defective merchandise was $40.

Problems

MyAccountingLab

Set A

10A-1. Robert Chase recently opened Robert's Skate Shop. As the bookkeeper of the company, use the periodic method to journalize, record, and post when appropriate the following transactions (account numbers are Store Supplies 115; Store Equipment 121; Accounts Payable 210; Purchases 510):

LO1,2 *(30 min)*

201X		
May	4	Bought $600 of merchandise on account from Wales Co., invoice no. 442, dated May 5; terms 3/10, n/30.
	5	Bought $4,600 of store equipment on account from Kingston Co., invoice no. 502, dated May 6.
	8	Bought $1,700 of merchandise on account from Rolo Co., invoice no. 401, dated May 9; terms 3/10, n/30.
	14	Bought $1,000 of store supplies on account from Wales Co., invoice no. 419, dated May 14.

Check Figure:
Accounts payable ending bal. $7,900

10A-2. As the accountant for Riley's Natural Food Store, (1) journalize the following transactions into the general journal (p. 2), (2) record and post as appropriate, and (3) prepare a schedule of accounts payable. If using working papers, be sure to put in the following balances: Aris Co., $350; Brown Co., $800; Moose Co., $1,350; Ready Co., $700; Accounts Payable, $3,200; Purchases, $19,000. Use the periodic method.

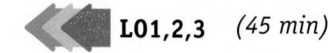 **LO1,2,3** *(45 min)*

201X		
April	8	Purchased $750 of merchandise on account from Aris Co., invoice no. 400, dated April 9; terms 5/10, n/60.
	10	Purchased $1,350 of merchandise on account from Brown Co., invoice no. 420, dated April 11; terms 5/10, n/60.
	12	Purchased $400 of store supplies on account from Moose Co., invoice no. 510, dated April 13.
	14	Issued debit memo no. 8 to Aris Co. for merchandise returned, $300, from invoice no. 400.
	17	Purchased $640 of office equipment on account from Ready Co., invoice no. 810, dated April 18.
	24	Purchased $850 of additional store supplies on account from Moose Co., invoice no. 516, dated April 25; terms 5/10, n/30.

Check Figure:
Total schedule of accounts payable $6,890

(45 min) **LO1,2,3**

Check Figure:
Total of schedule of accounts payable
$1,850

10A-3. Wendy Drew operates a wholesale computer center and has hired you as her bookkeeper to record the following transactions. She would like you to (1) journalize the following transactions, (2) record to the accounts payable subsidiary ledger and post to the general ledger as appropriate, and (3) prepare a schedule of accounts payable. If using working papers, be sure to put in the following beginning balances: Andersen Co., $1,200; Henderson Co., $400; Squash Co., $900; Xhosa Co., $1,300; Cash, $22,000; Accounts Payable, $3,800. Use the periodic method.

201X		
March	1	Paid half the amount owed Henderson Co. from previous purchases of computers on account, less a 7% purchases discount, check no. 21.
	3	Bought a delivery truck for $8,000 cash, check no. 22, payable to Bill Singer Co.
	6	Bought computer merchandise from Lossless Co., check no. 23, $2,500.
	18	Bought additional computer merchandise from Paced Co., check no. 24, $750.
	24	Paid Xhosa Co. the amount owed, less a 7% purchases discount, check no. 25.
	28	Paid rent expense to Viscount's Realty Trust, check no. 26, $2,200.
	29	Paid utilities expense to Granite Utility Co., check no. 27, $280.
	30	Paid half the amount owed Squash Co., no discount, check no. 28.

(130 min) **LO1,2,3**

S50 / QB

Check Figures:
Total of accounts receivable account
$9,400
Total of accounts payable account
$8,100

10A-4. Abby Gray opened Abby's Toy House. As her newly hired accountant, your tasks are to do the following:

1. Journalize the transactions for the month of December. Use the periodic method.
2. Record to subsidiary ledgers and post to the general ledger as appropriate.
3. Prepare a schedule of accounts receivable and a schedule of accounts payable.

The following is the partial chart of accounts for Abby's Toy House:

Abby's Toy House Chart of Accounts			
Assets		**Revenue**	
110	Cash	410	Toy Sales
112	Accounts Receivable	412	Sales Returns and Allowances
114	Prepaid Rent	414	Sales Discounts
121	Delivery Truck	**Cost of Goods**	
Liabilities		510	Toy Purchases
210	Accounts Payable	512	Purchases Returns and Allowances
Owner's Equity		514	Purchases Discount
310	A. Gray, Capital	**Expenses**	
		610	Salaries Expense
		612	Cleaning Expense

201X		
Dec.	1	Abby invested $7,000 in the toy store.
	1	Paid 3 months' rent in advance, check no. 1, $3,100.
	1	Purchased merchandise from Morris Curtis Company on account, $4,400, invoice no. 410, dated December 2; terms 5/10, n/30.
	3	Sold merchandise to David Plouffe on account, $500, invoice no. 1; terms 5/10, n/30.
	6	Sold merchandise to Robert Cooper on account, $400, invoice no. 2; terms 5/10, n/30.
	8	Purchased merchandise from Morris Curtis Co. on account, $1,300, invoice no. 415, dated December 9; terms 5/10, n/30.
	9	Sold merchandise to David Plouffe on account, $1,100, invoice no. 3; terms 5/10, n/30.
	9	Paid cleaning service, check no. 2, $275.
	10	Robert Cooper returned merchandise that cost $100 to Abby's Toy House. Abby issued credit memorandum no. 1 to Robert Cooper for $100.
	10	Purchased merchandise from Mildred Mann on account, $4,400, invoice no. 311, dated December 11; terms 1/15, n/60.
	12	Paid Morris Curtis Co., invoice no. 410, dated December 2, check no. 3.
	13	Sold $1,800 of toy merchandise for cash.
	13	Paid salaries, $1,100, check no. 4.
	14	Returned merchandise to Mildred Mann in the amount of $800. Abby's Toy House issued debit memorandum no. 1 to Mildred Mann.
	15	Sold merchandise for $3,900 cash.
	16	Received payment from Robert Cooper, invoice no. 2 (less returned merchandise), less discount.
	16	David Plouffe paid invoice no. 1.
	16	Sold toy merchandise to Alison Reach on account, $4,700, invoice no. 4; terms 5/10, n/30.
	20	Purchased delivery truck on account from Sam Katz Garage, $2,500, invoice no. 111, dated December 21 (no discount).
	22	Sold to David Plouffe merchandise on account, $1,200, invoice no. 5; terms 5/10, n/30.
	23	Paid Mildred Mann balance owed, check no. 5.
	24	Sold toy merchandise on account to Alison Reach, $600, invoice no. 6; terms 5/10, n/30.
	25	Purchased toy merchandise, $1,100, check no. 6.
	26	Purchased toy merchandise from Sanya Burger on account, $4,300, invoice no. 211, dated December 27; terms 5/10, n/30.
	28	David Plouffe paid invoice no. 5, dated December 22.
	28	Alison Reach paid invoice no. 6, dated December 24.
	28	Abby invested an additional $4,000 in the business.
	28	Purchased merchandise from Morris Curtis Co., $1,800, invoice no. 436, dated December 29; terms 5/10, n/30.
	30	Paid Morris Curtis Co. invoice no. 436, check no. 7.
	30	Sold merchandise to Bella Falco Company on account, $3,600, invoice no. 7; terms 5/10, n/30.

(40 min)   **LO4**   ➤

10A-5. Jackie's Toy Shop completed the following merchandise transactions in the month of April:

201X		
Apr.	2	Purchased merchandise on account from Irwin Suppliers, $2,500; terms 3/10, n/30.
	4	Sold merchandise on account, $500; terms 3/10, n/30. The cost of the merchandise sold was $330.
	4	Received credit from Irwin Suppliers for merchandise returned, $230.
	10	Received collection in full, less discounts, from April 4 sales.
	11	Paid Irwin Suppliers in full, less discount.
	14	Purchased store equipment for cash, $250.
	15	Purchased $1,000 of merchandise from Foley Distribution for cash.
	16	Received a refund due to defective merchandise from supplier on cash purchase of $90.
	17	Purchased merchandise on account from Thompson Corp., $3,600, F.O.B. shipping point (buyer pays freight); terms 3/10, n/30. Freight to be paid on April 21.
	18	Sold merchandise for $3,300 cash; the cost of merchandise sold was $1,550.
	21	Paid freight on April 17 purchase, $120.
	25	Purchased merchandise on account from Boute Co., $1,240, F.O.B. destination (seller pays freight); terms 3/10, n/30.
	26	Paid Thompson Corp. in full, less discount.
	27	Made refunds to cash customers for defective toys, $250. The cost of the defective toys was $110.

Check Figure:
Journal entry for Apr. 21 transaction
Dr. Merchandise inventory   120
  Cr. Cash   120

Jackie's Toy Shop accounts included the following: Cash 101; Accounts Receivable 112; Merchandise Inventory 120; Store Equipment 124; Accounts Payable 201; J. Jackie, Capital 301; Sales 401; Sales Discounts 412; Sales Returns and Allowances 414; Cost of Goods Sold 501.

Assignment

Journalize the transactions using a perpetual inventory system.

Set B

(30 min)   **LO1,2**   ➤

10B-1. Rasheed Chase recently opened Rasheed's Skate Shop. As the bookkeeper of the company, use the periodic method to journalize, record, and post when appropriate the following transactions (account numbers are Store Supplies 115; Store Equipment 121; Accounts Payable 210; Purchases 510):

201X		
Mar.	4	Bought $1,200 of merchandise on account from Newbury Co., invoice no. 442, dated March 5; terms 2/10, n/30.
	5	Bought $5,400 of store equipment on account from Andover Co., invoice no. 502, dated March 6.
	8	Bought $1,200 of merchandise on account from Lakeville Co., invoice no. 401, dated March 9, terms 2/10, n/30.
	14	Bought $1,300 of store supplies on account from Newbury Co., invoice no. 419, dated March 14.

Check Figure:
Accounts payable ending balance
$9,100

10B-2. As the accountant of Trina's Natural Food Store, (1) journalize the following transactions into the general journal (p. 2), (2) record and post as appropriate, and (3) prepare a schedule of accounts payable. If using working papers, be sure to put in the following balances: Antion Co., $450; Block Co., $500; Midden Co., $1,150; Rex Co., $250; Accounts Payable, $2,350; Purchases, $18,000. Use the periodic method.

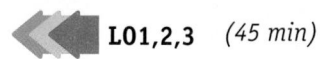 **LO1,2,3**   *(45 min)*

201X		
Oct.	8	Purchased $650 of merchandise on account from Antion Co., invoice no. 400, dated October 9; terms 9/10, n/60.
	10	Purchased $1,250 of merchandise on account from Block Co., invoice no. 420, dated October 11; terms 9/10, n/60.
	12	Purchased $700 of store supplies on account from Midden Co., invoice no. 510, dated October 13.
	14	Issued debit memo no. 8 to Antion Co. for merchandise returned, $500, from invoice no. 400.
	17	Purchased $620 of office equipment on account from Rex Co., invoice no. 810, dated October 18.
	24	Purchased $400 of additional store supplies on account from Midden Co., invoice no. 516, dated October 25; terms 9/10, n/30.

Check Figure:
Total of schedule of accounts payable
$5,470

10B-3. Wendy Johnson operates a wholesale computer center and has hired you as her bookkeeper to record the following transactions. She would like you to (1) journalize the following transactions, (2) record to the accounts payable subsidiary ledger and post to the general ledger as appropriate, and (3) prepare a schedule of accounts payable. If using working papers, be sure to put in the following beginning balances: Andersen Co., $1,050; Hack Co., $1,400; Soil Co., $850; Xydias Co., $1,000; Cash, $20,000; Accounts Payable, $4,300. Use the periodic method.

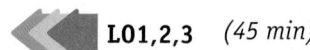 **LO1,2,3**   *(45 min)*

201X		
May	1	Paid half the amount owed Hack Co. from previous purchases of computers on account, less a 7% purchases discount, check no. 21.
	3	Bought a delivery truck for $7,500 cash, check no. 22, payable to Bill Brown Co.
	6	Bought computer merchandise from Lectro Co., check no. 23, $2,700.
	18	Bought additional computer merchandise from Pink Co., check no. 24, $600.
	24	Paid Xydias Co. the amount owed, less a 7% purchases discount, check no. 25.
	28	Paid rent expense to Queen's Realty Trust, check no. 26, $1,600.
	29	Paid utilities expense to Stone Utility Co., check no. 27, $360.
	30	Paid half the amount owed to Soil Co., no discount, check no. 28.

Check Figure:
Total of schedule of accounts payable
$2,175

10B-4. Abby Ellen opened Abby's Toy House. As her newly hired accountant, your tasks are to do the following:

1. Journalize the transactions for the month of March. Use the periodic method.
2. Record to subsidiary ledgers and post to the general ledger as appropriate.
3. Prepare a schedule of accounts receivable and a schedule of accounts payable.

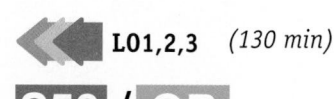 **LO1,2,3**   *(130 min)*

(Use the same chart of accounts as in Problem 10A-4, but now capital is Abby Ellen. The working papers that accompany this text have all the forms you need to complete this problem.)

201X		
Mar.	1	Abby Ellen invested $7,800 in the toy store.
	1	Paid 3 months' rent in advance, check no. 1, $3,400.
	1	Purchased merchandise from Morris Curtis Company on account, $4,300, invoice no. 410, dated March 2; terms 3/10, n/30.
	3	Sold merchandise to David Plouffe on account, $1,300, invoice no. 1; terms 3/10, n/30.
	6	Sold merchandise to John Drayton on account, $1,100, invoice no. 2; terms 3/10, n/30.
	8	Purchased merchandise from Morris Curtis Co. on account, $1,300, invoice no. 415, dated March 9; terms 3/10, n/30.
	9	Sold merchandise to David Plouffe on account, $400, invoice no. 3; terms 3/10, n/30.
	9	Paid cleaning service, check no. 2, $400.
	10	John Drayton returned merchandise that cost $500 to Abby's Toy House. Abby issued credit memorandum no. 1 to John Drayton for $500.
	10	Purchased merchandise from Michael Keiser on account, $4,500, invoice no. 311, dated March 11; terms 1/15, n/60.
	12	Paid Morris Curtis Co. invoice no. 410, dated March 2, check no. 3.
	13	Sold $900 of toy merchandise for cash.
	13	Paid salaries, $1,100, check no. 4.
	14	Returned merchandise to Michael Keiser in the amount of $600. Abby's Toy House issued debit memorandum no. 1 to Michael Keiser.
	15	Sold merchandise for $4,200 cash.
	16	Received payment from John Drayton, invoice no. 2 (less returned merchandise), less discount.
	16	David Plouffe paid invoice no. 1.
	16	Sold toy merchandise to Aimee Raypole on account, $4,000, invoice no. 4; terms 3/10, n/30.
	20	Purchased delivery truck on account from Sam Katz Garage, $3,300, invoice no. 111, dated March 21 (no discount).
	22	Sold merchandise to David Plouffe on account, $400, invoice no. 5; terms 3/10, n/30.
	23	Paid Michael Keiser balance owed, check no. 5.
	24	Sold toy merchandise to Aimee Raypole on account, $1,600, invoice no. 6; terms 3/10, n/30.
	25	Purchased toy merchandise, $500, check no. 6.
	26	Purchased toy merchandise from Millard Filmore on account, $4,100, invoice no. 211, dated March 27; terms 3/10, n/30.
	28	David Plouffe paid invoice no. 5, dated March 22.
	28	Aimee Raypole paid invoice no. 6, dated March 24.
	28	Abby invested an additional $8,500 in the business.
	28	Purchased merchandise from Morris Curtis Co., $2,000, invoice no. 436, dated March 29; terms 3/10, n/30.
	30	Paid Morris Curtis Co. invoice no. 436, check no. 7.
	30	Sold merchandise to Bella Falco Company on account, $3,400, invoice no. 7; terms 3/10, n/30.

Check Figures:
Total of schedule of accounts receivable $7,800; of accounts payable $8,700

10B-5. Jeanne's Toy Shop completed the following merchandise transactions in the month of April:

L04 *(40 min)*

201X		
Apr.	2	Purchased merchandise on account from Beech Suppliers, $3,500; terms 2/10, n/30.
	4	Sold merchandise on account $520; terms 2/10, n/30. The cost of the merchandise sold was $260.
	4	Received credit from Beech Suppliers for merchandise returned, $160.
	10	Received collection in full, less discounts, from April 4 sales.
	11	Paid Beech Suppliers in full, less discount.
	14	Purchased store equipment for cash, $290.
	15	Purchased $1,700 of merchandise from Soucy Distribution for cash.
	16	Received a refund due for defective merchandise from supplier on cash purchase of $80.
	17	Purchased merchandise on account from Tustin Corp., $3,700, F.O.B. shipping point (buyer pays freight); terms 2/10, n/30. Freight to be paid on April 21.
	18	Sold merchandise for $2,700 cash; the cost of the merchandise sold was $1,650.
	21	Paid freight on April 17 purchase, $130.
	25	Purchased merchandise on account from Oak Co., $1,040, F.O.B. destination (seller pays freight); terms 2/10, n/30.
	26	Paid Tustin Corp., in full, less discount.
	27	Made refunds to cash customers for defective toys, $190. The cost of the defective toys was $100.

Check Figure:
Journal entry for Apr. 21 transaction
Dr. Merchandise inventory   130
   Cr. Cash   130

Jeanne's Toy Shop accounts included the following: Cash 101; Accounts Receivable 112; Merchandise Inventory 120; Office Equipment 124; Accounts Payable 201; B. Jeanne, Capital 301; Sales 401; Sales Discounts 412; Sales Returns and Allowances 414; Cost of Goods Sold 501.

Assignment

Journalize the transactions using the perpetual inventory system.

Financial Report Problem

L01 *(15 min)*

Reading the Kellogg's Annual Report

Go to http://investor.kelloggs.com/investor-relations/annual-reports to access the Kellogg's 2013 Annual Report, and locate the balance sheet. How much has merchandise inventory increased or decreased from 2012 to 2013?

ON THE JOB SMITH COMPUTER CENTER

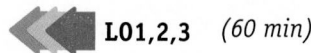
MyAccountingLab

The following is an updated schedule of accounts payable as of January 31, 201X.

L01,2,3 *(60 min)*

Schedule of Accounts Payable	
The Staple Store	50
Quality Office Furniture	1,800
Pacific Bell	170
A-Tech, Inc.	550
Total Accounts Payable	$2,570

Assignment

1. Journalize the transactions. Use the periodic method.
2. Record in the accounts payable subsidiary ledger and post to the general ledger as appropriate. A partial general ledger is included in the working papers that accompany this text.
3. The following accounts have been added to the chart of accounts: Purchases 6000, Purchase Returns and Allowances 6010, and Purchase Discounts 6020.
4. Prepare a schedule of accounts payable as of February 28, 201X.

The transactions for the month of February are as follows:

201X		
Feb.	1	Prepaid the rent for the months of February, March, and April, $1,500, check #2585.
	4	Bought merchandise on account from A-Tech, Inc., purchase order no. 4010, $480; terms 3/10, n/30.
	8	Bought office supplies on account from The Staple Store, purchase order no. 4011, $300; terms n/30.
	9	Purchased merchandise on account from Computers R Us, purchase order no. 4012, $450; terms 2/10, n/60.
	15	Paid purchase order no. 4010 in full to A-Tech, Inc., check #2586.
	21	Issued debit memorandum no. 10 to Computers R Us for merchandise returned from purchase order no. 4012, $150.
	27	Paid for office supplies, $120, check #2587.

S50 SAGE 50 COMPUTER WORKSHOP

Computerized Accounting Application for Chapter 10

Refresher on using Sage 50 Complete Accounting

Before starting this assignment, you may want to refresh your memory by reading the following PDF documents in the multimedia library of the MyAccountingLab Web site. Remember to choose the PDF document for your version of Sage 50.

1. An Introduction to Sage 50
2. Correcting Sage 50 Transactions
3. How to Repeat or Restart a Sage 50 Assignment
4. Backing Up and Restoring Your Work in Sage 50

You also should have completed the following workshops:

1. Workshop 1 Atlas Company from Chapter 3
2. Workshop 2 Zell Company from Chapter 4
3. Workshop 3 Sousa Realty from Chapter 5
4. Workshop 4 Pete's Market from Chapter 8

Workshop 5:

Part A: Recording Transactions in the Sales, Receipts, Purchases, and Payments Journals

Part B: Accounting Cycle Mini Practice Set with Sales and Purchasing

Part A: In this part of the workshop, you will learn to record customer sales on account, customer credit memos, customer cash receipts, purchases from vendors on account, and payments to vendors for Mars Company using Sage 50. You will also print the aged receivables and aged payables reports and the sales journal, cash receipts journal, purchasing journal, and cash disbursement journals.

Instructions and the data file for completing Part A of the assignment are in the multimedia library of the MyAccountingLab Web site. Open the *Workshop 5 Part A Mars Company* PDF document for your version of Sage 50 and download the *Mars Company* data file for your version of Sage 50.

Part B: In this part of the workshop, you will complete a mini practice set of March accounting transactions for Abby's Toy House using Sage 50. Transactions include customer sales on account, customer credit memos, customer cash receipts, purchases from vendors on account, payments to vendors, and general journal entries in Sage 50. You will also print the aged receivables and aged payables reports and the general journal and general ledger reports.

Instructions and the data file for completing Part B of the assignment are in the multimedia library of the MyAccountingLab Web site. Open the *Workshop 5 Part B Abby's Toy House* PDF document for your version of Sage 50 and download the *Abby's Toy House* data file for your version of Sage 50.

QUICKBOOKS COMPUTER WORKSHOP

QB

Computerized Accounting Application for Chapter 10

Refresher on using QuickBooks Accountant

Before starting this assignment, you may want to refresh your memory by reading the following PDF documents in the multimedia library of the MyAccountingLab Web site. Remember to choose the PDF document for your version of QuickBooks.

1. An Introduction to QuickBooks
2. Correcting QuickBooks Transactions
3. How to Repeat or Restart a QuickBooks Assignment
4. Backing Up and Restoring Your Work in QuickBooks

You also should have completed the following workshops:

1. Workshop 1 Atlas Company from Chapter 3
2. Workshop 2 Zell Company from Chapter 4
3. Workshop 3 Sousa Realty from Chapter 5
4. Workshop 4 Pete's Market from Chapter 8

Workshop 5:

Part A: Recording Transactions in the Sales, Receipts, Purchases, and Payments Journals

Part B: Accounting Cycle Mini Practice Set with Sales and Purchasing

Part A: In this part of the workshop, you will learn to record customer sales on account, customer credit memos, customer cash receipts, purchases from vendors on account, and payments to vendors for Mars Company using QuickBooks. You will also print the aged receivables and aged payables reports and the sales journal, cash receipts journal, purchasing journal, and cash disbursement journals.

Instructions and the data file for completing Part A of the assignment are in the multimedia library of the MyAccountingLab Web site. Open the *Workshop 5 Part A Mars Company* PDF document for your version of QuickBooks and download the *Mars Company* data file for your version of QuickBooks.

Part B: In this part of the workshop, you will complete a mini practice set of March accounting transactions for Abby's Toy House using QuickBooks. Transactions include customer sales on account, customer credit memos, customer cash receipts, purchases from vendors on account, payments to vendors, and general journal entries in QuickBooks. You will also print the aged receivables and aged payables reports and the general journal and general ledger reports.

Instructions and the data file for completing Part B of the assignment are in the multimedia library of the MyAccountingLab Web site. *Open the Workshop 5 Part B Abby's Toy House* PDF document for your version of QuickBooks and download the *Abby's Toy House* data file for your version of QuickBooks.

Appendix A

SPECIAL JOURNALS WITH PROBLEM MATERIAL

Learning Objectives

LO1   Identify Which Special Journal or General Journal Will Record a Transaction

LO2   Record Transactions in Special Journals or a General Journal and Post to Subsidiary and General Ledger Accounts

DEMONSTRATION SUMMARY PROBLEM  LO1,2

Journalizing Transactions to Special Journals*; Posting to Subsidiary and General Ledger Accounts from Special Journals: A Periodic Approach

All credit sales are 2/10, n/30. All merchandise purchased on account has 3/10, n/30 credit terms. Assume Periodic Inventory System. Ignore Sales Tax. The company uses Sales Journal, Purchases Journal, and Cash Receipt and Cash Payment Journals, as well as a General Journal.

Requirements

1. Identify journals to record transactions.
2. Record transactions in special journals or a general journal and post to subsidiary and general ledger accounts.

201X

Mar.		
	1	J. Ling invested $2,000 into the business.
	1	Sold merchandise on account to Balder Co., $500, invoice no. 1.
	2	Purchased merchandise on account from Case Co., $500.
	4	Sold $2,000 of merchandise for cash.
	6	Paid Case Co. from previous purchase on account, check no. 1.
	8	Sold merchandise on account to Lewis Co., $1,000, invoice no. 2.
	10	Received payment from Balder Co. for invoice no. 1.
	12	Issued a credit memorandum to Lewis Co. for $200 for faulty merchandise.
	14	Received payment from Lewis Co.
	16	Purchased merchandise on account from Noone Co., $1,000.
	17	Purchased equipment on account from Case Co., $300.
	18	Issued a debit memorandum to Noone Co. for $500 for defective merchandise.
	20	Paid salaries, $300, check no. 2.
	24	Paid Noone balance owed, check no. 3.

*All sales on account will go in a Sales Journal. Purchases on account will go in a Purchases Journal. Cash received will go in the Cash Receipts Journal and money paid out will go in the Cash Payments Journal.
Transactions that do not fit into these special journals will go into the General Journal.

Solutions

Requirement 1

Transaction	What to Do Step-by-Step
201X	
Mar. 1	*Money Received:* Record in cash receipts journal. Post immediately to J. Ling, Capital, because it is in sundry.
1	*Sale on Account:* Record in sales journal. Record immediately to Balder Co. in accounts receivable subsidiary ledger. Place a ✓ in Post. Ref. column of sales journal when subsidiary is updated.
2	*Buy Merchandise on Account:* Record in purchases journal. Record to Case Co. immediately in the accounts payable subsidiary ledger.
4	*Money In:* Record in cash receipts journal. No posting needed (put an × in Post. Ref. column).
6	*Money Out:* Record in cash payments journal. Save $15, which is a Purchases Discount. Record immediately to Case Co. in accounts payable subsidiary ledger (the full amount of $500).
8	*Sales on Account:* Record in sales journal. Update immediately to Lewis Co. in accounts receivable subsidiary ledger.
10	*Money In:* Record in cash receipts journal. Because Balder pays within 10 days, it gets a $10 discount. Record the full amount immediately to Balder in the accounts receivable subsidiary ledger.
12	*Returns:* Record in general journal. Seller issues credit memo resulting in higher sales returns and customers owing less. All postings and recordings are done immediately.
14	*Money In:* Record in cash receipts journal:

$$\$1,000 - \$200 \text{ returns} = \$800$$
$$\underline{\times\ 0.02}$$
$$\$\ 16 \text{ discount}$$

	Record immediately the $800 to Lewis Co. in the accounts receivable subsidiary ledger.
16	*Buy Now, Pay Later:* Record in purchases journal. Record immediately to Noone Co. in the accounts payable subsidiary ledger.
17	*Buy Now, Pay Later:* Record in purchases journal in Sundry. This item is not merchandise for resale. Record and post immediately.
18	*Returns:* Record in general ledger. Buyer issues a debit memo reducing the Accounts Payable due to purchases return and allowances. Post and record immediately.
20	*Salaries:* Record in cash payments journal, sundry column. Post immediately to Salaries Expense.
24	*Money Out:* Record in cash payments journal. Save 3% ($15), a purchases discount. Record immediately to accounts payable subsidiary ledger that you reduce Noone by $500.

Requirement 2

Record transactions in special journals or general journal and record to subsidiary and post to general ledger accounts.

Record accounts receivable
subsidiary ledger immediately.

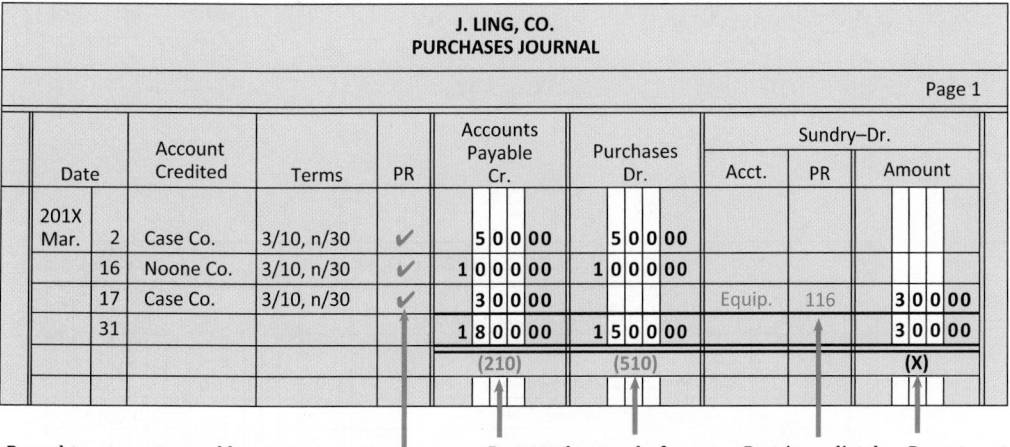

J. LING, CO.
SALES JOURNAL

Page 1

Date		Account Debited	Terms	Invoice No.	PR	Dr. Accts. Rec Cr. Sales
201X Mar.	1	Balder Co.	2/10, n/30	1	✔	5 0 0 00
	8	Lewis Co.	2/10, n/30	2	✔	1 0 0 0 00
	31					1 5 0 0 00
						(112) (410)

Total posted at end of
month to these accounts.

FIGURE 10A.1
Sales Journal

COACHING TIP

Remember, the sales journal only
records sales on account.

J. LING, CO.
PURCHASES JOURNAL

Page 1

Date		Account Credited	Terms	PR	Accounts Payable Cr.	Purchases Dr.	Sundry–Dr. Acct.	PR	Amount
201X Mar.	2	Case Co.	3/10, n/30	✔	5 0 0 00	5 0 0 00			
	16	Noone Co.	3/10, n/30	✔	1 0 0 0 00	1 0 0 0 00			
	17	Case Co.	3/10, n/30	✔	3 0 0 00		Equip.	116	3 0 0 00
	31				1 8 0 0 00	1 5 0 0 00			3 0 0 00
					(210)	(510)			(X)

Record to accounts payable
subsidiary ledger immediately.

Post totals at end of
month to general ledger.

Post immediately
to Equipment in
general ledger.

Do not post
total.

FIGURE 10A.2
Purchases Journal

COACHING TIP

Remember, the purchases
journal records buy now, pay
later transactions. Purchases
are merchandise for resale,
while equipment is not for
resale.

Post to capital immediately.

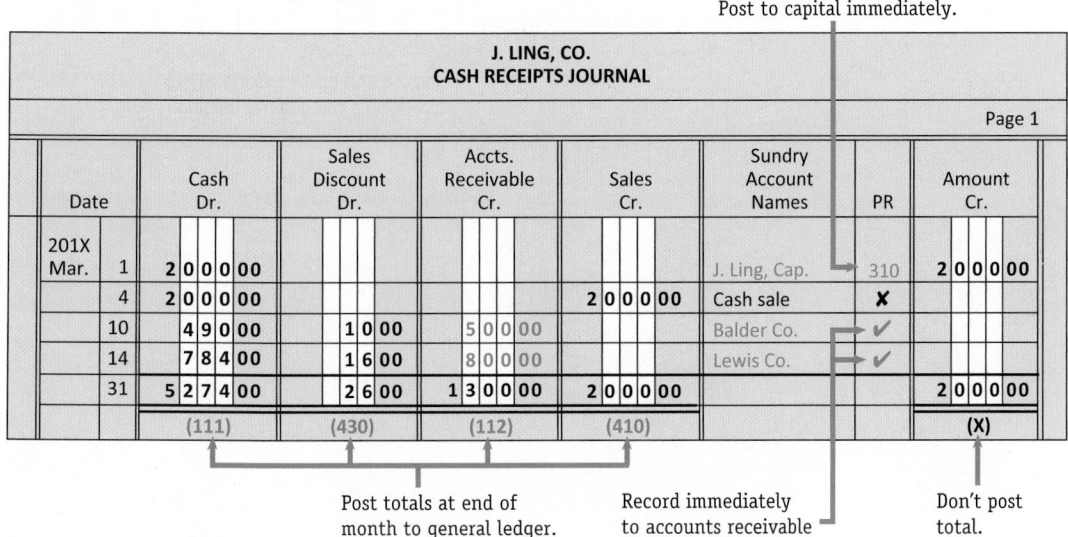

J. LING, CO.
CASH RECEIPTS JOURNAL

Page 1

Date		Cash Dr.	Sales Discount Dr.	Accts. Receivable Cr.	Sales Cr.	Sundry Account Names	PR	Amount Cr.
201X Mar.	1	2 0 0 0 00				J. Ling, Cap.	310	2 0 0 0 00
	4	2 0 0 0 00			2 0 0 0 00	Cash sale	✘	
	10	4 9 0 00	1 0 00	5 0 0 00		Balder Co.	✔	
	14	7 8 4 00	1 6 00	8 0 0 00		Lewis Co.	✔	
	31	5 2 7 4 00	2 6 00	1 3 0 0 00	2 0 0 0 00			2 0 0 0 00
		(111)	(430)	(112)	(410)			(X)

Post totals at end of
month to general ledger.

Record immediately
to accounts receivable
subsidiary ledger.

Don't post
total.

FIGURE 10A.3
Cash Receipts Journal

COACHING TIP

Remember, the cash
receipts journal records
any transaction that
involves the receipt
of cash.

FIGURE 10A.4

Cash Payments Journal

COACHING TIP

Remember, the cash payment journal records only transactions that result in the payment of cash.

Record immediately to accounts payable subsidiary ledger.

J. LING, CO. CASH PAYMENTS JOURNAL

Page 1

Date		Ck. No.	Account Debited	PR	Sundry Dr.	Accounts Payable Dr.	Purchases Discount Cr.	Cash Cr.
201X Mar.	6	1	Case Co.	✔		5 0 0 00	1 5 00	4 8 5 00
	20	2	Salaries Expense	610	3 0 0 00			3 0 0 00
	24	3	Noone Co.	✔		5 0 0 00	1 5 00	4 8 5 00
	31				3 0 0 00	1 0 0 0 00	3 0 00	1 2 7 0 00
					(X)	(210)	(530)	(111)

Post immediately to Salaries Expense.

Do not post total.

Post totals at end of month to the general ledger.

FIGURE 10A.5

General Journal

COACHING TIP

Remember, transactions not fitting into the four special journals are recorded in the general journal.

J. LING, CO. GENERAL JOURNAL

Page 1

Date		Account Titles and Description	PR	Dr.	Cr.
201X Mar.	12	Sales Returns and Allowances	420	2 0 0 00	
		Accounts Receivable, Lewis Co.	112 ✔		2 0 0 00
		Issued credit memo			
	18	Accounts Payable, Noone Co.	210 ✔	5 0 0 00	
		Purchases Returns and Allowances	520		5 0 0 00
		Issued debit memo			

Record and post immediately to subsidiary and general ledgers.

ACCOUNTS RECEIVABLE
SUBSIDIARY LEDGER

Balder Company

Date	PR	Dr.	Cr.	Dr. Bal.
201X 3/1	SJ1	500		500
3/10	CRJ1		500	—

Lewis Company

Date	PR	Dr.	Cr.	Dr. Bal.
201X 3/8	SJ1	1,000		1,000
3/12	GJ1		200	800
3/14	CRJ1		800	—

ACCOUNTS PAYABLE
SUBSIDIARY LEDGER

Case Company

Date	PR	Dr.	Cr.	Cr. Bal.
201X 3/2	PJ1		500	500
3/6	CPJ1	500		—
3/17	PJ1		300	300

Noone Company

Date	PR	Dr.	Cr.	Cr. Bal.
201X 3/16	PJ1		1,000	1,000
3/18	GJ1	500		500
3/24	CPJ1	500		—

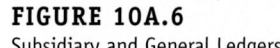

FIGURE 10A.6
Subsidiary and General Ledgers

COACHING TIP

Note that in the accounts receivable subsidiary ledger (Dr. balance) customers owe the seller, whereas in the accounts payable subsidiary ledger (Cr. balance) the seller owes the vendors it purchased items from.

GENERAL LEDGER

Cash 111

3/31 CRJ1 5,274	1,270 3/31 CPJ1
Bal. 4,004	

Accounts Receivable 112

3/31 SJ1 1,500	200 3/12 GJ1
	1,300 3/31 CRJ1
Bal. 0	

Equipment 116

3/17 PJ1 300	

Accounts Payable 210

3/18 GJ1 500	1,800 3/31 PJ1
3/31 CPJ1 1,000	
	300 Bal.

J. Ling, Capital 310

	2,000 3/1 CRJ1

Sales 410

	1,500 3/31 SJ1
	2,000 3/31 CRJ1
	3,500 Bal.

Sales Returns and Allowances 420

3/12 GJ1 200	

Sales Discount 430

3/31 CRJ1 26	

Purchases 510

3/31 PJ1 1,500	

Purchases Returns and Allowances 520

	500 3/18 GJ1

Purchases Discount 530

	30 3/31 CPJ1

Salaries Expense 610

3/20 CPJ1 300	

COACHING TIP

Remember, in the General Ledger Accounts Receivable and Accounts Payable are the controlling accounts.

Tips for Journalizing, Recording, and Posting from Special Journals

Seller	Buyer
Sales journal	Purchases journal
Cash receipts journal	Cash payments journal
Sales (Cr.)	Purchases (Dr.)
Sales Returns and Allowances (Dr.)	Purchase Returns and Allowances (Cr.)
Sales Discounts (Dr.)	Purchase Discounts (Cr.)
Accounts Receivable (Dr.)	Accounts Payable (Cr.)
Accounts receivable subsidiary ledger	Accounts payable subsidiary ledger
Schedule of accounts receivable	Schedule of accounts payable
Issue a credit memo or receive a debit memo	Receive a credit memo or issue a debit memo

End of Month Post totals (except sundry) of special journals to the general ledger.

Note: In this problem at the end of the month, (1) Accounts Receivable in the general ledger, the controlling account, has a zero balance, as does each title in the accounts receivable subsidiary ledger, and (2) the balance in Accounts Payable (the controlling account) is $300. In the accounts payable subsidiary ledger, J. Ling owes Case Co. $300. The sum of the accounts payable subsidiary ledger does equal the balance in the controlling account at the end of the month.

Appendix A Problems (Assume Periodic Method)

A-1. Jackie Red opened Yummy.com, a wholesale grocery and pizza company. Since Jackie only sells to retailers, she does not have to charge sales tax to her customers. Jackie uses a sales journal for sales on account. The following transactions occurred in April:

201X

Apr.	1	Sold grocery merchandise to Dabney Co. on account, $900, invoice no. 1.
	4	Sold pizza merchandise to Sally Drought Co. on account, $1,300, invoice no. 2.
	8	Sold grocery merchandise to Luxury Co. on account, $1,500, invoice no. 3.
	10	Issued credit memorandum no. 1 to Dabney Co. for $100 of grocery merchandise returned due to spoilage.
	15	Sold pizza merchandise to Sally Drought Co. on account, $220, invoice no. 4.
	19	Sold grocery merchandise to Luxury Co. on account, $700, invoice no. 5.
	25	Sold pizza merchandise to Dabney Co. on account, $800, invoice no. 6.

Required

1. Journalize the transactions in the appropriate journals.
2. Record to the accounts receivable subsidiary ledger and post to the general ledger as appropriate.
3. Prepare a schedule of accounts receivable.

Check Figure:
Schedule of accounts
receivable $5,320

A-2. The following transactions of David's Auto Supply occurred in June. David uses a sales journal to record sales on account. The balances as of June 1 for the accounts receivable subsidiary ledger are Graham Carter, $600; J. Sanders, $500; and R. Victor, $800. Other balances on June 1 are Accounts Receivable $1,900 and Sales Taxes Payable $1,900.

201X

June 1   Sold auto parts merchandise to R. Victor on account, $800, invoice no. 60, plus 4% sales tax.

     5   Sold auto parts merchandise to J. Sanders on account, $400, invoice no. 61, plus 4% sales tax.

     8   Sold auto parts merchandise to Graham Carter on account, $17,000, invoice no. 62, plus 4% sales tax.

   10   Issued credit memorandum no. 12 to R. Victor for $700 for defective auto parts merchandise returned from June 1 transaction. (Be careful to record the reduction in Sales Tax Payable as well.)

   12   Sold auto parts merchandise to J. Sanders on account, $1,200, invoice no. 63, plus 4% sales tax.

Required

1. Journalize the transactions in the appropriate journals.
2. Record to the accounts receivable subsidiary ledger and post to the general ledger as appropriate.
3. Prepare a schedule of accounts receivable.

Check Figure:
Schedule of accounts receivable
$21,348

A-3. Alison Murphy recently opened Tennis.com. Alison uses a purchases journal to record purchases on account. As the bookkeeper of her company, please journalize, record, and post when appropriate the following transactions (account numbers are Store Supplies, 115; Store Equipment, 121; Accounts Payable, 210; Purchases, 510):

201X

Nov. 4   Bought $600 of merchandise on account from Miller.com, invoice no. 442, dated November 5; terms 9/10, n/30.

     5   Bought $4,100 of store equipment on account from Newburg Co., invoice no. 502, dated November 6.

     8   Bought $1,200 of merchandise on account from Rapone Co., invoice no. 401, dated November 9; terms 9/10, n/30.

   14   Bought $700 of store supplies on account from Miller.com, invoice no. 419, dated November 14.

Check Figure:
Total of purchases column
in purchases journal: $1,800

A-4. Marion's Natural Food Store uses a purchases journal and a general journal to record the following transactions. The balances as of March 1 for the accounts payable subsidiary ledger are Alden Co., $300; Bullman Co., $800; Mott Co., $1,000; and Reynold Co., $500. Other balances on March 1 are Accounts Payable $2,600 and Purchases $18,000.

201X

Mar. 8   Purchased $1,400 of merchandise on account from Alden Co., invoice no. 400, dated March 9; terms 5/10, n/60.

   10   Purchased $2,000 of merchandise on account from Bullman Co., invoice no. 420, dated March 11; terms 5/10, n/60.

   12   Purchased $1,200 of store supplies on account from Mott Co., invoice no. 510, dated March 13.

   14   Issued debit memo no. 8 to Alden Co., for merchandise returned, $350, from invoice no. 400.

   17   Purchased $510 of office equipment on account from Reynold Co., invoice no. 810, dated March 18.

   24   Purchased $680 of additional store supplies on account from Mott Co., invoice no. 516, dated March 25; terms 5/10, n/30.

Check Figure:
Total schedule of accounts payable
$8,040

The food store decided to keep a separate column for the purchases of supplies in the purchases journal. Your tasks are to do the following:

1. Journalize the transactions.

2. Post and record as appropriate.

3. Prepare a schedule of accounts payable.

A-5. Andrea Richardson opened Andrea's Toy House. As her newly hired accountant, your tasks are to do the following:

1. Journalize the transactions for the month of December. Andrea uses special journals for sales on account, purchases on account, and cash receipts and cash payments, as well as a general journal.

2. Record to subsidiary ledgers and post to the general ledger as appropriate.

3. Total and rule the journals.

4. Prepare a schedule of accounts receivable and a schedule of accounts payable.

5. Ignore Sales Tax.

The following is the partial chart of accounts for Andrea's Toy House:

Andrea's Toy House Chart of Accounts

Assets		Revenue	
110	Cash	410	Toy Sales
112	Accounts Receivable	412	Sales Returns and Allowances
114	Prepaid Rent	414	Sales Discounts
121	Delivery Truck	**Cost of Goods**	
Liabilities		510	Toy Purchases
210	Accounts Payable	512	Purchases Returns and Allowances
Owner's Equity		514	Purchases Discount
310	A. Richardson, Capital	**Expenses**	
		610	Salaries Expense
		612	Cleaning Expense

201X

Dec. 1   Andrea Richardson invested $7,200 in the toy store.

1   Paid 3 months' rent in advance, check no. 1, $4,500.

1   Purchased merchandise from Morris Curtis Company on account, $3,500, invoice no. 410, dated December 2; terms 9/10, n/30.

3   Sold merchandise to Bill Burton on account, $900, invoice no. 1; terms 9/10, n/30.

6   Sold merchandise to David Muldrow Beasley on account, $1,200, invoice no. 2; terms 9/10, n/30.

8   Purchased merchandise from Morris Curtis Co. on account, $1,500, invoice no. 415, dated December 9; terms 9/10, n/30.

9   Sold merchandise to Bill Burton on account, $900, invoice no. 3; terms 9/10, n/30.

9   Paid cleaning service, check no. 2, $400.

10   David Muldrow Beasley returned merchandise with a selling price of $200 to Andrea's Toy House. Andrea issued credit memorandum no. 1 to David Muldrow Beasley for $200.

10   Purchased merchandise from Rose Kaufman on account, $4,300, invoice no. 311, dated December 11; terms 2/15, n/60.

12   Paid Morris Curtis Co. invoice no. 410, dated December 2, check no. 3.

13   Sold $800 of toy merchandise for cash.

13   Paid salaries, $500, check no. 4.

14   Returned merchandise to Rose Kaufman in the amount of $1,000. Andrea's Toy House issued debit memorandum no. 1 to Rose Kaufman.

15 Sold merchandise for $4,500 cash.

16 Received payment from David Muldrow Beasley, invoice no. 2 (less returned merchandise), less discount.

16 Bill Burton paid invoice no. 1.

16 Sold toy merchandise to Andrea Reagen on account, $4,000, invoice no. 4; terms 9/10, n/30.

20 Purchased delivery truck on account from Sam Katz Garage, $2,500, invoice no. 111, dated December 21 (no discount).

22 Sold to Bill Burton merchandise on account, $1,100, invoice no. 5; terms 9/10, n/30.

23 Paid Rose Kaufman balance owed, check no. 5.

24 Sold toy merchandise on account to Andrea Reagen, $900, invoice no. 6; terms 9/10, n/30.

25 Purchased toy merchandise, $900, check no. 6.

26 Purchased toy merchandise from Adam Graves on account, $5,100, invoice no. 211, dated December 27; terms 9/10, n/30.

28 Bill Burton paid invoice no. 5, dated December 22.

28 Andrea Reagen paid invoice no. 6, dated December 24.

28 Andrea Richardson invested an additional $4,500 in the business.

28 Purchased merchandise from Morris Curtis Co. on account, $1,300, invoice no. 436, dated December 29; terms 9/10, n/30.

30 Paid Morris Curtis Co. invoice no. 436, check no. 7.

30 Sold merchandise to Bella Falco Company on account, $2,900, invoice no. 7; terms 9/10, n/30.

Sales and Cash Receipts Journal Using a Perpetual Inventory System for Art's Wholesale Clothing

FIGURE 10A.7
A Sales Journal Under a Perpetual System

							Cost of Goods Sold Dr.	
Date	Account Debited	Terms	·	Invoice No.	Post. Ref.	Dr. Acc. Rec Cr. Sales	Merchandise Inventory Cr.	
201X Apr. 3	Hal's Clothing	2/10, n/30		1	✔	8 0 0 00	5 6 0 00	
6	Bevans Company	2/10, n/30		2	✔	1 6 0 0 00	1 1 2 0 00	
18	Roe Company	2/10, n/30		3	✔	2 0 0 0 00	1 4 0 0 00	
24	Roe Company	2/10, n/30		4	✔	5 0 0 00	3 5 0 00	
28	Mel's Dept. Store	2/10, n/30		5	✔	9 0 0 00	6 3 0 00	
29	Mel's Dept. Store	2/10, n/30		6	✔	7 0 0 00	4 9 0 00	
30								
						6 5 0 0 00	4 5 5 0 00	
						(113) (411)	(510) (114)	

ART'S WHOLESALE CLOTHING COMPANY
SALES JOURNAL
Page 1

What's new:

In the sales journal: New columns for Cost of Goods Sold (Dr.) and Merchandise Inventory (Cr.). Each time a charge sale is earned, the Cost of Goods Sold increases and the amount of Merchandise Inventory at cost is reduced.

In the general ledger: New ledger accounts for Inventory and Cost of Goods Sold. Example: On April 3, Art's Wholesale sold Hal's Clothing $800 of merchandise on account. This sale cost Art's $560 to bring this merchandise into the store.

FIGURE 10A.8 A Cash Receipts Journal Under a Perpetual System

Date		Cash Dr.	Sales Discount Dr.	Accounts Receivable Cr.	Sales Cr.	Sundry			Cost of Goods Sold Dr. Merchandise Inventory Cr.
						Account Name	Post. Ref.	Amount Cr.	
201X Apr.	1	8 0 0 0 00				Art Newner, Capital	311	8 0 0 0 00	
	4	7 8 4 00	1 6 00	8 0 0 00		Hal's Clothing	✔		
	15	9 0 0 00			9 0 0 00	Cash Sales	X		6 3 0 00
	16	9 8 0 00	2 0 00	1 0 0 0 00		Bevans Company	✔		
	22	1 9 6 0 00	4 0 00	2 0 0 0 00		Roe Company	✔		
	27	5 0 0 00				Store Equipment	121	5 0 0 00	
	30	1 2 0 0 00			1 2 0 0 00	Cash Sales	X		8 4 0 00
		1 4 3 2 4 00	7 6 00	3 8 0 0 00	2 1 0 0 00			8 5 0 0 00	1 4 7 0 00
		(111)	(413)	(113)	(411)			(X)	(510) (114)

What's new:

In the cash receipts journal: New columns for Cost of Goods Sold (Dr.) and Merchandise Inventory (Cr.). Each time a cash sale is earned, the Cost of Goods Sold increases and the amount of Inventory at cost is reduced.

CHAPTER 11

Preparing a Worksheet for a Merchandise Company

CHAPTER PREVIEW: THE BIG PICTURE

Roger Floss is planning to go to the Apple Store to buy the latest version of the iPad. He wonders if they may be out of stock. Apple Stores and its suppliers make adjustments to the inventory so customer demand can be met. In addition, Apple makes other adjustments that customers may not be aware of. These adjustments include supplies, rent, the wages of employees, and depreciation. Like the preparation of worksheets of nonmerchandising companies that you learned about in Chapter 4, to make these adjustments, many merchandise companies will also use a worksheet with some differences. In this chapter, you learn how a merchandising company prepares a worksheet and how it flows to the financial statements.

Learning Objectives

LO1   Figuring Adjustments for Merchandise Inventory, Unearned Rent, Supplies Used, Insurance Expired, Depreciation Expense, and Salaries Accrued

LO2   Preparing a Worksheet for a Merchandise Company

When you shop at the Apple Store, do you ever wonder how Apple controls its inventory? In Chapters 9 and 10 we discussed the subsidiary ledgers as well as entries for a merchandise company. Additional material provided an introduction to perpetual inventory. Now we shift our attention to recording adjustments and completing a worksheet for a merchandise company. Note that the appendix at the end of the chapter shows worksheets for a perpetual system.

LEARNING UNIT 11-1

L01 ▶

Adjustments for Merchandise Inventory, Unearned Rent, Supplies Used, Insurance Expired, Depreciation Expense, and Salaries Accrued

The Merchandise Inventory account shows the goods that a merchandise company has available to sell to customers. Companies have several ways to keep track of the cost of goods sold (the total cost of the goods sold to customers) and the quantity of inventory on hand. In this chapter we discuss the periodic inventory system, in which the balance in inventory is updated only at the end of the accounting period.* This system is used by companies, such as Art's Wholesale Clothing Company, that sell a variety of merchandise with low unit prices.

Assume that Art's Wholesale Clothing Company started the year with $19,000 worth of merchandise. This merchandise is called beginning merchandise inventory or simply beginning inventory. The balance of beginning inventory in the merchandise inventory account never changes during the accounting period. Any purchases of merchandise are recorded in a separate account, the Purchases account. During the accounting period $52,000 worth of such purchases were made and recorded in the Purchases account by Art's Wholesale.

At the end of the period, the company takes a physical count of the merchandise in stock; this amount is called ending merchandise inventory or simply ending inventory. It is calculated on an inventory sheet as shown in Figure 11.1. This $4,000 is the ending inventory for this period and will become the beginning inventory for the next period.

When the income statement is prepared, the cost of goods sold section requires two distinct numbers for inventory. The beginning inventory adds to the cost of goods sold, and the ending inventory is subtracted from the cost of goods sold. Remember that the two figures for beginning and ending inventory were calculated months apart. Thus, combining these amounts to come up with one inventory figure would not be accurate.

Note that in the calculation of cost of goods sold on the next page a title called Freight-In is shown.

Cost of goods sold Total cost of the goods which were sold to customers.

Periodic inventory system An inventory system that, at the *end* of each accounting period, calculates the cost of the unsold goods on hand by taking the cost of each unit times the number of units on hand of each product.

Beginning merchandise inventory (beginning inventory) The cost of goods on hand in a company to *begin* an accounting period.

Ending merchandise inventory (ending inventory) The cost of goods that remain unsold at the *end* of the accounting period. It is an asset on the new balance sheet.

Freight-In A cost of goods sold account that records the shipping cost to the buyer.

FIGURE 11.1
Ending Inventory Sheet

ART'S WHOLESALE CLOTHING COMPANY ENDING INVENTORY SHEET AS OF DECEMBER 31, 201X				
Amount	Explanation	Unit Cost	Total	
20	Ladies' Jackets code 14-0	$50	$1,000	
10	Men's Hats code 327	10	100	
90	Men's Shirts code 423	10	900	
100	Ladies' Blouses code 481	20	2,000	
			$4,000	
Counted by _____	Checked and priced by _____			

Perpetual inventory system An inventory system that keeps *continual track* of each type of inventory by recording units on hand at the beginning, units sold, and the current balance after each sale or purchase.

*For a discussion of the perpetual inventory system, see Chapter 10, Learning Unit 10-4.

Cost of goods sold

	Beginning inventory
+	Net purchases
+	Freight-in
−	Ending inventory
=	Cost of goods sold

Freight-In is a cost of goods sold account that records the shipping cost to the buyer. Note that net sales (gross sales less sales returns and allowances and sales discounts) less cost of goods sold equals gross profit. Subtracting operating expenses from gross profit equals net income.

Adjustments A and B: Merchandise Inventory, $19,000. Adjusting the Merchandise Inventory account is a two-step process because we must record the beginning inventory and ending inventory amounts separately. The first step deals with beginning merchandise inventory.

Given: Beginning Inventory, $19,000. Our first adjustment removes the old outdated beginning inventory from the asset account (Merchandise Inventory) and transfers it to Income Summary. We do so by crediting Merchandise Inventory for $19,000 and debiting Income Summary for the same amount. This adjustment (A) is shown in the following T account form and on a transaction analysis chart.

Gross profit Net sales less cost of goods sold.

COACHING TIP

Note that Income Summary has no normal balance of debit or credit.

Merchandise Inventory 114			Income Summary 313	
Bal.	19,000	Adj.	19,000	Adj.	19,000

Adjustment (A)

Accounts Affected	Category	↑↓	Rules
Income Summary	—	—	Dr.
Merchandise Inventory	Asset	↓	Cr.

(This, as well as the following adjusting entries, would be recorded first on the worksheet and then in the general journal.)

The second step is entering the amount of ending inventory ($4,000) in the Merchandise Inventory account. This step is done to record the up-to-date amount of goods on hand at the end of the period as an asset and to subtract this amount from the cost of goods sold (because we have not sold this inventory yet). To do so, we debit Merchandise Inventory for $4,000 and credit Income Summary for the same amount. This adjustment (B) is shown in the following T account form.

COACHING TIP

Second adjustment updates Inventory account with a new figure for ending inventory.

Merchandise Inventory 114				Income Summary 313			
Bal.	19,000	Adj.	19,000	Adj.	19,000	Adj.	4,000
Adj.	4,000						

Adjustment (B)

Let's look at how this process or method of recording merchandise inventory is reflected in the balance sheet and income statement (see Figure 11.2, page 408). Note that the $19,000 of beginning inventory is assumed sold and is shown on the income statement as part of the cost of goods sold. The ending inventory of $4,000 is assumed not to be sold and is subtracted from the cost of goods sold on the income statement. The ending inventory becomes next month's beginning inventory on the

COACHING TIP

Beginning inventory	$19,000
+ Net cost of purchases*	50,910
= Cost of goods available for sale	$69,910
− Ending inventory	4,000
= Cost of goods sold	$65,910

*$52,000 Purchases − $860 PD − $680 PRA + $450 Freight-In

FIGURE 11.2
Reporting Inventory on a Partial
Balance Sheet and Income
Statement

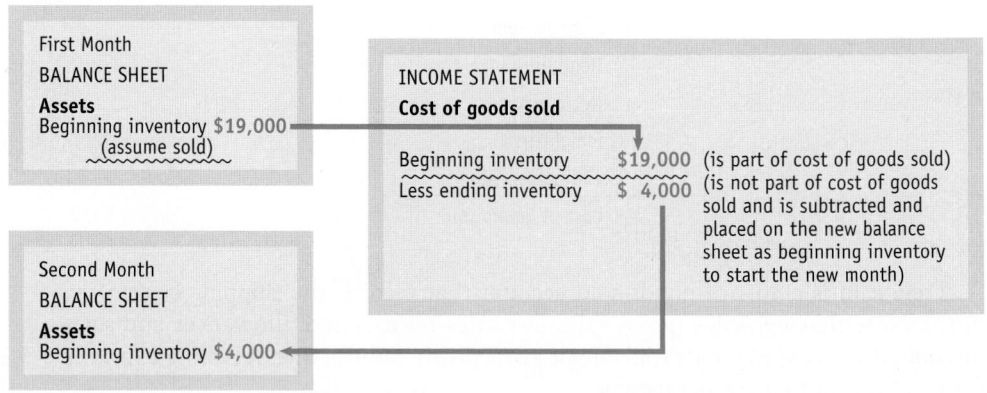

balance sheet. When the income statement is prepared, we will need a figure for beginning inventory as well as a figure for ending inventory. The goal of this adjustment is to wipe out the old inventory (a cost) and show the new inventory (not yet a cost).

Adjustment C: Unearned Rent. Another new account we have not seen before is a liability called Unearned Rent or Rent Received in Advance. This account records the amount collected for rent before the service (renting the space) has been provided.

Suppose Art's Wholesale Clothing Company is subletting a portion of its space to Jesse Company for $200 per month. Jesse Company sends Art's cash for $600 for 3 months' rent paid in advance. This unearned rent ($600) is a liability on the balance sheet because Art's Wholesale owes Jesse Company 3 months' worth of occupancy.

When Art's Wholesale fulfills a portion of the rental agreement—when Jesse Company has been in the space for a period of time—this liability account will be reduced and the Rental Income account will be increased. Rental income is another type of revenue for Art's Wholesale.

Remember that under accrual accounting, revenue is recognized when it is earned, whether payment is received then or not. Here, Art's Wholesale collected cash in advance for a service that it has not yet performed. A liability called Unearned Rent is the result. Art's Wholesale may have the cash, but the rental income is not recorded until it is earned. Examples of other types of unearned revenue besides unearned rent include prepaid subscriptions for magazines, legal fees collected before the work is performed, and prepaid insurance.

Now let's check your progress.

COACHING TIP

Received cash for renting space in future:

| Cash | Asset | ↑ | Dr. |
| Unearned Rent | Liab. | ↑ | Cr. |

COACHING TIP

The adjustment when rental income is earned:

| Unearned Rent | Liab. | ↓ | Dr. |
| Rental Income | Rev. | ↑ | Cr. |

 TRY IT!   Learning Unit 11-1

Jones Co. has calculated Merchandise Inventory to have a $30,000 balance at the end of the month. Jones also stated that the amount of unearned legal fees has been reduced by $4,000

Please update the following accounts to reflect the adjustment data for merchandise inventory and unearned legal fees.

Merchandise Inventory 114	
Dr.	Cr.
65,000	

Unearned Legal Fees 310

Dr.	Cr.
	8,000

Income Summary 313

Dr.	Cr.

Earned Legal Fees 410

Dr.	Cr.

Worksheets for Merchandise Companies

LEARNING UNIT 11-2

LO2

In this unit, we prepare a worksheet for Art's Wholesale Clothing Company. For convenience, we reproduce the company's chart of accounts in Figure 11.3.

CHART OF ACCOUNTS	
Assets 100–199	**Revenue 400–499**
111 Cash	411 Sales
112 Petty Cash	412 Sales Returns and Allowances
113 Accounts Receivable	413 Sales Discount
114 Merchandise Inventory	414 Rental Income
115 Supplies	**Cost of Goods Sold 500–599**
116 Prepaid Insurance	511 Purchases
121 Store Equipment	512 Purchases Discount
122 Accum. Depreciation, Store Equipment	513 Purchases Returns and Allowances
Liabilities 200–299	514 Freight-In
211 Accounts Payable	**Expenses 600–699**
212 Salaries Payable	611 Salaries Expense
213 Federal Income Tax Payable	612 Payroll Tax Expense
214 FICA—Social Security Payable	613 Depreciation Expense, Store Equipment
215 FICA—Medicare Payable	614 Supplies Expense
216 State Income Tax Payable	615 Insurance Expense
217 SUTA Tax Payable	616 Postage Expense
218 FUTA Tax Payable	617 Miscellaneous Expense
219 Unearned Rent*	618 Interest Expense
220 Mortgage Payable	619 Cleaning Expense
Owner's Equity 300–399	620 Delivery Expense
311 Art Newner, Capital	
312 Art Newner, Withdrawals	
313 Income Summary	
*Although Unearned Rent is the only term under Liabilities not using payable, it is a liability.	

FIGURE 11.3
Art's Wholesale Clothing Company Chart of Accounts

Figure 11.4 (page 410) shows the trial balance that was prepared on December 31, 201X, from Art's Wholesale ledger. (Note that it is placed directly in the first two columns of the worksheet.)

FIGURE 11.4
Trial Balance Section
of the Worksheet

		Trial Balance	
		Dr.	Cr.
Cash		12 9 2 0 00	
Petty Cash		1 0 0 00	
Accounts Receivable		14 5 0 0 00	
Merchandise Inventory		19 0 0 0 00	
Supplies		8 0 0 00	
Prepaid Insurance		9 0 0 00	
Store Equipment		4 0 0 0 00	
Acc. Dep., Store Equipment			4 0 0 00
Accounts Payable			17 9 0 0 00
Federal Income Tax Payable			8 0 0 00
FICA—Soc. Sec. Payable			4 5 4 00
FICA—Medicare Payable			1 0 6 00
State Income Tax Payable			2 0 0 00
SUTA Tax Payable			1 0 8 00
FUTA Tax Payable			3 2 00
Unearned Rent			6 0 0 00
Mortgage Payable			2 3 2 0 00
Art Newner, Capital			7 9 0 5 00
Art Newner, Withdrawals		8 6 0 0 00	
Income Summary			
Sales			95 0 0 0 00
Sales Returns and Allowances		9 5 0 00	
Sales Discount		6 7 0 00	
Purchases		52 0 0 0 00	
Purchases Discount			8 6 0 00
Purchases Returns and Allowances			6 8 0 00
Freight-In		4 5 0 00	
Salaries Expense		11 7 0 0 00	
Payroll Tax Expense		4 2 0 00	
Postage Expense		2 5 00	
Miscellaneous Expense		3 0 00	
Interest Expense		3 0 0 00	
Totals		127 3 6 5 00	127 3 6 5 00

In looking at the trial balance, we see many new titles that did not appear in the trial balance that we completed for a service company in Chapter 5. Let's look specifically at these new titles shown in Table 11.1.

Note the following:

Mortgage Payable A liability account showing amount owed on a mortgage.

- Mortgage Payable is a liability account that records the increases and decreases in the amount of debt owed on a mortgage. We discuss this account more in the next chapter, when financial statements are prepared.

Interest Expense The cost of borrowing money.

- Interest Expense represents a nonoperating expense for Art's Wholesale and thus is categorized as Other Expense. We look at this expense in the next chapter.

Unearned Revenue A liability account that records amount owed for goods or services in advance of delivery. The Cash account would record the receipt of cash.

- Unearned Revenue is a liability account that records receipt of payment for goods and services in advance of delivery. Unearned Rent is a particular example of this general type of account.

We already discussed the adjustments that make up the two-step process involved in adjusting Merchandise Inventory at the end of the accounting period. Now we show T accounts and transaction analysis charts for other adjustments that need to be made at this point for a merchandise firm, just as they must be made for a service company.

TABLE 11.1 Summary of New Account Titles

Title	Category	Account Reported on	Normal Balance	Temporary or Permanent
Petty Cash	Asset	Balance Sheet	Dr.	Permanent
Merchandise Inventory* (When sold)	Asset	Balance Sheet from prior period	Dr.	Permanent
	Cost of Goods Sold	Income Statement of current period		
Federal Income Tax Payable	Liability	Balance Sheet	Cr.	Permanent
FICA—Social Security Payable	Liability	Balance Sheet	Cr.	Permanent
FICA—Medicare Payable	Liability	Balance Sheet	Cr.	Permanent
State Income Tax Payable	Liability	Balance Sheet	Cr.	Permanent
SUTA Tax Payable	Liability	Balance Sheet	Cr.	Permanent
FUTA Tax Payable	Liability	Balance Sheet	Cr.	Permanent
Unearned Rent†	Liability	Balance Sheet	Cr.	Permanent
Mortgage Payable	Liability	Balance Sheet	Cr.	Permanent
Sales	Revenue	Income Statement	Cr.	Temporary
Sales Returns and Allowances	Contra-Revenue	Income Statement	Dr.	Temporary
Sales Discount	Contra-Revenue	Income Statement	Dr.	Temporary
Purchases§	Cost of Goods Sold	Income Statement	Dr.	Temporary
Purchases Discount	Contra-Cost of Goods Sold	Income Statement	Cr.	Temporary
Purchases Returns and Allowances	Contra-Cost of Goods Sold	Income Statement	Cr.	Temporary
Freight-In	Cost of Goods Sold	Income Statement	Dr.	Temporary
Payroll Tax Expense	Expense	Income Statement	Dr.	Temporary
Postage Expense	Expense	Income Statement	Dr.	Temporary
Interest Expense	Other Expense	Income Statement	Dr.	Temporary

*The ending inventory of current period is a contra-cost of goods sold on the income statement and will be an asset on the balance sheet for the next period.

†Referred to as Unearned Revenue.

§Note that the categories for Purchases and Freight-In are Cost of Goods Sold, whereas Purchases Discounts and Purchases Returns and Allowances are Contra-Cost of Goods Sold.

Adjustment C: Rental Income Earned by Art's Wholesale, $200. A month ago, Cash was increased by $600, as was a liability, Unearned Rent. Art's Wholesale received payment in advance but had not earned the rental income. Now, because $200 has been earned, the liability is reduced and Rental Income can be recorded for the $200. This step is shown as follows:

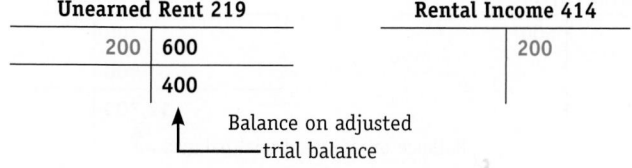

Unearned Rent	Liability	↓	Dr.	$200
Rental Income	Revenue	↑	Cr.	$200

Adjustment D: Supplies on Hand, $300. Because $500 worth of supplies were used up, Supplies Expense is increased, and the asset Supplies is decreased.

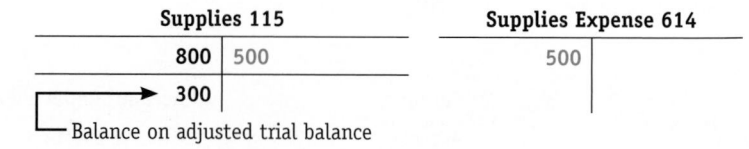

Supplies Expense	Expense	↑	Dr.	$500
Supplies	Asset	↓	Cr.	$500

Adjustment E: Insurance Expired, $300. Because insurance has expired by $300, Insurance Expense is increased by $300 and the asset Prepaid Insurance is decreased by $300.

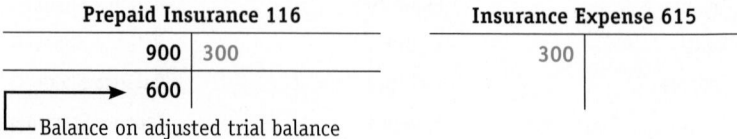

Insurance Expense	Expense	↑	Dr.	$300
Prepaid Insurance	Asset	↓	Cr.	$300

Adjustment F: Depreciation Expense, $50. When depreciation is taken, Depreciation Expense and Accumulated Depreciation are both increased by $50. Note that the cost of the store equipment remains the same.

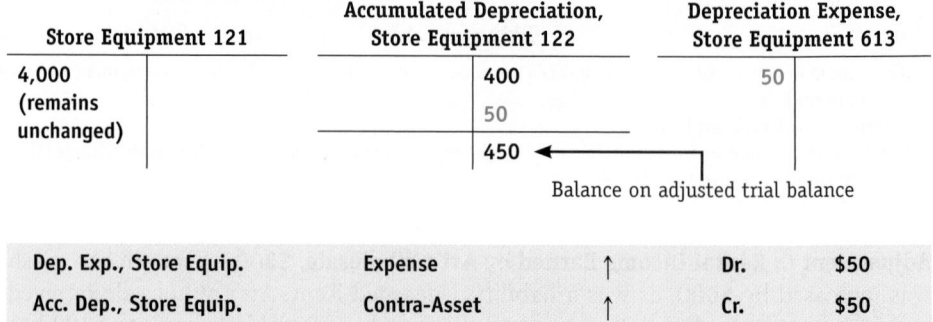

Dep. Exp., Store Equip.	Expense	↑	Dr.	$50
Acc. Dep., Store Equip.	Contra-Asset	↑	Cr.	$50

Adjustment G: Salaries Accrued, $600. The $600 in accrued salaries causes an increase in Salaries Expense and Salaries Payable.

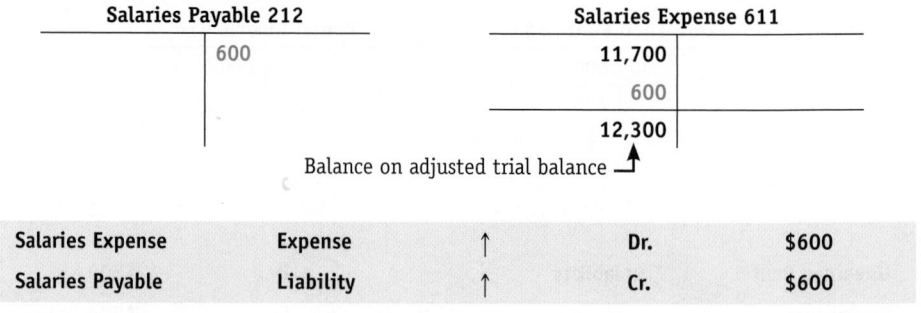

Salaries Expense	Expense	↑	Dr.	$600
Salaries Payable	Liability	↑	Cr.	$600

Figure 11.5 shows the worksheet with the adjustments and adjusted trial balance columns filled out. Note that the adjustment numbers in the Income Summary from beginning and ending inventory are also carried over to the adjusted trial balance and are not combined.

FIGURE 11.5 Worksheet with Six Columns

	Trial Balance Dr.	Trial Balance Cr.	Adjustments Dr.	Adjustments Cr.	Adjusted Trial Balance Dr.	Adjusted Trial Balance Cr.
Cash	12 9 2 0 00				12 9 2 0 00	
Petty Cash	1 0 0 00				1 0 0 00	
Accounts Receivable	14 5 0 0 00				14 5 0 0 00	
Merchandise Inventory	19 0 0 0 00		(B) 4 0 0 0 00	(A) 19 0 0 0 00	4 0 0 0 00	
Supplies	8 0 0 00			(D) 5 0 0 00	3 0 0 00	
Prepaid Insurance	9 0 0 00			(E) 3 0 0 00	6 0 0 00	
Store Equipment	4 0 0 0 00				4 0 0 0 00	
Acc. Dep., Store Equipment		4 0 0 00		(F) 5 0 00		4 5 0 00
Accounts Payable		17 9 0 0 00				17 9 0 0 00
Federal Income Tax Payable		8 0 0 00				8 0 0 00
FICA—Soc. Sec. Payable		4 5 4 00				4 5 4 00
FICA—Medicare Payable		1 0 6 00				1 0 6 00
State Income Tax Payable		2 0 0 00				2 0 0 00
SUTA Tax Payable		1 0 8 00				1 0 8 00
FUTA Tax Payable		3 2 00				3 2 00
Unearned Rent		6 0 0 00	(C) 2 0 0 00			4 0 0 00
Mortgage Payable		2 3 2 0 00				2 3 2 0 00
Art Newner, Capital		7 9 0 5 00				7 9 0 5 00
Art Newner, Withdrawals	8 6 0 0 00				8 6 0 0 00	
Income Summary			(A) 19 0 0 0 00	(B) 4 0 0 0 00	19 0 0 0 00	4 0 0 0 00
Sales		95 0 0 0 00				95 0 0 0 00
Sales Returns and Allowances	9 5 0 00				9 5 0 00	
Sales Discount	6 7 0 00				6 7 0 00	
Purchases	52 0 0 0 00				52 0 0 0 00	
Purchases Discount		8 6 0 00				8 6 0 00
Purchases Returns and Allowances		6 8 0 00				6 8 0 00
Freight-In	4 5 0 00				4 5 0 00	
Salaries Expense	11 7 0 0 00		(G) 6 0 0 00		12 3 0 0 00	
Payroll Tax Expense	4 2 0 00				4 2 0 00	
Postage Expense	2 5 00				2 5 00	
Miscellaneous Expense	3 0 00				3 0 00	
Interest Expense	3 0 0 00				3 0 0 00	
Totals	127 3 6 5 00	127 3 6 5 00				
Rental Income				(C) 2 0 0 00		2 0 0 00
Supplies Expense			(D) 5 0 0 00		5 0 0 00	
Insurance Expense			(E) 3 0 0 00		3 0 0 00	
Depreciation Expense, Store Equip.			(F) 5 0 00		5 0 00	
Salaries Payable				(G) 6 0 0 00		6 0 0 00
Totals			24 6 5 0 00	24 6 5 0 00	132 0 1 5 00	132 0 1 5 00

The next step in completing the worksheet is to fill out the income statement columns from the adjusted trial balance, as shown in Figure 11.6 (page 414).

COACHING TIP

Remember: We do not combine the $19,000 and $4,000 in Income Summary. When we prepare the cost of goods sold section for the formal income statement, we will need both a beginning and an ending figure for inventory.

FIGURE 11.6 Income Statement Section of the Worksheet

$19,000 of beginning inventory is assumed sold during the period and thus is part of the cost of goods sold. By placing it in the debit column of Income Summary we increase the cost of goods sold.

$4,000 is the cost of ending inventory at the end of the period. It is assumed to be unsold and therefore is not part of the cost of goods sold. By placing it in the credit column of Income Summary, we reduce the cost of goods sold.

$95,000 is the credit balance of Sales. The Sales Returns and Allowances, $950, and Sales Discount, $670, are placed on the debit side, which represents a reduction to total sales:

(Cr.) Sales
(Dr.) Less: Sales Returns and Allowances
(Dr.) Less: Sales Discount

The Purchases account, $52,000, is on the debit side, reflecting an increase in costs due to purchasing additional merchandise. The Purchases Discount, $860, and Purchases Returns and Allowances, $680, are on the credit side, which reduces cost of purchases:

(Dr.) Purchases
(Cr.) Less: Purchases Returns and Allowances
(Cr.) Less: Purchases Discount

Freight-In adds to the cost of goods sold.

Rental Income, which falls under the category "other income" for Art's Wholesale, is increased by $200, because the first month's rental agreement has been fulfilled.

	Income Statement	
	Dr.	Cr.
Income Summary	19 0 0 0 00	4 0 0 0 00
Sales		95 0 0 0 00
Sales Returns and Allowances	9 5 0 00	
Sales Discount	6 7 0 00	
Purchases	52 0 0 0 00	
Purchases Discount		8 6 0 00
Purchases Returns and Allowances		6 8 0 00
Freight-In	4 5 0 00	
Salaries Expense	12 3 0 0 00	
Payroll Tax Expense	4 2 0 00	
Postage Expense	2 5 00	
Miscellaneous Expense	3 0 00	
Interest Expense	3 0 0 00	
Rental Income		2 0 0 00
Supplies Expense	5 0 0 00	
Insurance Expense	3 0 0 00	
Depreciation Expense, Store Equip.	5 0 00	
Salaries Payable		
	86 9 9 5 00	100 7 4 0 00
Net Income	13 7 4 5 00	
Totals	100 7 4 0 00	100 7 4 0 00

The next step in completing the worksheet is to fill out the balance sheet columns (Figure 11.7). Note how ending inventory is carried over to the balance sheet from the adjusted trial balance column. Take time also to look at the placement of the payroll tax liabilities as well as Unearned Rent on the worksheet.

FIGURE 11.7 Balance Sheet Section of the Worksheet

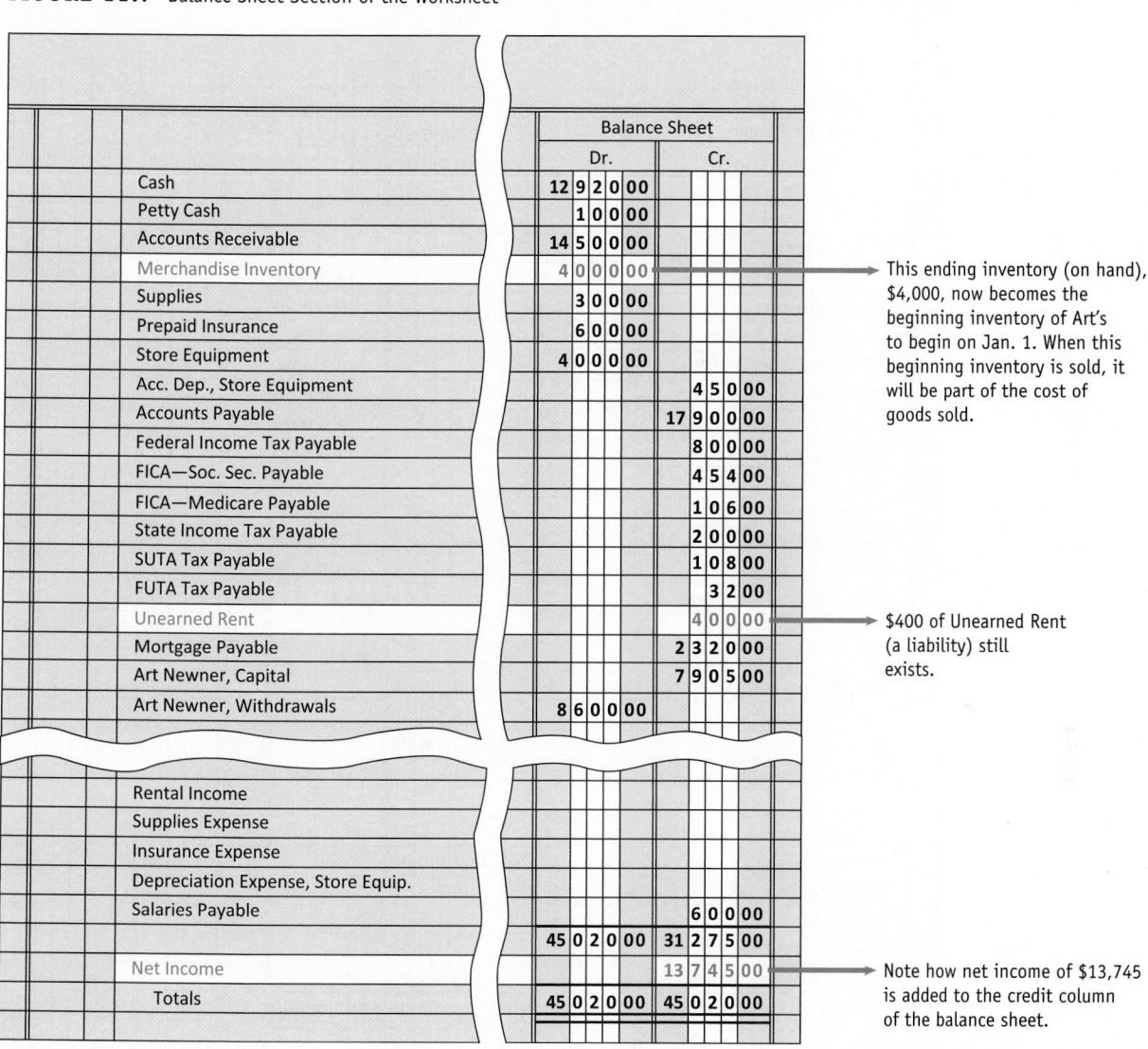

	Balance Sheet Dr.	Balance Sheet Cr.
Cash	12 9 2 0 00	
Petty Cash	1 0 0 00	
Accounts Receivable	14 5 0 0 00	
Merchandise Inventory	4 0 0 0 00	
Supplies	3 0 0 00	
Prepaid Insurance	6 0 0 00	
Store Equipment	4 0 0 0 00	
Acc. Dep., Store Equipment		4 5 0 00
Accounts Payable		17 9 0 0 00
Federal Income Tax Payable		8 0 0 00
FICA—Soc. Sec. Payable		4 5 4 00
FICA—Medicare Payable		1 0 6 00
State Income Tax Payable		2 0 0 00
SUTA Tax Payable		1 0 8 00
FUTA Tax Payable		3 2 00
Unearned Rent		4 0 0 00
Mortgage Payable		2 3 2 0 00
Art Newner, Capital		7 9 0 5 00
Art Newner, Withdrawals	8 6 0 0 00	
Rental Income		
Supplies Expense		
Insurance Expense		
Depreciation Expense, Store Equip.		
Salaries Payable		6 0 0 00
	45 0 2 0 00	31 2 7 5 00
Net Income		13 7 4 5 00
Totals	45 0 2 0 00	45 0 2 0 00

This ending inventory (on hand), $4,000, now becomes the beginning inventory of Art's to begin on Jan. 1. When this beginning inventory is sold, it will be part of the cost of goods sold.

$400 of Unearned Rent (a liability) still exists.

Note how net income of $13,745 is added to the credit column of the balance sheet.

Figure 11.8 is the completed worksheet.

FIGURE 11.8 Completed Worksheet

	Trial Balance		Adjustments	
	Dr.	Cr.	Dr.	Cr.
Cash	12 9 2 0 00			
Petty Cash	1 0 0 00			
Accounts Receivable	14 5 0 0 00			
Merchandise Inventory	19 0 0 0 00		(B) 4 0 0 0 00	(A)19 0 0 0 00
Supplies	8 0 0 00			(D) 5 0 0 00
Prepaid Insurance	9 0 0 00			(E) 3 0 0 00
Store Equipment	4 0 0 0 00			
Acc. Dep., Store Equipment		4 0 0 00		(F) 5 0 00
Accounts Payable		17 9 0 0 00		
Federal Income Tax Payable		8 0 0 00		
FICA—Social Security Payable		4 5 4 00		
FICA—Medicare Payable		1 0 6 00		
State Income Tax Payable		2 0 0 00		
SUTA Tax Payable		1 0 8 00		
FUTA Tax Payable		3 2 00		
Unearned Rent		6 0 0 00	(C) 2 0 0 00	
Mortgage Payable		2 3 2 0 00		
Art Newner, Capital		7 9 0 5 00		
Art Newner, Withdrawals	8 6 0 0 00			
Income Summary			(A)19 0 0 0 00	(B) 4 0 0 0 00
Sales		95 0 0 0 00		
Sales Returns and Allowances	9 5 0 00			
Sales Discount	6 7 0 00			
Purchases	52 0 0 0 00			
Purchases Discount		8 6 0 00		
Purchases Returns and Allowances		6 8 0 00		
Freight-In	4 5 0 00			
Salaries Expense	11 7 0 0 00		(G) 6 0 0 00	
Payroll Tax Expense	4 2 0 00			
Postage Expense	2 5 00			
Miscellaneous Expense	3 0 00			
Interest Expense	3 0 0 00			
Totals	127 3 6 5 00	127 3 6 5 00		
Rental Income				(C) 2 0 0 00
Supplies Expense			(D) 5 0 0 00	
Insurance Expense			(E) 3 0 0 00	
Depreciation Expense, Store Equip.			(F) 5 0 00	
Salaries Payable				(G) 6 0 0 00
Totals			24 6 5 0 00	24 6 5 0 00
Net Income				
Totals				

WORKSHEET
FOR YEAR ENDED DECEMBER 31, 201X

FIGURE 11.8 (continued)

Adjusted Trial Bal. Dr.	Adjusted Trial Bal. Cr.	Income Statement Dr.	Income Statement Cr.	Balance Sheet Dr.	Balance Sheet Cr.
12 9 2 0 00				12 9 2 0 00	
1 0 0 00				1 0 0 00	
14 5 0 0 00				14 5 0 0 00	
4 0 0 0 00				4 0 0 0 00	
3 0 0 00				3 0 0 00	
6 0 0 00				6 0 0 00	
4 0 0 0 00				4 0 0 0 00	
	4 5 0 00				4 5 0 00
	17 9 0 0 00				17 9 0 0 00
	8 0 0 00				8 0 0 00
	4 5 4 00				4 5 4 00
	1 0 6 00				1 0 6 00
	2 0 0 00				2 0 0 00
	1 0 8 00				1 0 8 00
	3 2 00				3 2 00
	4 0 0 00				4 0 0 00
	2 3 2 0 00				2 3 2 0 00
	7 9 0 5 00				7 9 0 5 00
8 6 0 0 00				8 6 0 0 00	
19 0 0 0 00	4 0 0 0 00	19 0 0 0 00	4 0 0 0 00		
	95 0 0 0 00		9 5 0 0 0 00		
9 5 0 00		9 5 0 00			
6 7 0 00		6 7 0 00			
52 0 0 0 00		52 0 0 0 00			
	8 6 0 00		8 6 0 00		
	6 8 0 00		6 8 0 00		
4 5 0 00		4 5 0 00			
12 3 0 0 00		12 3 0 0 00			
4 2 0 00		4 2 0 00			
2 5 00		2 5 00			
3 0 00		3 0 00			
3 0 0 00		3 0 0 00			
	2 0 0 00		2 0 0 00		
5 0 0 00		5 0 0 00			
3 0 0 00		3 0 0 00			
5 0 00		5 0 00			
	6 0 0 00				6 0 0 00
132 0 1 5 00	132 0 1 5 00	86 9 9 5 00	100 7 4 0 00	45 0 2 0 00	31 2 7 5 00
		13 7 4 5 00			13 7 4 5 00
		100 7 4 0 00	100 7 4 0 00	45 0 2 0 00	45 0 2 0 00

Now let's check your progress.

 **TRY IT!**   Learning Unit 11-2

The following is a partial trial balance along with adjustment data. Complete a partial worksheet for Blue Company.

Partial Worksheet

	Trial Balance		Adjustments		Adjusted Trial Balance		Income Statement		Balance Sheet	
	Dr.	Cr.	Dr.	Cr.	Dr.	Cr.	Dr.	Cr.	Dr.	Cr.
Cash	4,000									
Merchandise Inventory	2,000									
Prepaid Rent	600									
Prepaid Insurance	900									
Pet Equipment	3,000									
Accum. Dep., Pet Equipment		1,000								
Unearned Pet Training Fees		700								
Accounts Payable		4,800								
P. Blue, Capital		3,500								
Income Summary										
Pet Training Fees Earned		1,800								

Adjustment Data:

Rent Expired	$100
Insurance Expired	200
Depreciation Expense	300
Earned Pet Training Fees	400
Ending Merchandise Inventory	500

LO1,2  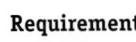   # DEMONSTRATION SUMMARY PROBLEM

Requirement

From the following trial balance of Ledger Sport Shop for March 31 and adjustment data, complete the worksheet:

Ledger Sport Shop
Trial Balance
March 31, 201X

	Dr.	Cr.
Cash	6,000	
Merchandise Inventory	2,000	
Prepaid Rent	600	
Prepaid Insurance	500	
Display Equipment	3,000	
Accumulated Depr., Display Equip.		2,000
Unearned Training Fees		3,000
Accounts Payable		7,000
J. Loy, Capital		7,000
Income Summary		
Sales		9,600
Sales Returns and Allowances	500	
Sales Discount	300	
Purchases	15,000	
Purchases Returns and Allowances		400
Purchases Discounts		800
Salary Expense	1,400	
Plumbing Expense	200	
Utilities Expense	300	
Totals	29,800	29,800

Additional Data (March 31, 201X)

a. and **b.** Ending Merchandise Inventory $400
c. Training Fees Earned $200
d. Insurance Expired $100
e. Prepaid Rent Expired $300
f. Depreciation Expense, Display Equip. $100
g. Salaries Accrued $500

Tips for Adjustments

Merchandise Inventory line: Wipe out old inventory with a credit and debit new inventory. Ending Inventory will end up in the debit column of the balance sheet.

Income Summary line: Ending inventory not sold and not a cost goes in the credit column on the income summary. Beginning inventory assumed sold and thus a cost goes in the debit column of the income summary.

These numbers for beginning and ending inventories are carried over to the income statement columns of the worksheet. Beginning Inventory goes in the debit column and ending inventory (not a cost) goes in the credit column.

Unearned Training Fees line: The amount earned will reduce the Unearned Training Fees account with a debit in the adjustment column. Whatever is earned goes to Training Fees Earned as a credit in the adjustments column. Eventually the Unearned Training Fees goes in the credit column of the balance sheet and the Training Fees Earned goes in the credit column of the income statement.

Solutions

The Completed Worksheet:

Ledger Sport Shop
Worksheet
For month ended March 31, 201X

Account Titles	Trial Balance Dr.	Trial Balance Cr.	Adjustments Dr.	Adjustments Cr.	Adjusted Trial Balance Dr.	Adjusted Trial Balance Cr.	Income Statement Dr.	Income Statement Cr.	Balance Sheet Dr.	Balance Sheet Cr.
Cash	6,000				6,000				6,000	
Merchandise Inv.	2,000		(B) 400	(A) 2,000	400				400	
Prepaid Rent	600			(E) 300	300				300	
Prepaid Insurance	500			(D) 100	400				400	
Display Equipment	3,000				3,000				3,000	
Acc. Dep., Disp. Eq.		2,000		(F) 100		2,100				2,100
Unearned Training Fees		3,000	(C) 200			2,800				2,800
Accounts Payable		7,000				7,000				7,000
J. Loy, Capital		7,000				7,000				7,000
Income Summary			(A) 2,000	(B) 400	2,000	400	2,000	400		
Sales		9,600				9,600		9,600		
Sales Returns and Allowances	500				500		500			
Sales Discounts	300				300		300			
Purchases	15,000				15,000		15,000			
Purchases Returns and Allowances		400				400		400		
Purchases Discounts		800				800		800		
Salary Expense	1,400		(G) 500		1,900		1,900			
Plumbing Expense	200				200		200			
Utilities Expense	300				300		300			
Totals	29,800	29,800								
Training Fees Earned				(C) 200		200		200		
Insurance Expense			(D) 100		100		100			
Rent Expense			(E) 300		300		300			
Depreciation Expense, Display Equipment			(F) 100		100		100			
Salaries Payable				(G) 500		500				500
Totals			3,600	3,600	30,800	30,800	20,700	11,400	10,100	19,400
Net Loss								9,300	9,300	
Totals							20,700	20,700	19,400	19,400

Tip to Complete a Worksheet

Note that we have a net loss. If we had a net income, the 9,300 would have been in the debit column of the income statement and the credit column of the balance sheet.

BLUEPRINT: A WORKSHEET FOR A MERCHANDISE COMPANY

Account Titles	Adjustments Dr.	Adjustments Cr.	Adjusted Trial Balance Dr.	Adjusted Trial Balance Cr.	Income Statement Dr.	Income Statement Cr.	Balance Sheet Dr.	Balance Sheet Cr.
Cash			X				X	
Petty Cash			X				X	
Accounts Receivable			X				X	
Merchandise Inventory	X-E	X-B	X-E				X-E	
Supplies			X				X	
Equipment			X				X	
Acc. Dep., Store Equipment				X				X
Accounts Payable				X				X
Federal Income Tax Payable				X				X
FICA—Social Security Payable				X				X
FICA—Medicare Payable				X				X
State Income Tax Payable				X				X
SUTA Tax Payable				X				X
FUTA Tax Payable				X				X
Unearned Sales				X				X
Mortgage Payable				X				X
A. Flynn, Capital				X				X
A. Flynn, Withdrawals			X				X	
Income Summary*	X-B	X-E	X-B	X-E	X-B	X-E		
Sales				X		X		
Sales Returns and Allow.			X		X			
Sales Discount			X		X			
Purchases			X		X			
Purchases Ret. and Allow.				X		X		
Purchases Discount				X		X		
Freight-In			X		X			
Salaries Expense			X		X			
Payroll Tax Expense			X		X			
Insurance Expense			X		X			
Depreciation Expense			X		X			
Salaries Payable				X				X
Rental Income				X		X		

*Note that the figures for beginning (X-B) and ending inventory (X-E) are never combined on the Income Summary line of the worksheet. When the formal income statement is prepared, two distinct figures for inventory will be used to explain and calculate cost of goods sold. Beginning inventory adds to cost of goods sold; ending inventory reduces cost of goods sold.

 **TRY IT!**

Solutions MyAccountingLab

Learning Unit 11-1

Merchandise Inventory 114 Dr.	Merchandise Inventory 114 Cr.	Unearned Legal Fees 310 Dr.	Unearned Legal Fees 310 Cr.	Income Summary 313 Dr.	Income Summary 313 Cr.	Earned Legal Fees 410 Dr.	Earned Legal Fees 410 Cr.
65,000	65,000	4,000	8,000	65,000	30,000		4,000
30,000							

Learning Unit 11-2

Accounts	Trial Balance Dr.	Trial Balance Cr.	Adjustments Dr.	Adjustments Cr.	Adjusted Trial Balance Dr.	Adjusted Trial Balance Cr	Income Statement Dr.	Income Statement Cr.	Balance Sheet Dr.	Balance Sheet Cr.
Cash	4,000				4,000				4,000	
Merchandise Inv.	2,000		500	2,000	500				500	
Prepaid Rent	600			100	500				500	
Prepaid Insurance	900			200	700				700	
Pet Equipment	3,000				3,000				3,000	
Acc. Dep., Pet Equip.		1,000		300		1,300				1,300
Unearned Pet Training Fees		700	400			300				300
Accounts Payable		4,800				4,800				4,800
P. Blue, Capital		3,500				3,500				3,500
Income Summary			2,000	500	2,000	500	2,000	500		
Pet Training Fees Earned		1,800		400		2,200		2,200		

ACCOUNTING COACH

The following Coaching Tips are from Learning Units 11-1 and 11-2. Take the Pre-Game Checkup and use the Check Your Score at the bottom of the page to see how you are doing. The Accounting Coach provides tips before each Checkup to help you avoid common accounting errors.

LU 11-1 Adjustments for Merchandise Inventory, Unearned Rent, Supplies Used, Insurance Expired, Depreciation Expense, and Salaries Accrued

Pre-Game Tips: The purpose of the adjustment for Merchandise Inventory is to wipe out the beginning inventory and bring on the ending inventory. We assume that the beginning inventory is sold and is part of the cost of goods sold. The ending inventory is not sold and is not part of the cost of goods sold. The ending inventory becomes the new figure for beginning inventory in the next accounting period. Unearned Rent is not a revenue account. It is a liability. Revenue will only be recognized when it is earned.

Pre-Game Checkup: Answer true or false to the following statements.

1. Freight-In is a cost of goods sold account.
2. Beginning inventory is subtracted from cost of goods sold.
3. Income Summary is not used to adjust Merchandise Inventory.
4. When unearned rent is earned the liability will go up.
5. The ending inventory of one period can never be the new inventory of the next period.

LU 11-2 Worksheets for Merchandise Companies

Pre-Game Tips: Before you complete the worksheet, make sure you review this table:

Account	Category	Normal Balance	Financial Statement
Sales	Revenue	Credit Balance	Income Statement
SRA	Contra-Revenue	Debit Balance	Income Statement
Unearned Revenue	Liability	Credit Balance	Balance Sheet
Purchases	Cost	Debit Balance	Income Statement
PRA	Contra-Cost	Credit Balance	Income Statement

Pre-Game Checkup: Answer true or false to the following statements.

1. Ending inventory goes in the credit column of the balance sheet section of the worksheet.
2. Freight-In goes in the debit column of the balance sheet section of the worksheet.
3. Unearned Rent goes in the debit column of the balance sheet section of the worksheet.
4. Accumulated Depreciation goes in the credit column of the balance sheet section of the worksheet.
5. Beginning inventory on the Income Summary line of the worksheet goes in the credit column of the income statement.

CHECK YOUR SCORE: Answers to the Pre-Game Checkup

LU 11-1
1. True
2. False—Beginning inventory is added to cost of goods sold.
3. False—Income Summary is used to adjust Merchandise Inventory.
4. False—When unearned rent is earned the liability will go down.
5. False—The ending inventory of one period always becomes new inventory of the next period.

LU 11-2
1. False—Ending inventory goes in the debit column of the balance sheet section of the worksheet.
2. False—Freight-In goes in the debit column of the income statement.

3. False—Unearned Rent goes in the credit column of the balance sheet section of the worksheet.
4. True
5. False—Beginning inventory on the Income Summary line of the worksheet goes in the debit column of the income statement.

Chapter Summary

Here are all the key terms and equations to help you understand the concepts of this chapter and prepare you for your exam. After completing this review, go to MyAccountingLab for more practice opportunities.

Concepts You Should Know	Key Terms

L01

Figure Adjustments for Merchandise Inventory, Unearned Rent, Supplies Used, Insurance Expired, Depreciation Expense, and Salaries Accrued

1. The periodic inventory system updates the record of goods on hand only at the end of the accounting period.

2. In the periodic inventory system, additional purchases of merchandise during the accounting period will be recorded in the Purchases account. The amount in beginning inventory will remain unchanged during the accounting period. At the end of the period, a new figure for ending inventory will be calculated.

3. Beginning inventory from the start of the accounting period becomes part of the cost of goods sold, whereas ending inventory is a reduction to cost of goods sold.

4. The perpetual inventory system keeps a continuous record of inventory.

5. Net sales less cost of goods sold equals gross profit. Gross profit less operating expenses equals net income.

6. Unearned Revenue is a liability account that accumulates revenue that has not been earned yet, although the cash has been received. It represents a liability to the seller until the service or product is performed or delivered.

Key Terms:

Beginning merchandise inventory (beginning inventory) (p. 406)

Cost of goods sold (p. 406)

Ending merchandise inventory (ending inventory) (p. 406)

Freight-In (p. 406)

Gross profit (p. 407)

Periodic inventory system (p. 406)

Perpetual inventory system (p. 406)

L02

Prepare a Worksheet for a Merchandise Company

1. Both the beginning and ending figures for merchandise inventory are shown in the Merchandise Inventory account and Income Summary. The balance sheet debit column shows the ending figure for inventory.

2. Unearned Revenue is a liability on the balance sheet credit column.

Key Terms:

Interest Expense (p. 410)

Mortgage Payable (p. 410)

Unearned Revenue (p. 410)

Discussion Questions and Critical Thinking/Ethical Case

1. What is the function of the Purchases account?

2. Explain why Unearned Revenue is a liability account.

3. In a periodic system of inventory, the balance of beginning inventory will remain unchanged during the period. True or false?

4. What is the purpose of an inventory sheet?

5. Why do many Unearned Revenue accounts have to be adjusted?

6. Explain why figures for beginning and ending inventory are not combined on the Income Summary line of the worksheet.

7. Jim Heary is the custodian of petty cash. Jim, who is short of personal cash, decided to pay his home electrical and phone bills from petty cash. He plans to pay it back next month. Do you feel Jim should do so? You make the call. Write down your specific recommendations to Jim.

Concept Checks

MyAccountingLab

Adjustment for Merchandise Inventory

◀ L01   *(10 min)*

1. Given the following, journalize the adjusting entries for Merchandise Inventory. Note that ending inventory has a balance of $13,000.

Merchandise Inventory 114	Income Summary 313
62,000	

Adjustment for Unearned Fees

◀ L01   *(15 min)*

2. **a.** Given the following, journalize the adjusting entry. By December 31, $200 of the unearned dog walking fees were earned.

Unearned Dog Walking Fees 225		Earned Dog Walking Fees 441	
940	12/1/1X	4,800	12/1/1X

   b. What is the category of unearned dog walking fees?

Worksheet

◀ L02   *(10 min)*

3. Match the following:
   1. Located on the Income Statement debit column of the worksheet.
   2. Located on the Income Statement credit column of the worksheet.
   3. Located on the Balance Sheet debit column of the worksheet.
   4. Located on the Balance Sheet credit column of the worksheet.

   _____ **a.** Beginning Merchandise Inventory (amount)
   _____ **b.** Sales Returns and Allowances
   _____ **c.** Salaries Payable
   _____ **d.** Sales
   _____ **e.** Accounts Receivable

(10 min)   **LO1** ▶   **Merchandise Inventory Adjustment**

4.   Given beginning merchandise inventory of $2,100 and ending merchandise inventory of $50, what would be the adjusting entries?

(10 min)   **LO2** ▶   **Income Summary on the Worksheet**

5.   Given a figure of beginning inventory of $390 and an $850 figure for ending inventory, place these numbers on the Income Summary line of this partial worksheet.

	Adjustments		Adjusted Trial Balance		Income Statement	
	Dr.	Cr.	Dr.	Cr.	Dr.	Cr.
Income Summary	A	B	C	D	E	F

MyAccountingLab   **Exercises**

Set A

(10 min)   **LO1** ▶   **11A-1.**   Indicate the normal balance and category of each of the following accounts:
   a.   Unearned Revenue
   b.   Merchandise Inventory (beginning of period)
   c.   Freight-In
   d.   Payroll Tax Expense
   e.   Purchases Discount
   f.   Sales Discount
   g.   FICA—Social Security Payable
   h.   Purchases Returns and Allowances

(15 min)   **LO1** ▶   **11A-2.**   From the following, calculate (a) net sales, (b) cost of goods sold, (c) gross profit, and (d) net income: Sales, $22,000; Sales Discount, $470; Sales Returns and Allowances, $240; Beginning Inventory, $640; Net Purchases, $13,500; Ending Inventory, $510; Operating Expenses, $3,300.

(10 min)   **LO1** ▶   **11A-3.**   Little Co. had the following balances on December 31, 201X:

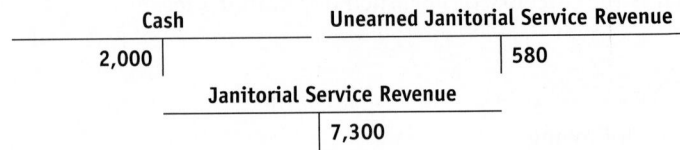

Cash	Unearned Janitorial Service Revenue
2,000	580

Janitorial Service Revenue
7,300

The accountant for Little has asked you to make an adjustment because $420 of janitorial services has just been performed for customers who had paid for 2 months. Construct a transaction analysis chart.

(15 min)   **LO1,2** ▶   **11A-4.**   Oak Co. purchased merchandise costing $380,000. Calculate the cost of goods sold under the following situations:
   a.   Beginning inventory $40,000 and no ending inventory
   b.   Beginning inventory $54,000 and a $56,000 ending inventory
   c.   No beginning inventory and a $33,000 ending inventory

11A-5. Prepare a worksheet for Mannon Co. from the following information using Figure 11.9:   **L02** *(20 min)*

a./b.	Merchandise Inventory, ending	15
c.	Store Supplies on hand	4
d.	Depreciation on Store Equipment	4
e.	Accrued Salaries	1

FIGURE 11.9
Trial Balance for Mannon Co.

MANNON CO. TRIAL BALANCE DECEMBER 31, 201X	Dr.	Cr.
Cash	9 00	
Accounts Receivable	5 00	
Merchandise Inventory	1 1 00	
Store Supplies	9 00	
Store Equipment	1 6 00	
Accumulated Depreciation, Store Equipment		7 00
Accounts Payable		3 00
J. Mannon, Capital		3 9 00
Income Summary	—	—
Sales		5 4 00
Sales Returns and Allowances	1 1 00	
Purchases	2 6 00	
Purchases Discount		4 00
Freight-In	1 00	
Salaries Expense	8 00	
Advertising Expense	1 1 00	
Totals	1 0 7 00	1 0 7 00

Set B

11B-1. Indicate the normal balance and category of each of the following accounts: **L01** *(10 min)*
   a. Salaries Payable
   b. Merchandise Inventory (beginning of period)
   c. Freight-In
   d. Payroll Tax Expense
   e. Purchases Returns and Allowances
   f. Sales Returns and Allowances
   g. FICA—Social Security Payable
   h. Purchases Discounts

11B-2. From the following, calculate (a) net sales, (b) cost of goods sold, (c) gross profit, and (d) net income: Sales, $21,700; Sales Discount, $480; Sales Returns and Allowances, $250; Beginning Inventory, $680; Net Purchases, $13,800; Ending Inventory, $500; Operating Expenses, $3,000.   **L01** *(15 min)*

11B-3. Bates Co. had the following balances on December 31, 201X: **L01** *(10 min)*

Cash	Unearned Janitorial Service Revenue
1,700	610

Janitorial Service Revenue
7,400

The accountant for Bates has asked you to make an adjustment because $430 of janitorial services has just been performed for customers who had paid for 2 months. Construct a transaction analysis chart.

(15 min) **LO1,2** ▶ **11B-4.** Maple Co. purchased merchandise costing $360,000. Calculate the cost of goods sold under the following situations:

    a. Beginning inventory $42,000 and no ending inventory

    b. Beginning inventory $49,000 and a $57,000 ending inventory

    c. No beginning inventory and a $27,000 ending inventory

(20 min) **LO2** ▶ **11B-5.** Prepare a worksheet for Michaud Co. from the following information using Figure 11.10:

a./b.	Merchandise Inventory, ending	13
c.	Store Supplies on hand	3
d.	Depreciation on Store Equipment	6
e.	Accrued Salaries	4

FIGURE 11.10
Trial Balance for Michaud Co.

MICHAUD CO. TRIAL BALANCE DECEMBER 31, 201X	Dr.	Cr.
Cash	10 00	
Accounts Receivable	6 00	
Merchandise Inventory	12 00	
Store Supplies	10 00	
Store Equipment	18 00	
Accumulated Depreciation, Store Equipment		7 00
Accounts Payable		4 00
J. Michaud, Capital		35 00
Income Summary		
Sales		56 00
Sales Returns and Allowances	10 00	
Purchases	18 00	
Purchases Discount		5 00
Freight-In	1 00	
Salaries Expense	8 00	
Advertising Expense	14 00	
Totals	107 00	107 00

Problems

Set A

You can also use the foldout worksheets at the end of the working papers that accompany this text.

(30 min) **LO1** ▶ **11A-1.** Based on the following accounts, calculate (a) net sales, (b) cost of goods sold, (c) gross profit, and (d) net income.

Accounts Payable	$ 6,300
Operating Expenses	1,600
Market Co., Capital	19,700
Purchases	1,100
Freight-In	85
Ending Merchandise Inventory, Dec. 31, 201X	68
Sales	6,400
Accounts Receivable	450
Cash	780
Purchases Discount	47
Sales Returns and Allowances	340
Beg. Merchandise Inventory, Jan. 1, 201X	83
Purchases Returns and Allowances	71
Sales Discount	85

Check Figure:
Net income $3,293

11A-2. From the trial balance in Figure 11.11, complete a worksheet for Jim's Hardware. Assume the following:

a./b. Ending inventory on December 31 is calculated at $340.
 c. Insurance expired, $110.
 d. Depreciation on store equipment, $70.
 e. Accrued wages, $80.

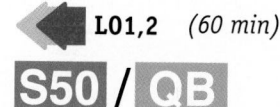
L01,2 *(60 min)*

S50 / QB

JIM'S HARDWARE
TRIAL BALANCE
DECEMBER 31, 201X

Account	Balance Dr.	Balance Cr.
Cash	7 9 1 00	
Accounts Receivable	1 2 5 2 00	
Merchandise Inventory	6 0 0 00	
Prepaid Insurance	6 6 6 00	
Store Equipment	2 1 9 0 00	
Accumulated Depreciation, Store Equipment		6 3 0 00
Accounts Payable		4 8 5 00
Jim Spool, Capital		1 6 0 8 00
Income Summary		
Hardware Sales		11 6 1 0 00
Hardware Sales Returns and Allowances	8 9 1 00	
Hardware Sales Discount	2 0 8 00	
Purchases	5 2 6 4 00	
Purchases Discount		1 6 8 00
Purchases Returns and Allowances		9 0 00
Wages Expense	1 7 0 8 00	
Rent Expense	7 9 2 00	
Telephone Expense	1 4 9 00	
Miscellaneous Expense	8 0 00	
Totals	14 5 9 1 00	14 5 9 1 00

FIGURE 11.11
Trial Balance for Jim's Hardware

Check Figure:
Net income $2,256

(60 min)   **LO1,2** ▶▶   **11A-3.** The owner of Carol Company asked you to prepare a worksheet from the trial balance in Figure 11.12 and additional data.

Additional Data

a./b. Ending merchandise inventory on December 31, $1,825.
   c. Office supplies used up, $210.
   d. Rent expired, $205.
   e. Depreciation expense on office equipment, $500.
   f. Office salaries earned but not paid, $300.

FIGURE 11.12
Trial Balance for Carol Company

Check Figure:
Net income $5,649

CAROL COMPANY
TRIAL BALANCE
DECEMBER 31, 201X

Account	Dr.	Cr.
Cash	5 3 7 2 00	
Petty Cash	2 6 0 00	
Accounts Receivable	2 5 1 2 00	
Beginning Merchandise Inventory, Jan. 1	4 9 5 1 00	
Prepaid Rent	6 0 2 00	
Office Supplies	8 7 9 00	
Office Equipment	9 4 1 0 00	
Accumulated Depreciation, Office Equipment		7 2 0 0 00
Accounts Payable		6 0 3 8 00
K. Carol, Capital		5 5 5 8 00
K. Carol, Withdrawals	4 8 0 0 00	
Income Summary		
Sales		5 3 1 1 4 00
Sales Returns and Allowances	9 6 00	
Sales Discount	2 5 5 0 00	
Purchases	29 3 1 6 00	
Purchases Discount		1 6 00
Purchases Returns and Allowances		3 7 2 00
Office Salaries Expense	7 8 2 4 00	
Insurance Expense	2 3 2 5 00	
Advertising Expense	8 2 5 00	
Utilities Expense	5 7 6 00	
Totals	72 2 9 8 00	72 2 9 8 00

(60 min)   **LO1,2** ▶▶   **11A-4.** From the trial balance in Figure 11.13 and additional data, complete the worksheet for Ron's Wholesale Clothing Company.

Additional Data

a./b. Ending merchandise inventory on December 31, $5,100.
   c. Supplies on hand, $650.
   d. Insurance expired, $550.
   e. Depreciation on store equipment, $650.
   f. Storage fees earned, $145.

RON'S WHOLESALE CLOTHING COMPANY TRIAL BALANCE DECEMBER 31, 201X																		
	Balance										
Account	Dr.						Cr.				
Cash	4	2	3	0	0	0					
Petty Cash		2	0	0	0	0					
Accounts Receivable	7	4	0	0	0	0					
Merchandise Inventory	9	3	0	0	0	0					
Supplies	1	3	0	0	0	0					
Prepaid Insurance		8	2	0	0	0					
Store Equipment	2	1	0	0	0	0					
Accumulated Depreciation, Store Equipment							1	0	0	0	0
Accounts Payable							11	2	0	5	0	0
Federal Income Tax Payable							1	0	0	0	0
FICA—Social Security Payable								4	5	4	0	0
FICA—Medicare Payable								1	1	2	0	0
State Income Tax Payable								1	9	0	0	0
SUTA Tax Payable								1	0	2	0	0
FUTA Tax Payable									3	0	0	0
Unearned Storage Fees								2	5	0	0	0
Ron Win, Capital							14	5	0	0	0	0
Ron Win, Withdrawals	3	9	0	0	0	0					
Income Summary			—						—			
Sales							40	1	5	2	0	0
Sales Returns and Allowances	1	4	5	0	0	0					
Sales Discount	1	3	5	5	0	0					
Purchases	25	0	0	0	0	0					
Purchases Discount								5	5	0	0	0
Purchases Returns and Allowances								5	0	0	0	0
Freight-In		1	7	5	0	0					
Salaries Expense	11	5	0	0	0	0					
Payroll Tax Expense		3	9	0	0	0					
Interest Expense		9	2	5	0	0					
Totals	70	0	4	5	0	0	70	0	4	5	0	0

FIGURE 11.13
Trial Balance for Ron's Wholesale
Clothing Company

Check Figure:
Net loss $5,498

Set B

11B-1. Based on the following accounts, calculate (a) net sales, (b) cost of goods
sold, (c) gross profit, and (d) net income.

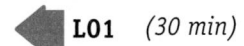 **LO1**   *(30 min)*

Accounts Payable	$ 5,600
Operating Expenses	1,800
Walker Co., Capital	19,300
Purchases	1,200
Freight-In	86
Ending Merchandise Inventory, Dec. 31, 201X	62
Sales	6,000
Accounts Receivable	490
Cash	840
Purchases Discounts	52
Sales Returns and Allowances	290
Beginning Merchandise Inventory, Jan. 1, 201X	77
Purchases Returns and Allowances	73
Sales Discount	88

Check Figure:
Net income $2,646

(60 min)   **LO1,2**

S50 / QB

11B-2. From the trial balance in Figure 11.14, complete a worksheet for Jabar's Hardware. Assume the following:

   a./b. Ending inventory on December 31 is calculated at $270.
   c. Insurance expired, $180.
   d. Depreciation on store equipment, $90.
   e. Accrued wages, $100.

FIGURE 11.14
Trial Balance for Jabar's Hardware

Check Figure:
Net income $1,917

JABAR'S HARDWARE TRIAL BALANCE DECEMBER 31, 201X		
	Balance	
Account	Dr.	Cr.
Cash	7 7 1 00	
Accounts Receivable	1 2 2 7 00	
Merchandise Inventory	5 7 5 00	
Prepaid Insurance	6 9 3 00	
Store Equipment	2 1 6 0 00	
Accumulated Depreciation, Store Equipment		6 8 0 00
Accounts Payable		5 5 8 00
Jabar Spool, Capital		1 5 9 6 00
Income Summary		
Hardware Sales		1 1 0 6 0 00
Hardware Sales Returns and Allowances	5 1 3 00	
Hardware Sales Discount	2 2 4 00	
Purchases	5 2 7 2 00	
Purchases Discounts		1 8 4 00
Purchases Returns and Allowances		1 0 8 00
Wages Expense	1 7 4 0 00	
Rent Expense	7 9 2 00	
Telephone Expense	1 3 5 00	
Miscellaneous Expense	8 4 00	
Totals	14 1 8 6 00	14 1 8 6 00

(60 min)   **LO1,2**

11B-3. The owner of Cannon Company asked you to prepare a worksheet from the trial balance shown in Figure 11.15 and additional data.

Additional Data

   a./b. Ending merchandise inventory on December 31, $1,835.
   c. Office supplies used up, $210.
   d. Rent expired, $195.
   e. Depreciation expense on office equipment, $525.
   f. Office salaries earned but not paid, $270.

CANNON COMPANY TRIAL BALANCE DECEMBER 31, 201X									
	Balance								
Account	Dr.				Cr.				
Cash	5	3 7 2	00						
Petty Cash		2 1 0	00						
Accounts Receivable	2	4 0 9	00						
Beginning Merchandise Inventory, Jan. 1	5	1 8 2	00						
Prepaid Rent		6 1 6	00						
Office Supplies		9 8 8	00						
Office Equipment	9	4 1 0	00						
Accumulated Depreciation, Office Equipment						7 2 0 0	00		
Accounts Payable						6 0 5 0	00		
K. Cannon, Capital						5 4 5 5	00		
K. Cannon, Withdrawals	4	8 0 0	00						
Income Summary		—				—			
Sales					52	6 7 7	00		
Sales Returns and Allowances		9 4	00						
Sales Discount	2	5 5 0	00						
Purchases	28	8 6 4	00						
Purchases Discount						1 6	00		
Purchases Returns and Allowances						3 3 6	00		
Office Salaries Expense	7	6 1 6	00						
Insurance Expense	2	3 2 5	00						
Advertising Expense		7 5 0	00						
Utilities Expense		5 4 8	00						
Totals	71	7 3 4	00		71	7 3 4	00		

FIGURE 11.15
Trial Balance for Cannon Company

Check Figure:
Net income $5,735

11B-4. From the trial balance in Figure 11.16 and additional data, complete the worksheet for Jack's Wholesale Clothing Company. **LO1,2** *(60 min)*

Additional Data

a./b. Ending merchandise inventory on December 31, $5,200.
  c. Supplies on hand, $450.
  d. Insurance expired, $450.
  e. Depreciation on store equipment, $350.
  f. Storage fees earned, $135.

FIGURE 11.16
Trial Balance for Jack's Wholesale Clothing Company

Check Figure:
Net loss $4,539

	JACK'S WHOLESALE CLOTHING COMPANY TRIAL BALANCE DECEMBER 31, 201X		
Account	**Balance**		
	Dr.	**Cr.**	
Cash	4 2 3 0 00		
Petty Cash	3 0 0 00		
Accounts Receivable	7 6 0 0 00		
Merchandise Inventory	9 2 0 0 00		
Supplies	8 0 0 00		
Prepaid Insurance	8 7 0 00		
Store Equipment	2 6 0 0 00		
Accumulated Depreciation, Store Equipment		1 6 0 0 00	
Accounts Payable		11 6 7 5 00	
Federal Income Tax Payable		7 0 0 00	
FICA—Social Security Payable		4 6 2 00	
FICA—Medicare Payable		1 1 6 00	
State Income Tax Payable		1 5 0 00	
SUTA Tax Payable		1 1 4 00	
FUTA Tax Payable		3 2 00	
Unearned Storage Fees		3 7 5 00	
Jack Win, Capital		13 5 0 0 00	
Jack Win, Withdrawals	3 6 0 0 00		
Income Summary			
Sales		42 0 3 1 00	
Sales Returns and Allowances	1 4 5 0 00		
Sales Discount	1 4 3 5 00		
Purchases	27 0 0 0 00		
Purchases Discount		3 5 0 00	
Purchases Returns and Allowances		5 0 0 00	
Freight-In	2 2 5 00		
Salaries Expense	11 0 0 0 00		
Payroll Tax Expense	4 4 0 00		
Interest Expense	8 5 5 00		
Totals	71 6 0 5 00	71 6 0 5 00	

  Financial Report Problem

(10 min)   **LO1**

Reading the Kellogg's Annual Report

Go to http://investor.kelloggs.com/investor-relations/annual-reports to access the Kellogg's 2013 Annual Report and find the Consolidated Statement of Income. What is the cost of goods sold in 2013?

  # ON THE JOB   SMITH COMPUTER CENTER

(60 min)   **LO1,2**

The first 6 months of the year have concluded for Smith Computer Center, and Thad wants to make the necessary adjustments to his accounts to prepare accurate financial statements.

Assignment

To prepare these adjustments, use the trial balance in Figure 11.17 and the following inventory that Thad took at the end of March:

Supplies

15 dozen $^1/_4$-inch screws at a cost of $15 a dozen

8 dozen $^1/_2$-inch screws at a cost of $10 a dozen

4 feet of coaxial cable at a cost of $8 per foot

<table>
<tr><td colspan="3" align="center">SMITH COMPUTER CENTER
TRIAL BALANCE
MARCH 31, 201X</td></tr>
<tr><td rowspan="2" align="center">Account Titles</td><td colspan="2" align="center">Trial Balance</td></tr>
<tr><td align="center">Dr.</td><td align="center">Cr.</td></tr>
<tr><td>Cash</td><td>17 2 6 3 76</td><td></td></tr>
<tr><td>Petty Cash</td><td>3 0 0 00</td><td></td></tr>
<tr><td>Accounts Receivable</td><td>13 0 9 5 00</td><td></td></tr>
<tr><td>Prepaid Rent</td><td>3 5 0 0 00</td><td></td></tr>
<tr><td>Supplies</td><td>6 1 2 00</td><td></td></tr>
<tr><td>Computer Shop Equipment</td><td>5 7 0 0 00</td><td></td></tr>
<tr><td>Accumulated Depreciation, C. S. Equipment</td><td></td><td>1 5 0 00</td></tr>
<tr><td>Office Equipment</td><td>3 8 5 0 00</td><td></td></tr>
<tr><td>Accumulated Depreciation, Office Equipment</td><td></td><td>1 1 0 00</td></tr>
<tr><td>Accounts Payable</td><td></td><td>3 1 7 0 00</td></tr>
<tr><td>T. Feldman, Capital</td><td></td><td>12 2 8 2 00</td></tr>
<tr><td>T. Feldman, Withdrawals</td><td>9 1 5 00</td><td></td></tr>
<tr><td>Income Summary</td><td>—</td><td>—</td></tr>
<tr><td>Service Revenue</td><td></td><td>21 8 0 0 00</td></tr>
<tr><td>Sales</td><td></td><td>11 6 8 0 00</td></tr>
<tr><td>Sales Returns and Allowances</td><td>4 6 0 00</td><td></td></tr>
<tr><td>Sales Discounts</td><td>1 9 8 00</td><td></td></tr>
<tr><td>Advertising Expense</td><td>—</td><td>—</td></tr>
<tr><td>Rent Expense</td><td>—</td><td>—</td></tr>
<tr><td>Utilities Expense</td><td>—</td><td>—</td></tr>
<tr><td>Phone Expense</td><td>1 7 0 00</td><td></td></tr>
<tr><td>Supplies Expense</td><td>4 5 00</td><td></td></tr>
<tr><td>Insurance Expense</td><td>—</td><td>—</td></tr>
<tr><td>Postage Expense</td><td>4 0 00</td><td></td></tr>
<tr><td>Miscellaneous Expense</td><td>1 5 00</td><td></td></tr>
<tr><td>Wage Expense</td><td>2 0 3 0 00</td><td></td></tr>
<tr><td>Payroll Tax Expense</td><td>2 1 8 24</td><td></td></tr>
<tr><td>Purchases</td><td>9 3 0 00</td><td></td></tr>
<tr><td>Purchases Returns</td><td></td><td>1 5 0 00</td></tr>
<tr><td>Totals</td><td>49 3 4 2 00</td><td>49 3 4 2 00</td></tr>
</table>

FIGURE 11.17
Trial Balance for Smith Computer Center

Merchandise Inventory

A physical inventory taken on March 31 indicated that merchandise inventory was valued at $400.

Depreciation of Computer Equipment

Computer depreciates at $50 a month; purchased July 5.

Computer workstations depreciate at $35 per month; purchased September 17.

Shop benches depreciate at $30 per month; purchased November 5.

Depreciation of Office Equipment

Office equipment depreciates at $55 per month; purchased July 17.

Fax machine depreciates at $15 per month; purchased November 20.

Expiration of Prepaid Rent

Six months' worth of rent at a rental rate of $500 per month has expired. The following accounts have been added to the chart of accounts: Merchandise Inventory 1050, and Income Summary 3020.

Remember: If any long-term asset is purchased in the first 15 days of the month, Thad will charge depreciation for the full month. If an asset is purchased later than the 15th, he will not charge depreciation in the month it was purchased.

Complete the 10-column worksheet for the 6 months ended March 31, 201X.

Appendix

A WORKSHEET FOR ART'S WHOLESALE CLOTHING CO. USING A PERPETUAL INVENTORY SYSTEM

This appendix shows how the worksheet for Art's Wholesale Clothing (periodic in the chapter) would look if a perpetual system was used. Take a moment to look at the major differences.

What's New: The Merchandise Inventory account (in Figure 11A.1) does not need to be adjusted. The $4,000 figure for merchandise is the up-to-date balance in the account. The difference between beginning inventory and ending inventory will be part of a new account called *Cost of Goods Sold* on the worksheet.

How the $65,910 of Cost of Goods Sold was calculated from a periodic setup:

	Purchases	$52,000	←	**Assumed sold; part of cost**
+	Merchandise Inventory	$15,000	←	**Beg. Inv. – Ending Inv. $19,000 – $4,000**
−	Purchases Discount	860	→	**Reduces costs**
−	Purchases Returns and Allowances	680		
+	Freight-In	450	→	**Adds to cost**
		$65,910		**Cost of Goods Sold**

What's Deleted from the Periodic Worksheet: Account titles for Purchases, Purchases Discounts, Purchases Returns and Allowances, and Freight-In.

Note: Net income is the same on the periodic and the perpetual worksheets.

FIGURE 11A.1 Worksheet for Art's Wholesale Clothing Company Using a Perpetual Inventory System

ART'S WHOLESALE CLOTHING CO.
WORKSHEET
FOR YEAR ENDED DECEMBER 31, 201X

Account Titles	Trial Balance Dr.	Trial Balance Cr.	Adjustments Dr.	Adjustments Cr.	Adjusted Trial Balance Dr.	Adjusted Trial Balance Cr.	Income Statement Dr.	Income Statement Cr.	Balance Sheet Dr.	Balance Sheet Cr.
Cash	12 9 2 0 00				12 9 2 0 00				12 9 2 0 00	
Petty Cash	1 0 0 00				1 0 0 00				1 0 0 00	
Accounts Receivable	14 5 0 0 00				14 5 0 0 00				14 5 0 0 00	
Merchandise Inventory	4 0 0 0 00				4 0 0 0 00				4 0 0 0 00	
Supplies	8 0 0 00			(B) 5 0 0 00	3 0 0 00				3 0 0 00	
Prepaid Insurance	9 0 0 00			(C) 3 0 0 00	6 0 0 00				6 0 0 00	
Store Equipment	4 0 0 0 00				4 0 0 0 00				4 0 0 0 00	
Acc. Dep., Store Equip.		4 0 0 00		(D) 5 00		4 5 00				4 5 00
Accounts Payable		17 9 0 0 00				17 9 0 0 00				17 9 0 0 00
Federal Income Tax Payable		8 0 0 00				8 0 0 00				8 0 0 00
FICA—Social Security Payable		4 5 4 00				4 5 4 00				4 5 4 00
FICA—Medicare Payable		1 0 6 00				1 0 6 00				1 0 6 00
State Income Tax Payable		2 0 0 00				2 0 0 00				2 0 0 00
SUTA Tax Payable		1 0 8 00				1 0 8 00				1 0 8 00
FUTA Tax Payable		3 2 00				3 2 00				3 2 00
Unearned Rent		6 0 0 00	(A) 2 0 0 00			4 0 0 00				4 0 0 00
Mortgage Payable		2 3 2 0 00				2 3 2 0 00				2 3 2 0 00
Art Newner, Capital		7 9 0 5 00				7 9 0 5 00				7 9 0 5 00
Art Newner, Withdrawal	8 6 0 0 00				8 6 0 0 00				8 6 0 0 00	
Sales		95 0 0 0 00				95 0 0 0 00		95 0 0 0 00		
Sales Returns and Allow.	9 5 0 00				9 5 0 00		9 5 0 00			
Sales Discount	6 7 0 00				6 7 0 00		6 7 0 00			
Cost of Goods Sold	65 9 1 0 00				65 9 1 0 00		65 9 1 0 00			
Salaries Expense	11 7 0 0 00		(E) 6 0 0 00		12 3 0 0 00		12 3 0 0 00			
Payroll Tax Expense	4 2 0 00				4 2 0 00		4 2 0 00			
Postage Expense	2 5 00				2 5 00		2 5 00			
Miscellaneous Expense	3 0 00				3 0 00		3 0 00			
Interest Expense	3 0 0 00				3 0 0 00		3 0 0 00			
Totals	125 8 2 5 00	125 8 2 5 00								
Rental Income				(A) 2 0 0 00		2 0 0 00		2 0 0 00		
Supplies Expense			(B) 5 0 0 00		5 0 0 00		5 0 0 00			
Insurance Expense			(C) 3 0 0 00		3 0 0 00		3 0 0 00			
Dep. Exp., Store Equip.			(D) 5 00		5 00		5 00			
Salaries Payable				(E) 6 0 0 00		6 0 0 00				6 0 0 00
Totals			1 6 5 0 00	1 6 5 0 00	126 4 7 5 00	126 4 7 5 00	81 4 5 5 00	95 2 0 0 00	45 0 2 0 00	31 2 7 5 00
Net Income							13 7 4 5 00			13 7 4 5 00
Totals							95 2 0 0 00	95 2 0 0 00	45 0 2 0 00	45 0 2 0 00

437

Completion of the Accounting Cycle for a Merchandise Company

CHAPTER PREVIEW: THE BIG PICTURE

Jason Frey took his son to see a Disney movie. After the show, Jason decided to go to Toys"R"Us to get a stuffed animal from the film. He knew the Disney toy would be in stock. Stores like Toys"R"Us try to be competitive but they have to make sure that they make a profit as well. Each year, companies prepare financial statements to see how their profit-making operations are performing. Two of the financial statements that they prepare are called the income statement and the balance sheet. In this chapter, you learn to prepare these two financial statements. The income statement will look at the company's revenues, amount of returns, cost of goods sold, and operating expenses. The balance sheet will provide a look at the company's assets, liabilities, and stockholders' equity on a certain date.

Learning Objectives

LO1   Prepare Financial Statements for a Merchandise Company

LO2   Complete Adjusting Entries, Closing Entries, and a Post-Closing Trial Balance for a Merchandise Company

LO3   Complete Reversing Entries

When you buy a toy at Toys"R"Us just keep in mind all the steps the company must take to complete its accounting cycle. In this chapter, we discuss the steps involved in completing the accounting cycle for a merchandise company. These steps include preparing financial reports, journalizing and posting adjusting and closing entries, preparing a post-closing trial balance, and reversing entries.

LEARNING UNIT 12-1

L01

Financial Statements for Merchandise Companies

As we discussed in Chapter 5, when we were dealing with a service company rather than a merchandise company, the three financial statements can be prepared from the worksheet. Let's begin by looking at how Art's Wholesale Clothing Company prepares the income statement.

The Income Statement

Art is interested in knowing how well his shop performed for the year ended December 31, 201X. What were its net sales? What was the level of returns of goods from dissatisfied customers? What was the cost of the goods brought into the store versus the selling price received? How many goods were returned to suppliers? What is the cost of the goods that have not been sold? What was the cost of the Freight-In? The income statement in Figure 12.1 is prepared from the income statement columns of the worksheet. Note that no debit or credit columns appear on the formal income statement; the inside columns in financial reports are used for subtotaling, not for debit and credit.

The income statement is broken down into several sections. Remembering the sections can help you set it up correctly on your own. The income statement shows the following:

	Net Sales
−	Cost of Goods Sold
=	Gross Profit
−	Operating Expenses
=	Net Income from Operations
+	Other Income
−	Other Expenses
=	Net Income

Let's take these sections one at a time and see where the figures come from on the worksheet.

Revenue Section: Net Sales. The first major category of the income statement shows net sales. The figure here—$93,380—is not on the worksheet. Instead, the accountant must combine the amounts for gross sales, sales returns and allowances, and sales discount found on the worksheet to arrive at a figure for net sales. Thus these individual amounts are not summarized in a single figure for net sales until the formal income statement is prepared.

Cost of Goods Sold Section. The figures for Merchandise Inventory are shown separately on the worksheet. The $19,000 represents the beginning inventory of the period, and the $4,000, calculated from an inventory sheet, is the ending inventory. Note that on the financial report the cost of goods sold section uses two separate figures for inventory.

COACHING TIP

	Sales
−	Sales Ret. & Allow.
−	Sales Discount
=	Net Sales

COACHING TIP

	Beg. Inventory
+	Net Cost of Purchases
−	Ending Inventory
=	Cost of Goods Sold

FIGURE 12.1 Partial Worksheet and Income Statement

ART'S WHOLESALE CLOTHING COMPANY
PARTIAL WORKSHEET
FOR YEAR ENDED DECEMBER 31, 201X

	Income Statement Dr.	Income Statement Cr.
Income Summary	19 0 0 0 00	4 0 0 0 00
Sales		95 0 0 0 00
Sales Returns and Allowances	9 5 0 00	
Sales Discount	6 7 0 00	
Purchases	52 0 0 0 00	
Purchases Discount		8 6 0 00
Purchases Returns and Allowances		6 8 0 00
Freight-In	4 5 0 00	
Salaries Expense	12 3 0 0 00	
Payroll Tax Expense	4 2 0 00	
Postage Expense	2 5 00	
Miscellaneous Expense	3 0 00	
Interest Expense	3 0 0 00	
Rental Income		2 0 0 00
Supplies Expense	5 0 0 00	
Insurance Expense	3 0 0 00	
Depreciation Expense, Store Equip.	5 0 00	
Salaries Payable		
	86 9 9 5 00	100 7 4 0 00
Net Income	13 7 4 5 00	
Totals	100 7 4 0 00	100 7 4 0 00

ART'S WHOLESALE CLOTHING COMPANY
INCOME STATEMENT
FOR YEAR ENDED DECEMBER 31, 201X

Revenue:			
Gross Sales			$95 0 0 0 00
Less: Sales Ret. and Allow.		$ 9 5 0 00	
Sales Discount		6 7 0 00	1 6 2 0 00
Net Sales			$93 3 8 0 00
Cost of Goods Sold:			
Merchandise Inventory, 1/1/1X		$19 0 0 0 00	
Purchases	$52 0 0 0 00		
Less: Purch. Discount	$ 8 6 0 00		
Purch. Ret. and Allow.	6 8 0 00	1 5 4 0 00	
Net Purchases	$50 4 6 0 00		
Add: Freight-In	4 5 0 00		
Net Cost of Purchases		50 9 1 0 00	
Cost of Goods Available for Sale		$69 9 1 0 00	
Less: Merch. Inv, 12/31/1X		4 0 0 0 00	
Cost of Goods Sold			65 9 1 0 00
Gross Profit			$27 4 7 0 00
Operating Expenses:			
Salaries Expense		$12 3 0 0 00	
Payroll Tax Expense		4 2 0 00	
Dep. Exp., Store Equip.		5 0 00	
Supplies Expense		5 0 0 00	
Insurance Expense		3 0 0 00	
Postage Expense		2 5 00	
Miscellaneous Expense		3 0 00	
Total Operating Expenses			13 6 2 5 00
Net Income from Operations			$13 8 4 5 00
Other Income:			
Rental Income		$ 2 0 0 00	
Other Expenses:			
Interest Expense		3 0 0 00	1 0 0 00
Net Income			$13 7 4 5 00

Note that the following numbers are not found on the worksheet but are shown on the formal income statement (they are combined by the accountant in preparing the income statement):

- Net Purchases: $50,460 (Purchases − Purchases Discount − Purchases Returns and Allowances)
- Net Cost of Purchases: $50,910 (Net Purchases + Freight-In)
- Cost of Goods Available for Sale: $69,910 (Beginning Inventory + Net Cost of Purchases)
- Cost of Goods Sold: $65,910 (Cost of Goods Available for Sale − Ending Inventory)

Gross Profit. Gross profit ($27,470) is calculated by subtracting the cost of goods sold from net sales ($93,380 – $65,910). This amount is not found on the worksheet.

Operating Expenses Section. Like the other figures we have discussed, the business's total operating expenses do not appear on the worksheet. To get this figure ($13,625), the accountant adds up all the operating expenses (excluding other expenses) from the worksheet.

Many operating companies break expenses down into those directly related to the selling activity of the company (selling expenses) and those related to administrative or office activity (administrative expenses or general expenses). Here's a sample list (not connected to the example for Art's Wholesale) broken down into these two categories:

Operating Expenses

- **Selling Expenses:**

    Sales Salaries Expense
    Delivery Expense
    Advertising Expense
    Depreciation Expense, Store Equipment
    Insurance Expense
        Total Selling Expenses

- **Administrative Expenses:**

    Rent Expense
    Office Salaries Expense
    Utilities Expense
    Office Supplies Expense
    Depreciation Expense, Office Equipment
        Total Administrative Expenses
            Total Operating Expenses

Selling expenses Operating expenses directly related to the sale of goods excluding Cost of Goods Sold.

Administrative expenses (general expenses) Operating expenses such as general office expenses that are incurred indirectly in the selling of goods.

Other income Any revenue other than revenue from sales and service revenue. It appears in a separate section on the income statement. Examples: Rental Income and Storage Fees.

Other expenses Nonoperating expenses that do not relate to the main operating activities of the business; they appear in a separate section on the income statement. One example given in the text is Interest Expense, interest owed on money borrowed by the company.

Other Income (or Other Revenue) Section. The other income, or other revenue, section is used to record any revenue other than revenue from sales and service revenue. For example, Art's Wholesale makes a profit from subletting a portion of a building. The $200 of rental income the company earns from this is reported in the other income section.

Other Expenses Section. The other expenses section is used to record nonoperating expenses, that is, expenses that are not related to the main operating activities of the business. For example, Art's Wholesale owes $300 interest on money it has borrowed. That expense is shown in the other expenses section.

Statement of Owner's Equity. The information used to prepare the statement of owner's equity comes from the balance sheet columns of the worksheet. Keep in mind that the capital account in the ledger should be checked to see whether any additional investments occurred during the period. Figure 12.2 shows how the worksheet aids

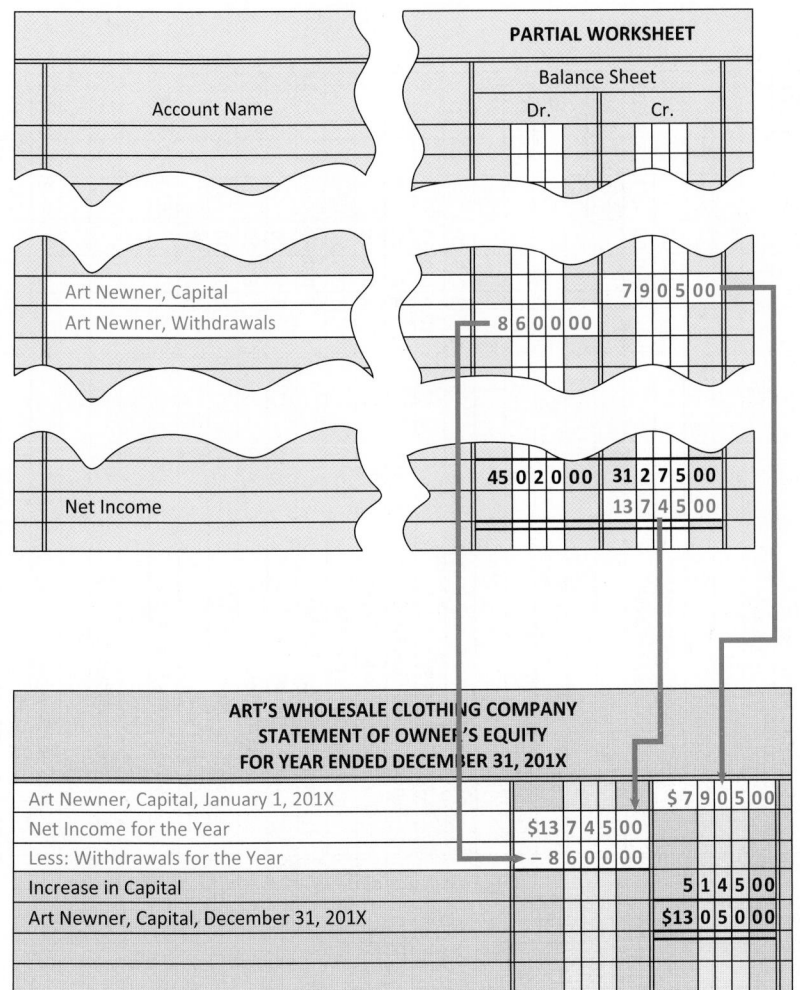

FIGURE 12.2
Preparing a Statement of Owner's Equity from the Worksheet

COACHING TIP

Any additional investment by the owner would be added to his or her beginning capital amount.

in this step. The ending figure of $13,050 for Art Newner, Capital is carried over to the balance sheet, which is the final report we look at in this chapter.

The Balance Sheet

Figure 12.3 (page 444) shows how a worksheet is used to aid in the preparation of a classified balance sheet. A classified balance sheet breaks down the assets and liabilities into more detail. Classified balance sheets provide management, owners, creditors, and suppliers with more information about the company's ability to pay current and long-term debts. They also provide a more complete financial picture of the firm.

The categories on the classified balance sheet are as follows:

- Current assets are defined as cash and assets that will be converted into cash or used up during the normal operating cycle of the company or 1 year, whichever is longer. (Think of the operating cycle as the time period it takes a company to buy and sell merchandise and then collect accounts receivable.)

  Accountants list current assets in order of how easily they can be converted into cash (called *liquidity*). In most cases, Accounts Receivable can be turned into cash more quickly than Merchandise Inventory. For example, it can be quite difficult to sell an outdated computer in a computer store or to sell last year's model car this year.

- Plant and equipment are long-lived assets that are used in the production or sale of goods or services. Art's Wholesale has only one plant asset, store equipment; other plant assets could include buildings and land. The assets are usually listed in order according to how long they will last; the shortest-lived

Classified balance sheet A balance sheet that categorizes assets as current assets or plant and equipment and groups liabilities as current or long-term liabilities.

Current assets Assets that can be converted into cash or used within 1 year or the normal operating cycle of the business, whichever is longer.

Operating cycle Average time it takes to buy and sell merchandise and then collect accounts receivable.

Plant and equipment Long-lived assets such as equipment, buildings, or land that are used in the production or sale of goods or services.

FIGURE 12.3 Partial Worksheet and Classified Balance Sheet

ART'S WHOLESALE CLOTHING COMPANY
WORKSHEET
FOR YEAR ENDED DECEMBER 31, 200X

	Balance Sheet Dr.	Balance Sheet Cr.
Cash	12 9 2 0 00	
Petty Cash	1 0 0 00	
Accounts Receivable	14 5 0 0 00	
Merchandise Inventory	4 0 0 0 00	
Supplies	3 0 0 00	
Prepaid Insurance	6 0 0 00	
Store Equipment	4 0 0 0 00	
Acc. Dep., Store Equipment		4 5 0 00
Accounts Payable		17 9 0 0 00
Federal Income Tax Payable		8 0 0 00
FICA—Social Security Payable		4 5 4 00
FICA—Medicare Payable		1 0 6 00
State Income Tax Payable		2 0 0 00
SUTA Tax Payable		1 0 8 00
FUTA Tax Payable		3 2 00
Unearned Rent		4 0 0 00
Mortgage Payable		2 3 2 0 00
Art Newner, Capital		7 9 0 5 00
Salaries Payable		6 0 0 00
Totals	45 0 2 0 00	31 2 7 5 00
Net Income		13 7 4 5 00
Totals	45 0 2 0 00	45 0 2 0 00

ART'S WHOLESALE CLOTHING COMPANY
CLASSIFIED BALANCE SHEET
DECEMBER 31, 201X

Assets

Current Assets:			
Cash		$12 9 2 0 00	
Petty Cash		1 0 0 00	
Accounts Receivable		14 5 0 0 00	
Merchandise Inventory		4 0 0 0 00	
Supplies		3 0 0 00	
Prepaid Insurance		6 0 0 00	
Total Current Assets			$32 4 2 0 00
Plant and Equipment:			
Store Equipment		$ 4 0 0 0 00	
Less: Accum. Depreciation		4 5 0 00	3 5 5 0 00
Total Assets			$35 9 7 0 00

Liabilities

Current Liabilities:			
Mortgage Payable (current portion)	$	3 2 0 00	
Accounts Payable	17	9 0 0 00	
Federal Income Tax Payable		8 0 0 00	
FICA—Social Security Payable		4 5 4 00	
FICA—Medicare Payable		1 0 6 00	
State Income Tax Payable		2 0 0 00	
SUTA Tax Payable		1 0 8 00	
FUTA Tax Payable		3 2 00	
Salaries Payable		6 0 0 00	
Unearned Rent		4 0 0 00	
Total Current Liabilities			$20 9 2 0 00
Long-Term Liabilities			
Mortgage Payable			2 0 0 0 00
Total Liabilities			$22 9 2 0 00

Owner's Equity

Art Newner, Capital, December 31, 201X			13 0 5 0 00
Total Liabilities and Owner's Equity			$35 9 7 0 00

assets are listed first. Land is always the last asset listed (and—keep in mind—land is never depreciated). Note that we still show the cost of the asset less its accumulated depreciation.

- Current liabilities are the debts or obligations of Art's Wholesale that must be paid within 1 year or one operating cycle. The order of listing accounts in this section is not always the same; many times companies will list their liabilities in the order they expect to pay them off. Note that the current portion of the mortgage, $320 (that portion due within 1 year), is listed before Accounts Payable.

- Long-term liabilities are debts or obligations that are not due and payable for a comparatively long period, usually for more than 1 year. For Art's Wholesale the only long-term liability is Mortgage Payable. The long-term portion of the mortgage is listed here; the current portion, due within 1 year, is listed under current liabilities.

Now it's time to check your progress.

Current liabilities Obligations that will come due within 1 year or within the operating cycle, whichever is longer.

COACHING TIP

Mortgage Payable:

$2,320
− 320 current portion
$2,000 long-term liability

Long-term liabilities Obligations that are not due or payable for a long time, usually for more than a year.

 TRY IT!   Learning Unit 12-1

Complete the following chart by placing an (X) in the appropriate column(s).

Account Title	IS	SOE	BS	Curr. Asset	Curr. Liab.	Pl. + Eq.
Purchases Discount						
Sales Discount						
Ending Merch. Inventory						
Unearned Storage Fees						
Accum. Dep., Store Equip.						
Prepaid Insurance						
Ending Capital						
Sales Ret. and Allow.						
Store Equipment						
Sales						
Accounts Payable						

Adjusting and Closing Entries and the Post-Closing Trial Balance for a Merchandise Company

LEARNING UNIT 12-2
 L02

Journalizing and Posting Adjusting Entries

From the worksheet of Art's Wholesale (repeated in Figure 12.4, pages 446 and 447, for your convenience), the adjusting entries can be journalized from the adjustments column and posted to the ledger. Keep in mind that the adjustments have been placed only on the worksheet, not in the journal or in the ledger. At this point, the journal does not reflect adjustments and the ledger still contains only unadjusted amounts.

Partial Ledger

Merchandise Inventory 114			Income Summary 313	
Dr.	Cr.		Dr.	Cr.
19,000	19,000 (A)		(A) 19,000	4,000 (B)
(B) 4,000				

FIGURE 12.4 Completed Worksheet

	Trial Balance Dr.	Trial Balance Cr.	Adjustments Dr.	Adjustments Cr.
ART'S WHOLESALE CLOTHING CO. WORKSHEET FOR YEAR ENDED DECEMBER 31, 201X				
Cash	12 9 2 0 00			
Petty Cash	1 0 0 00			
Accounts Receivable	14 5 0 0 00			
Merchandise Inventory	19 0 0 0 00		(B) 4 0 0 0 00	(A)19 0 0 0 00
Supplies	8 0 0 00			(D) 5 0 0 00
Prepaid Insurance	9 0 0 00			(E) 3 0 0 00
Store Equipment	4 0 0 0 00			
Acc. Dep., Store Equipment		4 0 0 00		(F) 5 0 00
Accounts Payable		17 9 0 0 00		
Federal Income Tax Payable		8 0 0 00		
FICA—Social Security Payable		4 5 4 00		
FICA—Medicare Payable		1 0 6 00		
State Income Tax Payable		2 0 0 00		
SUTA Tax Payable		1 0 8 00		
FUTA Tax Payable		3 2 00		
Unearned Rent		6 0 0 00	(C) 2 0 0 00	
Mortgage Payable		2 3 2 0 00		
Art Newner, Capital		7 9 0 5 5 00		
Art Newner, Withdrawals	8 6 0 0 00			
Income Summary			(A)19 0 0 0 00	(B) 4 0 0 0 00
Sales		95 0 0 0 00		
Sales Returns and Allowances	9 5 0 00			
Sales Discount	6 7 0 00			
Purchases	52 0 0 0 00			
Purchases Discount		8 6 0 00		
Purchases Returns and Allowances		6 8 0 00		
Freight-In	4 5 0 00			
Salaries Expense	11 7 0 0 00		(G) 6 0 0 00	
Payroll Tax Expense	4 2 0 00			
Postage Expense	2 5 00			
Miscellaneous Expense	3 0 00			
Interest Expense	3 0 0 00			
Totals	127 3 6 5 00	127 3 6 5 00		
Rental Income				(C) 2 0 0 00
Supplies Expense			(D) 5 0 0 00	
Insurance Expense			(E) 3 0 0 00	
Depreciation Expense, Store Equip.			(F) 5 0 00	
Salaries Payable				(G) 6 0 0 00
Totals			24 6 5 0 00	24 6 5 0 00
Net Income				
Totals				

FIGURE 12.4 *(concluded)*

	Adjusted Trial Bal.		Income Statement		Balance Sheet	
	Dr.	Cr.	Dr.	Cr.	Dr.	Cr.
Cash	12 9 2 0 00				12 9 2 0 00	
Petty Cash	1 0 0 00				1 0 0 00	
Accounts Receivable	14 5 0 0 00				14 5 0 0 00	
Merchandise Inventory	4 0 0 0 00				4 0 0 0 00	
Supplies	3 0 0 00				3 0 0 00	
Prepaid Insurance	6 0 0 00				6 0 0 00	
Store Equipment	4 0 0 0 00				4 0 0 0 00	
Acc. Dep., Store Equipment		4 5 0 00				4 5 0 00
Accounts Payable		17 9 0 0 00				17 9 0 0 00
Federal Income Tax Payable		8 0 0 00				8 0 0 00
FICA—Social Security Payable		4 5 4 00				4 5 4 00
FICA—Medicare Payable		1 0 6 00				1 0 6 00
State Income Tax Payable		2 0 0 00				2 0 0 00
SUTA Tax Payable		1 0 8 00				1 0 8 00
FUTA Tax Payable		3 2 00				3 2 00
Unearned Rent		4 0 0 00				4 0 0 00
Mortgage Payable		2 3 2 0 00				2 3 2 0 00
Art Newner, Capital		7 9 0 5 00				7 9 0 5 00
Art Newner, Withdrawals	8 6 0 0 00				8 6 0 0 00	
Income Summary	19 0 0 0 00	4 0 0 0 00	19 0 0 0 00	4 0 0 0 00		
Sales		95 0 0 0 00		95 0 0 0 00		
Sales Returns and Allowances	9 5 0 00		9 5 0 00			
Sales Discount	6 7 0 00		6 7 0 00			
Purchases	52 0 0 0 00		52 0 0 0 00			
Purchases Discount		8 6 0 00		8 6 0 00		
Purchases Returns and Allowances		6 8 0 00		6 8 0 00		
Freight-In	4 5 0 00		4 5 0 00			
Salaries Expense	12 3 0 0 00		12 3 0 0 00			
Payroll Tax Expense	4 2 0 00		4 2 0 00			
Postage Expense	2 5 00		2 5 00			
Miscellaneous Expense	3 0 00		3 0 00			
Interest Expense	3 0 0 00		3 0 0 00			
Rental Income		2 0 0 00		2 0 0 00		
Supplies Expense	5 0 0 00		5 0 0 00			
Insurance Expense	3 0 0 00		3 0 0 00			
Depreciation Expense, Store Equip.	5 0 00		5 0 00			
Salaries Payable		6 0 0 00				6 0 0 00
Totals	132 0 1 5 00	132 0 1 5 00	86 9 9 5 00	100 7 4 0 00	45 0 2 0 00	31 2 7 5 00
Net Income			13 7 4 5 00			13 7 4 5 00
Totals			100 7 4 0 00	100 7 4 0 00	45 0 2 0 00	45 0 2 0 00

Unearned Rent 219			Rental Income 414	
Dr.	Cr.		Dr.	Cr.
(C) 200	600			200 (C)

Supplies 115			Supplies Expense 614	
Dr.	Cr.		Dr.	Cr.
800	500 (D)		(D) 500	

Prepaid Insurance 116			Insurance Expense 615	
Dr.	Cr.		Dr.	Cr.
900	300 (E)		(E) 300	

Accum. Dep., Store Equipment 122			Dep. Expense, Store Equip. 613	
Dr.	Cr.		Dr.	Cr.
	400		(F) 50	
	50 (F)			

Salaries Payable 212			Salaries Exp. 611	
Dr.	Cr.		Dr.	Cr.
	600 (G)		11,700	
			(G) 600	

The journalized and posted adjusting entries are shown in Figure 12.5. Note that the liability Unearned Rent is reduced by $200 and Rental Income has increased by $200.

FIGURE 12.5
Journalized and Posted Adjusting Entries

			ART'S WHOLESALE CLOTHING CO. GENERAL JOURNAL				
							Page 2
	Date		Account Titles and Description	PR	Dr.	Cr.	
			Adjusting Entries				
	31		Income Summary	313	19 0 0 0 00		
			Merchandise Inventory	114		19 0 0 0 00	
			Transferred beginning inventory				
			to Income Summary				
	31		Merchandise Inventory	114	4 0 0 0 00		
			Income Summary	313		4 0 0 0 00	
			Records cost of ending inventory				
	31		Unearned Rent	219	2 0 0 00		
			Rental Income	414		2 0 0 00	
			Rental income earned				
	31		Supplies Expense	614	5 0 0 00		
			Supplies	115		5 0 0 00	
			Supplies consumed				
	31		Insurance Expense	615	3 0 0 00		
			Prepaid Insurance	116		3 0 0 00	
			Insurance expired				
	31		Dep. Exp., Store Equipment	613	5 0 00		
			Acc. Dep., Store Equipment	122		5 0 00	
			Depreciation on equipment				
	31		Salaries Expense	611	6 0 0 00		
			Salaries Payable	212		6 0 0 00	
			Accrued salaries				

Journalizing and Posting Closing Entries

In Chapter 5, we discussed the closing process for a service company. The goals of closing are the same for a merchandise company. These goals are (1) to clear all temporary accounts in the ledger to zero and (2) to update capital in the ledger to its latest balance. The company must use the worksheet and the steps listed here to complete the closing process.

STEP 1   Close all balances on the income statement credit column of the worksheet, except Income Summary, by debits.
Then credit the total to the Income Summary account.

STEP 2   Close all balances on the income statement debit column of the worksheet, except Income Summary, by credits.
Then debit the total to the Income Summary account.

STEP 3   Transfer the balance of the Income Summary account to the Capital account.

STEP 4   Transfer the balance of the owner's Withdrawals account to the Capital account.

Let's look now at the journalized closing entries in Figure 12.6 (page 450). When these entries are posted, all the temporary accounts will have zero balances in the ledger, and the Capital account will be updated with a new balance.

Let's take a moment to look at the Income Summary account in T account form.

	Income Summary 313		
	Dr.	Cr.	
Adj.	19,000	4,000	Adj.
Clos.	67,995	96,740	Clos.
	86,995	100,740	
Closing	13,745	13,745	Net Income

COACHING TIP

Note that Income Summary before the closing process contains the adjustments for Merchandise Inventory. The end result is that the net income of $13,745 is closed to the Capital account.

The Post-Closing Trial Balance

The post-closing trial balance shown in Figure 12.7 (page 451) is prepared from the general ledger. Note first that all temporary accounts have been closed and thus are not shown on this post-closing trial balance. Note also that the ending inventory figure of the last accounting period, $4,000, becomes the beginning inventory figure on January 1, 201Y. In a computerized accounting system, the post-closing trial balance can be created by a click of a key in the main menu.

FIGURE 12.6
General Journal Closing Entries

			ART'S WHOLESALE CLOTHING CO. GENERAL JOURNAL																

Page 2

Date		Account Titles and Description	PR	Dr.						Cr.					
		Closing Entries													
	31	Sales	411	95	0	0	0	00							
		Rental Income	414		2	0	0	00							
		Purchases Discount	512		8	6	0	00							
		Purchases Ret. and Allow.	513		6	8	0	00							
		Income Summary	313							96	7	4	0	00	
		Transfers credit account balances													
		on income statement column of													
		worksheet to Income Summary													
	31	Income Summary	313	67	9	9	5	00							
		Sales Returns and Allowances	412								9	5	0	00	
		Sales Discount	413								6	7	0	00	
		Purchases	511							52	0	0	0	00	
		Freight-In	514								4	5	0	00	
		Salaries Expense	611							12	3	0	0	00	
		Payroll Tax Expense	612								4	2	0	00	
		Postage Expense	616									2	5	00	
		Miscellaneous Expense	617									3	0	00	
		Interest Expense	618								3	0	0	00	
		Supplies Expense	614								5	0	0	00	
		Insurance Expense	615								3	0	0	00	
		Depreciation Expense, Store Equip.	613									5	0	00	
		Transfers all expenses, and													
		deductions to Sales are													
		closed to Income Summary													
	31	Income Summary	313	13	7	4	5	00							
		A. Newner, Capital	311							13	7	4	5	00	
		Transfer of net income to													
		Capital from Income Summary													
	31	A. Newner, Capital	311	8	6	0	0	00							
		A. Newner, Withdrawals	312								8	6	0	0	00
		Closes withdrawals to													
		Capital Account													

ART'S WHOLESALE CLOTHING COMPANY POSTCLOSING TRIAL BALANCE DECEMBER 31, 201X	Dr.	Cr.
Cash	12 9 2 0 00	
Petty Cash	1 0 0 00	
Accounts Receivable	14 5 0 0 00	
Merchandise Inventory	4 0 0 0 00	
Supplies	3 0 0 00	
Prepaid Insurance	6 0 0 00	
Store Equipment	4 0 0 0 00	
Accum. Depreciation, Store Equipment		4 5 0 00
Accounts Payable		17 9 0 0 00
Federal Income Tax Payable		8 0 0 00
FICA—Social Security Payable		4 5 4 00
FICA—Medicare Payable		1 0 6 00
State Income Tax Payable		2 0 0 00
SUTA Tax Payable		1 0 8 00
FUTA Tax Payable		3 2 00
Salary Payable		6 0 0 00
Unearned Rent		4 0 0 00
Mortgage Payable		2 3 2 0 00
Art Newner, Capital		13 0 5 0 00
Totals	36 4 2 0 00	36 4 2 0 00

FIGURE 12.7
Post-Closing Trial Balance for Art's Wholesale Clothing Company

Now let's check your progress.

 TRY IT!   Learning Unit 12-2

Complete the following table by placing an (X) in the appropriate column(s).

Accounts	Temp.	Perm.	Closed to Inc. Sum.	Ending Balance Listed on Post-Closing Trial Balance
Cash				
Petty Cash				
Accounts Receivable				
Sales				
Purchases Discounts				
Purchases Returns and Allowances				
Sales Returns and Allowances				
Sales Discounts				
Purchases				
Accounts Payable				
Merchandise Inventory				
Depreciation Expense				
Accumulated Depreciation				
FICA Medicare Payable				
Capital				
Unearned Rent				

What will the ending balance in Income Summary be when net income or net loss is closed to capital?

Reversing entries Optional bookkeeping technique in which certain adjusting entries are reversed or switched on the first day of the new accounting period so that transactions in the new period can be recorded without referring back to prior adjusting entries.

Reversing Entries (Optional Section)

The accounting cycle for Art's Wholesale Clothing Company is completed. Now let's look at reversing entries, an optional way of handling some adjusting entries. Reversing entries are general journal entries that are the opposite of adjusting entries. Reversing entries help reduce potential errors and simplify the recordkeeping process. If Art's accountant makes reversing entries, routine transactions can be made in the usual steps.

To help explain the concept of reversing entries, let's look at these two adjustments that could be reversed:

1. When an increase occurs in an asset account (no previous balance).

   Example: Interest Receivable

   Interest Income

   (Interest earned but not collected is covered in later chapters.)

2. When an increase occurs in a liability account (no previous balance).

   Example: Salaries Expense

   Salaries Payable

With the exception of businesses in their first year of operation, accounts such as Accumulated Depreciation or Inventory cannot be reduced because they have previous balances.

Art's bookkeeper handles an entry without reversing for salaries at the end of the year (see Figure 12.8). Note that the permanent account, Salaries Payable, carries over to the new accounting period a $600 balance. Remember that the $600 was an expense of the prior year.

FIGURE 12.8 Reversing Entries Not Used

❶ On December 31, an adjusting entry was journalized and posted for $600 of salaries incurred but not paid.

❷ On January 1, after closing entries have been journalized and posted, Salaries Expense has a zero balance.

On January 8 of the new year, the payroll to be paid is $2,000. If the optional reversing entry is *not* used, the bookkeeper must make the following compound journal entry as shown in Figure 12.9.

FIGURE 12.9 Entry When Optional Reversing Entry Is Not Used

To do so, the bookkeeper has to refer back to the adjustment on December 31 to determine how much of the salary of $2,000 is indeed a new salary expense and what portion was shown in the old year although not paid. It is easy to see how potential errors can result if the bookkeeper pays the payroll but forgets about the adjustment in the previous year. In this way, reversing entries can help avoid potential errors.

Figure 12.10 shows the four steps the bookkeeper would take if reversing entries were used. Note that steps 1 and 2 are the same whether the accountant uses reversing entries or not.

Note that the balance of Salaries Expense is indeed only $1,400, the *true* expense in the new year. Reversing results in switching the adjustment the first day of the new period. Also note that each of the accounts ends up with the same balance no matter which method is chosen. Using a reversing entry for salaries, however, allows the accountant to make the normal entry when it is time to pay salaries.

FIGURE 12.10 Reversing Entries Used

① On December 31, an adjustment for salary was recorded.

ADJUSTING JOURNAL ENTRY

Dec.	31	Salaries Expense	6 0 0 00		
		Salaries Payable		6 0 0 00	

Salaries Exp.
11,700
600
12,300

Salaries Pay.
600

② Closing entry on December 31.

CLOSING JOURNAL ENTRY

Dec.	31	Income Summary	12 3 0 0 00		
		Salaries Expense		12 3 0 0 00	

Salaries Exp.
11,700
600
12,300 | 12,300 Closing

Salaries Pay.
600

③ On January 1 (first day of the following fiscal period), a reversing entry was made for salary on December 31 (by "flipping" the previous adjustment).

Jan.	1	Salaries Payable	6 0 0 00		
		Salaries Expense		6 0 0 00	

Salaries Exp.
| 600

Salaries Pay.
600 | 600

This way, the liability is reduced to 0. We know it will be paid in this new period, but the Salaries Expense has a credit balance of $600 until the payroll is paid. When the payroll of $2,000 is paid, the following results:

④ Paid Payroll $2,000.

Jan.	8	Salaries Expense	2 0 0 0 00		
		Cash		2 0 0 0 00	

Salaries Exp.
2,000 | 600
1,400 |

Cash
| 2,000

Now let's check your progress.

 TRY IT!   **Learning Unit 12-3**

Journalize the following transactions:

2013
Dec. 31   Salaries were adjusted for $500 (beg. balance of salary expense was $400).
  31   Closing entry was prepared.

2014
Jan. 1   A reversing entry for salaries was made.
  6   New salary expense is paid $1,200.

DEMONSTRATION SUMMARY PROBLEM   LO1,2,3

Requirements

Using the completed worksheet in Chapter 11 for Ledger Sport Shop (p. 424):

1. Journalize (p. 9) and post the adjusting and closing entries (omit explanations).
2. Prepare a post-closing trial balance.

The Chart of Accounts is as follows:

> Cash 110; Merchandise Inventory 120; Prepaid Rent 130; Prepaid Insurance 140; Display Equipment 150; Accumulated Depreciation, Display Equipment 160; Unearned Training Fees 210; Accounts Payable 220; Salaries Payable 230; J. Loy, Capital 310; Income Summary 320; Sales 410; Sales Returns and Allowances 412; Sales Discounts 414; Training Fees Earned 420; Purchases 540; Purchases Returns and Allowances 550; Purchases Discounts 560; Salary Expense 600; Plumbing Expense 610; Utilities Expense 620; Insurance Expense 630; Rent Expense 640; Depreciation Expense, Display Equipment 650.

Solutions

Requirement 1

page 9

Date	Account Titles	PR	Dr.	Cr.
	Adjusting Entries			
201X				
March 31	Income Summary	320	2,000	
	Merchandise Inventory	120		2,000
31	Merchandise Inventory	120	400	
	Income Summary	320		400
31	Unearned Training Fees	210	200	
	Training Fees Earned	420		200
31	Insurance Expense	630	100	
	Prepaid Insurance	140		100
31	Rent Expense	640	300	
	Prepaid Rent	130		300
31	Depreciation Expense, Display Equip.	650	100	
	Accum. Depreciation, Display Equip.	160		100
31	Salary Expense	600	500	
	Salaries Payable	230		500
	Closing Entries			
31	Sales	410	9,600	
	Purchases Returns and Allowances	550	400	
	Purchases Discounts	560	800	
	Training Fees Earned	420	200	
	Income Summary	320		11,000
31	Income Summary	320	18,700	
	Sales Returns and Allowances	412		500
	Sales Discounts	414		300
	Purchases	540		15,000
	Salary Expense	600		1,900
	Plumbing Expense	610		200
	Utilities Expense	620		300
	Insurance Expense	630		100
	Rent Expense	640		300
	Depreciation Expense, Display Equip.	650		100
31	J. Loy, Capital	310	9,300	
	Income Summary	320		9,300

General Ledger After Posting Adjusting and Closing Entries

Cash 110	
Dr.	Cr.
Bal. 6,000	

Merchandise Inventory 120	
Dr.	Cr.
Bal. 2,000	2,000 3/31 GJ9
3/31 GJ9 400	

Prepaid Rent 130	
Dr.	Cr.
Bal. 600	300 3/31 GJ9

Prepaid Insurance 140	
Dr.	Cr.
Bal. 500	100 3/31 GJ9

Display Equipment 150	
Dr.	Cr.
Bal 3,000	

Accum. Depreciation, Display Equip. 160	
Dr.	Cr.
	2,000 Bal.
	100 3/31 GJ9

Unearned Training Fees 210	
Dr.	Cr.
3/31 GJ9 200	3,000 Bal.

Accounts Payable 220	
Dr.	Cr.
	7,000 Bal.

Salaries Payable 230	
Dr.	Cr.
	500 3/31 GJ9

J. Loy, Capital 310	
Dr.	Cr.
3/31 GJ9 9,300	7,000 Bal.

Income Summary 320	
Dr.	Cr.
3/31 GJ9 2,000	400 3/31 GJ9
3/31 GJ9 18,700	11,000 3/31 GJ9
Bal. 9,300	9,300 3/31 GJ9 Closing

Sales 410	
Dr.	Cr.
3/31 GJ9 9,600	9,600 Bal.

Sales Returns and Allowances 412	
Dr.	Cr.
Bal. 500	500 3/31 GJ9

Sales Discounts 414	
Dr.	Cr.
Bal. 300	300 3/31 GJ9

Training Fees Earned 420	
Dr.	Cr.
3/31 GJ9 200	200 3/31 GJ9

Purchases 540	
Dr.	Cr.
Bal. 15,000	15,000 3/31 GJ9

Purchases Returns and Allowances 550	
Dr.	Cr.
3/31 GJ9 400	400 Bal.

Purchases Discount 560	
Dr.	Cr.
3/31 GJ9 800	800 Bal.

Salary Expense 600	
Dr.	Cr.
Bal. 1,400	1,900 3/31 GJ9
3/31 GJ9 500	

General Ledger After Posting Adjusting and Closing Entries

Plumbing Expense 610

Dr.	Cr.
Bal. 200	200 3/31 GJ9

Utilities Expense 620

Dr.	Cr.
Bal. 300	300 3/31 GJ9

Insurance Expense 630

Dr.	Cr.
3/31 GJ9 100	100 3/31 GJ9

Rent Expense 640

Dr.	Cr.
3/31 GJ9 300	300 3/31 GJ9

Depreciation Expense, Display Equip. 650

Dr.	Cr.
3/31 GJ9 100	100 3/31 GJ9

Requirement 2

Ledger Sport Shop
Post-Closing Trial Balance
March 31, 201X

	Dr.	Cr.
Cash	6,000	
Merchandise Inventory	400	
Prepaid Rent	300	
Prepaid Insurance	400	
Display Equipment	3,000	
Accum. Depreciation, Display Equip.		2,100
Unearned Training Fees		2,800
Accounts Payable		7,000
Salaries Payable		500
J. Loy, Capital	2,300	
Totals	12,400	12,400

Tips for Adjusting and Closing Entries

Note that the Merchandise Inventory is an adjustment that was accumulated in the Income Summary account. When closing is complete, all the temporary accounts will be closed to Income Summary (except if you had a withdrawal). Note in the ledger that after adjusting and closing entries were posted only permanent accounts have balances. From these permanent accounts with balances, a Post-Closing Trial Balance is prepared.

A key point is that this problem had a net loss instead of a net income. The end result is that the capital account has an unusual debit balance of $2,300.

BLUEPRINT: FINANCIAL STATEMENTS

(1) INCOME STATEMENT					
Revenue:					
Sales				$ XXX	
Less: Sales Ret. and Allow.			$ XXX		
Sales Discount			XXX	XXX	
Net Sales				$ XXXX	
Cost of Goods Sold:					
Merchandise Inventory, 1/1/1X			$ XXX		
Purchases		$XXX			
Less: Purchases Discount	$XXX				
Purch. Ret. and Allow.	XXX	XXX			
Net Purchases		XXX			
Add: Freight-In		XXX			
Net Cost of Purchases			XXX		
Cost of Goods Avail. for Sale			$XXXX		
Less: Merch. Inv., 12/31/1X			XXX		
Cost of Goods Sold				XXXX	
Gross Profit				$ XXXX	
Operating Expenses:					
~~			$ XXX		
~~			XXX		
~~			XXX		
Total Operating Expenses				XXX	
Net Income from Operations				$ XXX	
Other Income:					
Rental Income			$ XXX		
Storage Fees Income			XXX		
Total Other Income			$ XXX		
Other Expenses:					
Interest Expenses			XXX	XXX	
Net Income				$ XXX	

(2) STATEMENT OF OWNER'S EQUITY			
Beginning Capital			$ XXX
Additional Investments			XXX
Total Investment			$ XXX
Net Income		$ XXX	
Less: Withdrawals		XXX	
Increase in Capital			XXX
Ending Capital			$ XXX

(3) BALANCE SHEET				
Assets				
Current Assets:				
Cash		$ XXXX		
Acccounts Receivable		XXXX		
Merchandise Inventory		XXXX		
Prepaid Insurance		XXX		
Total Current Assets			$ XXXX	
Plant and Equipment:				
Store Equipment	$XXXX			
Less Accumulated Depreciation	XXXX	$XXXX		
Office Equipment	$XXXX			
Less Accumulated Depreciation	XXX	XXX		
Total Plant and Equipment			XXXX	
Total Assets			$XXXX	
Liabilities				
Current Liabilities:				
Unearned Revenue		$XXX		
Mortgage Payable (current portion)		XXX		
Accounts Payable		XXX		
Salaries Payable		XX		
FICA—Social Security Payable		XX		
FICA—Medicare Payable		XX		
Income Taxes Payable		XX		
Total Current Liabilities			$XXX	
Long-Term Liabilities				
Mortgage Payable			$XXX	
Total Liabilities			$XXXX	
Owner's Equity				
Capital*			XXXX	
Total Liabilities and Owner's Equity			$XXXX	

*From statement of owner's equity

 **TRY IT!**   **Solutions**   MyAccountingLab

Learning Unit 12-1

Account Title	IS	SOE	BS	Curr. Asset	Curr. Liab.	Pl.+Eq.
Purchases Discount	X					
Sales Discount	X					
Ending Merch. Inv.	X		X	X		
Unearned Storage Fees			X		X	
Accumulated Dep., Store Equipment			X			X
Prepaid Insurance			X	X		
Ending Capital		X	X			
Sales Returns and Allowances	X					
Store Equipment			X			X
Sales	X					
Accounts Payable			X		X	

Learning Unit 12-2

Account	Temp.	Perm.	Closed to Income Summary	Ending Balance Listed on Post-Closing Trial Balance
Cash		X		X
Petty Cash		X		X
Accounts Receivable		X		X
Sales	X		X	
Purchases Discounts	X		X	
Purchases Returns and Allowances	X		X	
Sales Returns and Allowances	X		X	
Sales Discounts	X		X	
Purchases	X		X	
Accounts Payable		X		X
Merchandise Inventory		X		X
Depreciation Expense	X		X	
Accumulated Depreciation		X		X
FICA-Medicare Payable		X		X
Capital		X		X
Unearned Rent		X		X

Balance in Income Summary will be zero when it is closed to capital.

Learning Unit 12-3

Date		Accounts	Dr.	Cr.
2013				
Dec.	31	Salaries Expense	500	
		Salaries Payable		500
	31	Income Summary	900	
		Salaries Expense		900
2014				
Jan.	1	Salaries Payable	500	
		Salaries Expense		500
	6	Salaries Expense	1,200	
		Cash		1,200

ACCOUNTING COACH

The following Coaching Tips are from Learning Units 12-1 to 12-3. Take the Pre-Game Checkup and use the Check Your Score at the bottom of the page to see how you are doing. The Accounting Coach provides tips before each Checkup to help you avoid common accounting errors.

LU 12-1 Financial Statements for Merchandise Companies

Pre-Game Tips: The financial statements do not have debits and credits. The inside columns are for subtotaling. The totals on the financial statements will not always equal the same total amounts on the worksheet. Net Income will always be the same on the worksheet and income statement.

Purchases along with Beginning Merchandise Inventory will be added to Cost of Goods Sold, while Ending Inventory will be subtracted. Revenue less Cost of Goods Sold equals Gross Profit. To get Net Income from Operations, we subtract Operating Expenses from Gross Profit.

Pre-Game Checkup: Answer true or false to the following statements.

1. Freight-In is subtracted from Net Purchases.
2. Sales on the formal income statement has a credit balance.
3. Rental Income is shown on the balance sheet.
4. Accumulated Depreciation is a contra-asset on the balance sheet.
5. Unearned Rent is a revenue on the income statement.

LU 12-2 Adjusting and Closing Entries and the Post-Closing Trial Balance for a Merchandise Company

Pre-Game Tips: All adjustments can be taken from the adjustments column on the worksheet. Keep in mind that we adjust Inventory through Income Summary. We assume that old inventory is sold and is a cost and that the ending inventory is not a cost until it is sold. Income Summary is a temporary account and will not appear on the post-closing trial balance. The closing process transfers all temporary accounts through Income Summary except Withdrawals, which is closed directly to Capital.

Pre-Game Checkup: Answer true or false to the following statements.

1. Some temporary accounts will go on the post-closing trial balance.
2. Merchandise Inventory (ending) is listed as a debit on the post-closing trial balance.
3. Unearned Rent is a permanent account.
4. The Capital amount on the post-closing trial balance is listed before the closing process.
5. Purchases is listed on the post-closing trial balance.

LU 12-3 Reversing Entries (Optional Section)

Pre-Game Tips: Reversing entries is a way of handling some adjusting entries. By making a reversing entry, the accountant does not have to worry about the past adjustment and will make the normal entry when a transaction occurs. Reversing entries can be done when an increase occurs in an asset (no previous balance) or when an increase occurs in a liability account (no previous balance).

Pre-Game Checkup: Answer true or false to the following statements.

1. Reversing entries are required.
2. Interest Income and Interest Receivables may sometimes use a reversing entry.
3. Reversing entries are made in the old year, not the new.
4. Reversing entries for Salary will show true salary expense in the new year.
5. Regardless of whether reversing entries are used, the same balances will end up in each account.

CHECK YOUR SCORE: Answers to the Pre-Game Checkup

LU 12-1
1. False—Freight-In is added to Net Purchases.
2. False—Sales on the formal income statement has no debits or credits.
3. False—Rental Income is shown on the income statement.
4. True
5. False—Unearned Rent is a liability on the balance sheet.

LU 12-2
1. False—No temporary accounts will go on the post-closing trial balance.
2. True
3. True

4. False—The Capital account on the post-closing trial balance is listed after the closing process.
5. False—Purchases is a temporary account and will not appear on the post-closing trial balance.

LU 12-3
1. False—Reversing entries are optional.
2. True
3. False—Reversing entries are made in the new year.
4. True
5. True

Chapter Summary

MyAccountingLab

Here are all the key terms and equations to help you understand the concepts of this chapter and prepare you for your exam. After completing this review, go to MyAccountingLab for more practice opportunities.

Concepts You Should Know	Key Terms
L01 **Prepare Financial Statements for a Merchandise Company** 1. The formal income statement can be prepared from the income statement columns of the worksheet. 2. No debit or credit columns are used on the formal income statement. 3. The cost of goods sold section has a figure for beginning inventory and a separate figure for ending inventory. 4. Operating expenses could be broken down into selling and administrative expenses. 5. A classified balance sheet breaks assets into current assets and plant and equipment. Liabilities are broken down into current and long-term liabilities.	Administrative expenses (general expenses) (p. 442) Classified balance sheet (p. 443) Current assets (p. 443) Current liabilities (p. 445) Long-term liabilities (p. 445) Operating cycle (p. 443) Other expenses (p. 442) Other income (p. 442) Plant and equipment (p. 443) Selling expenses (p. 442)
L02 **Complete Adjusting Entries, Closing Entries, and a Post-Closing Trial Balance for a Merchandise Company** 1. The information for journalizing, adjusting, and closing entries can be obtained from the worksheet. 2. In the closing process, the balances of all temporary accounts will be zero and the Capital account is brought up to its new balance. 3. Inventory is not a temporary account. 4. The ending inventory, along with other permanent accounts, will be listed in the post-closing trial balance.	
L03 **Complete Reversing Entries** 1. Reversing entries are optional. They can aid in reducing potential errors and simplify the recordkeeping process. 2. The reversing entry "flips" the previous adjustment on the first day of a new fiscal period. 3. Reversing entries are only used if (a) assets are increasing and have no previous balance or (b) liabilities are increasing and have no previous balance.	Reversing entries (p. 452)

Discussion Questions and Critical Thinking/Ethical Case

1. Which columns of the worksheet aid in the preparation of the income statement?

2. Explain the components of cost of goods sold.

3. Explain how operating expenses can be broken down into different categories.

4. What is the difference between current assets and plant and equipment?

5. What is an operating cycle?

6. Why journalize adjusting entries *after* the formal reports in a manual system have been prepared?

7. Explain the steps of closing for a merchandise company.

8. Temporary accounts could appear on a post-closing trial balance. Agree or disagree?

9. What is the purpose of using reversing entries? Are they mandatory? When should they be used?

10. Janet Flynn, owner of Reel Company, plans to apply for a bank loan at Petro National Bank. Because the company has a lot of debt on its balance sheet, Janet does not plan to show it to the loan officer. She plans only to bring the income statement. Do you feel that this move is a sound financial move by Janet? You make the call. Write down your specific recommendations to Janet.

Concept Checks

MyAccountingLab

Calculate Net Sales

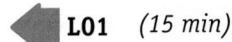 **L01**   *(5 min)*

1. From the following, calculate net sales:

Purchases	$ 99	Sales Discount	$15
Gross Sales	179	Operating Expenses	45
Sales Returns and Allowances	13		

Calculate Cost of Goods Sold

L01   *(5 min)*

2. Calculate Cost of Goods Sold:

Freight-In	$3	Ending Inventory	$ 2
Beginning Inventory	6	Net Purchases	65

Calculate Gross Profit and Net Income

L01   *(15 min)*

3. From the following information, calculate:
   a. Gross profit
   b. Net income or net loss

   Purchases, $98; Gross Sales, $180; Sales Returns and Allowances, $17; Sales Discounts, $23; Operating Expenses, $46; Net Sales, $140; Freight-In, $8; Beginning Inventory, $16; Ending Inventory, $5; Net Purchases, $65; Cost of Goods Sold, $84

(15 min)   **LO1**   **Classification of Accounts**

4.   Match the following categories to each account listed.

1. Current Asset
2. Plant and Equipment
3. Current Liabilities
4. Long-Term Liabilities

_____ **a.** Petty Cash
_____ **b.** Accounts Receivable
_____ **c.** Prepaid Rent
_____ **d.** FICA Payable
_____ **e.** Store Supplies
_____ **f.** Mortgage Payable (Current)
_____ **g.** SUTA Payable
_____ **h.** Accumulated Depreciation
_____ **i.** Computer Equipment
_____ **j.** Unearned Rent

(10 min)   **LO3**   **Reversing Entries**

5.   **a.** On January 1, prepare a reversing entry. On January 8, journalize the entry to record the paying of Salaries Expense, $760.
      b. What will be the balance in Salaries Expense on January 8 (after posting)?

December 31:

Salaries Expense				Salaries Payable	
Dr.	Cr.			Dr.	Cr.
760					380 Adj.
Adj. 380					
1,140	1,140 closing				

    Exercises

Set A

(15 min)   **LO1**   **12A-1.** From the following accounts, prepare a cost of goods sold section in proper form: Merchandise Inventory, 12/31/1X, $9,000; Purchases Discount, $920; Merchandise Inventory, 12/01/1X, $4,000; Purchases, $62,000; Purchases Returns and Allowances, $970; Freight-In, $250.

(10 min)   **LO1**   **12A-2.** Give the category, the classification, and the report(s) on which each of the following appears (for example: Cash—asset, current asset, balance sheet):

a. Salaries Payable
b. Accounts Payable
c. Mortgage Payable
d. Unearned Legal Fees
e. SIT Payable
f. Office Equipment
g. Land

12A-3. From the partial worksheet in Figure 12.11, journalize the closing entries for December 31 for F. Henry Co.

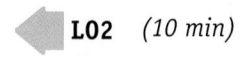 **L02**   *(10 min)*

FIGURE 12.11
Worksheet for F. Henry Co.

Account	Income Statement Dr.	Income Statement Cr.	Balance Sheet Dr.	Balance Sheet Cr.
Cash			1 8 9 00	
Merchandise Inventory			4 4 9 00	
Prepaid Advertising			5 6 3 00	
Prepaid Insurance			3 2 00	
Office Equipment			1 0 7 9 00	
Accum. Dep., Office Equip.				2 0 6 00
Accounts Payable				2 5 7 00
F. Henry, Capital				9 6 7 00
Income Summary	3 5 6 00	4 4 9 00		
Sales		5 5 0 4 00		
Sales Returns and Allowances	2 2 8 00			
Sales Discount	1 0 6 00			
Purchases	2 6 2 2 00			
Purchases Returns and Allowances		3 6 00		
Purchases Discount		5 4 00		
Salaries Expense	1 0 8 7 00			
Insurance Expense	6 9 5 00			
Utilities Expense	4 2 00			
Plumbing Expense	5 9 00			
Advertising Expense	1 6 00			
Dep. Expenses, Office Equip.	2 5 00			
Salaries Payable				7 5 00
Totals	5 2 3 6 00	6 0 4 3 00	2 3 1 2 00	1 5 0 5 00
Net Income	8 0 7 00			8 0 7 00
Totals	6 0 4 3 00	6 0 4 3 00	2 3 1 2 00	2 3 1 2 00

F. HENRY CO.
WORKSHEET
FOR YEAR ENDED DECEMBER 31, 201X

12A-4. From the worksheet in Exercise 12A-3, prepare the assets section of a classified balance sheet.

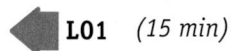 **L01**   *(15 min)*

12A-5. On December 31, 2012, $290 of salaries has been accrued. (Salaries before the accrued amount totaled $24,500.) The next payroll to be paid will be on February 3, 2013, for $6,200. Please do the following:

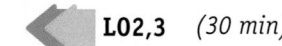 **L02,3**   *(30 min)*

   a. Journalize and post the adjusting entry (use T accounts).
   b. Journalize and post the reversing entry on January 1.
   c. Journalize and post the payment of the payroll. Cash has a balance of $15,500 before the payment of payroll on February 3.

Set B

12B-1. From the following accounts, prepare a cost of goods sold section in proper form: Merchandise Inventory, 12/31/1X, $8,950; Purchases Discount, $920; Merchandise Inventory, 12/01/1X, $4,100; Purchases, $62,000; Purchases Returns and Allowances, $960; Freight-In, $320.

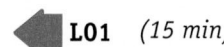 **L01**   *(15 min)*

12B-2. Give the category, the classification, and the report(s) on which each of the following appears (for example: Cash—asset, current asset, balance sheet):

L01   *(10 min)*

   a. Wages Payable
   b. Accounts Payable
   c. Notes Payable

    d. Unearned Revenue
    e. FIT Payable
    f. Office Furniture
    g. Land

(10 min) **L02** ▶ **12B-3.** From the partial worksheet in Figure 12.12, journalize the closing entries for December 31 for C. Blossom Co.

FIGURE 12.12
Worksheet for C. Blossom Co.

	C. BLOSSOM CO. WORKSHEET FOR YEAR ENDED DECEMBER 31, 201X				
	Income Statement		Balance Sheet		
Account	Dr.	Cr.	Dr.	Cr.	
Cash			1 9 6 00		
Merchandise Inventory			4 5 3 00		
Prepaid Advertising			5 5 9 00		
Prepaid Insurance			2 6 00		
Office Equipment			1 0 8 6 00		
Accum. Dep., Office Equipment				2 0 8 00	
Accounts Payable				2 6 0 00	
C. Blossom, Capital				9 6 9 00	
Income Summary	3 5 6 00	4 5 3 00			
Sales		5 5 0 7 00			
Sales Returns and Allowances	2 2 4 00				
Sales Discounts	1 0 3 00				
Purchases	2 6 2 5 00				
Purchases Returns and Allowances		3 1 00			
Purchases Discount		4 9 00			
Salaries Expense	1 0 8 7 00				
Insurance Expense	6 9 6 00				
Utilities Expense	4 9 00				
Plumbing Expenses	5 7 00				
Advertising Expense	8 00				
Dep. Expenses, Office Equip.	2 9 00				
Salaries Payable				7 7 00	
Totals	5 2 3 4 00	6 0 4 0 00	2 3 2 0 00	1 5 1 4 00	
Net Income	8 0 6 00			8 0 6 00	
Totals	6 0 4 0 00	6 0 4 0 00	2 3 2 0 00	2 3 2 0 00	

(15 min) **L01** ▶ **12B-4.** From the worksheet in Exercise 12B-3, prepare the assets section of a classified balance sheet.

(30 min) **L02,3** ▶ **12B-5.** On December 31, 2012, $300 of salaries has been accrued. (Salaries before the accrued amount totaled $24,000.) The next payroll to be paid will be on February 3, 2013, for $6,300. Please do the following:

    a. Journalize and post the adjusting entry (use T accounts).
    b. Journalize and post the reversing entry on January 1.
    c. Journalize and post the payment of the payroll. Cash has a balance of $12,500 before the payment of payroll on February 3.

MyAccountingLab **Problems**

(30 min) **L01** ▶ **Set A**

12A-1. Prepare a formal income statement from the partial worksheet for Nelson Company in Figure 12.13.

NELSON CO. PARTIAL WORKSHEET FOR YEAR ENDED DECEMBER 31, 201X		
	Income Statement	
Account Titles	Dr.	Cr.
Income Summary	3 6 0 00	2 7 0 00
Sales		2 9 0 0 00
Sales Returns and Allowances	1 1 5 00	
Sales Discount	7 0 00	
Purchases	8 9 0 00	
Purchases Returns and Allow.		1 6 5 00
Purchases Discount		1 2 3 00
Freight-In	1 0 8 00	
Salaries Expense	3 5 0 00	
Insurance Expense	1 8 0 00	
Advertising Expense	1 4 5 00	
Rental Income		2 4 0 00
Rent Expense	2 2 5 00	
Dep. Exp., Store Equip.	2 2 0 00	
Salaries Payable		
Totals	2 6 6 3 00	3 6 9 8 00
Net Income	1 0 3 5 00	
Totals	3 6 9 8 00	3 6 9 8 00

FIGURE 12.13
Partial Worksheet for Nelson Company

Check Figure:
Net Income from operations $795

12A-2. Prepare a statement of owner's equity and a classified balance sheet from the worksheet for James Company in Figure 12.14. (*Note:* Of the Mortgage Payable, $240 is due within 1 year.)

L01 *(40 min)*

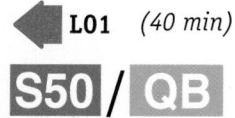

FIGURE 12.14
Partial Worksheet for James Company

JAMES COMPANY PARTIAL WORKSHEET FOR YEAR ENDED DECEMBER 31, 201X		
	Balance Sheet	
Account Titles	Dr.	Cr.
Cash	24 0 0 0 00	
Petty Cash	6 0 00	
Accounts Receivable	1 5 5 0 00	
Merchandise Inventory	4 2 0 0 00	
Supplies	3 2 5 00	
Prepaid Insurance	5 0 0 00	
Store Equipment	3 0 0 0 00	
Acc. Dep., Store Eq.		7 5 0 00
Automobile	2 0 0 0 00	
Acc. Dep., Auto.		1 7 5 00
Accounts Payable		3 0 0 0 00
Taxes Payable		2 4 0 0 00
Unearned Rent		20 5 0 0 00
Mortgage Payable		5 5 0 00
H. James, Capital		12 1 0 0 00
H. James, Withdrawals	2 5 0 00	
Salaries Payable		6 5 0 00
Totals	35 8 8 5 00	40 1 2 5 00
Net Loss	4 2 4 0 00	
Totals	40 1 2 5 00	40 1 2 5 00

Check Figure:
Total Assets $34,710

(90 min)   **LO1,2**

Check Figure:
Net Income $4,930

12A-3. From the partial worksheet for Josh's Supplies in Figure 12.15, do the following:

1. Complete the worksheet.
2. Prepare an income statement, a statement of owner's equity, and a classified balance sheet. (*Note:* The amount of the mortgage due the first year is $890.)
3. Journalize the adjusting and closing entries.

FIGURE 12.15 Worksheet for Josh's Supplies

JOSH'S SUPPLIES WORKSHEET FOR YEAR ENDED DECEMBER 31, 201X								
	Trial Balance				**Adjustments**			
Account Titles	**Dr.**		**Cr.**		**Dr.**		**Cr.**	
Cash	2 5 0 0 00							
Accounts Receivable	2 7 0 0 00							
Merch. Inventory, 1/01/1X	11 2 0 0 00				(B)10 6 0 0 00		(A)11 2 0 0 00	
Prepaid Insurance	1 9 1 0 00						(E) 5 4 0 00	
Equipment	3 5 0 0 00							
Accum. Dep., Equipment			1 0 4 0 00				(D) 3 7 0 00	
Accounts Payable			5 0 5 0 00					
Unearned Training Fees			2 1 8 0 00		(C) 3 5 0 00			
Mortgage Payable			1 2 6 0 00					
P. Josh, Capital			10 5 0 0 00					
P. Josh, Withdrawals	4 3 1 0 00							
Income Summary					(A)11 2 0 0 00		(B)10 6 0 0 00	
Sales			96 2 5 0 00					
Sales Returns and Allowances	3 2 4 0 00							
Sales Discount	2 5 9 0 00							
Purchases	63 8 0 0 00							
Purchases Returns and Allow.			13 6 0 0 00					
Purchases Discounts			3 1 7 0 00					
Freight-In	2 7 0 0 00							
Advertising Expense	10 9 0 0 00							
Rent Expense	10 1 0 0 00							
Salaries Expense	13 6 0 0 00							
Totals	133 0 5 0 00		133 0 5 0 00					
Training Fees Earned							(C) 3 5 0 00	
Dep. Exp., Equipment					(D) 3 7 0 00			
Insurance Expense					(E) 5 4 0 00			
Totals					23 0 6 0 00		23 0 6 0 00	

(150 min)   **LO1,2,3**

Check Figure:
Net Income $4,923

12A-4. Using the ledger balances and additional data given, do the following for Cullen Lumber for the year ended December 31, 201X:

1. Prepare the worksheet.
2. Prepare the income statement, statement of owner's equity, and balance sheet.
3. Journalize and post adjusting and closing entries. (Be sure to put beginning balances in the ledger first.)
4. Prepare a post-closing trial balance.
5. Journalize the reversing entry for wages accrued.

Account Balances for Cullen Lumber

Acct. No.		
110	Cash	$ 1,370
111	Accounts Receivable	1,260
112	Merchandise Inventory	4,450
113	Lumber Supplies	277
114	Prepaid Insurance	212
121	Lumber Equipment	2,600
122	Accum. Dep., Lumber Equipment	530
220	Accounts Payable	1,180
221	Wages Payable	—
330	J. Cullen, Capital	6,544
331	J. Cullen, Withdrawals	3,300
332	Income Summary	—
440	Sales	23,100
441	Sales Returns and Allowances	220
550	Purchases	14,600
551	Purchases Discount	285
552	Purchases Returns and Allowances	290
660	Wages Expense	2,480
661	Advertising Expense	370
662	Rent Expense	790
663	Dep. Expense, Lumber Equipment	—
664	Lumber Supplies Expense	—
665	Insurance Expense	—

Additional Data

a./b.	Merchandise inventory, December 31	$4,800
c.	Lumber supplies on hand, December 31	100
d.	Insurance expired	180
e.	Depreciation for the year	200
f.	Accrued wages on December 31	85

Set B

(70 min)   **L01**

12B-1.   Prepare a formal income statement from the partial worksheet for Wright Co. in Figure 12.16.

FIGURE 12.16
Partial Worksheet for Wright Co.

Check Figure:
Net income from operations $637

	Income Statement	
WRIGHT CO. PARTIAL WORKSHEET FOR YEAR ENDED DECEMBER 31, 201X		
Account Titles	Dr.	Cr.
Income Summary	4 1 0 00	2 3 0 00
Sales		2 8 5 0 00
Sales Returns and Allowances	1 1 9 00	
Sales Discount	6 4 00	
Purchases	8 9 0 00	
Purchases Returns and Allow.		1 7 5 00
Purchases Discount		1 3 5 00
Freight-In	1 1 0 00	
Salaries Expense	4 0 0 00	
Insurance Expense	1 9 0 00	
Advertising Expense	1 7 5 00	
Rental Income		2 2 0 00
Rent Expense	2 2 5 00	
Dep. Exp., Store Equip.	1 7 0 00	
Salaries Payable		
Totals	$ 2 7 5 3 00	3 6 1 0 00
Net Income	8 5 7 00	
Totals	3 6 1 0 00	3 6 1 0 00

12B-2. Prepare a statement of owner's equity and a classified balance sheet from the worksheet shown for Jager Company in Figure 12.17. (*Note:* Of the Mortgage Payable, $200 is due within 1 year.)

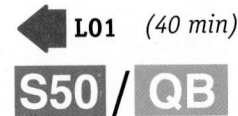

L01 *(40 min)*

S50 / **QB**

FIGURE 12.17
Partial Worksheet for Jager Company

Check Figure:
Total assets $31,960

		JAGER COMPANY PARTIAL WORKSHEET FOR YEAR ENDED DECEMBER 31, 201X		
	Account Titles	**Balance Sheet**		
		Dr.	Cr.	
	Cash	22 0 0 0 00		
	Petty Cash	1 1 0 00		
	Accounts Receivable	1 5 5 0 00		
	Merchandise Inventory	4 1 0 0 00		
	Supplies	3 2 5 00		
	Prepaid Insurance	4 5 0 00		
	Store Equipment	2 5 0 0 00		
	Acc. Dep., Store Eq.		7 5 0 00	
	Automobile	1 8 0 0 00		
	Acc. Dep., Auto.		1 2 5 00	
	Accounts Payable		2 6 0 0 00	
	Taxes Payable		2 5 0 0 00	
	Unearned Rent		19 0 0 0 00	
	Mortgage Payable		7 5 0 00	
	H. Jager, Capital		12 6 0 0 00	
	H. Jager, With.	5 0 00		
	Salaries Payable		8 0 0 00	
	Totals	32 8 8 5 00	39 1 2 5 00	
	Net Loss	6 2 4 0 00		
	Totals	39 1 2 5 00	39 1 2 5 00	

(90 min)　**LO1,2**

12B-3. From the partial worksheet for Justin's Supplies in Figure 12.18, do the following:

1. Complete the worksheet.
2. Prepare the income statement, statement of owner's equity, and classified balance sheet. (*Note:* The amount of the mortgage due the first year is $820.)
3. Journalize the adjusting and closing entries.

FIGURE 12.18

Worksheet for Justin's Supplies

	JUSTIN'S SUPPLIES WORKSHEET FOR YEAR ENDED DECEMBER 31, 201X							
	Trial Balance				Adjustments			
Account Titles	Dr.		Cr.		Dr.		Cr.	
Cash	2 3 0 0 00							
Accounts Receivable	3 3 0 0 00							
Merch. Inventory, 1/01/1X	10 9 0 0 00				(B) 10 2 0 0 00		(A) 10 9 0 0 00	
Prepaid Insurance	1 8 6 0 00						(E) 5 1 0 00	
Equipment	3 7 0 0 00							
Accum. Dep., Equipment			1 0 8 0 00				(D) 3 9 0 00	
Accounts Payable			5 0 6 0 00					
Unearned Training Fees			2 1 0 0 00		(C) 2 9 0 00			
Mortgage Payable			1 2 1 0 00					
P. Justin, Capital			10 5 8 0 00					
P. Justin, Withdrawals	4 3 0 0 00							
Income Summary					(A) 10 9 0 0 00		(B) 10 2 0 0 00	
Sales			96 4 4 0 00					
Sales Returns and Allowances	3 1 5 0 00							
Sales Discount	2 6 3 0 00							
Purchases	63 7 0 0 00							
Purchases Returns and Allow.			13 3 0 0 00					
Purchases Discounts			3 1 8 0 00					
Freight-In	2 6 1 0 00							
Advertising Expense	11 0 0 0 00							
Rent Expense	10 3 0 0 00							
Salaries Expense	13 2 0 0 00							
Totals	132 9 5 0 00		132 9 5 0 00					
Training Fees Earned							(C) 2 9 0 00	
Dep. Exp., Equipment					(D) 3 9 0 00			
Insurance Expense					(E) 5 1 0 00			
Totals					22 2 9 0 00		22 2 9 0 00	

12B-4. Using the ledger balances and additional data given, do the following for Crew Lumber for the year ended December 31, 201X.

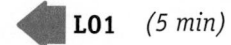

L01,2,3 *(150 min)*

Check Figure:
Net income $4,230

1. Prepare the worksheet.
2. Prepare the income statement, statement of owner's equity, and balance sheet.
3. Journalize and post adjusting and closing entries. (Be sure to put beginning balances in the ledger first.)
4. Prepare a post-closing trial balance.
5. Journalize the reversing entry for wages accrued.

Account Balances of Crew Lumber

Acct. No.		
110	Cash	$ 1,340
111	Accounts Receivable	1,210
112	Merchandise Inventory	4,350
113	Lumber Supplies	275
114	Prepaid Insurance	215
121	Lumber Equipment	3,300
122	Acc. Dep., Lumber Equipment	470
220	Accounts Payable	1,170
221	Wages Payable	—
330	J. Crew, Capital	8,405
331	J. Crew, Withdrawals	3,300
332	Income Summary	—
440	Sales	22,400
441	Sales Returns and Allowances	190
550	Purchases	15,200
551	Purchases Discount	235
552	Purchases Returns and Allowances	280
660	Wages Expense	2,390
661	Advertising Expense	350
662	Rent Expense	840
663	Dep. Exp., Lumber Equipment	—
664	Lumber Supplies Expense	—
665	Insurance Expense	—

Additional Data

a./b.	Merchandise inventory, December 31	$5,300
c.	Lumber supplies on hand, December 31	65
d.	Insurance expired	150
e.	Depreciation for the year	240
f.	Accrued wages on December 31	65

Financial Report Problem

L01 *(5 min)*

Reading the Kellogg's Annual Report

Go to http://investor.kelloggs.com/investor-relations/annual-reports to access the Kellogg's 2013 Annual Report and locate the consolidated statement of Income. How much has Selling and General Administrative Expense decreased from 2012 to 2013?

MyAccountingLab

ON THE JOB SMITH COMPUTER CENTER

(60 min) **LO1,2** ➤ Using the worksheet in Chapter 11 for Smith Computer Center, journalize and post the adjusting entries and prepare the financial statements.

Mini Practice Set

The Elegant Dress Shop

Reviewing the Accounting Cycle for a Merchandise Company

This practice set will help you review all the key concepts of a merchandise company, along with the integration of payroll, including the preparation of Form 941.

Because you are the bookkeeper for the Elegant Dress Shop, we have gathered the following information for you. It will be your task to complete the accounting cycle for March. The company uses the periodic inventory method.

THE ELEGANT DRESS SHOP POST-CLOSING TRIAL BALANCE FEBRUARY 28, 201X	1	2
Cash	2 3 6 4 80	
Petty Cash	5 5 00	
Accounts Receivable	1 8 0 0 00	
Merchandise Inventory	4 9 0 0 00	
Prepaid Rent	1 6 5 0 00	
Delivery Truck	12 0 0 0 00	
Accumulated Depreciation, Truck		3 0 0 0 00
Accounts Payable		2 0 0 0 00
FIT Payable		7 4 2 00
FICA—OASDI Payable		1 1 5 3 20
FICA—Medicare Payable		2 6 9 70
SIT Payable		6 5 1 00
SUTA Payable		8 5 4 40
FUTA Payable		1 0 6 80
Unearned Rent		1 0 0 0 00
B. Duval, Capital		12 9 9 2 70
Totals	22 7 6 9 80	22 7 6 9 80

Balances in subsidiary ledgers as of March 1 are as follows:

Accounts Receivable		Accounts Payable	
Bach Co.	$1,800	Danmark Co.	$2,000
Danmark Co.	—	Johnsons Co.	—
Young Co.	—	Manny's Garage	—
		Thomas Co.	—

Payroll is paid monthly:

FICA rate	OASDI 6.2% on $117,000
	Medicare 1.45% on all earnings
SUTA rate	4.8% on $7,000
FUTA rate	0.6% on $7,000
SIT rate	7%
FIT	Use the table provided at the end of this practice set.

The payroll register for January and February is provided. In March, salaries are as follows:

Jim Reed	$3,860
Emma Hyde	4,580
Sue Bolton	4,530

Your tasks are to do the following:

1. Set up a general ledger, accounts receivable subsidiary ledger, accounts payable subsidiary ledger, auxiliary petty cash record, and payroll register. (Be sure to update ledger accounts based on information given in the post-closing trial balance for February 28 before beginning.)

2. Journalize the transactions, prepare the payroll register, and prepare the auxiliary petty cash record.

3. Update the accounts payable and accounts receivable subsidiary ledgers.

4. Post to the general ledger.

5. Prepare a trial balance on a worksheet and complete the worksheet.

6. Prepare an income statement, statement of owner's equity, and classified balance sheet.

7. Journalize the adjusting and closing entries.

8. Post the adjusting and closing entries to the ledger.

9. Prepare a post-closing trial balance.

10. Complete Form 941 and sign it for the quarter ending March 31, 201X.

Chart of Accounts for the
Elegant Dress Shop

Assets
110 Cash
111 Petty Cash
112 Accounts Receivable
114 Merchandise Inventory
116 Prepaid Rent
120 Delivery Truck
121 Accumulated Depreciation, Truck

Liabilities
210 Accounts Payable
212 Salaries Payable
214 Federal Income Tax Payable
216 FICA—OASDI Payable
218 FICA—Medicare Payable
220 State Income Tax Payable
222 SUTA Tax Payable
224 FUTA Tax Payable
226 Unearned Rent

Owner's Equity
310 B. Duval, Capital
320 B. Duval, Withdrawals
330 Income Summary

Revenue
410 Sales
412 Sales Returns and Allowances
414 Sales Discount
416 Rental Income

Cost of Goods Sold
510 Purchases
512 Purchases Returns and Allowances
514 Purchases Discount

Expenses
610 Sales Salaries Expense
611 Office Salaries Expense
612 Payroll Tax Expense
614 Cleaning Expense
616 Depreciation Expense, Truck
618 Rent Expense
620 Postage Expense
622 Delivery Expense
624 Miscellaneous Expense

THE ELEGANT DRESS SHOP
PAYROLL REGISTER
JANUARY AND FEBRUARY 201X

Employees	Allow. and Marital Status	Cum. Earnings	Salary	Earnings Reg.	O/T	Gross	Cum. Earnings
Jim Reed	M – 2		2 1 0 0 00	2 1 0 0 00		2 1 0 0 00	2 1 0 0 00
Emma Hyde	M – 1		3 3 0 0 00	3 3 0 0 00		3 3 0 0 00	3 3 0 0 00
Sue Bolton	M – 0		3 9 0 0 00	3 9 0 0 00		3 9 0 0 00	3 9 0 0 00
Totals for Jan.			9 3 0 0 00	9 3 0 0 00		9 3 0 0 00	9 3 0 0 00
Jim Reed	M – 2	2 1 0 0 00	2 1 0 0 00	2 1 0 0 00		2 1 0 0 00	4 2 0 0 00
Emma Hyde	M – 1	3 3 0 0 00	3 3 0 0 00	3 3 0 0 00		3 3 0 0 00	6 6 0 0 00
Sue Bolton	M – 0	3 9 0 0 00	3 9 0 0 00	3 9 0 0 00		3 9 0 0 00	7 8 0 0 00
Totals for Feb.		9 3 0 0 00	9 3 0 0 00	9 3 0 0 00		9 3 0 0 00	18 6 0 0 00

PAYROLL REGISTER

Taxable Earnings Unemp.	FICA OASDI	FICA Medicare	Deductions FICA OASDI	FICA Medicare	FIT	SIT	Net Pay	Ck. No.	Distribution Office Salary Expense	Sales Salary Expense
2 1 0 0 00	2 1 0 0 00	2 1 0 0 00	1 3 0 20	3 0 45	7 4 00	1 4 7 00	1 7 1 8 35		2 1 0 0 00	
3 3 0 0 00	3 3 0 0 00	3 3 0 0 00	2 0 4 60	4 7 85	2 6 4 00	2 3 1 00	2 5 5 2 55			3 3 0 0 00
3 9 0 0 00	3 9 0 0 00	3 9 0 0 00	2 4 1 80	5 6 55	4 0 4 00	2 7 3 00	2 9 2 4 65			3 9 0 0 00
9 3 0 0 00	9 3 0 0 00	9 3 0 0 00	5 7 6 60	1 3 4 85	7 4 2 00	6 5 1 00	7 1 9 5 55		2 1 0 0 00	7 2 0 0 00
2 1 0 0 00	2 1 0 0 00	2 1 0 0 00	1 3 0 20	3 0 45	7 4 00	1 4 7 00	1 7 1 8 35		2 1 0 0 00	
3 3 0 0 00	3 3 0 0 00	3 3 0 0 00	2 0 4 60	4 7 85	2 6 4 00	2 3 1 00	2 5 5 2 55			3 3 0 0 00
3 1 0 0 00	3 9 0 0 00	3 9 0 0 00	2 4 1 80	5 6 55	4 0 4 00	2 7 3 00	2 9 2 4 65			3 9 0 0 00
8 5 0 0 00	9 3 0 0 00	9 3 0 0 00	5 7 6 60	1 3 4 85	7 4 2 00	6 5 1 00	7 1 9 5 55		2 1 0 0 00	7 2 0 0 00

201X

Mar.   1   Bach paid balance owed, no discount.

2   Purchased merchandise from Thomas Company on account, $8,000; terms 1/10, n/30.

2   Paid $10 from the petty cash fund for cleaning package, voucher no. 18 (consider it a cleaning expense).

3   Sold merchandise to Young Company on account, $8,000, invoice no. 51; terms 3/10, n/30.

5   Paid $7 from the petty cash fund for postage, voucher no. 19.

6   Sold merchandise to Young Company on account, $8,000, invoice no. 52; terms 3/10, n/30.

8   Paid $11 from the petty cash fund for first aid emergency, voucher no. 20.

9   Purchased merchandise from Thomas Company on account, $4,000; terms 1/10, n/30.

9   Paid $9 for delivery expense from petty cash fund, voucher no. 21.

9   Sold more merchandise to Young Company on account, $6,000, invoice no. 53; terms 3/10, n/30.

9   Paid cleaning service, $100, check no. 110.

10 Young Company returned merchandise costing $3,200 from invoice no. 52; the Elegant Dress Shop issued credit memo no. 10 to Young Company for $3,200.

11 Purchased merchandise from Johnsons Company on account, $14,000; terms 3/15, n/60.

12 Sold merchandise for $30,000 cash.

12 Paid Thomas Company invoice dated March 2, check no. 111.

13 Sold $5,000 of merchandise for cash.

14 Returned merchandise to Johnsons Company in the amount of $1,000; the Elegant Dress Shop issued debit memo no. 4 to Johnsons Company.

14 Paid $2 from the petty cash fund for delivery expense, voucher no. 22.

15 Paid taxes due for FICA (OASDI and Medicare) and FIT for February payroll, check no. 112.

15 Bridget withdrew $250 for her own personal expenses, check no. 113.

15 Paid state income tax for February payroll, check no. 114.

16 Received payment from Young Company for invoice no. 52, less discount.

16 Young Company paid invoice no. 51, $8,000.

16 Sold merchandise to Bach Company on account, $4,600, invoice no. 54; terms 3/10, n/30.

21 Purchased delivery truck on account from Manny's Garage, $19,700.

22 Sold merchandise to Young Company on account, $5,000, invoice no. 55; terms 3/10, n/30.

23 Paid Johnsons Company the balance owed, check no. 115.

24 Sold merchandise to Bach Company on account, $1,400, invoice no. 56; terms 3/10, n/30.

25 Purchased merchandise for $1,800, check no. 116.

27 Purchased merchandise from Danmark Company on account, $5,000; terms 1/10, n/30.

27 Paid $3 postage from the petty cash fund, voucher no. 23.

28 Young Company paid invoice no. 55 dated March 22, less discount.

28 Bach Company paid invoice no. 54 dated March 16.

29 Purchased merchandise from Thomas Company on account, $13,000; terms 1/10, n/30.

30 Sold merchandise to Danmark Company on account, $9,000, invoice no. 57; terms 3/10, n/30.

30 Issued check no. 117 to replenish the petty cash fund to the same level. Assume no shortage or overage.

30 Recorded payroll in payroll register.

30 Journalized payroll entry (to be paid on 31st).

30 Journalized employer's payroll tax expense.

31 Paid payroll checks no. 118, no. 119, and no. 120.

Additional Data

a./b. Ending merchandise inventory, $14,580.

c. During March, rent expired, $550.

d. Truck depreciated, $300.

e. Rental income earned, $250 (one month's rent from subletting).

f. Bridget Duval's dress shop is located at 1 Milgate Rd., Marblehead, MA 01945. Its identification number is 33-4158215.

MARRIED Persons-**MONTHLY** Payroll Period

(For Wages Paid through December 2014)

And the wages are—		And the number of withholding allowances claimed is—										
At least	But less than	0	1	2	3	4	5	6	7	8	9	10
		The amount of income tax to be withheld is—										
$0	$720	$0	$0	$0	$0	$0	$0	$0	$0	$0	$0	$0
720	760	4	0	0	0	0	0	0	0	0	0	0
760	800	8	0	0	0	0	0	0	0	0	0	0
2,000	2,040	132	99	66	33	0	0	0	0	0	0	0
2,040	2,080	132	103	70	37	4	0	0	0	0	0	0
2,080	2,120	140	107	74	41	8	0	0	0	0	0	0
2,120	2,160	144	111	78	45	12	0	0	0	0	0	0
2,160	2,200	148	115	82	49	16	0	0	0	0	0	0
2,200	2,240	152	119	86	53	20	0	0	0	0	0	0
2,240	2,280	158	123	90	57	24	0	0	0	0	0	0
2,280	2,320	164	127	94	61	28	0	0	0	0	0	0
2,320	2,360	170	131	98	65	32	0	0	0	0	0	0
2,360	2,400	176	135	102	69	36	3	0	0	0	0	0
2,400	2,440	182	139	106	73	40	7	0	0	0	0	0
2,440	2,480	188	143	110	77	44	11	0	0	0	0	0
2,480	2,520	194	147	114	81	48	15	0	0	0	0	0
2,520	2,560	200	151	118	85	52	19	0	0	0	0	0
2,560	2,600	206	156	122	89	56	23	0	0	0	0	0
2,600	2,640	212	162	126	93	60	27	0	0	0	0	0
2,640	2,680	218	168	130	97	64	31	0	0	0	0	0
2,680	2,720	224	174	134	101	68	35	2	0	0	0	0
2,720	2,760	230	180	138	105	72	39	6	0	0	0	0
2,760	2,800	236	186	142	109	76	43	10	0	0	0	0
2,800	2,840	242	192	146	113	80	47	14	0	0	0	0
2,840	2,880	248	198	150	117	84	51	18	0	0	0	0
2,880	2,920	254	204	155	121	88	55	22	0	0	0	0
2,920	2,960	260	210	161	125	92	59	26	0	0	0	0
2,960	3,000	266	216	167	129	96	63	30	0	0	0	0
3,000	3,040	272	222	173	133	100	67	34	1	0	0	0
3,040	3,080	278	228	179	137	104	71	38	5	0	0	0
3,080	3,120	284	234	185	141	108	75	42	9	0	0	0
3,120	3,160	290	240	191	145	112	79	46	13	0	0	0
3,160	3,200	296	246	197	149	116	83	50	17	0	0	0
3,200	3,240	302	252	203	154	120	87	54	21	0	0	0
3,240	3,280	308	258	209	160	124	91	58	25	0	0	0
3,280	3,320	314	264	215	166	128	95	62	29	0	0	0
3,320	3,360	320	270	221	172	132	99	66	33	0	0	0
3,360	3,400	326	276	227	178	136	103	70	37	4	0	0
3,400	3,440	332	282	233	184	140	107	74	41	8	0	0
3,440	3,480	338	288	239	190	144	111	78	45	12	0	0
3,480	3,520	344	294	245	196	148	115	82	49	16	0	0
3,520	3,560	350	300	251	202	152	119	86	53	20	0	0
3,560	3,600	356	306	257	208	158	123	90	57	24	0	0
3,600	3,640	362	312	263	214	164	127	94	61	28	0	0
3,640	3,680	368	318	269	220	170	131	98	65	32	0	0
3,680	3,720	374	324	275	226	176	135	102	69	36	3	0
3,720	3,760	380	330	281	232	182	139	106	73	40	7	0
3,760	3,800	386	336	287	238	186	143	110	77	44	11	0
3,800	3,840	392	342	293	244	194	147	114	81	48	15	0
3,840	3,880	398	348	299	250	200	151	118	85	52	19	0
3,880	3,920	404	354	305	256	206	157	122	89	56	23	0
3,920	3,960	410	360	311	262	212	163	126	93	60	27	0
3,960	4,000	416	366	317	268	218	169	130	97	64	31	0
4,000	4,040	422	372	323	274	224	175	134	101	68	35	2
4,040	4,080	428	378	329	280	230	181	138	105	72	39	6
4,080	4,120	434	384	335	286	236	187	142	109	76	43	10
4,120	4,160	440	390	341	292	242	193	146	113	80	47	14
4,160	4,200	446	396	347	298	248	199	150	117	84	51	18
4,200	4,240	452	402	353	304	254	205	156	121	88	55	22
4,240	4,280	458	408	359	310	260	211	162	125	92	59	26
4,280	4,320	464	414	365	316	266	217	168	129	96	63	30
4,320	4,360	470	420	371	322	272	223	174	133	100	67	34
4,360	4,400	476	426	377	328	278	229	180	137	104	71	36
4,400	4,440	482	432	383	334	284	235	186	141	108	75	42
4,440	4,480	488	438	389	340	290	241	192	145	112	79	46
4,480	4,520	494	444	395	346	296	247	198	149	116	83	50
4,520	4,560	500	450	401	352	302	253	204	154	120	87	54
4,560	4,600	506	456	407	358	308	259	210	160	124	91	58

SAGE 50 COMPUTER WORKSHOP

Computerized Accounting Application for Chapter 12

Refresher on using Sage 50 Complete Accounting

Before starting this assignment, you may want to refresh your memory by reading the following PDF documents in the multimedia library of the MyAccountingLab Web site. Remember to choose the PDF document for your version of Sage 50.

1. An Introduction to Sage 50
2. Correcting Sage 50 Transactions
3. How to Repeat or Restart a Sage 50 Assignment
4. Backing Up and Restoring Your Work in Sage 50

   You also should have completed the following workshops:

1. Workshop 1 Atlas Company from Chapter 3
2. Workshop 2 Zell Company from Chapter 4
3. Workshop 3 Sousa Realty from Chapter 5
4. Workshop 4 Pete's Market from Chapter 8
5. Workshop 5 Part A Mars Company from Chapter 10
6. Workshop 5 Part B Abby's Toy House from Chapter 10

Workshop 6:

Accounting Cycle for a Merchandising Company

In this workshop, you complete an accounting cycle for a merchandising business owned by the Elegant Dress Shop using Sage 50. Tasks include maintaining inventory, recording sales on account, merchandise returns, merchandise purchases, vendor payments, and payroll. You will also prepare inventory reports, aged receivables and aged payable reports, general journal and general ledger reports, a trial balance, and financial statements. Finally, you will close the accounting period.

Instructions and the data file for completing this assignment are in the multimedia library of the MyAccountingLab Web site. Open the *Workshop 6 The Elegant Dress Shop* PDF document for your version of Sage 50 and download *The Elegant Dress Shop* data file for your version of Sage 50.

QUICKBOOKS COMPUTER WORKSHOP

Computerized Accounting Application for Chapter 12

Refresher on using QuickBooks Accountant

Before starting this assignment, you may want to refresh your memory by reading the following PDF documents in the multimedia library of the MyAccountingLab Web site. Remember to choose the PDF document for your version of QuickBooks.

1. An Introduction to QuickBooks
2. Correcting QuickBooks Transactions
3. How to Repeat or Restart a QuickBooks Assignment
4. Backing Up and Restoring Your Work in QuickBooks

   You also should have completed the following workshops:

1. Workshop 1 Atlas Company from Chapter 3
2. Workshop 2 Zell Company from Chapter 4
3. Workshop 3 Sousa Realty from Chapter 5

4. Workshop 4 Pete's Market from Chapter 8
5. Workshop 5 Part A Mars Company from Chapter 10
6. Workshop 5 Part B Abby's Toy House from Chapter 10

Workshop 6:

Accounting Cycle for a Merchandising Company

In this workshop, you complete an accounting cycle for a merchandising business owned by the Elegant Dress Shop using QuickBooks. Tasks include maintaining inventory, recording sales on account, merchandise returns, merchandise purchases, vendor payments, and payroll. You will also prepare inventory reports, aged receivables and aged payable reports, general journal and general ledger reports, a trial balance, and financial statements. Finally, you will close the accounting period.

Instructions and the data file for completing this assignment are in the multimedia library of the MyAccountingLab Web site. Open the *Workshop 6 The Elegant Dress Shop* PDF document for your version of Quickbooks and download the *The Elegant Dress Shop* data file for your version of Quickbooks.

Glindex

A Combined Glossary and Subject Index

A

Accounting, A system that measures the business's activities in financial terms, provides written reports and financial statements about those activities, and communicates these reports to decision makers and others, 2–4

Accounting cycle, For each accounting period, the process that begins with the recording of business transactions or procedures into a journal and ends with the completion of a post-closing trial balance, 68
  adjusting entries, 146–148, 160–167, 171–174
  adjustments, 108–117, 132–135
  blueprint for first four steps, 89
  closing entries, 148–158, 166–167, 174
  completing. *See* Merchandise company
  journalizing transactions, 68–74, 91–93
  post-closing trial balance, 158–159, 168
  posting to ledger, 75–80, 91–94
  preparing financial statements from worksheet, 120–124, 132–133, 135
  preparing trial balance, 80–85, 91–94
  preparing worksheet, 117–120, 132–136

Accounting equation, Assets = Liabilities + Owner's Equity, 4–7, 36–37. *See also* Expanded accounting equation

Accounting period, The period of time for which an income statement is prepared, 68

Accounts, An accounting device used in bookkeeping to record increases and decreases of business transactions relating to individual assets, liabilities, capital, withdrawals, revenue, expenses, and so on, 34, 35
  account categories, 34
  Accounts Receivable, 9
  Accumulated Depreciation, 112
  adjustments to. *See* Adjustments
  balancing, 34–37
  Capital, 5–6
  Cash, 74–78
  Cash Short and Over, 221–223
  chart of. *See* Chart of accounts
  Cost of Goods Sold, 364, 368
  Income Summary, 149
  Merchandise Inventory, 364, 368
  Mortgage Payable, 410
  Office Salaries, 72–73, 77–78
  Payroll Cash, 254
  Prepaid Rent, 110–111
  Purchases, 350, 354
  Purchases Returns and Allowances, 350, 354
  Revenue, 9
  Salaries Accrued, 115–117
  Sales Discount, 315–316, 319–320
  Sales Returns and Allowances, 314–315, 318–319
  Sales Tax Payable, 316–317, 320–321
  Standard, 34–35
  Supplies on Hand, 109–110, 132, 411
  T accounts, 34–35, 53–54
  Unearned Rent, 408–411, 413, 415

Accounts payable, Amounts owed to creditors that result from the purchase of goods or services on account—a liability, 7

Accounts payable subsidiary ledger, A book or file that contains, in alphabetical order, the name of the creditor and amount owed from purchases on account, 355–358, 359–367
  posting transactions to, 375–376, 379–380
  recording purchases, 350–351, 354–355

Accounts receivable, An asset that indicates amounts owed by customers, 9
  recording collection of cash, 205
  schedule of, 327, 331

Accounts receivable subsidiary ledger, A book or file that contains the individual records, in alphabetical order, of amounts owed by various credit customers, 319–326, 323–331, 333–335

Accrual basis, An accounting system that matches revenues when earned with expenses that are incurred, 9

Accrued salaries payable, Salaries that are earned by employees but unpaid and unrecorded during the period (and thus need to be recorded by an adjustment) and will not come due for payment until the next accounting period, 115–117

Accumulated Depreciation, A contra-asset account that summarizes or accumulates the amount of depreciation that has been taken on an asset, 112–114, 117

Adjusting, The process of calculating the latest up-to-date balance of each account at the end of an accounting period, 109
  journal entries, 146–148, 166–167, 171–174

Adjustments, worksheet
  accrued salaries, 114–117, 135
  computer supplies, 109–110, 134
  depreciation, 112–114, 135
  example of, 116
  journalizing and posting entries, 146–148, 173–174
  overview of, 108–109
  prepaid rent, 110–111, 134
  preparing financial statements from, 127–131
  preparing worksheet, 125–127
  trial balance, 117–119, 121, 135

Administrative expenses (general expenses), Operating expenses such as general office expenses that are incurred indirectly in the selling of goods, 442

Advertising expenses, 72

Allowances (*exemptions*), Certain dollar amounts of a person's income tax that will be considered nontaxable for income tax withholding purposes, 242–243, 259, 261

Allowances, Sales Returns and, 314–316, 318–320

Assets, Properties (resources) of value owned by a business (cash, supplies, equipment, land), 4
  accounting rules, 36
  prepaid rents as, 71
  recording, 4–8, 10–13
  in transaction analysis, 38–44

ATMs (automatic teller machines), Machine that allows for depositing, withdrawal, and advanced banking transactions, 212–214

Auxiliary petty cash record, A supplementary record for summarizing petty cash information, 218–220

Photo Credits

STUDY GUIDE
& WORKING PAPERS
CHAPTERS 1-12
for

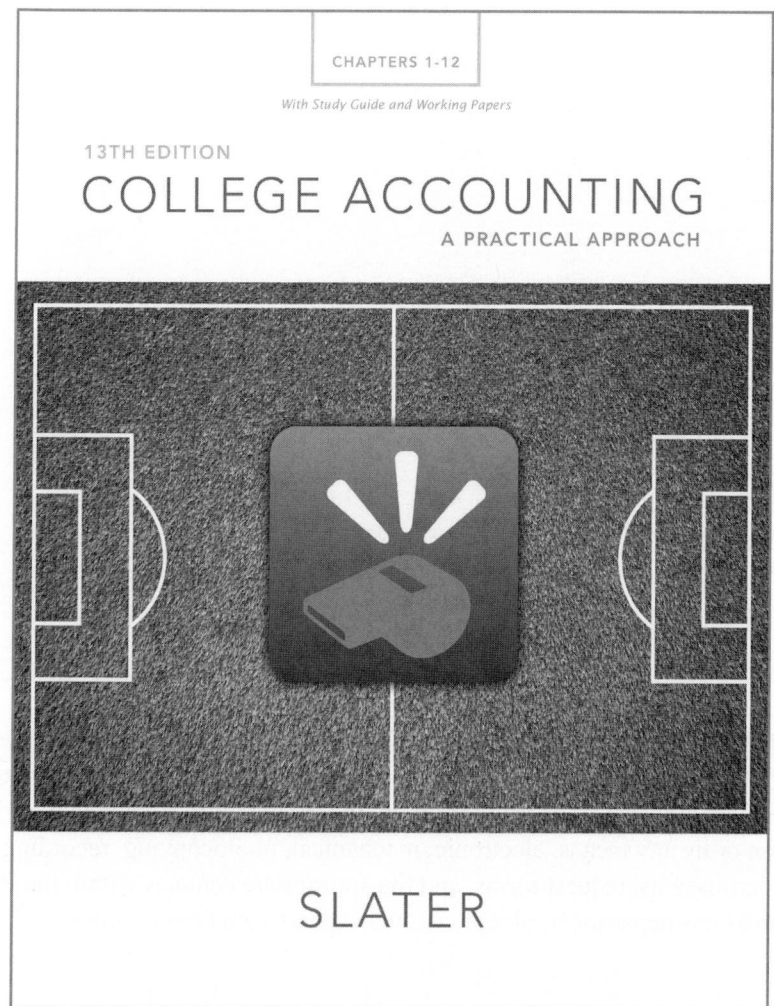

CHAPTERS 1-12

With Study Guide and Working Papers

13TH EDITION

COLLEGE ACCOUNTING

A PRACTICAL APPROACH

SLATER

Carolyn Streuly

PEARSON

Boston Columbus Hoboken Indianapolis New York San Francisco
Amsterdam Cape Town Dubai London Madrid Milan Munich Paris Montréal Toronto
Delhi Mexico City São Paulo Sydney Hong Kong Seoul Singapore Taipei Tokyo

Acquisitions Editor: Ellen Geary
Program Managers: Erin McDonagh, Nancy Freihofer
Project Manager: Heather Pagano
Operations Specialist: Carol Melville
Cover Art: Arcady/Shutterstock and Bubaone/iStockphoto

10 9 8 7 6 5 4 3 2 1

PEARSON

ISBN-10:   0-13-379150-5
ISBN-13:   978-0-13-379150-1

Contents

STUDY GUIDE AND WORKING PAPERS CHAPTERS 1–12

Contents

Accounting Concepts and Procedures

FORMS FOR DEMONSTRATION PROBLEM

(1)

MICHAEL BROWN, ATTORNEY AT LAW

	ASSETS			=	LIABILITIES	+	OWNER'S EQUITY				
	Cash	+	Accounts Receivable	+	Office Equipment	=	Accounts Payable	+	M. Brown, Capital	–	M. Brown, Withd.	+	Legal fees	–	Expenses
a.											
Balance											
b.											
Balance											
c.											
Balance											
d.											
Balance											
e.											
Balance											
f.											
Balance											
g.											
Balance											
h.											
Balance											
i.											
Ending Balance											

DEMONSTRATION PROBLEM (CONTINUED)

(2A)

MICHAEL BROWN, ATTORNEY AT LAW
INCOME STATEMENT
FOR MONTH ENDED JUNE 30, 201X

(2B)

MICHAEL BROWN, ATTORNEY AT LAW
STATEMENT OF OWNER'S EQUITY
FOR MONTH ENDED JUNE 30, 201X

(2C)

MICHAEL BROWN, ATTORNEY AT LAW
BALANCE SHEET
JUNE 30, 201X

ASSETS	LIABILITIES AND OWNER'S EQUITY

FORMS FOR SET A EXERCISES

1A-1

a._____

b._____

c._____

1A-2

	ASSETS	= LIABILITIES	+	OWNER'S EQUITY
a.				
b.				
c.				

1A-3

RIDEOUT CO. CLEANERS
BALANCE SHEET
NOVEMBER 30, 201X

ASSETS				LIABILITIES AND OWNER'S EQUITY			

SET A EXERCISES

1A-4

	ASSETS			= LIABILITIES +	OWNER'S EQUITY			
Cash	+ Accounts Receivable	+ Computer Equipment	= Accounts Payable	+ B. Black, Capital	− B. Black, Withd.	+ Revenues	− Expenses
a.							
b.							
c.							
d.							
e.							
f.							
g.							
Ending Balance							

SET A EXERCISES

1A-5

(a)

FREDERICK REALTY
INCOME STATEMENT
FOR MONTH ENDED NOVEMBER 30, 201X

(b)

FREDERICK REALTY
STATEMENT OF OWNER'S EQUITY
FOR MONTH ENDED NOVEMBER 30, 201X

(c)

FREDERICK REALTY
BALANCE SHEET
NOVEMBER 30, 201X

ASSETS	LIABILITIES AND OWNER'S EQUITY

FORMS FOR SET B EXERCISES

1B-1

a. _____

b. _____

c. _____

1B-2

ASSETS	= LIABILITIES	+	OWNER'S EQUITY
a.			
b.			
c.			

1B-3

ROLAND CO. CLEANERS
BALANCE SHEET
JUNE 30, 201X

ASSETS				LIABILITIES AND OWNER'S EQUITY				

SET B EXERCISES

1B-4

	ASSETS				=	LIABILITIES	+			OWNER'S EQUITY				
	Cash	+	Accounts Receivable	+	Computer Equipment	=	Accounts Payable	+	B. Bell, Capital	−	B. Bell, Withd.	+	Revenues	−	Expenses
a.															
b.															
c.															
d.															
e.															
f.															
g.															
Ending Balance															

SET B EXERCISES

1B-5

(a)

FRENCH REALTY
INCOME STATEMENT
FOR MONTH ENDED SEPTEMBER 30, 201X

(b)

FRENCH REALTY
STATEMENT OF OWNER'S EQUITY
FOR MONTH ENDED SEPTEMBER 30, 201X

(c)

FRENCH REALTY
BALANCE SHEET
SEPTEMBER 30, 201X

ASSETS   **LIABILITIES AND OWNER'S EQUITY**

FORMS FOR SET A PROBLEMS

PROBLEM 1A-1

MORGAN'S NAIL SPA

	ASSETS			=	LIABILITIES	+	OWNER'S EQUITY
	Cash	+	Store Equipment	=	Accounts Payable	+	M. Amberson, Capital
TRANSACTION a							
NEW BALANCE							
TRANSACTION b							
NEW BALANCE							
TRANSACTION c							
NEW BALANCE							
TRANSACTION d							
ENDING BALANCE							

PROBLEM 1A-2

SHEA'S INTERNET SERVICE
BALANCE SHEET
JUNE 30, 201X

ASSETS			LIABILITIES AND OWNER'S EQUITY		

PROBLEM 1A-3

RICK FONTAN
COMPUTER SERVICE

	Cash	+	Accounts Receivable	+	Office Equipment	=	Accounts Payable	+	R. Fontan, Capital	−	R. Fontan, Withd.	+	Computer Service Revenue	−	Expenses
				ASSETS			= LIABILITIES +				OWNER'S EQUITY				
a.																
BALANCE																
b.																
BALANCE																
c.																
BALANCE																
d.																
BALANCE																
e.																
BALANCE																
f.																
BALANCE																
g.																
BALANCE																
h.																
ENDING BALANCE																

PROBLEM 1A-4

(a)

WILLIAMS HOME DECORATING SERVICE
INCOME STATEMENT
FOR MONTH ENDED SEPTEMBER 30, 201X

(b)

WILLIAMS HOME DECORATING SERVICE
STATEMENT OF OWNER'S EQUITY
FOR MONTH ENDED SEPTEMBER 30, 201X

PROBLEM 1A-4 (CONCLUDED)

(c)

WILLIAMS HOME DECORATING SERVICE
BALANCE SHEET
SEPTEMBER 30, 201X

ASSETS			LIABILITIES AND OWNER'S EQUITY		

PROBLEM 1A-5

TANSON'S CATERING SERVICE

	ASSETS			=	LIABILITIES +		OWNER'S EQUITY				
	Cash +	Accounts Receivable +	Equipment	=	Accounts Payable +	J. Tanson, Capital −	J. Tanson, Withd. +	Catering Revenue −	Expenses
10/25									
BALANCE									
10/27									
BALANCE									
10/28									
BALANCE									
10/29									
BALANCE									
11/1									
BALANCE									
11/5									
BALANCE									
11/8									
BALANCE									
11/10									
BALANCE									
11/15									
BALANCE									
11/17									
BALANCE									
11/20									
BALANCE									
11/25									
BALANCE									
11/28									
BALANCE									
11/30									
END. BAL.									

(a)

PROBLEM 1A-5 (CONTINUED)

(b)

TANSON'S CATERING SERVICE
BALANCE SHEET
OCTOBER 31, 201X

ASSETS				LIABILITIES AND OWNER'S EQUITY				

(c)

TANSON'S CATERING SERVICE
INCOME STATEMENT
FOR MONTH ENDED NOVEMBER 30, 201X

PROBLEM 1A-5 (CONCLUDED)

(d)

TANSON'S CATERING SERVICE
STATEMENT OF OWNER'S EQUITY
FOR MONTH ENDED NOVEMBER 30, 201X

(e)

TANSON'S CATERING SERVICE
BALANCE SHEET
NOVEMBER 30, 201X

ASSETS		LIABILITIES AND OWNER'S EQUITY	

FORMS FOR SET B PROBLEMS

PROBLEM 1B-1

MANDY'S NAIL SPA

	ASSETS			=	LIABILITIES	+	OWNER'S EQUITY
	Cash	+	Store Equipment	=	Accounts Payable	+	M. Anabelle, Capital
TRANSACTION a							
NEW BALANCE							
TRANSACTION b							
NEW BALANCE							
TRANSACTION c							
NEW BALANCE							
TRANSACTION d							
ENDING BALANCE							

PROBLEM 1B-2

SEALY'S INTERNET SERVICE
BALANCE SHEET
NOVEMBER 30, 201X

ASSETS			LIABILITIES AND OWNER'S EQUITY		

PROBLEM 1B-3

**RED FUMAN
COMPUTER SERVICE**

	ASSETS			=	LIABILITIES	+		OWNER'S EQUITY		
Cash	+	Accounts Receivable	+	Office Equipment	=	Accounts Payable	+	R. Fuman, Capital	−	R. Fuman, Withd.	+	Computer Service Revenue	−	Expenses

a.
BALANCE
b.
BALANCE
c.
BALANCE
d.
BALANCE
e.
BALANCE
f.
BALANCE
g.
BALANCE
h.
ENDING BALANCE

PROBLEM 1B-4

(a)

WU HOME DECORATING SERVICE
INCOME STATEMENT
FOR MONTH ENDED JUNE 30, 201X

(b)

WU HOME DECORATING SERVICE
STATEMENT OF OWNER'S EQUITY
FOR MONTH ENDED JUNE 30, 201X

PROBLEM 1B-4 (CONCLUDED)

(c)

WU HOME DECORATING SERVICE
BALANCE SHEET
JUNE 30, 201X

ASSETS				LIABILITIES AND OWNER'S EQUITY			

PROBLEM 1B-5

THILDORE'S CATERING SERVICE

(a)

	ASSETS			=	LIABILITIES	+			OWNER'S EQUITY			
	Cash	+	Accounts Receivable	+	Equipment	=	Accounts Payable	+	J. Thildore, Capital	−	J. Thildore, Withd.	+	Catering Revenue	−	Expenses
10/25												
BALANCE												
10/27												
BALANCE												
10/28												
BALANCE												
10/29												
BALANCE												
11/1												
BALANCE												
11/5												
BALANCE												
11/8												
BALANCE												
11/10												
BALANCE												
11/15												
BALANCE												
11/17												
BALANCE												
11/20												
BALANCE												
11/25												
BALANCE												
11/28												
BALANCE												
11/30												
END. BAL.												

PROBLEM 1B-5 (CONTINUED)

(b)

**THILDORE'S CATERING SERVICE
BALANCE SHEET
OCTOBER 31, 201X**

ASSETS	LIABILITIES AND OWNER'S EQUITY

(c)

**THILDORE'S CATERING SERVICE
INCOME STATEMENT
FOR MONTH ENDED NOVEMBER 30, 201X**

PROBLEM 1B-5 (CONCLUDED)

(d)

THILDORE'S CATERING SERVICE
STATEMENT OF OWNER'S EQUITY
FOR MONTH ENDED NOVEMBER 30, 201X

(e)

THILDORE'S CATERING SERVICE
BALANCE SHEET
NOVEMBER 30, 201X

ASSETS			LIABILITIES AND OWNER'S EQUITY		

ON THE JOB CONTINUING PROBLEM

ASSIGNMENTS 1 AND 2

SMITH COMPUTER CENTER

	Cash	+	Supplies	+	Computer Shop Equipment	+	Office Equipment	=	Accounts Payable	+	Feldman, Capital	−	Feldman, Withdrawals	+	Service Revenue	−	Expenses
a																	
BALANCE																	
b																	
BALANCE																	
c																	
BALANCE																	
d																	
BALANCE																	
e																	
BALANCE																	
f																	
BALANCE																	
g																	
BALANCE																	
h																	
BALANCE																	
i																	
BALANCE																	
j																	
END BAL.																	

ASSETS = LIABILITIES + OWNER'S EQUITY

ASSIGNMENT 3

SMITH COMPUTER CENTER
INCOME STATEMENT
FOR THE MONTH ENDED JULY 31, 201X

SMITH COMPUTER CENTER
STATEMENT OF OWNER'S EQUITY
FOR MONTH ENDED JULY 31, 201X

SMITH COMPUTER CENTER
BALANCE SHEET
JULY 31, 201X

ASSETS			LIABILITIES AND OWNER'S EQUITY		

CHAPTER 1
SUMMARY PRACTICE TEST:
ACCOUNTING CONCEPTS AND PROCEDURES

Part I

Fill in the blank(s) to complete the statement.

1. _____ was passed to prevent corporate fraud.

2. _____ – Liabilities = Owner's Equity

3. The owner's current investment or equity in the assets of a business is called _____.

4. A list of assets, liabilities, and owner's equity as of a particular date is reported on a(n) _____ _____.

5. _____ create an outward or potential outward flow of assets.

6. Revenue earned not on account creates an asset entitled _____.

7. _____ record personal expenses that are not related to the business. They are a subdivision of owner's equity.

8. The _____ _____ reports how well a business performs for a period of time.

9. The _____ _____ _____ _____ is a report that shows changes in capital.

10. The ending figure for capital from the statement of owner's equity is placed on the _____ _____.

Part II

Answer true or false to the following statements.

1. Accounts Receivable is a liability.
2. Liabilities produce revenue.
3. Revenue is an asset.
4. Capital means cash.
5. Bookkeeping is 50% of accounting.
6. The balance sheet lists assets, revenue, and owner's equity.
7. The balance sheet shows where we are now for a specific period of time.
8. Revenue creates an outward flow of assets.
9. Expenses are a subdivision of owner's equity.
10. Withdrawals are the only subdivision of owner's equity.
11. Withdrawals are listed on the income statement.
12. Revenue is a subdivision of owner's equity.
13. Revenues and withdrawals are listed on the income statement.
14. The income statement helps update the statement of owner's equity, and the statement of owner's equity helps update the balance sheet.
15. Withdrawals are listed on the statement of owner's equity.

Part III

In column B, record the appropriate code(s) that result from recording the transaction in column A.

1.	Increase in assets	**5.**	Increase in capital
2.	Decrease in assets	**6.**	Increase in revenues
3.	Increase in liabilities	**7.**	Increase in expenses
4.	Decrease in liabilities	**8.**	Increase in withdrawals

	COLUMN A	COLUMN B
1.	EXAMPLE: Pete Smith invested $5,000 in his business.	1,5
2.	Bought computer equipment on account for $600.	_____
3.	Paid salaries of $70.	_____
4.	Bought additional computer equipment for $750 cash.	_____
5.	Paid rent expense of $90.	_____
6.	Received $5,000 in cash from revenue earned.	_____
7.	Paid heat expense of $15.	_____
8.	Earned revenue of $500 that will not be received until next month.	_____
9.	Paid amount owed on equipment previously purchased on account.	_____
10.	Paid for cleaning supplies expense, $15.	_____
11.	Customers paid $10 of amount previously owed.	_____
12.	Bought additional equipment of $1,000, half paid in cash and half charged.	_____
13.	Charged customer $100 for services performed.	_____
14.	Pete paid home phone bill from the company's cash.	_____
15.	Advertising expense incurred but not to be paid until next month.	_____

SOLUTIONS

Part I

1.	The Sarbanes-Oxley Act	**5.**	Expenses	**9.**	statement of owner's equity
2.	Assets	**6.**	Cash		
3.	capital	**7.**	Withdrawals	**10.**	balance sheet
4.	balance sheet	**8.**	income statement		

Part II

1.	false	**6.**	false	**11.**	false
2.	false	**7.**	false	**12.**	true
3.	false	**8.**	false	**13.**	false
4.	false	**9.**	true	**14.**	true
5.	false	**10.**	false	**15.**	true

Part III

1.	1,5	**6.**	1,6	**11.**	1,2
2.	1,3	**7.**	7,2	**12.**	1,2,3
3.	7,2	**8.**	1,6	**13.**	1,6
4.	1,2	**9.**	4,2	**14.**	8,2
5.	7,2	**10.**	7,2	**15.**	7,3

Debits and Credits: Analyzing and Recording Business Transactions

FORMS FOR DEMONSTRATION PROBLEM

(1,2,3)

Advertising Expense 511

Gas Expense 512

Salaries Expense 513

Telephone Expense 514

Accounts Payable 211

Mel Free, Capital 311

Mel Free, Withdrawals 312

Delivery Fees Earned 411

Cash 111

Accounts Receivable 112

Office Equipment 121

Delivery Trucks 122

FORMS FOR DEMONSTRATION PROBLEM (CONTINUED)

(4)

MEL'S DELIVERY SERVICE
TRIAL BALANCE
JULY 31, 201X

	Dr.	Cr.

(5a)

MEL'S DELIVERY SERVICE
INCOME STATEMENT
FOR MONTH ENDED JULY 31, 201X

FORMS FOR DEMONSTRATION PROBLEM (CONCLUDED)

(5b)

MEL'S DELIVERY SERVICE
STATEMENT OF OWNER'S EQUITY
FOR MONTH ENDED JULY 31, 201X

(5c)

MEL'S DELIVERY SERVICE
BALANCE SHEET
JULY 31, 201X

ASSETS	LIABILITIES AND OWNER'S EQUITY

FORMS FOR SET A EXERCISES

2A-1

_____

_____

_____

_____

_____

_____

_____

_____

_____

_____

_____

_____

_____

_____

_____

_____

_____

_____

_____

_____

_____

2A-2

1. Accounts Affected	2. Category	3. ↑ ↓	4. Rules	5. T Account Update

2A-3

Account	Category	↑↓	Financial Statement
Computer Supplies			
Legal Fees Earned			
R. Roy, Withdrawals			
Accounts Payable			
Salaries Expense			
Auto			

SET A EXERCISES

2A-4

Transaction	Dr.	Cr.
A. Paid salaries expense.	8	1
B. Bob paid personal utilities bill from the company checkbook.		
C. Advertising bill received but unpaid.		
D. Received cash from plumbing fees.		
E. Paid supplies expense.		
F. Bob invested in additional equipment for the business.		
G. Billed customers for plumbing services rendered.		
H. Received one-half the balance from transaction G.		
I. Bought equipment on account.		

2A-5

(1)

HUGO'S CLEANERS
INCOME STATEMENT
FOR MONTH ENDED JULY 31, 201X

(2)

HUGO'S CLEANERS
STATEMENT OF OWNER'S EQUITY
FOR MONTH ENDED JULY 31, 201X

SET A EXERCISES

(3)

HUGO'S CLEANERS
BALANCE SHEET
JULY 31, 201X

ASSETS					LIABILITIES AND OWNER'S EQUITY				

FORMS FOR SET B EXERCISES

2B-1

_____
_____
_____
_____

_____
_____
_____
_____
_____
_____
_____
_____
_____
_____
_____
_____
_____
_____

2B-2

1. Accounts Affected	2. Category	3. ↑ ↓	4. Rules	5. T Account Update

2B-3

Account	Category	↑↓	Financial Statement
Office Supplies			
Rental Fees Earned			
A. Troy, Withdrawals			
Accounts Payable			
Wage Expense			
Computer			

SET B EXERCISES

2B-4

Transaction	Dr.	Cr.
A. Paid salaries expense.	_____	
B. Bill paid personal utilities bill from the company checkbook.	_____	
C. Advertising bill received but unpaid.	_____	
D. Received cash from photography fees.	_____	
E. Paid supplies expense.	_____	
F. Bill invested in additional furniture for the business.	_____	
G. Billed customers for photography services rendered.	_____	
H. Received one-half the balance from transaction G.	_____	
I. Bought furniture on account.	_____	

2B-5

(1)

HELM'S CLEANERS
INCOME STATEMENT
FOR MONTH ENDED MAY 31, 201X

(2)

HELM'S CLEANERS
STATEMENT OF OWNER'S EQUITY
FOR MONTH ENDED MAY 31, 201X

SET B EXERCISES

(3)

HELM'S CLEANERS
BALANCE SHEET
MAY 31, 201X

ASSETS					LIABILITIES AND OWNER'S EQUITY				

FORMS FOR SET A PROBLEMS

PROBLEM 2A-1

Accounts Affected	Category	Inc. Dec. ↑ →	Rules	T Account Update
A.				
B.				
C.				
D.				
E.				
F.				

PROBLEM 2A-2

	Cash	111

	Brett Pillows, Withdrawals	312

	Office Equipment	121

	Consulting Fees Earned	411

	Accounts Payable	211

	Advertising Expense	511

	Brett Pillows, Capital	311

	Rent Expense	512

PROBLEM 2A-3

(a)

	Cash		111		Accounts Payable		211		Cleaning Fees Earned		411
(A)	12,000	(D)	700	(D)	700	(C)	1,300			(B)	9,000
(G)	2,500	(E)	250								
		(F)	300								
		(H)	350								
		(I)	300								

	Accounts Receivable		112		Bill Jolt, Capital		311		Rent Expense		511
(B)	9,000	(G)	2,500			(A)	12,000	(F)	300		

	Office Equipment		121		Bill Jolt, Withdrawals		312		Utilities Expense		512
(C)	1,300			(I)	300			(E)	250		
(H)	350										

(b)

BILL'S CLEANING SERVICE
TRIAL BALANCE
DECEMBER 31, 201X

	Dr.	Cr.

PROBLEM 2A-4

(a)

GIRTIE LILLIS, ATTORNEY AT LAW
INCOME STATEMENT
FOR MONTH ENDED MAY 31, 201X

(b)

GIRTIE LILLIS, ATTORNEY AT LAW
STATEMENT OF OWNER'S EQUITY
FOR MONTH ENDED MAY 31, 201X

PROBLEM 2A-4 (CONCLUDED)

(c)

GIRTIE LILLIS, ATTORNEY AT LAW
BALANCE SHEET
MAY 31, 201X

ASSETS

LIABILITIES AND OWNER'S EQUITY

PROBLEM 2A-5

(1,2)

Advertising Expense	511

Gas Expense	512

Salaries Expense	513

Telephone Expense	514

Accounts Payable	211

Andrea Adler, Capital	311

Andrea Adler, Withdrawals	312

Delivery Fees Earned	411

Cash	111

Accounts Receivable	112

Office Equipment	121

Delivery Trucks	122

PROBLEM 2A-5 (CONTINUED)

(3)

ADLER'S DELIVERY SERVICE
TRIAL BALANCE
JULY 31, 201X

		Dr.	Cr.

(4a)

ADLER'S DELIVERY SERVICE
INCOME STATEMENT
FOR MONTH ENDED JULY 31, 201X

PROBLEM 2A-5 (CONCLUDED)

(4b)

ADLER'S DELIVERY SERVICE
STATEMENT OF OWNER'S EQUITY
FOR MONTH ENDED JULY 31, 201X

(4c)

ADLER'S DELIVERY SERVICE
BALANCE SHEET
JULY 31, 201X

ASSETS   LIABILITIES AND OWNER'S EQUITY

FORMS FOR SET B PROBLEMS

PROBLEM 2B-1

Accounts Affected	Category	Inc. Dec. ↑ →	Rules	T Account Update
A.				
B.				
C.				
D.				
E.				
F.				

PROBLEM 2B-2

| Cash | 111 | | Bill Palu, Withdrawals | 312 |

| Office Equipment | 121 | | Consulting Fees Earned | 411 |

| Accounts Payable | 211 | | Advertising Expense | 511 |

| Bill Palu, Capital | 311 | | Rent Expense | 512 |

PROBLEM 2B-3

(a)

	Cash		111
(A)	15,000	(D)	800
(G)	1,000	(E)	200
		(F)	250
		(H)	200
		(I)	1,100

	Accounts Payable		211
(D)	800	(C)	1,900

	Cleaning Fees Earned		411
		(B)	15,000

	Accounts Receivable		112
(B)	15,000	(G)	1,000

	Breck Jal, Capital		311
		(A)	15,000

	Rent Expense		511
(F)	250		

	Office Equipment		121
(C)	1,900		
(H)	200		

	Breck Jal, Withdrawals		312
(I)	1,100		

	Utilities Expense		512
(E)	200		

(b)

BRECK'S CLEANING SERVICE
TRIAL BALANCE
MAY 31, 201X

	Dr.	Cr.

PROBLEM 2B-4

(a)

GRETCHEN LYMAN, ATTORNEY AT LAW
INCOME STATEMENT
FOR MONTH ENDED JANUARY 31, 201X

(b)

GRETCHEN LYMAN, ATTORNEY AT LAW
STATEMENT OF OWNER'S EQUITY
FOR MONTH ENDED JANUARY 31, 201X

PROBLEM 2B-4 (CONCLUDED)

(c)

GRETCHEN LYMAN, ATTORNEY AT LAW
BALANCE SHEET
JANUARY 31, 201X

ASSETS

LIABILITIES AND OWNER'S EQUITY

PROBLEM 2B-5

(1,2)

Advertising Expense 511	Gas Expense 512	Salaries Expense 513	Telephone Expense 514

Accounts Payable 211	Andrea Aikman, Capital 311	Andrea Aikman, Withdrawals 312	Delivery Fees Earned 411

Cash 111	Accounts Receivable 112	Office Equipment 121	Delivery Trucks 122

PROBLEM 2B-5 (CONTINUED)

(3)

AIKMAN'S DELIVERY SERVICE
TRIAL BALANCE
MAY 31, 201X

	Dr.	Cr.

(4a)

AIKMAN'S DELIVERY SERVICE
INCOME STATEMENT
FOR MONTH ENDED MAY 31, 201X

PROBLEM 2B-5 (CONCLUDED)

(4b)

AIKMAN'S DELIVERY SERVICE
STATEMENT OF OWNER'S EQUITY
FOR MONTH ENDED MAY 31, 201X

(4c)

AIKMAN'S DELIVERY SERVICE
BALANCE SHEET
MAY 31, 201X

ASSETS	LIABILITIES AND OWNER'S EQUITY

ON THE JOB CONTINUING PROBLEM

ASSIGNMENTS 1, 2, 3

Cash 1000	Accounts Receivable 1020	Supplies 1030	Computer Shop Equipment 1080
Bal. 3,425		Bal. 200	Bal. 1,800

Feldman, Withdrawals 3010	Office Equipment 1090	Accounts Payable 2000	Feldman, Capital 3000
Bal. 175	Bal. 3,300	275 Bal.	6,000 Bal.

Utilities Expense 5030	Service Revenue 4000	Advertising Expense 5010	Rent Expense 5020
Bal. 75	3,200 Bal.		Bal. 500

Postage Expense 5070	Phone Expense 5040	Supplies Expense 5050	Insurance Expense 5060

ASSIGNMENT 4

SMITH COMPUTER CENTER
TRIAL BALANCE
AUGUST 31, 201X

	Dr.	Cr.

ASSIGNMENT 5

SMITH COMPUTER CENTER
INCOME STATEMENT
FOR THE TWO MONTHS ENDED AUGUST 31, 201X

SMITH COMPUTER CENTER
STATEMENT OF OWNER'S EQUITY
FOR THE TWO MONTHS ENDED AUGUST 31, 201X

SMITH COMPUTER CENTER
BALANCE SHEET
AUGUST 31, 201X

ASSETS	LIABILITIES AND OWNER'S EQUITY

CHAPTER 2
SUMMARY PRACTICE TEST:
DEBITS AND CREDITS: ANALYZING AND RECORDING
BUSINESS TRANSACTIONS

Part I

Fill in the blank(s) to complete the statement.

1. Financial reports do not contain _____ or _____.
2. The right side of any T account is called the _____ _____.
3. Assets are increased by _____.
4. The process of balancing an account involves _____.
5. Transaction analysis charts are an aid in recording _____ _____.
6. The _____ _____ _____ indicates the names and numbering system of accounts.
7. A(n) _____ is a group of accounts.
8. A(n) _____ _____ is an informal report that lists accounts and their balances.
9. Withdrawals are increased by _____.
10. The income statement, statement of owner's equity, and balance sheet may be prepared from a(n) _____ _____.
11. Cash, Accounts Receivable, and Equipment are examples of _____.
12. Increasing expenses ultimately cause owner's equity to _____.
13. An increase in rent expense is a(n) _____ by the rules of debits and credits.
14. A debit to one asset and a credit to another asset for the same transaction reflect a(n) _____ in assets.
15. The category of accounts receivable is a(n) _____.

Part II

Bea Paul opened a shuttle service company. From the following chart of accounts, indicate in column B (by account number) which account (s) will be debited or credited as related to the transaction in column A.

Chart of Accounts

ASSETS	LIABILITIES	EXPENSES
10 Cash	50 Accounts Payable	80 Advertising Expense
20 Accounts Receivable		90 Gas Expense
30 Equipment	OWNER'S EQUITY	100 Salaries Expense
40 Shuttle Bus	60 B. Paul, Capital	110 Telephone Expense
	62 B. Paul, Withdrawals	
	REVENUE	
	70 Shuttle Fees Earned	

COLUMN A

COLUMN B

		DEBIT(S)	CREDIT(S)
1.	EXAMPLE: Bea Paul invested $40,000 in the shuttle service.	10	60
2.	Purchased a shuttle bus on account for $25,000.		
3.	Bought equipment on account for $3,000.		
4.	Advertising bill received, but not paid until next month, $60.		
5.	Bea paid home telephone bill from company checkbook, $20.		
6.	Collected $100 in cash from daily shuttle fees earned.		
7.	Customer charged a shuttle ride of $20.		
8.	Received partial payment for Transaction #7 of $10.		
9.	Paid business telephone bill, $32.		
10.	Purchased additional equipment for cash, $550.		
11.	Paid shuttle driver salaries of $150.		
12.	Drove customer on account to local train station for $6.		
13.	Received $5 from customer who hired a shuttle for ride across town.		
14.	Collected from past charged revenue, $15.		
15.	Bought office equipment on account for $110.		

Part III

Answer true or false to the following statements.

1. There are no debit and credit columns found on the three financial statements.
2. A trial balance could balance but be wrong.
3. Withdrawals are listed on the credit column of the trial balance.
4. Double entry bookkeeping results in a system where the sum of all the debits is equal to the sum of all the credits.
5. The ledger is numbered like a textbook.

6. Withdrawals are always increased by credits.

7. An expense could create a liability.

8. A shift in assets means the total of assets must change.

9. The rules of debit and credit are constantly changing.

10. The transaction analysis chart is a teaching device.

11. The chart of accounts makes locating and identifying accounts easier.

12. The left side of any account is a credit.

13. A debit means all accounts are decreasing.

14. Financial statements are prepared from a trial balance.

15. The statement of owner's equity is prepared before the income statement.

16. Liabilities increase by credits.

17. Footings aid in balancing accounts.

18. Withdrawals are listed on the income statement.

19. The balance sheet contains the old figure for capital.

20. Think of a credit as always meaning something good.

SOLUTIONS

Part I

1. debits/credits
2. credit side
3. debits
4. footings
5. journal entries
6. chart of accounts
7. ledger (general)
8. trial balance
9. debits
10. trial balance
11. assets
12. decrease
13. debit
14. shift
15. asset

Part II

	Debit	Credit		Debit	Credit		Debit	Credit
1.	10	60	6.	10	70	11.	100	10
2.	40	50	7.	20	70	12.	20	70
3.	30	50	8.	10	20	13.	10	70
4.	80	50	9.	110	10	14.	10	20
5.	62	10	10.	30	10	15.	30	50

Part III

1. true
2. true
3. false
4. true
5. false
6. false
7. true
8. false
9. false
10. true
11. true
12. false
13. false
14. true
15. false
16. true
17. true
18. false
19. false
20. false

Beginning the Accounting Cycle

FORMS FOR DEMONSTRATION PROBLEM
(1)

ABBY'S EMPLOYMENT AGENCY
GENERAL JOURNAL

PAGE 1

Date	Account Titles and Description	PR	Dr.	Cr.

FORMS FOR DEMONSTRATION PROBLEM (CONTINUED)
(2, 3)

GENERAL LEDGER OF ABBY'S EMPLOYMENT AGENCY

CASH   **ACCOUNT NO. 111**

Date	Explanation	Post Ref.	Debit	Credit	Balance	
					Debit	Credit

ACCOUNTS RECEIVABLE   **ACCOUNT NO. 112**

Date	Explanation	Post Ref.	Debit	Credit	Balance	
					Debit	Credit

SUPPLIES   **ACCOUNT NO. 131**

Date	Explanation	Post Ref.	Debit	Credit	Balance	
					Debit	Credit

EQUIPMENT   **ACCOUNT NO. 141**

Date	Explanation	Post Ref.	Debit	Credit	Balance	
					Debit	Credit

FORMS FOR DEMONSTRATION PROBLEM (CONTINUED)

ACCOUNTS PAYABLE — ACCOUNT NO. 211

Date		Explanation	Post Ref.	Debit	Credit	Balance	
						Debit	Credit

A. TODD, CAPITAL — ACCOUNT NO. 311

Date		Explanation	Post Ref.	Debit	Credit	Balance	
						Debit	Credit

A. TODD, WITHDRAWALS — ACCOUNT NO. 321

Date		Explanation	Post Ref.	Debit	Credit	Balance	
						Debit	Credit

EMPLOYMENT FEES EARNED — ACCOUNT NO. 411

Date		Explanation	Post Ref.	Debit	Credit	Balance	
						Debit	Credit

FORMS FOR DEMONSTRATION PROBLEM (CONTINUED)

WAGE EXPENSE ACCOUNT NO. <u>511</u>

Date	Explanation	Post Ref.	Debit	Credit	Balance	
					Debit	Credit

TELEPHONE EXPENSE ACCOUNT NO. 521

Date	Explanation	Post Ref.	Debit	Credit	Balance	
					Debit	Credit

ADVERTISING EXPENSE ACCOUNT NO. 531

Date	Explanation	Post Ref.	Debit	Credit	Balance	
					Debit	Credit

FORMS FOR DEMONSTRATION PROBLEM (CONCLUDED)
(4)

ABBY'S EMPLOYMENT AGENCY
TRIAL BALANCE
MARCH 31, 201X

	Dr.	Cr.

FORMS FOR SET A EXERCISES

3A-1

Date		Account Titles and Description	PR		Dr.				Cr.			

SET A EXERCISES

3A-2

Date		Account Titles and Description	PR		Dr.			Cr.		

SET A EXERCISES

3A-3

Date 201X		Account Titles and Description	PR	Dr.						Cr.					
Feb.	6	Cash		12	0	0	0	00							
		A. Kramer, Capital								12	0	0	0	00	
		Cash investment													
	14	Equipment		8	0	0	0	00							
		Cash								5	0	0	0	00	
		Accounts Payable								3	0	0	0	00	
		Purchase of equipment													

CASH   ACCOUNT NO. <u>111</u>

Date	Explanation	Post Ref.	Debit	Credit	Balance Debit	Balance Credit

EQUIPMENT   ACCOUNT NO. <u>121</u>

Date	Explanation	Post Ref.	Debit	Credit	Balance Debit	Balance Credit

ACCOUNTS PAYABLE   ACCOUNT NO. <u>211</u>

Date	Explanation	Post Ref.	Debit	Credit	Balance Debit	Balance Credit

A. KRAMER, CAPITAL   ACCOUNT NO. <u>311</u>

Date	Explanation	Post Ref.	Debit	Credit	Balance Debit	Balance Credit

SET A EXERCISES

3A-4

(a)   PAGE 1

Date	Account Titles and Description	PR	Dr.	Cr.

(b)   **CASH**   **ACCOUNT NO. 111**

Date	Explanation	Post Ref.	Debit	Credit	Balance Debit	Balance Credit

ACCOUNTS RECEIVABLE   **ACCOUNT NO. 112**

Date	Explanation	Post Ref.	Debit	Credit	Balance Debit	Balance Credit

SET A EXERCISES

EQUIPMENT   **ACCOUNT NO. 121**

Date	Explanation	Post Ref.	Debit	Credit	Balance	
					Debit	Credit

ACCOUNTS PAYABLE   **ACCOUNT NO. 211**

Date	Explanation	Post Ref.	Debit	Credit	Balance	
					Debit	Credit

J. LUCAS, CAPITAL   **ACCOUNT NO. 311**

Date	Explanation	Post Ref.	Debit	Credit	Balance	
					Debit	Credit

J. LUCAS, WITHDRAWALS   **ACCOUNT NO. 312**

Date	Explanation	Post Ref.	Debit	Credit	Balance	
					Debit	Credit

FEES EARNED   **ACCOUNT NO. 411**

Date	Explanation	Post Ref.	Debit	Credit	Balance	
					Debit	Credit

SALARIES EXPENSE   **ACCOUNT NO. 511**

Date	Explanation	Post Ref.	Debit	Credit	Balance	
					Debit	Credit

SET A EXERCISES

(c)

LUCAS COMPANY
TRIAL BALANCE
MAY 31, 201X

		Dr.	Cr.

3A-5

SALT LAKE CO.
TRIAL BALANCE
OCTOBER 31, 201X

		Dr.	Cr.

3A-6

Date 201X	Account Titles and Description	PR	Dr.	Cr.
Feb. 6	Office Equipment		8 0 0 00	
	Accounts Payable			8 0 0 00
	Purchase of office equip. on account			

FORMS FOR SET B EXERCISES

3B-1

Date	Account Titles and Description	PR	Dr.	Cr.

SET B EXERCISES

3B-2

Date		Account Titles and Description	PR		Dr.				Cr.		

SET B EXERCISES

3B-3

Date 201X		Account Titles and Description	PR	Dr.					Cr.				
Nov.	6	Cash		52	0	0	0	00					
		A. Kingston, Capital							52	0	0	0	00
		Cash investment											
	14	Equipment		3	0	0	0	00					
		Cash							1	0	0	0	00
		Accounts Payable							2	0	0	0	00
		Purchase of equipment											

CASH　　　　　　　　　　　　　　　　ACCOUNT NO. 111

Date	Explanation	Post Ref.	Debit	Credit	Balance Debit	Balance Credit

EQUIPMENT　　　　　　　　　　　　　ACCOUNT NO. 121

Date	Explanation	Post Ref.	Debit	Credit	Balance Debit	Balance Credit

ACCOUNTS PAYABLE　　　　　　　　ACCOUNT NO. 211

Date	Explanation	Post Ref.	Debit	Credit	Balance Debit	Balance Credit

A. KINGSTON, CAPITAL　　　　　　ACCOUNT NO. 311

Date	Explanation	Post Ref.	Debit	Credit	Balance Debit	Balance Credit

SET B EXERCISES

3B-4

(a)   PAGE 1

Date	Account Titles and Description	PR	Dr.	Cr.

(b)

CASH   **ACCOUNT NO. 111**

Date	Explanation	Post Ref.	Debit	Credit	Balance Debit	Balance Credit

ACCOUNTS RECEIVABLE   **ACCOUNT NO. 112**

Date	Explanation	Post Ref.	Debit	Credit	Balance Debit	Balance Credit

SET B EXERCISES

EQUIPMENT   ACCOUNT NO. 121

Date	Explanation	Post Ref.	Debit	Credit	Balance Debit	Balance Credit

ACCOUNTS PAYABLE   ACCOUNT NO. 211

Date	Explanation	Post Ref.	Debit	Credit	Balance Debit	Balance Credit

J. LOWE, CAPITAL   ACCOUNT NO. 311

Date	Explanation	Post Ref.	Debit	Credit	Balance Debit	Balance Credit

J. LOWE, WITHDRAWALS   ACCOUNT NO. 312

Date	Explanation	Post Ref.	Debit	Credit	Balance Debit	Balance Credit

FEES EARNED   ACCOUNT NO. 411

Date	Explanation	Post Ref.	Debit	Credit	Balance Debit	Balance Credit

SALARIES EXPENSE   ACCOUNT NO. 511

Date	Explanation	Post Ref.	Debit	Credit	Balance Debit	Balance Credit

SET B EXERCISES

(c)

LOWE COMPANY
TRIAL BALANCE
DECEMBER 31, 201X

		Dr.	Cr.

3B-5

SUNG CO.
TRIAL BALANCE
AUGUST 31, 201X

		Dr.	Cr.

3B-6

Date 201X	Account Titles and Description	PR	Dr.	Cr.
Feb. 6	Office Equipment		9 00	
	Accounts Payable			9 00
	Purchase of office equip. on account			

FORMS FOR SET A PROBLEMS

PROBLEM 3A-1

JASON'S CLEANING SERVICE
GENERAL JOURNAL

PAGE 1

Date	Account Titles and Description	PR	Dr.	Cr.

PROBLEM 3A-1 (CONCLUDED)

JASON'S CLEANING SERVICE
GENERAL JOURNAL

PAGE 2

Date	Account Titles and Description	PR	Dr.	Cr.

PROBLEM 3A-2
(a, b)

BRENDA'S ART STUDIO
GENERAL JOURNAL

Date	Account Titles and Description	PR	Dr.	Cr.

PROBLEM 3A-2 (CONTINUED)

GENERAL LEDGER OF BRENDA'S ART STUDIO

CASH   **ACCOUNT NO. 111**

Date	Explanation	Post Ref.	Debit	Credit	Balance Debit	Balance Credit

ACCOUNTS RECEIVABLE   **ACCOUNT NO. 112**

Date	Explanation	Post Ref.	Debit	Credit	Balance Debit	Balance Credit

PREPAID RENT   **ACCOUNT NO. 114**

Date	Explanation	Post Ref.	Debit	Credit	Balance Debit	Balance Credit

ART SUPPLIES   **ACCOUNT NO. 121**

Date	Explanation	Post Ref.	Debit	Credit	Balance Debit	Balance Credit

PROBLEM 3A-2 (CONTINUED)

EQUIPMENT   ACCOUNT NO. 131

Date	Explanation	Post Ref.	Debit	Credit	Balance Debit	Balance Credit

ACCOUNTS PAYABLE   ACCOUNT NO. 211

Date	Explanation	Post Ref.	Debit	Credit	Balance Debit	Balance Credit

B. RENNICKE, CAPITAL   ACCOUNT NO. 311

Date	Explanation	Post Ref.	Debit	Credit	Balance Debit	Balance Credit

B. RENNICKE, WITHDRAWALS   ACCOUNT NO. 312

Date	Explanation	Post Ref.	Debit	Credit	Balance Debit	Balance Credit

PROBLEM 3A-2 (CONTINUED)

ART FEES EARNED   ACCOUNT NO. <u>411</u>

Date		Explanation	Post Ref.	Debit	Credit	Balance	
						Debit	Credit

ELECTRICAL EXPENSE   ACCOUNT NO. <u>511</u>

Date		Explanation	Post Ref.	Debit	Credit	Balance	
						Debit	Credit

SALARIES EXPENSE   ACCOUNT NO. <u>521</u>

Date		Explanation	Post Ref.	Debit	Credit	Balance	
						Debit	Credit

TELEPHONE EXPENSE   ACCOUNT NO. <u>531</u>

Date		Explanation	Post Ref.	Debit	Credit	Balance	
						Debit	Credit

PROBLEM 3A-2 (CONCLUDED)

(c)

BRENDA'S ART STUDIO
TRIAL BALANCE
JUNE 30, 201X

		Dr.	Cr.

PROBLEM 3A-3
(a, b)

A. ONE'S PLACEMENT AGENCY
GENERAL JOURNAL

PAGE 1

Date		Account Titles and Description	PR	Dr.		Cr.	

PROBLEM 3A-3 (CONTINUED)

GENERAL LEDGER OF A. ONE'S PLACEMENT AGENCY

CASH   ACCOUNT NO. **111**

Date	Explanation	Post Ref.	Debit	Credit	Balance Debit	Balance Credit

ACCOUNTS RECEIVABLE   ACCOUNT NO. **112**

Date	Explanation	Post Ref.	Debit	Credit	Balance Debit	Balance Credit

SUPPLIES   ACCOUNT NO. **131**

Date	Explanation	Post Ref.	Debit	Credit	Balance Debit	Balance Credit

EQUIPMENT   ACCOUNT NO. **141**

Date	Explanation	Post Ref.	Debit	Credit	Balance Debit	Balance Credit

PROBLEM 3A-3 (CONTINUED)

ACCOUNTS PAYABLE   ACCOUNT NO. 211

Date	Explanation	Post Ref.	Debit	Credit	Balance Debit	Balance Credit

A. ONE, CAPITAL   ACCOUNT NO. 311

Date	Explanation	Post Ref.	Debit	Credit	Balance Debit	Balance Credit

A. ONE, WITHDRAWALS   ACCOUNT NO. 312

Date	Explanation	Post Ref.	Debit	Credit	Balance Debit	Balance Credit

PLACEMENT FEES EARNED   ACCOUNT NO. 411

Date	Explanation	Post Ref.	Debit	Credit	Balance Debit	Balance Credit

PROBLEM 3A-3 (CONTINUED)

WAGE EXPENSE   ACCOUNT NO. **511**

Date		Explanation	Post Ref.	Debit	Credit	Balance	
						Debit	Credit

TELEPHONE EXPENSE   ACCOUNT NO. **521**

Date		Explanation	Post Ref.	Debit	Credit	Balance	
						Debit	Credit

ADVERTISING EXPENSE   ACCOUNT NO. **531**

Date		Explanation	Post Ref.	Debit	Credit	Balance	
						Debit	Credit

PROBLEM 3A-3 (CONCLUDED)

(c)

A. ONE'S PLACEMENT AGENCY
TRIAL BALANCE
JUNE 30, 201X

		Dr.		Cr.	

FORMS FOR SET B PROBLEMS

PROBLEM 3B-1

JIMMY'S CLEANING SERVICE
GENERAL JOURNAL

PAGE 1

Date	Account Titles and Description	PR	Dr.	Cr.

PROBLEM 3B-1 (CONCLUDED)

JIMMY'S CLEANING SERVICE
GENERAL JOURNAL

PAGE 2

Date		Account Titles and Description	PR	Dr.		Cr.	

PROBLEM 3B-2
(a, b)

BETH'S ART STUDIO
GENERAL JOURNAL

PAGE 1

Date	Account Titles and Description	PR	Dr.	Cr.

PROBLEM 3B-2 (CONTINUED)

GENERAL LEDGER OF BETH'S ART STUDIO

CASH   **ACCOUNT NO. 111**

Date	Explanation	Post Ref.	Debit	Credit	Balance Debit	Balance Credit

ACCOUNTS RECEIVABLE   **ACCOUNT NO. 112**

Date	Explanation	Post Ref.	Debit	Credit	Balance Debit	Balance Credit

PREPAID RENT   **ACCOUNT NO. 114**

Date	Explanation	Post Ref.	Debit	Credit	Balance Debit	Balance Credit

ART SUPPLIES   **ACCOUNT NO. 121**

Date	Explanation	Post Ref.	Debit	Credit	Balance Debit	Balance Credit

PROBLEM 3B-2 (CONTINUED)

EQUIPMENT   ACCOUNT NO. 131

Date		Explanation	Post Ref.	Debit	Credit	Balance	
						Debit	Credit

ACCOUNTS PAYABLE   ACCOUNT NO. 211

Date		Explanation	Post Ref.	Debit	Credit	Balance	
						Debit	Credit

BETH ORTH, CAPITAL   ACCOUNT NO. 311

Date		Explanation	Post Ref.	Debit	Credit	Balance	
						Debit	Credit

BETH ORTH, WITHDRAWALS   ACCOUNT NO. 312

Date		Explanation	Post Ref.	Debit	Credit	Balance	
						Debit	Credit

PROBLEM 3B-2 (CONTINUED)

ART FEES EARNED   ACCOUNT NO. 411

Date	Explanation	Post Ref.	Debit	Credit	Balance	
					Debit	Credit

ELECTRICAL EXPENSE   ACCOUNT NO. 511

Date	Explanation	Post Ref.	Debit	Credit	Balance	
					Debit	Credit

SALARIES EXPENSE   ACCOUNT NO. 521

Date	Explanation	Post Ref.	Debit	Credit	Balance	
					Debit	Credit

TELEPHONE EXPENSE   ACCOUNT NO. 531

Date	Explanation	Post Ref.	Debit	Credit	Balance	
					Debit	Credit

PROBLEM 3B-2 (CONCLUDED)

(c)

BETH'S ART STUDIO
TRIAL BALANCE
APRIL 30, 201X

	Dr.	Cr.

PROBLEM 3B-3
(a, b)

A. FRENCH'S PLACEMENT AGENCY
GENERAL JOURNAL

PAGE 1

Date	Account Titles and Description	PR	Dr.	Cr.

PROBLEM 3B-3 (CONTINUED)

GENERAL LEDGER OF A. FRENCH'S PLACEMENT AGENCY

CASH   ACCOUNT NO. 111

Date	Explanation	Post Ref.	Debit	Credit	Balance Debit	Credit

ACCOUNTS RECEIVABLE   ACCOUNT NO. 112

Date	Explanation	Post Ref.	Debit	Credit	Balance Debit	Credit

SUPPLIES   ACCOUNT NO. 131

Date	Explanation	Post Ref.	Debit	Credit	Balance Debit	Credit

EQUIPMENT   ACCOUNT NO. 141

Date	Explanation	Post Ref.	Debit	Credit	Balance Debit	Credit

PROBLEM 3B-3 (CONTINUED)

ACCOUNTS PAYABLE   ACCOUNT NO. 211

Date		Explanation	Post Ref.	Debit	Credit	Balance	
						Debit	Credit

A. FRENCH, CAPITAL   ACCOUNT NO. 311

Date		Explanation	Post Ref.	Debit	Credit	Balance	
						Debit	Credit

A. FRENCH, WITHDRAWALS   ACCOUNT NO. 312

Date		Explanation	Post Ref.	Debit	Credit	Balance	
						Debit	Credit

PLACEMENT FEES EARNED   ACCOUNT NO. 411

Date		Explanation	Post Ref.	Debit	Credit	Balance	
						Debit	Credit

PROBLEM 3B-3 (CONTINUED)

WAGE EXPENSE   ACCOUNT NO. <u>511</u>

Date	Explanation	Post Ref.	Debit	Credit	Balance Debit	Balance Credit

TELEPHONE EXPENSE   ACCOUNT NO. <u>521</u>

Date	Explanation	Post Ref.	Debit	Credit	Balance Debit	Balance Credit

ADVERTISING EXPENSE   ACCOUNT NO. <u>531</u>

Date	Explanation	Post Ref.	Debit	Credit	Balance Debit	Balance Credit

PROBLEM 3B-3 (CONCLUDED)

(c)

A. FRENCH'S PLACEMENT AGENCY
TRIAL BALANCE
APRIL 30, 201X

	Dr.	Cr.

ON THE JOB CONTINUING PROBLEM
ASSIGNMENT 1

SMITH COMPUTER CENTER
GENERAL JOURNAL

PAGE 1

Date	Account Titles and Description	PR	Dr.	Cr.

SMITH COMPUTER CENTER
GENERAL JOURNAL

PAGE 1 (Cont.)

Date	Account Titles and Description	PR	Dr.	Cr.

ASSIGNMENT 2

		CASH				ACCOUNT NO. <u>1000</u>	

Date		Explanation	Post Ref.	Debit	Credit	Balance	
						Debit	Credit
9/1	1X	Balance forward	✔			3 0 8 0 00	

ACCOUNTS RECEIVABLE   ACCOUNT NO. 1020

Date		Explanation	Post Ref.	Debit	Credit	Balance Debit	Balance Credit
9/1	1X	Balance forward	✔			1 7 0 0 00	

PREPAID RENT   ACCOUNT NO. 1025

Date	Explanation	Post Ref.	Debit	Credit	Balance Debit	Balance Credit

SUPPLIES   ACCOUNT NO. 1030

Date	Explanation	Post Ref.	Debit	Credit	Balance Debit	Balance Credit
9/1	Balance forward	✔			5 0 0 00	

COMPUTER SHOP EQUIPMENT   ACCOUNT NO. 1080

Date		Explanation	Post Ref.	Debit	Credit	Balance Debit	Balance Credit
9/1	1X	Balance forward	✔			1 8 0 0 00	

OFFICE EQUIPMENT   ACCOUNT NO. 1090

Date		Explanation	Post Ref.	Debit	Credit	Balance Debit	Credit
9/1	1X	Balance forward	✔			3 3 0 0 00	

ACCOUNTS PAYABLE   ACCOUNT NO. 2000

Date		Explanation	Post Ref.	Debit	Credit	Balance Debit	Credit
9/1	1X	Balance forward	✔				4 3 0 00

FELDMAN, CAPITAL   ACCOUNT NO. 3000

Date		Explanation	Post Ref.	Debit	Credit	Balance Debit	Credit
9/1	1X	Balance forward	✔				6 0 0 0 00

FELDMAN, WITHDRAWALS   ACCOUNT NO. 3010

Date		Explanation	Post Ref.	Debit	Credit	Balance Debit	Credit
9/1	1X	Balance forward	✔			1 7 5 00	

SERVICE REVENUE   ACCOUNT NO. 4000

Date		Explanation	Post Ref.	Debit	Credit	Balance	
						Debit	Credit
9/1	1X	Balance forward	✔				6 2 0 0 00

ADVERTISING EXPENSE   ACCOUNT NO. 5010

Date		Explanation	Post Ref.	Debit	Credit	Balance	
						Debit	Credit
9/1	1X	Balance forward	✔			9 0 0 00	

RENT EXPENSE   ACCOUNT NO. 5020

Date		Explanation	Post Ref.	Debit	Credit	Balance	
						Debit	Credit
9/1	1X	Balance forward	✔			5 0 0 00	

UTILITIES EXPENSE   ACCOUNT NO. <u>5030</u>

Date		Explanation	Post Ref.	Debit	Credit	Balance Debit	Balance Credit
9/1	1X	Balance forward	✔			7 5 00	

PHONE EXPENSE   ACCOUNT NO. <u>5040</u>

Date		Explanation	Post Ref.	Debit	Credit	Balance Debit	Balance Credit
9/1	1X	Balance forward	✔			8 0 00	

SUPPLIES EXPENSE   ACCOUNT NO. <u>5050</u>

Date		Explanation	Post Ref.	Debit	Credit	Balance Debit	Balance Credit

INSURANCE EXPENSE   ACCOUNT NO. 5060

Date		Explanation	Post Ref.	Debit	Credit	Balance	
						Debit	Credit
9/1	1X	Balance forward	✔			4 5 0 00	

POSTAGE EXPENSE   ACCOUNT NO. 5070

Date		Explanation	Post Ref.	Debit	Credit	Balance	
						Debit	Credit
9/1	1X	Balance forward	✔			7 0 00	

ASSIGNMENT 3

SMITH COMPUTER CENTER
TRIAL BALANCE
SEPTEMBER 30, 201X

		Dr.		Cr.	

ASSIGNMENT 4

SMITH COMPUTER CENTER
INCOME STATEMENT
FOR THE QUARTER ENDED 9/30/1X

SMITH COMPUTER CENTER
STATEMENT OF OWNER'S EQUITY
FOR THE QUARTER ENDED 9/30/1X

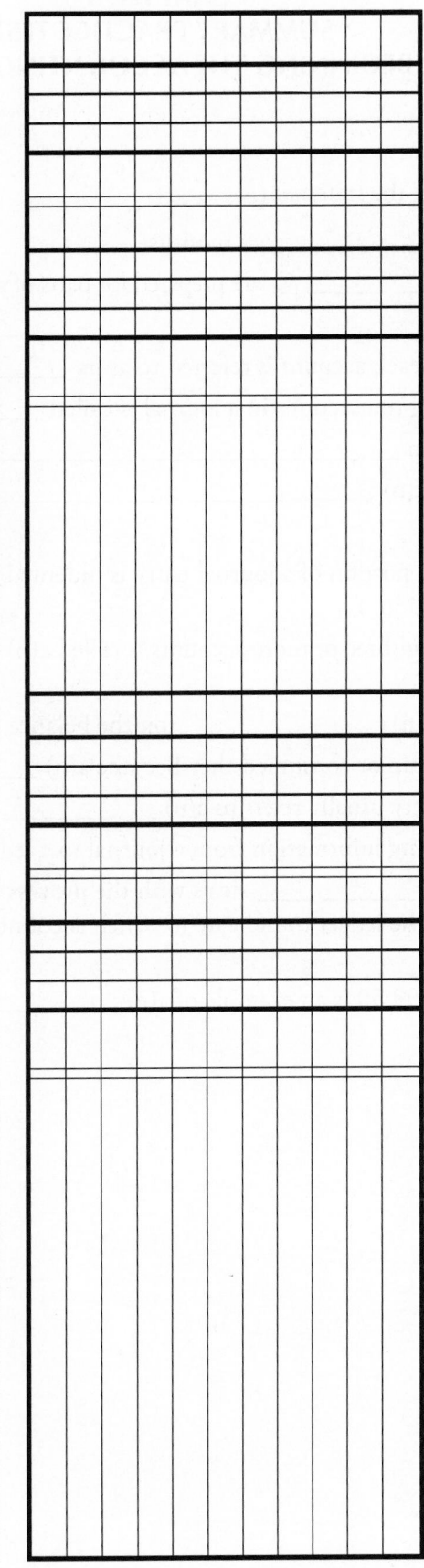

SMITH COMPUTER CENTER
BALANCE SHEET
9/30/1X

ASSETS

LIABILITIES AND OWNER'S EQUITY

CHAPTER 3
SUMMARY PRACTICE TEST:
BEGINNING THE ACCOUNTING CYCLE

Part I

Fill in the blank(s) to complete the statement.

1. A fiscal year runs for _____ months.

2. _____ _____ are prepared for parts of a fiscal year (monthly, quarterly, etc.).

3. The _____ _____ _____ eliminates the need for footings.

4. The positive balance of each account is referred to as its _____ _____.

5. The process of recording transactions in a journal is called _____.

6. Entries are journalized in _____ _____.

7. A ledger is often called a(n) _____ _____ _____

   _____ .

8. The _____ portion of a journal entry is indented and placed below the _____ portion.

9. A journal entry requiring three or more accounts is called a(n) _____ _____

   _____.

10. Accounts receivable is a(n) _____ on the balance sheet.

11. When supplies are used up or consumed they become a(n) _____.

12. The book of original entry usually refers to a(n) _____.

13. The process of transferring information from a journal to a ledger is called _____.

14. _____ _____ deals with the process of updating the PR of the journal from the account number of the ledger to indicate to which account in the ledger information has been posted.

15. Recording $995.00 as $99.50 is an example of a(n) _____.

Part II

Match the term in column A to the definition, example, or phrase in column B. Be sure to use a letter only once.

COLUMN A

__g__ **1.** EXAMPLE: Book of original entry

_____ **2.** Non-Business Expense

_____ **3.** Slide

_____ **4.** Transposition

_____ **5.** Posting

_____ **6.** General Journal

_____ **7.** Cross-reference

_____ **8.** Journalizing

_____ **9.** Balance Sheet prepared monthly

_____ **10.** A fiscal year

COLUMN B

a. 243 — 2430

b. Transferring information from a general journal to a ledger

c. Chronological order

d. Increased by a credit

e. Withdrawal

f. Compound journal entry

g. General journal

h. Rearrangement of digits of a number by accident

i. Updating PR column of journal from ledger account

j. Trial balance

k. Place to record transactions

l. Accounting cycle

m. Accounting period

n. Interim statements

Part III

Answer true or false to the following statements.

1. A slide results in a rearrangement of digits in a number by error.

2. The totals of a trial balance may possibly not balance due to transpositions.

3. Withdrawals has a normal balance of a credit.

4. The running balance of an account can be kept in a four-column account.

5. The journal links debits and credits in alphabetical order.

6. The ledger accumulates information from the journal.

7. The post reference column of a ledger records the account number of that account.

8. An accounting cycle must be from January 1 to December 31.

9. The ledger is the book of original entry.

10. The income statement is prepared for a specific accounting period.

11. Interim statements are prepared for an entire fiscal year.

12. A calendar year could be a fiscal year.

13. 390 written by mistake as 3,900 is an example of a slide.

14. If the totals of a trial balance balance, the individual balance of items must be correct.

15. The equality of debits and credits on a trial balance does not guarantee that transactions have been properly recorded.

16. The trial balance is prepared from the journal.

17. Cross-referencing means never updating the post reference column of the journal.

18. Journals and ledgers are always in the same book.

19. The normal balance of each account is located on the same side that increases the acccount.

20. To increase the Capital account, we credit the Capital account.

SOLUTIONS

Part I

1. 12
2. Interim statements
3. four-column account
4. normal balance
5. journalizing

6. chronological order
7. book of final entry
8. credit, debit
9. compound journal entry
10. asset

11. expense
12. journal
13. posting
14. Cross-reference
15. slide

Part II

1. g
2. e
3. a
4. h
5. b

6. k
7. i
8. c
9. n
10. m

Part III

1. false
2. true
3. false
4. true
5. false

6. true
7. false
8. false
9. false
10. true

11. false
12. true
13. true
14. false
15. true

16. false
17. false
18. false
19. true
20. true

The Accounting Cycle Continued

FORMS FOR DEMONSTRATION PROBLEM

(1) Worksheet

Use one of the blank fold-out worksheets that accompanied your textbook.

(2)

FROST COMPANY
INCOME STATEMENT
FOR MONTH ENDED DECEMBER 31, 201X

FROST COMPANY
STATEMENT OF OWNER'S EQUITY
FOR MONTH ENDED DECEMBER 31, 201X

DEMONSTRATION PROBLEM (CONCLUDED)

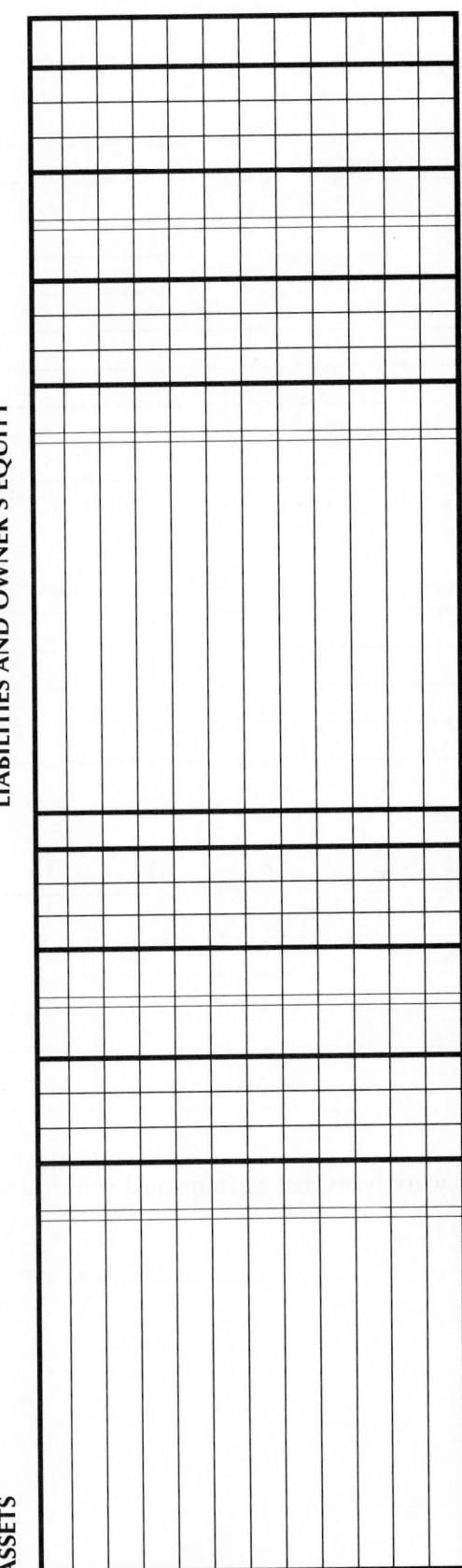

FROST COMPANY
BALANCE SHEET
DECEMBER 31, 201X

ASSETS

LIABILITIES AND OWNER'S EQUITY

FORMS FOR SET A EXERCISES

4A-1

Account	Category	Normal Balance	Financial Statement(s) Found on
Accumulated Depreciation, Office Equipment			
Prepaid Rent			
Office Equipment			
Depreciation Expense, Office Equipment			
B. Reel, Capital			
B. Reel, Withdrawals			
Wages Payable			

4A-2

	Accounts Affected	Category	↑ ↓	Rules	Amount
a.					
b.					

4A-3

	Accounts	Dr.	Cr.
a.			
b.			

4A-4

Use one of the blank fold-out worksheets that accompanied your textbook.

SET A EXERCISES

4A-5

(a)

J. REVERE
INCOME STATEMENT
FOR MONTH ENDED JANUARY 31, 201X

(b)

J. REVERE
STATEMENT OF OWNER'S EQUITY
FOR MONTH ENDED JANUARY 31, 201X

SET A EXERCISES

(c)

J. REVERE
BALANCE SHEET
JANUARY 31, 201X

ASSETS

LIABILITIES AND OWNER'S EQUITY

FORMS FOR SET B EXERCISES

4B-1

Account	Category	Normal Balance	Financial Statement(s) Found on
Accounts Payable			
Prepaid Insurance			
Computer Equipment			
Depreciation Expense, Computer Equipment			
B. Free, Capital			
B. Free, Withdrawals			
Salaries Payable			
Accumulated Depreciation, Computer Equipment			

4B-2

Accounts Affected	Category	↑ ↓ Rules	Amount
a.			
b.			

4B-3

Accounts	Dr.	Cr.
a.		
b.		

4B-4

Use one of the blank fold-out worksheets that accompanied your textbook.

SET B EXERCISES

4B-5

(a)

J. TUTLE
INCOME STATEMENT
FOR MONTH ENDED MARCH 31, 201X

(b)

J. TUTLE
STATEMENT OF OWNER'S EQUITY
FOR MONTH ENDED MARCH 31, 201X

SET B EXERCISES
(c)

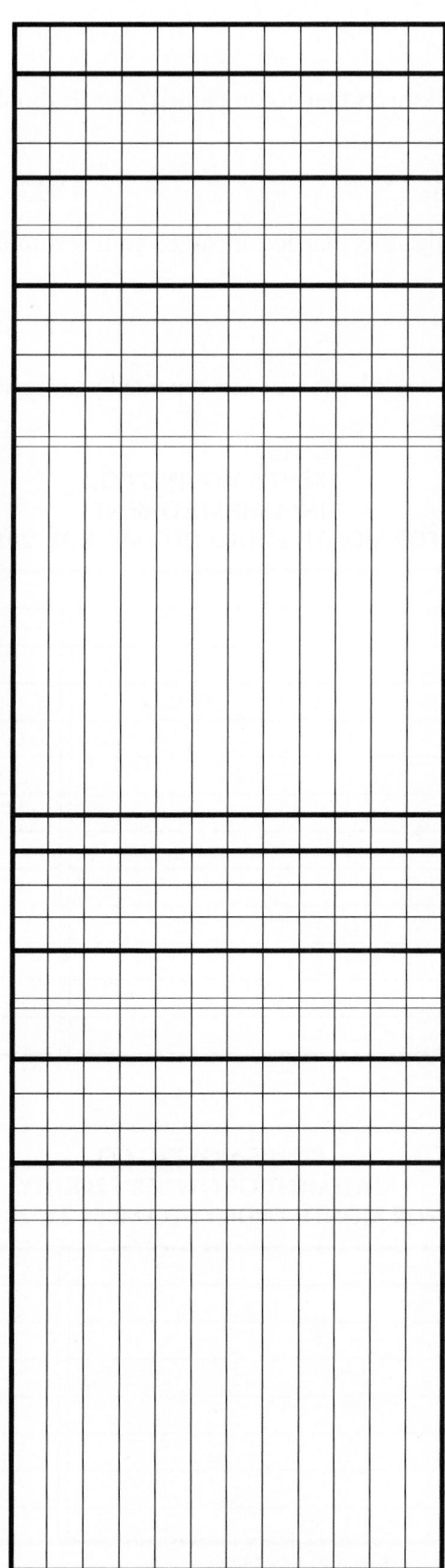

J. TUTLE
BALANCE SHEET
MARCH 31, 201X

LIABILITIES AND OWNER'S EQUITY

ASSETS

FORMS FOR SET A PROBLEMS

PROBLEM 4A-1

Use one of the blank fold-out worksheets that accompanied your textbook.

PROBLEM 4A-2

Use one of the blank fold-out worksheets that accompanied your textbook.

PROBLEM 4A-3

(1) Use one of the blank fold-out worksheets that accompanied your textbook.

(2)

KENT'S MOVING CO.
INCOME STATEMENT
FOR MONTH ENDED DECEMBER 31, 201X

KENT'S MOVING CO.
STATEMENT OF OWNER'S EQUITY
FOR MONTH ENDED DECEMBER 31, 201X

PROBLEM 4A-3 (CONCLUDED)

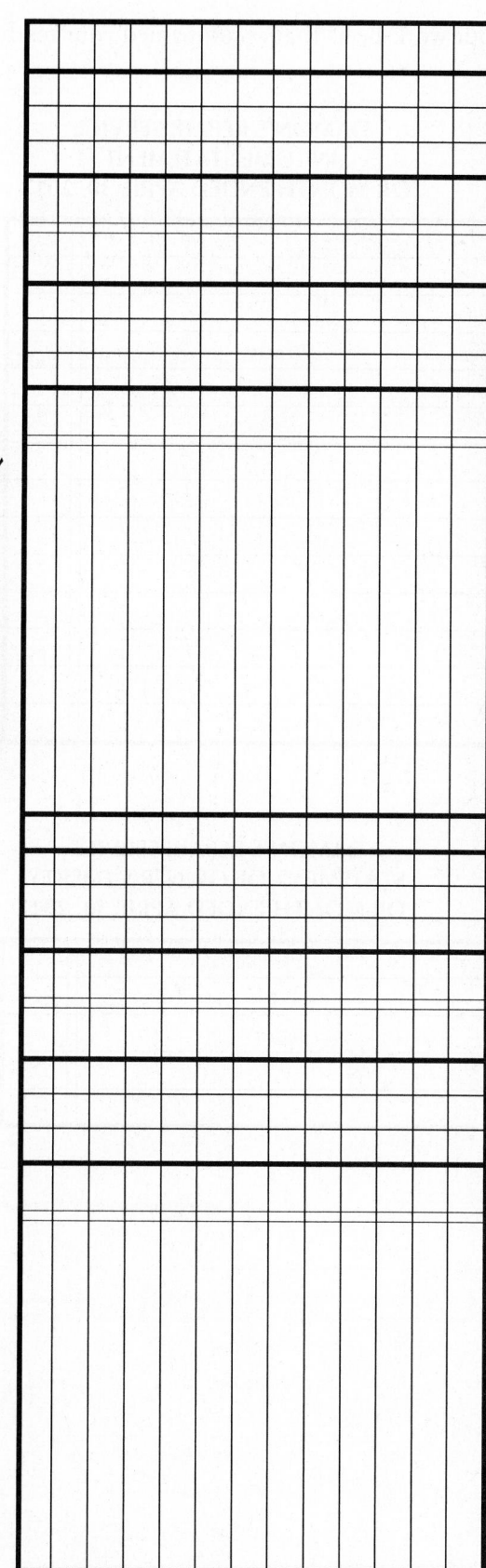

KENT'S MOVING CO.
BALANCE SHEET
DECEMBER 31, 201X

LIABILITIES AND OWNER'S EQUITY

ASSETS

PROBLEM 4A-4

(1) Use one of the blank fold-out worksheets that accompanied your textbook.

(2)

DAMON'S REPAIR SERVICE
INCOME STATEMENT
FOR MONTH ENDED APRIL 30, 201X

DAMON'S REPAIR SERVICE
STATEMENT OF OWNER'S EQUITY
FOR MONTH ENDED APRIL 30, 201X

PROBLEM 4A-4 (CONCLUDED)

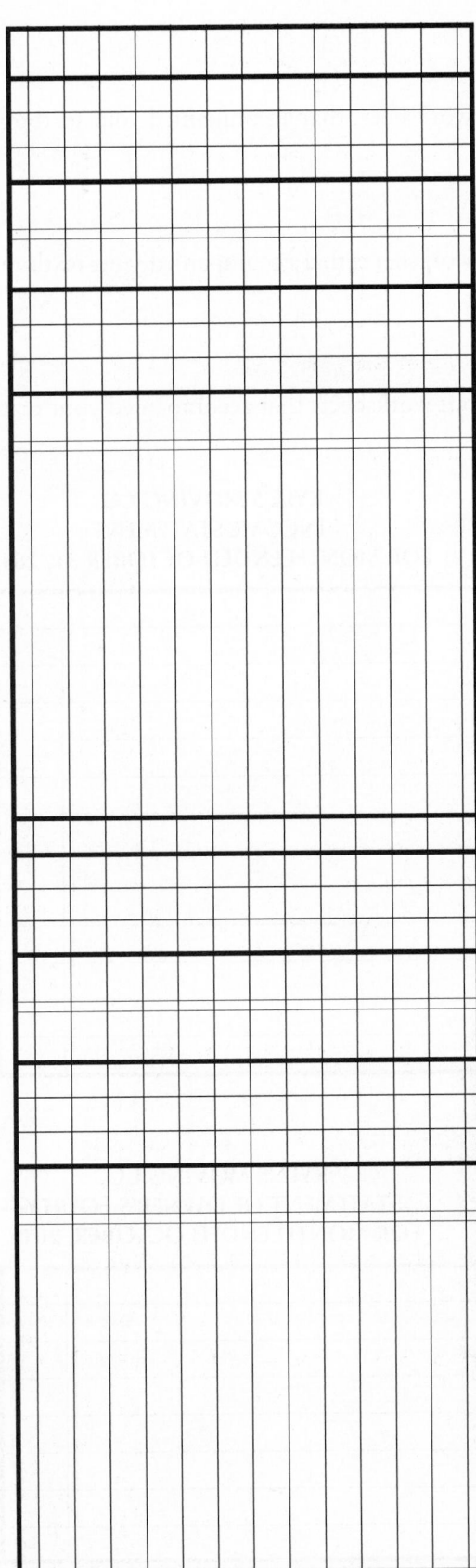

DAMON'S REPAIR SERVICE
BALANCE SHEET
APRIL 30, 201X

ASSETS

LIABILITIES AND OWNER'S EQUITY

FORMS FOR SET B PROBLEMS

PROBLEM 4B-1

Use one of the blank fold-out worksheets that accompanied your textbook.

PROBLEM 4B-2

Use one of the blank fold-out worksheets that accompanied your textbook.

PROBLEM 4B-3

(1) Use one of the blank fold-out worksheets that accompanied your textbook.

(2)

KYLE'S MOVING CO.
INCOME STATEMENT
FOR MONTH ENDED OCTOBER 31, 201X

KYLE'S MOVING CO.
STATEMENT OF OWNER'S EQUITY
FOR MONTH ENDED OCTOBER, 201X

PROBLEM 4B-3 (CONCLUDED)

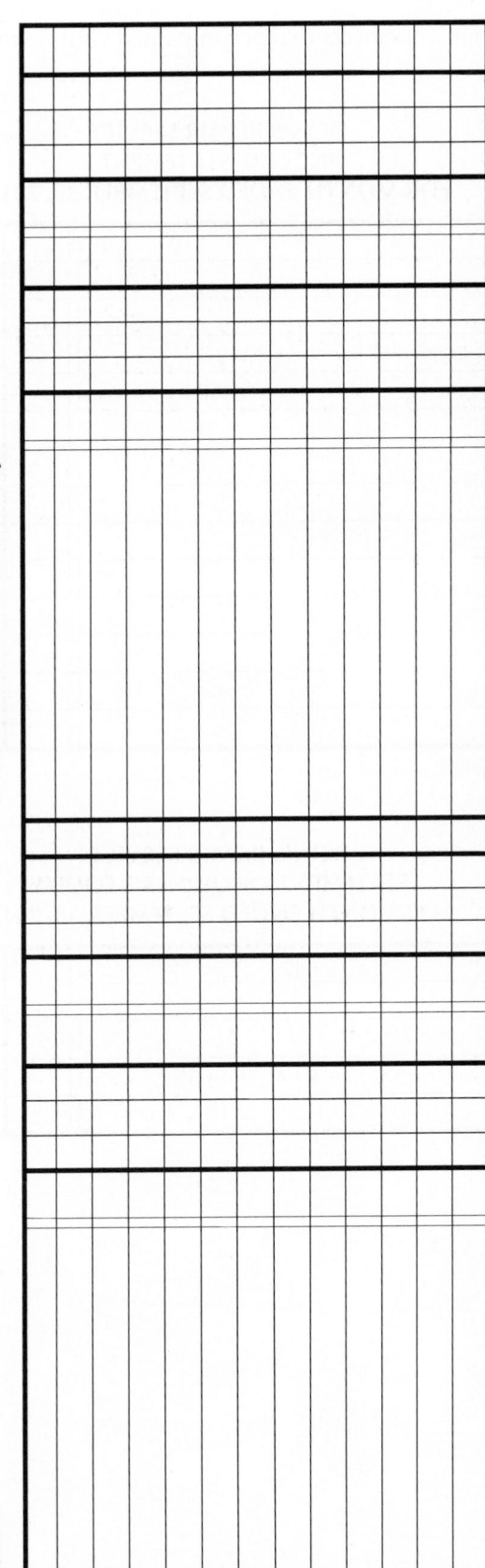

KYLE'S MOVING CO.
BALANCE SHEET
OCTOBER 31, 201X

LIABILITIES AND OWNER'S EQUITY

ASSETS

PROBLEM 4B-4

(1) Use one of the blank fold-out worksheets that accompanied your textbook.

(2)

DON'S REPAIR SERVICE
INCOME STATEMENT
FOR MONTH ENDED SEPTEMBER 30, 201X

DON'S REPAIR SERVICE
STATEMENT OF OWNER'S EQUITY
FOR MONTH ENDED SEPTEMBER 30, 201X

PROBLEM 4B-4 (CONCLUDED)

DON'S REPAIR SERVICE
BALANCE SHEET
SEPTEMBER 30, 201X

ASSETS

LIABILITIES AND OWNER'S EQUITY

ON THE JOB CONTINUING PROBLEM

ASSIGNMENT

Use the blank fold-out worksheet for Chapter 4 that accompanied your textbook. Complete the worksheet using the trial balance below.

SMITH COMPUTER CENTER
TRIAL BALANCE
SEPTEMBER 30, 201X

		Dr.					Cr.			
Cash	2	1	2	0	00					
Accounts Receivable	2	7	0	0	00					
Prepaid Rent	1	5	0	0	00					
Supplies		5	0	0	00					
Computer Shop Equipment	3	9	0	0	00					
Office Equipment	3	3	0	0	00					
Accounts Payable							1	7	0	00
Feldman, Capital						6	0	0	0	00
Feldman, Withdrawals		1	7	5	00					
Service Revenue						10	2	2	0	00
Advertising Expense		9	0	0	00					
Rent Expense		5	0	0	00					
Utilities Expense		1	6	0	00					
Phone Expense		1	1	5	00					
Insurance Expense		4	5	0	00					
Postage Expense			7	0	00					
Totals	16	3	9	0	00	16	3	9	0	00

ON THE JOB CONTINUING PROBLEM

SMITH COMPUTER CENTER
INCOME STATEMENT
FOR THE THREE MONTHS ENDED SEPTEMBER 30, 201X

SMITH COMPUTER CENTER
STATEMENT OF OWNER'S EQUITY
FOR THE THREE MONTHS ENDED SEPTEMBER 30, 201X

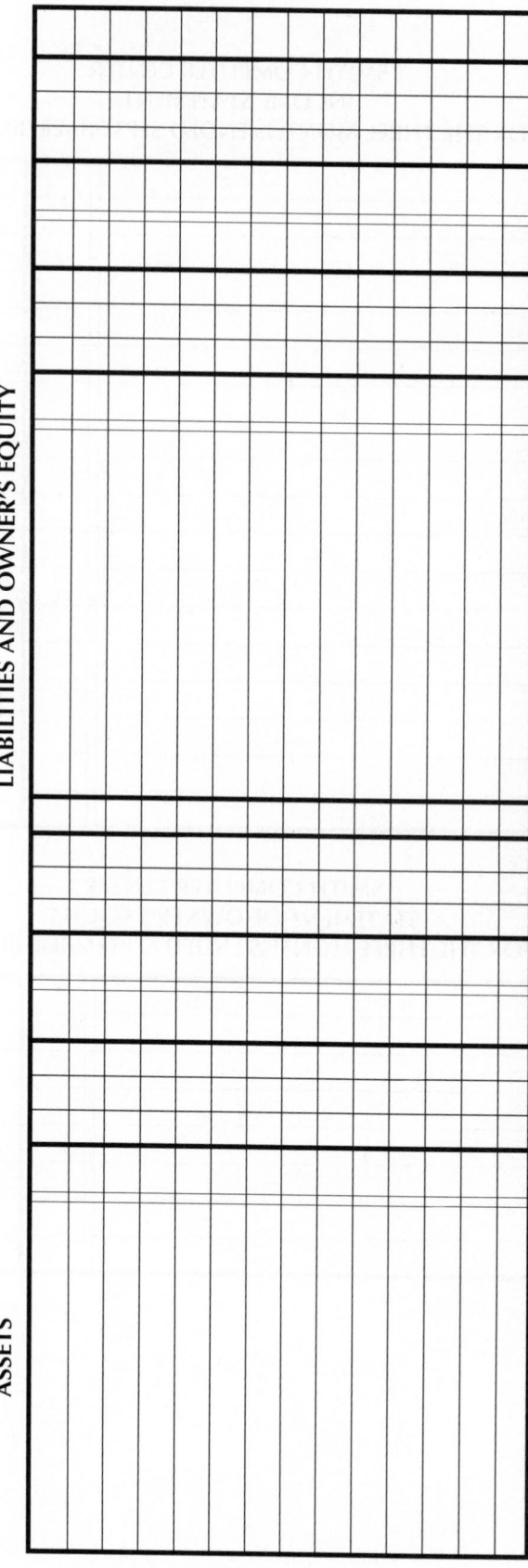

SMITH COMPUTER CENTER
BALANCE SHEET
SEPTEMBER 30, 201X

ASSETS

LIABILITIES AND OWNER'S EQUITY

CHAPTER 4
SUMMARY PRACTICE TEST:
THE ACCOUNTING CYCLE CONTINUED

Part I

Fill in the blank(s) to complete the statement.

1. _____ is an estimate.
2. A(n) _____ will decrease accumulated depreciation.
3. _____ affect both the income statement and balance sheet.
4. The adjustment for supplies reflects the amount of supplies _____ _____.
5. Supplies Expense is found on the income statement. Supplies are found on the _____ _____.
6. _____ _____ reflects the cost of equipment at time of purchase.
7. Depreciation Expense is found on the _____ _____.
8. _____ _____ is a contra asset that has a credit balance.
9. Accumulated Depreciation, a contra asset, is found on the _____ _____.
10. Historical or original cost of an auto less _____ _____ reflects the unused amount of the auto on the accounting books.
11. Withdrawals are found in the _____ column of the balance sheet section of the worksheet.
12. Salaries Payable is a liability that will appear in the _____ _____ _____ _____ of the worksheet.
13. The figure for net income on the worksheet is carried over to the _____ column of the balance sheet.
14. A worksheet is a(n) _____ report.
15. _____ _____ are prepared after the completion of the worksheet.

Part II

Complete the following statements by circling the letter of the appropriate answer.

1. The adjustment for depreciation results in Accumulated Depreciation
   a. decreasing.
   b. staying the same.
   c. increasing.

2. The historical or original cost of an asset on the worksheet
   a. never changes.
   b. sometimes changes.
   c. continually changes.

3. Net income on the worksheet is carried over to the
   a. trial balance.
   b. adjusted trial balance.
   c. balance sheet column.

4. Accumulated Depreciation is found on
   a. a worksheet.
   b. an income statement.
   c. both a worksheet and an income statement.

5. Accumulated Depreciation, a contra asset, is increased by a
   a. debit.
   b. credit.
   c. both a and b.

6. A worksheet is usually completed
   a. one column at a time.
   b. two columns at a time.
   c. three columns at a time.

7. Withdrawals on the worksheet are found in the
   a. debit column of the income statement.
   b. debit column of the balance sheet.
   c. both a and b.

8. The worksheet specifically shows the
   a. beginning figure for owner's capital.
   b. ending figure for owner's capital.
   c. average figure for owner's capital.

9. The balance sheet will report Depreciation Expense and Accumulated Depreciation.
   a. always
   b. sometimes
   c. never

10. The adjustment for depreciation affects
    a. the income statement.
    b. the balance sheet.
    c. both a and b.

11. The adjustment for supplies requires one to know
    a. beginning supplies plus supplies purchased.
    b. supplies on hand.
    c. both a and b.

12. The purpose of adjustments is to

    a. adjust accounts on the balance sheet.

    b. adjust accounts on the income statement.

    c. both a. and b.

13. The book value of equipment equals cost less

    a. expenses.

    b. accumulated depreciation.

    c. neither a nor b.

14. The _____ is an informal report.

    a. income statement

    b. balance sheet

    c. worksheet

Part III

Answer true or false to the following statements.

1. The normal balance of accumulated depreciation is a credit.
2. Liabilities are only income statement accounts.
3. The total of the adjustments columns on the worksheet may balance but be incorrect.
4. Prepaid rent is found on the income statement.
5. Rent expense is found on the income statement.
6. Debits and credits are found on financial statements.
7. Historical cost relates only to automobiles.
8. Accumulated Depreciation is found on the income statement.
9. As Accumulated Depreciation increases, the historical cost changes.
10. The adjustment for depreciation directly affects cash.
11. An expense is only recorded when it is paid.
12. The ending figure for owner's capital is found in the trial balance columns of the worksheet.
13. Withdrawals have the same balance as Accumulated Depreciation.
14. Salaries Payable is an asset on the income statement.
15. Net loss would never be shown on a worksheet.
16. The net income on the worksheet is the same amount on the income statement.
17. Worksheets must use dollar signs.
18. The worksheet eliminates the need to prepare financial statements.
19. Cost less accumulated depreciation equals book value.
20. Accrued salaries payable are an asset on the balance sheet.

SOLUTIONS

Part I

1.	Depreciation Expense	9.	balance sheet
2.	sale of a plant asset	10.	accumulated depreciation
3.	Adjustments	11.	debit
4.	used up	12.	balance sheet credit column
5.	balance sheet	13.	credit
6.	Historical (original) cost	14.	informal
7.	income statement	15.	Financial statements
8.	Accumulated Depreciation		

Part II

1.	c	6.	b	11.	c		
2.	a	7.	b	12.	c		
3.	c	8.	a	13.	b		
4.	a	9.	c	14.	c		
5.	b	10.	c				

Part III

1.	true	6.	false	11.	false	16.	true
2.	false	7.	false	12.	false	17.	false
3.	true	8.	false	13.	false	18.	false
4.	false	9.	false	14.	false	19.	true
5.	true	10.	false	15.	false	20.	false

The Accounting Cycle Completed

CHAPTER 5

FORMS FOR DEMONSTRATION PROBLEM

(1)

ROLO COMPANY
GENERAL JOURNAL

PAGE 1

Date	Account Titles and Description	PR	Dr.	Cr.

FORMS FOR DEMONSTRATION PROBLEM (CONTINUED)

ROLO COMPANY
GENERAL JOURNAL

PAGE 2

Date		Account Titles and Description	PR	Dr.		Cr.	

FORMS FOR DEMONSTRATION PROBLEM (CONTINUED)

CASH   ACCOUNT NO. 111

Date	Explanation	Post Ref.	Debit	Credit	Balance Debit	Balance Credit

ACCOUNTS RECEIVABLE   ACCOUNT NO. 112

Date	Explanation	Post Ref.	Debit	Credit	Balance Debit	Balance Credit

PREPAID RENT   ACCOUNT NO. 114

Date	Explanation	Post Ref.	Debit	Credit	Balance Debit	Balance Credit

OFFICE SUPPLIES   ACCOUNT NO. 115

Date	Explanation	Post Ref.	Debit	Credit	Balance Debit	Balance Credit

FORMS FOR DEMONSTRATION PROBLEM (CONTINUED)

OFFICE EQUIPMENT   **ACCOUNT NO. 121**

Date		Explanation	Post Ref.	Debit	Credit	Balance	
						Debit	Credit

ACCUMULATED DEPRECIATION, OFFICE EQUIPMENT   ACCOUNT NO. 122

Date		Explanation	Post Ref.	Debit	Credit	Balance	
						Debit	Credit

ACCOUNTS PAYABLE   **ACCOUNT NO. 211**

Date		Explanation	Post Ref.	Debit	Credit	Balance	
						Debit	Credit

FORMS FOR DEMONSTRATION PROBLEM (CONTINUED)

SALARIES PAYABLE   **ACCOUNT NO. 212**

Date		Explanation	Post Ref.	Debit	Credit	Balance Debit	Balance Credit

R. KERN, CAPITAL   **ACCOUNT NO. 311**

Date		Explanation	Post Ref.	Debit	Credit	Balance Debit	Balance Credit

R. KERN, WITHDRAWALS   **ACCOUNT NO. 312**

Date		Explanation	Post Ref.	Debit	Credit	Balance Debit	Balance Credit

INCOME SUMMARY   **ACCOUNT NO. 313**

Date		Explanation	Post Ref.	Debit	Credit	Balance Debit	Balance Credit

FEES EARNED   **ACCOUNT NO. 411**

Date		Explanation	Post Ref.	Debit	Credit	Balance Debit	Balance Credit

FORMS FOR DEMONSTRATION PROBLEM (CONTINUED)

SALARIES EXPENSE   ACCOUNT NO. 511

Date	Explanation	Post Ref.	Debit	Credit	Balance	
					Debit	Credit

ADVERTISING EXPENSE   ACCOUNT NO. 512

Date	Explanation	Post Ref.	Debit	Credit	Balance	
					Debit	Credit

RENT EXPENSE   ACCOUNT NO. 513

Date	Explanation	Post Ref.	Debit	Credit	Balance	
					Debit	Credit

OFFICE SUPPLIES EXPENSE   ACCOUNT NO. 514

Date	Explanation	Post Ref.	Debit	Credit	Balance	
					Debit	Credit

DEPRECIATION EXPENSE, OFFICE EQUIPMENT   ACCOUNT NO. 515

Date	Explanation	Post Ref.	Debit	Credit	Balance	
					Debit	Credit

FORMS FOR DEMONSTRATION PROBLEM (CONTINUED)

(2)   Use one of the blank fold-out worksheets that accompanied your textbook.

(3)

ROLO COMPANY
INCOME STATEMENT
FOR MONTH ENDED JANUARY 31, 201X

ROLO COMPANY
STATEMENT OF OWNER'S EQUITY
FOR MONTH ENDED JANUARY 31, 201X

FORMS FOR DEMONSTRATION PROBLEM (CONTINUED)

ROLO COMPANY
BALANCE SHEET
JANUARY 31, 201X

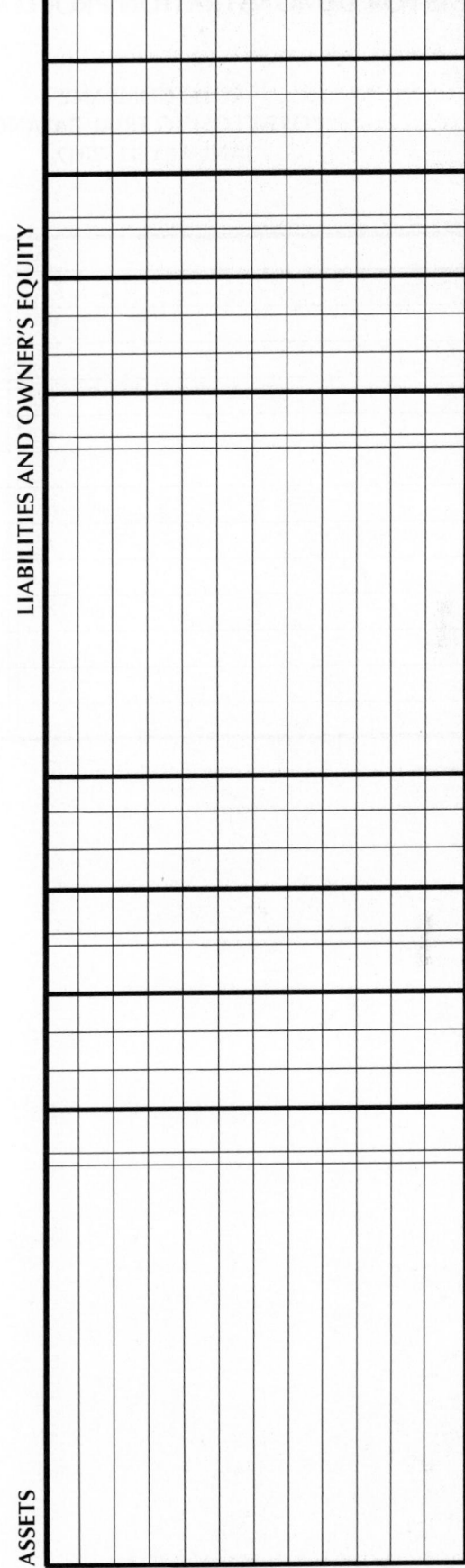

ASSETS

LIABILITIES AND OWNER'S EQUITY

FORMS FOR DEMONSTRATION PROBLEM (CONCLUDED)

(4)

ROLO COMPANY
POST-CLOSING TRIAL BALANCE
JANUARY 31, 201X

	Dr.	Cr.

FORMS FOR SET A EXERCISES

5A-1

Date		Account Titles and Description	PR		Dr.		Cr.

5A-2

	TEMPORARY	PERMANENT	WILL BE CLOSED
1. Income Summary			
2. Jan Ralls, Capital			
3. Rent Expense			
4. Jan Ralls, Withdrawals			
5. Fees Earned			
6. Accounts Payable			
7. Cash			

SET A EXERCISES

5A-3

Date		Account Titles and Description	PR		Dr.		Cr.

SET A EXERCISES

5A-4

Date	Account Titles and Description	PR	Dr.	Cr.

5A-5

WURLEY CO.
POST-CLOSING TRIAL BALANCE
MARCH 31, 201X

	Dr.	Cr.

FORMS FOR SET B EXERCISES

5B-1

Date	Account Titles and Description	PR	Dr.	Cr.

5B-2

	TEMPORARY	PERMANENT	WILL BE CLOSED
1. Income Summary			
2. Jen Rich, Capital			
3. Salary Expense			
4. Jen Rich, Withdrawals			
5. Fees Earned			
6. Accounts Payable			
7. Cash			

SET B EXERCISES

5B-3

Date	Account Titles and Description	PR	Dr.	Cr.

SET B EXERCISES

5B-4

Date		Account Titles and Description	PR	Dr.	Cr.

5B-5

WASHINGTON CO.
POST-CLOSING TRIAL BALANCE
DECEMBER 31, 201X

	Dr.	Cr.

FORMS FOR SET A PROBLEMS

PROBLEM 5A-1

(1)   Use one of the blank fold-out worksheets that accompanied your textbook.

(2)

DREW'S DANCE STUDIO
GENERAL JOURNAL

PAGE 3

Date	Account Titles and Description	PR	Dr.	Cr.

PROBLEM 5A-2

(1)

PARKHOUSE'S CLEANING SERVICE
GENERAL JOURNAL

PAGE 2

Date	Account Titles and Description	PR	Dr.	Cr.

PROBLEM 5A-2 (CONTINUED)

CASH   ACCOUNT NO. 112

Date	Explanation	Post Ref.	Debit	Credit	Balance	
					Debit	Credit

PREPAID INSURANCE   ACCOUNT NO. 114

Date	Explanation	Post Ref.	Debit	Credit	Balance	
					Debit	Credit

CLEANING SUPPLIES   ACCOUNT NO. 115

Date	Explanation	Post Ref.	Debit	Credit	Balance	
					Debit	Credit

AUTO   ACCOUNT NO. 121

Date	Explanation	Post Ref.	Debit	Credit	Balance	
					Debit	Credit

ACCUMULATED DEPRECIATION, AUTO   ACCOUNT NO. 122

Date	Explanation	Post Ref.	Debit	Credit	Balance	
					Debit	Credit

PROBLEM 5A-2 (CONTINUED)

ACCOUNTS PAYABLE   ACCOUNT NO. 212

Date	Explanation	Post Ref.	Debit	Credit	Balance Debit	Balance Credit

SALARIES PAYABLE   ACCOUNT NO. 213

Date	Explanation	Post Ref.	Debit	Credit	Balance Debit	Balance Credit

B. PARKHOUSE, CAPITAL   ACCOUNT NO. 312

Date	Explanation	Post Ref.	Debit	Credit	Balance Debit	Balance Credit

B. PARKHOUSE, WITHDRAWALS   ACCOUNT NO. 313

Date	Explanation	Post Ref.	Debit	Credit	Balance Debit	Balance Credit

INCOME SUMMARY   ACCOUNT NO. 314

Date	Explanation	Post Ref.	Debit	Credit	Balance Debit	Balance Credit

PROBLEM 5A-2 (CONTINUED)

CLEANING FEES   ACCOUNT NO. 412

Date	Explanation	Post Ref.	Debit	Credit	Balance Debit	Balance Credit

SALARIES EXPENSE   ACCOUNT NO. 513

Date	Explanation	Post Ref.	Debit	Credit	Balance Debit	Balance Credit

TELEPHONE EXPENSE   ACCOUNT NO. 514

Date	Explanation	Post Ref.	Debit	Credit	Balance Debit	Balance Credit

ADVERTISING EXPENSE   ACCOUNT NO. 515

Date	Explanation	Post Ref.	Debit	Credit	Balance Debit	Balance Credit

GAS EXPENSE   ACCOUNT NO. 516

Date	Explanation	Post Ref.	Debit	Credit	Balance Debit	Balance Credit

PROBLEM 5A-2 (CONTINUED)

INSURANCE EXPENSE **ACCOUNT NO. 517**

Date	Explanation	Post Ref.	Debit	Credit	Balance Debit	Balance Credit

CLEANING SUPPLIES EXPENSE **ACCOUNT NO. 518**

Date	Explanation	Post Ref.	Debit	Credit	Balance Debit	Balance Credit

DEPRECIATION EXPENSE, AUTO **ACCOUNT NO. 519**

Date	Explanation	Post Ref.	Debit	Credit	Balance Debit	Balance Credit

PROBLEM 5A-2 (CONCLUDED)

(2)

PARKHOUSE'S CLEANING SERVICE
POST-CLOSING TRIAL BALANCE
DECEMBER 31, 201X

	Dr.	Cr.

PROBLEM 5A-3

Use one of the blank fold-out worksheets that accompanied your textbook.

PROBLEM 5A-3 (CONTINUED)

PAT'S PLOWING
GENERAL JOURNAL

PAGE 1

Date	Account Titles and Description	PR	Dr.	Cr.

PROBLEM 5A-3 (CONTINUED)

PAT'S PLOWING
GENERAL JOURNAL

PAGE 2

Date	Account Titles and Description	PR	Dr.	Cr.

PROBLEM 5A-3 (CONTINUED)

PAT'S PLOWING
GENERAL JOURNAL

PAGE 3

Date	Account Titles and Description	PR	Dr.	Cr.

PROBLEM 5A-3 (CONTINUED)

CASH   ACCOUNT NO. 111

Date	Explanation	Post Ref.	Debit	Credit	Balance	
					Debit	Credit

ACCOUNTS RECEIVABLE   ACCOUNT NO. 112

Date	Explanation	Post Ref.	Debit	Credit	Balance	
					Debit	Credit

PREPAID RENT   ACCOUNT NO. 114

Date	Explanation	Post Ref.	Debit	Credit	Balance	
					Debit	Credit

SNOW SUPPLIES   ACCOUNT NO. 115

Date	Explanation	Post Ref.	Debit	Credit	Balance	
					Debit	Credit

PROBLEM 5A-3 (CONTINUED)

OFFICE EQUIPMENT   ACCOUNT NO. 121

Date		Explanation	Post Ref.	Debit	Credit	Balance	
						Debit	Credit

ACCUMULATED DEPRECIATION, OFFICE EQUIPMENT   ACCOUNT NO. 122

Date		Explanation	Post Ref.	Debit	Credit	Balance	
						Debit	Credit

SNOW EQUIPMENT   ACCOUNT NO. 123

Date		Explanation	Post Ref.	Debit	Credit	Balance	
						Debit	Credit

ACCUMULATED DEPRECIATION, SNOW EQUIPMENT   ACCOUNT NO. 124

Date		Explanation	Post Ref.	Debit	Credit	Balance	
						Debit	Credit

ACCOUNTS PAYABLE   ACCOUNT NO. 211

Date		Explanation	Post Ref.	Debit	Credit	Balance	
						Debit	Credit

PROBLEM 5A-3 (CONTINUED)

SALARIES PAYABLE   ACCOUNT NO. 212

Date	Explanation	Post Ref.	Debit	Credit	Balance Debit	Balance Credit

P. MUNRO, CAPITAL   ACCOUNT NO. 311

Date	Explanation	Post Ref.	Debit	Credit	Balance Debit	Balance Credit

P. MUNRO, WITHDRAWALS   ACCOUNT NO. 312

Date	Explanation	Post Ref.	Debit	Credit	Balance Debit	Balance Credit

INCOME SUMMARY   ACCOUNT NO. 313

Date	Explanation	Post Ref.	Debit	Credit	Balance Debit	Balance Credit

PLOWING FEES   ACCOUNT NO. 411

Date	Explanation	Post Ref.	Debit	Credit	Balance Debit	Balance Credit

PROBLEM 5A-3 (CONTINUED)

SALARIES EXPENSE   ACCOUNT NO. 511

Date	Explanation	Post Ref.	Debit	Credit	Balance	
					Debit	Credit

ADVERTISING EXPENSE   ACCOUNT NO. 512

Date	Explanation	Post Ref.	Debit	Credit	Balance	
					Debit	Credit

TELEPHONE EXPENSE   ACCOUNT NO. 513

Date	Explanation	Post Ref.	Debit	Credit	Balance	
					Debit	Credit

RENT EXPENSE   ACCOUNT NO. 514

Date	Explanation	Post Ref.	Debit	Credit	Balance	
					Debit	Credit

SNOW SUPPLIES EXPENSE   ACCOUNT NO. 515

Date	Explanation	Post Ref.	Debit	Credit	Balance	
					Debit	Credit

PROBLEM 5A-3 (CONTINUED)

DEPRECIATION EXPENSE, OFFICE EQUIPMENT   ACCOUNT NO. 516

Date	Explanation	Post Ref.	Debit	Credit	Balance Debit	Balance Credit

DEPRECIATION EXPENSE, SNOW EQUIPMENT   ACCOUNT NO. 517

Date	Explanation	Post Ref.	Debit	Credit	Balance Debit	Balance Credit

PROBLEM 5A-3 (CONTINUED)

PAT'S PLOWING
INCOME STATEMENT
FOR MONTH ENDED JANUARY 31, 201X

PAT'S PLOWING
STATEMENT OF OWNER'S EQUITY
FOR MONTH ENDED JANUARY 31, 201X

PROBLEM 5A-3 (CONTINUED)

PAT'S PLOWING
BALANCE SHEET
JANUARY 31, 201X

ASSETS

LIABILITIES AND OWNER'S EQUITY

PROBLEM 5A-3 (CONCLUDED)

PAT'S PLOWING
POST-CLOSING TRIAL BALANCE
JANUARY 31, 201X

		Dr.		Cr.	

FORMS FOR SET B PROBLEMS

PROBLEM 5B-1

(1)   Use one of the blank fold-out worksheets that accompanied your textbook.

(2)

DEB'S DANCE STUDIO
GENERAL JOURNAL

PAGE 3

Date	Account Titles and Description	PR	Dr.	Cr.

PROBLEM 5B-2

(1)

POTTER'S CLEANING SERVICE
GENERAL JOURNAL

PAGE 2

Date	Account Titles and Description	PR	Dr.	Cr.

PROBLEM 5B-2 (CONTINUED)

CASH   **ACCOUNT NO. 112**

Date	Explanation	Post Ref.	Debit	Credit	Balance Debit	Balance Credit

PREPAID INSURANCE   **ACCOUNT NO. 114**

Date	Explanation	Post Ref.	Debit	Credit	Balance Debit	Balance Credit

CLEANING SUPPLIES   **ACCOUNT NO. 115**

Date	Explanation	Post Ref.	Debit	Credit	Balance Debit	Balance Credit

AUTO   **ACCOUNT NO. 121**

Date	Explanation	Post Ref.	Debit	Credit	Balance Debit	Balance Credit

ACCUMULATED DEPRECIATION, AUTO   **ACCOUNT NO. 122**

Date	Explanation	Post Ref.	Debit	Credit	Balance Debit	Balance Credit

PROBLEM 5B-2 (CONTINUED)

ACCOUNTS PAYABLE   ACCOUNT NO. 212

Date		Explanation	Post Ref.	Debit	Credit	Balance	
						Debit	Credit

SALARIES PAYABLE   ACCOUNT NO. 213

Date		Explanation	Post Ref.	Debit	Credit	Balance	
						Debit	Credit

B. POTTER, CAPITAL   ACCOUNT NO. 312

Date		Explanation	Post Ref.	Debit	Credit	Balance	
						Debit	Credit

B. POTTER, WITHDRAWALS   ACCOUNT NO. 313

Date		Explanation	Post Ref.	Debit	Credit	Balance	
						Debit	Credit

INCOME SUMMARY   ACCOUNT NO. 314

Date		Explanation	Post Ref.	Debit	Credit	Balance	
						Debit	Credit

PROBLEM 5B-2 (CONTINUED)

CLEANING FEES   ACCOUNT NO. 412

Date	Explanation	Post Ref.	Debit	Credit	Balance Debit	Balance Credit

SALARIES EXPENSE   ACCOUNT NO. 513

Date	Explanation	Post Ref.	Debit	Credit	Balance Debit	Balance Credit

TELEPHONE EXPENSE   ACCOUNT NO. 514

Date	Explanation	Post Ref.	Debit	Credit	Balance Debit	Balance Credit

ADVERTISING EXPENSE   ACCOUNT NO. 515

Date	Explanation	Post Ref.	Debit	Credit	Balance Debit	Balance Credit

GAS EXPENSE   ACCOUNT NO. 516

Date	Explanation	Post Ref.	Debit	Credit	Balance Debit	Balance Credit

PROBLEM 5B-2 (CONTINUED)

INSURANCE EXPENSE   ACCOUNT NO. 517

Date	Explanation	Post Ref.	Debit	Credit	Balance Debit	Balance Credit

CLEANING SUPPLIES EXPENSE   ACCOUNT NO. 518

Date	Explanation	Post Ref.	Debit	Credit	Balance Debit	Balance Credit

DEPRECIATION EXPENSE, AUTO   ACCOUNT NO. 519

Date	Explanation	Post Ref.	Debit	Credit	Balance Debit	Balance Credit

PROBLEM 5B-2 (CONCLUDED)

(2)

POTTER'S CLEANING SERVICE
POST-CLOSING TRIAL BALANCE
JULY 31, 201X

		Dr.	Cr.

PROBLEM 5B-3

Use one of the blank fold-out worksheets that accompanied your textbook.

PROBLEM 5B-3 (CONTINUED)

PALMER'S PLOWING
GENERAL JOURNAL

PAGE 1

Date	Account Titles and Description	PR	Dr.	Cr.

PROBLEM 5B-3 (CONTINUED)

PALMER'S PLOWING
GENERAL JOURNAL

PAGE 2

Date	Account Titles and Description	PR	Dr.	Cr.

PROBLEM 5B-3 (CONTINUED)

PALMER'S PLOWING
GENERAL JOURNAL

PAGE 3

Date	Account Titles and Description	PR		Dr.			Cr.	

PROBLEM 5B-3 (CONTINUED)

CASH   ACCOUNT NO. 111

Date	Explanation	Post Ref.	Debit	Credit	Balance Debit	Balance Credit

ACCOUNTS RECEIVABLE   ACCOUNT NO. 112

Date	Explanation	Post Ref.	Debit	Credit	Balance Debit	Balance Credit

PREPAID RENT   ACCOUNT NO. 114

Date	Explanation	Post Ref.	Debit	Credit	Balance Debit	Balance Credit

SNOW SUPPLIES   ACCOUNT NO. 115

Date	Explanation	Post Ref.	Debit	Credit	Balance Debit	Balance Credit

PROBLEM 5B-3 (CONTINUED)

OFFICE EQUIPMENT   ACCOUNT NO. 121

Date	Explanation	Post Ref.	Debit	Credit	Balance Debit	Balance Credit

ACCUMULATED DEPRECIATION, OFFICE EQUIPMENT   ACCOUNT NO. 122

Date	Explanation	Post Ref.	Debit	Credit	Balance Debit	Balance Credit

SNOW EQUIPMENT   ACCOUNT NO. 123

Date	Explanation	Post Ref.	Debit	Credit	Balance Debit	Balance Credit

ACCUMULATED DEPRECIATION, SNOW EQUIPMENT   ACCOUNT NO. 124

Date	Explanation	Post Ref.	Debit	Credit	Balance Debit	Balance Credit

ACCOUNTS PAYABLE   ACCOUNT NO. 211

Date	Explanation	Post Ref.	Debit	Credit	Balance Debit	Balance Credit

PROBLEM 5B-3 (CONTINUED)

SALARIES PAYABLE   **ACCOUNT NO. 212**

Date		Explanation	Post Ref.	Debit	Credit	Balance	
						Debit	Credit

P. MAO, CAPITAL   **ACCOUNT NO. 311**

Date		Explanation	Post Ref.	Debit	Credit	Balance	
						Debit	Credit

P. MAO, WITHDRAWALS   **ACCOUNT NO. 312**

Date		Explanation	Post Ref.	Debit	Credit	Balance	
						Debit	Credit

INCOME SUMMARY   **ACCOUNT NO. 313**

Date		Explanation	Post Ref.	Debit	Credit	Balance	
						Debit	Credit

PLOWING FEES   **ACCOUNT NO. 411**

Date		Explanation	Post Ref.	Debit	Credit	Balance	
						Debit	Credit

PROBLEM 5B-3 (CONTINUED)

SALARIES EXPENSE   ACCOUNT NO. 511

Date	Explanation	Post Ref.	Debit	Credit	Balance Debit	Balance Credit

ADVERTISING EXPENSE   ACCOUNT NO. 512

Date	Explanation	Post Ref.	Debit	Credit	Balance Debit	Balance Credit

TELEPHONE EXPENSE   ACCOUNT NO. 513

Date	Explanation	Post Ref.	Debit	Credit	Balance Debit	Balance Credit

RENT EXPENSE   ACCOUNT NO. 514

Date	Explanation	Post Ref.	Debit	Credit	Balance Debit	Balance Credit

SNOW SUPPLIES EXPENSE   ACCOUNT NO. 515

Date	Explanation	Post Ref.	Debit	Credit	Balance Debit	Balance Credit

PROBLEM 5B-3 (CONTINUED)

DEPRECIATION EXPENSE, OFFICE EQUIPMENT   ACCOUNT NO. 516

Date	Explanation	Post Ref.	Debit	Credit	Balance Debit	Balance Credit

DEPRECIATION EXPENSE, SNOW EQUIPMENT   ACCOUNT NO. 517

Date	Explanation	Post Ref.	Debit	Credit	Balance Debit	Balance Credit

PROBLEM 5B-3 (CONTINUED)

PALMER'S PLOWING
INCOME STATEMENT
FOR MONTH ENDED JANUARY 31, 201X

PALMER'S PLOWING
STATEMENT OF OWNER'S EQUITY
FOR MONTH ENDED JANUARY 31, 201X

PROBLEM 5B-3 (CONTINUED)

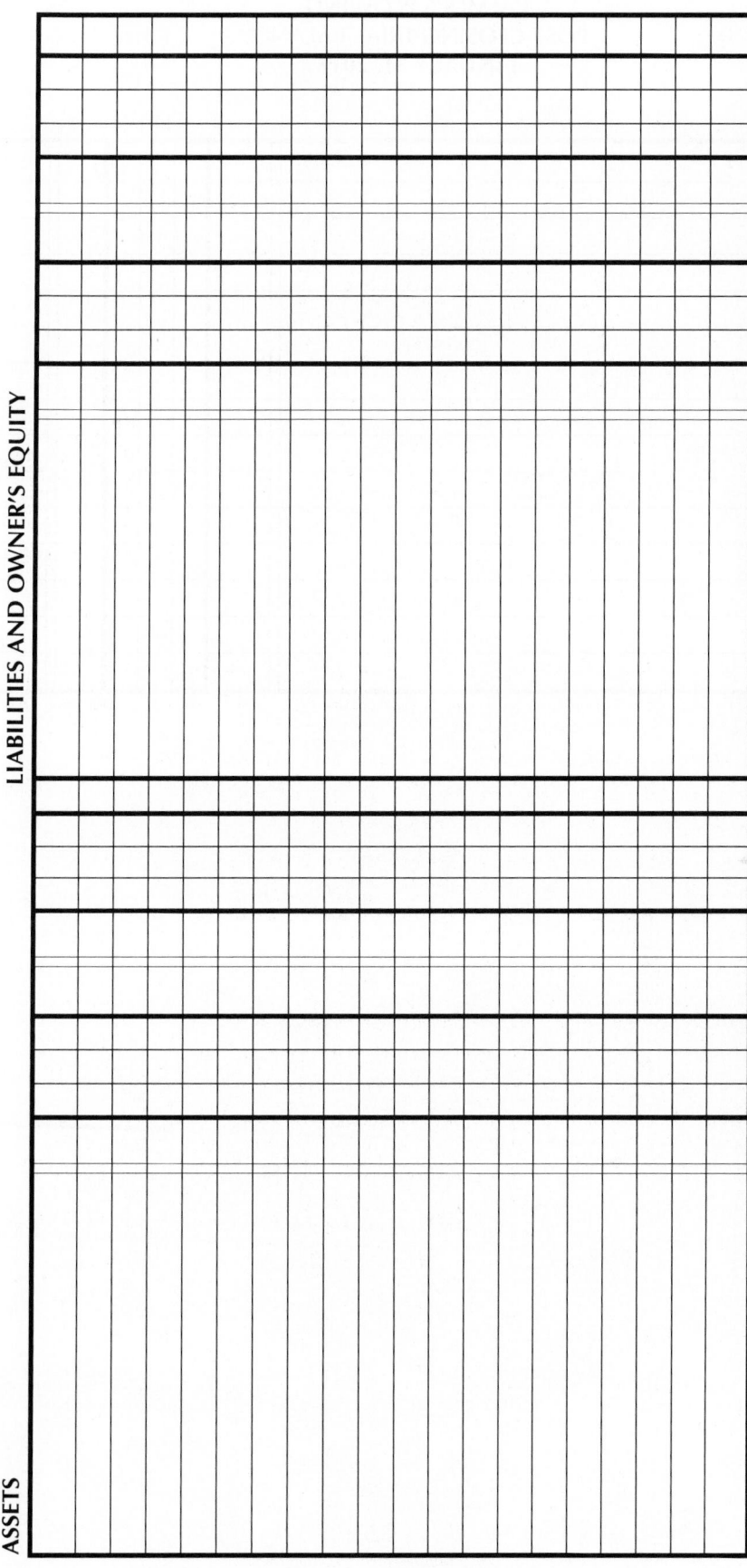

PALMER'S PLOWING
BALANCE SHEET
JANUARY 31, 201X

LIABILITIES AND OWNER'S EQUITY

ASSETS

PROBLEM 5B-3 (CONCLUDED)

PALMER'S PLOWING
POST-CLOSING TRIAL BALANCE
JANUARY 31, 201X

	Dr.	Cr.

ON THE JOB CONTINUING PROBLEM

ASSIGNMENTS 1, 3

SMITH COMPUTER CENTER
GENERAL JOURNAL

PAGE 2

Date	Account Titles and Description	PR	Dr.	Cr.

ASSIGNMENTS 2, 4

CASH — ACCOUNT NO. 1000

Date		Explanation	Post Ref.	Debit	Credit	Balance Debit	Balance Credit
9/30	1X	Balance forward	✔			2 1 2 0 00	

ACCOUNTS RECEIVABLE — ACCOUNT NO. 1020

Date		Explanation	Post Ref.	Debit	Credit	Balance Debit	Balance Credit
9/30	1X	Balance forward	✔			2 7 0 0 00	

PREPAID RENT — ACCOUNT NO. 1025

Date		Explanation	Post Ref.	Debit	Credit	Balance Debit	Balance Credit
9/30	1X	Balance forward	✔			1 5 0 0 00	

SUPPLIES — ACCOUNT NO. 1030

Date		Explanation	Post Ref.	Debit	Credit	Balance Debit	Balance Credit
9/30	1X	Balance forward	✔			5 0 0 00	

COMPUTER SHOP EQUIPMENT   ACCOUNT NO. 1080

Date		Explanation	Post Ref.	Debit	Credit	Balance	
						Debit	Credit
9/30	1X	Balance forward	✔			3 9 0 0 00	

ACCUMULATED DEPRECIATION, COMPUTER SHOP EQUIPMENT   ACCOUNT NO. 1081

Date		Explanation	Post Ref.	Debit	Credit	Balance	
						Debit	Credit

OFFICE EQUIPMENT   ACCOUNT NO. 1090

Date		Explanation	Post Ref.	Debit	Credit	Balance	
						Debit	Credit
9/30	1X	Balance forward	✔			3 3 0 0 00	

ACCUMULATED DEPRECIATION, OFFICE EQUIPMENT   ACCOUNT NO. 1091

Date		Explanation	Post Ref.	Debit	Credit	Balance	
						Debit	Credit

ACCOUNTS PAYABLE   ACCOUNT NO. 2000

Date		Explanation	Post Ref.	Debit	Credit	Balance	
						Debit	Credit
9/30	1X	Balance forward	✔				1 7 0 00

T. FELDMAN, CAPITAL   ACCOUNT NO. 3000

Date		Explanation	Post Ref.	Debit	Credit	Balance	
						Debit	Credit
9/30	1X	Balance forward	✔				6 0 0 0 00

T. FELDMAN, WITHDRAWALS   ACCOUNT NO. 3010

Date		Explanation	Post Ref.	Debit	Credit	Balance	
						Debit	Credit
9/30	1X	Balance forward	✔			1 7 5 00	

INCOME SUMMARY   ACCOUNT NO. <u>3020</u>

Date		Explanation	Post Ref.	Debit	Credit	Balance Debit	Balance Credit

SERVICE REVENUE   ACCOUNT NO. <u>4000</u>

Date		Explanation	Post Ref.	Debit	Credit	Balance Debit	Balance Credit
9/30	1X	Balance forward	✔				10 2 2 0 00

ADVERTISING EXPENSE   ACCOUNT NO. <u>5010</u>

Date		Explanation	Post Ref.	Debit	Credit	Balance Debit	Balance Credit
9/30	1X	Balance forward	✔			9 0 0 00	

RENT EXPENSE   ACCOUNT NO. <u>5020</u>

Date		Explanation	Post Ref.	Debit	Credit	Balance Debit	Balance Credit
9/30	1X	Balance forward	✔			5 0 0 00	

UTILITIES EXPENSE   ACCOUNT NO. 5030

Date		Explanation	Post Ref.	Debit	Credit	Balance	
						Debit	Credit
9/30	1X	Balance forward	✔			1 6 0 00	

PHONE EXPENSE   ACCOUNT NO. 5040

Date		Explanation	Post Ref.	Debit	Credit	Balance	
						Debit	Credit
9/30	1X	Balance forward	✔			1 1 5 00	

SUPPLIES EXPENSE   ACCOUNT NO. 5050

Date		Explanation	Post Ref.	Debit	Credit	Balance	
						Debit	Credit

INSURANCE EXPENSE   ACCOUNT NO. 5060

Date		Explanation	Post Ref.	Debit	Credit	Balance	
						Debit	Credit
9/30	1X	Balance forward	✔			4 5 0 00	

POSTAGE EXPENSE   ACCOUNT NO. 5070

Date		Explanation	Post Ref.	Debit	Credit	Balance	
						Debit	Credit
9/30	1X	Balance forward	✔			7 0 00	

DEPRECIATION EXPENSE, C.S. EQUIPMENT   ACCOUNT NO. 5080

Date		Explanation	Post Ref.	Debit	Credit	Balance	
						Debit	Credit

DEPRECIATION EXPENSE, OFFICE EQUIPMENT   ACCOUNT NO. 5090

Date		Explanation	Post Ref.	Debit	Credit	Balance	
						Debit	Credit

ASSIGNMENT 5

SMITH COMPUTER CENTER
POST-CLOSING TRIAL BALANCE
SEPTEMBER 30, 201X

	Dr.	Cr.

MINI PRACTICE SET
SOUSA REALTY

(1)

SOUSA REALTY
GENERAL JOURNAL

PAGE 1

Date	Account Titles and Description	PR	Dr.	Cr.

MINI PRACTICE SET
SOUSA REALTY

SOUSA REALTY
GENERAL JOURNAL

PAGE 2

Date	Account Titles and Description	PR	Dr.	Cr.

MINI PRACTICE SET
SOUSA REALTY

SOUSA REALTY
GENERAL JOURNAL

PAGE 3

Date	Account Titles and Description	PR	Dr.	Cr.

MINI PRACTICE SET
SOUSA REALTY

SOUSA REALTY
GENERAL JOURNAL

PAGE 4

Date	Account Titles and Description	PR	Dr.	Cr.

MINI PRACTICE SET
SOUSA REALTY

SOUSA REALTY
GENERAL JOURNAL

PAGE 5

Date	Account Titles and Description	PR	Dr.	Cr.

MINI PRACTICE SET
SOUSA REALTY

SOUSA REALTY
GENERAL JOURNAL

PAGE 6

Date	Account Titles and Description	PR	Dr.	Cr.

MINI PRACTICE SET
SOUSA REALTY

CASH   ACCOUNT NO. <u>111</u>

Date	Explanation	Post Ref.	Debit	Credit	Balance	
					Debit	Credit

MINI PRACTICE SET
SOUSA REALTY

ACCOUNTS RECEIVABLE   ACCOUNT NO. 112

Date	Explanation	Post Ref.	Debit	Credit	Balance Debit	Balance Credit

PREPAID RENT   ACCOUNT NO. 114

Date	Explanation	Post Ref.	Debit	Credit	Balance Debit	Balance Credit

OFFICE SUPPLIES   ACCOUNT NO. 115

Date	Explanation	Post Ref.	Debit	Credit	Balance Debit	Balance Credit

OFFICE EQUIPMENT   ACCOUNT NO. 121

Date	Explanation	Post Ref.	Debit	Credit	Balance Debit	Balance Credit

MINI PRACTICE SET: SOUSA REALTY

ACCUMULATED DEPRECIATION, OFFICE EQUIPMENT   ACCOUNT NO. 122

Date	Explanation	Post Ref.	Debit	Credit	Balance Debit	Balance Credit

AUTOMOBILE   ACCOUNT NO. 123

Date	Explanation	Post Ref.	Debit	Credit	Balance Debit	Balance Credit

ACCUMULATED DEPRECIATION, AUTOMOBILE   ACCOUNT NO. 124

Date	Explanation	Post Ref.	Debit	Credit	Balance Debit	Balance Credit

ACCOUNTS PAYABLE   ACCOUNT NO. 211

Date	Explanation	Post Ref.	Debit	Credit	Balance Debit	Balance Credit

SALARIES PAYABLE   ACCOUNT NO. 212

Date	Explanation	Post Ref.	Debit	Credit	Balance Debit	Balance Credit

MINI PRACTICE SET
SOUSA REALTY

JAMES SOUSA, CAPITAL   ACCOUNT NO. 311

Date	Explanation	Post Ref.	Debit	Credit	Balance Debit	Balance Credit

JAMES SOUSA, WITHDRAWALS   ACCOUNT NO. 312

Date	Explanation	Post Ref.	Debit	Credit	Balance Debit	Balance Credit

INCOME SUMMARY   ACCOUNT NO. 313

Date	Explanation	Post Ref.	Debit	Credit	Balance Debit	Balance Credit

MINI PRACTICE SET
SOUSA REALTY

COMMISSIONS EARNED   ACCOUNT NO. 411

Date	Explanation	Post Ref.	Debit	Credit	Balance Debit	Balance Credit

RENT EXPENSE   ACCOUNT NO. 511

Date	Explanation	Post Ref.	Debit	Credit	Balance Debit	Balance Credit

SALARIES EXPENSE   ACCOUNT NO. 512

Date	Explanation	Post Ref.	Debit	Credit	Balance Debit	Balance Credit

MINI PRACTICE SET
SOUSA REALTY

GAS EXPENSE   ACCOUNT NO. 513

Date		Explanation	Post Ref.	Debit	Credit	Balance	
						Debit	Credit

REPAIRS EXPENSE   ACCOUNT NO. 514

Date		Explanation	Post Ref.	Debit	Credit	Balance	
						Debit	Credit

TELEPHONE EXPENSE   ACCOUNT NO. 515

Date		Explanation	Post Ref.	Debit	Credit	Balance	
						Debit	Credit

ADVERTISING EXPENSE   ACCOUNT NO. 516

Date		Explanation	Post Ref.	Debit	Credit	Balance	
						Debit	Credit

MINI PRACTICE SET
SOUSA REALTY

OFFICE SUPPLIES EXPENSE   ACCOUNT NO. 517

Date	Explanation	Post Ref.	Debit	Credit	Balance Debit	Balance Credit

DEPRECIATION EXPENSE, OFFICE EQUIPMENT   ACCOUNT NO. 518

Date	Explanation	Post Ref.	Debit	Credit	Balance Debit	Balance Credit

DEPRECIATION EXPENSE, AUTOMOBILE   ACCOUNT NO. 519

Date	Explanation	Post Ref.	Debit	Credit	Balance Debit	Balance Credit

MISCELLANEOUS EXPENSE   ACCOUNT NO. 524

Date	Explanation	Post Ref.	Debit	Credit	Balance Debit	Balance Credit

MINI PRACTICE SET
SOUSA REALTY

(2) Use one of the blank fold-out worksheets that accompanied your textbook.

(3)

SOUSA REALTY
INCOME STATEMENT
FOR MONTH ENDED SEPTEMBER 30, 201X

**MINI PRACTICE SET
SOUSA REALTY**

SOUSA REALTY
STATEMENT OF OWNER'S EQUITY
FOR MONTH ENDED SEPTEMBER 30, 201X

MINI PRACTICE SET
SOUSA REALTY

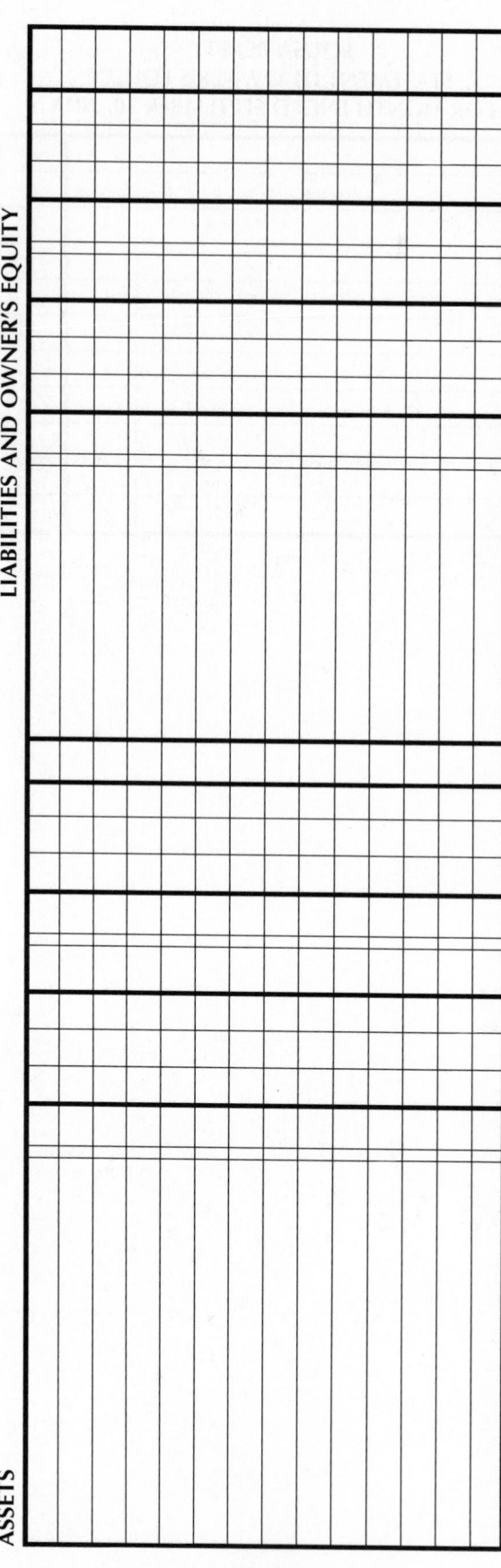

SOUSA REALTY
BALANCE SHEET
SEPTEMBER 30, 201X

ASSETS

LIABILITIES AND OWNER'S EQUITY

MINI PRACTICE SET
SOUSA REALTY

(5)

SOUSA REALTY
POST-CLOSING TRIAL BALANCE
SEPTEMBER 30, 201X

		Dr.	Cr.

MINI PRACTICE SET
SOUSA REALTY

(3)

SOUSA REALTY
INCOME STATEMENT
FOR MONTH ENDED OCTOBER 31, 201X

MINI PRACTICE SET
SOUSA REALTY

SOUSA REALTY
STATEMENT OF OWNER'S EQUITY
FOR MONTH ENDED OCTOBER 31, 201X

MINI PRACTICE SET
SOUSA REALTY

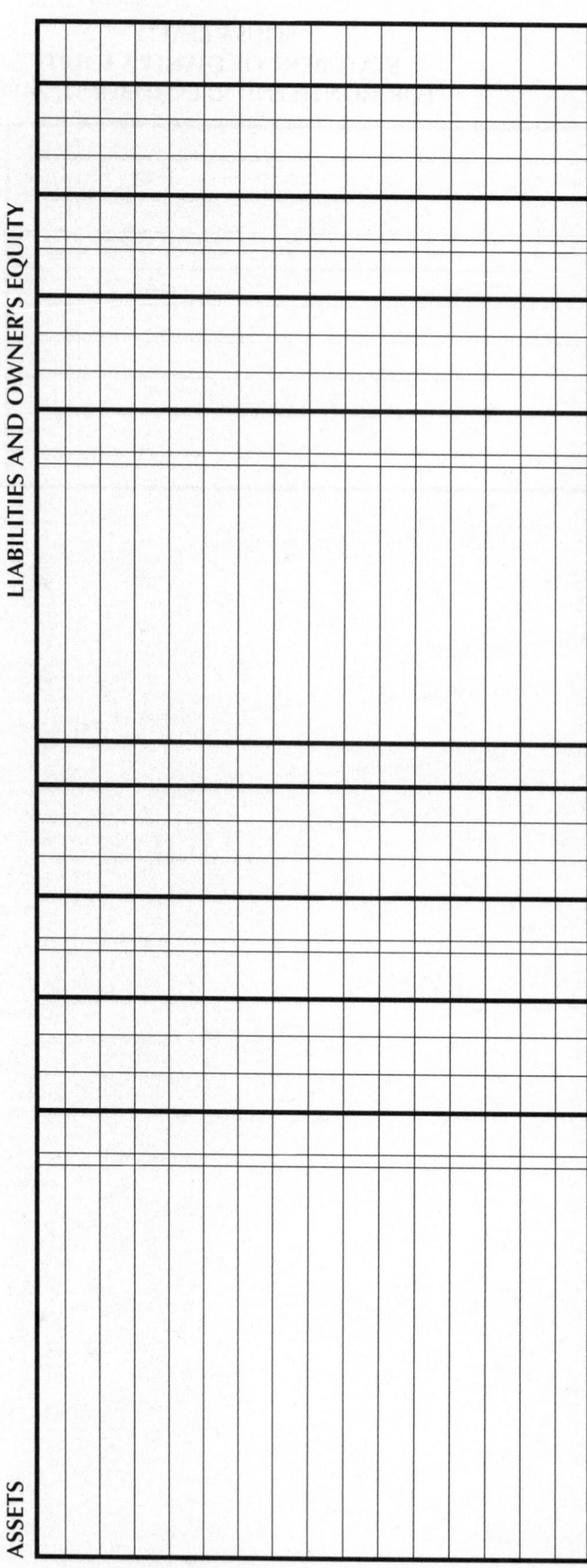

SOUSA REALTY
BALANCE SHEET
OCTOBER 31, 201X

ASSETS

LIABILITIES AND OWNER'S EQUITY

MINI PRACTICE SET
SOUSA REALTY

(5)

SOUSA REALTY
POST-CLOSING TRIAL BALANCE
OCTOBER 31, 201X

	Dr.	Cr.

CHAPTER 5
SUMMARY PRACTICE TEST:
THE ACCOUNTING CYCLE COMPLETED

Part I

Fill in the blank(s) to complete the statement.

1. After the closing process only _____ accounts remain with balances.
2. Revenue, Expenses, and Withdrawals are examples of _____ _____.
3. _____ in temporary accounts will not be carried over to the next accounting period.
4. After closing entries are posted, owner's Capital in the ledger will contain the _____ _____.
5. Revenue is closed to Income Summary by a(n) _____ to each revenue account and a(n) _____ to Income Summary.
6. Expenses are closed to Income Summary by _____ the individual expenses and _____ Income Summary.
7. If the balance of Income Summary is a credit, it will be closed by _____ Income Summary and _____ owner's Capital.
8. The balance of Withdrawals is closed by a(n) _____ and the amount transferred to owner's Capital by a(n) _____.
9. At the end of the closing process, all temporary accounts in the ledger will have a(n) _____ balance.
10. The _____ _____ _____ _____ contains a list of permanent accounts after the adjusting and closing entries have been posted to the ledger from a journal.
11. Closing entries can be prepared from a(n) _____.
12. After closing entries are posted, Income Summary will have a(n) _____ balance.
13. Journalizing adjustments can be done from the _____.
14. Cash, Equipment, and Supplies are not part of the _____ process.
15. Income Summary is a(n) _____ account.

Part II

The following is a chart of accounts for Al's Auto Shop. From the chart, indicate in Column B (by account number) which accounts will be debited or credited as related to the transactions in Column A.

CHART OF ACCOUNTS

ASSETS

112 Cash

114 Accounts Receivable

116 Prepaid Rent

118 Auto Supplies

120 Delivery Truck

121 Accumulated Depreciation, Delivery Truck

LIABILITIES

230 Accounts Payable

232 Salaries Payable

OWNER'S EQUITY

340 A. Jones, Capital

341 A. Jones, Withdrawals

342 Income Summary

REVENUE

450 Fees Earned

EXPENSES

560 Salaries Expense

562 Advertising Expense

564 Rent Expense

566 Auto Supplies Expense

568 Depreciation Expense, Delivery Truck

COLUMN A	COLUMN B Debit(s)	Credit(s)
1. Closed balance in revenue account to Income Summary.	_____	_____
2. Closed balances in individual expenses to Income Summary.	_____	_____
3. Closed balance in Income Summary to owner's Capital. (Assume that it is a net income.)	_____	_____
4. Closed Withdrawals to owner's Capital.	_____	_____
5. Recorded auto supplies used up.	_____	_____
6. Recorded depreciation on delivery truck.	_____	_____
7. Brought Salaries Expense up to date (an adjustment).	_____	_____

Part III

Answer true or false to the following statements.

1. Closing entries are done every other month.
2. Adjustments are journalized before preparing the worksheet.
3. Closing entries can only clear permanent accounts.
4. Income summary is a temporary account.
5. Interim statements can be prepared from worksheets.
6. To close expenses in the closing process, a compound entry is appropriate.
7. Withdrawals is a temporary account on the income statement.
8. Income Summary helps update withdrawals.

9. Accumulated Depreciation is a permanent account on the income statement.

10. Cash, Rent Expense, and Accounts Receivable need to be closed at the end of the period.

11. Closing entries do not relate to the worksheet.

12. Revenue is closed by a credit.

13. Expenses are placed on the debit side of the Income Summary account.

14. A post-closing trial balance closely resembles the ending balance sheet.

15. Accumulated Depreciation never has to be adjusted.

16. Interim statements are always prepared monthly.

17. A post-closing trial balance is prepared before adjustments are journalized.

18. Income Summary is shown on the balance sheet.

19. The process of closing entries will help update owner's Capital.

20. The normal balance of the Income Summary is a debit.

21. The normal balance of the Income Summary is a credit.

22. The income statement is listed in terms of debits and credits.

23. Closing updates only permanent accounts.

24. After the closing process, the balance in Service Revenue is zero.

25. Withdrawals is closed to Income Summary.

SOLUTIONS

Part I

1.	permanent	9.	zero
2.	temporary accounts	10.	post-closing trial balance
3.	Balances	11.	worksheet
4.	ending figure (balance)	12.	zero
5.	debit, credit	13.	worksheet
6.	crediting, debiting	14.	closing
7.	debiting, crediting	15.	temporary
8.	credit, debit		

Part II

	Debit	Credit
1.	450	342
2.	342	560, 562, 564, 566, 568
3.	342	340
4.	340	341
5.	566	118
6.	568	121
7.	560	232

Part III

1.	false	**7.**	false	**13.**	true	**19.**	true	**25.** false
2.	false	**8.**	false	**14.**	true	**20.**	false	
3.	false	**9.**	false	**15.**	false	**21.**	false	
4.	true	**10.**	false	**16.**	false	**22.**	false	
5.	true	**11.**	false	**17.**	false	**23.**	false	
6.	true	**12.**	false	**18.**	false	**24.**	true	

Banking Procedures and Control of Cash

FORMS FOR DEMONSTRATION PROBLEM

(1)

LEE CO.
BANK RECONCILIATION AS OF MARCH 31, 201X

Checkbook Balance		Bank Balance	
Add:		Add:	
Deduct:		Deduct:	
Reconciled Bal.		Reconciled Bal.	

(2)

Date	Account Titles and Description	PR	Dr.	Cr.

FORMS FOR SET A EXERCISES

6A-1

BANG CO.
BANK RECONCILIATION AS OF FEBRUARY 28, 201X

CHECKBOOK BALANCE

Ending Checkbook Balance _____
   Add: _____

_____
_____

Deduct: _____

_____

Reconciled Balance _____

BALANCE PER BANK

Ending Bank Statement Balance _____
   Add: _____

_____
_____

Deduct: _____

_____

Reconciled Balance _____

Date	Account			Dr.	Cr.

6A-2

Date	Account			Dr.	Cr.

6A-3

Date	Account			Dr.	Cr.

SET A EXERCISES

6A-4

Date		Account			Dr.				Cr.		

6A-5

Beg. Change Fund
+Cash Register Total
=Cash should have on hand
– Counted Cash
= Cash Shortage

Date		Account			Dr.				Cr.		

FORMS FOR SET B EXERCISES

6B-1

ZOOM CO.
BANK RECONCILIATION AS OF OCTOBER 31, 201X

CHECKBOOK BALANCE	BALANCE PER BANK
Ending Checkbook Balance _____	Ending Bank Statement Balance _____
Add: _____	Add: _____
_____	_____
_____	_____
Deduct: _____	Deduct: _____
_____	_____
Reconciled Balance _____	Reconciled Balance _____

Date	Account			Dr.		Cr.	

6B-2

Date	Account			Dr.		Cr.	

6B-3

Date	Account			Dr.		Cr.	

SET B EXERCISES

6B-4

Date		Account			Dr.			Cr.		

6B-5

   Beg. Change Fund
+Cash Register Total
=Cash should have on hand
−Counted Cash
= Cash Shortage

Date		Account			Dr.			Cr.		

FORMS FOR SET A PROBLEMS

PROBLEM 6A-1

DENIM.COM
BANK RECONCILIATION AS OF JULY 31, 201X

CHECKBOOK BALANCE

Checkbook Balance

Add:

Deduct:

Reconciled Balance

BALANCE PER BANK

Bank Statement Balance

Add:

Deduct:

Reconciled Balance

PROBLEM 6A-1 (CONCLUDED)

Date		Account Titles and Description	PR		Dr.	Cr.

PROBLEM 6A-2

JOSH'S DELI
BANK RECONCILIATION AS OF FEBRUARY 28, 201X

<u>**CHECKBOOK BALANCE**</u>   <u>**BALANCE PER BANK**</u>

Checkbook Balance   Bank Statement Balance

  Add: Add:

_____   Deduct: _____

Deduct:

_____   _____

Reconciled Balance   ═══════════   Reconciled Balance   ═══════════

PROBLEM 6A-2 (CONCLUDED)

(2)

GENERAL JOURNAL

Date	Account Titles and Description	PR	Dr.	Cr.

PROBLEM 6A-3

(a, b)

EXULTANT CO.
GENERAL JOURNAL

Date		Account Titles and Description	PR	Dr.		Cr.	

PROBLEM 6A-3 (CONCLUDED)

EXULTANT CO.
AUXILIARY PETTY CASH RECORD

Date	Voucher No.	Description	Receipts	Payment	Category of Payment				
					Postage Expense	Office Supplies Expense	Account	Sundry Amount	

PROBLEM 6A-4

ROCHESTER CO.
GENERAL JOURNAL

Date		Account Titles and Description	PR		Dr.				Cr.	

PROBLEM 6A-4 (CONCLUDED)

ROCHESTER CO.
AUXILIARY PETTY CASH RECORD

Date	Voucher No.	Description	Receipts	Payment	Category of Payment				
					Postage Expense	Delivery Expense	Account	Sundry Amount	

FORMS FOR SET B PROBLEMS

PROBLEM 6B-1

WORK.COM
BANK RECONCILIATION AS OF JULY 31, 201X

CHECKBOOK BALANCE   **BALANCE PER BANK**

Checkbook Balance   Bank Statement Balance

  Add: Add:

                            _____   Deduct: _____

  Deduct:

                            _____   _____

Reconciled Balance   _____   Reconciled Balance   _____

PROBLEM 6B-1 (CONCLUDED)

Date	Account Titles and Description	PR	Dr.	Cr.

PROBLEM 6B-2

JACKIE'S DELI
BANK RECONCILIATION AS OF FEBRUARY 28, 201X

CHECKBOOK BALANCE   **BALANCE PER BANK**

Checkbook Balance   Bank Statement Balance

  Add: Add:

                            _____   Deduct: _____

  Deduct:

                            _____   _____

Reconciled Balance   _____   Reconciled Balance   _____

PROBLEM 6B-2 (CONCLUDED)

(2)

GENERAL JOURNAL

Date	Account Titles and Description	PR	Dr.	Cr.

PROBLEM 6B-3

(a, b)

JOLLY CO.
GENERAL JOURNAL

Date		Account Titles and Description	PR		Dr.			Cr.	

PROBLEM 6B-3 (CONCLUDED)

JOLLY CO.
AUXILIARY PETTY CASH RECORD

Date	Voucher No.	Description	Receipts	Payment	Category of Payment				
					Postage Expense	Office Supplies Expense	Sundry Account	Amount	

PROBLEM 6B-4

KONA CO.
GENERAL JOURNAL

Date		Account Titles and Description	PR	Dr.	Cr.

PROBLEM 6B-4 (CONCLUDED)

KONA CO.
AUXILIARY PETTY CASH RECORD

Date	Voucher No.	Description	Receipts	Payment	Category of Payment				
					Postage Expense	Delivery Expense	Account (Sundry)		Amount (Sundry)

ON THE JOB CONTINUING PROBLEM
ASSIGNMENT 1

SMITH COMPUTER CENTER
GENERAL JOURNAL

PAGE 3

Date	Account Titles and Description	PR	Dr.	Cr.

AUXILIARY PETTY CASH RECORD

Date	Voucher No.	Description	Receipts	Payment	Category of Payment				
					Postage Expense	Supplies Expense	Account	Sundry	Amount

ASSIGNMENT 2

CASH   ACCOUNT NO. **1000**

Date		Explanation	Post Ref.	Debit	Credit	Balance	
						Debit	Credit
9/30	1X	Balance forward	✔			2 1 2 0 00	

PETTY CASH   ACCOUNT NO. **1010**

Date		Explanation	Post Ref.	Debit	Credit	Balance	
						Debit	Credit

ACCOUNTS RECEIVABLE   ACCOUNT NO. 1020

Date		Explanation	Post Ref.	Debit	Credit	Balance	
						Debit	Credit
9/30	1X	Balance forward	✔			2 7 0 0 00	

PREPAID RENT   ACCOUNT NO. 1025

Date		Explanation	Post Ref.	Debit	Credit	Balance	
						Debit	Credit
9/30	1X	Balance forward	✔			5 0 0 00	

SUPPLIES   ACCOUNT NO. 1030

Date		Explanation	Post Ref.	Debit	Credit	Balance	
						Debit	Credit
9/30	1X	Balance forward	✔			1 9 2 00	

COMPUTER SHOP EQUIPMENT   ACCOUNT NO. 1080

Date		Explanation	Post Ref.	Debit	Credit	Balance	
						Debit	Credit
9/30	1X	Balance forward	✔			3 9 0 0 00	

ACCUMULATED DEPRECIATION, COMPUTER SHOP EQUIPMENT   ACCOUNT NO. 1081

Date		Explanation	Post Ref.	Debit	Credit	Balance	
						Debit	Credit
9/30	1X	Balance forward	✔				1 5 0 00

OFFICE EQUIPMENT   ACCOUNT NO. 1090

Date		Explanation	Post Ref.	Debit	Credit	Balance	
						Debit	Credit
9/30	1X	Balance forward	✔			3 3 0 0 00	

ACCUMULATED DEPRECIATION, OFFICE EQUIPMENT   ACCOUNT NO. 1091

Date		Explanation	Post Ref.	Debit	Credit	Balance	
						Debit	Credit
9/30	1X	Balance forward	✔				1 1 0 00

ACCOUNTS PAYABLE   ACCOUNT NO. 2000

Date		Explanation	Post Ref.	Debit	Credit	Balance	
						Debit	Credit
9/30	1X	Balance forward	✔				1 7 0 00

T. FELDMAN, CAPITAL ACCOUNT NO. 3000

Date		Explanation	Post Ref.	Debit	Credit	Balance	
						Debit	Credit
9/30	1X	Balance forward	✔				12 2 8 2 00

T. FELDMAN, WITHDRAWALS ACCOUNT NO. 3010

Date		Explanation	Post Ref.	Debit	Credit	Balance	
						Debit	Credit

INCOME SUMMARY ACCOUNT NO. 3020

Date		Explanation	Post Ref.	Debit	Credit	Balance	
						Debit	Credit

SERVICE REVENUE   **ACCOUNT NO. 4000**

Date	Explanation	Post Ref.	Debit	Credit	Balance	
					Debit	Credit

ADVERTISING EXPENSE   **ACCOUNT NO. 5010**

Date	Explanation	Post Ref.	Debit	Credit	Balance	
					Debit	Credit

RENT EXPENSE   **ACCOUNT NO. 5020**

Date	Explanation	Post Ref.	Debit	Credit	Balance	
					Debit	Credit

UTILITIES EXPENSE   ACCOUNT NO. <u>5030</u>

Date		Explanation	Post Ref.	Debit	Credit	Balance	
						Debit	Credit

PHONE EXPENSE   ACCOUNT NO. <u>5040</u>

Date	Explanation	Post Ref.	Debit	Credit	Balance	
					Debit	Credit

SUPPLIES EXPENSE   ACCOUNT NO. <u>5050</u>

Date		Explanation	Post Ref.	Debit	Credit	Balance	
						Debit	Credit

INSURANCE EXPENSE   ACCOUNT NO. <u>5060</u>

Date		Explanation	Post Ref.	Debit	Credit	Balance	
						Debit	Credit

POSTAGE EXPENSE — ACCOUNT NO. 5070

Date		Explanation	Post Ref.	Debit	Credit	Balance Debit	Balance Credit

DEPRECIATION EXPENSE, COMPUTER SHOP EQUIPMENT — ACCOUNT NO. 5080

Date		Explanation	Post Ref.	Debit	Credit	Balance Debit	Balance Credit

DEPRECIATION EXPENSE, OFFICE EQUIPMENT — ACCOUNT NO. 5090

Date		Explanation	Post Ref.	Debit	Credit	Balance Debit	Balance Credit

MISCELLANEOUS EXPENSE — ACCOUNT NO. 5100

Date		Explanation	Post Ref.	Debit	Credit	Balance Debit	Balance Credit

ASSIGNMENT 3

SMITH COMPUTER CENTER
TRIAL BALANCE
OCTOBER 31, 201X

ASSIGNMENT 4

SMITH COMPUTER CENTER
BANK RECONCILIATION AS OF SEPTEMBER 30, 201X

CHECKBOOK BALANCE   **BALANCE PER BANK**

Checkbook Balance   Bank Statement Balance

  Add: Add:

                            _____   Deduct: _____

Deduct:

                            _____   _____

Reconciled Balance   ================   Reconciled Balance   ================

CHAPTER 6
SUMMARY PRACTICE TEST
BANKING PROCEDURES AND CONTROL OF CASH

Part I

Fill in the blank(s) to complete the statement.

1. Online banking is _____ due to the internet.
2. Today, use of the _____ _____ has greatly increased.
3. All adjustments to the checkbook balance in the reconciliation process will require _____ _____.
4. Petty cash is a(n) _____ found on the balance sheet.
5. The auxiliary petty cash record is not a(n) _____.
6. A(n) _____ _____ is an asset used to make change for customer.
7. A cash overage will be _____ _____ on the income statement.
8. _____ _____ represents checks not processed by the bank at the time the bank statement was prepared.
9. When a bank credits your account, your balance will _____.
10. _____ is a procedure whereby the bank does not return the processed checks.

Part II

Indicate which of the following procedures are involved in each of the transactions below.

a. Recorded in General Journal
b. Recorded in both general journal and auxiliary petty cash record
c. Recorded only in auxiliary petty cash record
d. New check is written
e. Account petty cash is increased

1. EXAMPLE: Check issued to establish petty cash   <u>b,d,e</u>
2. Paid donation from petty cash   _____
3. Paid postage from petty cash   _____
4. Paid past purchases previously charged   _____
5. Paid for business luncheon with petty cash   _____
6. Issued check to pay for office supplies   _____
7. Replenished petty cash   _____
8. Paid local donation from petty cash   _____
9. Paid for past purchases bought on account   _____
10. Replenished petty cash   _____

Part III

Answer true or false to the following statements.

1.   Online banking is decreasing today.

2.   Petty cash is a liability found on the balance sheet.

3.   Checks returned from the bank are placed in alphabetical order.

4.   ATMs are being used less today than in the past.

5.   Bank service charges represent an expense to the business.

6.   The bank statement is the same as the bank reconciliation.

7.   The balance in the company cash account will always equal the bank balance before the bank statement is received.

8.   Deposit slips are needed in writing checks.

9.   A bank uses the signature card when cashing a check.

10.   The auxiliary petty cash record is posted monthly.

11.   The petty cash account has a debit balance.

12.   Replenishment of petty cash requires a new check.

13.   The expenses paid from petty cash are journalized at time of replenishment.

14.   Internal control only affects large companies.

15.   A petty cash voucher records the expense into the ledger.

16.   The petty cash fund must be replenished monthly.

17.   The petty cash voucher identifies the account that will be charged.

18.   The establishment of petty cash may require some judgment as to the amount of petty cash needed.

19.   EFT is the same as safekeeping.

20.   The drawer is the person who receives the check.

21.   A debit memo issued by a bank will increase the depositor's balance.

22.   A change fund uses only one denomination.

23.   The payer is the person or company the check is payable to.

Part IV

Based on the following situation, prepare a bank reconciliation.

The checkbook balance of Miller Company is $5,263.08. The bank statement shows a bank balance of $7,980. The bank statement shows interest earned of $42 and a service charge of $29.76. There is a deposit in transit of $2,558.22. Outstanding checks total $3,762.90. The bank collected a note for Miller for $4,200. Miller Company forgot to deduct a check for $2,700 during the month.

SOLUTIONS

Part I

1. increasing
2. debit card
3. journal entries
4. asset
5. journal
6. change fund
7. miscellaneous income
8. Checks outstanding
9. increase
10. Truncation

Part II

1. b, d, e
2. c
3. c
4. a, d
5. c
6. a, d
7. b, d
8. c
9. a, d
10. b, d

Part III

1. false	6. false	11. true	16. false	21. false
2. false	7. false	12. true	17. true	22. false
3. false	8. false	13. true	18. true	23. false
4. false	9. true	14. false	19. false	
5. true	10. false	15. false	20. false	

Part IV

MILLER COMPANY
BANK RECONCILIATION

Checkbook Balance			$5,263.08	Bank Balance		$7,980.00
ADD:				ADD:		
				Deposit		
Interest	$	42		in Transit		2,558.22
Collection of note		4,200	4,242.00			$10,538.22
			9,505.08			
DEDUCT:				DEDUCT:		
Service Chg.	$	29.76		Check outstanding		$3,762.90
Error		2,700.00	2,729.76			
Reconciled Balance			$6,775.32	Reconciled Balance		$6,775.32

Calculating Pay and Recording Payroll Taxes: The Beginning of the Payroll Process

CHAPTER 7

FORMS FOR DEMONSTRATION PROBLEM

REQUIREMENT 1

Use fold-out worksheet for Chapter 7 Demonstration Problem

REQUIREMENTS 2 AND 3

DAVIDSON COMPANY
GENERAL JOURNAL

PAGE 1

Date	Account Titles and Description	PR	Dr.	Cr.

FORMS FOR SET A EXERCISES

7A-1   Total Wages   Biweekly Earnings

a. Paula Anderson _____   **b.** John Smith _____
       Olivia Turner _____   Jane Doe _____

       _____

       Kellen Gates _____

       _____

7A-2

Xu Daoning	William Pierce
Gross Pay $1,650	Gross Pay $1,630
OASDI:	OASDI:
Medicare:	Medicare:
FIT:	FIT:
Net Pay	Net Pay

7A-3

Employee	FICA–OASDI	FICA–Medicare	FUTA Tax	SUTA Tax
O. Barns				
C. Hart				
Q. Roberts				
Total				

7A-4

Employee	FICA–OASDI	FICA–Medicare	FUTA Tax	SUTA Tax
O. Barns				
C. Hart				
Q. Roberts				
Total				

SET A EXERCISES

7A-5

Employee	FICA–OASDI	FICA–Medicare	FUTA Tax	SUTA Tax
O. Barns				
C. Hart				
Q. Roberts				
Total				

7A-6

Date	Account	Debit	Credit

7A-7

Employee	Weekly Pay	Weeks	Total	FUTA Taxable Earnings	FUTA Tax Rate	FUTA Tax
W. Duncan	$690					
S. Ivan	780					
V. North	560					
H. Young	430					
Total						

7A-8

FORMS FOR SET B EXERCISES

7B-1

	Total Wages			Biweekly Earnings

a. Marie Norris _____   **b.** George Day _____

Heidi Rodes _____   Min Lee _____

_____

Norman Duncan _____

_____

7B-2

Alvin Pang

Gross Pay $1,680 _____

OASDI: _____

_____

Medicare: _____

_____

FIT: _____

_____

Net Pay _____

David Parker

Gross Pay $1,600 _____

OASDI: _____

_____

Medicare: _____

_____

FIT: _____

_____

Net Pay _____

7B-3

Employee	FICA–OASDI	FICA–Medicare	FUTA Tax	SUTA Tax
I. Benson				
K. Larry				
Q. Roberts				
Total				

7B-4

Employee	FICA–OASDI	FICA–Medicare	FUTA Tax	SUTA Tax
I. Benson				
K. Larry				
Q. Roberts				
Total				

SET B EXERCISES

7B-5

Employee	FICA–OASDI	FICA–Medicare	FUTA Tax	SUTA Tax
I. Benson				
K. Larry				
Q. Roberts				
Total				

7B-6

Date	Account	Debit	Credit

7B-7

Employee	Weekly Pay	Weeks	Total	FUTA Taxable Earnings	FUTA Tax Rate	FUTA Tax
O. Barn	$650					
Z. Grande	790					
J. Mathison	580					
E. Walsh	460					
Total						

7B-8

FORMS FOR SET A PROBLEMS

PROBLEM 7A-1

Employee	Number of Hours Worked	Number of Regular Hours	Hourly Rate	Total Regular Earnings	Overtime Hours	Overtime Rate	Total Overtime Earnings
Jade Martina							
Lauren McBride							
Natala Polino							
Dmitri Wittman							

	Gross Earnings
Jade Martina	
Lauren McBride	
Natala Polino	
Dmitri Wittman	

PROBLEM 7A-2

Use the fold-out payroll register for Problem 7A-2 that accompanied your textbook.

PROBLEM 7A-3

Use the fold-out payroll register for Problem 7A-3 that accompanied your textbook.

PROBLEM 7A-4

REQUIREMENT 1

Use the fold-out payroll register for Problem 7A-4 that accompanied your textbook.

REQUIREMENT 2

Employee	FICA–OASDI	FICA–Medicare	FUTA Tax	SUTA Tax
Avery, Joanna				
Garth, Natashia				
Martinez, Joan				
Seward, Peter				
Total				

PROBLEM 7A-4 (CONCLUDED)

REQUIREMENT 3

GENERAL JOURNAL

Date	Account Titles and Description	PR	Dr.	Cr.

FORMS FOR SET B PROBLEMS

PROBLEM 7B-1

Employee	Number of Hours Worked	Number of Regular Hours	Hourly Rate	Total Regular Earnings	Overtime Hours	Overtime Rate	Total Overtime Earnings
Jag Valleria							
Lara Harrison							
Natalie Whittier							
Dmitri Jacobson							

Employee	Gross Earnings
Jag Valleria	
Lara Harrison	
Natalie Whittier	
Dmitri Jacobson	

PROBLEM 7B-2

Use the fold-out payroll register for Problem 7B-2 that accompanied your textbook.

PROBLEM 7B-3

Use the fold-out payroll register for Problem 7B-3 that accompanied your textbook.

PROBLEM 7B-4

REQUIREMENT 1

Use the fold-out payroll register for Problem 7B-4 that accompanied your textbook.

REQUIREMENT 2

Employee	FICA–OASDI	FICA–Medicare	FUTA Tax	SUTA Tax
Ackery, John				
Geary, Nicki				
Martin, Jeff				
Sherard, Paul				
Total				

PROBLEM 7B-4 (CONCLUDED)

REQUIREMENT 3

GENERAL JOURNAL

Date	Account Titles and Description	PR	Dr.	Cr.

ON THE JOB CONTINUING PROBLEM

ASSIGNMENT 1

SMITH COMPUTER CENTER
GENERAL JOURNAL

PAGE 4

Date	Account Titles and Description	PR	Dr.	Cr.

SMITH COMPUTER CENTER
GENERAL JOURNAL

Date	Account Titles and Description	PR	Dr.	Cr.

CASH   ACCOUNT NO. 1000

Date		Explanation	Post Ref.	Debit	Credit	Balance	
						Debit	Credit
10/31	1X	Balance forward	✔			6 4 8 5 00	

PETTY CASH   ACCOUNT NO. 1010

Date		Explanation	Post Ref.	Debit	Credit	Balance	
						Debit	Credit
10/31	1X	Balance forward	✔			3 0 0 00	

ACCOUNTS RECEIVABLE   ACCOUNT NO. 1020

Date		Explanation	Post Ref.	Debit	Credit	Balance	
						Debit	Credit
10/31	1X	Balance forward	✔			5 4 0 0 00	

PREPAID RENT   ACCOUNT NO. <u>1025</u>

Date		Explanation	Post Ref.	Debit	Credit	Balance				
						Debit			Credit	
10/31	1X	Balance forward	✔			2	0 0 0 00			

SUPPLIES   ACCOUNT NO. <u>1030</u>

Date		Explanation	Post Ref.	Debit	Credit	Balance				
						Debit			Credit	
10/31	1X	Balance forward	✔				1 9 2 00			

COMPUTER SHOP EQUIPMENT   ACCOUNT NO. <u>1080</u>

Date		Explanation	Post Ref.	Debit	Credit	Balance				
						Debit			Credit	
10/31	1X	Balance forward	✔			3	9 0 0 00			

ACCUMULATED DEPRECIATION, COMPUTER SHOP EQUIPMENT   ACCOUNT NO. <u>1081</u>

Date		Explanation	Post Ref.	Debit	Credit	Balance				
						Debit			Credit	
10/31	1X	Balance forward	✔					1	5 0 00	

OFFICE EQUIPMENT

ACCOUNT NO. 1090

Date		Explanation	Post Ref.	Debit	Credit	Balance	
						Debit	Credit
10/31	1X	Balance forward	✔			3 3 0 0 00	

ACCUMULATED DEPRECIATION, OFFICE EQUIPMENT

ACCOUNT NO. 1091

Date		Explanation	Post Ref.	Debit	Credit	Balance	
						Debit	Credit
10/31	1X	Balance forward	✔				1 1 0 00

ACCOUNTS PAYABLE

ACCOUNT NO. 2000

Date		Explanation	Post Ref.	Debit	Credit	Balance	
						Debit	Credit
10/31	1X	Balance forward	✔				5 0 00

WAGES PAYABLE

ACCOUNT NO. 2010

Date	Explanation	Post Ref.	Debit	Credit	Balance	
					Debit	Credit

FICA—OASDI PAYABLE

ACCOUNT NO. <u>2020</u>

Date	Explanation	Post Ref.	Debit	Credit	Balance	
					Debit	Credit

FICA—MEDICARE PAYABLE

ACCOUNT NO. <u>2030</u>

Date	Explanation	Post Ref.	Debit	Credit	Balance	
					Debit	Credit

FIT PAYABLE

ACCOUNT NO. <u>2040</u>

Date	Explanation	Post Ref.	Debit	Credit	Balance	
					Debit	Credit

SIT PAYABLE

ACCOUNT NO. <u>2050</u>

Date	Explanation	Post Ref.	Debit	Credit	Balance	
					Debit	Credit

T. FELDMAN, CAPITAL   ACCOUNT NO. 3000

Date		Explanation	Post Ref.	Debit	Credit	Balance Debit	Balance Credit
10/31	1X	Balance forward	✔				12 2 8 2 00

T. FELDMAN, WITHDRAWALS   ACCOUNT NO. 3010

Date		Explanation	Post Ref.	Debit	Credit	Balance Debit	Balance Credit
10/31	1X	Balance forward	✔			9 1 5 00	

SERVICE REVENUE   ACCOUNT NO. 4000

Date		Explanation	Post Ref.	Debit	Credit	Balance Debit	Balance Credit
10/31	1X	Balance forward	✔				10 0 0 0 00

ADVERTISING EXPENSE   ACCOUNT NO. 5010

Date		Explanation	Post Ref.	Debit	Credit	Balance Debit	Balance Credit

RENT EXPENSE   ACCOUNT NO. 5020

Date		Explanation	Post Ref.	Debit	Credit	Balance Debit	Balance Credit

UTILITIES EXPENSE

ACCOUNT NO. 5030

Date		Explanation	Post Ref.	Debit	Credit	Balance	
						Debit	Credit

PHONE EXPENSE

ACCOUNT NO. 5040

Date		Explanation	Post Ref.	Debit	Credit	Balance	
						Debit	Credit

SUPPLIES EXPENSE

ACCOUNT NO. 5050

Date		Explanation	Post Ref.	Debit	Credit	Balance	
						Debit	Credit
10/31	1X	Balance forward	✔			4 5 00	

INSURANCE EXPENSE

ACCOUNT NO. 5060

Date		Explanation	Post Ref.	Debit	Credit	Balance	
						Debit	Credit

POSTAGE EXPENSE

ACCOUNT NO. 5070

Date		Explanation	Post Ref.	Debit	Credit	Balance	
						Debit	Credit
10/31	1X	Balance forward	✔			4 0 00	

DEPRECIATION EXPENSE C. S. EQUIPMENT   ACCOUNT NO. 5080

Date		Explanation	Post Ref.	Debit	Credit	Balance Debit	Credit

DEPRECIATION EXPENSE OFFICE EQUIPMENT   ACCOUNT NO. 5090

Date		Explanation	Post Ref.	Debit	Credit	Balance Debit	Credit

MISCELLANEOUS EXPENSE   ACCOUNT NO. 5100

Date		Explanation	Post Ref.	Debit	Credit	Balance Debit	Credit
10/31	1X	Balance forward	✔			1 5 00	

WAGES EXPENSE   ACCOUNT NO. 5110

Date		Explanation	Post Ref.	Debit	Credit	Balance Debit	Credit

ASSIGNMENT 2

SMITH COMPUTER CENTER
TRIAL BALANCE
NOVEMBER 30, 201X

	Dr.	Cr.

CHAPTER 7
SUMMARY PRACTICE TEST:
CALCULATING PAY AND RECORDING PAYROLL TAXES:
THE BEGINNING OF THE PAYROLL PROCESS

PART I

Fill in the blank(s) to complete the statement.

1. _____ _____ is gross pay less deductions.

2. Form _____ aids the employer in knowing how much to deduct for federal income tax.

3. The base for OASDI-Medicare will _____ _____ from year to year.

4. _____ _____ of the employer's tax guide has tables available for deductions for FIT.

5. _____ _____ _____ protects employees against losses due to injury or death incurred while on the job.

6. The two primary records used to keep track of payroll information are the _____ _____ and _____ _____ _____.

7. Payroll tax expense includes _____, _____, _____, and _____.

8. _____ _____ is paid every two weeks.

9. A(n) _____ employee will only be paid for the hours actually worked.

10. An employer must pay FUTA on wages earned by each employee up to a maximum of $_____.

Part II

Answer true or false to the following.

1. OASDI is the tax form for SUTA.
2. Employers only pay FUTA and SUTA.
3. Employers pay a higher FICA-OASDI tax rate than employees do.
4. Gross pay plus deductions equals net pay.
5. Form W-4 aids in calculating FICA-OASDI.
6. The employer will match the employee's contribution for FICA (OASDI and Medicare).
7. The maximum tax credit for state unemployment tax is .8%.
8. A company may have different types of employees.
9. The Wage-Bracket Table makes it more difficult to calculate the amount of deductions for FIT.
10. A calendar year has no effect on taxes for FICA-Social Security.

Part III

Complete the chart below (use table in text as needed). Use the following information: Before this payroll Pete Bloom had earned $105,800. This week Pete earned $2,000 for the past two weeks. Assume an OASDI rate of Social Security of 6.2% up to $117,000. Medicare, 1.45%. FIT is $246.00. The state income tax is 7 percent.

GROSS PAY	TAXABLE FICA	DEDUCTIONS		FIT	SIT	NET PAY
		FICA				
		OASDI	Med.			

SOLUTIONS

Part I

1. Net Pay
2. W-4
3. not change
4. Circular E
5. Workers' Compensation Insurance

6. payroll register, employee earnings record
7. FICA-OASDI, FICA-Medicare, FUTA, SUTA
8. Biweekly payroll
9. hourly
10. 7,000

Part II

1. false
2. true
3. false
4. false
5. false

6. true
7. false
8. true
9. false
10. false

Part III

OASDI	$2,000 x .062 =	$124.00	
Medicare	2,000 x .0145 =	29.00	
FIT		246.00	$2,000.00
SIT	2,000 x .07	140.00	– 539.00
Total deductions		$539.00	$1,461.00

CHAPTER

8

Paying the Payroll, Depositing Payroll Taxes, and Filing the Required Quarterly and Annual Tax Forms: The Conclusion of the Payroll Process

FORMS FOR DEMONSTRATION PROBLEM

REQUIREMENT 1

FORMS FOR DEMONSTRATION PROBLEM

REQUIREMENT 2

Form **941 for 201X:** Employer's QUARTERLY Federal Tax Return

950114

(Rev. January 2014)   Department of the Treasury — Internal Revenue Service

OMB No. 1545-0029

Employer identification number (EIN) ☐☐ — ☐☐☐☐☐☐☐

Name *(not your trade name)* _____

Trade name *(if any)* _____

Address _____

Number   Street   Suite or room number

_____

City   State   ZIP code

_____

Foreign country name   Foreign province/county   Foreign postal code

Report for this Quarter of 201X
(Check one.)

☐ **1:** January, February, March

☐ **2:** April, May, June

☐ **3:** July, August, September

☐ **4:** October, November, December

Instructions and prior year forms are available at *www.irs.gov/form941.*

Read the separate instructions before you complete Form 941. Type or print within the boxes.

Part 1:   Answer these questions for this quarter.

1   Number of employees who received wages, tips, or other compensation for the pay period including: *Mar. 12* (Quarter 1), *June 12* (Quarter 2), *Sept. 12* (Quarter 3), or *Dec. 12* (Quarter 4)   **1** ☐

2   Wages, tips, and other compensation . . . .   **2** ☐ .

3   Federal income tax withheld from wages, tips, and other compensation . . . . . .   **3** ☐ .

4   If no wages, tips, and other compensation are subject to social security or Medicare tax   ☐ Check and go to line 6.

	Column 1		Column 2	
5a Taxable social security wages . .	☐ .	× .124 =	☐ .	
5b Taxable social security tips . . .	☐ .	× .124 =	☐ .	
5c Taxable Medicare wages & tips. .	☐ .	× .029 =	☐ .	
5d Taxable wages & tips subject to Additional Medicare Tax withholding	☐ .	× .009 =	☐ .	

5e   Add Column 2 from lines 5a, 5b, 5c, and 5d . . . .   **5e** ☐ .

5f   Section 3121(q) Notice and Demand—Tax due on unreported tips (see instructions) . .   **5f** ☐ .

6   Total taxes before adjustments. Add lines 3, 5e, and 5f . . . .   **6** ☐ .

7   Current quarter's adjustment for fractions of cents . . . .   **7** ☐ .

8   Current quarter's adjustment for sick pay . . . .   **8** ☐ .

9   Current quarter's adjustments for tips and group-term life insurance . . . . .   **9** ☐ .

10   Total taxes after adjustments. Combine lines 6 through 9 . . . .   **10** ☐ .

11   Total deposits for this quarter, including overpayment applied from a prior quarter and overpayments applied from Form 941-X, 941-X (PR), 944-X, 944-X (PR), or 944-X (SP) filed in the current quarter . . . .   **11** ☐ .

12   Balance due. If line 10 is more than line 11, enter the difference and see instructions . . .   **12** 0 .

13   Overpayment. If line 11 is more than line 10, enter the difference ☐ . Check one: ☐ Apply to next return.   ☐ Send a refund.

▶ **You MUST complete both pages of Form 941 and SIGN it.**

Next ▶

For Privacy Act and Paperwork Reduction Act Notice, see the back of the Payment Voucher.   Cat. No. 17001Z   Form **941** (Rev. 1-2014)

FORMS FOR DEMONSTRATION PROBLEM
REQUIREMENT 2 (CONCLUDED)

950214

Name *(not your trade name)*	Employer identification number (EIN)

Part 2: Tell us about your deposit schedule and tax liability for this quarter.

If you are unsure about whether you are a monthly schedule depositor or a semiweekly schedule depositor, see Pub. 15 (Circular E), section 11.

14 Check one: ☐ Line 10 on this return is less than $2,500 or line 10 on the return for the prior quarter was less than $2,500, and you did not incur a $100,000 next-day deposit obligation during the current quarter. If line 10 for the prior quarter was less than $2,500 but line 10 on this return is $100,000 or more, you must provide a record of your federal tax liability. If you are a monthly schedule depositor, complete the deposit schedule below; if you are a semiweekly schedule depositor, attach Schedule B (Form 941). Go to Part 3.

☐ **You were a monthly schedule depositor for the entire quarter.** Enter your tax liability for each month and total liability for the quarter, then go to Part 3.

Tax liability: Month 1 [.   ]

Month 2 [.   ]

Month 3 [.   ]

Total liability for quarter [.   ]   Total must equal line 10.

☐ **You were a semiweekly schedule depositor for any part of this quarter.** Complete Schedule B (Form 941), Report of Tax Liability for Semiweekly Schedule Depositors, and attach it to Form 941.

Part 3: Tell us about your business. If a question does NOT apply to your business, leave it blank.

15 If your business has closed or you stopped paying wages . . . . ☐ Check here, and

enter the final date you paid wages [/   /   ] .

16 If you are a seasonal employer and you do not have to file a return for every quarter of the year . . ☐ Check here.

Part 4: May we speak with your third-party designee?

Do you want to allow an employee, a paid tax preparer, or another person to discuss this return with the IRS? See the instructions for details.

☐ Yes. Designee's name and phone number [   ] [   ]

Select a 5-digit Personal Identification Number (PIN) to use when talking to the IRS. [ ] [ ] [ ] [ ] [ ]

☐ No.

Part 5: Sign here. You MUST complete both pages of Form 941 and SIGN it.

Under penalties of perjury, I declare that I have examined this return, including accompanying schedules and statements, and to the best of my knowledge and belief, it is true, correct, and complete. Declaration of preparer (other than taxpayer) is based on all information of which preparer has any knowledge.

X   **Sign your name here** [   ]

Print your name here [   ]

Print your title here [   ]

Date [/   /   ]

Best daytime phone [   ]

Paid Preparer Use Only   Check if you are self-employed . . . ☐

Preparer's name		PTIN	
Preparer's signature		Date	[/ /]
Firm's name (or yours if self-employed)		EIN	
Address		Phone	
City		State	ZIP code	

FORMS FOR DEMONSTRATION PROBLEM

REQUIREMENT 3

Form **940 for 201X:** **Employer's Annual Federal Unemployment (FUTA) Tax Return**

Department of the Treasury — Internal Revenue Service

850113

OMB No. 1545-0028

Employer identification number (EIN) ☐☐ – ☐☐☐☐☐☐☐

Name *(not your trade name)* _____

Trade name *(if any)* _____

Address

_____

Number   Street   Suite or room number

_____

City   State   ZIP code

_____

Foreign country name   Foreign province/county   Foreign postal code

Type of Return
(Check all that apply.)

☐ **a.** Amended

☐ **b.** Successor employer

☐ **c.** No payments to employees in 201X

☐ **d.** Final: Business closed or stopped paying wages

Instructions and prior-year forms are available at *www.irs.gov/form940*.

Read the separate instructions before you complete this form. Please type or print within the boxes.

Part 1:   **Tell us about your return. If any line does NOT apply, leave it blank.**

1a	If you had to pay state unemployment tax in one state only, enter the state abbreviation .	1a	☐☐
1b	If you had to pay state unemployment tax in more than one state, you are a multi-state employer	1b	☐ Check here. Complete Schedule A (Form 940).
2	If you paid wages in a state that is subject to CREDIT REDUCTION	2	☐ Check here. Complete Schedule A (Form 940).

Part 2:   **Determine your FUTA tax before adjustments for 201X. If any line does NOT apply, leave it blank.**

| 3 | Total payments to all employees . . . . | 3 | . |
| 4 | Payments exempt from FUTA tax . . . . | 4 | . | | |

Check all that apply: **4a** ☐ Fringe benefits   **4c** ☐ Retirement/Pension   **4e** ☐ Other

4b ☐ Group-term life insurance   **4d** ☐ Dependent care

5	Total of payments made to each employee in excess of $7,000	5	.		
6	Subtotal (line 4 + line 5 = line 6)	6	.
7	Total taxable FUTA wages (line 3 – line 6 = line 7) (see instructions)	7	.
8	FUTA tax before adjustments (line 7 × .006 = line 8)	8	.

Part 3:   **Determine your adjustments. If any line does NOT apply, leave it blank.**

9	If ALL of the taxable FUTA wages you paid were excluded from state unemployment tax, multiply line 7 by .054 (line 7 × .054 = line 9). Go to line 12	9	.
10	If SOME of the taxable FUTA wages you paid were excluded from state unemployment tax, OR you paid ANY state unemployment tax late (after the due date for filing Form 940), complete the worksheet in the instructions. Enter the amount from line 7 of the worksheet . .	10	.
11	If credit reduction applies, enter the total from Schedule A (Form 940)	11	.

Part 4:   **Determine your FUTA tax and balance due or overpayment for 201X. If any line does NOT apply, leave it blank.**

12	Total FUTA tax after adjustments (lines 8 + 9 + 10 + 11 = line 12)	12	.
13	FUTA tax deposited for the year, including any overpayment applied from a prior year .	13	.
14	Balance due (If line 12 is more than line 13, enter the excess on line 14.)		
	• If line 14 is more than $500, you must deposit your tax.		
	• If line 14 is $500 or less, you may pay with this return. (see instructions)	14	.
15	Overpayment (If line 13 is more than line 12, enter the excess on line 15 and check a box below.)	15	.

▶ You **MUST** complete both pages of this form and **SIGN** it.   Check one: ☐ Apply to next return.   ☐ Send a refund.

Next ▶

For Privacy Act and Paperwork Reduction Act Notice, see the back of Form 940-V, Payment Voucher.   Cat. No. 11234O   Form **940** (2013)

FORMS FOR DEMONSTRATION PROBLEM

REQUIREMENT 3 (CONCLUDED)

850212

Name (not your trade name)	**Employer identification number (EIN)**

Part 5: Report your FUTA tax liability by quarter only if line 12 is more than $500. If not, go to Part 6.

16 Report the amount of your FUTA tax liability for each quarter; do NOT enter the amount you deposited. If you had no liability for a quarter, leave the line blank.

    16a **1st quarter** (January 1 – March 31) . . . . **16a** [.]

    16b **2nd quarter** (April 1 – June 30) . . . . **16b** [.]

    16c **3rd quarter** (July 1 – September 30) . . . . **16c** [.]

    16d **4th quarter** (October 1 – December 31) . . . . **16d** [.]

17 Total tax liability for the year (lines 16a + 16b + 16c + 16d = line 17) **17** [.] **Total must equal line 12.**

Part 6: May we speak with your third-party designee?

Do you want to allow an employee, a paid tax preparer, or another person to discuss this return with the IRS? See the instructions for details.

[ ] **Yes.**   Designee's name and phone number [   ] [   ]

          Select a 5-digit Personal Identification Number (PIN) to use when talking to IRS [ ][ ][ ][ ][ ]

[ ] **No.**

Part 7: Sign here. You MUST complete both pages of this form and SIGN it.

Under penalties of perjury, I declare that I have examined this return, including accompanying schedules and statements, and to the best of my knowledge and belief, it is true, correct, and complete, and that no part of any payment made to a state unemployment fund claimed as a credit was, or is to be, deducted from the payments made to employees. Declaration of preparer (other than taxpayer) is based on all information of which preparer has any knowledge.

X Sign your name here [   ]   Print your name here [   ]

                           Print your title here [   ]

    Date [/ /]   Best daytime phone [   ]

Paid Preparer Use Only   Check if you are self-employed . [ ]

Preparer's name		PTIN
Preparer's signature		Date / /
Firm's name (or yours if self-employed)		EIN
Address		Phone
City	State	ZIP code

FORMS FOR SET A EXERCISES

8A-1

Date	Account			Debit	Credit

8A-2

                                                941 Tax Deposit Due Date

a. Monthly depositor, owing $1,500 tax for the first quarter. _____

b. Monthly depositor, owing $5,000 tax for the month of July. _____

c. Monthly depositor, owing $110,000 tax as of Tuesday. _____

d. Semiweekly depositor, owing $110,000 tax as of Tuesday. _____

e. Semiweekly depositor, owing $20,000 tax as of Friday. _____

8A-3

Line 1 Number of employees who received wages, tips, or other compensation _____

Line 2 Wages, tips, and other compensation _____

Line 3 Federal income tax withheld from wages, tips, and other compensation _____

Line 4 If no wages, tips, and other compensation are subject to social security
        or Medicare tax ___ Check

Line 5a Taxable social security wages _____ x .124 = _____

Line 5b Taxable social security tips _____ x .124 = _____

Line 5c Taxable Medicare wages & tips _____ x .029 = _____

Line 5d Taxable wages & tips subject
        to additional Medicare Tax _____ x .009 = _____

Line 5e Add Column 2 from Lines 5a, 5b, 5c, and 5d _____

Line 5f Section 3121(q) Notice and Demand—Tax due on unreported tips _____

Line 6 Total taxes before adjustments. Add lines 3, 5e, and 5f _____

SET A EXERCISES

8A-4

_____
_____
_____
_____
_____
_____
_____
_____
_____
_____

Date		Account			Debit	Credit

8A-5

Line 3 Total payments to all employees   _____

Line 4 Payments exempt from FUTA tax   _____

Line 5 Total of payments made to each employee
       in excess of $7,000   _____

Line 6 Subtotal (line 4 + line 5 = line 6)   _____

Line 7 Total taxable FUTA wages (line 3 – line 6 = line 7)   _____

Line 8 FUTA tax before adjustments (line 7 x .006 = line 8)   _____

Total annual payroll for the year   _____

Payments made in excess of $7,000 FUTA tax limit   _____

Total FUTA liability before any adjustments   _____

8A-6

Monthly or semiweekly for 201C?   _____

8A-7

Monthly or semiweekly for 201C?   _____

8A-8

Date		Account			Debit	Credit

FORMS FOR SET B EXERCISES

8B-1

Date		Account			Debit			Credit	

8B-2

941 Tax Deposit Due Date

a. Monthly depositor, owing $1,850 tax for the third quarter. _____

b. Monthly depositor, owing $4,100 tax for the month of May. _____

c. Monthly depositor, owing $121,000 tax as of Thursday. _____

d. Semiweekly depositor, owing $121,000 tax as of Friday. _____

e. Semiweekly depositor, owing $32,000 tax as of Friday. _____

8B-3

Line 1   Number of employees who received wages, tips, or other compensation _____

Line 2   Wages, tips, and other compensation _____

Line 3   Federal income tax withheld from wages, tips, and other compensation _____

Line 4   If no wages, tips, and other compensation are subject to social security
or Medicare tax   ___ Check

Line 5a Taxable social security wages   _____ x .124 = _____

Line 5b Taxable social security tips   _____ x .124 = _____

Line 5c Taxable Medicare wages & tips _____ x .029 = _____

Line 5d Taxable wages & tips subject
to additional Medicare Tax   _____ x .009 = _____

Line 5e Add Column 2 from Lines 5a, 5b, 5c, and 5d   _____

Line 5f Section 3121(q) Notice and Demand—Tax due on unreported tips   _____

Line 6   Total taxes before adjustments. Add lines 3, 5e, and 5f   _____

SET B EXERCISES

8B-4

_____
_____
_____
_____
_____
_____
_____
_____
_____
_____

Date		Account			Debit		Credit	

8B-5

Line 3 Total payments to all employees   _____

Line 4 Payments exempt from FUTA tax   _____

Line 5 Total of payments made to each employee
in excess of $7,000   _____

Line 6 Subtotal (line 4 + line 5 = line 6)   _____

Line 7 Total taxable FUTA wages (line 3 − line 6 = line 7)   _____

Line 8 FUTA tax before adjustments (line 7 x .006 = line 8)   _____

Total annual payroll for the year   _____

Payments made in excess of $7,000 FUTA limit   _____

Total FUTA liability before any adjustments   _____

8B-6

Monthly or semiweekly for 201C?   _____

8B-7

Monthly or semiweekly for 201C?   _____

8B-8

Date		Account			Debit		Credit	

FORMS FOR SET A PROBLEMS

PROBLEM 8A-1

Employee	Taxable FUTA Earnings	Taxable SUTA Earnings	FUTA Tax	SUTA Tax
January				
Steven Koy				
Juanita Lane				
Alison Pickens				
February				
Steven Koy				
Juanita Lane				
Alison Pickens				
March				
Steven Koy				
Juanita Lane				
Alison Pickens				

PROBLEM 8A-1 (CONTINUED)

REQUIREMENT 1

Record payroll tax expense.

Date		Account Titles and Description	PR		Dr.			Cr.	

PROBLEM 8A-1 (CONCLUDED)

REQUIREMENT 2

Record payment of each tax liability.

Date		Account Titles and Description	PR	Dr.	Cr.

PROBLEM 8A-2

Form **941 for 201X:** Employer's **QUARTERLY** Federal Tax Return
(Rev. January 2014) Department of the Treasury — Internal Revenue Service

950114

OMB No. 1545-0029

Employer identification number (EIN) ☐☐ – ☐☐☐☐☐☐☐

Name *(not your trade name)* _____

Trade name *(if any)* _____

Address _____
Number   Street   Suite or room number

_____
City   State   ZIP code

_____
Foreign country name   Foreign province/county   Foreign postal code

Report for this Quarter of 201X
(Check one.)

☐ **1:** January, February, March

☐ **2:** April, May, June

☐ **3:** July, August, September

☐ **4:** October, November, December

Instructions and prior year forms are available at *www.irs.gov/form941.*

Read the separate instructions before you complete Form 941. Type or print within the boxes.

Part 1: **Answer these questions for this quarter.**

1 Number of employees who received wages, tips, or other compensation for the pay period including: *Mar. 12* (Quarter 1), *June 12* (Quarter 2), *Sept. 12* (Quarter 3), or *Dec. 12* (Quarter 4) **1** ☐

2 Wages, tips, and other compensation . . . . **2** ☐

3 Federal income tax withheld from wages, tips, and other compensation . . . . . . **3** ☐

4 If no wages, tips, and other compensation are subject to social security or Medicare tax ☐ Check and go to line 6.

	Column 1		Column 2
5a Taxable social security wages . .	☐	× .124 =	☐
5b Taxable social security tips . . .	☐	× .124 =	☐
5c Taxable Medicare wages & tips. .	☐	× .029 =	☐
5d Taxable wages & tips subject to Additional Medicare Tax withholding	☐	× .009 =	☐

5e Add Column 2 from lines 5a, 5b, 5c, and 5d . . . . **5e** ☐

5f Section 3121(q) Notice and Demand—Tax due on unreported tips (see instructions) . . **5f** ☐

6 Total taxes before adjustments. Add lines 3, 5e, and 5f . . . . . . **6** ☐

7 Current quarter's adjustment for fractions of cents . . . . **7** ☐

8 Current quarter's adjustment for sick pay . . . . **8** ☐

9 Current quarter's adjustments for tips and group-term life insurance . . . . . **9** ☐

10 Total taxes after adjustments. Combine lines 6 through 9 . . . . . . **10** ☐

11 Total deposits for this quarter, including overpayment applied from a prior quarter and overpayments applied from Form 941-X, 941-X (PR), 944-X, 944-X (PR), or 944-X (SP) filed in the current quarter . . . . **11** ☐

12 Balance due. If line 10 is more than line 11, enter the difference and see instructions . . . **12** 0 ☐

13 Overpayment. If line 11 is more than line 10, enter the difference ☐ Check one: ☐ Apply to next return. ☐ Send a refund.

▶ **You MUST complete both pages of Form 941 and SIGN it.**

Next ▶

For Privacy Act and Paperwork Reduction Act Notice, see the back of the Payment Voucher.   Cat. No. 17001Z   Form **941** (Rev. 1-2014)

PROBLEM 8A-2 (CONCLUDED)

Name *(not your trade name)*

950214

Employer identification number (EIN)

Part 2: Tell us about your deposit schedule and tax liability for this quarter.

If you are unsure about whether you are a monthly schedule depositor or a semiweekly schedule depositor, see Pub. 15 (Circular E), section 11.

14 Check one: ☐ Line 10 on this return is less than $2,500 or line 10 on the return for the prior quarter was less than $2,500, and you did not incur a $100,000 next-day deposit obligation during the current quarter. If line 10 for the prior quarter was less than $2,500 but line 10 on this return is $100,000 or more, you must provide a record of your federal tax liability. If you are a monthly schedule depositor, complete the deposit schedule below; if you are a semiweekly schedule depositor, attach Schedule B (Form 941). Go to Part 3.

☐ **You were a monthly schedule depositor for the entire quarter.** Enter your tax liability for each month and total liability for the quarter, then go to Part 3.

Tax liability:	Month 1	_____ . ____
	Month 2	_____ . ____
	Month 3	_____ . ____
Total liability for quarter		_____ . ____ Total must equal line 10.

☐ **You were a semiweekly schedule depositor for any part of this quarter.** Complete Schedule B (Form 941), Report of Tax Liability for Semiweekly Schedule Depositors, and attach it to Form 941.

Part 3: Tell us about your business. If a question does **NOT** apply to your business, leave it blank.

15 If your business has closed or you stopped paying wages . . . . ☐ Check here, and

enter the final date you paid wages [___ / ___ / ___] .

16 If you are a seasonal employer and you do not have to file a return for every quarter of the year . . ☐ Check here.

Part 4: May we speak with your third-party designee?

Do you want to allow an employee, a paid tax preparer, or another person to discuss this return with the IRS? See the instructions for details.

☐ Yes. Designee's name and phone number _____ _____

Select a 5-digit Personal Identification Number (PIN) to use when talking to the IRS. ☐ ☐ ☐ ☐ ☐

☐ No.

Part 5: Sign here. You MUST complete both pages of Form 941 and SIGN it.

Under penalties of perjury, I declare that I have examined this return, including accompanying schedules and statements, and to the best of my knowledge and belief, it is true, correct, and complete. Declaration of preparer (other than taxpayer) is based on all information of which preparer has any knowledge.

X **Sign your name here** _____

Print your name here _____

Print your title here _____

Date [___ / ___ / ___]

Best daytime phone _____

Paid Preparer Use Only

Check if you are self-employed . . . ☐

Preparer's name	_____	PTIN	_____
Preparer's signature	_____	Date	[___ / ___ / ___]
Firm's name (or yours if self-employed)	_____	EIN	_____
Address	_____	Phone	_____
City	_____ State _____	ZIP code	_____

PROBLEM 8A-3

REQUIREMENT 1

Karen Becker

Calculation for December OASDI tax _____

REQUIREMENT 2

Date	Account			Debit			Credit	

PROBLEM 8A-3 (CONTINUED)

REQUIREMENT 3

Date	Account			Debit		Credit	

Name _____ Class _____ Date _____

PROBLEM 8A-3 (CONTINUED)

REQUIREMENT 4

Form **941 for 201X:** **Employer's QUARTERLY Federal Tax Return**

Form (Rev. January 2014)

Department of the Treasury — Internal Revenue Service

950114

OMB No. 1545-0029

Employer identification number (EIN) ☐☐ – ☐☐☐☐☐☐☐

Name *(not your trade name)* _____

Trade name *(if any)* _____

Address _____

Number   Street   Suite or room number

_____

City   State   ZIP code

_____

Foreign country name   Foreign province/county   Foreign postal code

Report for this Quarter of 201X
(Check one.)

☐ **1:** January, February, March

☐ **2:** April, May, June

☐ **3:** July, August, September

☐ **4:** October, November, December

Instructions and prior year forms are available at *www.irs.gov/form941*.

Read the separate instructions before you complete Form 941. Type or print within the boxes.

Part 1:   **Answer these questions for this quarter.**

1   Number of employees who received wages, tips, or other compensation for the pay period including: *Mar. 12* (Quarter 1), *June 12* (Quarter 2), *Sept. 12* (Quarter 3), or *Dec. 12* (Quarter 4)   **1** ☐

2   Wages, tips, and other compensation . . . .   **2** ☐.

3   Federal income tax withheld from wages, tips, and other compensation . . . . .   **3** ☐.

4   If no wages, tips, and other compensation are subject to social security or Medicare tax   ☐ Check and go to line 6.

	Column 1		Column 2
5a Taxable social security wages . .	☐ .	× .124 =	☐ .
5b Taxable social security tips . . .	☐ .	× .124 =	☐ .
5c Taxable Medicare wages & tips. .	☐ .	× .029 =	☐ .
5d Taxable wages & tips subject to Additional Medicare Tax withholding	☐ .	× .009 =	☐ .

5e   Add Column 2 from lines 5a, 5b, 5c, and 5d . . . .   **5e** ☐.

5f   Section 3121(q) Notice and Demand—Tax due on unreported tips (see instructions) . .   **5f** ☐.

6   Total taxes before adjustments. Add lines 3, 5e, and 5f . . . .   **6** ☐.

7   Current quarter's adjustment for fractions of cents . . . .   **7** ☐.

8   Current quarter's adjustment for sick pay . . . .   **8** ☐.

9   Current quarter's adjustments for tips and group-term life insurance . . . . .   **9** ☐.

10   Total taxes after adjustments. Combine lines 6 through 9 . . . .   **10** ☐.

11   Total deposits for this quarter, including overpayment applied from a prior quarter and overpayments applied from Form 941-X, 941-X (PR), 944-X, 944-X (PR), or 944-X (SP) filed in the current quarter . . . .   **11** ☐.

12   Balance due. If line 10 is more than line 11, enter the difference and see instructions   **12** | 0 .

13   Overpayment. If line 11 is more than line 10, enter the difference ☐ .   Check one: ☐ Apply to next return. ☐ Send a refund.

▶ **You MUST complete both pages of Form 941 and SIGN it.**

Next ▶

For Privacy Act and Paperwork Reduction Act Notice, see the back of the Payment Voucher.   Cat. No. 17001Z   Form **941** (Rev. 1-2014)

PROBLEM 8A-3 (CONCLUDED)

950214

Name *(not your trade name)* | **Employer identification number (EIN)**

Part 2: Tell us about your deposit schedule and tax liability for this quarter.

If you are unsure about whether you are a monthly schedule depositor or a semiweekly schedule depositor, see Pub. 15 (Circular E), section 11.

14 Check one: ☐ Line 10 on this return is less than $2,500 or line 10 on the return for the prior quarter was less than $2,500, and you did not incur a $100,000 next-day deposit obligation during the current quarter. If line 10 for the prior quarter was less than $2,500 but line 10 on this return is $100,000 or more, you must provide a record of your federal tax liability. If you are a monthly schedule depositor, complete the deposit schedule below; if you are a semiweekly schedule depositor, attach Schedule B (Form 941). Go to Part 3.

☐ **You were a monthly schedule depositor for the entire quarter.** Enter your tax liability for each month and total liability for the quarter, then go to Part 3.

Tax liability: Month 1 [.]

Month 2 [.]

Month 3 [.]

Total liability for quarter [.] **Total must equal line 10.**

☐ **You were a semiweekly schedule depositor for any part of this quarter.** Complete Schedule B (Form 941), Report of Tax Liability for Semiweekly Schedule Depositors, and attach it to Form 941.

Part 3: Tell us about your business. If a question does NOT apply to your business, leave it blank.

15 If your business has closed or you stopped paying wages . . . . ☐ Check here, and

enter the final date you paid wages [/ /] .

16 If you are a seasonal employer and you do not have to file a return for every quarter of the year . . ☐ Check here.

Part 4: May we speak with your third-party designee?

Do you want to allow an employee, a paid tax preparer, or another person to discuss this return with the IRS? See the instructions for details.

☐ Yes. Designee's name and phone number [ ] [ ]

Select a 5-digit Personal Identification Number (PIN) to use when talking to the IRS. [ ][ ][ ][ ][ ]

☐ No.

Part 5: Sign here. You MUST complete both pages of Form 941 and SIGN it.

Under penalties of perjury, I declare that I have examined this return, including accompanying schedules and statements, and to the best of my knowledge and belief, it is true, correct, and complete. Declaration of preparer (other than taxpayer) is based on all information of which preparer has any knowledge.

X **Sign your name here** [ ] | Print your name here [ ]

| Print your title here [ ]

Date [/ /] | Best daytime phone [ ]

Paid Preparer Use Only | Check if you are self-employed . . . ☐

Preparer's name [ ] | PTIN [ ]

Preparer's signature [ ] | Date [/ /]

Firm's name (or yours if self-employed) [ ] | EIN [ ]

Address [ ] | Phone [ ]

City [ ] State [ ] | ZIP code [ ]

PROBLEM 8A-4

Form **940 for 201X:** **Employer's Annual Federal Unemployment (FUTA) Tax Return**

Department of the Treasury — Internal Revenue Service

850113

OMB No. 1545-0028

Employer identification number (EIN) ☐☐ – ☐☐☐☐☐☐☐

Name (not your trade name) _____

Trade name (if any) _____

Address _____

Number   Street   Suite or room number

_____

City   State   ZIP code

_____

Foreign country name   Foreign province/county   Foreign postal code

Type of Return
(Check all that apply.)

☐ **a.** Amended

☐ **b.** Successor employer

☐ **c.** No payments to employees in 201X

☐ **d.** Final: Business closed or stopped paying wages

Instructions and prior-year forms are available at *www.irs.gov/form940.*

Read the separate instructions before you complete this form. Please type or print within the boxes.

Part 1:   Tell us about your return. If any line does NOT apply, leave it blank.

1a If you had to pay state unemployment tax in one state only, enter the state abbreviation . **1a** ☐ ☐

1b If you had to pay state unemployment tax in more than one state, you are a multi-state employer . . . . **1b** ☐ Check here. Complete Schedule A (Form 940).

2 If you paid wages in a state that is subject to CREDIT REDUCTION . . . . **2** ☐ Check here. Complete Schedule A (Form 940).

Part 2:   Determine your FUTA tax before adjustments for 201X. If any line does NOT apply, leave it blank.

3 Total payments to all employees . . . . **3** ☐ .

4 Payments exempt from FUTA tax . . . . **4** ☐ .

Check all that apply: **4a** ☐ Fringe benefits   **4c** ☐ Retirement/Pension   **4e** ☐ Other
4b ☐ Group-term life insurance   **4d** ☐ Dependent care

5 Total of payments made to each employee in excess of $7,000 . . . . **5** ☐ .

6 Subtotal (line 4 + line 5 = line 6) . . . . **6** ☐ .

7 Total taxable FUTA wages (line 3 – line 6 = line 7) (see instructions) . . . . **7** ☐ .

8 FUTA tax before adjustments (line 7 x .006 = line 8) . . . . **8** ☐ .

Part 3:   Determine your adjustments. If any line does NOT apply, leave it blank.

9 If ALL of the taxable FUTA wages you paid were excluded from state unemployment tax, multiply line 7 by .054 (line 7 × .054 = line 9). Go to line 12 . . . . **9** ☐ .

10 If SOME of the taxable FUTA wages you paid were excluded from state unemployment tax, OR you paid ANY state unemployment tax late (after the due date for filing Form 940), complete the worksheet in the instructions. Enter the amount from line 7 of the worksheet . . **10** ☐ .

11 If credit reduction applies, enter the total from Schedule A (Form 940) . . . . . . **11** ☐ .

Part 4:   Determine your FUTA tax and balance due or overpayment for 201X. If any line does NOT apply, leave it blank.

12 Total FUTA tax after adjustments (lines 8 + 9 + 10 + 11 = line 12) . . . . **12** ☐ .

13 FUTA tax deposited for the year, including any overpayment applied from a prior year . **13** ☐ .

14 Balance due (If line 12 is more than line 13, enter the excess on line 14.)
• If line 14 is more than $500, you must deposit your tax.
• If line 14 is $500 or less, you may pay with this return. (see instructions) . . . . . . **14** ☐ .

15 Overpayment (If line 13 is more than line 12, enter the excess on line 15 and check a box below.) . . . . **15** ☐ .

▶ You **MUST** complete both pages of this form and **SIGN** it.

Check one: ☐ Apply to next return.   ☐ Send a refund.

Next ▶

For Privacy Act and Paperwork Reduction Act Notice, see the back of Form 940-V, Payment Voucher.   Cat. No. 11234O   Form **940** (2013)

PROBLEM 8A-4 (CONCLUDED)

850212

Name (not your trade name)	Employer identification number (EIN)

Part 5: Report your FUTA tax liability by quarter only if line 12 is more than $500. If not, go to Part 6.

16 Report the amount of your FUTA tax liability for each quarter; do NOT enter the amount you deposited. If you had no liability for a quarter, leave the line blank.

16a **1st quarter** (January 1 – March 31) . . . . **16a** [.   ]

16b **2nd quarter** (April 1 – June 30) . . . . **16b** [.   ]

16c **3rd quarter** (July 1 – September 30) . . . . **16c** [.   ]

16d **4th quarter** (October 1 – December 31) . . . . **16d** [.   ]

17 Total tax liability for the year (lines 16a + 16b + 16c + 16d = line 17) **17** [.   ] **Total must equal line 12.**

Part 6: May we speak with your third-party designee?

Do you want to allow an employee, a paid tax preparer, or another person to discuss this return with the IRS? See the instructions for details.

☐ **Yes.** Designee's name and phone number [   ] [   ]

Select a 5-digit Personal Identification Number (PIN) to use when talking to IRS [ ] [ ] [ ] [ ] [ ]

☐ **No.**

Part 7: Sign here. You MUST complete both pages of this form and SIGN it.

Under penalties of perjury, I declare that I have examined this return, including accompanying schedules and statements, and to the best of my knowledge and belief, it is true, correct, and complete, and that no part of any payment made to a state unemployment fund claimed as a credit was, or is to be, deducted from the payments made to employees. Declaration of preparer (other than taxpayer) is based on all information of which preparer has any knowledge.

X **Sign your name here** [   ]   Print your name here [   ]

Print your title here [   ]

Date [/   /   ]   Best daytime phone [   ]

Paid Preparer Use Only   Check if you are self-employed . ☐

Preparer's name	[ ]	PTIN [ ]
Preparer's signature	[ ]	Date [/ /]
Firm's name (or yours if self-employed)	[ ]	EIN [ ]
Address	[ ]	Phone [ ]
City	[ ] State [ ]	ZIP code [ ]

FORMS FOR SET B PROBLEMS

PROBLEM 8B-1

Employee	Taxable FUTA Earnings	Taxable SUTA Earnings	FUTA Tax	SUTA Tax
January				
Saul Hantona				
Jade Alaymo				
Ariana Santana				
February				
Saul Hantona				
Jade Alaymo				
Ariana Santana				
March				
Saul Hantona				
Jade Alaymo				
Ariana Santana				

PROBLEM 8B-1 (CONTINUED)

REQUIREMENT 1

Record payroll tax expense.

Date	Account Titles and Description	PR	Dr.	Cr.

PROBLEM 8B-1 (CONCLUDED)

REQUIREMENT 2

Record payment of each tax liability.

Date		Account Titles and Description	PR	Dr.	Cr.

PROBLEM 8B-2

Form **941 for 201X:** **Employer's QUARTERLY Federal Tax Return**
(Rev. January 2014)   Department of the Treasury — Internal Revenue Service

950114

OMB No. 1545-0029

Employer identification number (EIN) ☐☐ — ☐☐☐☐☐☐☐

Name *(not your trade name)* _____

Trade name *(if any)* _____

Address _____
Number   Street   Suite or room number

_____
City   State   ZIP code

_____
Foreign country name   Foreign province/county   Foreign postal code

Report for this Quarter of 201X
(Check one.)

☐ **1:** January, February, March

☐ **2:** April, May, June

☐ **3:** July, August, September

☐ **4:** October, November, December

Instructions and prior year forms are available at *www.irs.gov/form941*.

Read the separate instructions before you complete Form 941. Type or print within the boxes.

Part 1:   **Answer these questions for this quarter.**

1 Number of employees who received wages, tips, or other compensation for the pay period
   including: *Mar. 12* (Quarter 1), *June 12* (Quarter 2), *Sept. 12* (Quarter 3), or *Dec. 12* (Quarter 4)   **1** ☐

2 Wages, tips, and other compensation . . . .   **2** ☐ .

3 Federal income tax withheld from wages, tips, and other compensation . . . .   **3** ☐ .

4 If no wages, tips, and other compensation are subject to social security or Medicare tax   ☐ Check and go to line 6.

	Column 1		Column 2
5a Taxable social security wages . .	☐ .	× .124 =	☐ .
5b Taxable social security tips . . .	☐ .	× .124 =	☐ .
5c Taxable Medicare wages & tips. .	☐ .	× .029 =	☐ .
5d Taxable wages & tips subject to Additional Medicare Tax withholding	☐ .	× .009 =	☐ .

5e Add Column 2 from lines 5a, 5b, 5c, and 5d . . . .   **5e** ☐ .

5f Section 3121(q) Notice and Demand—Tax due on unreported tips (see instructions) . .   **5f** ☐ .

6 Total taxes before adjustments. Add lines 3, 5e, and 5f . . . .   **6** ☐ .

7 Current quarter's adjustment for fractions of cents . . . .   **7** ☐ .

8 Current quarter's adjustment for sick pay . . . .   **8** ☐ .

9 Current quarter's adjustments for tips and group-term life insurance . . . .   **9** ☐ .

10 Total taxes after adjustments. Combine lines 6 through 9 . . . .   **10** ☐ .

11 Total deposits for this quarter, including overpayment applied from a prior quarter and
    overpayments applied from Form 941-X, 941-X (PR), 944-X, 944-X (PR), or 944-X (SP) filed
    in the current quarter . . . .   **11** ☐ .

12 Balance due. If line 10 is more than line 11, enter the difference and see instructions . . .   **12** ☐ 0 .

13 Overpayment. If line 11 is more than line 10, enter the difference ☐ .   Check one: ☐ Apply to next return. ☐ Send a refund.

▶ **You MUST complete both pages of Form 941 and SIGN it.**   Next ▶

For Privacy Act and Paperwork Reduction Act Notice, see the back of the Payment Voucher.   Cat. No. 17001Z   Form **941** (Rev. 1-2014)

PROBLEM 8B-2 (CONCLUDED)

950214

Name (not your trade name)	Employer identification number (EIN)

Part 2: Tell us about your deposit schedule and tax liability for this quarter.

If you are unsure about whether you are a monthly schedule depositor or a semiweekly schedule depositor, see Pub. 15 (Circular E), section 11.

14 Check one: ☐ Line 10 on this return is less than $2,500 or line 10 on the return for the prior quarter was less than $2,500, and you did not incur a $100,000 next-day deposit obligation during the current quarter. If line 10 for the prior quarter was less than $2,500 but line 10 on this return is $100,000 or more, you must provide a record of your federal tax liability. If you are a monthly schedule depositor, complete the deposit schedule below; if you are a semiweekly schedule depositor, attach Schedule B (Form 941). Go to Part 3.

☐ **You were a monthly schedule depositor for the entire quarter.** Enter your tax liability for each month and total liability for the quarter, then go to Part 3.

Tax liability: Month 1 [.   ]

Month 2 [.   ]

Month 3 [.   ]

Total liability for quarter [.   ] **Total must equal line 10.**

☐ **You were a semiweekly schedule depositor for any part of this quarter.** Complete Schedule B (Form 941), Report of Tax Liability for Semiweekly Schedule Depositors, and attach it to Form 941.

Part 3: Tell us about your business. If a question does NOT apply to your business, leave it blank.

15 If your business has closed or you stopped paying wages . . . . ☐ Check here, and

enter the final date you paid wages [/   /].

16 If you are a seasonal employer and you do not have to file a return for every quarter of the year . . ☐ Check here.

Part 4: May we speak with your third-party designee?

Do you want to allow an employee, a paid tax preparer, or another person to discuss this return with the IRS? See the instructions for details.

☐ Yes. Designee's name and phone number [   ] [   ]

Select a 5-digit Personal Identification Number (PIN) to use when talking to the IRS. [ ][ ][ ][ ][ ]

☐ No.

Part 5: Sign here. You MUST complete both pages of Form 941 and SIGN it.

Under penalties of perjury, I declare that I have examined this return, including accompanying schedules and statements, and to the best of my knowledge and belief, it is true, correct, and complete. Declaration of preparer (other than taxpayer) is based on all information of which preparer has any knowledge.

X **Sign your name here** [   ]

Print your name here [   ]

Print your title here [   ]

Date [/   /]

Best daytime phone [   ]

Paid Preparer Use Only	Check if you are self-employed . . . ☐
Preparer's name [ ]	PTIN [ ]
Preparer's signature [ ]	Date [/ /]
Firm's name (or yours if self-employed) [ ]	EIN [ ]
Address [ ]	Phone [ ]
City [ ] State [ ]	ZIP code [ ]

PROBLEM 8B-3

REQUIREMENT 1

Amber Bixby

Calculation for December OASDI tax _____

REQUIREMENT 2

Date		Account			Debit		Credit

PROBLEM 8B-3 (CONTINUED)

REQUIREMENT 3

Date	Account			Debit		Credit	

PROBLEM 8B-3 (CONTINUED)

REQUIREMENT 4

Form **941 for 201X:** **Employer's QUARTERLY Federal Tax Return**
(Rev. January 2014)   Department of the Treasury — Internal Revenue Service

950114

OMB No. 1545-0029

Employer identification number (EIN) ☐☐ – ☐☐☐☐☐☐☐

Name *(not your trade name)* _____

Trade name *(if any)* _____

Address _____
　　　　　Number　　　　Street　　　　　　　　　　Suite or room number

_____
City　　　　　　　　　　　State　　　ZIP code

_____
Foreign country name　　　Foreign province/county　　Foreign postal code

Report for this Quarter of 201X
(Check one.)

☐ **1:** January, February, March

☐ **2:** April, May, June

☐ **3:** July, August, September

☐ **4:** October, November, December

Instructions and prior year forms are available at *www.irs.gov/form941.*

Read the separate instructions before you complete Form 941. Type or print within the boxes.

Part 1:	**Answer these questions for this quarter.**

1　Number of employees who received wages, tips, or other compensation for the pay period including: *Mar. 12* (Quarter 1), *June 12* (Quarter 2), *Sept. 12* (Quarter 3), or *Dec. 12* (Quarter 4) **1** ☐

2　Wages, tips, and other compensation . . . . **2** ☐.

3　Federal income tax withheld from wages, tips, and other compensation . . . . **3** ☐.

4　If no wages, tips, and other compensation are subject to social security or Medicare tax ☐ Check and go to line 6.

		Column 1		**Column 2**
5a	Taxable social security wages . .	☐.	× .124 =	☐.
5b	Taxable social security tips . . .	☐.	× .124 =	☐.
5c	Taxable Medicare wages & tips. .	☐.	× .029 =	☐.
5d	Taxable wages & tips subject to Additional Medicare Tax withholding	☐.	× .009 =	☐.

5e　Add Column 2 from lines 5a, 5b, 5c, and 5d . . . . **5e** ☐.

5f　Section 3121(q) Notice and Demand—Tax due on unreported tips (see instructions) . . **5f** ☐.

6　Total taxes before adjustments. Add lines 3, 5e, and 5f . . . . **6** ☐.

7　Current quarter's adjustment for fractions of cents . . . . **7** ☐.

8　Current quarter's adjustment for sick pay . . . . **8** ☐.

9　Current quarter's adjustments for tips and group-term life insurance . . . . **9** ☐.

10　Total taxes after adjustments. Combine lines 6 through 9 . . . . . . **10** ☐.

11　Total deposits for this quarter, including overpayment applied from a prior quarter and overpayments applied from Form 941-X, 941-X (PR), 944-X, 944-X (PR), or 944-X (SP) filed in the current quarter . . . . **11** ☐.

12　Balance due. If line 10 is more than line 11, enter the difference and see instructions . . . **12** ☐ 0.

13　Overpayment. If line 11 is more than line 10, enter the difference ☐. Check one: ☐ Apply to next return. ☐ Send a refund.

▶ **You MUST complete both pages of Form 941 and SIGN it.**　　　　　　　　　　　　　　　Next ▶

For Privacy Act and Paperwork Reduction Act Notice, see the back of the Payment Voucher.　　Cat. No. 17001Z　　Form **941** (Rev. 1-2014)

PROBLEM 8B-3 (CONCLUDED)

950214

Name *(not your trade name)*	Employer identification number (EIN)

Part 2: Tell us about your deposit schedule and tax liability for this quarter.

If you are unsure about whether you are a monthly schedule depositor or a semiweekly schedule depositor, see Pub. 15 (Circular E), section 11.

14 Check one: ☐ Line 10 on this return is less than $2,500 or line 10 on the return for the prior quarter was less than $2,500, and you did not incur a $100,000 next-day deposit obligation during the current quarter. If line 10 for the prior quarter was less than $2,500 but line 10 on this return is $100,000 or more, you must provide a record of your federal tax liability. If you are a monthly schedule depositor, complete the deposit schedule below; if you are a semiweekly schedule depositor, attach Schedule B (Form 941). Go to Part 3.

☐ **You were a monthly schedule depositor for the entire quarter.** Enter your tax liability for each month and total liability for the quarter, then go to Part 3.

Tax liability: Month 1 ☐.

Month 2 ☐.

Month 3 ☐.

Total liability for quarter ☐. **Total must equal line 10.**

☐ **You were a semiweekly schedule depositor for any part of this quarter.** Complete Schedule B (Form 941), Report of Tax Liability for Semiweekly Schedule Depositors, and attach it to Form 941.

Part 3: Tell us about your business. If a question does NOT apply to your business, leave it blank.

15 If your business has closed or you stopped paying wages . . . . ☐ Check here, and

enter the final date you paid wages [/ /] .

16 If you are a seasonal employer and you do not have to file a return for every quarter of the year . . ☐ Check here.

Part 4: May we speak with your third-party designee?

Do you want to allow an employee, a paid tax preparer, or another person to discuss this return with the IRS? See the instructions for details.

☐ Yes. Designee's name and phone number [ ] [ ]

Select a 5-digit Personal Identification Number (PIN) to use when talking to the IRS. ☐ ☐ ☐ ☐ ☐

☐ No.

Part 5: Sign here. You MUST complete both pages of Form 941 and SIGN it.

Under penalties of perjury, I declare that I have examined this return, including accompanying schedules and statements, and to the best of my knowledge and belief, it is true, correct, and complete. Declaration of preparer (other than taxpayer) is based on all information of which preparer has any knowledge.

X **Sign your name here** [ ]

Print your name here [ ]

Print your title here [ ]

Date [/ /]

Best daytime phone [ ]

Paid Preparer Use Only

Check if you are self-employed . . . ☐

Preparer's name		PTIN	
Preparer's signature		Date	/ /
Firm's name (or yours if self-employed)		EIN	
Address		Phone	
City	State	ZIP code	

PROBLEM 8B-4

Form **940** for **201X**: **Employer's Annual Federal Unemployment (FUTA) Tax Return**

850113

Department of the Treasury — Internal Revenue Service

OMB No. 1545-0028

Employer identification number (EIN)

☐☐ – ☐☐☐☐☐☐☐

Name *(not your trade name)* _____

Trade name *(if any)* _____

Address _____

Number   Street   Suite or room number

_____

City   State   ZIP code

_____

Foreign country name   Foreign province/county   Foreign postal code

Type of Return
(Check all that apply.)

☐ **a.** Amended

☐ **b.** Successor employer

☐ **c.** No payments to employees in 201X

☐ **d.** Final: Business closed or stopped paying wages

Instructions and prior-year forms are available at *www.irs.gov/form940*.

Read the separate instructions before you complete this form. Please type or print within the boxes.

Part 1: **Tell us about your return. If any line does NOT apply, leave it blank.**

1a If you had to pay state unemployment tax in one state only, enter the state abbreviation . **1a** ☐☐

1b If you had to pay state unemployment tax in more than one state, you are a multi-state employer . . . . **1b** ☐ Check here. Complete Schedule A (Form 940).

2 If you paid wages in a state that is subject to **CREDIT REDUCTION** . . . . **2** ☐ Check here. Complete Schedule A (Form 940).

Part 2: **Determine your FUTA tax before adjustments for 201X. If any line does NOT apply, leave it blank.**

3 Total payments to all employees . . . . **3** ☐ .

4 Payments exempt from FUTA tax . . . . **4** ☐ .

Check all that apply: **4a** ☐ Fringe benefits   **4c** ☐ Retirement/Pension   **4e** ☐ Other
                      4b ☐ Group-term life insurance   **4d** ☐ Dependent care

5 Total of payments made to each employee in excess of $7,000 . . . . **5** ☐ .

6 Subtotal (line 4 + line 5 = line 6) . . . . **6** ☐ .

7 Total taxable FUTA wages (line 3 – line 6 = line 7) (see instructions) . . . . **7** ☐ .

8 FUTA tax before adjustments (line 7 x .006 = line 8) . . . . **8** ☐ .

Part 3: **Determine your adjustments. If any line does NOT apply, leave it blank.**

9 If ALL of the taxable FUTA wages you paid were excluded from state unemployment tax, multiply line 7 by **.054** (line 7 × .054 = line 9). Go to line 12 . . . . . . **9** ☐ .

10 If SOME of the taxable FUTA wages you paid were excluded from state unemployment tax, **OR** you paid ANY state unemployment tax late (after the due date for filing Form 940), complete the worksheet in the instructions. Enter the amount from line 7 of the worksheet . . **10** ☐ .

11 If credit reduction applies, enter the total from Schedule A (Form 940) . . . . **11** ☐ .

Part 4: **Determine your FUTA tax and balance due or overpayment for 201X. If any line does NOT apply, leave it blank.**

12 Total FUTA tax after adjustments (lines 8 + 9 + 10 + 11 = line 12) . . . . **12** ☐ .

13 FUTA tax deposited for the year, including any overpayment applied from a prior year . **13** ☐ .

14 Balance due (If line 12 is more than line 13, enter the excess on line 14.)
   • If line 14 is more than $500, you must deposit your tax.
   • If line 14 is $500 or less, you may pay with this return. (see instructions) . . . . . . **14** ☐ .

15 Overpayment (If line 13 is more than line 12, enter the excess on line 15 and check a box below.) . . . . **15** ☐ .

▶ You **MUST** complete both pages of this form and **SIGN** it.   Check one: ☐ Apply to next return.   ☐ Send a refund.

Next ▶

For **Privacy Act and Paperwork Reduction Act Notice, see the back of Form 940-V, Payment Voucher.**   Cat. No. 11234O   Form **940** (2013)

PROBLEM 8B-4 (CONCLUDED)

850212

Name *(not your trade name)*	Employer identification number (EIN)

Part 5:   Report your FUTA tax liability by quarter only if line 12 is more than $500. If not, go to Part 6.

16   Report the amount of your FUTA tax liability for each quarter; do NOT enter the amount you deposited. If you had no liability for a quarter, leave the line blank.

    16a   **1st quarter** (January 1 – March 31) . . . . **16a**   ☐ . ☐

    16b   **2nd quarter** (April 1 – June 30) . . . . **16b**   ☐ . ☐

    16c   **3rd quarter** (July 1 – September 30) . . . . **16c**   ☐ . ☐

    16d   **4th quarter** (October 1 – December 31) . . . . . . **16d**   ☐ . ☐

17   Total tax liability for the year (lines 16a + 16b + 16c + 16d = line 17) **17**   ☐ . ☐   **Total must equal line 12.**

Part 6:   May we speak with your third-party designee?

Do you want to allow an employee, a paid tax preparer, or another person to discuss this return with the IRS? See the instructions for details.

☐ **Yes.**   Designee's name and phone number   [_____]   [_____]

      Select a 5-digit Personal Identification Number (PIN) to use when talking to IRS   ☐ ☐ ☐ ☐ ☐

☐ **No.**

Part 7:   Sign here. You MUST complete both pages of this form and SIGN it.

Under penalties of perjury, I declare that I have examined this return, including accompanying schedules and statements, and to the best of my knowledge and belief, it is true, correct, and complete, and that no part of any payment made to a state unemployment fund claimed as a credit was, or is to be, deducted from the payments made to employees. Declaration of preparer (other than taxpayer) is based on all information of which preparer has any knowledge.

✗ **Sign your name here**   [_____]

    Print your name here   [_____]

    Print your title here   [_____]

Date   [/   /   ]

Best daytime phone   [_____]

Paid Preparer Use Only   Check if you are self-employed . ☐

Preparer's name	[_____]	PTIN	[_____]
Preparer's signature	[_____]	Date	[/ /]
Firm's name (or yours if self-employed)	[_____]	EIN	[_____]
Address	[_____]	Phone	[_____]
City	[_____] State [_____]	ZIP code	[_____]

ON THE JOB CONTINUING PROBLEM
SMITH COMPUTER CENTER

ASSIGNMENT 1

Use the fold-out payroll register provided for this assignment, which includes the first three pay periods. Prepare the payroll register.

ASSIGNMENT 2

Record the December payrolls and the payment of the payrolls in the general journal. Post journal entries to the general ledger.

SMITH COMPUTER CENTER
GENERAL JOURNAL

PAGE 5

Date	Account Titles and Description	PR	Dr.	Cr.

ON THE JOB CONTINUING PROBLEM
SMITH COMPUTER CENTER

ASSIGNMENT 3
Record payroll tax expense for the fourth quarter in the general journal. Post to the ledger.

ASSIGNMENT 4
Record the payment of each tax liability in the general journal and post to the ledger.

SMITH COMPUTER CENTER
GENERAL JOURNAL

PAGE 6

Date	Account Titles and Description	PR	Dr.	Cr.

CASH   ACCOUNT NO. **1000**

Date		Explanation	Post Ref.	Debit	Credit	Balance	
						Debit	Credit
11/30	1X	Balance forward	✔			8 1 1 0 00	

PETTY CASH   ACCOUNT NO. **1010**

Date		Explanation	Post Ref.	Debit	Credit	Balance	
						Debit	Credit
11/30	1X	Balance forward	✔			3 0 0 00	

ACCOUNTS RECEIVABLE   ACCOUNT NO. **1020**

Date		Explanation	Post Ref.	Debit	Credit	Balance	
						Debit	Credit
11/30	1X	Balance forward	✔			15 5 7 5 00	

PREPAID RENT   **ACCOUNT NO. 1025**

Date		Explanation	Post Ref.	Debit	Credit	Balance	
						Debit	Credit
11/30	1X	Balance forward	✔			2 0 0 0 00	

SUPPLIES   **ACCOUNT NO. 1030**

Date		Explanation	Post Ref.	Debit	Credit	Balance	
						Debit	Credit
11/30	1X	Balance forward	✔			1 9 2 00	

COMPUTER SHOP EQUIPMENT   **ACCOUNT NO. 1080**

Date		Explanation	Post Ref.	Debit	Credit	Balance	
						Debit	Credit
11/30	1X	Balance forward	✔			5 7 0 0 00	

ACCUMULATED DEPRECIATION, COMPUTER SHOP EQUIPMENT   **ACCOUNT NO. 1081**

Date		Explanation	Post Ref.	Debit	Credit	Balance	
						Debit	Credit
11/30	1X	Balance forward	✔				1 5 0 00

OFFICE EQUIPMENT   ACCOUNT NO. **1090**

Date		Explanation	Post Ref.	Debit	Credit	Balance Debit	Balance Credit
11/30	1X	Balance forward	✔			3 8 5 0 00	

ACCUMULATED DEPRECIATION, OFFICE EQUIPMENT   ACCOUNT NO. **1091**

Date		Explanation	Post Ref.	Debit	Credit	Balance Debit	Balance Credit
11/30	1X	Balance forward	✔				1 1 0 00

ACCOUNTS PAYABLE   ACCOUNT NO. **2000**

Date		Explanation	Post Ref.	Debit	Credit	Balance Debit	Balance Credit
11/30	1X	Balance forward	✔				2 5 7 0 00

WAGES PAYABLE   ACCOUNT NO. **2010**

Date		Explanation	Post Ref.	Debit	Credit	Balance Debit	Balance Credit

FICA—OASDI PAYABLE   ACCOUNT NO. <u>2020</u>

Date		Explanation	Post Ref.	Debit	Credit	Balance	
						Debit	Credit

FICA—MEDICARE PAYABLE   ACCOUNT NO. <u>2030</u>

Date		Explanation	Post Ref.	Debit	Credit	Balance	
						Debit	Credit

FIT PAYABLE   ACCOUNT NO. <u>2040</u>

Date		Explanation	Post Ref.	Debit	Credit	Balance	
						Debit	Credit

SIT PAYABLE   ACCOUNT NO. <u>2050</u>

Date		Explanation	Post Ref.	Debit	Credit	Balance	
						Debit	Credit

FUTA TAX PAYABLE   **ACCOUNT NO. 2060**

Date	Explanation	Post Ref.	Debit	Credit	Balance	
					Debit	Credit

SUTA TAX PAYABLE   **ACCOUNT NO. 2070**

Date	Explanation	Post Ref.	Debit	Credit	Balance	
					Debit	Credit

T. FELDMAN, CAPITAL   ACCOUNT NO. 3000

Date		Explanation	Post Ref.	Debit	Credit	Balance	
						Debit	Credit
11/30	1X	Balance forward	✔				12 2 8 2 00

T. FELDMAN, WITHDRAWALS   ACCOUNT NO. 3010

Date		Explanation	Post Ref.	Debit	Credit	Balance	
						Debit	Credit
11/30	1X	Balance forward	✔			9 1 5 00	

SERVICE REVENUE   ACCOUNT NO. 4000

Date		Explanation	Post Ref.	Debit	Credit	Balance	
						Debit	Credit
11/30	1X	Balance forward	✔				21 8 0 0 00

ADVERTISING EXPENSE   ACCOUNT NO. 5010

Date		Explanation	Post Ref.	Debit	Credit	Balance	
						Debit	Credit

RENT EXPENSE   ACCOUNT NO. 5020

Date		Explanation	Post Ref.	Debit	Credit	Balance	
						Debit	Credit

UTILITIES EXPENSE

ACCOUNT NO. 5030

Date	Explanation	Post Ref.	Debit	Credit	Balance Debit	Balance Credit

PHONE EXPENSE

ACCOUNT NO. 5040

Date	Explanation	Post Ref.	Debit	Credit	Balance Debit	Balance Credit
11/30 1X	Balance forward	✔			1 7 0 00	

SUPPLIES EXPENSE

ACCOUNT NO. 5050

Date	Explanation	Post Ref.	Debit	Credit	Balance Debit	Balance Credit
11/30 1X	Balance forward	✔			4 5 00	

INSURANCE EXPENSE

ACCOUNT NO. 5060

Date	Explanation	Post Ref.	Debit	Credit	Balance Debit	Balance Credit

POSTAGE EXPENSE

ACCOUNT NO. 5070

Date	Explanation	Post Ref.	Debit	Credit	Balance Debit	Balance Credit
11/30 1X	Balance forward	✔			4 0 00	

DEPRECIATION EXPENSE C. S. EQUIPMENT

ACCOUNT NO. 5080

Date		Explanation	Post Ref.	Debit	Credit	Balance Debit	Balance Credit

DEPRECIATION EXPENSE OFFICE EQUIPMENT

ACCOUNT NO. 5090

Date		Explanation	Post Ref.	Debit	Credit	Balance Debit	Balance Credit

MISCELLANEOUS EXPENSE

ACCOUNT NO. 5100

Date		Explanation	Post Ref.	Debit	Credit	Balance Debit	Balance Credit
11/30	1X	Balance forward	✔			1 5 00	

WAGES EXPENSE

ACCOUNT NO. 5110

Date		Explanation	Post Ref.	Debit	Credit	Balance Debit	Balance Credit

PAYROLL TAX EXPENSE

ACCOUNT NO. 5120

Date		Explanation	Post Ref.	Debit	Credit	Balance Debit	Balance Credit

Name _____ Class _____ Date _____

ON THE JOB CONTINUING PROBLEM

ASSIGNMENT 5

Form **941 for 201X:** **Employer's QUARTERLY Federal Tax Return**
(Rev. January 2014)   Department of the Treasury — Internal Revenue Service

950114

OMB No. 1545-0029

Employer identification number (EIN) [ ] [ ] — [ ] [ ] [ ] [ ] [ ] [ ] [ ]

Name *(not your trade name)* [_____]

Trade name *(if any)* [_____]

Address [_____]
Number   Street   Suite or room number

[_____] [_____] [_____]
City   State   ZIP code

[_____] [_____] [_____]
Foreign country name   Foreign province/county   Foreign postal code

Report for this Quarter of 201X
(Check one.)

[ ] **1:** January, February, March

[ ] **2:** April, May, June

[ ] **3:** July, August, September

[ ] **4:** October, November, December

Instructions and prior year forms are available at *www.irs.gov/form941.*

Read the separate instructions before you complete Form 941. Type or print within the boxes.

| Part 1: | Answer these questions for this quarter. |

1 Number of employees who received wages, tips, or other compensation for the pay period including: *Mar. 12* (Quarter 1), *June 12* (Quarter 2), *Sept. 12* (Quarter 3), or *Dec. 12* (Quarter 4)   **1** [_____]

2 Wages, tips, and other compensation . . . .   **2** [_____ . __]

3 Federal income tax withheld from wages, tips, and other compensation . . . . . .   **3** [_____ . __]

4 If no wages, tips, and other compensation are subject to social security or Medicare tax   [ ] Check and go to line 6.

	Column 1		Column 2
5a Taxable social security wages . .	[____ . _]	× .124 =	[____ . _]
5b Taxable social security tips . . .	[____ . _]	× .124 =	[____ . _]
5c Taxable Medicare wages & tips. .	[____ . _]	× .029 =	[____ . _]
5d Taxable wages & tips subject to Additional Medicare Tax withholding	[____ . _]	× .009 =	[____ . _]

5e Add Column 2 from lines 5a, 5b, 5c, and 5d . . . .   **5e** [_____ . __]

5f Section 3121(q) Notice and Demand—Tax due on unreported tips (see instructions) . .   **5f** [_____ . __]

6 Total taxes before adjustments. Add lines 3, 5e, and 5f . . . .   **6** [_____ . __]

7 Current quarter's adjustment for fractions of cents . . . .   **7** [_____ . __]

8 Current quarter's adjustment for sick pay . . . .   **8** [_____ . __]

9 Current quarter's adjustments for tips and group-term life insurance . . . . . .   **9** [_____ . __]

10 Total taxes after adjustments. Combine lines 6 through 9 . . . .   **10** [_____ . __]

11 Total deposits for this quarter, including overpayment applied from a prior quarter and overpayments applied from Form 941-X, 941-X (PR), 944-X, 944-X (PR), or 944-X (SP) filed in the current quarter . . . .   **11** [_____ . __]

12 Balance due. If line 10 is more than line 11, enter the difference and see instructions . . .   **12** [_____ 0 . __]

13 Overpayment. If line 11 is more than line 10, enter the difference [_____ . __] Check one: [ ] Apply to next return. [ ] Send a refund.

▶ You MUST complete both pages of Form 941 and SIGN it.

Next ▶

For Privacy Act and Paperwork Reduction Act Notice, see the back of the Payment Voucher.   Cat. No. 17001Z   Form **941** (Rev. 1-2014)

ON THE JOB CONTINUING PROBLEM

ASSIGNMENT 5 (CONCLUDED)

950214

Name *(not your trade name)*	Employer identification number (EIN)

Part 2:   **Tell us about your deposit schedule and tax liability for this quarter.**

If you are unsure about whether you are a monthly schedule depositor or a semiweekly schedule depositor, see Pub. 15 (Circular E), section 11.

14 Check one: ☐ Line 10 on this return is less than $2,500 or line 10 on the return for the prior quarter was less than $2,500, and you did not incur a $100,000 next-day deposit obligation during the current quarter. If line 10 for the prior quarter was less than $2,500 but line 10 on this return is $100,000 or more, you must provide a record of your federal tax liability. If you are a monthly schedule depositor, complete the deposit schedule below; if you are a semiweekly schedule depositor, attach Schedule B (Form 941). Go to Part 3.

☐ **You were a monthly schedule depositor for the entire quarter.** Enter your tax liability for each month and total liability for the quarter, then go to Part 3.

Tax liability: **Month 1**   [.   ]

                           Month 2   [.   ]

                           Month 3   [.   ]

Total liability for quarter   [.   ]   **Total must equal line 10.**

☐ **You were a semiweekly schedule depositor for any part of this quarter.** Complete Schedule B (Form 941), Report of Tax Liability for Semiweekly Schedule Depositors, and attach it to Form 941.

Part 3:   **Tell us about your business. If a question does NOT apply to your business, leave it blank.**

15 If your business has closed or you stopped paying wages . . . . ☐ Check here, and

enter the final date you paid wages   [/ /   ] .

16 If you are a seasonal employer and you do not have to file a return for every quarter of the year . . ☐ Check here.

Part 4:   **May we speak with your third-party designee?**

Do you want to allow an employee, a paid tax preparer, or another person to discuss this return with the IRS? See the instructions for details.

☐ Yes. Designee's name and phone number   [   ]   [   ]

Select a 5-digit Personal Identification Number (PIN) to use when talking to the IRS.   ☐ ☐ ☐ ☐ ☐

☐ No.

Part 5:   **Sign here. You MUST complete both pages of Form 941 and SIGN it.**

Under penalties of perjury, I declare that I have examined this return, including accompanying schedules and statements, and to the best of my knowledge and belief, it is true, correct, and complete. Declaration of preparer (other than taxpayer) is based on all information of which preparer has any knowledge.

X   **Sign your name here**   [   ]   Print your name here   [   ]

                           Print your title here   [   ]

Date   [/ /   ]   Best daytime phone   [   ]

Paid Preparer Use Only   Check if you are self-employed . . . ☐

Preparer's name		PTIN	
Preparer's signature		Date	/ /
Firm's name (or yours if self-employed)		EIN	
Address		Phone	
City	State	ZIP code	

ON THE JOB CONTINUING PROBLEM

ASSIGNMENT 6

Form **940 for 201X:** **Employer's Annual Federal Unemployment (FUTA) Tax Return**

850113

Department of the Treasury — Internal Revenue Service

OMB No. 1545-0028

Employer identification number (EIN) ☐☐ – ☐☐☐☐☐☐☐

Name *(not your trade name)* _____

Trade name *(if any)* _____

Address _____

Number   Street   Suite or room number

_____

City   State   ZIP code

_____

Foreign country name   Foreign province/county   Foreign postal code

Type of Return
(Check all that apply.)

☐ **a.** Amended

☐ **b.** Successor employer

☐ **c.** No payments to employees in 201X

☐ **d.** Final: Business closed or stopped paying wages

Instructions and prior-year forms are available at *www.irs.gov/form940*.

Read the separate instructions before you complete this form. Please type or print within the boxes.

Part 1: Tell us about your return. If any line does NOT apply, leave it blank.

1a If you had to pay state unemployment tax in one state only, enter the state abbreviation . **1a** ☐ ☐

1b If you had to pay state unemployment tax in more than one state, you are a multi-state employer . . . . **1b** ☐ Check here. Complete Schedule A (Form 940).

2 If you paid wages in a state that is subject to CREDIT REDUCTION . . . . **2** ☐ Check here. Complete Schedule A (Form 940).

Part 2: Determine your FUTA tax before adjustments for 201X. If any line does NOT apply, leave it blank.

3 Total payments to all employees . . . . **3** _____ .

4 Payments exempt from FUTA tax . . . . . . **4** _____ .

Check all that apply: **4a** ☐ Fringe benefits   **4c** ☐ Retirement/Pension   **4e** ☐ Other
            4b ☐ Group-term life insurance   **4d** ☐ Dependent care

5 Total of payments made to each employee in excess of $7,000 . . . . **5** _____ .

6 **Subtotal** (line 4 + line 5 = line 6) . . . . **6** _____ .

7 Total taxable FUTA wages (line 3 – line 6 = line 7) (see instructions) . . . . . . **7** _____ .

8 FUTA tax before adjustments (line 7 × .006 = line 8) . . . . . . **8** _____ .

Part 3: Determine your adjustments. If any line does NOT apply, leave it blank.

9 If ALL of the taxable FUTA wages you paid were excluded from state unemployment tax, multiply line 7 by .054 (line 7 × .054 = line 9). Go to line 12 . . . . **9** _____ .

10 If SOME of the taxable FUTA wages you paid were excluded from state unemployment tax, OR you paid ANY state unemployment tax late (after the due date for filing Form 940), complete the worksheet in the instructions. Enter the amount from line 7 of the worksheet . . **10** _____ .

11 If credit reduction applies, enter the total from Schedule A (Form 940) . . . . **11** _____ .

Part 4: Determine your FUTA tax and balance due or overpayment for 201X. If any line does NOT apply, leave it blank.

12 Total FUTA tax after adjustments (lines 8 + 9 + 10 + 11 = line 12) . . . . **12** _____ .

13 FUTA tax deposited for the year, including any overpayment applied from a prior year . **13** _____ .

14 Balance due (If line 12 is more than line 13, enter the excess on line 14.)
• If line 14 is more than $500, you must deposit your tax.
• If line 14 is $500 or less, you may pay with this return. (see instructions) . . . . . . **14** _____ .

15 Overpayment (If line 13 is more than line 12, enter the excess on line 15 and check a box below.) . . . . **15** _____ .

▶ You **MUST** complete both pages of this form and **SIGN** it.   Check one: ☐ Apply to next return.   ☐ Send a refund.

Next ➡

For Privacy Act and Paperwork Reduction Act Notice, see the back of Form 940-V, Payment Voucher.   Cat. No. 11234O   Form **940** (2013)

ON THE JOB CONTINUING PROBLEM (CONCLUDED)

ASSIGNMENT 6 (CONCLUDED)

850212

Name (not your trade name)	Employer identification number (EIN)

Part 5: Report your FUTA tax liability by quarter only if line 12 is more than $500. If not, go to Part 6.

16 Report the amount of your FUTA tax liability for each quarter; do NOT enter the amount you deposited. If you had no liability for a quarter, leave the line blank.

16a **1st quarter** (January 1 – March 31) . . . . 16a [.   ]

16b **2nd quarter** (April 1 – June 30) . . . . 16b [.   ]

16c **3rd quarter** (July 1 – September 30) . . . . 16c [.   ]

16d **4th quarter** (October 1 – December 31) . . . . . . 16d [.   ]

17 **Total tax liability for the year** (lines 16a + 16b + 16c + 16d = line 17) 17 [.   ] **Total must equal line 12.**

Part 6: May we speak with your third-party designee?

Do you want to allow an employee, a paid tax preparer, or another person to discuss this return with the IRS? See the instructions for details.

☐ **Yes.**   Designee's name and phone number [   ] [   ]

Select a 5-digit Personal Identification Number (PIN) to use when talking to IRS [ ] [ ] [ ] [ ] [ ]

☐ **No.**

Part 7: Sign here. You MUST complete both pages of this form and SIGN it.

Under penalties of perjury, I declare that I have examined this return, including accompanying schedules and statements, and to the best of my knowledge and belief, it is true, correct, and complete, and that no part of any payment made to a state unemployment fund claimed as a credit was, or is to be, deducted from the payments made to employees. Declaration of preparer (other than taxpayer) is based on all information of which preparer has any knowledge.

X Sign your name here [   ]

Print your name here [   ]

Print your title here [   ]

Date [/   /   ]

Best daytime phone [   ]

Paid Preparer Use Only

Check if you are self-employed . ☐

Preparer's name	[ ]	PTIN	[ ]
Preparer's signature	[ ]	Date	[/ /]
Firm's name (or yours if self-employed)	[ ]	EIN	[ ]
Address	[ ]	Phone	[ ]
City	[ ] State	[ ] ZIP code	[ ]

CHAPTER 8
SUMMARY PRACTICE TEST:
PAYING THE PAYROLL, DEPOSITING PAYROLL TAXES, AND FILING
THE REQUIRED QUARTERLY AND ANNUAL TAX FORMS

Part I

Fill in the blank(s) to complete the statement.

1. Form 941 is completed _____.
2. The payroll tax expense for the employer is made up of _____, _____, _____, and FUTA.
3. Data from the _____ _____ will provide the needed information to record the payroll in the general journal.
4. SUTA is usually paid _____.
5. FUTA Payable is a _____ found on the _____ _____.
6. Form 941 summarizes the taxes owed for _____ and _____.
7. _____ _____ _____ will tell if a deposit is to be made monthly or semiweekly for FIT and Social Security.
8. Form _____ is prepared quarterly to summarize tax liabilities for FICA (Social Security and Medicare) and FIT.
9. The _____ _____ _____ _____ is required to be given to employees by January 31 following the year employed.
10. _____ does not have a merit rating like SUTA.

Part II

Answer true or false to the following.

1. Prepaid Workers' Compensation Insurance is a liability.
2. Payroll taxes are recorded as assets for a business.
3. Payroll Tax Expense is made up of FICA, SUTA, and FIT.
4. The frequency of deposits relating to Form 941 is based on the amount of payroll tax liability in the look-back period.
5. The normal balance of FIT payable is a debit.
6. The individual earnings record provides the data to prepare W-2s.
7. A tax calendar provides little help to the employer involving the payment of tax liabilities.
8. Form 941 is completed twice a year.
9. A year-end adjusting entry is needed for workers' compensation.
10. Form 940 reports state unemployment taxes payable for all employees.

Part III

Complete the following table:

ACCOUNT	CATEGORY	FOUND ON WHICH REPORT
1. Salaries Payable		
2. FUTA Payable		
3. SUTA Payable		
4. OASDI Tax Payable—Medicare		
5. FIT Payable		
6. Office Salaries Expense		

Part IV

Complete the following table:

	4 QUARTERS LOOK-BACK PERIOD LIABILITY	PAYROLL PAID WEEKLY	TAX PAID BY:
Sit. A	$40,000	October	?
Sit. B	75,000		
		on Wed.	?
		on Thurs.	?
		on Fri.	?
		on Sat.	?
		on Sun.	?
		on Mon.	?
		on Tues.	?

Why is the depositor in situation A classified as a monthly depositor while in situation B the depositor is classified as semiweekly?

SOLUTIONS

Part I

1. quarterly
2. FICA (OASDI), FICA (Medicare), SUTA
3. payroll register
4. quarterly
5. liability, balance sheet
6. FICA (OASDI and Medicare), FIT
7. Payroll tax liability in look-back period
8. 941
9. Wage and Tax Statement
10. FUTA

Part II

1. false
2. false
3. false
4. true
5. false

6. true
7. false
8. false
9. true
10. false

Part III

1. Liability; Balance Sheet
2. Liability; Balance Sheet
3. Liability; Balance Sheet
4. Liability; Balance Sheet
5. Liability; Balance Sheet
6. Expense; Income Statement

Part IV

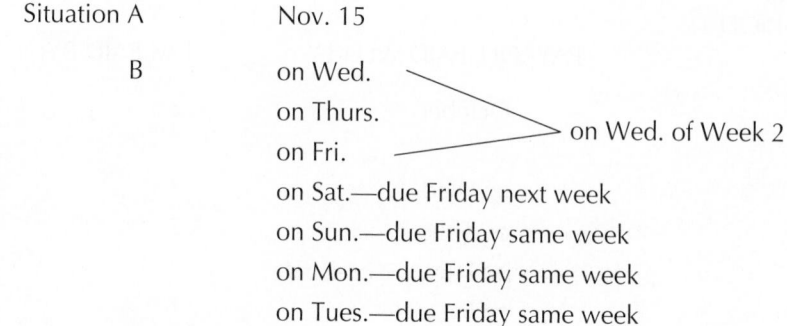

Situation A   Nov. 15

B   on Wed.
     on Thurs.
     on Fri.   on Wed. of Week 2
     on Sat.—due Friday next week
     on Sun.—due Friday same week
     on Mon.—due Friday same week
     on Tues.—due Friday same week

The depositor in situation A is classified as a monthly depositor because its tax liability of $40,000 during the look-back period was less than the $50,000 limit.

On the other hand, the depositor in situation B owed $75,000 during the look-back period. Since this is greater than the $50,000 limit, it was classified as a semiweekly depositor.

Sales and Cash Receipts

CHAPTER
9

FORMS FOR DEMONSTRATION PROBLEM
REQUIREMENT 1

KIM'S RUNNING SHOP
GENERAL JOURNAL

PAGE 6

Date	Account Titles and Description	PR	Dr.	Cr.

FORMS FOR DEMONSTRATION PROBLEM
REQUIREMENT 2

PARTIAL GENERAL LEDGER

CASH   ACCOUNT NO. 110

Date 201X		Explanation	Post Ref.	Debit	Credit	Balance Debit	Balance Credit
June	1	Balance	✔			4 0 0 0 00	

ACCOUNTS RECEIVABLE   ACCOUNT NO. 120

Date 201X		Explanation	Post Ref.	Debit	Credit	Balance Debit	Balance Credit
June	1	Balance	✔			1 4 0 0 00	

DISPLAY EQUIPMENT   ACCOUNT NO. 130

Date 201X		Explanation	Post Ref.	Debit	Credit	Balance Debit	Balance Credit
June	1	Balance	✔			9 0 0 00	

M. KIM, CAPITAL   ACCOUNT NO. 310

Date 201X		Explanation	Post Ref.	Debit	Credit	Balance Debit	Balance Credit
June	1	Balance	✔				8 0 0 0 00

FORMS FOR DEMONSTRATION PROBLEM

PARTIAL GENERAL LEDGER

SALES   ACCOUNT NO. 410

Date 201X		Explanation	Post Ref.	Debit	Credit	Balance	
						Debit	Credit
June	1	Balance	✔				2 000 00

SALES DISCOUNTS   ACCOUNT NO. 420

Date 201X	Explanation	Post Ref.	Debit	Credit	Balance	
					Debit	Credit

SALES RETURNS AND ALLOWANCES   ACCOUNT NO. 440

Date 201X	Explanation	Post Ref.	Debit	Credit	Balance	
					Debit	Credit

FORMS FOR DEMONSTRATION PROBLEM

ACCOUNTS RECEIVABLE SUBSIDIARY LEDGER

NAME   ROGER FLYNN

ADDRESS   81 FOSTER RD., BEVERLY, MA 09125

Date 201X		Explanation	Post Ref.	Debit	Credit	Dr. Balance
June	1	Balance	✔			2 0 0 00

NAME   BOB JEY

ADDRESS   10 RONG RD., BEVERLY, MA 01215

Date 201X		Explanation	Post Ref.	Debit	Credit	Dr. Balance
June	1	Balance	✔			4 0 0 00

FORMS FOR DEMONSTRATION PROBLEM

ACCOUNTS RECEIVABLE SUBSIDIARY LEDGER

NAME JOE LANTZ

ADDRESS 81 FOSTER RD., BEVERLY, MA 09125

Date 201X		Explanation	Post Ref.	Debit	Credit	Dr. Balance
June	1	Balance	✔			8 0 0 00

NAME VALERIE TOG

ADDRESS 10 RONG RD., BEVERLY, MA 01215

Date 201X		Explanation	Post Ref.	Debit	Credit	Dr. Balance

FORMS FOR DEMONSTRATION PROBLEM

REQUIREMENT 3

KIM'S RUNNING SHOP
SCHEDULE OF ACCOUNTS RECEIVABLE
JUNE 30, 201X

FORMS FOR SET A EXERCISES

9A-1

GENERAL JOURNAL

PAGE 1

Date 201X		Account Titles and Description	PR	Dr.					Cr.				
Sept.	18	Accounts Receivable, Twilight Co.			6	4	0	00					
		Sales								6	4	0	00
		Sold merchandise to Twilight Co.											
	19	Accounts Receivable, Falcon Co.			8	5	0	00					
		Sales								8	5	0	00
		Sold merchandise to Falcon Co.											

Twilight Co.

Accounts Receivable 112

Falcon Co.

Sales   411

9A-2

GENERAL JOURNAL

PAGE 1

Date	Account Titles and Description	PR	Dr.	Cr.

Cart Co.

Accounts Receivable   112

Sales   411

French Co.

Sales Returns & Allowances   412

Sales Discounts   413

SET A EXERCISES

9A-3

Date		Account	PR	Dr.				Cr.			

9A-4

AVA CO.
GENERAL JOURNAL

PAGE 1

Date		Account Titles and Description	PR	Dr.				Cr.			

SET A EXERCISES

9A-4 (CONCLUDED)

GENERAL JOURNAL (CONTINUED)   PAGE 1

Date		Account Titles and Description	PR	Dr.	Cr.

ACCOUNTS RECEIVABLE SUBSIDIARY LEDGER   **PARTIAL GENERAL LEDGER**

Charleston Co.

William Co.

Cash   111

Accounts Receivable   113

Ava Roberts, Capital   311

Sales   411

Sales Returns & Allowances   412

Sales Discount   413

AVA CO.
SCHEDULE OF ACCOUNTS RECEIVABLE
October 31, 201X

9A-5

FORMS FOR SET B EXERCISES

9B-1

GENERAL JOURNAL

PAGE 1

Date 201X		Account Titles and Description	PR	Dr.				Cr.			
May	18	Accounts Receivable, Henry Co.		5	9	0	00				
		Sales						5	9	0	00
		Sold merchandise to Henry Co.									
	19	Accounts Receivable, Lincoln Co.		8	9	0	00				
		Sales						8	9	0	00
		Sold merchandise to Lincoln Co.									

Henry Co.

Accounts Receivable 112

Lincoln Co.

Sales   411

9B-2

GENERAL JOURNAL

PAGE 1

Date	Account Titles and Description	PR	Dr.	Cr.

Market Co.

Accounts Receivable   112

Sales   411

Ralph Co.

Sales Returns & Allowances   412

Sales Discounts   413

SET B EXERCISES

9B-3

Date		Account	PR	Dr.	Cr.

9B-4

AUTUMN CO.
GENERAL JOURNAL

PAGE 1

Date		Account Titles and Description	PR	Dr.	Cr.

SET B EXERCISES

9B-4 (CONCLUDED)

GENERAL JOURNAL (CONTINUED)   PAGE 1

Date	Account Titles and Description	PR	Dr.	Cr.

ACCOUNTS RECEIVABLE SUBSIDIARY LEDGER   **PARTIAL GENERAL LEDGER**

Clearview Co.   Cash   111

Nathan Co.   Accounts Receivable   113

Andrew Rodgers, Capital 311

Sales   411

Sales Returns & Allowances   412

Sales Discount   413

AUTUMN CO.
SCHEDULE OF ACCOUNTS RECEIVABLE
August 31, 201X

9B-5

FORMS FOR SET A PROBLEMS

PROBLEM 9A-1

REQUIREMENT 1

FONTINA AND STUFF
GENERAL JOURNAL

PAGE 1

Date	Account Titles and Description	PR	Dr.	Cr.

PROBLEM 9A-1 (CONTINUED)
REQUIREMENT 2

ACCOUNTS RECEIVABLE SUBSIDIARY LEDGER

NAME   DUTCH CO.

ADDRESS   942 MOSE ST., REVERE, MA 01938

Date	Explanation	Post Ref.	Debit	Credit	Dr. Balance

NAME   FRAN CO.

ADDRESS   8 JOSS AVE., LYNN, MA 01947

Date	Explanation	Post Ref.	Debit	Credit	Dr. Balance

NAME   GROOM CO.

ADDRESS   10 LOST RD., TOPSFIELD, MA 01998

Date	Explanation	Post Ref.	Debit	Credit	Dr. Balance

PROBLEM 9A-1 (CONTINUED)

FONTINA AND STUFF
GENERAL LEDGER

ACCOUNTS RECEIVABLE ACCOUNT NO. 112

Date	Explanation	Post Ref.	Debit	Credit	Balance Debit	Balance Credit

CHEESE SALES ACCOUNT NO. 410

Date	Explanation	Post Ref.	Debit	Credit	Balance Debit	Balance Credit

GROCERY SALES ACCOUNT NO. 411

Date	Explanation	Post Ref.	Debit	Credit	Balance Debit	Balance Credit

SALES RETURNS AND ALLOWANCES ACCOUNT NO. 412

Date	Explanation	Post Ref.	Debit	Credit	Balance Debit	Balance Credit

PROBLEM 9A-1 (CONCLUDED)

REQUIREMENT 3

FONTINA AND STUFF
SCHEDULE OF ACCOUNTS RECEIVABLE
FEBRUARY 28, 201X

PROBLEM 9A-2

REQUIREMENT 1

JEFF'S AUTO SUPPLY
GENERAL JOURNAL

PAGE 2

Date		Account Titles and Description	PR	Dr.		Cr.	

PROBLEM 9A-2 (CONTINUED)

REQUIREMENT 2

ACCOUNTS RECEIVABLE SUBSIDIARY LEDGER

NAME   **LANCE BLACK**

ADDRESS   **9 ROE ST., BARTLETT, NH 01382**

Date		Explanation	Post Ref.	Debit	Credit	Dr. Balance
		Balance				

NAME   **R. DICK**

ADDRESS   **22 REESE ST., LACONIA, NH 04321**

Date		Explanation	Post Ref.	Debit	Credit	Dr. Balance

NAME   **J. METCALF**

ADDRESS   **12 ASTER RD., MERRIMACK, NH 02134**

Date		Explanation	Post Ref.	Debit	Credit	Dr. Balance

PROBLEM 9A-2 (CONTINUED)

JEFF'S AUTO SUPPLY
PARTIAL GENERAL LEDGER

ACCOUNTS RECEIVABLE   **ACCOUNT NO. 110**

Date	Explanation	Post Ref.	Debit	Credit	Balance Debit	Balance Credit

SALES TAX PAYABLE   **ACCOUNT NO. 210**

Date	Explanation	Post Ref.	Debit	Credit	Balance Debit	Balance Credit

AUTO PARTS SALES   **ACCOUNT NO. 410**

Date	Explanation	Post Ref.	Debit	Credit	Balance Debit	Balance Credit

SALES RETURNS AND ALLOWANCES   **ACCOUNT NO. 420**

Date	Explanation	Post Ref.	Debit	Credit	Balance Debit	Balance Credit

PROBLEM 9A-2 (CONCLUDED)

REQUIREMENT 3

JEFF'S AUTO SUPPLY
SCHEDULE OF ACCOUNTS RECEIVABLE
FEBRUARY 28, 201X

PROBLEM 9A-3

REQUIREMENT 1

PAYNE'S SNEAKER SHOP
GENERAL JOURNAL

PAGE 2

Date	Account Titles and Description	PR	Dr.	Cr.

PROBLEM 9A-3 (CONTINUED)

PAYNE'S SNEAKER SHOP
GENERAL JOURNAL

PAGE 3

Date	Account Titles and Description	PR	Dr.	Cr.

PROBLEM 9A-3 (CONTINUED)
REQUIREMENT 2

ACCOUNTS RECEIVABLE SUBSIDIARY LEDGER

NAME   B. DURANT

ADDRESS   1822 RIVER RD., MEMPHIS, TN 09111

Date		Explanation	Post Ref.	Debit	Credit	Dr. Balance

NAME   RON LANHAM

ADDRESS   18 MASS. AVE., SAN DIEGO, CA 01999

Date		Explanation	Post Ref.	Debit	Credit	Dr. Balance

NAME   PENNY PRY

ADDRESS   918 MOORE DR., HOMEWOOD, IL 60430

Date		Explanation	Post Ref.	Debit	Credit	Dr. Balance

PROBLEM 9A-3 (CONTINUED)

NAME   JIM ZAMARA

ADDRESS   2 CHESTNUT ST., SWAMPSCOTT, MA 01970

Date	Explanation	Post Ref.	Debit	Credit	Dr. Balance

PAYNE'S SNEAKER SHOP
PARTIAL GENERAL LEDGER

CASH   **ACCOUNT NO. 10**

Date	Explanation	Post Ref.	Debit	Credit	Balance Debit	Balance Credit

PROBLEM 9A-3 (CONTINUED)

ACCOUNTS RECEIVABLE   **ACCOUNT NO. 12**

Date	Explanation	Post Ref.	Debit	Credit	Balance Debit	Balance Credit

SNEAKER RACK EQUIPMENT   **ACCOUNT NO. 14**

Date	Explanation	Post Ref.	Debit	Credit	Balance Debit	Balance Credit

JARED PAYNE, CAPITAL   **ACCOUNT NO. 30**

Date	Explanation	Post Ref.	Debit	Credit	Balance Debit	Balance Credit

PROBLEM 9A-3 (CONTINUED)

SALES   **ACCOUNT NO. 40**

Date	Explanation	Post Ref.	Debit	Credit	Balance Debit	Balance Credit

SALES DISCOUNT   **ACCOUNT NO. 42**

Date 201X	Explanation	Post Ref.	Debit	Credit	Balance Debit	Balance Credit

SALES RETURNS & ALLOWANCES   **ACCOUNT NO. 44**

Date 201X	Explanation	Post Ref.	Debit	Credit	Balance Debit	Balance Credit

PROBLEM 9A-3 (CONCLUDED)

REQUIREMENT 3

PAYNE'S SNEAKER SHOP
SCHEDULE OF ACCOUNTS RECEIVABLE
MARCH 31, 201X

PROBLEM 9A-4

REQUIREMENT 1

CHEVY'S COSMETIC MARKET
GENERAL JOURNAL

PAGE 1

Date	Account Titles and Description	PR	Dr.	Cr.

PROBLEM 9A-4 (CONTINUED)

CHEVY'S COSMETIC MARKET
GENERAL JOURNAL

Date		Account Titles and Description	PR	Dr.	Cr.

PROBLEM 9A-4 (CONTINUED)

ACCOUNTS RECEIVABLE SUBSIDIARY LEDGER

NAME   LOIS KOZAK CO.

ADDRESS   2 RYAN RD., BUFFALO, NY 09113

Date	Explanation	Post Ref.	Debit	Credit	Debit Balance

PROBLEM 9A-4 (CONTINUED)

ACCOUNTS RECEIVABLE SUBSIDIARY LEDGER

NAME   ANN MARIE MAXWELL CO.

ADDRESS   4 REEL RD., LANCASTER, PA 04332

Date	Explanation	Post Ref.	Debit	Credit	Debit Balance

NAME   DAVID PARNELL CO.

ADDRESS   14 BONE DR., ENGLEWOOD CLIFFS, NJ 07632

Date	Explanation	Post Ref.	Debit	Credit	Debit Balance

NAME   EVERETTE TENNIS CO.

ADDRESS   2 MARION RD., BOSTON, MA 01981

Date	Explanation	Post Ref.	Debit	Credit	Debit Balance

PROBLEM 9A-4 (CONTINUED)

CHEVY'S COSMETIC MARKET
GENERAL LEDGER

CASH ACCOUNT NO. 10

Date	Explanation	Post Ref.	Debit	Credit	Balance Debit	Balance Credit

ACCOUNTS RECEIVABLE ACCOUNT NO. 12

Date	Explanation	Post Ref.	Debit	Credit	Balance Debit	Balance Credit

PROBLEM 9A-4 (CONTINUED)

SALES TAX PAYABLE   ACCOUNT NO. <u>20</u>

Date	Explanation	Post Ref.	Debit	Credit	Balance Debit	Balance Credit

CHEVY CANTON, CAPITAL   ACCOUNT NO. <u>30</u>

Date	Explanation	Post Ref.	Debit	Credit	Balance Debit	Balance Credit

LIPSTICK SALES   ACCOUNT NO. <u>40</u>

Date	Explanation	Post Ref.	Debit	Credit	Balance Debit	Balance Credit

PROBLEM 9A-4 (CONCLUDED)

SALES RETURNS & ALLOWANCES, LIPSTICK   ACCOUNT NO. 42

Date	Explanation	Post Ref.	Debit	Credit	Balance Debit	Balance Credit

EYE SHADOW SALES   ACCOUNT NO. 44

Date	Explanation	Post Ref.	Debit	Credit	Balance Debit	Balance Credit

REQUIREMENT 2

CHEVY'S COSMETIC MARKET
SCHEDULE OF ACCOUNTS RECEIVABLE
MAY 31, 201X

FORMS FOR SET B PROBLEMS

PROBLEM 9B-1

REQUIREMENT 1

MACCHIATO AND MORE
GENERAL JOURNAL

PAGE 1

Date	Account Titles and Description	PR	Dr.	Cr.

PROBLEM 9B-1 (CONTINUED)
REQUIREMENT 2

ACCOUNTS RECEIVABLE SUBSIDIARY LEDGER

NAME   DUTCH CO.

ADDRESS   942 MOSE ST., REVERE, MA 01938

Date		Explanation	Post Ref.	Debit	Credit	Dr. Balance

NAME   FRAN CO.

ADDRESS   8 JOSS AVE., LYNN, MA 01947

Date		Explanation	Post Ref.	Debit	Credit	Dr. Balance

NAME   GROOM CO.

ADDRESS   10 LOST RD., TOPSFIELD, MA 01998

Date		Explanation	Post Ref.	Debit	Credit	Dr. Balance

PROBLEM 9B-1 (CONTINUED)

MACCHIATO AND MORE
GENERAL LEDGER

ACCOUNTS RECEIVABLE   **ACCOUNT NO. 112**

Date	Explanation	Post Ref.	Debit	Credit	Balance Debit	Balance Credit

COFFEE SALES   **ACCOUNT NO. 410**

Date	Explanation	Post Ref.	Debit	Credit	Balance Debit	Balance Credit

GROCERY SALES   **ACCOUNT NO. 411**

Date	Explanation	Post Ref.	Debit	Credit	Balance Debit	Balance Credit

SALES RETURNS AND ALLOWANCES   **ACCOUNT NO. 412**

Date	Explanation	Post Ref.	Debit	Credit	Balance Debit	Balance Credit

PROBLEM 9B-1 (CONCLUDED)

REQUIREMENT 3

MACCHIATO AND MORE
SCHEDULE OF ACCOUNTS RECEIVABLE
JUNE 30, 201X

PROBLEM 9B-2

REQUIREMENT 1

JACK'S AUTO SUPPLY
GENERAL JOURNAL

PAGE 2

Date	Account Titles and Description	PR	Dr.	Cr.

PROBLEM 9B-2 (CONTINUED)

REQUIREMENT 2

ACCOUNTS RECEIVABLE SUBSIDIARY LEDGER

NAME   LANCE CORNER

ADDRESS   9 ROE ST., BARTLETT, NH 01382

Date	Explanation	Post Ref.	Debit	Credit	Dr. Balance
	Balance				

NAME   R. NONACK

ADDRESS   22 REESE ST., LACONIA, NH 04321

Date	Explanation	Post Ref.	Debit	Credit	Dr. Balance

NAME   J. SETH

ADDRESS   12 ASTER RD., MERRIMACK, NH 02134

Date	Explanation	Post Ref.	Debit	Credit	Dr. Balance

PROBLEM 9B-2 (CONTINUED)

JACK'S AUTO SUPPLY
PARTIAL GENERAL LEDGER

ACCOUNTS RECEIVABLE   ACCOUNT NO. **110**

Date	Explanation	Post Ref.	Debit	Credit	Balance Debit	Balance Credit

SALES TAX PAYABLE   ACCOUNT NO. **210**

Date	Explanation	Post Ref.	Debit	Credit	Balance Debit	Balance Credit

AUTO PARTS SALES   ACCOUNT NO. **410**

Date	Explanation	Post Ref.	Debit	Credit	Balance Debit	Balance Credit

SALES RETURNS AND ALLOWANCES   ACCOUNT NO. **420**

Date	Explanation	Post Ref.	Debit	Credit	Balance Debit	Balance Credit

PROBLEM 9B-2 (CONCLUDED)

REQUIREMENT 3

JACK'S AUTO SUPPLY
SCHEDULE OF ACCOUNTS RECEIVABLE
JANUARY 31, 201X

PROBLEM 9B-3

REQUIREMENT 1

PENEY'S SNEAKER SHOP
GENERAL JOURNAL

PAGE 2

Date	Account Titles and Description	PR	Dr.	Cr.

PROBLEM 9B-3 (CONTINUED)

PENEY'S SNEAKER SHOP
GENERAL JOURNAL

PAGE 3

Date	Account Titles and Description	PR	Dr.	Cr.

PROBLEM 9B-3 (CONTINUED)

REQUIREMENT 2

ACCOUNTS RECEIVABLE SUBSIDIARY LEDGER

NAME   **B. DONOVAN**

ADDRESS   **1822 RIVER RD., MEMPHIS, TN 09111**

Date	Explanation	Post Ref.	Debit	Credit	Dr. Balance

NAME   **RON LITTLER**

ADDRESS   **18 MASS. AVE., SAN DIEGO, CA 01999**

Date	Explanation	Post Ref.	Debit	Credit	Dr. Balance

NAME   **PAGE PRY**

ADDRESS   **918 MOORE DR., HOMEWOOD, IL 60430**

Date	Explanation	Post Ref.	Debit	Credit	Dr. Balance

PROBLEM 9B-3 (CONTINUED)

NAME   JIM ZAMORA

ADDRESS   2 CHESTNUT ST., SWAMPSCOTT, MA 01970

Date	Explanation	Post Ref.	Debit	Credit	Dr. Balance

PENEY'S SNEAKER SHOP
PARTIAL GENERAL LEDGER

CASH   ACCOUNT NO. **10**

Date	Explanation	Post Ref.	Debit	Credit	Balance Debit	Balance Credit

PROBLEM 9B-3 (CONTINUED)

ACCOUNTS RECEIVABLE   **ACCOUNT NO. 12**

Date	Explanation	Post Ref.	Debit	Credit	Balance Debit	Balance Credit

SNEAKER RACK EQUIPMENT   **ACCOUNT NO. 14**

Date	Explanation	Post Ref.	Debit	Credit	Balance Debit	Balance Credit

MAX PENEY, CAPITAL   **ACCOUNT NO. 30**

Date	Explanation	Post Ref.	Debit	Credit	Balance Debit	Balance Credit

PROBLEM 9B-3 (CONTINUED)

SALES   ACCOUNT NO. 40

Date	Explanation	Post Ref.	Debit	Credit	Balance	
					Debit	Credit

SALES DISCOUNT   ACCOUNT NO. 42

Date 201X	Explanation	Post Ref.	Debit	Credit	Balance	
					Debit	Credit

SALES RETURNS & ALLOWANCES   ACCOUNT NO. 44

Date 201X	Explanation	Post Ref.	Debit	Credit	Balance	
					Debit	Credit

PROBLEM 9B-3 (CONCLUDED)

REQUIREMENT 3

PENEY'S SNEAKER SHOP
SCHEDULE OF ACCOUNTS RECEIVABLE
AUGUST 31, 201X

PROBLEM 9B-4
REQUIREMENT 1

AL'S COSMETIC MARKET
GENERAL JOURNAL

PAGE 1

Date	Account Titles and Description	PR	Dr.	Cr.

PROBLEM 9B-4 (CONTINUED)

AL'S COSMETIC MARKET
GENERAL JOURNAL

PAGE 2

Date		Account Titles and Description	PR		Dr.		Cr.

PROBLEM 9B-4 (CONTINUED)

ACCOUNTS RECEIVABLE SUBSIDIARY LEDGER

NAME   ALEXANDER KOZLOSKY CO.

ADDRESS   2 RYAN RD., BUFFALO, NY 09113

Date	Explanation	Post Ref.	Debit	Credit	Debit Balance

PROBLEM 9B-4 (CONTINUED)

ACCOUNTS RECEIVABLE SUBSIDIARY LEDGER

NAME   DOUGLAS SABIN CO.

ADDRESS   4 REEL RD., LANCASTER, PA 04332

Date		Explanation	Post Ref.	Debit	Credit	Debit Balance

NAME   JOHN TOBIN CO.

ADDRESS   14 BONE DR., ENGLEWOOD CLIFFS, NJ 07632

Date		Explanation	Post Ref.	Debit	Credit	Debit Balance

NAME   EDWARD WEASE CO.

ADDRESS   2 MARION RD., BOSTON, MA 01981

Date		Explanation	Post Ref.	Debit	Credit	Debit Balance

PROBLEM 9B-4 (CONTINUED)

AL'S COSMETIC MARKET
GENERAL LEDGER

CASH   ACCOUNT NO. <u>10</u>

Date	Explanation	Post Ref.	Debit	Credit	Balance	
					Debit	Credit

ACCOUNTS RECEIVABLE   ACCOUNT NO. <u>12</u>

Date	Explanation	Post Ref.	Debit	Credit	Balance	
					Debit	Credit

PROBLEM 9B-4 (CONTINUED)

SALES TAX PAYABLE ACCOUNT NO. 20

Date	Explanation	Post Ref.	Debit	Credit	Balance Debit	Balance Credit

AL FRANKLIN, CAPITAL ACCOUNT NO. 30

Date	Explanation	Post Ref.	Debit	Credit	Balance Debit	Balance Credit

LIPSTICK SALES ACCOUNT NO. 40

Date	Explanation	Post Ref.	Debit	Credit	Balance Debit	Balance Credit

PROBLEM 9B-4 (CONCLUDED)

SALES RETURNS & ALLOWANCES, LIPSTICK
ACCOUNT NO. 42

Date		Explanation	Post Ref.	Debit	Credit	Balance	
						Debit	Credit

EYE SHADOW SALES
ACCOUNT NO. 44

Date		Explanation	Post Ref.	Debit	Credit	Balance	
						Debit	Credit

REQUIREMENT 2

AL'S COSMETIC MARKET
SCHEDULE OF ACCOUNTS RECEIVABLE
DECEMBER 31, 201X

ON THE JOB CONTINUING PROBLEM
ASSIGNMENT 1

SMITH COMPUTER CENTER
GENERAL JOURNAL

PAGE 4

Date	Account Titles and Description	PR	Dr.	Cr.

ASSIGNMENT 2

CASH   ACCOUNT NO. **1000**

Date		Explanation	Post Ref.	Debit	Credit	Balance	
						Debit	Credit
1/1	1X	Balance Forward	✔			5 8 6 1 76	

SMITH COMPUTER CENTER
PARTIAL GENERAL LEDGER

ACCOUNTS RECEIVABLE   **ACCOUNT NO. 1020**

Date		Explanation	Post Ref.	Debit	Credit	Balance	
						Debit	Credit
1/1	1X	Balance Forward	✔			15 5 7 5 00	

SALES   **ACCOUNT NO. 4010**

Date		Explanation	Post Ref.	Debit	Credit	Balance	
						Debit	Credit

SALES RETURNS & ALLOWANCES   **ACCOUNT NO. 4020**

Date		Explanation	Post Ref.	Debit	Credit	Balance	
						Debit	Credit

SALES DISCOUNTS   ACCOUNT NO. __4030__

Date		Explanation	Post Ref.	Debit	Credit	Balance	
						Debit	Credit

ACCOUNTS RECEIVABLE
SUBSIDIARY LEDGER

NAME   PHIL'S PHOTOGRAPHY   ACCOUNT NO. __100__

ADDRESS   1010 MOCKINGBIRD LANE, CARLSBAD, CA 92008

Date		Explanation	Post Ref.	Debit	Credit	Dr. Balance
1/1	1X	Balance forward	✔			3 7 7 5 00

NAME   WORLDWIDE PROFESSIONALS   ACCOUNT NO. __101__

ADDRESS   144 CANTATA, IRVINE, CA 92606

Date		Explanation	Post Ref.	Debit	Credit	Dr. Balance
1/1	1X	Balance	✔			7 4 0 0 00

ACCOUNTS RECEIVABLE SUBSIDIARY LEDGER

NAME   ALL STAR SPORTS, INC.   **ACCOUNT NO. 103**

ADDRESS   1717 JORDAN ST., SAN CLEMENTE, CA 91607

Date		Explanation	Post Ref.	Debit	Credit	Dr. Balance
1/1	1X	Balance	✔			4 4 0 0 00

NAME   DR. MICHAEL TURIONO   **ACCOUNT NO. 104**

ADDRESS   600 NEWPORT BEACH, NEWPORT, CA 91600

Date		Explanation	Post Ref.	Debit	Credit	Dr. Balance

ASSIGNMENT 3

SMITH COMPUTER CENTER
SCHEDULE OF ACCOUNTS RECEIVABLE
1/31/1X

CHAPTER 9
SUMMARY PRACTICE TEST
SALES AND CASH RECEIPTS

Part I

Fill in the blank(s) to complete the statement.

1. The normal balance of sales returns and allowances is _____.
2. _____ _____ and _____ is a contra-revenue account.
3. Sales is a(n) _____ account.
4. A discount period is less time than the _____ _____.
5. A debit to accounts receivable and a credit to sales records the sale of merchandise _____ _____.
6. The _____ _____ _____ _____ lists in alphabetical order an account for each customer.
7. _____ _____ in the general ledger is called the controlling account.
8. The collection of a sale on account is posted to the _____ and _____.
9. Issuing _____ _____ results in a debit to sales returns and allowancs and a credit to accounts receivable.
10. The normal balance of Sales Discounts is _____.
11. Sales Tax Payable is a(n) _____ in the general ledger.
12. Cash sales result in a(n) _____ to cash and a _____ to sales.
13. Sales Returns and Allowances is a(n) _____ _____ account.
14. A sale on account is posted to the _____ and the _____.
15. No _____ _____ are taken on sales tax.
16. A(n) _____ _____ _____ _____ lists the ending balances from the accounts receivable ledger.

Part II

Complete the following chart:

Transaction	Dr.	Cr.
1. Sale for cash	_____	_____
2. Issued credit memo	_____	_____
3. Sale on account	_____	_____
4. Received cash payment less discount	_____	_____

Partial Chart of Accounts

10 Cash
20 Accounts Receivable

40 Sales
42 Sales Discount
44 Sales Returns and Allowances

Part III

Answer true or false to the following statements.

1. A schedule of accounts receivable shows what customers do not owe.
2. A perpetual system would keep continual track of inventory.
3. Sales Discount policies can never change.
4. Sales Tax Payable is an asset.
5. Sales Discount is a contra asset.
6. Issuing a credit memorandum results in Sales Returns and Allowances decreasing with Accounts Receivable increasing.
7. The sum of the accounts in the accounts receivable subsidiary ledger is equal to the balance in the controlling account at the end of the month.
8. The buyer issues the credit memo.
9. The accounts receivable subsidiary ledger is listed in numerical order.
10. Sales Discount is a contra-revenue account.
11. Net sales = gross sales − SRA − SD.
12. The normal balance of Accounts Receivable is a debit.
13. Discounts are taken on sales tax.
14. 2/10, N/30 means a cash discount is good for 30 days.
15. The accounts receivable subsidiary ledger is always located in the general ledger.
16. Gross profit plus operating expenses equals net income.
17. A credit period is longer than the discount period.
18. In the accounts receivable subsidiary ledger each account is debited to record amounts customers owe.
19. Sales Tax Payable is an asset.

SOLUTIONS

Part I

1. debit
2. Sales Returns, Allowances
3. revenue
4. credit period
5. on account
6. accounts receivable subsidiary ledger
7. Accounts Receivable
8. general ledger, accounts receivable subsidiary ledger
9. credit memorandum
10. debit
11. liability
12. debit, credit
13. contra-revenue
14. general ledger, accounts receivable subsidiary ledger
15. sales discounts
16. schedule of accounts receivable

Part II

	Dr.	Cr.
1.	10	40
2.	44	20
3.	20	40
4.	10	20
	42	

Part III

1.	false	11.	true
2.	true	12.	true
3.	false	13.	false
4.	false	14.	false
5.	false	15.	false
6.	false	16.	false
7.	true	17.	true
8.	false	18.	true
9.	false	19.	false
10.	true		

Purchases and Cash Payments

FORMS FOR DEMONSTRATION PROBLEM

REQUIREMENT 1

DALE'S ELECTRONICS SHOP
GENERAL JOURNAL

PAGE 2

Date	Account Titles and Description	PR	Dr.	Cr.

FORMS FOR DEMONSTRATION PROBLEM

PARTIAL GENERAL LEDGER

ELECTRONIC SUPPLIES   ACCOUNT NO. 112

Date	Explanation	Post Ref.	Debit	Credit	Balance	
					Debit	Credit

ELECTRONIC EQUIPMENT   ACCOUNT NO. 120

Date	Explanation	Post Ref.	Debit	Credit	Balance	
					Debit	Credit

ACCOUNTS PAYABLE   ACCOUNT NO. 210

Date	Explanation	Post Ref.	Debit	Credit	Balance	
					Debit	Credit

PURCHASES   ACCOUNT NO. 510

Date	Explanation	Post Ref.	Debit	Credit	Balance	
					Debit	Credit

PURCHASES RETURNS AND ALLOWANCES   ACCOUNT NO. 512

Date	Explanation	Post Ref.	Debit	Credit	Balance	
					Debit	Credit

FORMS FOR DEMONSTRATION PROBLEM

ACCOUNTS PAYABLE SUBSIDARY LEDGER

NAME   HOPE CO.

ADDRESS   112 FLYING HIGHWAY, TRENTON, NJ 00861

Date 201X	Explanation	Post Ref.	Debit	Credit	Cr. Balance

NAME   MATTY CO.

ADDRESS   118 WANG RD., SAUGUS, MA 01432

Date 201X	Explanation	Post Ref.	Debit	Credit	Cr. Balance

NAME   MIA CO.

ADDRESS   112 FLYING HIGHWAY, TRENTON, NJ 00861

Date 201X	Explanation	Post Ref.	Debit	Credit	Cr. Balance

NAME   SAM CO.

ADDRESS   118 WANG RD., SAUGUS, MA 01432

Date 201X	Explanation	Post Ref.	Debit	Credit	Cr. Balance

FORMS FOR DEMONSTRATION PROBLEM
REQUIREMENT 2

DALE'S ELECTRONICS SHOP
SCHEDULE OF ACCOUNTS PAYABLE
NOVEMBER 30, 201X

REQUIREMENT 3

Date	Account Titles and Description	PR	Dr.	Cr.

FORMS FOR SET A EXERCISES

10A-1

Date 201X		Account Titles and Description	PR		Dr.					Cr.			
Jun.	3	Purchases			9	4	0	00					
		Accounts Payable, Cortland.com								9	4	0	00
		Purchased merchandise on account											
	4	Purchases			6	2	0	00					
		Accounts Payable, Harold.com								6	2	0	00
		Purchased merchandise on account											
	8	Equipment			1	9	0	00					
		Accounts Payable, Nickel.com								1	9	0	00
		Bought equipment on account											

Cortland.com   Equipment   120

Harold.com   Accounts Payable   210

Nickel.com   Purchases   510

10A-2

Date		Accounts			Debit					Credit			

Roger Co.

Accounts Payable 211

Purchases Returns and
Allowances 513

SET A EXERCISES

10A-3   PAGE 2

Date		Account Titles and Description	PR		Dr.			Cr.	

ACCOUNTS PAYABLE SUBSIDIARY LEDGER

A. Jordan
	500

B. Thomas
	200

J. Wright
	400

B. Campbell
	100

PARTIAL GENERAL LEDGER

Cash   110
3,100	

Accounts Payable   210
	1,200

Purchases Discount   511

Advertising Expense   610

SET A EXERCISES

10A-4

JACOB'S CLOTHING
SCHEDULE OF ACCOUNTS PAYABLE
APRIL 30, 201X

_____

_____

_____

_____

_____
Accounts Payable   210

10A-5

Accounts Affected	Category	↑↓	Rules

10A-6

_____

_____

_____

_____

_____

_____

FORM FOR EXERCISES 10A-7, 10A-8, 10A-9, 10A-10

Date		Account Titles and Description	PR	Dr.	Cr.

FORM FOR EXERCISES 10A-7, 10A-8, 10A-9, 10A-10

Date		Account Titles and Description	PR	Dr.			Cr.		

CALCULATIONS PAGE

Name _____ Class _____ Date _____

FORMS FOR SET B EXERCISES

10B-1

Date 201X		Account Titles and Description	PR		Dr.					Cr.			
Jun.	3	Purchases			9	3	0	00					
		Accounts Payable, Eve.com								9	3	0	00
		Purchased merchandise on account											
	4	Purchases			6	1	0	00					
		Accounts Payable, Jack.com								6	1	0	00
		Purchased merchandise on account											
	8	Equipment			2	2	0	00					
		Accounts Payable, Noel.com								2	2	0	00
		Bought equipment on account											

Eve.com

Equipment   120

Jack.com

Accounts Payable   210

Noel.com

Purchases   510

10B-2   PAGE 1

Date	Accounts			Debit					Credit				

                                                    Purchases Returns and
          Line Co.   Accounts Payable   211   Allowances   513
_____   _____   _____
            | | |
            | | |
            | | |

SET B EXERCISES

10B-3

Date	Account Titles and Description	PR	Dr.	Cr.

ACCOUNTS PAYABLE SUBSIDIARY LEDGER

A. Jae
	1,400

B. Miller
	800

J. Hall
	1,100

B. Parker
	250

PARTIAL GENERAL LEDGER

Cash   110
3,600	

Accounts Payable   210
	3,550

Purchases Discount   511

Advertising Expense   610

SET B EXERCISES

10B-4

**CODY'S CLOTHING
SCHEDULE OF ACCOUNTS PAYABLE
APRIL 30, 201X**

_____

_____

_____

_____

Accounts Payable   210

10B-5

Accounts Affected	Category	↑↓	Rules

10B-6

_____

_____

_____

_____

_____

_____

FORM FOR EXERCISES 10B-7, 10B-8, 10B-9, 10B-10

Date		Account Titles and Description	PR	Dr.			Cr.		

FORM FOR EXERCISES 10B-7, 10B-8, 10B-9, 10B-10

Date	Account Titles and Description	PR	Dr.	Cr.

CALCULATIONS PAGE

FORMS FOR SET A PROBLEMS

PROBLEM 10A-1

ROBERT'S SKATE SHOP
GENERAL JOURNAL

Date	Account Titles and Description	PR	Dr.	Cr.

PROBLEM 10A-1 (CONTINUED)

ACCOUNTS PAYABLE SUBSIDIARY LEDGER

NAME   KINGSTON CO.

ADDRESS   12 SMITH ST., DEARBORN, MI 09113

Date		Explanation	Post Ref.	Debit	Credit	Cr. Balance

NAME   ROLO CO.

ADDRESS   1 RANTOUL RD., CHARLOTTE, NC 01114

Date		Explanation	Post Ref.	Debit	Credit	Cr. Balance

NAME   WALES CO.

ADDRESS   2 WEST RD., LYNN, MA 01471

Date		Explanation	Post Ref.	Debit	Credit	Cr. Balance

PARTIAL GENERAL LEDGER

STORE SUPPLIES   **ACCOUNT NO. 115**

Date		Explanation	Post Ref.	Debit	Credit	Balance	
						Debit	Credit

PROBLEM 10A-1 (CONCLUDED)

STORE EQUIPMENT   ACCOUNT NO. 121

Date		Explanation	Post Ref.	Debit	Credit	Balance	
						Debit	Credit

ACCOUNTS PAYABLE   ACCOUNT NO. 210

Date		Explanation	Post Ref.	Debit	Credit	Balance	
						Debit	Credit

PURCHASES   ACCOUNT NO. 510

Date		Explanation	Post Ref.	Debit	Credit	Balance	
						Debit	Credit

PROBLEM 10A-2

REQUIREMENT 1

RILEY'S NATURAL FOOD STORE

PAGE 2

Date	Account Titles and Description	PR	Dr.	Cr.

PROBLEM 10A-2 (CONTINUED)
REQUIREMENT 2

ACCOUNTS PAYABLE SUBSIDIARY LEDGER

NAME ARIS CO.

ADDRESS 11 LYNNWAY AVE., NEWPORT, RI 03112

Date		Explanation	Post Ref.	Debit	Credit	Cr. Balance

NAME BROWN CO.

ADDRESS 21 RIVER ST., ANAHEIM, CA 43110

Date		Explanation	Post Ref.	Debit	Credit	Cr. Balance

NAME MOOSE CO.

ADDRESS 10 ASTER RD., DUBUQUE, IA 80021

Date		Explanation	Post Ref.	Debit	Credit	Cr. Balance

NAME READY CO.

ADDRESS 22 GERALD RD., SMITH, CO 43138

Date		Explanation	Post Ref.	Debit	Credit	Cr. Balance

PROBLEM 10A-2 (CONTINUED)

PARTIAL GENERAL LEDGER

STORE SUPPLIES   **ACCOUNT NO. 110**

Date	Explanation	Post Ref.	Debit	Credit	Balance	
					Debit	Credit

OFFICE EQUIPMENT   **ACCOUNT NO. 120**

Date	Explanation	Post Ref.	Debit	Credit	Balance	
					Debit	Credit

ACCOUNTS PAYABLE   **ACCOUNT NO. 210**

Date	Explanation	Post Ref.	Debit	Credit	Balance	
					Debit	Credit

PURCHASES   **ACCOUNT NO. 510**

Date	Explanation	Post Ref.	Debit	Credit	Balance	
					Debit	Credit

PROBLEM 10A-2 (CONCLUDED)

PURCHASES RETURNS AND ALLOWANCES   ACCOUNT NO. 512

Date		Explanation	Post Ref.	Debit	Credit	Balance Debit	Balance Credit

REQUIREMENT 3

RILEY'S NATURAL FOOD STORE
SCHEDULE OF ACCOUNTS PAYABLE
APRIL 30, 201X

PROBLEM 10A-3

REQUIREMENT 1

Date		Account Titles and Description	PR	Dr.			Cr.		

PROBLEM 10A-3 (CONTINUED)
REQUIREMENT 2

ACCOUNTS PAYABLE SUBSIDIARY LEDGER

NAME   ANDERSEN CO.

ADDRESS   1 REACH RD., IPSWICH, MA 01932

Date		Explanation	Post Ref.	Debit	Credit	Cr. Balance

NAME   HENDERSON CO.

ADDRESS   1 RALPH RD., REVERE, MA 01321

Date		Explanation	Post Ref.	Debit	Credit	Cr. Balance

NAME   SQUASH CO.

ADDRESS   7 PLYMOUTH AVE., GLENN, NH 01218

Date		Explanation	Post Ref.	Debit	Credit	Cr. Balance

NAME   XHOSA CO.

ADDRESS   22 REY RD., BOCA RATON, FL 99132

Date		Explanation	Post Ref.	Debit	Credit	Cr. Balance

PROBLEM 10A-3 (CONTINUED)

PARTIAL GENERAL LEDGER

CASH   **ACCOUNT NO. 110**

Date	Explanation	Post Ref.	Debit	Credit	Balance Debit	Balance Credit

DELIVERY TRUCK   **ACCOUNT NO. 150**

Date 201X	Explanation	Post Ref.	Debit	Credit	Balance Debit	Balance Credit

ACCOUNTS PAYABLE   **ACCOUNT NO. 210**

Date	Explanation	Post Ref.	Debit	Credit	Balance Debit	Balance Credit

COMPUTER PURCHASES   **ACCOUNT NO. 510**

Date 201X	Explanation	Post Ref.	Debit	Credit	Balance Debit	Balance Credit

PROBLEM 10A-3 (CONCLUDED)

COMPUTER PURCHASES DISCOUNT   ACCOUNT NO. <u>511</u>

Date	Explanation	Post Ref.	Debit	Credit	Balance Debit	Balance Credit

RENT EXPENSE   ACCOUNT NO. <u>610</u>

Date	Explanation	Post Ref.	Debit	Credit	Balance Debit	Balance Credit

UTILITIES EXPENSE   ACCOUNT NO. <u>620</u>

Date	Explanation	Post Ref.	Debit	Credit	Balance Debit	Balance Credit

REQUIREMENT 3

DREW COMPUTER CENTER
SCHEDULE OF ACCOUNTS PAYABLE
MARCH 31, 201X

PROBLEM 10A-4

REQUIREMENT 1

ABBY'S TOY HOUSE
GENERAL JOURNAL

PAGE 1

Date	Account Titles and Description	PR	Dr.	Cr.

PROBLEM 10A-4 (CONTINUED)

Date		Account Titles and Description	PR		Dr.			Cr.	

PROBLEM 10A-4 (CONTINUED)

Date		Account Titles and Description	PR	Dr.			Cr.		

PROBLEM 10A-4 (CONTINUED)

Date		Account Titles and Description	PR	Dr.	Cr.

PROBLEM 10A-4 (CONTINUED)

Date		Account Titles and Description	PR	Dr.		Cr.	

PROBLEM 10A-4 (CONTINUED)

REQUIREMENT 2

ACCOUNTS PAYABLE SUBSIDIARY LEDGER

NAME   MORRIS CURTIS COMPANY

ADDRESS   87 GARFIELD AVE., REVERE, MA 01245

Date	Explanation	Post Ref.	Debit	Credit	Cr. Balance

NAME   SAM KATZ GARAGE

ADDRESS   22 REGIS RD., BOSTON, MA 01950

Date	Explanation	Post Ref.	Debit	Credit	Cr. Balance

NAME   MILDRED MANN

ADDRESS   22 RETTER ST., SAN DIEGO, CA 01211

Date	Explanation	Post Ref.	Debit	Credit	Cr. Balance

NAME   SANYA BURGER

ADDRESS   2 SPRING ST., WEERS, ND 02118

Date	Explanation	Post Ref.	Debit	Credit	Cr. Balance

PROBLEM 10A-4 (CONTINUED)

ACCOUNTS RECEIVABLE SUBSIDIARY LEDGER

NAME   DAVID PLOUFFE

ADDRESS   24 RYAN RD., BUIKE, OH 02183

Date	Explanation	Post Ref.	Debit	Credit	Dr. Balance

NAME   ROBERT COOPER

ADDRESS   2 SMITH RD., DALLAS, TX 22210

Date	Explanation	Post Ref.	Debit	Credit	Dr. Balance

NAME   ALISON REACH

ADDRESS   1 SCHOOL ST., CLEVELAND, OH 22441

Date	Explanation	Post Ref.	Debit	Credit	Dr. Balance

PROBLEM 10A-4 (CONTINUED)

NAME   **BELLA FALCO COMPANY**

ADDRESS   **18 VEEK RD., CHESTER, CT 80111**

Date		Explanation	Post Ref.	Debit	Credit	Dr. Balance

GENERAL LEDGER

CASH   **ACCOUNT NO. 110**

Date		Explanation	Post Ref.	Debit	Credit	Balance	
						Debit	Credit

PROBLEM 10A-4 (CONTINUED)

ACCOUNTS RECEIVABLE   ACCOUNT NO. 112

Date	Explanation	Post Ref.	Debit	Credit	Balance Debit	Balance Credit

PREPAID RENT   ACCOUNT NO. 114

Date	Explanation	Post Ref.	Debit	Credit	Balance Debit	Balance Credit

DELIVERY TRUCK   ACCOUNT NO. 121

Date	Explanation	Post Ref.	Debit	Credit	Balance Debit	Balance Credit

PROBLEM 10A-4 (CONTINUED)

ACCOUNTS PAYABLE   ACCOUNT NO. 210

Date		Explanation	Post Ref.	Debit	Credit	Balance	
						Debit	Credit

A. GRAY, CAPITAL   ACCOUNT NO. 310

Date		Explanation	Post Ref.	Debit	Credit	Balance	
						Debit	Credit

TOY SALES   ACCOUNT NO. 410

Date		Explanation	Post Ref.	Debit	Credit	Balance	
						Debit	Credit

PROBLEM 10A-4 (CONTINUED)

SALES RETURNS AND ALLOWANCES   ACCOUNT NO. 412

Date	Explanation	Post Ref.	Debit	Credit	Balance Debit	Balance Credit

SALES DISCOUNTS   ACCOUNT NO. 414

Date	Explanation	Post Ref.	Debit	Credit	Balance Debit	Balance Credit

TOY PURCHASES   ACCOUNT NO. 510

Date	Explanation	Post Ref.	Debit	Credit	Balance Debit	Balance Credit

PURCHASES RETURNS AND ALLOWANCES   ACCOUNT NO. 512

Date	Explanation	Post Ref.	Debit	Credit	Balance Debit	Balance Credit

PROBLEM 10A-4 (CONTINUED)

PURCHASES DISCOUNT ACCOUNT NO. 514

Date	Explanation	Post Ref.	Debit	Credit	Balance Debit	Credit

SALARIES EXPENSE ACCOUNT NO. 610

Date	Explanation	Post Ref.	Debit	Credit	Balance Debit	Credit

CLEANING EXPENSE ACCOUNT NO. 612

Date	Explanation	Post Ref.	Debit	Credit	Balance Debit	Credit

PROBLEM 10A-4 (CONCLUDED)

REQUIREMENT 3

ABBY'S TOY HOUSE
SCHEDULE OF ACCOUNTS RECEIVABLE
DECEMBER 31, 201X

ABBY'S TOY HOUSE
SCHEDULE OF ACCOUNTS PAYABLE
DECEMBER 31, 201X

PROBLEM 10A-5

Date		Account Titles and Description	PR	Dr.			Cr.		

PROBLEM 10A-5 (CONCLUDED)

Date	Account Titles and Description	PR	Dr.		Cr.	

FORMS FOR SET B PROBLEMS

PROBLEM 10B-1

RASHEED'S SKATE SHOP
GENERAL JOURNAL

Date	Account Titles and Description	PR	Dr.	Cr.

PROBLEM 10B-1 (CONTINUED)

ACCOUNTS PAYABLE SUBSIDIARY LEDGER

NAME   ANDOVER CO.

ADDRESS   12 SMITH ST., DEARBORN, MI 09113

Date		Explanation	Post Ref.	Debit	Credit	Cr. Balance

NAME   LAKEVILLE CO.

ADDRESS   1 RANTOUL RD., CHARLOTTE, NC 01114

Date		Explanation	Post Ref.	Debit	Credit	Cr. Balance

NAME   NEWBURY CO.

ADDRESS   2 WEST RD., LYNN, MA 01471

Date		Explanation	Post Ref.	Debit	Credit	Cr. Balance

PARTIAL GENERAL LEDGER

STORE SUPPLIES   ACCOUNT NO. 115

Date		Explanation	Post Ref.	Debit	Credit	Balance	
						Debit	Credit

PROBLEM 10B-1 (CONCLUDED)

STORE EQUIPMENT ACCOUNT NO. <u>121</u>

Date		Explanation	Post Ref.	Debit	Credit	Balance	
						Debit	Credit

ACCOUNTS PAYABLE ACCOUNT NO. <u>210</u>

Date		Explanation	Post Ref.	Debit	Credit	Balance	
						Debit	Credit

PURCHASES ACCOUNT NO. <u>510</u>

Date		Explanation	Post Ref.	Debit	Credit	Balance	
						Debit	Credit

PROBLEM 10B-2

REQUIREMENT 1

TRINA'S NATURAL FOOD STORE

PAGE 2

Date		Account Titles and Description	PR		Dr.			Cr.	

PROBLEM 10B-2 (CONTINUED)

REQUIREMENT 2

ACCOUNTS PAYABLE SUBSIDIARY LEDGER

NAME ANTION CO.

ADDRESS 11 LYNNWAY AVE., NEWPORT, RI 03112

Date		Explanation	Post Ref.	Debit	Credit	Cr. Balance

NAME BLOCK CO.

ADDRESS 21 RIVER ST., ANAHEIM, CA 43110

Date		Explanation	Post Ref.	Debit	Credit	Cr. Balance

NAME MIDDEN CO.

ADDRESS 10 ASTER RD., DUBUQUE, IA 80021

Date		Explanation	Post Ref.	Debit	Credit	Cr. Balance

NAME REX CO.

ADDRESS 22 GERALD RD., SMITH, CO 43138

Date		Explanation	Post Ref.	Debit	Credit	Cr. Balance

PROBLEM 10B-2 (CONTINUED)

PARTIAL GENERAL LEDGER

STORE SUPPLIES   **ACCOUNT NO. 110**

Date	Explanation	Post Ref.	Debit	Credit	Balance Debit	Balance Credit

OFFICE EQUIPMENT   **ACCOUNT NO. 120**

Date	Explanation	Post Ref.	Debit	Credit	Balance Debit	Balance Credit

ACCOUNTS PAYABLE   **ACCOUNT NO. 210**

Date	Explanation	Post Ref.	Debit	Credit	Balance Debit	Balance Credit

PURCHASES   **ACCOUNT NO. 510**

Date	Explanation	Post Ref.	Debit	Credit	Balance Debit	Balance Credit

PROBLEM 10B-2 (CONCLUDED)

PURCHASES RETURNS AND ALLOWANCES **ACCOUNT NO. 512**

Date	Explanation	Post Ref.	Debit	Credit	Balance Debit	Balance Credit

REQUIREMENT 3

TRINA'S NATURAL FOOD STORE
SCHEDULE OF ACCOUNTS PAYABLE
OCTOBER 31, 201X

PROBLEM 10B-3

REQUIREMENT 1

Date	Account Titles and Description	PR	Dr.	Cr.

PROBLEM 10B-3 (CONTINUED)
REQUIREMENT 2

ACCOUNTS PAYABLE SUBSIDIARY LEDGER

NAME   ANDERSEN CO.

ADDRESS   1 REACH RD., IPSWICH, MA 01932

Date	Explanation	Post Ref.	Debit	Credit	Cr. Balance

NAME   HACK CO.

ADDRESS   1 RALPH RD., REVERE, MA 01321

Date	Explanation	Post Ref.	Debit	Credit	Cr. Balance

NAME   SOIL CO.

ADDRESS   7 PLYMOUTH AVE., GLENN, NH 01218

Date	Explanation	Post Ref.	Debit	Credit	Cr. Balance

NAME   XYDIAS CO.

ADDRESS   22 REY RD., BOCA RATON, FL 99132

Date	Explanation	Post Ref.	Debit	Credit	Cr. Balance

PROBLEM 10B-3 (CONTINUED)

PARTIAL GENERAL LEDGER

CASH   **ACCOUNT NO. 110**

Date	Explanation	Post Ref.	Debit	Credit	Balance Debit	Balance Credit

DELIVERY TRUCK   **ACCOUNT NO. 150**

Date 201X	Explanation	Post Ref.	Debit	Credit	Balance Debit	Balance Credit

ACCOUNTS PAYABLE   **ACCOUNT NO. 210**

Date	Explanation	Post Ref.	Debit	Credit	Balance Debit	Balance Credit

COMPUTER PURCHASES   **ACCOUNT NO. 510**

Date 201X	Explanation	Post Ref.	Debit	Credit	Balance Debit	Balance Credit

PROBLEM 10B-3 (CONCLUDED)

COMPUTER PURCHASES DISCOUNT **ACCOUNT NO. 511**

Date		Explanation	Post Ref.	Debit	Credit	Balance	
						Debit	Credit

RENT EXPENSE **ACCOUNT NO. 610**

Date		Explanation	Post Ref.	Debit	Credit	Balance	
						Debit	Credit

UTILITIES EXPENSE **ACCOUNT NO. 620**

Date		Explanation	Post Ref.	Debit	Credit	Balance	
						Debit	Credit

REQUIREMENT 3

JOHNSON COMPUTER CENTER
SCHEDULE OF ACCOUNTS PAYABLE
MAY 31, 201X

PROBLEM 10B-4

REQUIREMENT 1

ABBY'S TOY HOUSE
GENERAL JOURNAL

PAGE 1

Date	Account Titles and Description	PR	Dr.	Cr.

PROBLEM 10B-4 (CONTINUED)

Date		Account Titles and Description	PR		Dr.			Cr.	

PROBLEM 10B-4 (CONTINUED)

Date		Account Titles and Description	PR	Dr.	Cr.

PROBLEM 10B-4 (CONTINUED)

Date	Account Titles and Description	PR	Dr.	Cr.

PROBLEM 10B-4 (CONTINUED)

Date		Account Titles and Description	PR	Dr.			Cr.		

PROBLEM 10B-4 (CONTINUED)

REQUIREMENT 2

ACCOUNTS PAYABLE SUBSIDIARY LEDGER

NAME   MORRIS CURTIS COMPANY

ADDRESS   87 GARFIELD AVE., REVERE, MA 01245

Date	Explanation	Post Ref.	Debit	Credit	Cr. Balance

NAME   SAM KATZ GARAGE

ADDRESS   22 REGIS RD., BOSTON, MA 01950

Date	Explanation	Post Ref.	Debit	Credit	Cr. Balance

NAME   MICHAEL KEISER

ADDRESS   22 RETTER ST., SAN DIEGO, CA 01211

Date	Explanation	Post Ref.	Debit	Credit	Cr. Balance

NAME   MILLARD FILMORE

ADDRESS   2 SPRING ST., WEERS, ND 02118

Date	Explanation	Post Ref.	Debit	Credit	Cr. Balance

PROBLEM 10B-4 (CONTINUED)

ACCOUNTS RECEIVABLE SUBSIDIARY LEDGER

NAME   DAVID PLOUFFE

ADDRESS   24 RYAN RD., BUIKE, OH 02183

Date	Explanation	Post Ref.	Debit	Credit	Dr. Balance

NAME   JOHN DRAYTON

ADDRESS   2 SMITH RD., DALLAS, TX 22210

Date	Explanation	Post Ref.	Debit	Credit	Dr. Balance

NAME   AIMEE RAYPOLE

ADDRESS   1 SCHOOL ST., CLEVELAND, OH 22441

Date	Explanation	Post Ref.	Debit	Credit	Dr. Balance

PROBLEM 10B-4 (CONTINUED)

NAME   BELLA FALCO COMPANY

ADDRESS   18 VEEK RD., CHESTER, CT 80111

Date	Explanation	Post Ref.	Debit	Credit	Dr. Balance

GENERAL LEDGER

CASH   ACCOUNT NO. <u>110</u>

Date	Explanation	Post Ref.	Debit	Credit	Balance Debit	Balance Credit

PROBLEM 10B-4 (CONTINUED)

ACCOUNTS RECEIVABLE   ACCOUNT NO. 112

Date		Explanation	Post Ref.	Debit	Credit	Balance	
						Debit	Credit

PREPAID RENT   ACCOUNT NO. 114

Date		Explanation	Post Ref.	Debit	Credit	Balance	
						Debit	Credit

DELIVERY TRUCK   ACCOUNT NO. 121

Date		Explanation	Post Ref.	Debit	Credit	Balance	
						Debit	Credit

PROBLEM 10B-4 (CONTINUED)

ACCOUNTS PAYABLE   ACCOUNT NO. 210

Date	Explanation	Post Ref.	Debit	Credit	Balance Debit	Balance Credit

A. ELLEN, CAPITAL   ACCOUNT NO. 310

Date	Explanation	Post Ref.	Debit	Credit	Balance Debit	Balance Credit

TOY SALES   ACCOUNT NO. 410

Date	Explanation	Post Ref.	Debit	Credit	Balance Debit	Balance Credit

PROBLEM 10B-4 (CONTINUED)

SALES RETURNS AND ALLOWANCES   ACCOUNT NO. 412

Date	Explanation	Post Ref.	Debit	Credit	Balance Debit	Balance Credit

SALES DISCOUNTS   ACCOUNT NO. 414

Date	Explanation	Post Ref.	Debit	Credit	Balance Debit	Balance Credit

TOY PURCHASES   ACCOUNT NO. 510

Date	Explanation	Post Ref.	Debit	Credit	Balance Debit	Balance Credit

PURCHASES RETURNS AND ALLOWANCES   ACCOUNT NO. 512

Date	Explanation	Post Ref.	Debit	Credit	Balance Debit	Balance Credit

PROBLEM 10B-4 (CONTINUED)

PURCHASES DISCOUNT   ACCOUNT NO. 514

Date		Explanation	Post Ref.	Debit	Credit	Balance	
						Debit	Credit

SALARIES EXPENSE   ACCOUNT NO. 610

Date		Explanation	Post Ref.	Debit	Credit	Balance	
						Debit	Credit

CLEANING EXPENSE   ACCOUNT NO. 612

Date		Explanation	Post Ref.	Debit	Credit	Balance	
						Debit	Credit

PROBLEM 10B-4 (CONCLUDED)
REQUIREMENT 3

ABBY'S TOY HOUSE
SCHEDULE OF ACCOUNTS RECEIVABLE
MARCH 31, 201X

ABBY'S TOY HOUSE
SCHEDULE OF ACCOUNTS PAYABLE
MARCH 31, 201X

PROBLEM 10B-5

Date	Account Titles and Description	PR	Dr.	Cr.

PROBLEM 10B-5 (CONCLUDED)

Date		Account Titles and Description	PR	Dr.			Cr.		

ON THE JOB CONTINUING PROBLEM
ASSIGNMENT 1

SMITH COMPUTER CENTER
GENERAL JOURNAL

PAGE 7

Date	Account Titles and Description	PR	Dr.	Cr.

ASSIGNMENT 2

PARTIAL GENERAL LEDGER

CASH   **ACCOUNT NO. 1000**

Date		Explanation	Post Ref.	Debit	Credit	Balance Debit	Balance Credit
2/1	1X	Balance forward	✔			19 3 6 3 76	

MERCHANDISE INVENTORY   **ACCOUNT NO. 1021**

Date		Explanation	Post Ref.	Debit	Credit	Balance Debit	Balance Credit

PREPAID RENT   **ACCOUNT NO. 1025**

Date		Explanation	Post Ref.	Debit	Credit	Balance Debit	Balance Credit
2/1	1X	Balance forward	✔			2 0 0 0 00	

SUPPLIES ACCOUNT NO. <u>1030</u>

Date		Explanation	Post Ref.	Debit	Credit	Balance	
						Debit	Credit
2/1	1X	Balance forward	✔			1 9 2 00	

ACCOUNTS PAYABLE ACCOUNT NO. <u>2000</u>

Date		Explanation	Post Ref.	Debit	Credit	Balance	
						Debit	Credit
2/1	1X	Balance forward	✔				2 5 7 0 00

PURCHASES ACCOUNT NO. <u>6000</u>

Date		Explanation	Post Ref.	Debit	Credit	Balance	
						Debit	Credit

PURCHASE RETURNS AND ALLOWANCES ACCOUNT NO. <u>6010</u>

Date		Explanation	Post Ref.	Debit	Credit	Balance	
						Debit	Credit

PURCHASE DISCOUNTS ACCOUNT NO. <u>6020</u>

Date		Explanation	Post Ref.	Debit	Credit	Balance	
						Debit	Credit

ACCOUNTS PAYABLE SUBSIDIARY LEDGER

NAME   THE STAPLE STORE   # 6A3

ADDRESS   1919 MORAN ST., ANAHEIM, CA 92606

Date		Explanation	Post Ref.	Debit	Credit	Cr. Balance
2/1	1X	Balance forward	✔			5 0 00

NAME   QUALITY OFFICE FURNITURE   # 6A4

ADDRESS   460 ESCONDIDO BLVD., ESCONDIDO, CA 92025

Date		Explanation	Post Ref.	Debit	Credit	Cr. Balance
2/1	1X	Balance forward	✔			1 8 0 0 00

NAME   PACIFIC BELL   # 6A5

ADDRESS   606 INDUSTRIAL ST., SAN DIEGO, CA 92121

Date		Explanation	Post Ref.	Debit	Credit	Cr. Balance
2/1	1X	Balance forward	✔			1 7 0 00

NAME   A-TECH, INC.   # 6A6

ADDRESS   101 BELL AVE., SAN DIEGO, CA 92101

Date		Explanation	Post Ref.	Debit	Credit	Cr. Balance
2/1	1X	Balance forward	✓			5 5 0 00

NAME   COMPUTERS R US   # 6A7

ADDRESS   1020 WIL LANE, LOS ANGELES, CA 92405

Date		Explanation	Post Ref.	Debit	Credit	Cr. Balance

ASSIGNMENT 4

SMITH COMPUTER CENTER
SCHEDULE OF ACCOUNTS PAYABLE
2/28/1X

APPENDIX 10A
FORMS FOR DEMONSTRATION PROBLEM — SPECIAL JOURNALS

J. LING CO.
SALES JOURNAL

PAGE 1

Date	Account Debited	Terms	Invoice No.	Post Ref.	Dr. Acc. Receivable Cr. Sales

CASH RECEIPTS JOURNAL

PAGE 1

Date	Cash Dr.	Sales Discounts Dr.	Accounts Receivable Cr.	Sales Cr.	Sundry Account Name	PR	Sundry Amount Cr.

PURCHASES JOURNAL

PAGE 1

Date	Account Credited	Terms	PR	Accounts Payable Cr.	Purchases Dr.	Sundry Dr. Account	PR	Amount

CASH PAYMENTS JOURNAL

PAGE 1

Date	Check No.	Account Debited	PR	Sundry Account Dr.	Accounts Payable Dr.	Purchases Discounts Cr.	Cash Cr.

FORMS FOR DEMONSTRATION PROBLEM (CONTINUED)

GENERAL JOURNAL

PAGE 1

Date	Account Titles and Description	PR	Dr.	Cr.

ACCOUNTS RECEIVABLE SUBSIDIARY LEDGER

NAME   **BALDER CO.**

ADDRESS   **1 ROCK RD., DENVER, CO 66083**

Date	Explanation	Post Ref.	Debit	Credit	Dr. Balance

NAME   **LEWIS CO.**

ADDRESS   **15 SMITH AVE., REVERE, MA 01545**

Date	Explanation	Post Ref.	Debit	Credit	Dr. Balance

FORMS FOR DEMONSTRATION PROBLEM (CONCLUDED)

ACCOUNTS PAYABLE SUBSIDIARY LEDGER

NAME　　CASE CO.

ADDRESS　　1 LONG RD., MARLBOROUGH, MA 01545

Date	Explanation	Post Ref.	Debit	Credit	Cr. Balance

NAME　　NOONE CO.

ADDRESS　　11 MILL RD., MALDEN, OK 01143

Date	Explanation	Post Ref.	Debit	Credit	Cr. Balance

PARTIAL GENERAL LEDGER

Cash　　111

Sales　　410

Purchases Discounts　　530

Accounts Receivable　　112

Sales Returns & Allowances　　420

Salaries Expense　　610

Equipment　　116

Sales Discount　　430

Accounts Payable　　210

Purchases　　510

J. Ling, Capital　　310

Purchases Returns & Allowances　　520

CHAPTER 10A APPENDIX FORMS

PROBLEM A-1

(1, 2)

YUMMY.COM
SALES JOURNAL

PAGE 1

Date		Account Debited	Invoice No.	PR	Accounts Receivable Dr.			Pizza Sales Cr.			Grocery Sales Cr.		

(1, 2)

YUMMY.COM
GENERAL JOURNAL

PAGE 1

Date		Account Titles and Description	PR		Dr.			Cr.		

PROBLEM A-1 (CONTINUED)

ACCOUNTS RECEIVABLE SUBSIDIARY LEDGER

NAME   DABNEY CO.

ADDRESS   942 MOSE ST., REVERE, MA 01938

Date	Explanation	Post Ref.	Debit	Credit	Dr. Balance

NAME   LUXURY CO.

ADDRESS   8 JOSS AVE., LYNN, MA 01947

Date	Explanation	Post Ref.	Debit	Credit	Dr. Balance

NAME   SALLY DROUGHT CO.

ADDRESS   10 LOST RD., TOPSFIELD, MA 01998

Date	Explanation	Post Ref.	Debit	Credit	Dr. Balance

PROBLEM A-1 (CONTINUED)

YUMMY.COM
GENERAL LEDGER

ACCOUNTS RECEIVABLE   ACCOUNT NO. 112

Date	Explanation	Post Ref.	Debit	Credit	Balance Debit	Balance Credit

PIZZA SALES   ACCOUNT NO. 410

Date	Explanation	Post Ref.	Debit	Credit	Balance Debit	Balance Credit

GROCERY SALES   ACCOUNT NO. 411

Date	Explanation	Post Ref.	Debit	Credit	Balance Debit	Balance Credit

SALES RETURNS AND ALLOWANCES   ACCOUNT NO. 412

Date	Explanation	Post Ref.	Debit	Credit	Balance Debit	Balance Credit

PROBLEM A-1 (CONCLUDED)

(3)

YUMMY.COM
SCHEDULE OF ACCOUNTS RECEIVABLE
APRIL 30, 201X

PROBLEM A-2

(1,2)

DAVID'S AUTO SUPPLY
SALES JOURNAL

PAGE 1

Date	Account Debited	Invoice No.	PR	Accounts Receivable Dr.	Sales Tax Payable Cr.	Auto Parts Sales Cr.

PROBLEM A-2 (CONTINUED)

(1,2)

DAVID'S AUTO SUPPLY
GENERAL JOURNAL

PAGE 1

Date	Account Titles and Description	PR	Dr.	Cr.

PROBLEM A-2 (CONTINUED)

ACCOUNTS RECEIVABLE SUBSIDIARY LEDGER

NAME   GRAHAM CARTER

ADDRESS   9 ROE ST., BARTLETT, NH 01382

Date 201X		Explanation	Post Ref.	Debit	Credit	Dr. Balance
Jun	1	Balance	✔			6 0 0 00

NAME   J. SANDERS

ADDRESS   22 REESE ST., LACONIA, NH 04321

Date 201X		Explanation	Post Ref.	Debit	Credit	Dr. Balance
Jun	1	Balance	✔			5 0 0 00

NAME   R. VICTOR

ADDRESS   12 ASTER RD., MERRIMACK, NH 02134

Date 201X		Explanation	Post Ref.	Debit	Credit	Dr. Balance
Jun	1	Balance	✔			8 0 0 00

PROBLEM A-2 (CONTINUED)

DAVID'S AUTO SUPPLY
GENERAL JOURNAL

ACCOUNTS RECEIVABLE   ACCOUNT NO. 110

Date 201X		Explanation	Post Ref.	Debit	Credit	Balance Debit	Balance Credit
Jun	1	Balance	✔			1 9 0 0 00	

SALES TAX PAYABLE   ACCOUNT NO. 210

Date 201X		Explanation	Post Ref.	Debit	Credit	Balance Debit	Balance Credit
Jun	1	Balance	✔				1 9 0 0 00

AUTO PARTS SALES   ACCOUNT NO. 410

Date	Explanation	Post Ref.	Debit	Credit	Balance Debit	Balance Credit

SALES RETURNS AND ALLOWANCES   ACCOUNT NO. 420

Date	Explanation	Post Ref.	Debit	Credit	Balance Debit	Balance Credit

PROBLEM A-2 (CONCLUDED)

(3)

DAVID'S AUTO SUPPLY
SCHEDULE OF ACCOUNTS RECEIVABLE
JUNE 30, 201X

PROBLEM A-3

TENNIS.COM
PURCHASES JOURNAL

Date	Account Credited	Date of Invoice	Inv. No.	Terms	PR	Accounts Payable Cr.	Purchases Dr.	Sundry Dr.		
								Account	PR	Amount

PROBLEM A-3 (CONTINUED)

ACCOUNTS PAYABLE SUBSIDIARY LEDGER

NAME MILLER.COM

ADDRESS 12 SMITH ST., DEARBORN, MI 09113

Date	Explanation	Post Ref.	Debit	Credit	Cr. Balance

NAME NEWBURG CO.

ADDRESS 1 RANTOUL RD., CHARLOTTE, NC 01114

Date	Explanation	Post Ref.	Debit	Credit	Cr. Balance

NAME RAPONE CO.

ADDRESS 2 WEST RD., LYNN, MA 01471

Date	Explanation	Post Ref.	Debit	Credit	Cr. Balance

PARTIAL GENERAL LEDGER

STORE SUPPLIES   **ACCOUNT NO. 115**

Date	Explanation	Post Ref.	Debit	Credit	Balance Debit	Balance Credit

PROBLEM A-3 (CONCLUDED)

STORE EQUIPMENT   **ACCOUNT NO. 121**

Date		Explanation	Post Ref.	Debit	Credit	Balance	
						Debit	Credit

ACCOUNTS PAYABLE   **ACCOUNT NO. 210**

Date		Explanation	Post Ref.	Debit	Credit	Balance	
						Debit	Credit

PURCHASES   **ACCOUNT NO. 510**

Date		Explanation	Post Ref.	Debit	Credit	Balance	
						Debit	Credit

PROBLEM A-4

(1)

MARION'S NATURAL FOOD STORE
PURCHASES JOURNAL

PAGE 1

Date	Account Credited	Date of Invoice	Inv. No.	Terms	PR	Accounts Payable Cr.	Purchases Dr.	Store Supplies Dr.	Sundry Dr.		
									Account	PR	Amount

PROBLEM A-4 (CONTINUED)

(2)

ACCOUNTS PAYABLE SUBSIDIARY LEDGER

NAME   ALDEN CO.

ADDRESS   11 LYNNWAY AVE., NEWPORT, RI 03112

Date 201X		Explanation	Post Ref.	Debit	Credit	Cr. Balance
Mar.	1	Balance	✔			3 0 0 00

NAME   BULLMAN CO.

ADDRESS   21 RIVER ST., ANAHEIM, CA 43110

Date 201X		Explanation	Post Ref.	Debit	Credit	Cr. Balance
Mar.	1	Balance	✔			8 0 0 00

NAME   MOTT CO.

ADDRESS   10 ASTER RD., DUBUQUE, IA 80021

Date 201X		Explanation	Post Ref.	Debit	Credit	Cr. Balance
Mar.	1	Balance	✔			1 0 0 0 00

NAME   REYNOLD CO.

ADDRESS   22 GERALD RD., SMITH, CO 43138

Date 201X		Explanation	Post Ref.	Debit	Credit	Cr. Balance
Mar.	1	Balance	✔			5 0 0 00

PROBLEM A-4 (CONTINUED)

PARTIAL GENERAL LEDGER

STORE SUPPLIES   **ACCOUNT NO. 110**

Date	Explanation	Post Ref.	Debit	Credit	Balance Debit	Balance Credit

OFFICE EQUIPMENT   **ACCOUNT NO. 120**

Date	Explanation	Post Ref.	Debit	Credit	Balance Debit	Balance Credit

ACCOUNTS PAYABLE   **ACCOUNT NO. 210**

Date 201X	Explanation	Post Ref.	Debit	Credit	Balance Debit	Balance Credit
Mar. 1	Balance	✔				2 6 0 0 00

PURCHASES   **ACCOUNT NO. 510**

Date 201X	Explanation	Post Ref.	Debit	Credit	Balance Debit	Balance Credit
Mar. 1	Balance	✔			18 0 0 0 00	

PROBLEM A-4 (CONCLUDED)

PURCHASES RETURNS AND ALLOWANCES   **ACCOUNT NO. 512**

Date		Explanation	Post Ref.	Debit	Credit	Balance	
						Debit	Credit

GENERAL JOURNAL   PAGE 1

Date		Account Titles and Description	PR	Dr.	Cr.

(3)

MARION'S NATURAL FOOD STORE
SCHEDULE OF ACCOUNTS PAYABLE
MARCH 31, 201X

PROBLEM A-5

(1, 3)

ANDREA'S TOY HOUSE
PURCHASES JOURNAL

PAGE 1

Date	Account Credited	Date of Inv.	Inv. No.	Terms	PR	Accounts Payable Cr.	Toy Purchases Dr.	Sundry Dr.		
								Accounts	PR	Amount

PROBLEM A-5 (CONTINUED)

ANDREA'S TOY HOUSE
CASH RECEIPTS JOURNAL

PAGE 1

Date	Cash Dr.	Sales Discounts Dr.	Accounts Receivable Cr.	Toy Sales Cr.	Sundry Account	PR	Amount Cr.

PROBLEM A-5 (CONTINUED)

ANDREA'S TOY HOUSE
CASH PAYMENTS JOURNAL

PAGE 1

Date	Check No.	Account Debited	PR	Sundry Dr.	Accounts Payable Dr.	Purchases Discount Cr.	Cash Cr.

PROBLEM A-5 (CONTINUED)

ANDREA'S TOY HOUSE
SALES JOURNAL

Date	Account Debited	Invoice No.	Terms	PR	Accounts Rec. – Dr. Toy Sales – Cr.

ANDREA'S TOY HOUSE
GENERAL JOURNAL

Date	Account Titles and Description	PR	Dr.	Cr.

PROBLEM A-5 (CONTINUED)

(2)   ACCOUNTS PAYABLE SUBSIDIARY LEDGER

NAME   ROSE KAUFMAN

ADDRESS   87 GARFIELD AVE., REVERE, MA 01245

Date		Explanation	Post Ref.	Debit	Credit	Cr. Balance

NAME   SAM KATZ GARAGE

ADDRESS   22 REGIS RD., BOSTON, MA 01950

Date		Explanation	Post Ref.	Debit	Credit	Cr. Balance

NAME   MORRIS CURTIS CO.

ADDRESS   22 RETTER ST., SAN DIEGO, CA 01211

Date		Explanation	Post Ref.	Debit	Credit	Cr. Balance

NAME   ADAM GRAVES

ADDRESS   2 SPRING ST., WEERS, ND 02118

Date		Explanation	Post Ref.	Debit	Credit	Cr. Balance

PROBLEM A-5 (CONTINUED)

ACCOUNTS RECEIVABLE SUBSIDIARY LEDGER

NAME   BILL BURTON

ADDRESS   24 RYAN RD., BUIKE, OH 02183

Date	Explanation	Post Ref.	Debit	Credit	Dr. Balance

NAME   BELLA FALCO CO.

ADDRESS   2 SMITH RD., DALLAS, TX 22210

Date	Explanation	Post Ref.	Debit	Credit	Dr. Balance

NAME   DAVID MULDROW BEASLEY

ADDRESS   1 SCHOOL ST., CLEVELAND, OH 22441

Date	Explanation	Post Ref.	Debit	Credit	Dr. Balance

PROBLEM A-5 (CONTINUED)

NAME   ANDREA REAGAN

ADDRESS   18 VEEK RD., CHESTER, CT 80111

Date		Explanation	Post Ref.	Debit	Credit	Dr. Balance

GENERAL LEDGER

CASH   **ACCOUNT NO. 110**

Date		Explanation	Post Ref.	Debit	Credit	Balance	
						Debit	Credit

ACCOUNTS RECEIVABLE   **ACCOUNT NO. 112**

Date		Explanation	Post Ref.	Debit	Credit	Balance	
						Debit	Credit

PREPAID RENT   **ACCOUNT NO. 114**

Date		Explanation	Post Ref.	Debit	Credit	Balance	
						Debit	Credit

PROBLEM A-5 (CONTINUED)

DELIVERY TRUCK　　　　　　　　　　　**ACCOUNT NO. 121**

Date	Explanation	Post Ref.	Debit	Credit	Balance Debit	Balance Credit

ACCOUNTS PAYABLE　　　　　　　　　　**ACCOUNT NO. 210**

Date	Explanation	Post Ref.	Debit	Credit	Balance Debit	Balance Credit

A. RICHARDSON, CAPITAL　　　　　　　**ACCOUNT NO. 310**

Date	Explanation	Post Ref.	Debit	Credit	Balance Debit	Balance Credit

TOY SALES　　　　　　　　　　　　　　**ACCOUNT NO. 410**

Date	Explanation	Post Ref.	Debit	Credit	Balance Debit	Balance Credit

PROBLEM A-5 (CONTINUED)

SALES RETURNS AND ALLOWANCES — ACCOUNT NO. 412

Date	Explanation	Post Ref.	Debit	Credit	Balance Debit	Balance Credit

SALES DISCOUNTS — ACCOUNT NO. 414

Date	Explanation	Post Ref.	Debit	Credit	Balance Debit	Balance Credit

TOY PURCHASES — ACCOUNT NO. 510

Date	Explanation	Post Ref.	Debit	Credit	Balance Debit	Balance Credit

PURCHASES RETURNS AND ALLOWANCES — ACCOUNT NO. 512

Date	Explanation	Post Ref.	Debit	Credit	Balance Debit	Balance Credit

PROBLEM A-5 (CONTINUED)

PURCHASES DISCOUNT   **ACCOUNT NO. 514**

Date	Explanation	Post Ref.	Debit	Credit	Balance Debit	Balance Credit

SALARIES EXPENSE   **ACCOUNT NO. 610**

Date	Explanation	Post Ref.	Debit	Credit	Balance Debit	Balance Credit

CLEANING EXPENSE   **ACCOUNT NO. 612**

Date	Explanation	Post Ref.	Debit	Credit	Balance Debit	Balance Credit

PROBLEM A-5 (CONCLUDED)

(4)

ANDREA'S TOY HOUSE
SCHEDULE OF ACCOUNTS RECEIVABLE
DECEMBER 31, 201X

(4)

ANDREA'S TOY HOUSE
SCHEDULE OF ACCOUNTS PAYABLE
DECEMBER 31, 201X

CHAPTER 10
SUMMARY PRACTICE TEST
PURCHASES AND CASH PAYMENTS

Part I

Fill in the blank(s) to complete the statement.

1. The trend in accounting is more to _____ inventory rather than _____ inventory.

2. Purchase discounts are categorized as a(n) _____ _____ account.

3. The Purchases account has a _____ balance.

4. Purchases are defined as merchandise for _____ to customers.

5. The accounts payable subsidiary ledger represents a potential _____ of cash.

6. The controlling account in the general ledger for the accounts payable subsidiary ledger is called _____ _____.

7. The accounts payable subsidiary ledger would be recorded _____.

8. The balance in the Accounts Payable controlling account should be equal to the sum of the accounts in the _____ _____ _____ _____.

9. In perpetual inventory, purchases are recorded as _____ _____.

10. Changes in individual accounts payable should be posted _____.

11. A(n) _____ _____ that is issued means the buyer owes less money, as merchandise is being returned or an allowance received.

12. A debit memorandum issued or a credit memorandum received results in a(n) _____ to Accounts Payable and a credit to Purchases Returns and Allowances.

13. A sales discount is a _____ _____ to a buyer.

14. The accounts payable subsidiary ledger is listed in _____ _____.

15. Purchases Returns and Allowances is increased by a(n) _____.

16. Cost of goods sold is classified as a(n) _____.

17. In a perpetual inventory system, freight is recorded in the _____ _____ account.

18. Purchases Discounts is increased by _____.

19. A(n) _____ _____ provides the purchasing department the information to then prepare a purchase order.

20. A(n) _____ _____ is made out after a company inspects received shipments.

Part II

Complete the following table:

	Account Title	Category	↑↓	Financial Statement
1.	Purchases			
2.	Purchase Discount			
3.	Accounts Receivable			
4.	Cost of Goods Sold			
5.	Salary Expenses			
6.	Accounts Payable			
7.	Purchase Returns and Allowances			
8.	Cash			
9.	Supplies			
10.	Sale Discount			

Part III

Answer true or false to the following statements.

1. F.O.B. shipping point means the seller is responsible to cover shipping costs.
2. The Purchases account is a contra-cost of goods sold account.
3. Purchases discounts are the result of paying for merchandise inventory within the discount period.
4. F.O.B. Destination means the seller is responsible to cover shipping costs.
5. Purchases discounts are taken on freight.
6. Merchandise inventory is an asset.
7. The account Cost of Goods Sold is a cost.
8. The balance in Accounts Payable, the controlling account, will be equal to the sum of the accounts receivable subsidiary ledger at the end of the month.
9. A purchase order is completed after the purchase requisition.
10. On receiving a purchase order, the seller may issue a sales invoice.
11. The normal balance of Purchases Discount is a debit balance.
12. The seller will often issue a debit memorandum to the buyer.
13. The account Cost of Goods Sold is used in a periodic inventory system.
14. Returned merchandise inventory by a buyer results in a change in Purchases Returns and Allowances.
15. Trade discounts do not occur because of early payments of one's bills.
16. A seller's sales discount on sales is the buyer's purchases discount.
17. Buying of equipment on account is only recorded in the general ledger.
18. On receiving a debit memorandum, the seller will issue a credit memorandum.
19. Returns in a perpetual accounting system are recorded in the merchandise inventory account.
20. Purchases are contra costs.

SOLUTIONS

Part I

1. perpetual, periodic
2. contra-cost
3. debit
4. resale
5. outflow or payment
6. accounts payable
7. daily
8. accounts payable subsidiary ledger
9. merchandise inventory
10. daily
11. debit memorandum
12. debit
13. purchase discount
14. alphabetical order
15. credit
16. cost
17. merchandise inventory
18. credits
19. purchase requisition
20. receiving report

Part II

	Category	Increase	Decrease	Financial Statement
1.	cost	Dr	Cr	Income Statement
2.	contra-cost	Cr	Dr	Income Statement
3.	asset	Dr	Cr	Balance Sheet
4.	cost	Dr	Cr	Income Statement
5.	expense	Dr	Cr	Income Statement
6.	liability	Cr	Dr	Balance Sheet
7.	contra-cost	Cr	Dr	Income Statement
8.	asset	Dr	Cr	Balance Sheet
9.	asset	Dr	Cr	Balance Sheet
10.	contra-revenue	Dr	Cr	Income Statement

Part III

1. false
2. false
3. true
4. true
5. false
6. true
7. true
8. false
9. true
10. true
11. false
12. false
13. false
14. true
15. true
16. true
17. false
18. true
19. true
20. false

Preparing a Worksheet for a Merchandise Company

CHAPTER
11

FORMS FOR DEMONSTRATION PROBLEM

Use one of the blank fold-out worksheets that accompanied your textbook.

FORMS FOR SET A EXERCISES

11A-1

Account	Category	Normal Balance
a. Unearned Revenue		
b. Merch. Inventory (beg.)		
c. Freight-In		
d. Payroll Tax Expense		
e. Purchases Discount		
f. Sales Discount		
g. FICA—Social Security Payable		
h. Purchases Returns and Allowances		

11A-2

a. Net Sales

b. Cost of Goods Sold

c. Gross Profit

d. Net Income

11A-3

Accounts Affected	Category	↑↓	Rules

11A-4

a.

b.

c.

11A-5

Use one of the blank fold-out worksheets that accompanied your textbook.

FORMS FOR SET B EXERCISES

11B-1

Account	Category	Normal Balance
a. Salaries Payable		
b. Merch. Inventory (beg.)		
c. Freight-In		
d. Payroll Tax Expense		
e. Purchases Returns and Allowances		
f. Sales Returns and Allowances		
g. FICA—Social Security Payable		
h. Purchases Discounts		

11B-2

a. Net Sales

_____

_____

b. Cost of Goods Sold

_____

_____

c. Gross Profit

_____

_____

d. Net Income

_____

_____

11B-3

Accounts Affected	Category	↑↓	Rules

11B-4

a. _____

b. _____

c. _____

11B-5

Use one of the blank fold-out worksheets that accompanied your textbook.

FORMS FOR SET A PROBLEMS

PROBLEM 11A-1

a.	Net sales	
b.	Cost of goods sold	
c.	Gross profit	
d.	Net income	

PROBLEM 11A-2;
PROBLEM 11A-3;
PROBLEM 11A-4

Use one of the blank fold-out worksheets that accompanied your textbook.

FORMS FOR SET B PROBLEMS

PROBLEM 11B-1

a.	Net sales	
b.	Cost of goods sold	
c.	Gross profit	
d.	Net income	

PROBLEM 11B-2;
PROBLEM 11B-3;
PROBLEM 11B-4

Use one of the blank fold-out worksheets that accompanied your textbook.

ON THE JOB CONTINUING PROBLEM

Use the blank fold-out worksheet for this problem that accompanied your textbook.

CHAPTER 11
SUMMARY PRACTICE TEST:
PREPARING A WORKSHEET
FOR A MERCHANDISE COMPANY

Part I

Fill in the blank(s) to complete the statement.

1. The _____ _____ system keeps a continual track of the quantity and cost of the inventory on hand.

2. In the periodic inventory system, new inventories bought is recorded in the _____ account.

3. A continuous record of inventory is kept in a(n) _____ _____ system.

4. When using the periodic system, _____ _____ will remain unchanged.

5. _____ _____ represents a liability on the balance sheet and records money received for a sale or service not yet performed.

6. Freight-in is _____ to the cost of goods sold.

7. Net Sales less Cost of Goods Sold equals _____ _____.

8. _____ _____ equals Gross Sales less Sales Discounts and Sales Returns and Allowances.

9. Net Purchases equals Purchases less _____ _____ and _____ _____ _____ _____.

10. A(n) _____ _____ helps calculate ending inventory.

11. Ending inventory is _____ from the cost of goods available for sale.

12. Net purchases are _____ to Beginning Inventory to get the cost of goods available for sale.

13. Gross Profit less _____ equals Net Income.

14. Purchase discounts _____ the total cost of merchandise sold.

15. Beginning inventory at the end of the period is assumed to be _____, and thus a _____.

16. The ending inventory of one period becomes the _____ _____ next period.

17. Ending inventory represents goods not _____.

18. Net income is put in the _____ column of the balance sheet on the worksheet.

19. Purchases are increased by a(n) _____.

20. Sales returns and allowances are used in calculating _____ _____.

21. Net income is put in the _____ column of the income statement on the worksheet.

22. Beginning Inventory and Ending Inventory are never _____ on the worksheet.

Part II

Answer true or false to the following statements.

1. Unearned Revenue is a liability.
2. Perpetual inventory keeps a continuous record of inventory.
3. Purchases increase cost of goods sold.
4. Freight-in is added to Purchases in the schedule of cost of goods sold.
5. Figures for Beginning and Ending Inventory are combined on the worksheet.
6. A periodic system is used by companies with low volume and high unit prices.
7. Merchandise Inventory is an asset.
8. Unearned Revenue is a liability on the income statement.
9. Inventory is always taken 10 times per year.
10. Purchases replace ending inventory in a periodic system.
11. A trial balance may be placed directly on a worksheet.
12. The adjustment process updates the inventory account.
13. A post-closing trial balance has no temporary accounts.
14. Sales Discounts is a permanent account.
15. Gross sales are located on the balance sheet.
16. The Sales Returns and Allowances account has a normal balance of a credit.
17. Ending inventory of one period is the beginning inventory of the following period.
18. Net income always means cash.
19. Ending inventory increases cost of goods sold.
20. Net purchases is always the same as total purchases.
21. Gross profit plus expenses equals net income.
22. Unearned Storage Fees is a liability.
23. Merchandise inventory that is sold is assumed to be a cost.
24. Accumulated Depreciation is increased by a debit.
25. Merchandise Inventory can never be listed on a trial balance.
26. Ending Merchandise Inventory can only be found on a balance sheet.
27. The amount of rent expired is used in the adjustment process.
28. Adjustments help update individual ledger accounts.
29. Purchases Returns and Allowances is found on a balance sheet.
30. Beginning Merchandise Inventory found on the balance sheet from the prior period will also be placed in the cost of goods sold section of the balance sheet.
31. Sales always means cash received.
32. Ending Merchandise Inventory of the current period is found only on the balance sheet.
33. Purchases adds to the cost of goods sold.
34. Purchases discounts reduce the cost of purchases on the balance sheet.
35. Beginning inventory can never be assumed sold by the end of a period.

36. Ending inventory in one period becomes beginning inventory for the next two periods.
37. The ending inventory may be calculated from an inventory sheet.
38. Income Summary is used in the adjustment of merchandise inventory.
39. Ending inventory not sold is only placed in the credit column of the balance sheet section on the worksheet.
40. Purchases Discount is recorded in the credit column of the income statement section on the worksheet.
41. Gross profit and net income mean the same.
42. All companies must give sales discounts.
43. A merchandise company does not need a cost of goods sold section on the income statement.
44. Cost of goods available for sale less ending inventory equals cost of goods sold.

SOLUTIONS

Part I

1. perpetual inventory
2. Purchases
3. perpetual inventory
4. beginning inventory
5. Unearned Revenue
6. added
7. Gross Profit
8. Net sales
9. Purchases Discounts, Purchases Returns and Allowances
10. Inventory sheet (record)
11. subtracted
12. added
13. Expenses
14. reduce
15. sold, cost
16. begining inventory
17. sold
18. credit
19. debit
20. net sales
21. debit
22. combined

Part II

1. true	**12.** true	**23.** true	**34.** false
2. true	**13.** true	**24.** false	**35.** false
3. true	**14.** false	**25.** false	**36.** false
4. true	**15.** false	**26.** false	**37.** true
5. false	**16.** false	**27.** true	**38.** true
6. false	**17.** true	**28.** true	**39.** false
7. true	**18.** false	**29.** false	**40.** true
8. false	**19.** false	**30.** false	**41.** false
9. false	**20.** false	**31.** false	**42.** false
10. false	**21.** false	**32.** false	**43.** false
11. true	**22.** true	**33.** true	**44.** true

Completion of the Accounting Cycle for a Merchandise Company

CHAPTER 12

Name _____ Class _____ Date _____

FORMS FOR DEMONSTRATION PROBLEM
REQUIREMENT 1

GENERAL JOURNAL   PAGE 9

Date	Account Titles and Description	PR	Dr.	Cr.

FORMS FOR DEMONSTRATION PROBLEM

REQUIREMENT 1

GENERAL JOURNAL

Date	Account Titles and Description	PR	Dr.	Cr.

FORMS FOR DEMONSTRATION PROBLEM

GENERAL LEDGER

CASH   ACCOUNT NO. 110

Date		Explanation	Post Ref.	Debit	Credit	Balance	
						Debit	Credit
3/31	1X	Balance forward	✔			6 0 0 0 00	

MERCHANDISE INVENTORY   ACCOUNT NO. 120

Date		Explanation	Post Ref.	Debit	Credit	Balance	
						Debit	Credit
3/31	1X	Balance forward	✔			2 0 0 0 00	

PREPAID RENT   ACCOUNT NO. 130

Date		Explanation	Post Ref.	Debit	Credit	Balance	
						Debit	Credit
3/31	1X	Balance forward	✔			6 0 0 00	

PREPAID INSURANCE   ACCOUNT NO. 140

Date		Explanation	Post Ref.	Debit	Credit	Balance	
						Debit	Credit
3/31	1X	Balance forward	✔			5 0 0 00	

FORMS FOR DEMONSTRATION PROBLEM

DISPLAY EQUIPMENT   ACCOUNT NO. 150

Date	Explanation	Post Ref.	Debit	Credit	Balance Debit	Balance Credit
3/31 1X	Balance forward	✔			3 000 00	

ACCUMULATED DEPRECIATION, DISPLAY EQUIPMENT   ACCOUNT NO. 160

Date	Explanation	Post Ref.	Debit	Credit	Balance Debit	Balance Credit
3/31 1X	Balance forward	✔				2 000 00

UNEARNED TRAINING FEES   ACCOUNT NO. 210

Date	Explanation	Post Ref.	Debit	Credit	Balance Debit	Balance Credit
3/31 1X	Balance forward	✔				3 000 00

ACCOUNTS PAYABLE   ACCOUNT NO. 220

Date	Explanation	Post Ref.	Debit	Credit	Balance Debit	Balance Credit
3/31 1X	Balance forward	✔				7 000 00

SALARIES PAYABLE   ACCOUNT NO. 230

Date	Explanation	Post Ref.	Debit	Credit	Balance Debit	Balance Credit

FORMS FOR DEMONSTRATION PROBLEM

J. LOY, CAPITAL   ACCOUNT NO. 310

Date		Explanation	Post Ref.	Debit	Credit	Balance Debit	Balance Credit
3/31	1X	Balance forward	✔				7 000 00

INCOME SUMMARY   ACCOUNT NO. 320

Date	Explanation	Post Ref.	Debit	Credit	Balance Debit	Balance Credit

SALES   ACCOUNT NO. 410

Date		Explanation	Post Ref.	Debit	Credit	Balance Debit	Balance Credit
3/31	1X	Balance forward					9 600 00

SALES RETURNS AND ALLOWANCES   ACCOUNT NO. 412

Date		Explanation	Post Ref.	Debit	Credit	Balance Debit	Balance Credit
3/31	1X	Balance forward				5 00 00	

SALES DISCOUNTS   ACCOUNT NO. 414

Date		Explanation	Post Ref.	Debit	Credit	Balance Debit	Balance Credit
3/31	1X	Balance forward				3 00 00	

FORMS FOR DEMONSTRATION PROBLEM

TRAINING FEES EARNED   ACCOUNT NO. 420

Date	Explanation	Post Ref.	Debit	Credit	Balance Debit	Balance Credit

PURCHASES   ACCOUNT NO. 540

Date	Explanation	Post Ref.	Debit	Credit	Balance Debit	Balance Credit
3/31 1X	Balance forward				15 0 0 0 00	

PURCHASES RETURNS AND ALLOWANCES   ACCOUNT NO. 550

Date	Explanation	Post Ref.	Debit	Credit	Balance Debit	Balance Credit
3/31 1X	Balance forward					4 0 0 00

PURCHASES DISCOUNTS   ACCOUNT NO. 560

Date	Explanation	Post Ref.	Debit	Credit	Balance Debit	Balance Credit
3/31 1X	Balance forward					8 0 0 00

SALARY EXPENSE   ACCOUNT NO. 600

Date	Explanation	Post Ref.	Debit	Credit	Balance Debit	Balance Credit
3/31 1X	Balance forward	✓			1 4 0 0 00	

FORMS FOR DEMONSTRATION PROBLEM

PLUMBING EXPENSE — ACCOUNT NO. 610

Date		Explanation	Post Ref.	Debit	Credit	Balance Debit	Balance Credit
3/31	1X	Balance forward	✓			2 0 0 00	

UTILITIES EXPENSE — ACCOUNT NO. 620

Date		Explanation	Post Ref.	Debit	Credit	Balance Debit	Balance Credit
3/31	1X	Balance forward				3 0 0 00	

INSURANCE EXPENSE — ACCOUNT NO. 630

Date		Explanation	Post Ref.	Debit	Credit	Balance Debit	Balance Credit

RENT EXPENSE — ACCOUNT NO. 640

Date		Explanation	Post Ref.	Debit	Credit	Balance Debit	Balance Credit

FORMS FOR DEMONSTRATION PROBLEM

GENERAL LEDGER

DEPRECIATION EXPENSE, DISPLAY EQUIPMENT   **ACCOUNT NO. 650**

Date	Explanation	Post Ref.	Debit	Credit	Balance	
					Debit	Credit

FORMS FOR DEMONSTRATION PROBLEM

REQUIREMENT 2

LEDGER SPORT SHOP
POST-CLOSING TRIAL BALANCE
MARCH 31, 201X

FORMS FOR SET A EXERCISES

12A-1

COST OF GOODS SOLD

Merchandise Inv. 12/01/1X	_____
Purchases	_____
Less: Purchases Disc.	_____
Purch. R. & A.	_____
	_____
Net Purchases	_____
Add: Freight-in	_____
Net Cost of Purchases	_____
Cost of Goods Available for Sale	_____
Less: Merchandise Inv. 12/31/1X	_____
Cost of Goods Sold	_____

12A-2

	Account	Category	Classification	Financial Statement
a.	Salaries Payable			
b.	Accounts Payable			
c.	Mortgage Payable			
d.	Unearned Legal Fees			
e.	SIT Payable			
f.	Office Equipment			
g.	Land			

12A-3

Date	Account		Debit	Credit

SET A EXERCISES

12A-4

F. HENRY CO.
PARTIAL BALANCE SHEET
DECEMBER 31, 201X

12A-5

(a)

Date	Account		Debit	Credit

_____ Salaries Expense _____   _____ Salaries Payable _____

(b)

Date	Account		Debit	Credit

_____ Salaries Expense _____   _____ Salaries Payable _____

(c)

Date	Account		Debit	Credit

_____ Salaries Expense _____   _____ Cash _____

FORMS FOR SET B EXERCISES

12B-1

COST OF GOODS SOLD

Merchandise Inv. 12/01/1X	_____
Purchases	_____
Less: Purchases Disc.	_____
Purch. R. & A.	_____
	_____
Net Purchases	_____
Add: Freight-in	_____
Net Cost of Purchases	_____
Cost of Goods Available for Sale	_____
Less: Merchandise Inv. 12/31/1X	_____
Cost of Goods Sold	_____

12B-2

	Account	Category	Classification	Financial Statement
a.	Wages Payable			
b.	Accounts Payable			
c.	Notes Payable			
d.	Unearned Revenue			
e.	FIT Payable			
f.	Office Furniture			
g.	Land			

12B-3

Date	Account		Debit	Credit

SET B EXERCISES

12B-4

C. BLOSSOM CO.
PARTIAL BALANCE SHEET
DECEMBER 31, 201X

12B-5

(a)

Date	Account	Debit	Credit

_____ Salaries Expense _____   _____ Salaries Payable _____

(b)

Date	Account	Debit	Credit

_____ Salaries Expense _____   _____ Salaries Payable _____

(c)

Date	Account	Debit	Credit

_____ Salaries Expense _____   _____ Cash _____

FORMS FOR SET A PROBLEMS

PROBLEM 12A-1

NELSON CO.
INCOME STATEMENT
FOR YEAR ENDED DECEMBER 31, 201X

PROBLEM 12A-2

JAMES CO.
STATEMENT OF OWNER'S EQUITY
FOR YEAR ENDED DECEMBER 31, 201X

PROBLEM 12A-2 (CONCLUDED)

JAMES CO.
BALANCE SHEET
DECEMBER 31, 201X

PROBLEM 12A-3

(1) Use one of the blank fold-out worksheets that accompanied your textbook.

(2)

JOSH'S SUPPLIES
INCOME STATEMENT
FOR YEAR ENDED DECEMBER 31, 201X

PROBLEM 12A-3 (CONTINUED)

JOSH'S SUPPLIES
STATEMENT OF OWNER'S EQUITY
FOR YEAR ENDED DECEMBER 31, 201X

PROBLEM 12A-3 (CONTINUED)

JOSH'S SUPPLIES
BALANCE SHEET
DECEMBER 31, 201X

PROBLEM 12A-3 (CONTINUED)

(3)

GENERAL JOURNAL

PAGE 2

Date		Account Titles and Description	PR		Dr.			Cr.	

PROBLEM 12A-3 (CONCLUDED)

GENERAL JOURNAL

Date	Account Titles and Description	PR	Dr.	Cr.

PROBLEM 12A-4

(1) Use one of the blank fold-out worksheets that accompanied your textbook.

(2)

CULLEN LUMBER
INCOME STATEMENT
FOR YEAR ENDED DECEMBER 31, 201X

PROBLEM 12A-4 (CONTINUED)

CULLEN LUMBER
STATEMENT OF OWNER'S EQUITY
FOR YEAR ENDED DECEMBER 31, 201X

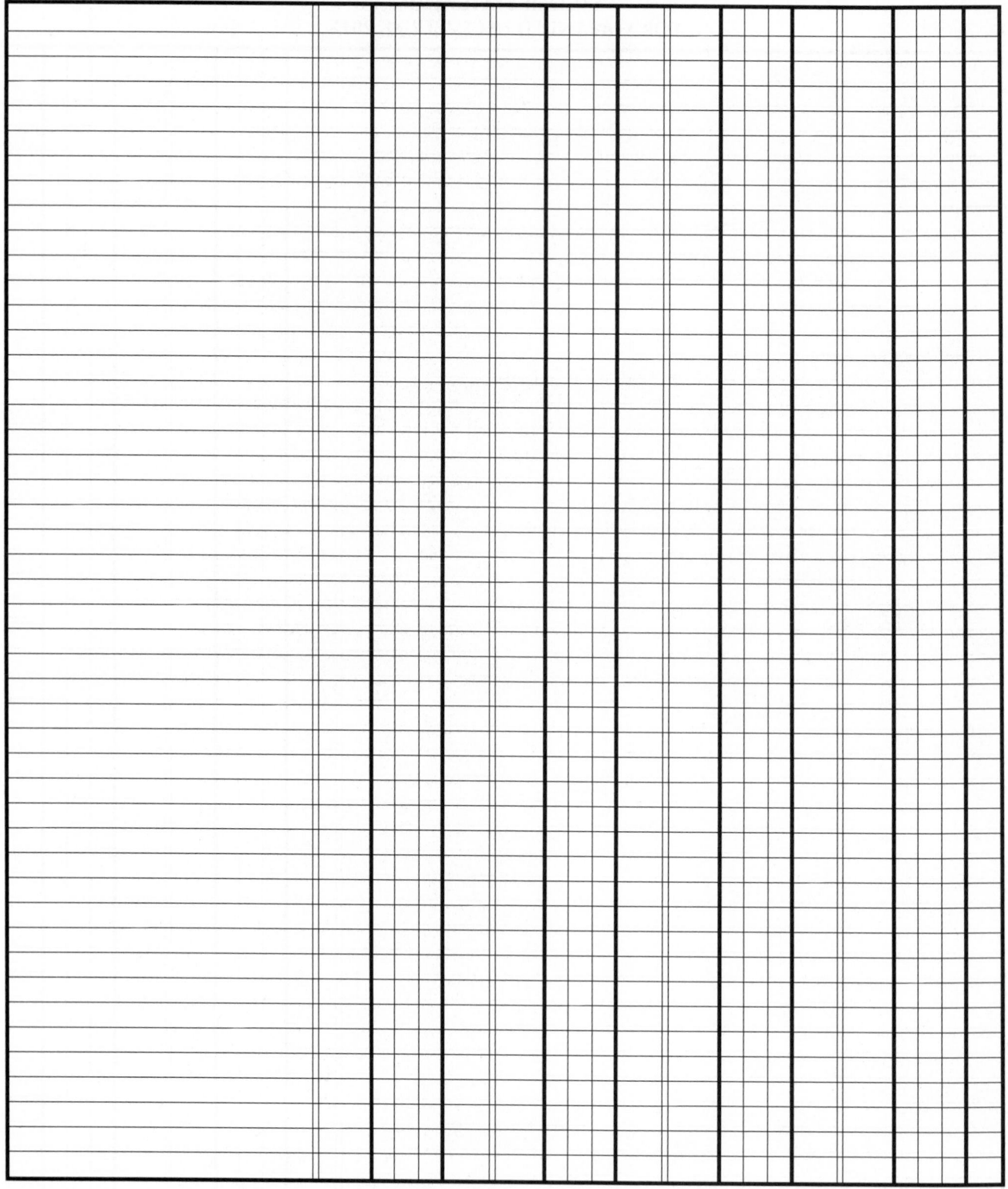

PROBLEM 12A-4 (CONTINUED)

CULLEN LUMBER
BALANCE SHEET
DECEMBER 31, 201X

PROBLEM 12A-4 (CONTINUED)

(3)

GENERAL JOURNAL

Date	Account Titles and Description	PR	Dr.	Cr.

PROBLEM 12A-4 (CONTINUED)

**CULLEN LUMBER
GENERAL LEDGER**

CASH   **ACCOUNT NO. 110**

Date	Explanation	Post Ref.	Debit	Credit	Balance Debit	Balance Credit

ACCOUNTS RECEIVABLE   **ACCOUNT NO. 111**

Date	Explanation	Post Ref.	Debit	Credit	Balance Debit	Balance Credit

MERCHANDISE INVENTORY   **ACCOUNT NO. 112**

Date	Explanation	Post Ref.	Debit	Credit	Balance Debit	Balance Credit

LUMBER SUPPLIES   **ACCOUNT NO. 113**

Date	Explanation	Post Ref.	Debit	Credit	Balance Debit	Balance Credit

PROBLEM 12A-4 (CONTINUED)

PREPAID INSURANCE   ACCOUNT NO. 114

Date	Explanation	Post Ref.	Debit	Credit	Balance Debit	Balance Credit

LUMBER EQUIPMENT   ACCOUNT NO. 121

Date	Explanation	Post Ref.	Debit	Credit	Balance Debit	Balance Credit

ACCUMULATED DEPRECIATION, LUMBER EQUIPMENT   ACCOUNT NO. 122

Date	Explanation	Post Ref.	Debit	Credit	Balance Debit	Balance Credit

ACCOUNTS PAYABLE   ACCOUNT NO. 220

Date	Explanation	Post Ref.	Debit	Credit	Balance Debit	Balance Credit

WAGES PAYABLE   ACCOUNT NO. 221

Date	Explanation	Post Ref.	Debit	Credit	Balance Debit	Balance Credit

PROBLEM 12A-4 (CONTINUED)

J. CULLEN, CAPITAL   ACCOUNT NO. 330

Date	Explanation	Post Ref.	Debit	Credit	Balance Debit	Balance Credit

J. CULLEN, WITHDRAWALS   ACCOUNT NO. 331

Date	Explanation	Post Ref.	Debit	Credit	Balance Debit	Balance Credit

INCOME SUMMARY   ACCOUNT NO. 332

Date	Explanation	Post Ref.	Debit	Credit	Balance Debit	Balance Credit

SALES   ACCOUNT NO. 440

Date	Explanation	Post Ref.	Debit	Credit	Balance Debit	Balance Credit

SALES RETURNS AND ALLOWANCES   ACCOUNT NO. 441

Date	Explanation	Post Ref.	Debit	Credit	Balance Debit	Balance Credit

PROBLEM 12A-4 (CONTINUED)

PURCHASES   ACCOUNT NO. 550

Date	Explanation	Post Ref.	Debit	Credit	Balance Debit	Balance Credit

PURCHASES DISCOUNT   ACCOUNT NO. 551

Date	Explanation	Post Ref.	Debit	Credit	Balance Debit	Balance Credit

PURCHASES RETURNS AND ALLOWANCES   ACCOUNT NO. 552

Date	Explanation	Post Ref.	Debit	Credit	Balance Debit	Balance Credit

WAGES EXPENSE   ACCOUNT NO. 660

Date	Explanation	Post Ref.	Debit	Credit	Balance Debit	Balance Credit

ADVERTISING EXPENSE   ACCOUNT NO. 661

Date	Explanation	Post Ref.	Debit	Credit	Balance Debit	Balance Credit

PROBLEM 12A-4 (CONTINUED)

RENT EXPENSE   ACCOUNT NO. 662

Date	Explanation	Post Ref.	Debit	Credit	Balance Debit	Balance Credit

DEPRECIATION EXPENSE, LUMBER EQUIPMENT   ACCOUNT NO. 663

Date	Explanation	Post Ref.	Debit	Credit	Balance Debit	Balance Credit

LUMBER SUPPLIES EXPENSE   ACCOUNT NO. 664

Date	Explanation	Post Ref.	Debit	Credit	Balance Debit	Balance Credit

INSURANCE EXPENSE   ACCOUNT NO. 665

Date	Explanation	Post Ref.	Debit	Credit	Balance Debit	Balance Credit

PROBLEM 12A-4 (CONCLUDED)

(4)

CULLEN LUMBER
POST-CLOSING TRIAL BALANCE
DECEMBER 31, 201X

	Dr.	Cr.

(5)   **GENERAL JOURNAL**

Date	Account	Debit	Credit

FORMS FOR SET B PROBLEMS

PROBLEM 12B-1

WRIGHT CO.
INCOME STATEMENT
FOR YEAR ENDED DECEMBER 31, 201X

PROBLEM 12B-2

JAGER CO.
STATEMENT OF OWNER'S EQUITY
FOR YEAR ENDED DECEMBER 31, 201X

PROBLEM 12B-2 (CONCLUDED)

JAGER CO.
BALANCE SHEET
DECEMBER 31, 201X

PROBLEM 12B-3

(1) Use one of the blank fold-out worksheets that accompanied your textbook.

(2)

JUSTIN'S SUPPLIES
INCOME STATEMENT
FOR YEAR ENDED DECEMBER 31, 201X

PROBLEM 12B-3 (CONTINUED)

JUSTIN'S SUPPLIES
STATEMENT OF OWNER'S EQUITY
FOR YEAR ENDED DECEMBER 31, 201X

PROBLEM 12B-3 (CONTINUED)

JUSTIN'S SUPPLIES
BALANCE SHEET
DECEMBER 31, 201X

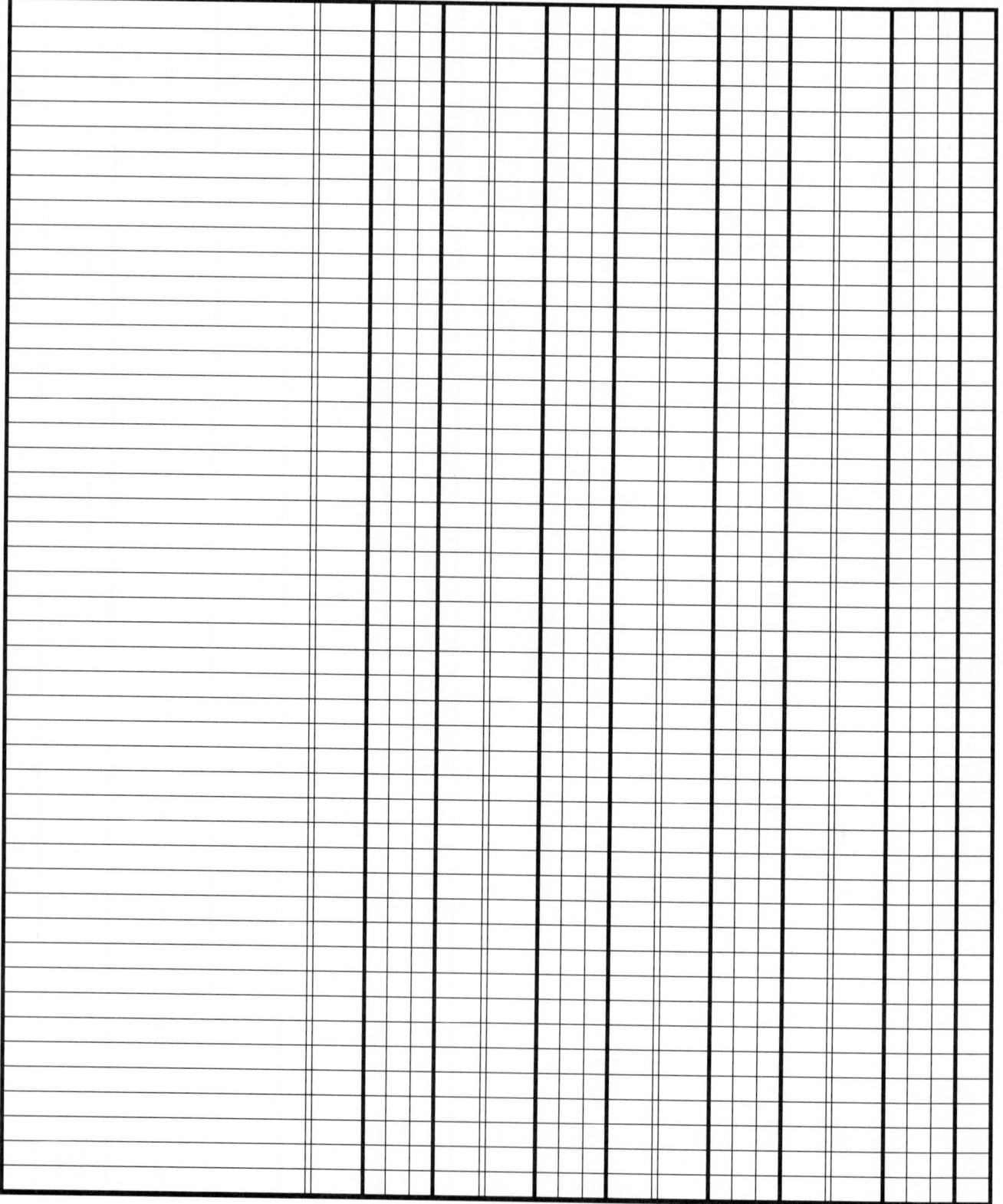

PROBLEM 12B-3 (CONTINUED)

(3)

GENERAL JOURNAL

PAGE 2

Date	Account Titles and Description	PR	Dr.	Cr.

PROBLEM 12B-3 (CONCLUDED)

GENERAL JOURNAL

Date	Account Titles and Description	PR	Dr.	Cr.

PROBLEM 12B-4

(1) Use one of the blank fold-out worksheets that accompanied your textbook.

(2)

CREW LUMBER
INCOME STATEMENT
FOR YEAR ENDED DECEMBER 31, 201X

PROBLEM 12B-4 (CONTINUED)

CREW LUMBER
STATEMENT OF OWNER'S EQUITY
FOR YEAR ENDED DECEMBER 31, 201X

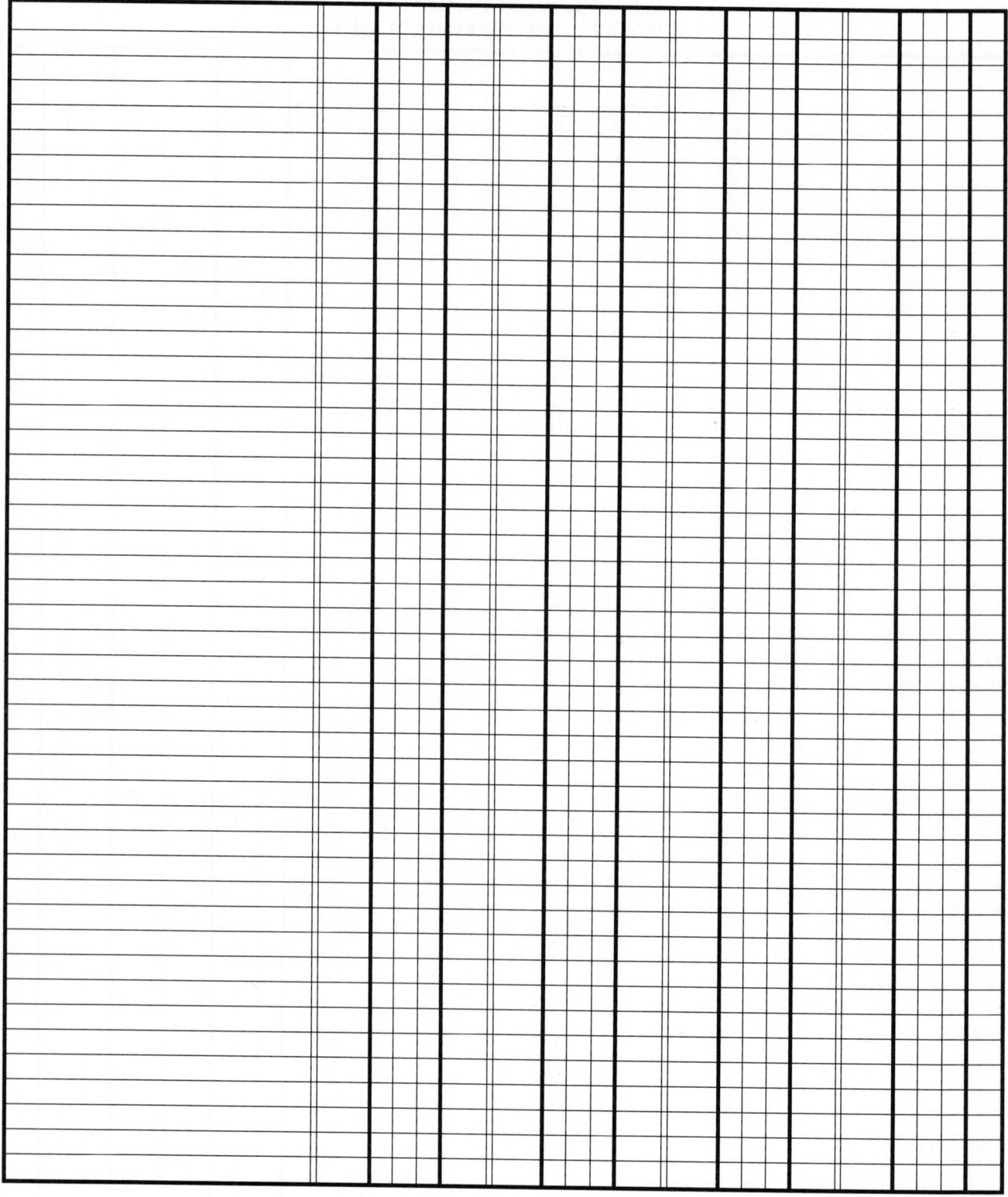

PROBLEM 12B-4 (CONTINUED)

CREW LUMBER
BALANCE SHEET
DECEMBER 31, 201X

PROBLEM 12B-4 (CONTINUED)

(3)

GENERAL JOURNAL

Date	Account Titles and Description	PR	Dr.	Cr.

PROBLEM 12B-4 (CONTINUED)

CREW LUMBER
GENERAL LEDGER

CASH   **ACCOUNT NO. 110**

Date	Explanation	Post Ref.	Debit	Credit	Balance Debit	Balance Credit

ACCOUNTS RECEIVABLE   **ACCOUNT NO. 111**

Date	Explanation	Post Ref.	Debit	Credit	Balance Debit	Balance Credit

MERCHANDISE INVENTORY   **ACCOUNT NO. 112**

Date	Explanation	Post Ref.	Debit	Credit	Balance Debit	Balance Credit

LUMBER SUPPLIES   **ACCOUNT NO. 113**

Date	Explanation	Post Ref.	Debit	Credit	Balance Debit	Balance Credit

PROBLEM 12B-4 (CONTINUED)

PREPAID INSURANCE   ACCOUNT NO. <u>114</u>

Date	Explanation	Post Ref.	Debit	Credit	Balance Debit	Balance Credit

LUMBER EQUIPMENT   ACCOUNT NO. <u>121</u>

Date	Explanation	Post Ref.	Debit	Credit	Balance Debit	Balance Credit

ACCUMULATED DEPRECIATION, LUMBER EQUIPMENT   ACCOUNT NO. <u>122</u>

Date	Explanation	Post Ref.	Debit	Credit	Balance Debit	Balance Credit

ACCOUNTS PAYABLE   ACCOUNT NO. <u>220</u>

Date	Explanation	Post Ref.	Debit	Credit	Balance Debit	Balance Credit

WAGES PAYABLE   ACCOUNT NO. <u>221</u>

Date	Explanation	Post Ref.	Debit	Credit	Balance Debit	Balance Credit

PROBLEM 12B-4 (CONTINUED)

J. CREW, CAPITAL   **ACCOUNT NO. 330**

Date	Explanation	Post Ref.	Debit	Credit	Balance Debit	Balance Credit

J. CREW, WITHDRAWALS   **ACCOUNT NO. 331**

Date	Explanation	Post Ref.	Debit	Credit	Balance Debit	Balance Credit

INCOME SUMMARY   **ACCOUNT NO. 332**

Date	Explanation	Post Ref.	Debit	Credit	Balance Debit	Balance Credit

SALES   **ACCOUNT NO. 440**

Date	Explanation	Post Ref.	Debit	Credit	Balance Debit	Balance Credit

SALES RETURNS AND ALLOWANCES   **ACCOUNT NO. 441**

Date	Explanation	Post Ref.	Debit	Credit	Balance Debit	Balance Credit

PROBLEM 12B-4 (CONTINUED)

PURCHASES   ACCOUNT NO. 550

Date		Explanation	Post Ref.	Debit	Credit	Balance	
						Debit	Credit

PURCHASES DISCOUNT   ACCOUNT NO. 551

Date		Explanation	Post Ref.	Debit	Credit	Balance	
						Debit	Credit

PURCHASES RETURNS AND ALLOWANCES   ACCOUNT NO. 552

Date		Explanation	Post Ref.	Debit	Credit	Balance	
						Debit	Credit

WAGES EXPENSE   ACCOUNT NO. 660

Date		Explanation	Post Ref.	Debit	Credit	Balance	
						Debit	Credit

ADVERTISING EXPENSE   ACCOUNT NO. 661

Date		Explanation	Post Ref.	Debit	Credit	Balance	
						Debit	Credit

PROBLEM 12B-4 (CONTINUED)

RENT EXPENSE   **ACCOUNT NO. 662**

Date	Explanation	Post Ref.	Debit	Credit	Balance	
					Debit	Credit

DEPRECIATION EXPENSE, LUMBER EQUIPMENT   **ACCOUNT NO. 663**

Date	Explanation	Post Ref.	Debit	Credit	Balance	
					Debit	Credit

LUMBER SUPPLIES EXPENSE   **ACCOUNT NO. 664**

Date	Explanation	Post Ref.	Debit	Credit	Balance	
					Debit	Credit

INSURANCE EXPENSE   **ACCOUNT NO. 665**

Date	Explanation	Post Ref.	Debit	Credit	Balance	
					Debit	Credit

PROBLEM 12B-4 (CONCLUDED)

(4)

CREW LUMBER
POST-CLOSING TRIAL BALANCE
DECEMBER 31, 201X

	Dr.	Cr.

(5)   **GENERAL JOURNAL**

Date	Account	Debit	Credit

ON THE JOB CONTINUING PROBLEM

SMITH COMPUTER CENTER
GENERAL JOURNAL

PAGE 12

Date		Account Titles and Description	PR	Dr.			Cr.		

SMITH COMPUTER CENTER
GENERAL LEDGER

CASH ACCOUNT NO. **1000**

Date		Explanation	Post Ref.	Debit	Credit	Balance	
						Debit	Credit
3/31	1X	Balance forward	✔			17 2 6 3 76	

PETTY CASH ACCOUNT NO. **1010**

Date		Explanation	Post Ref.	Debit	Credit	Balance	
						Debit	Credit
3/31	1X	Balance forward	✔			3 0 0 00	

ACCOUNTS RECEIVABLE ACCOUNT NO. **1020**

Date		Explanation	Post Ref.	Debit	Credit	Balance	
						Debit	Credit
3/31	1X	Balance forward	✔			13 0 9 5 00	

MERCHANDISE INVENTORY ACCOUNT NO. **1021**

Date	Explanation	Post Ref.	Debit	Credit	Balance	
					Debit	Credit

PREPAID RENT   ACCOUNT NO. 1025

Date		Explanation	Post Ref.	Debit	Credit	Balance	
						Debit	Credit
3/31	1X	Balance forward	✔			3 5 0 0 00	

SUPPLIES   ACCOUNT NO. 1030

Date		Explanation	Post Ref.	Debit	Credit	Balance	
						Debit	Credit
3/31	1X	Balance forward	✔			6 1 2 00	

COMPUTER SHOP EQUIPMENT   ACCOUNT NO. 1080

Date		Explanation	Post Ref.	Debit	Credit	Balance	
						Debit	Credit
3/31	1X	Balance forward	✔			5 7 0 0 00	

ACCUMULATED DEPRECIATION, C.S. EQUIPMENT   ACCOUNT NO. 1081

Date		Explanation	Post Ref.	Debit	Credit	Balance	
						Debit	Credit
3/31	1X	Balance forward	✔				1 5 0 00

OFFICE EQUIPMENT   ACCOUNT NO. 1090

Date		Explanation	Post Ref.	Debit	Credit	Balance	
						Debit	Credit
3/31	1X	Balance forward	✔			3 8 5 0 00	

ACCUMULATED DEPRECIATION,
OFFICE EQUIPMENT

ACCOUNT NO. 1091

Date		Explanation	Post Ref.	Debit	Credit	Balance	
						Debit	Credit
3/31	1X	Balance forward	✔				1 1 0 00

ACCOUNTS PAYABLE

ACCOUNT NO. 2000

Date		Explanation	Post Ref.	Debit	Credit	Balance	
						Debit	Credit
3/31	1X	Balance forward	✔				3 1 7 0 00

WAGES PAYABLE

ACCOUNT NO. 2010

Date	Explanation	Post Ref.	Debit	Credit	Balance	
					Debit	Credit

FICA OASDI PAYABLE

ACCOUNT NO. 2020

Date	Explanation	Post Ref.	Debit	Credit	Balance	
					Debit	Credit

FICA MEDICARE PAYABLE

ACCOUNT NO. 2030

Date	Explanation	Post Ref.	Debit	Credit	Balance	
					Debit	Credit

FIT PAYABLE   ACCOUNT NO. 2040

Date		Explanation	Post Ref.	Debit	Credit	Balance	
						Debit	Credit

SIT PAYABLE   ACCOUNT NO. 2050

Date		Explanation	Post Ref.	Debit	Credit	Balance	
						Debit	Credit

FUTA PAYABLE   ACCOUNT NO. 2060

Date		Explanation	Post Ref.	Debit	Credit	Balance	
						Debit	Credit

SUTA PAYABLE   ACCOUNT NO. 2070

Date		Explanation	Post Ref.	Debit	Credit	Balance	
						Debit	Credit

T. FELDMAN, CAPITAL   ACCOUNT NO. 3000

Date		Explanation	Post Ref.	Debit	Credit	Balance	
						Debit	Credit
3/31	1X	Balance forward	✔				12 2 8 2 00

T. FELDMAN, WITHDRAWALS   ACCOUNT NO. **3010**

Date		Explanation	Post Ref.	Debit	Credit	Balance Debit	Balance Credit
3/31	1X	Balance forward	✔			9 1 5 00	

INCOME SUMMARY   ACCOUNT NO. **3020**

Date		Explanation	Post Ref.	Debit	Credit	Balance Debit	Balance Credit

SERVICE REVENUE   ACCOUNT NO. **4000**

Date		Explanation	Post Ref.	Debit	Credit	Balance Debit	Balance Credit
3/31	1X	Balance forward	✔				21 8 0 0 00

SALES   ACCOUNT NO. **4010**

Date		Explanation	Post Ref.	Debit	Credit	Balance Debit	Balance Credit
3/31	1X	Balance forward	✔				11 6 8 0 00

GENERAL LEDGER

SALES RETURNS AND ALLOWANCES   **ACCOUNT NO. 4020**

Date		Explanation	Post Ref.	Debit	Credit	Balance	
						Debit	Credit
3/31	1X	Balance forward	✓			4 6 0 00	

SALES DISCOUNTS   **ACCOUNT NO. 4030**

Date		Explanation	Post Ref.	Debit	Credit	Balance	
						Debit	Credit
3/31	1X	Balance forward	✓			1 9 8 00	

ADVERTISING EXPENSE   **ACCOUNT NO. 5010**

Date	Explanation	Post Ref.	Debit	Credit	Balance	
					Debit	Credit

RENT EXPENSE   **ACCOUNT NO. 5020**

Date	Explanation	Post Ref.	Debit	Credit	Balance	
					Debit	Credit

UTILITIES EXPENSE   **ACCOUNT NO. 5030**

Date	Explanation	Post Ref.	Debit	Credit	Balance	
					Debit	Credit

PHONE EXPENSE   ACCOUNT NO. 5040

Date		Explanation	Post Ref.	Debit	Credit	Balance Debit	Balance Credit
3/31	1X	Balance forward	✔			1 7 0 00	

SUPPLIES EXPENSE   ACCOUNT NO. 5050

Date		Explanation	Post Ref.	Debit	Credit	Balance Debit	Balance Credit
3/31	1X	Balance forward	✔			4 5 00	

INSURANCE EXPENSE   ACCOUNT NO. 5060

Date		Explanation	Post Ref.	Debit	Credit	Balance Debit	Balance Credit

POSTAGE EXPENSE   ACCOUNT NO. 5070

Date		Explanation	Post Ref.	Debit	Credit	Balance Debit	Balance Credit
3/31	1X	Balance forward	✔			4 0 00	

DEPRECIATION EXPENSE C.S. EQUIPMENT   ACCOUNT NO. 5080

Date		Explanation	Post Ref.	Debit	Credit	Balance Debit	Balance Credit

DEPRECIATION EXPENSE OFFICE EQUIPMENT   ACCOUNT NO. 5090

Date	Explanation	Post Ref.	Debit	Credit	Balance Debit	Balance Credit

MISCELLANEOUS EXPENSE   ACCOUNT NO. 5100

Date	Explanation	Post Ref.	Debit	Credit	Balance Debit	Balance Credit
3/31 1X	Balance forward	✔			1 5 00	

WAGE EXPENSE   ACCOUNT NO. 5110

Date	Explanation	Post Ref.	Debit	Credit	Balance Debit	Balance Credit
3/31 1X	Balance forward	✔			2 0 3 0 00	

PAYROLL TAX EXPENSE   ACCOUNT NO. 5120

Date	Explanation	Post Ref.	Debit	Credit	Balance Debit	Balance Credit
3/31 1X	Balance forward	✔			2 1 8 24	

INTEREST EXPENSE   ACCOUNT NO. 5130

Date	Explanation	Post Ref.	Debit	Credit	Balance Debit	Balance Credit

BAD DEBT EXPENSE   ACCOUNT NO. 5140

Date		Explanation	Post Ref.	Debit	Credit	Balance	
						Debit	Credit

PURCHASES   ACCOUNT NO. 6000

Date		Explanation	Post Ref.	Debit	Credit	Balance	
						Debit	Credit
3/31	1X	Balance forward	✔			9 3 0 00	

PURCHASE RETURNS AND ALLOWANCES   ACCOUNT NO. 6010

Date		Explanation	Post Ref.	Debit	Credit	Balance	
						Debit	Credit
3/31	1X	Balance forward	✔				1 5 0 00

PURCHASE DISCOUNTS   ACCOUNT NO. 6020

Date		Explanation	Post Ref.	Debit	Credit	Balance	
						Debit	Credit

FREIGHT IN   ACCOUNT NO. 6030

Date		Explanation	Post Ref.	Debit	Credit	Balance	
						Debit	Credit

SMITH COMPUTER CENTER
INCOME STATEMENT
FOR THE SIX MONTHS ENDED MARCH 31, 201X

SMITH COMPUTER CENTER
STATEMENT OF OWNER'S EQUITY
FOR THE SIX MONTHS ENDED MARCH 31, 201X

Name _____ Class _____ Date _____

SMITH COMPUTER CENTER
BALANCE SHEET
MARCH 31, 201X

MINI PRACTICE SET

REQUIREMENTS 2, 7

THE ELEGANT DRESS SHOP
GENERAL JOURNAL

Date	Account Titles and Description	PR	Dr.	Cr.

THE ELEGANT DRESS SHOP

Use a blank payroll register for this problem that accompanied your textbook.

MINI PRACTICE SET

THE ELEGANT DRESS SHOP
GENERAL JOURNAL

Date	Account Titles and Description	PR	Dr.	Cr.

MINI PRACTICE SET

THE ELEGANT DRESS SHOP
GENERAL JOURNAL

Date	Account Titles and Description	PR	Dr.	Cr.

MINI PRACTICE SET

THE ELEGANT DRESS SHOP
GENERAL JOURNAL

Date	Account Titles and Description	PR	Dr.	Cr.

MINI PRACTICE SET

THE ELEGANT DRESS SHOP
GENERAL JOURNAL

Date	Account Titles and Description	PR	Dr.	Cr.

MINI PRACTICE SET

THE ELEGANT DRESS SHOP
GENERAL JOURNAL

Date		Account Titles and Description	PR	Dr.		Cr.	

MINI PRACTICE SET

THE ELEGANT DRESS SHOP
AUXILIARY PETTY CASH RECORD

Date	Voucher No.	Description	Receipts	Payment	Category of Payment				
					Postage Expense	Delivery Expense	Sundry		
							Account	Amount	

MINI PRACTICE SET
REQUIREMENT 3

ACCOUNTS PAYABLE SUBSIDIARY LEDGER

NAME   DANMARK CO.

Date 201X		Explanation	Post Ref.	Debit	Credit	Credit Balance
Mar	1	Balance	✔			2 0 0 0 00

NAME   JOHNSONS CO.

Date 201X		Explanation	Post Ref.	Debit	Credit	Credit Balance

NAME   MANNY'S GARAGE

Date 201X		Explanation	Post Ref.	Debit	Credit	Credit Balance

MINI PRACTICE SET

NAME   THOMAS CO.

Date 201X		Explanation	Post Ref.	Debit	Credit	Credit Balance

ACCOUNTS RECEIVABLE SUBSIDIARY LEDGER

NAME   BACH CO.

Date 201X		Explanation	Post Ref.	Debit	Credit	Debit Balance
Mar	1	Balance	✔			1 8 0 0 00

NAME   DANMARK CO.

Date 201X		Explanation	Post Ref.	Debit	Credit	Debit Balance

MINI PRACTICE SET

NAME   YOUNG CO.

Date 201X		Explanation	Post Ref.	Debit	Credit	Debit Balance

REQUIREMENT 4

GENERAL LEDGER

CASH   **ACCOUNT NO. 110**

Date 201X		Explanation	Post Ref.	Debit	Credit	Balance Debit	Balance Credit
Mar	1	Balance	✔			2 3 6 4 80	

MINI PRACTICE SET

PETTY CASH   ACCOUNT NO. 111

Date 201X		Explanation	Post Ref.	Debit	Credit	Balance Debit	Balance Credit
Mar	1	Balance	✓			5 5 00	

ACCOUNTS RECEIVABLE   ACCOUNT NO. 112

Date 201X		Explanation	Post Ref.	Debit	Credit	Balance Debit	Balance Credit
Mar	1	Balance	✓			1 8 0 0 00	

MERCHANDISE INVENTORY   ACCOUNT NO. 114

Date 201X		Explanation	Post Ref.	Debit	Credit	Balance Debit	Balance Credit
Mar	1	Balance	✓			4 9 0 0 00	

MINI PRACTICE SET

PREPAID RENT   ACCOUNT NO. 116

Date 201X	Explanation	Post Ref.	Debit	Credit	Balance Debit	Balance Credit
Mar 1	Balance	✔			1 6 5 0 00	

DELIVERY TRUCK   ACCOUNT NO. 120

Date 201X	Explanation	Post Ref.	Debit	Credit	Balance Debit	Balance Credit
Mar 1	Balance	✔			12 0 0 0 00	

ACCUMULATED DEPRECIATION, TRUCK   ACCOUNT NO. 121

Date 201X	Explanation	Post Ref.	Debit	Credit	Balance Debit	Balance Credit
Mar 1	Balance	✔				3 0 0 0 00

MINI PRACTICE SET

ACCOUNTS PAYABLE — ACCOUNT NO. 210

Date 201X		Explanation	Post Ref.	Debit	Credit	Balance Debit	Balance Credit
Mar	1	Balance	✔				2 000 00

SALARIES PAYABLE — ACCOUNT NO. 212

Date 201X	Explanation	Post Ref.	Debit	Credit	Balance Debit	Balance Credit

FIT PAYABLE — ACCOUNT NO. 214

Date 201X		Explanation	Post Ref.	Debit	Credit	Balance Debit	Balance Credit
Mar	1	Balance	✔				7 4 2 00

Name _____ Class _____ Date _____

MINI PRACTICE SET

FICA-OASDI PAYABLE   ACCOUNT NO. 216

Date 201X		Explanation	Post Ref.	Debit	Credit	Balance	
						Debit	Credit
Mar	1	Balance	✔				1 1 5 3 20

FICA-MEDICARE PAYABLE   ACCOUNT NO. 218

Date 201X		Explanation	Post Ref.	Debit	Credit	Balance	
						Debit	Credit
Mar	1	Balance	✔				2 6 9 70

SIT PAYABLE   ACCOUNT NO. 220

Date 201X		Explanation	Post Ref.	Debit	Credit	Balance	
						Debit	Credit
Mar	1	Balance	✔				6 5 1 00

SUTA TAX PAYABLE   ACCOUNT NO. 222

Date 201X		Explanation	Post Ref.	Debit	Credit	Balance	
						Debit	Credit
Mar	1	Balance	✔				8 5 4 40

FUTA TAX PAYABLE   ACCOUNT NO. 224

Date 201X		Explanation	Post Ref.	Debit	Credit	Balance	
						Debit	Credit
Mar	1	Balance	✔				1 0 6 80

UNEARNED RENT   ACCOUNT NO. 226

Date 201X		Explanation	Post Ref.	Debit	Credit	Balance	
						Debit	Credit
Mar	1	Balance	✔				1 0 0 0 00

MINI PRACTICE SET

B. DUVAL, CAPITAL   ACCOUNT NO. 310

Date 201X		Explanation	Post Ref.	Debit	Credit	Balance Debit	Balance Credit
Mar	1	Balance	✔				12 9 9 2 70

B. DUVAL, WITHDRAWALS   ACCOUNT NO. 320

Date 201X		Explanation	Post Ref.	Debit	Credit	Balance Debit	Balance Credit

INCOME SUMMARY   ACCOUNT NO. 330

Date 201X		Explanation	Post Ref.	Debit	Credit	Balance Debit	Balance Credit

SALES   ACCOUNT NO. 410

Date 201X		Explanation	Post Ref.	Debit	Credit	Balance Debit	Balance Credit

SALES RETURNS AND ALLOWANCES   ACCOUNT NO. 412

Date 201X		Explanation	Post Ref.	Debit	Credit	Balance Debit	Balance Credit

MINI PRACTICE SET

SALES DISCOUNT   ACCOUNT NO. 414

Date 201X	Explanation	Post Ref.	Debit	Credit	Balance Debit	Balance Credit

RENTAL INCOME   ACCOUNT NO. 416

Date 201X	Explanation	Post Ref.	Debit	Credit	Balance Debit	Balance Credit

PURCHASES   ACCOUNT NO. 510

Date 201X	Explanation	Post Ref.	Debit	Credit	Balance Debit	Balance Credit

PURCHASES RETURNS AND ALLOWANCES   ACCOUNT NO. 512

Date 201X	Explanation	Post Ref.	Debit	Credit	Balance Debit	Balance Credit

PURCHASES DISCOUNT   ACCOUNT NO. 514

Date 201X	Explanation	Post Ref.	Debit	Credit	Balance Debit	Balance Credit

MINI PRACTICE SET

SALES SALARY EXPENSE   ACCOUNT NO. 610

Date 201X	Explanation	Post Ref.	Debit	Credit	Balance Debit	Balance Credit

OFFICE SALARY EXPENSE   ACCOUNT NO. 611

Date 201X	Explanation	Post Ref.	Debit	Credit	Balance Debit	Balance Credit

PAYROLL TAX EXPENSE   ACCOUNT NO. 612

Date 201X	Explanation	Post Ref.	Debit	Credit	Balance Debit	Balance Credit

CLEANING EXPENSE   ACCOUNT NO. 614

Date 201X	Explanation	Post Ref.	Debit	Credit	Balance Debit	Balance Credit

DEPRECIATION EXPENSE, TRUCK   ACCOUNT NO. 616

Date 201X	Explanation	Post Ref.	Debit	Credit	Balance Debit	Balance Credit

MINI PRACTICE SET

RENT EXPENSE　　　　　　　　　　　　　　　　ACCOUNT NO. 618

Date 201X	Explanation	Post Ref.	Debit	Credit	Balance Debit	Balance Credit

POSTAGE EXPENSE　　　　　　　　　　　　　　ACCOUNT NO. 620

Date 201X	Explanation	Post Ref.	Debit	Credit	Balance Debit	Balance Credit

DELIVERY EXPENSE　　　　　　　　　　　　　ACCOUNT NO. 622

Date 201X	Explanation	Post Ref.	Debit	Credit	Balance Debit	Balance Credit

MISCELLANEOUS EXPENSE　　　　　　　　ACCOUNT NO. 624

Date 201X	Explanation	Post Ref.	Debit	Credit	Balance Debit	Balance Credit

MINI PRACTICE SET

REQUIREMENT 5

Using one of the blank fold-out worksheets that accompanied your textbook, enter the trial balance and complete the worksheet.

MINI PRACTICE SET
REQUIREMENT 6

THE ELEGANT DRESS SHOP
INCOME STATEMENT
FOR MONTH ENDED MARCH 31, 201X

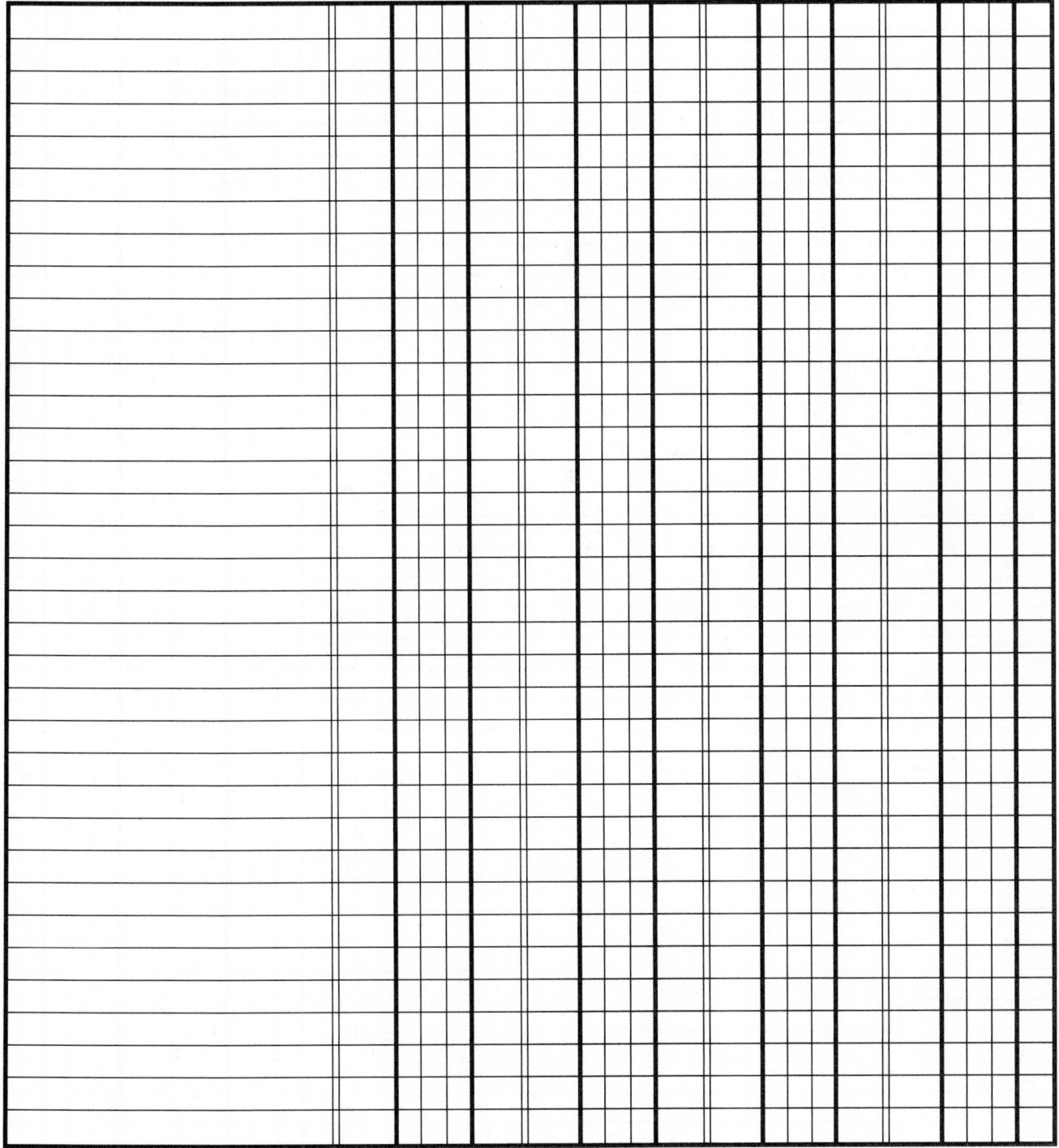

MINI PRACTICE SET

THE ELEGANT DRESS SHOP
STATEMENT OF OWNER'S EQUITY
FOR MONTH ENDED MARCH 31, 201X

MINI PRACTICE SET

THE ELEGANT DRESS SHOP
BALANCE SHEET
MARCH 31, 201X

MINI PRACTICE SET

REQUIREMENT 9

THE ELEGANT DRESS SHOP
POST-CLOSING TRIAL BALANCE
MARCH 31, 201X

MINI PRACTICE SET
REQUIREMENT 10

Form **941 for 201X:** **Employer's QUARTERLY Federal Tax Return**
(Rev. January 2014)   Department of the Treasury — Internal Revenue Service

950114

OMB No. 1545-0029

Employer identification number (EIN) ☐☐ – ☐☐☐☐☐☐☐

Name *(not your trade name)* _____

Trade name *(if any)* _____

Address _____
Number   Street   Suite or room number

_____
City   State   ZIP code

_____
Foreign country name   Foreign province/county   Foreign postal code

Report for this Quarter of 201X
(Check one.)

☐ **1:** January, February, March

☐ **2:** April, May, June

☐ **3:** July, August, September

☐ **4:** October, November, December

Instructions and prior year forms are available at *www.irs.gov/form941*.

Read the separate instructions before you complete Form 941. Type or print within the boxes.

Part 1: Answer these questions for this quarter.

1 Number of employees who received wages, tips, or other compensation for the pay period including: *Mar. 12* (Quarter 1), *June 12* (Quarter 2), *Sept. 12* (Quarter 3), or *Dec. 12* (Quarter 4) **1** ☐

2 Wages, tips, and other compensation . . . . **2** ☐ .

3 Federal income tax withheld from wages, tips, and other compensation . . . . . . **3** ☐ .

4 If no wages, tips, and other compensation are subject to social security or Medicare tax ☐ Check and go to line 6.

	Column 1		Column 2
5a Taxable social security wages . .	☐ .	× .124 =	☐ .
5b Taxable social security tips . . .	☐ .	× .124 =	☐ .
5c Taxable Medicare wages & tips. .	☐ .	× .029 =	☐ .
5d Taxable wages & tips subject to Additional Medicare Tax withholding	☐ .	× .009 =	☐ .

5e Add Column 2 from lines 5a, 5b, 5c, and 5d . . . . **5e** ☐ .

5f Section 3121(q) Notice and Demand—Tax due on unreported tips (see instructions) . . **5f** ☐ .

6 Total taxes before adjustments. Add lines 3, 5e, and 5f . . . . **6** ☐ .

7 Current quarter's adjustment for fractions of cents . . . . **7** ☐ .

8 Current quarter's adjustment for sick pay . . . . **8** ☐ .

9 Current quarter's adjustments for tips and group-term life insurance . . . . . . **9** ☐ .

10 Total taxes after adjustments. Combine lines 6 through 9 . . . . **10** ☐ .

11 Total deposits for this quarter, including overpayment applied from a prior quarter and overpayments applied from Form 941-X, 941-X (PR), 944-X, 944-X (PR), or 944-X (SP) filed in the current quarter . . . . **11** ☐ .

12 Balance due. If line 10 is more than line 11, enter the difference and see instructions . . . **12** 0 .

13 Overpayment. If line 11 is more than line 10, enter the difference ☐ . Check one: ☐ Apply to next return. ☐ Send a refund.

▶ **You MUST complete both pages of Form 941 and SIGN it.**   Next ▶

For Privacy Act and Paperwork Reduction Act Notice, see the back of the Payment Voucher.   Cat. No. 17001Z   Form **941** (Rev. 1-2014)

CTICE SET

950214

(...ur trade name) | Employer identification number (EIN)

Tell us about your deposit schedule and tax liability for this quarter.

...u are unsure about whether you are a monthly schedule depositor or a semiweekly schedule depositor, see Pub. 15 ...rcular E), section 11.

14 Check one: ☐ **Line 10 on this return is less than $2,500 or line 10 on the return for the prior quarter was less than $2,500, and you did not incur a $100,000 next-day deposit obligation during the current quarter.** If line 10 for the prior quarter was less than $2,500 but line 10 on this return is $100,000 or more, you must provide a record of your federal tax liability. If you are a monthly schedule depositor, complete the deposit schedule below; if you are a semiweekly schedule depositor, attach Schedule B (Form 941). Go to Part 3.

☐ **You were a monthly schedule depositor for the entire quarter.** Enter your tax liability for each month and total liability for the quarter, then go to Part 3.

Tax liability:	Month 1	⬚ .
	Month 2	⬚ .
	Month 3	⬚ .
	Total liability for quarter	⬚ .	**Total must equal line 10.**

☐ **You were a semiweekly schedule depositor for any part of this quarter.** Complete Schedule B (Form 941), Report of Tax Liability for Semiweekly Schedule Depositors, and attach it to Form 941.

Part 3: Tell us about your business. If a question does NOT apply to your business, leave it blank.

15 If your business has closed or you stopped paying wages . . . . ☐ Check here, and

enter the final date you paid wages ⬚ / / .

16 If you are a seasonal employer and you do not have to file a return for every quarter of the year . . ☐ Check here.

Part 4: May we speak with your third-party designee?

Do you want to allow an employee, a paid tax preparer, or another person to discuss this return with the IRS? See the instructions for details.

☐ Yes. Designee's name and phone number ⬚ ⬚

Select a 5-digit Personal Identification Number (PIN) to use when talking to the IRS. ☐ ☐ ☐ ☐ ☐

☐ No.

Part 5: Sign here. You MUST complete both pages of Form 941 and SIGN it.

Under penalties of perjury, I declare that I have examined this return, including accompanying schedules and statements, and to the best of my knowledge and belief, it is true, correct, and complete. Declaration of preparer (other than taxpayer) is based on all information of which preparer has any knowledge.

X **Sign your name here** ⬚

Print your name here ⬚

Print your title here ⬚

Date / /

Best daytime phone ⬚

Paid Preparer Use Only   Check if you are self-employed . . . ☐

Preparer's name	⬚	PTIN	⬚
Preparer's signature	⬚	Date	/ /
Firm's name (or yours if self-employed)	⬚	EIN	⬚
Address	⬚	Phone	⬚
City	⬚	State ⬚	ZIP code	⬚

Form **941** (Rev. 1-2014)

SG-604

SOLUTIONS

Part I

1. financial reports
2. two separate
3. is not
4. Gross profit
5. Administrative expenses
6. Operating expenses
7. ending
8. Current assets
9. Plant, Equipment
10. current liabilities
11. current liability
12. current asset
13. Income Summary
14. post-closing trial balance
15. adjusting
16. increasing, increasing

Part II

1. d
2. j
3. f
4. a
5. g
6. o
7. n
8. h
9. e
10. l
11. k
12. m
13. b
14. i

Part III

1. false
2. false
3. true
4. false
5. false
6. false
7. false
8. false
9. false
10. false
11. true
12. false
13. false
14. true
15. true
16. false
17. true
18. false
19. true
20. true